SOCIAL
JUSTICE
AND
PUBLIC
POLICY

By the same author

Poverty in Britain and the Reform of Social Security, Cambridge University Press.
Unequal Shares — Wealth in Britain, Penguin.
(ed.) *Wealth, Income and Inequality,* Oxford
The Tax Credit Scheme and the Redistribution of Income, Institute for Fiscal Studies.
The Economics of Inequality, Oxford University Press.
The Distribution of Personal Wealth in Britain (with A. J. Harrison), Cambridge University Press.
(ed.) *The Personal Distribution of Income,* Allen and Unwin.
Lectures on Public Economics (with J. E. Stiglitz), McGraw-Hill.
Parents and Children: Incomes in Two Generations (with A. K. Maynard and C. G. Trinder), Heinemann.

SOCIAL JUSTICE AND PUBLIC POLICY

A. B. ATKINSON

Professor of Economics,
London School of Economics

Wheatsheaf
Books

A MEMBER OF THE HARVESTER PRESS GROUP

First published in Great Britain in 1983 by
WHEATSHEAF BOOKS LTD
A MEMBER OF THE HARVESTER PRESS GROUP
Publisher: John Spiers
Director of Publications: Edward Elgar
16 Ship Street, Brighton, Sussex

© A. B. Atkinson, 1983

British Library Cataloguing in Publication Data
Atkinson, A. B.
    Social justice and public policy.
    1. Economic development—Addresses, essays, lectures
    I. Title
    339.5   HD82

    ISBN 0-7108-0134-3

Photoset by Unwin Brothers Limited in 10/11 pt Times
Printed by Unwin Brothers Limited

Handwritten: 39
tkinson

Contents

Acknowledgements

The author and publishers would like to thank the following for permission to reprint the essays in this volume:

Academic Press Inc. (Chapter 1), the Society of Economic Analysis Ltd (Chapters 2, 8, 13), Het Spectrum BV (Chapter 3), Physica Verlag (Chapter 4), The Brookings Institution (Chapter 5), Oxford University Press (Chapter 7), George Allen & Unwin (Chapter 9), Institut National de la Statistique et des Etudes Economiques (Chapter 6), North-Holland Publishing Co. (Chapters 10 and 11), Canadian Economics Association (Chapter 12), Cambridge University Press (Chapter 14), Association of University Teachers of Economics (Chapter 15), the Macmillan Press Ltd (Chapters 16 and 19), D. C. Heath & Co. (Chapter 18), Economica (Chapter 20), and Butterworths (Chapter 22).

Foreword

This volume contains a selection of my scientific papers in the fields of economic inequality and public policy.

The principal reason for collecting the papers together in this way is to bring out two important unifying themes in my research over the past fifteen years. The first theme is that of distributional justice. The material covered in the essays ranges from the theory of the measurement of inequality and mobility (Part I), through analysis of the extent and causes of inequality (Part II), to the design of public policy for taxation and public expenditure (Parts III and IV). In the area of public policy, the essays, at the level of both theory and application, attempt to redress the neglect by economists of distributional concerns. Issues such as the choice between direct and indirect taxation (Chapters 10–12), the progression of income tax (Chapter 15), the reform of housing finance (Chapters 16 and 17), or of unemployment insurance (Chapters 21 and 22), cannot sensibly be discussed without regard to the resulting distribution of gains and losses.

The second unifying theme is my belief in the value of economic analysis in clarifying and illuminating issues of public concern. In this respect, I am not seeking to establish a particular claim for economics as opposed to other social sciences. Indeed, the essays touch on common ground with moral philosophy, statistics, social administration and social medicine. Rather, at a time when the value of social inquiry is being questioned by those in authority, I should like to argue that informed analysis, drawing on one or more academic subjects, can contribute to our understanding of social problems and to more effective design of government policy. Economic research cannot ensure the solution of the problems that confront us, but – as I have tried to show in the fields such as taxation, housing, savings and social security – it can illuminate the nature of the difficulties and help us focus on the central issues. Certainly the alternative of relying on a blend of prejudice and anecdote is no substitute for the discipline of rigorous analysis and careful empirical investigation.

The attack on social science research is part of a wider campaign against academic endeavour, and this is a further major reason for the production of the present volume. The financial position of British universities has worsened dramatically in recent years, and the London School of Economics – with its high proportion of overseas students – has suffered particularly severely. All the royalties from this volume will go to the LSE 1980s Fund, established to help overcome these difficulties, by making scholarships available to students at the School. I am most grateful to my co-authors, and to the holders of the copyright in the essays, who have helped make this possible.

The essays have been reprinted as originally published, apart from minor corrections and editorial amendments. In some cases, there have been subsequent changes in policy, or more recent evidence has become available. The most important of these developments are discussed in the introductory notes to each of the four parts. In the case of one essay – on the measurement of inequality – I have appended a bibliography of the subsequent literature.

Finally, I should like to thank those who have assisted in the production of the essays. At the International Centre for Economics and Related Disciplines at the LSE, Jane Dickson, Prue Hutton and Angela Swain have all been most helpful. Frank Cowell and Tony Shorrocks made a number of useful suggestions for the Bibliography attached to Chapter 1. Jennifer Pinney and Patrick Davis have advised on the arrangements with the 1980s Fund. At Wheatsheaf Books, Edward Elgar and his staff have smoothed the process of publication.

A. B. Atkinson
London School of Economics

April 1982

PART I

INEQUALITY AND MOBILITY

Introduction to Part I

Chapter 1   On The Measurement of Inequality

The measurement of inequality has long concerned writers in the field of personal income distribution. Hugh Dalton, in the preface to *The Inequality of Incomes* (1920), referred to 'the ambiguity of the conception of "inequality" and the need to give it…a more precise definition and a logical measure' ([12], p. viii). This he proceeded to develop in his pioneering article [13] on the measurement of inequality, in which he took issue with earlier writers who had suggested that the position of an economist choosing a measure of inequality was identical to that of the biologist in determining the distribution of physical characteristics. Dalton argued that

this is clearly wrong. For the economist is primarily interested, not in the distribution of income as such, but in the effects of the distribution of income upon the distribution and total amount of economic welfare, which may be derived from income ([13], p. 348).

Dalton's article did not receive the attention which it deserved for many years. Empirical work on income and wealth inequality continued to use summary indicators of inequality, such as the mean deviation or the Gini coefficient, which were statistical in origin rather than derived from considerations of social welfare. It was indeed nearly a half century later that Serge Kolm [21] and I (Chapter 1 in this volume) independently returned to his approach, and argued for a reconsideration of the measurement of inequality. These contributions led in turn to a very substantial literature on the underlying conceptual issues.

Lorenz curves and dominance
Chapter 1, originally published in 1970, sought to develop Dalton's work in two respects. The first concerned the *comparison* of distributions, the idea being that this may place less demand on our knowledge about social values. In order to rank one distribution as 'less unequal' than another, we may need only to agree on a limited range of properties of the social welfare function. This limited agreement may only generate a partial ordering (e.g. we may be able to compare country A with country B, but not with country C), but even that may be an advance. It is here that the result in Chapter 1 on Lorenz dominance is of assistance. This shows that if we consider two distributions, A and B, with the same mean income, then if the Lorenz curve for A lies

everywhere inside that for B, then A gives a higher level of social welfare for all welfare functions which are symmetric, monotonically increasing, additive and strictly concave (the latter two conditions can be weakened to S–concavity – see, for example, Kolm [21], Dasgupta *et al.* [14], and Sen [31]). The fact that the Lorenz curve satisfies this condition means that the share in total income of the bottom x% of the population is greater in A than in B for all values of x. If the mean incomes differ, then the condition can be written in terms of the total income, rather than the *share* of income, received by the bottom x% of the population (Kolm [21]; Rothschild and Stiglitz [30]). The total income concept is referred to by Shorrocks [39] as a 'generalised Lorenz curve'.

The dominance condition given in Chapter 1 serves to rationalise the use of Lorenz curves. It also brings out the limitations on the comparisons which can be made without specifying further properties of the social welfare function. In the case of distributions A and B with the same mean, if the Lorenz curves intersect then we can always find two welfare functions, satisfying the general conditions for the theorem, which rank A and B differently. At this point, a natural way to proceed is to specify additional general properties of the class of welfare functions, and this is the second main way in which Chapter 1 attempted to extend Dalton's approach.

A new measure of inequality
In the second part of Chapter 1, the notion is introduced of 'equally distributed equivalent' income, Y_{EDE}, or the level of income per head which, if equally shared, would generate the same level of social welfare as the observed distribution. A new measure of inequality is then defined, equal to

$$I = 1 - \frac{Y_{EDE}}{\mu} \tag{1}$$

where μ is the mean income. This applies quite generally to any functional form for the social welfare function, but may provide help in narrowing the choice of such forms. In particular, it is suggested in Chapter 1 that we consider the case where the index I is invariant with respect to equal proportionate shifts in income: i.e. it is scale (or mean) independent. Coupled with our earlier assumptions of symmetry, monotonicity and additivity, this implies that the class of measures, I, is of the form:

$$I_\varepsilon = 1 - \left[\sum_i (y_i/\mu)^{1-\varepsilon} f_i \right]^{1/(1-\varepsilon)} \qquad \text{for } \varepsilon > 0 \text{ and } \varepsilon \neq 1 \tag{2}$$

and

$$I_1 = 1 - \prod_i (y_i/\mu)^{f_i} \qquad \text{where } \varepsilon = 1 \tag{3}$$

In these expressions y_i denotes the income of the i-th group, and f_i is the proportion of the population in that group. (The index I_1 is that proposed by Champernowne [8].)

By applying an index like I_ε, we can arrive at a complete ranking of distributions. In this sense it is no different from the conventional summary measures such as the Gini coefficient. However, there is the important difference that it has been reached via a process of considering the desirable properties of a measure of inequality. The assumptions may be debatable (see below), but they are explicit.

The fact that judgements are involved in the choice of measure is brought out by the presence of the parameter ε. We have narrowed consideration to a *class* of measures, but the choice of ε still leaves a great deal of scope for disagreement. Indeed some people have objected to the index I_ε on those very grounds: '[the measure I_ε] includes an additional parameter (ε) for which it is difficult to choose a generally acceptable value. The Gini coefficient, while it may involve an implicit value judgement, avoids this difficulty' (Nicholson [25], p. 91). It scarcely seems desirable to cover up disagreements in this way, not least with a measure whose creator claimed as an advantage for his approach that it was 'applicable not only to incomes and wealth, but to all other quantitative characteristics (economic, demographic, anatomical or physiological)' (Gini [16], p. 124).

At the same time, we must recognise that it is not easy to form a judgement about appropriate values of ε, and it may be helpful to give some intuitive feeling for the implications of different values. Suppose that we consider the following 'mental experiment'. (This mental experiment was described in Atkinson [2]; later it was christened by Okun [26] the 'leaky bucket experiment'.) There are two people, one with twice the income of the other, and the government takes £1 from the richer to transfer £x to the poorer, where £x is less than £1 because of the costs of the transfer. How far can £x fall below £1 before we cease to regard the transfer as desirable? (Clearly if we are at all concerned with inequality, then £x = £1 is desirable.) The answer to the question is one way of calibrating ε. For example, $\varepsilon = 1$ corresponds to stopping at £0.50, and $\varepsilon = 2$ to accepting a transfer of £0.25.

The approach to the measurement of inequality described in Chapter 1 is based on the concept of a welfare function. It should be stressed that the function is defined in terms of individual *incomes*, and not individual *utilities*. In contrast to Dalton's original contribution, there is nothing inherently *utilitarian* in the formulation (in retrospect, it would have been wiser to use a letter other than U in equation (1) in Chapter 1). The analysis is quite consistent with a variety of views about principles of economic justice. For example, the Rawlsian difference principle (Rawls [28]), where inequality is assessed in terms of the position of the least advantaged, is obtained as the limiting case of equation (2) above as $\varepsilon \to \infty$. Nevertheless, not all the principles of justice can be subsumed in this formulation. Most importantly, notions of 'distance' or 'egalitarian' principles need independent treatment. Despite assertions to the contrary (e.g. Okun [26]), the Rawlsian difference principle is not equivalent to egalitarianism. For example, the Rawlsian principle would rank society A with incomes (£6,000 and £25,000) above society B with incomes

(£5,000 and £5,000), whereas the latter may be preferred by those concerned with distance (see Atkinson and Stiglitz [4], p. 341). After all, society A does breach Plato's recommendation that the ratio of the top income to the bottom should not exceed four to one (quoted by Cowell [10], p. 26). For these reasons, I am prepared to go some way towards accepting the criticisms by Sen ([34] and [35]). The social welfare cost of income differences is only part of the story.

Subsequent developments

Since 1970, a great deal has been written on the measurement of inequality, and I have appended to Chapter 1 a bibliography of publications which have subsequently appeared. Although no attempt has been made to cover the field comprehensively, the bibliography contains around 150 items. It is evidently not possible to review all the contributions here. What follows is a selective and highly condensed description of some of the developments.

First, the results have been generalised in several directions. Reference has already been made to the extension of the Lorenz dominance result to symmetric, quasi-concave social welfare functions (or, still more generally, S-concave functions), and to the generalised Lorenz curve.

Secondly, there has been considerable discussion of different properties of the social welfare function. Kolm [22] has investigated the question of scale independence, contrasting the measure (2) above, which is invariant with respect to equal *proportionate* increases, with the index which is invariant with respect to equal *absolute* additions to income:

$$I_\alpha \equiv \frac{1}{\alpha} \log_e \left[\sum_i e^{\alpha(\mu - y_i)} f_i \right] \tag{4}$$

where $\alpha \geq 0$. He refers to this as a 'leftist' measure in contrast to the 'rightist' measure (2), citing in support the events of May 1968. At that time, an equal proportionate increase in pay was felt by radical students in France to have increased inequality. A rather different perspective is provided by a somewhat earlier historical event:

In the House of Commons on 12th September 1931, Sir Austen Chamberlain announced that a shilling a day reduction would be made in the pay of all naval ratings below the rank of a warrant officer. For the general rating this meant a cut of as much as twenty-five per cent. There followed on 15th September the world-startling news that trouble had arisen amongst the sailors of the British Navy, Atlantic Fleet, at Invergordon (Hannington [18], p. 222).

The manifesto of the mutineers made it clear that they were 'quite agreeable to accept a cut which they consider reasonable' (Labour Research, October 1931), but they did not regard it as fair that they should bear a bigger proportionate cut than the officers.

Thirdly, there has been extensive research concerned with a direct axiomatisation of inequality measures: i.e. considering the set of properties which an indicator I should possess. For example, Sen [32] has set out axioms which lead to a ranking of distributions based on the Gini coefficient, the essential feature being that the weight attached to each income is related to the person's rank order in the distribution. The axiomatic approach has been particularly developed in the analysis of the decomposability of inequality measures. This includes decomposition by population sub-groups (Bourguignon [7]; Cowell [11], Shorrocks [37]) and decomposition by income type (Shorrocks [38]). Suppose, in particular, that we consider an inequality index which is continuous, symmetric, non-negative (taking the value zero only where incomes are equal), satisfying a differentiability condition, scale independent with regard to income and population, and which is additively decomposable with respect to population sub-groups. Then it is characterised by:

$$I_c = \frac{1}{c(c-1)}\sum_i f_i \left[(y_i/\mu)^c - 1\right] \qquad \text{for } c \neq 0, 1 \qquad (5)$$

$$= -\sum_i f_i \log(y_i/\mu) \qquad \text{for } c = 0 \qquad (6)$$

$$= \sum_i f_i \frac{y_i}{\mu} \log\left(\frac{y_i}{\mu}\right) \qquad \text{for } c = 1 \qquad (7)$$

This class, referred to as the 'generalised entropy' class, includes (half) the square of the coefficient of variation ($c = 2$) and the Theil entropy measure ($c = 1$); the measures I_ε are monotonic transforms of I_c where $c < 1$.

Finally, reference should be made to the related literature on the measurement of poverty. In a pioneering paper, Sen [33] has pointed to the inadequacy of conventional measures of poverty, such as the head count or the poverty gap. To simply count the number of people below the poverty line is to ignore the extent of income short-fall; the income-gap considers only the aggregate short-fall, and not how it is distributed. He goes on to provide an axiomatic treatment of a poverty measure, based on rank order weights. The resulting measure is:

$$P = H[I + (1-I)G] \qquad (8)$$

where H is the proportion in poverty, I the average income short-fall expressed as a percentage of the poverty line, and G is the Gini coefficient of the distribution of income among the poor. The choice of rank order weights is debatable – see, for example, Clark, Hemming and Ulph [9] – but the issues raised are clearly important. We need, for example, to clarify the relation between measures of poverty and measures of inequality. Unless government objectives are assumed to be lexicographic, it is necessary to weigh concern about poverty with considerations of inequality.

Chapter 2   Multi-Dimensioned Inequality

One development of the literature on measuring inequality is concerned with the extension to more than one dimension, and this is the subject of Chapter 2, written jointly with François Bourguignon.

This raises once again the question of the raw ingredients for social judgements. It has been explained that the social welfare function of Chapter 1 is defined over individual incomes, not utilities, and the same is true in Chapter 2. The social judgement is based on the vector $\underset{\sim}{x}^i$ enjoyed by household i, and not on a utility function $U(\underset{\sim}{x}^i)$ (which would reduce the problem again to a single dimension). We are assuming no information about individual i's relative valuation of the different goods. This is an extreme situation, but one which may arise in a number of cases, including those where the government may reject private preferences (e.g. with merit goods), or where private preferences cannot readily be inferred (e.g. with respect to life expectancy).

The analysis in Chapter 2 is concerned with the development of *dominance* conditions, and in this sense may be seen as an extension of the first part of Chapter 1. (It may, incidentally, be noted that the covariance analogue of the Lorenz curve is of the 'generalised' type.) The construction of *measures*, analogous to I_ε, is touched on (equation (18)), but will be the subject of further work.

The dominance results as developed in Chapter 2 relate to the situation where $\underset{\sim}{x}$ has two dimensions, but even this case has a number of applications. The example given in the chapter is that where one variable is income, and the other is life expectancy. Although there is a substantial literature attempting to measure private valuation of life, this seems an example where social judgements may well override individual values. (See the discussion in the volume edited by Krelle and Shorrocks [23].)

A second potential application is to the distribution of income and the provision of public goods, where access to the latter varies across the population (e.g. by region). Consideration in terms of the social valuation of public goods, and their complementarity or substitutability for private consumption, would be an alternative approach to that based on estimates of the private value placed on public goods, as proposed originally by Aaron and McGuire [1].

Yet another application is where the variables are income, Y, and an indicator of needs, N. There are two common approaches to the treatment of needs. On the one hand, some investigators take readily observed characteristics, such as family size, and assume a simple valuation function, such as Y/N. This provides straightforward answers. Other writers emphasise that many aspects of need are unobservable, and conclude that little can be said. The approach adopted here allows intermediate positions to be adopted. We may, for example, have an observed index of need, but wish to consider a general class of valuation functions. The results given in Chapter 2 provide insight into the key properties. Alternatively, we may suppose that only certain features of the distribution of needs are known, and, by an extension of the results, seek to draw conclusions about the consequences of changes in the distribution of income.

Chapter 3 Economic Mobility

The application of the results on multi-dimensioned inequality which prompted my original interest in the subject was that to the measurement of mobility between generations. Suppose that X_1 denotes the income of consumption of generation 1, and X_2 that of the next generation. Of course, the income of one generation may enter the utility function of another (either older or younger), but there may be good reasons why the social valuation differs. It is on this interpretation that I concentrate in Chapter 3, written for a volume in honour of Jan Pen; the aim of the essay being to take up Pen's challenge of building a bridge between the figures on vertical mobility and those on income distribution (the latter subject being one in which Pen has made substantial advances).

The fact that the social valuation depends on the incomes of two or more generations does not in itself mean that the degree of mobility affects social welfare. Where the social welfare function is additive, mobility is irrelevant (Markandya [24]). It is solely the distribution within each generation which is of concern (the 'marginal' distributions, not the transition matrix). But if, for example, we allow concave transformations of the welfare function, then the degree of correlation of good or bad fortune across generations becomes relevant. We need to consider the extent of mobility.

The issue of the measurement of mobility has been much discussed in the statistical and sociological literature, and Bartholomew [5] and Boudon [6] provide reviews of this research. The discussion has however tended to concentrate on the construction of summary measures of mobility and examination of their properties. The same applies to the interesting axiomatic treatment of measures of economic mobility developed by Shorrocks [36]. The approach in Chapter 3 differs in that it is concerned with the development of dominance conditions. This line of attack can scarcely come as a surprise, given Chapters 1 and 2, but it provides considerable insight.

The basic question may be posed in terms of transition matrices. In what circumstances can we rank one matrix, A, relative to another, B, for all social valuation functions in a specified class? As in Chapters 1 and 2, this generates a partial ordering, and the extent of the ordering increases as we impose further conditions on the social valuation function.

The results in action are illustrated by the data collected in the course of the follow-up study of the families interviewed in the 1950 Rowntree survey of York. This follow-up, carried out jointly with Alan Maynard and Christopher Trinder, collected information on the earnings of the second generation, and their husbands and wives, to be compared with the earnings of the father in 1950. (The data, and their limitations, are discussed in Atkinson, Maynard and Trinder [3].) Table 1 shows the estimated transition proportions, where fathers and sons/sons-in-law are ranked according to their position in the national earnings distribution. How can the degree of mobility for fathers and sons be compared with that for fathers and sons-in-law? In Table 2 we show the matrix calculated by taking the differences between the individual transition proportions and cumulating from the top left-hand corner. This matrix, which corresponds to $\alpha - \alpha^*$ in Chapter 3, contains both positive and

Table 1 *Transitions between earnings ranges: Fathers and sons and fathers sons-in-law*

| | | Sons by range of national distribution | | | | |
		Bottom 20%	4	Middle 20%	2	Top 20%
Fathers by	Bottom 20%	44.9	10.3	14.1	17.9	12.8
range of	2	26.6	22.3	22.8	15.3	13.0
national	Middle 20%	12.2	29.7	17.6	24.3	16.2
distribution	4	16.2	21.6	21.6	16.2	24.4
	Top 20%	0.1	16.1	23.9	26.3	33.6
		Sons-in-law by range of national distribution				
		Bottom 20%	4	Middle 20%	2	Top 20%
Fathers by	Bottom 20%	32.7	42.8	10.2	10.2	4.1
range of	2	30.8	21.3	26.7	17.1	4.1
national	Middle 20%	16.9	22.4	32.6	16.9	11.2
distribution	4	19.6	13.5	25.7	9.8	31.4
	Top 20%	0	0	4.8	46.0	49.2

Notes: 1 The data are drawn from Atkinson, Maynard and Trinder ([3], Tables 6.1 and 6.3), and relate to hourly earnings in 1975–8 (adjusted to April 1977) in the case of sons/sons-in-law, weekly earnings in 1950 in the case of fathers. There are 373 observations for sons, and 335 for sons-in-law.

2 The transition proportions for the top 20% are obtained as residuals by imposing the condition that the column sums add to unity. In the case of the sons-in-law, this led to negative entries in two cases, and the matrix has been adjusted by transformations of the type (20) in Chapter 3, tending to shift weight away from the diagonal.

negative elements. It does not, therefore satisfy the condition for first degree dominance: but it does help clarify the differences. The matrix in Table 2 is largely negative, implying that if the social welfare function embodies a preference for mobility (it belongs to class U^-), this is in general higher for sons. At the same time, the 'advantage' for the sons-in-law is concentrated at the bottom (of the distribution), and social valuation functions giving sufficient weight to the lowest ranges will always be convinced by the fact that a smaller proportion of sons-in-law are estimated to stay in the bottom 20%. (The term 'estimated' should be emphasised, and the use of the data here is intended only to be illustrative.)

Chapter 4   Inequality of Opportunity

Economic mobility is discussed in Chapter 3 in terms of its implications for social welfare, but this is not the only reason why the extent of mobility may be of concern. A major reason for investigating occupational mobility has indeed been its relation with inequality of opportunity, and this is the subject of Chapter 4.

Equality of opportunity is a concept which occurs frequently in public debate, and it is widely accepted as a principle of justice: 'not many would

Table 2 *Difference between transition proportions for sons and sons-in-law cumulated from bottom 20%*

| | | Sons/sons-in-law | | | | |
		Bottom 20%		Middle 20%	4	Top 20%
	Bottom 20%	12.2	− 20.3	− 16.4	− 8.7	0
	2	8.0	− 23.5	− 23.5	− 17.6	0
Fathers	Middle 20%	3.3	− 20.9	− 35.9	− 22.6	0
	4	− 0.1	− 16.2	− 35.3	− 15.6	0
	Top 20%	0	0	0	0	0

Note: Constructed from Table 1.

argue that . . . the criterion of equality of opportunity is ethically invalid. There are some, indeed, who defend it as the paramount criterion of justice' (Gordon [17], p. 108). Yet its meaning has not been very fully analysed. It is often suggested that inequality of opportunity is a more straightforward principle than inequality of outcome, and this is one reason why writers, such as those referred to by Gordon, have given it primacy. But in Chapter 4 it is argued that the implementation of the concept of unequal opportunity is more complex than appears at first sight.

Of particular interest is the relation between the goals of reducing inequality of opportunity and inequality of outcome. Are measures to estimate the former consistent with reducing inequality of results? Some writers believe that the two go in tandem. Okun, for example, is 'confident that greater equality of opportunity would produce greater equality of income' (quoted in Chapter 4). In contrast, others see the goals as potentially in conflict:

they are to a considerable degree inharmonious with one another. In a world where people differ in their natural endowments or their preferences, or both, equality of opportunity will lead to inequality of resulting states (such as income); while if we insist on producing equality of resulting states, we will prevent the working of equality of opportunity (Gordon [17], p. 111).

The aim of Chapter 4 is to clarify these issues. To this end it takes a highly simplified distributional model. No particular claims are made for the realism of the assumptions (the modelling of the distribution is discussed further in Part II), but the use of explicit models of this type helps define more precisely the content of ethical judgements. By confronting principles – such as equality of opportunity – with concrete situations, we may be able to contribute to their development. This interaction between moral philosophy, on the one hand, and economic applications, on the other, has been a feature of much of modern welfare economics, and has enriched both. (This interaction is similarly illustrated by the optimum taxation literature in Part III.)

Chapter 5 Horizontal Equity

This chapter on horizontal equity and the distribution of the tax burden, written for a volume in honour of Joseph Pechman, could have been placed here, or in Part III on the design of taxation. The issue of horizontal equity, stressed in the public finance literature to which Pechman has made such a distinguished contribution, has been discussed in the context of the optimum design of taxation by Atkinson and Stiglitz (Chapter 11 below and [4]), Feldstein [15], and others. There are however a number of respects in which the analysis is parallel to that in Chapters 1–4. In particular, the primary aim is to clarify the meaning of a concept which is in widespread use, and to bring out the relationship with equality of outcome.

The approach adopted in Chapter 5, working through the 'tax mobility matrices', has evident similarity with that in Chapters 2 and 3. The treatment can indeed by interpreted in terms of two-variable inequality measurement, where the social valuation depends on the relationship between gross and net income. This leads naturally in the direction of partial orderings, with dominance results, an approach which has been developed by Plotnick [27]. Measures of horizontal inequity giving complete orderings have been proposed by, among others, Johnson and Mayer [19], Rosen [29] and King [20].

References

[1] Aaron, H. and McGuire, M. (1970), 'Public goods and income distribution', *Econometrica*, vol. 38, pp. 907–20.
[2] Atkinson, A. B. (1973), 'Non-technical addendum', in *Wealth, Income and Inequality*, Penguin, London.
[3] Atkinson, A. B., Maynard, A. K. and Trinder, C. G. (forthcoming), *Parents and Children*, London, Heinemann
[4] Atkinson, A. B. and Stiglitz, J. E. (1980), *Lectures on Public Economics*, London and New York, McGraw-Hill.
[5] Bartholomew, D. J. (1973), *Stochastic Models for Social Processes* (2nd edn), London, Wiley.
[6] Boudon, R. (1973), *Mathematical Structures of Social Mobility*, Amsterdam, Elsevier.
[7] Bourguignon, F. (1979), 'Decomposable income inequality measures', *Econometrica*, vol. 47, pp. 901–20.
[8] Champernowne, D. G. (1973), *The Distribution of Income Between Persons*, London, Cambridge University Press.
[9] Clark, S., Hemming, R. C. L. and Ulph, D. (1981), 'On indices for the measurement of poverty', *Economic Journal*, vol. 91, pp. 515–26.
[10] Cowell, F. A. (1977), *Measuring Inequality*, Deddington, Philip Allan.
[11] Cowell, F. A. (1980), 'On the structure of additive inequality measures', *Review of Economic Studies*, vol. 47, pp. 521–31.
[12] Dalton, H. (1920a), *The Inequality of Incomes*, London, Routledge.
[13] Dalton, H. (1920b), 'The measurement of the inequality of incomes', *Economic Journal*, vol. 30, pp. 348–61.
[14] Dasgupta, P., Sen, A. K. and Starrett, D. (1973), 'Notes on the measurement of inequality', *Journal of Economic Theory*, vol. 6, pp. 180–7.
[15] Feldstein, M. S. (1976), 'On the theory of tax reform', *Journal of Public Economics*, vol. 6, pp. 77–104.
[16] Gini, C. (1921), 'Measurement of inequality of incomes', *Economic Journal*, vol. 31, pp. 124–6.
[17] Gordon, S. (1980), *Welfare, Justice and Freedom*, New York, Columbia University Press.
[18] Hannington, W. (1977), *Unemployed Struggles 1919/1936*, Wakefield, EP Publishing.
[19] Johnson, S. B. and Mayer, T. (1962), 'An extension of Sidgwick's equity principle', *Quarterly Journal of Economics*, vol. 76, pp. 454–63.

[20] King, M. A. (forthcoming), 'An index of inequality: with applications to horizontal equity and social mobility', *Econometrica*.

[21] Kolm, S-Ch. (1969), 'The optimal production of social justice', in J. Margolis and H. Guitton (eds.), *Public Economics*, London, Macmillan.

[22] Kolm, S-Ch. (1976), 'Unequal inequalities', *Journal of Economic Theory*, vol. 12, pp. 416–42, and vol. 13, pp. 82–111.

[23] Krelle, W. and Shorrocks, A. F. (eds.) (1978), *Personal Income Distribution*, Amsterdam, North-Holland.

[24] Markandya, A. (1980), 'Toward a theory of intergenerational economic mobility', Discussion paper 13, University College, London.

[25] Nicholson, J. L. (1974), 'The distribution and redistribution of income in the United Kingdom', in D. Wedderburn (ed.), *Poverty, Inequality and Class Structure*, London, Cambridge University Press.

[26] Okun, A. M. (1975), *Equality and Efficiency*, Washington, DC, Brookings Institution.

[27] Plotnick, R. D. (forthcoming), 'The concept and measurement of horizontal inequity', *Journal of Public Economics*.

[28] Rawls, J. (1972), *A Theory of Justice*, London, Oxford University Press.

[29] Rosen, H. S. (1978), 'An approach to the study of income, utility and horizontal equity', *Quarterly Journal of Economics*, vol. 92, pp. 306–22.

[30] Rothschild, M. and Stiglitz, J. E. (1973), 'Some further results on the measurement of inequality', *Journal of Economic Theory*, vol. 6, pp. 188–204.

[31] Sen, A. K. (1973), *On Economic Inequality*, Oxford, Clarendon Press.

[32] Sen, A. K. (1974), 'Informational bases of alternative welfare approaches', *Journal of Public Economics*, vol. 3, pp. 387–403.

[33] Sen, A. K. (1976), 'Poverty: an ordinal approach to measurement', *Econometrica*, vol. 44, pp. 219–31.

[34] Sen, A. K. (1978), 'Ethical measurement of inequality: some difficulties', in W. Krelle and A. F. Shorrocks (eds.), *Personal Income Distribution*, Amsterdam, North-Holland.

[35] Sen, A. K. (1980), 'Description as choice', *Oxford Economic Papers*, vol. 32, pp. 353–69.

[36] Shorrocks, A. F. (1978), 'The measurement of mobility', *Econometrica*, vol. 46, pp. 1013–24.

[37] Shorrocks, A. F. (1980), 'The class of additively decomposable inequality measures', *Econometrica*, vol. 48, pp. 613–25.

[38] Shorrocks, A. F. (1982), 'Inequality decomposition by factor components', *Econometrica*, vol. 50, pp. 193–211.

[39] Shorrocks, A. F. (forthcoming), 'Ranking income distributions', *Economica*.

1 On the Measurement of Inequality*

1 Introduction

Measures of inequality are used by economists to answer a wide range of questions. Is the distribution of income more equal than it was in the past? Are underdeveloped countries characterised by greater inequality than advanced countries? Do taxes lead to greater equality in the distribution of income or wealth? However, despite the wide use of these measures, relatively little attention has been given to the conceptual problems involved in the measurement of inequality and there have been few contributions to the theoretical foundations of the subject. In this chapter, I try to clarify some of the basic issues, to examine the properties of the measures that are commonly employed, and to discuss a possible new approach. In the course of this, I draw on the parallel with the formally similar problem of measuring risk in the theory of decision-making under uncertainty and make use of recent results in this field.[1]

The problem with which we are concerned is basically that of comparing two frequency distributions $f(y)$ of an attribute y which for convenience I shall refer to as income. The conventional approach in nearly all empirical work is to adopt some summary statistic of inequality such as the variance, the coefficient of variation or the Gini coefficient – with no very explicit reason being given for preferring one measure rather than another. As, however, was pointed out by Dalton sixty years ago in his pioneering article [3], underlying any such measure is some concept of social welfare and it is with this concept that we should be concerned. He argued that we should approach the question by considering directly the form of the social welfare function to be employed. If we follow him in assuming that this would be an additively separable and symmetric function of individual incomes, then we would rank distributions according to[2]

$$W \equiv \int_0^{\bar{y}} U(y)f(y)dy. \tag{1}$$

My main concern in this chapter is to explore the implications of adopting this approach and its relationship to the conventional summary measures of inequality.

* Reprinted from *Journal of Economic Theory*, Vol. 2, 3, September 1970.

It may be helpful to distinguish two objectives that we may have in seeking to compare distributions. First, we may want simply to obtain a ranking of distributions – to be able to say, for example, that post-tax income is more equally distributed than pre-tax income. On the other hand, we may want to go further than this and to quantify the difference in inequality between two distributions. In particular, we may want to separate 'shifts' in the distribution from changes in its shape and confine the term inequality to the latter aspect. Now it is clear that the conventional summary measures are chiefly directed at the second of these problems. For the economist, however, it is more natural to begin by considering the ordinal problem of obtaining a ranking of distributions, since this may require less agreement about the form of the social welfare function.

2   The Ranking of Distributions

In order to arrive at any ranking of distributions, we clearly have to make some assumption about the form of the function $U(y)$. As a first step, let us consider what can be said if we restrict our attention to the class of functions $U(y)$ that are increasing and concave – which seem quite acceptable requirements. Under what conditions can we then rank two distributions without specifying any further the form of the function $U(y)$?

Fortunately, at this point we can draw on recent work on the economically unrelated but formally similar problem of decision-making under uncertainty. As should be quite clear, ranking income distributions according to (1) is formally identical to ranking probability distributions $f(y)$ according to expected utility, and the assumption that $U(y)$ is concave is equivalent to assuming that a person is risk averse. Since the field of decision-making under uncertainty has attracted more attention recently than that of measuring inequality, I intend to exploit the parallel by making use of the results that have been reached. In particular, a number of authors have proved the following result:[3]

A distribution $f(y)$ will be preferred to another distribution $f^*(y)$ according to criterion (1) for all $U(y)$ $(U' > 0, U^* \leqslant 0)$ *if and only if*:

$$\int_0^z [F(y) - F^*(y)] \, dy \leqslant 0 \qquad \text{for all } z, \qquad 0 \leqslant z \leqslant \bar{y}$$

and

$$F(y) \neq F^*(y) \qquad \text{for some } y \tag{2}$$

where $F(y) = \int_0^y f(x) dx$.

This condition (2) provides the answer to our question, but as it stands it is very difficult to interpret. It can, however, easily be shown to have a straightforward interpretation in terms of the familiar Lorenz curve – an interpretation which has been overlooked by those working in the field of uncertainty. Let us suppose for the moment that we are comparing distributions with the same mean – as when considering a redistribution of a given total income. The Lorenz curve (which shows the proportion of total income received by the bottom $x\%$) is defined implicitly by:

$$\phi(F)=\frac{1}{\mu}\int_0^{y_1} yf(y)dy, \qquad F=\int_0^{y_1} f(y)dy,$$

where μ denotes the mean of the distribution.

Integrating the expression for ϕ by parts, we obtain:

$$\mu\phi[F(y_1)]=y_1F(y_1)-\int_0^{y_1} F(y)dy. \qquad (3)$$

If we now compare the Lorenz curves for two distributions $f(y)$ and $f^*(y)$ at a point $\bar{F}=F(y_1)=F^*(y_1^*)$, then:

$$\mu[\phi(\bar{F})-\phi^*(\bar{F})]=[y_1-y_1^*]\bar{F}-\left[\int_0^{y_1} F(y)dy-\int_0^{y_1^*} F^*(y)dy\right]$$

$$=-\int_0^{y_1^*}(F(y)-F^*(y))dy$$

$$+\left[\int_{y_1}^{y_1^*} F(y)dy-(y_1^*-y_1)F(y_1)\right]$$

Applying the first mean-value theorem, the second term is positive, so that it follows that condition (2) implies that the Lorenz curve corresponding to $f(y)$ will lie everywhere above that corresponding to $f^*(y)$. From (3), we can also write:

$$-\int_0^{y_1}[F(y)-F^*(y)]dy =\mu[\phi(F\{y_1\})-\phi^*(F^*\{y_1\})]-y_1[F(y_1)-F^*(y_1)].$$

But from the definition of the Lorenz curve, $\mu\phi(\bar{F})=\int_0^F y\,dF$ so that:

$$-\int_0^{y_1}[F(y)-F^*(y)]dy$$

$$=\mu[\phi(F\{y_1\})-\phi^*(F\{y_1\})]+\left[\int_{F^*(y_1)}^{F(y_1)} y\,dF^*-y_1(F-F^*)\right]$$

Again applying the first mean-value theorem to the second term, we can see that it is positive, so that if the Lorenz curve for $f(y)$ lies above that for $f^*(y)$ for all F, then condition (2) will be satisfied. We have shown, therefore, that, when comparing distributions with the same mean, condition (2) is equivalent to the requirement that the Lorenz curves do not intersect. We can deduce that if the Lorenz curves of two distributions do not intersect, then we can judge between them without needing to agree on the form of $U(y)$ (except that it be increasing and concave); but that if they cross, we can always find two functions that will rank them differently. If we consider distributions with different means, then condition (2) clearly implies that the mean of $f(y)$ can be no lower than that of $f^*(y)$. Conversely, if $\mu \geqslant \mu^*$ and the Lorenz curve of $f(y)$ lies inside that of $f^*(y)$ then (2) will hold.

In the literature on decision-making under uncertainty it has been shown that there are a number of conditions equivalent to (2), and by making use of one of these equivalences we can throw further light on the problem of ranking income distributions. In his article, Dalton argued that any ranking of distributions should satisfy what he called *the principle of transfers*: If we make a transfer of income d from a person with income y_1 to a person with a lower income y_2 (where $y_2 \leqslant y_1 - d$), then the new distribution should be preferred. In terms of Figure 1, the distribution $f(y)$ should be preferred to $f^*(y)$. This

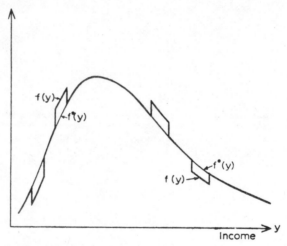

Figure 1   *The principle of transfers.*

principle of transfers turns out, however, to be identical to the concept of a mean preserving spread introduced by Rothschild and Stiglitz.[4] Now they have shown that where two distributions satisfy condition (2), then $f^*(y)$ could have been reached from $f(y)$ to any desired degree of approximation by a sequence of mean preserving spreads, and the converse is also true (two distributions differing by a mean preserving spread satisfy (2)). (The effect of a mean preserving spread on the Lorenz curve is illustrated in Figure 2.) This gives, therefore, an alternative interpretation of condition (2): a necessary and sufficient condition for us to be able to rank two distributions independently of the utility function (other than that it be increasing and concave) is that one

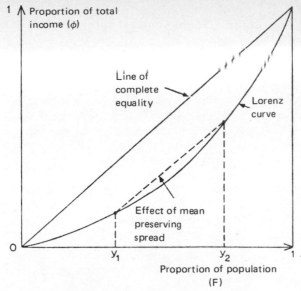

Figure 2   *Effect of mean-preserving spread on Lorenz curve.*

can be obtained from the other by redistributing income from the richer to the poorer. That the concavity of $U(y)$ is sufficient to guarantee that the principle of transfers holds is hardly surprising; however, it is not so obvious that this is the widest class of distributions that can be ranked without any further restriction of the form of $U(y)$.

3   Complete Ranking and Equally Distributed Equivalent Income

The results of section 2 demonstrate that we cannot obtain a complete ordering of distributions according to (1) unless we are prepared to specify more precisely the form of the function $U(y)$. It is in fact clear that for a complete ranking we need to specify $U(y)$ up to a (monotonic) linear transformation. In the rest of this chapter, I consider the implications of alternative social welfare functions and their relation to the summary measures that are commonly used.

The specification of the function $U(y)$ will provide a ranking of all distributions; it will also, however, allow us to meet the second objective of quantifying the degree of inequality. Dalton, for example, suggested that we should use as a measure of inequality the ratio of the actual level of social welfare to that which would be achieved if income were equally distributed:

$$\frac{\int_0^{\bar{y}} U(y)f(y)\,dy}{U(\mu)} \tag{4}$$

This normalisation is not, however, invariant with respect to linear transformations of the function $U(y)$; for example, in the case of the logarithmic utility function, Dalton's measure is:

$$\frac{\int_0^y \log(y)f(y)\,dy + c}{\log(\mu) + c}$$

the value of which clearly depends on c. So that although two people might agree that the social welfare function should be logarithmic – and hence agree on the ranking of distributions – their measures of inequality would only coincide if they agreed also about the value of c. For this reason, the measure suggested by Dalton is not very useful.[5]

We can, however, obtain a measure of inequality that is invariant with respect to linear transformations by introducing the concept of the *equally distributed equivalent* level of income (y_{EDE}) or the level of income per head which if equally distributed would give the same level of social welfare as the present distribution,[6] that is:

$$U(y_{EDE}) \int_0^y f(y)\,dy = \int_0^y U(y)f(y)\,dy.$$

We can then define as our new measure of inequality:

$$I = 1 - \frac{y_{EDE}}{\mu}$$

or 1 minus the ratio of the equally distributed equivalent level of income to the mean of the actual distribution. If I falls, then the distribution has become more equal – we would require a higher level of equally distributed income (relative to the mean) to achieve the same level of social welfare as the actual distribution. The measure I has, of course, the convenient property of lying between 0 (complete equality) and 1 (complete inequality). Moreover, this new measure has considerable intuitive appeal. If $I = 0.3$, for example, it allows us to say that if incomes were equally distributed, then we should need only 70% of the present national income to achieve the same level of social welfare (according to the particular social welfare function). Or we could say that a certain plan for redistributing income would raise social welfare by an amount equivalent to an increase of 5% in equally distributed income. This facilitates comparison of the gains from redistribution with the costs that it might impose – such as any disincentive effect of income taxation – and with the benefits from alternative economic measures. Finally, it should be clear that the concept of equally distributed equivalent income is closely related to that of a risk premium or certainty equivalent in the theory of decision-making under uncertainty. y_{EDE} is simply the analogue of the certainty equivalent and I is equal to the proportional risk premium as defined by Pratt [11].[7] This parallel conveniently allows us once more to borrow results.

Before examining the implications of specific measures, it may be helpful to discuss some of the general properties that we should like such measures to possess. In particular, I should like to consider the relationship between inequality *per se* and general shifts in the distribution. Nearly all the measures conventionally used are concerned to measure inequality independently of the mean level of incomes so that if the distribution of income in country A is simply a scaled-up version of that in country B, $f_A(y) = f_B(\theta y)$, then we should regard them as characterised by the same degree of inequality. Now suppose that we were to require that the equally distributed measure I were invariant with respect to such proportional shifts, so that we could consider the degree of inequality independently of the mean level of incomes. Then by applying the results of Pratt [11], Arrow [2], and others, we can see that this requirement (which may be referred to as *constant (relative) inequality-aversion*) implies that $U(y)$ has the form:

$$U(y) = A + B\frac{y^{1-\varepsilon}}{1-\varepsilon} \qquad \varepsilon \neq 1$$

and (5)

$$U(y) = \log_e (y) \qquad \varepsilon = 1$$

where we require $\varepsilon \geqslant 0$ for concavity. On the other hand, it might quite reasonably be argued that as the general level of incomes rises we are more concerned about inequality – that I should rise with proportional additions to incomes. In other words, the social welfare function should exhibit *increasing (relative) inequality-aversion*. In that event, the measure of inequality I can only be interpreted with reference to the mean of the distribution.

The previous paragraph was concerned with the effect of equal *proportional* additions to income; we may also consider the effect of equal *absolute* additions to incomes (denoted by θ). We can then define a measure of *absolute* inequality-aversion (which is again parallel to the measure of risk-aversion in the theory of uncertainty):[8] Absolute inequality-aversion is increasing/constant/decreasing according as:

$$\partial y_{\text{EDE}}/\partial\theta \text{ is less than/equal to/greater than 1}$$

It has been argued by a number of writers that equal absolute additions to all incomes should reduce inequality; if one looks at the effect on I, this has the sign of:

$$(1-I) - \frac{\partial y_{\text{EDE}}}{\partial\theta}$$

From this we can see that I may fall with equal absolute additions to income even if absolute inequality-aversion is increasing.

4   Specific Measures of Inequality

So far I have discussed general principles without considering specific measures of inequality. In this section, I examine some of the implications of different measures, beginning with the conventional summary statistics.

The conventional summary measures
The measures most commonly used in empirical work include the following: (a) the variance, V^2; (b) the coefficient of variation, V/μ; (c) the relative mean deviation, $\int_0^y |y - \mu| f(y) dy$; (d) the Gini coefficient, $1/2\mu\int_0^y [yF(y) - \mu\phi(y)] f(y) dy$; (e) the standard deviation of logarithms, the square root of $\int_0^y [\log(y/\bar{\mu})]^2 f(y) dy$, where $\bar{\mu}$ is the geometric mean.

The implications of the earlier discussion for the use of these summary measures can be seen as follows. If we consider distributions with the same mean and apply one of the measures (a)–(d), then we are guaranteed to arrive at the same ranking as with an arbitrary concave social welfare function if and only if condition (2) is satisfied.[9] For example, if condition (2) holds (and the distributions have the same mean), then the Gini coefficient will give the same ranking as any concave social welfare function (this is clearly the case since it represents the area between the Lorenz curve and the line of complete equality); but if (2) does not hold, we can always find a function $U(y)$ such that the distribution with the *higher* Gini coefficient is preferred. With these measures it follows, therefore, that they will give the same ranking of distributions satisfying (2), but where this condition is not met, they may give conflicting results.[10] Dalton suggested that 'in most practical cases' the measures would in fact give the same ranking, so that we could rely on the 'corroboration of several'. However, as the work of Yntema [16], Ranadive [12] and others has demonstrated, this expectation is not borne out and in practice the measures give quite different rankings. Much of the early literature was in fact concerned with the problem of choosing between the different summary measures, and such properties were discussed as ease of computation, ease of interpretation, the range of variation, and whether they required information about the entire distribution. However, as I have emphasised earlier, the central issue clearly concerns the underlying assumption about the form of the social welfare function that is implicit in the choice of a particular summary measure. It is, therefore, on this aspect that I shall concentrate here.

The first issue is one discussed in the previous section – the dependence of the measures on the mean income. With the exception of the variance, all the measures listed above are defined relative to the mean, so that they are unaffected by equal proportional increases in all incomes. In the case of the variance, we know from the theory of uncertainty that ranking distributions according to mean and variance is equivalent to assuming that $U(y)$ is quadratic, and that this in turn implies increasing relative and absolute inequality-aversion. As argued earlier, increasing relative inequality-aversion may be a quite acceptable property of the social welfare function. Increasing absolute inequality-aversion, however, may be less reasonable: It means that equal absolute increases in all incomes cause the equally distributed equivalent income to rise by less than the same amount. While the objections to this property are less strong than the corresponding objections in the uncertainty case, it may be grounds for rejecting the quadratic. In any event, it is the mean independent measures (b) (c) that have received most attention, and for this reason I shall concentrate on them here.

The second point is one made by Dalton, but apparently neglected since then. He argued that if we make a strictly positive transfer from a richer person to a poorer person, this ought to lead to a strictly positive reduction in the index of inequality (and not merely leave it unchanged). If we accept this requirement, which seems quite reasonable, it provides grounds for rejecting measures which are not *strictly* concave – in particular the relative mean deviation – as well as other measures such as the interquartile range. As is clear from the definition of the relative mean deviation, it is unaffected by transfers between people on the same side of the mean. This is illustrated by Figure 3.

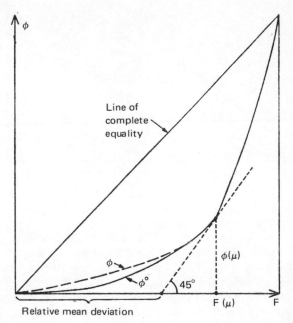

Figure 3 *Effect of transfers on the relative mean deviation* (*Note: the relative mean deviation is given by* $2[F(\mu) - \phi(\mu)]$).

The distributions characterised by ϕ and $\phi°$ have the same relative mean deviation, although ϕ would be preferred for all strictly concave utility functions (and has a lower Gini coefficient). This view is not, however, shared by two recent supporters of the relative mean deviation – Elteto and Frigyes [4]. In their article, these authors put forward three measures which are simple transforms of the relative mean deviation and argue that these are preferable to the Gini coefficient. They suggest, in particular, that their measure is more 'sensitive' than the Gini coefficient because it has a wider range of variation, but ignore the fact that it is completely insensitive to transfers between people on the same side of the mean.[11]

The three remaining measures – the coefficient of variation, the Gini coefficient, and the standard deviation of logarithms – are sensitive to transfers at all income levels; however, it is important to examine the *relative* sensitivity of the measures at different income levels. Suppose that the Lorenz curves for two distributions intersect once (as shown in Figure 4) so that country A has a

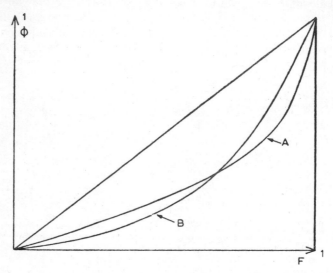

Figure 4.

more equal distribution at the bottom and country B is more equal at the top. Now it is clear that we could redistribute income in A in such a way that the distribution was the same as in B. We should (broadly) take some from the poor and give it to the middle income class and take some from the rich and give it to those in the middle. In this way, we can see the choice between distributions A and B in terms of the weight attached to redistributive transfers at different points of the income distribution. If we are ranking distributions according to $\int_0^{\bar{y}} V(y) f(y) \, dy$, then the effect of an infinitesimal redistribution from a person with income y_1 to a person with income $y_1 - h$ is given by $V'(y_1 - h) - V'(y_1)$. In the case of the coefficient of variation, this would be constant for all y_1. The effect of a transfer would be independent of the income level at which it was made. If, therefore, one wanted to give more weight to transfers at the lower end of the distribution than at the top, this measure would not be appropriate. In the case of the standard deviation of logarithms, $V' \sim \{\log (y/\bar{\mu})\}/(y/\bar{\mu})$, which does attach more weight to transfers at the lower end, but which also of course ceases to be concave at high incomes. Finally, in

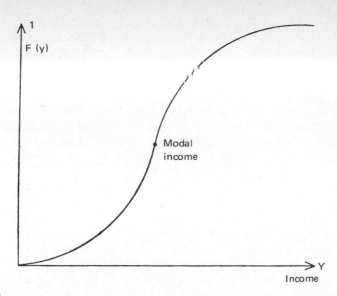

Figure 5.

the case of the Gini coefficient the effect of an infinitesimal transfer can be shown to be proportional to $F(y_1) - F(y_1 - h)$.[12] This suggests that for typical distributions more weight would be attached to transfers in the centre of the distribution than at the tails (see Figure 5). It is not clear that such a weighting would necessarily accord with social values.

The results of this examination of five of the conventional summary measures have shown that:

(a) The use of the variance implies increasing inequality-aversion; all the other measures imply constant (relative) inequality-aversion;
(b) The relative mean deviation is not strictly concave and is not sensitive to transfers on the same side of the mean;
(c) The coefficient of variation attaches equal weight to transfers at different income levels, the Gini coefficient attaches more weight to transfers affecting middle income classes and the standard deviation weights transfers at the lower end more heavily.

The social welfare function approach
In the previous section, I examined the implicit assumptions about the form of the social welfare function embodied in the conventional summary measures and suggested that a number of these assumptions were unlikely to command wide support. In any case, it seems more reasonable to approach the question directly by considering the social welfare function that we should like to employ rather than indirectly through these summary statistical measures. While there is undoubtedly a wide range of disagreement about the form that the social welfare function should take, this direct approach allows us to reject at once those that attract no supporters, and also serves to emphasise that *any*

measure of inequality involves judgements about social welfare.

The social welfare function considered here is assumed to be of the form (1) that we have been discussing throughout; that is, it is symmetric and additively separable in individual incomes – although this is, of course, restrictive. Now we have seen that nearly all the conventional measures are defined relative to the mean of the distribution, so that they are invariant with respect to proportional shifts. If we want the equally distributed equivalent measure to have this property, then this restricts us still further to the class of homothetic functions (5), which in the case of discrete distributions imply a measure:

$$I = 1 - \left[\sum_i \left(\frac{y_i}{\mu}\right)^{1-\varepsilon} f(y_i) \right]^{1/(1-\varepsilon)}$$

In this case, the question is narrowed to one of choosing ε, which is clearly a measure of the degree of inequality-aversion – or the relative sensititivy to transfers at different income levels. As ε rises, we attach more weight to transfers at the lower end of the distribution and less weight to transfers at the top. The limiting case at one extreme is $\varepsilon \to \infty$ giving the function $\min_i\{y_i\}$ which only takes account of transfers to the very lowest income group (and is therefore not strictly concave); at the other extreme we have $\varepsilon = 0$ giving the linear utility function which ranks distributions solely according to total income.[13]

5   An Illustration

To illustrate the points made in the previous section about the conventional summary measures and the use of the equally distributed equivalent measure, I have taken the data collected by Kuznets [8] covering the distribution of income in seven advanced and five developing countries. These data have been used by both sides in the recent controversy as to whether incomes are more unequally distributed in the developing countries – see, for example, Ranadive [12]. I should emphasise, however, that my use of the figures is purely illustrative; their well-recognised deficiencies make any concrete conclusion difficult to draw.

Our earlier discussion suggested that the first step in the analysis should be an examination of the Lorenz curves corresponding to the distributions. If we consider all the pairwise comparisons of the twelve countres, then in only sixteen out of sixty-six cases do the Lorenz curves not intersect, so that we can arrive at a ranking without specifying the form of the social welfare function in only some quarter of the cases.[14] This explains the finding of Kuznets and others that the application of the conventional summary measures yields conflicting results. In the first three columns of Table 1, I have summarised the results obtained by Ranadive using three of the conventional summary measures. This shows clearly the discrepancies that arise; for example, India would be ranked as more unequal than West Germany on the basis of the coefficient of variation, as less unequal on the basis of the standard deviation of the logarithms of income, and ranks equally when we take the Gini coefficient.

Table 1 Conventional and equally distributed equivalent measure of inequality

Country	Year	1[a] Gini coefficient	2[a] Standard deviation of logarithms	3[a] Coefficient of variation	Equally distributed equivalent measure: ε 4[b] ε=1.0	5[b] ε=1.5	5[b] ε=2.0
India	1950	0.410 (8=)	0.305 (3)	0.901 (11)	0.297 (7)	0.359 (5)	0.399 (3)
Ceylon	1952–3	0.427 (10)	0.341 (6)	0.876 (10)	0.311 (10)	0.395 (6)	0.457 (6)
Mexico	1957	0.498 (12)	0.395 (12)	1.058 (12)	0.401 (12)	0.492 (12)	0.550 (12)
Barbados	1951–2	0.436 (11)	0.383 (10)	0.842 (9)	0.315 (11)	0.433 (10)	0.524 (10)
Puerto Rico	1953	0.394 (4)	0.317 (4)	0.783 (8)	0.256 (4)	0.341 (4)	0.408 (4)
Italy	1948	0.378 (3)	0.301 (1)	0.748 (3)	0.241 (2)	0.319 (2)	0.379 (1)
Great Britain	1951–2	0.356 (1)	0.304 (2)	0.673 (1)	0.224 (1)	0.311 (1)	0.384 (2)
West Germany	1950	0.410 (8=)	0.369 (8)	0.773 (6)	0.299 (8)	0.411 (8)	0.498 (8)
Netherlands	1950	0.406 (6=)	0.355 (7)	0.781 (7)	0.290 (5)	0.395 (7)	0.478 (7)
Denmark	1952	0.401 (5)	0.381 (9)	0.751 (4)	0.292 (6)	0.418 (9)	0.521 (9)
Sweden	1948	0.406 (6=)	0.393 (11)	0.752 (5)	0.303 (9)	0.435 (11)	0.540 (11)
United States	1950	0.372 (2)	0.325 (5)	0.705 (2)	0.242 (3)	0.339 (3)	0.421 (5)

[a] Source of columns 1–3 is Ranadive [12], p. 122.
[b] Source of columns 4–6 is calculated from data in Kuznets [8], Table 3.

In fact the three measures agree in only forty out of sixty-six cases, which subtracting those where the Lorenz curves do not intersect means that no more than half the doubtful cases would be agreed. The differences in ranking are in fact such that no clear conclusion emerges with regard to the relative degree of inequality in advanced and developing countries. The Gini coefficient and the coefficient of variation suggest that income is more unequally distributed in developing countries (four out of five come right at the bottom), but this is not borne out by the standard deviation of logarithms.

The last three columns in Table 1 show the effect of adopting the equally distributed equivalent measure (for the iso-elastic function with different values of ε). If we look first at the absolute value of the measure, then in the United States, for example, the measure of inequality (I) for $\varepsilon = 1.5$ is 0.34. In other words, if incomes were equally distributed, the same level of social welfare could be achieved with only two-thirds of the present national income – which is a striking figure. For most other countries, the figure is even lower and in the case of Mexico it is only one-half. These figures relate to one particular value of ε and it is clearly important to examine their sensitivity to changes in ε. In Figure 6, I have shown how I varies with ε in the case of the United States. The range of variation is considerable, but I is less sensitive than

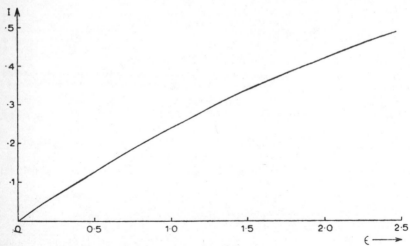

Figure 6   *Sensitivity of I to variation in ε – United States.*

one might at first have expected; for example, if we could agree that ε should be between 1.5 and 2.0, then I would lie between 0.42 and 0.34. It is also interesting to note that the potential gains from redistribution are considerable over most of the range: for $\varepsilon > 0.2$ they are greater than 5% of national income and for $\varepsilon > 0.8$ they are greater than 20%.

Turning to the relative ranking of different countries, we may note first of all that the last column ($\varepsilon = 2.0$) gives a ranking *identical* with that based on the standard deviation of logarithms, but one which is very different from that given by the Gini coefficient and the coefficient of variation. Of the fifty pairwise comparisons where the Lorenz curves intersect, the equally distributed equivalent measure with $\varepsilon = 2.0$ would disagree with the Gini coefficient in seventeen cases and with the coefficient of variation in no fewer than twenty-six cases. If we take $\varepsilon = 1.0$, which implies a lower degree of inequality-aversion, then the ranking is closer to that of the Gini coefficient (only in five cases would it be different), but is still quite a lot different from that of the coefficient of variation (fourteen disagree). The sensitivity of the ranking to ε is shown more clearly in Figure 7, which covers the range $\varepsilon = 1.0$ to $\varepsilon = 2.5$. This indicates that if we could agree, for example, that ε should lie between 1.5 and 2.0, then only five rankings would remain ambiguous.

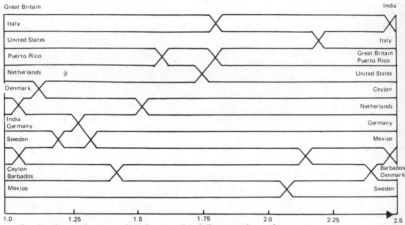

Figure 7   *Ranking of income distributions for different values of ε.*

It appears from this example that two of the conventional measures (the Gini coefficient and the coefficient of variation) tend to give rankings which are similar to those reached with a relatively low degree of inequality-aversion – ε of the order of 1.0 or less. This accords with the analysis of these measures in the previous section. It also appears that the conclusions reached about the relative degree of inequality in advanced and developing countries depends on the degree of inequality-aversion. It is clear why this is the case. The distribution of income in the developing countries is typically more equal at the bottom and less equal at the top than in the advanced countries, and as the degree of inequality-aversion increases, we attach more weight to the distribution at the lower end of the scale. It is striking that in Figure 7 none of the reversals of ranking as ε increases involves a developing country relative to an advanced country.

6   Concluding Comments

In this chapter I have examined the problem of measuring inequality in the distribution of income (alternatively consumption or wealth). At present this problem is usually approached through the use of such summary statistics as the Gini coefficient, the variance or the relative mean deviation. I have tried to argue, however, that this conventional method of approach is misleading. First, the use of these measures often serves to obscure the fact that a complete ranking of distributions cannot be reached without fully specifying the form of the social welfare function. Secondly, examination of the social welfare functions implicit in these measures shows that in a number of cases they have properties which are unlikely to be acceptable, and in general there are no grounds for believing that they would accord with social values. For these reasons, I hope that these conventional measures will be rejected in favour of direct consideration of the properties that we should like the social welfare function to display.

Acknowledgements

I am very grateful to P. Dasgupta, G. M. Heal, A. Klevorick, D. M. G. Newbery, M. Rothschild, J. E. Stiglitz, and the referees for their comments on earlier versions of this chapter, which have led to considerable improvements. After it was accepted for publication, I discovered that a number of the results have been proved independently in an important paper by S. Ch. Kolm [7]. However, I feel that the rather different approach adopted here may still be of interest.

Notes

1 My interest in the question of measuring inequality was originally stimulated by reading an early version of the paper by Rothschild and Stiglitz [13], to which I owe a great deal.
2 It is assumed throughout that $U(y)$ is twice continuously differentiable. The restriction of the incomes under consideration to a finite range $0 \leqslant y \leqslant \bar{y}$ is mathematically convenient and not very limiting as far as the problem is concerned.
3 See Rothschild and Stiglitz [13]; Hadar and Russell [5]; and Hanoch and Levy [6].
4 Using their notation, a mean preserving spread is equivalent to a tax of d on α of those with incomes between $a+d$ and $a+t+d$ which is used to give e to β of those with incomes between b and $b+t$.
5 Dalton's approach has been applied by Wedgwood [15], who calculated that in the case of the logarithmic function the level of welfare associated with the actual distribution of income in Great Britain in 1919–20 was only 77% of what it would have been had income been equally distributed.
   A similar approach has been adopted by Aigner and Heins [1]. For the reason described in the text, however, the particular numerical values calculated by these authors have no meaning.
6 This line of approach was suggested to me by discussions with David Newbery. It also resembles the work of Mirrlees and Stern in a quite different context [9].
7 The proportional risk premium is defined as the amount π^* such that a person with initial wealth W would be indifferent between accepting a risk Wz (where z is a random variable) and receiving the non-random amount $E(Wz) - W\pi^*$. In the present case, $W = \mu$ and $z = (y - \mu)/\mu$.
8 This definition can be seen to be parallel to that for the uncertainty case since y_{EDE} is equal to $\mu - \pi$, where π is the *absolute* risk premium (for an absolute gamble $y-\mu$ and initial assets μ).
9 In the case of the variance, this follows directly. See [13]. For the other measures, the restriction to distributions with the same mean is important. In the case of measures (b) and (c), we can write them in the form

$$\int_0^y V(y,\mu)f(y)\,dy$$

where V is convex, in y (Note: the integral is minimised to give the least inequality). While the Gini coefficient cannot in general be written in this form (as shown by the example of Newbery [10]), the same result can be shown to hold.

10 The relationship between cases where the conventional measures give conflicting rankings and the crossing of the Lorenz curves was suggested by Ranadive [12], the results given in section 3 provide a proof of this.

11 Schutz [14] also argued that the relative mean deviation is preferable to the Gini coefficient. He pointed out that 'the shape of the Lorenz curve may be infinitely varied without any change in the Gini coefficient'. However, as we have just seen, the same objection applies even more strongly to the relative mean deviation.

12 This does not follow directly, but can be shown by taking a discrete mean preserving spread (as defined in [13]) and allowing the size of the transfer to tend to zero.

13 It should be noted that the measure is readily decomposable if it is desired to measure the contribution of inequality *within* and inequality *between* sub-groups of the population.

14 I assume throughout this section that we are ranking distributions independently of the mean level of income.

References

[1] Aigner, D. J. and Heins, A. J. (1967), 'A social welfare view of the measurement of income inequality', *Rev. Income Wealth*, **13**, March.

[2] Arrow, K. J. (1965), *Aspects of the Theory of Risk Bearing*, Helsinki.

[3] Dalton, H. (1920), 'The measurement of the inequality of incomes', *Econ. J.*, **30**, September.

[4] Eltetö, O. and Frigyes, E. (1968), 'New income inequality measures as efficient tools for causal analysis and planning', *Econometrica*, **36**, April.

[5] Hadar, J. and Russell, W. R. (1969), 'Rules for ordering uncertain prospects', *Amer. Econ. Rev.*, **59**, March.

[6] Hanoch, G. and Levy, H. (1969), 'The efficiency analysis of choices involving risk', *Rev. Econ. Studies*, **36**, July.

[7] Kolm, S. Ch. (1969), 'The optimal production of social justice, *in* "Public Economics"', Margolis, J. and Guitton, H. (eds.), Macmillan, New York/London.

[8] Kuznets, S. (1963), 'Quantitative aspects of economic growth of nations: VIII Distribution of income by size', *Econ. Development Cultural Change*, **11**, January.

[9] Mirrlees, J. A. and Stern, N. H. (1972), 'On fairly good plans', *J. Econ. Theory*, **4**.

[10] Newbery, D. M. G. (1970), 'A theorem on the measurement of inequality', *J. Econ. Theory*, **2**, 264.

[11] Pratt, J. W. (1964), 'Risk aversion in the small and large', *Econometrica*, **32**, January–April.

[12] Ranadive, K. R. (1965), 'The equality of incomes in India', *Bull. Oxford Institute of Statistics*, **27**, May.

[13] Rothschild, M. and Stiglitz, J. E. (1970), 'Increasing risk: A definition and its economic consequences', *J. Econ. Theory*, **2**.

[14] Schutz, R. R. (1951), 'On the measurement of income inequality', *Amer. Econ. Rev.*, **41**, March.

[15] Wedgwood, J. (1939), *The Economics of Inheritance*, Penguin, London.

[16] Yntema, D. B. (1933), 'Measures of inequality in the personal distribution of income or wealth', *J. Amer. Statist. Assoc.*, **28**, December.

Bibliography 1970–82

Since the publication of Chapter 1, a great deal has been written on the measurement of inequality and poverty. This bibliography of published work is not intended to be comprehensive, but rather to give the reader an impression of the range of subsequent research. It covers the *theory* of measurement, and does not attempt to list all the very large number of studies which have been concerned with the empirical implementation of inequality measures. In constructing the bibliography I have drawn on a number of sources, including Cowell (1977), Chakravarty (1981), and Nygård and Sandström (1981).

The bibliography is arranged in the following sections:
Texts
General issues
Axiomatic treatment
Lorenz curves and specific distributions
Specific measures of inequality
Measurement of poverty
Multi-dimensioned inequality

Texts

Cowell, F. A. (1977), *Measuring Inequality*, Deddington, Philip Allan.
Kakwani, N. (1980), *Income Inequality and Poverty; Methods of Estimation and Policy Applications*, New York, Oxford University Press.
Kolm, S-Ch. (1972), *Justice et equité*, Paris, CNRS, (in French).
Lüthi, A. (1981), *Messung wirtschaftlicher Ungleichheit*, Berlin, Springer, (in German).
Meade, J. E. (1976), *The Just Economy*, London, Allen & Unwin.
Nygård, F. and Sandström, A. (1981), *Measuring Income Inequality*, Stockholm, Almqvist & Wiksell.
Sen, A. K. (1973), *On Economic Inequality*, London, Oxford University Press.

General issues

Alker, H. R. (1970), 'Measuring inequality', in E. R. Tufte (ed.), *The Quantitative Analysis of Social Problems*, Reading, Mass., Addison-Wesley.
Allais, M. (1971), 'Inégalité èt civilisations', in *Mélanges en l'honneur de Raymond Aron*, vol. II, Paris, Calmann-Levy, (in French).
Allison, P. D. (1967), 'Measures of inequality', *American Sociological Review*, 43, pp. 865–80.
Bartels, C. P. A. (1977), *Economic Aspects of Regional Welfare, Income Distribution and Unemployment*, Leiden, Martinus Nijhoff.
Benedetti, C. (1980), 'Di alcuni indici di disuguaglianza del benessere', *Statistica*, 40, pp. 7–12, (in Italian, with English summary).
Bentzel, R. (1970), 'The social significance of income distribution statistics', *Review of Income and Wealth*, 16, pp. 253–64.
Berrebi, Z. M. and Silber, J. (1981), 'Weighting income ranks and levels', *Economics Letters*, 7, pp. 391–7.
Chakravarty, S. R. (1981), *On Measurement of Income Inequality and Poverty*, PhD thesis, Indian Statistical Institute, Calcutta.
Champernowne, D. G. (1974), 'A comparison of measures of inequality of income distributions', *Economic Journal*, vol. 84, pp. 787–816.
Dagum, C. (1980), 'Inequality measures between income distributions with applications', *Econometrica*, vol. 48, pp. 1791–803.
Dasgupta, P., Sen, A. K. and Starrett, D. (1973), 'Notes on the measurement of inequality', *Journal of Economic Theory*, vol. 6, pp. 180–7.
Ferreri, C. (1978), 'Su un sistema di indicatori di concezione Daltoniana del grado di benessere economico individuale del reddito', *Statistica*, vol. 38, pp. 13–42, (in Italian, with English summary).
Fishburn, P. C. (1979), 'Evaluative comparisons of distributions of a social variable', *Social Indicators Research*, vol. 6, pp. 103–26.
Gastwirth, J. L. (1974), 'A new index of income inequality', *International Statistical Institute Bulletin*, vol. 45, book I, pp. 437–41.

Hansson, B. (1977), 'The measurement of social inequality', in R. Butts and J. Hintikka (eds.), *Logic, Methodology and Philosophy of Science*, Dordrecht, D. Reidel.

Hart, P. E. (1975), 'Moment distributions in economics: an exposition', *Journal of the Royal Statistical Society*, series A, vol. 138, pp. 423–34.

Hart, P. E. (1976), 'The comparative statics and dynamics of income distributions', *Journal of the Royal Statistical Society*, series A, vol. 139, pp. 108–125.

Hart, P. E. (1981), 'The statics and dynamics of income distributions: a survey', in N. A. Klevmarken and J. A. Lybeck (eds.), *The Statics and Dynamics of Income*, Clevedon, Tieto.

Jasso, G. (1980), 'A new theory of distributive justice', *American Sociological Review*, vol. 45, pp. 3–32.

Kolm, S-Ch. (1974), 'Sur les conséquences economiques des principes de justice et de justice pratique', *Revue d'economie politique*, vol. 84, pp. 80–107 (in French).

Kolm, S-Ch. (1976a), 'Unequal inequalities I', *Journal of Economic Theory*, vol. 12, pp. 416–42.

Kolm, S-Ch. (1976b), 'Unequal inequalities II', *Journal of Economic Theory*, vol. 13, pp. 82–111.

Kondor, Y. (1975), 'Value judgements implied by the use of various measures of income inequality', *Review of Income and Wealth*, vol. 21, pp. 309–21.

Kuga, K. (1979), 'Comparison of inequality measures: a Monte Carlo study', *Economic Studies Quarterly*, 30, pp. 219–35.

Lambert, P. J. (1980), 'Inequality and social choice', *Theory and Decision*, vol. 12, pp. 395–8.

Love, R. and Wolfson, M. C. (1976), 'Income inequality: statistical methodology and Canadian illustrations', *Statistics Canada*, Ottawa.

Mehran, F. (1976), 'Linear measures of income inequality', *Econometrica*, vol. 44, 805–9.

Muellbauer, J. (1974), 'Inequality measures, prices and household composition', *Review of Economic Studies*, vol. XLI, pp. 493–503.

Osmani, S. R. (1978), 'On the normative measurement of inequality', *Bangladesh Development Studies*, 6, pp. 417–42.

Piesch, W. (1975), *Statistische Konzentrationsmasse*, Tubingen, J. C. B. Mohr (in German).

Rothschild, M. and Stiglitz, J. E. (1973), 'Some further results on the measurement of inequality', *Journal of Economic Theory*, vol. 6, pp. 188–204.

Schwartz, J. E. and Winship, C. (1980), 'The welfare approach to measuring inequality', in K. F. Schuessler (ed.), *Sociological Methodology*.

Sen, A. K. (1978), 'Ethical measurement of inequality: some difficulties', in W. Krelle and A. F. Shorrocks (eds.), *Personal Income Distribution*, Amsterdam, North-Holland.

Sen, A. K. (1980), 'Description as choice', *Oxford Economic Papers*, vol. 32, pp. 353–69.

Shorrocks, A. F. (1978), 'Income inequality and income mobility', *Journal of Economic Theory*, 19, pp. 376–93.

Shorrocks, A. F. (1982a), 'On the distance between income distributions', *Econometrica* (forthcoming).

Shorrocks, A. F. (1982b), 'Ranking income distributions', *Economica* (forthcoming).

Suppes, P. (1977), 'The distributive justice of income inequality', in H. W. Gottinger and W. Leinfellner (eds.), *Decision Theory and Social Ethics*, Dordrecht, D. Reidel.

Szal, R. and Robinson, S. (1977), 'Measuring income inequality', in C. R. Frank and R. C. Webb (eds.), *Income Distribution and Growth in Less-Developed Countries*, Washington DC, The Brookings Institution.

Thurow, L. (1971), 'The income distribution as a pure public good', *Quarterly Journal of Economics*, vol. 85, pp. 327–36.

Toyoda, T. (1975), 'Income inequality: the measures and their comparisons', *Kokumin Keizai*, vol. 134, pp. 15–41 (in Japanese).

Van Praag, B. (1977), 'The perception of welfare inequality', *European Economic Review*, vol. 10, pp. 180–207.

Van Praag, B. (1978), 'The perception of income inequality', in W. Krelle and A. F. Shorrocks (eds.), *Personal Income Distribution*, Amsterdam, North-Holland.

Wiles, P. J. D. (1974), *Income Distribution, East and West*, Amsterdam, North-Holland.

Willig, R. D. (1981), 'Social welfare dominance', *American Economic Review*, Papers and Proceedings, vol. 71, pp. 200–4.

Axiomatic treatment

Blackorby, C. and Donaldson, D. (1977a), 'Utility vs. equity: some plausible quasi-orderings', *Journal of Public Economics*, vol. 7, pp. 365–82.

Blackorby, C. and Donaldson, D. (1977b), 'A theoretical treatment of indices of absolute inequality', *International Economic Review*, vol. 20, pp. 107–36.

Blackorby, C. and Donaldson, D. (1978), 'Measures of relative equality and their meaning in terms of social welfare', *Journal of Economic Theory*, vol. 18, pp. 59–80.

Cowell, F. A. and Kuga, K. (1981a), 'Inequality measurement: an axiomatic approach', *European Economic Review*, vol. 15, pp. 287–305.

Cowell, F. A. and Kuga, K. (1981b), 'Additivity and the entropy concept: an axiomatic approach to inequality measurement', *Journal of Economic Theory*, vol. 25, pp. 131–43.

Fields, G. S. and Fei, J. C. H. (1978), 'On inequality comparisons', *Econometrica*, vol. 46, pp. 303–16.

Hamada, K. (1973), 'A simple majority rule on the distribution of income', *Journal of Economic Theory*, vol. 6, pp. 243–64.

Hammond, P. J. (1975), 'A note on extreme inequality aversion', *Journal of Economic Theory*, vol. 11, pp. 465–7.

Hammond, P. J. (1976a), 'Why ethical measures of inequality need interpersonal comparisons', *Theory and Decision*, vol. 7, pp. 263–74.

Hammond, P. J. (1976b), 'Equity, Arrow's conditions and Rawls' difference principle', *Econometrica*, vol. 44, pp. 793–804.

Hammond, P. J. (1977), 'Dual interpersonal comparisons of utility and the welfare economics of income distribution', *Journal of Public Economics*, vol. 7, pp. 51–71.

Sen, A. K. (1974), 'Informational bases of alternative welfare approaches', *Journal of Public Economics*, vol. 3, pp. 387–403.

Sen, A. K. (1976), 'Welfare inequalities and Rawlsian axiomatics', *Theory and Decision*, vol. 7, pp. 243–62.

Sen, A. K. (1977), 'On weights and measures: informational constraints in social welfare analysis', *Econometrica*, vol. 45, pp. 1539–72.

Decomposition of inequality measures

Blackorby, C., Donaldson, D. and Auersperg, M. (1982), 'A new procedure for measurement of inequality within and among population subgroups', *Canadian Journal of Economics* (forthcoming).

Bourguignon, F. (1979), 'Decomposable income inequality measures', *Econometrica*, vol. 47, pp. 901–20.

Cowell, F. A. (1980), 'On the structure of additive inequality measures', *Review of Economic Studies*, vol. 48, pp. 521–31.

Das, T. and Parikh, A. (1981), 'Decompositions of Atkinson's measure of inequality', *Australian Economic Papers*, vol. 20, pp. 171–8.

Fei, J. C. H., Ranis, G. and Kuo, S. W. Y. (1978), 'Growth and the family distribution of income by factor components', *Quarterly Journal of Economics*, vol. 92, pp. 17–53.

Fields, G. S. (1979a), 'Income inequality in urban Colombia: a decomposition analysis', *Review of Income and Wealth*, vol. 25, pp. 325–41.

Fields, G. S. (1979b), 'Decomposing LDC inequality', *Oxford Economic Papers*, vol. 31, pp. 437–59.

Mookherjee, D. and Shorrocks, A. F. (1982), 'A decomposition analysis of the trend in UK income inequality', *Economic Journal* (forthcoming).

Pyatt, G., Chen-nan and Fei, J. C. H. (1980), 'The distribution of income by factor components', *Quarterly Journal of Economics*, vol. 95, pp. 451–73.

Shorrocks, A. F. (1980), 'The class of additively decomposable inequality measures', *Econometrica*, vol. 48, pp. 613–25.

Shorrocks, A. F. (1982), 'Inequality decomposition by factor components', *Econometrica*, vol. 50, pp. 193–211.

Theil, H. (1972), *Statistical Decomposition Analysis*, Amsterdam, North-Holland.

Theil, H. (1979a), 'World income inequality and its components', *Economics Letters*, vol. 2, pp. 99–102.

Theil, H. (1979b), 'The measurement of inequality by components of income', *Economics Letters*, vol. 2, pp. 197–9.

Toyoda, T. (1980) 'Decomposability of inequality measures', Economic Studies Quarterly, vol. 31, pp. 207 16.

Lorenz curves and specific distributions

Chipman, J. (1974), 'The welfare ranking of Pareto distributions', *Journal of Economic Theory*, vol. 9, pp. 275–82.

Fellman, J. (1976), 'The effect of transformations on Lorenz curves', *Econometrica*, vol. 44, pp. 823–4.

Gastwirth, J. L. (1971), 'A general definition of the Lorenz curve', *Econometrica*, vol. 39, pp. 1937–2039.

Gastwirth, J. L. (1972), 'The estimation of the Lorenz curve and the Gini index', *Review of Economics and Statistics*, vol. 54, pp. 306–16.

Levine, D. B. and Singer, N. M. (1970), 'The mathematical relation between the income density function and the measurement of income inequality', *Econometrica*, vol. 38, pp. 324–30.

McDonald, J. B. and Jensen, B. C. (1979), 'An analysis of alternative measures of income inequality based on the gamma distribution function', *Journal of the American Statistical Association*, vol. 74, pp. 856–60.

Specific measures of inequality

Creedy, J. (1977), 'The principle of transfers and the variance of logarithms', *Oxford Bulletin of Economics and Statistics*, vol. 39, pp. 153–8.

Danziger, S., Haveman, R. and Smolensky, E. (1977), 'Comment on Paglin (1975)', *American Economic Review*, vol. 67, pp. 505–12.

Donaldson, D. and Weymark, J. A. (1980), 'A single-parameter generalisation of the Gini indices of inequality', *Journal of Economic Theory*, vol. 22, pp. 67–86.

Dorfman, R. (1979), 'A formula for the Gini coefficient', *Review of Economics and Statistics*, vol. 61, pp. 146–9.

Foster, J. E. (1982), 'An axiomatic characterisation of the Theil measure of income inequality', *Journal of Economic Theory* (forthcoming).

Hey, J. D. and Lambert, P. J. (1980), 'Relative deprivation and the Gini coefficient: comment', *Quarterly Journal of Economics*, vol. 95, pp. 567–73.

Jasso, G. (1979), 'On Gini's mean difference and Gini's index of concentration', *American Sociological Review*, vol. 44, pp. 867–70.

Johnson, W. R. (1977), 'Comment on Paglin (1975)', *American Economic Review*, vol. 67, pp. 502–4.

Kats, A. (1972), 'On the social welfare function and the parameters of income distribution', *Journal of Economic Theory*, vol. 5, pp. 377–82.

Kondor, Y. (1971), 'An old-new measure of income inequality', *Econometrica*, vol. 39, pp. 1041–2.

Kondor, Y. (1975), 'The Gini coefficient of concentration and the Kuznets measure of inequality: a note', *Review of Income and Wealth*, vol. 21, p. 354.

Kuga, K. (1980), 'Gini index and the generalised entropy class: further results and a vindication', *Economic Studies Quarterly*, vol. 31, pp. 217–18.

Kurien, C. J. (1977), 'Comment on Paglin (1975)', *American Economic Review*, vol. 67, pp. 517–19.

Mehran, F. (1974), 'Decomposition of the Gini index: a statistical analysis of income inequality', Income Distribution and Employment Programme, Geneva, ILO.

Minarik, J. (1977), 'Comment on Paglin (1975)', *American Economic Review*, vol. 67, pp. 513–16.

Nelson, E. R. (1977), 'Comment on Paglin (1975)', *American Economic Review*, vol. 67, pp. 497–501.

Paglin, M. (1975), 'The measurement and trend of inequality: a basic revision', *American Economic Review*, vol. 65, pp. 598–609.

Paglin, M. (1977), 'Reply', *American Economic Review*, vol. 67, pp. 520–31.

Paglin, M. (1979), 'Reply to Wertz (1979)', *American Economic Review*, vol. 79, pp. 613–77.

Pyatt, G. (1976), 'On the interpretation and disaggregation of Gini coefficients', *Economic Journal*, vol. 86, pp. 243–55.
Sheshinski, E. (1972), 'Relation between a social welfare function and the Gini index of income inequality', *Journal of Economic Theory*, vol. 4, pp. 98–100.
Wertz, K. L. (1979), 'Comment on Paglin (1975)', *American Economic Review*, vol. 69, pp. 670–2.
Yitzhaki, S. (1979), 'Relative deprivation and the Gini coefficient', *Quarterly Journal of Economics*, vol. 93, pp. 321–4.
Yitzhaki, S. (1980), 'Relative deprivation and the Gini coefficient: reply', *Quarterly Journal of Economics*, vol. 95, pp. 575–6.

Measurement of poverty

Anand, S. (1977), 'Aspects of poverty in Malaysia', *Review of Income and Wealth*, vol. 23, pp. 1–16.
Blackorby, C. and Donaldson, D. (1980), 'Ethical indices for the measurement of poverty', *Econometrica*, vol. 48, pp. 1053–60.
Clark, S., Hemming, R. and Ulph, D. T. (1981), 'On indices for the measurement of poverty', *Economic Journal*, vol. 91, pp. 515–26.
Fields, G. S. (1980), *Poverty, Inequality and Development*, Cambridge, Cambridge University Press.
Goedhart, T., Halberstadt, V., Kapteyn, A. and Van Praag, B. (1977), 'The poverty line: concept and measurement', *Journal of Human Resources*, vol. XII, pp. 503–20.
Hamada, K. and Takayama, N. (1978), 'Censored income distributions and the measurement of poverty', *Bulletin of International Statistical Institute*, vol. 47, book I.
Kakwani, N. (1980), 'On a class of poverty measures', *Econometrica*, vol. 48, pp. 437–46.
Sen, A. K. (1976), 'Poverty: an ordinal approach to measurement', *Econometrica*, vol. 44, pp. 219–31.
Sen, A. K. (1979), 'Issues in the measurement of poverty', *Scandinavian Journal of Economics*, vol. 91, pp. 285–307.
Sen, A. K. (1981), *Poverty and Famines*, Oxford, Oxford University Press.
Srinivasan, T. N. (1977), 'Poverty: some measurement problems', *Bulletin of the International Statistical Institute*, vol. 47, book I.
Takayama, N. (1979), 'Poverty, income inequality and their measures: Professor Sen's axiomatic approach reconsidered', *Econometrica*, vol. 47, pp. 747–59.
Thon, D. (1979), 'On measuring poverty', *Review of Income and Wealth*, vol. 25, pp. 429–39.
Townsend, P. B. (1979), *Poverty in the United Kingdom*, London, Allen Lane.

Multi-dimensioned inequality

Allingham, M. G. (1972), 'The measurement of inequality', *Journal of Economic Theory*, vol. 5, pp. 163–96.
Kolm, S-Ch. (1973), 'More equal distributions of bundles of commodities', *CEPREMAP*, Paris.
Kolm, S-Ch. (1977), 'Multidimensional egalitarianisms', *Quarterly Journal of Economics*, vol. 91, pp. 1–13.
Roberts, K. W. S. (1980), 'Price-independent welfare prescriptions', *Journal of Public Economics*, vol. 13, pp. 277–97.
Sen, A. K. (1976), 'Real national income', *Review of Economic Studies*, vol. 43, pp. 19–39.
Ulph, D. (1978), 'On labour supply and the measurement of inequality', *Journal of Economic Theory*, vol. 19, pp. 492–512.

2 The Comparison of Multi-Dimensioned Distributions of Economic Status

1 Introduction

The literature on the measurement of inequality has been largely concerned with single-dimensioned indicators of economic status. Yet there are many situations in which there are several dimensions to inequality and where these are not readily reduced to a single index. In this chapter, we explore some of the issues which arise when inequality is multi-dimensioned, concentrating especially on the two-dimensioned case. We seek in particular the generalisation of results on Lorenz dominance, which allows us to make a partial ranking of distributions without knowledge of the precise form of the social welfare function. As in much of the literature, we assess inequality in terms of its implications for social welfare, a position which is clearly debatable (e.g. Sen [26]), but which appears to have considerable relevance to policy formation.

An illustration of the kind of multi-dimensioned problem we have in mind is provided by the case where the government is concerned both with monetary variables, such as income, and with non-monetary variables. Thus, to take the example used in this chapter, we may want to assess the extent of international inequality allowing for differences between countries both in incomes and in life expectancies, with the judgement depending on the distribution of each variable taken separately and on the way in which they vary together. Or, within a country, we may have characteristics, such as health, which vary between people and modify our valuation of a given income distribution. In the study of multiple deprivation, investigators have been concerned with the ways in which different forms of deprivation (such as low income, poor health, bad housing, etc.) tend to be associated, often drawing a contrast with what would be observed if they were independently distributed. A related example is that of private consumption and access to publicly-supplied goods. We may want to compare the degree of inequality in different countries taking account of both income and the provision, for example, of education or medical care.

Multi-dimensioned inequality was considered by Fisher [7], who intro-

A. B. Atkinson and F. Bourguignon.

duced the concept of a distribution matrix, giving the percentage of the total quantity of the i-th commodity allocated to the j-th individual (see his Appendix). As has been pointed out by Sen [24], this is similar to the term 'named good' employed by Hahn [9] in the analysis of transaction costs. As Sen notes, the standard procedure in real income comparisons is to use market prices to aggregate different goods going to the same person, these weights being 'anonymous'. It in effect replaces the social welfare function $W[U(x^i)]$, where x^i denotes the vector of goods received by person i, by $W[V(M^i, p)]$ where V is the indirect utility function defined over the income of person i, M^i, and the price vector, p. In this way, a multi-dimensioned comparison – of x^i – is reduced to a single dimention, V.

A multi-dimensioned treatment may become necessary for several reasons. First, the individual indirect utility functions may differ in more than one argument: for example, lump-sum income and the wage rate, or lump-sum income and the prices of commodities (e.g. they may vary by region). Roberts [21] has examined the conditions under which judgements can be made about the distribution of M^i independently of the price vector. Stiglitz [27] and Ulph [29] investigate the case where there are differences in the wage rate. In this case, the properties of the indirect utility function impose a particular structure on their interdependence in the social welfare function. Second, it may be that we cannot apply market aggregation. In the situation for which the term 'named goods' was introduced, when there are transaction costs, 'households face a sequence of budget constraints and there may be no unique set of discount rates applicable to all households which allows one to "amalgamate" all those constraints into a single present value budget constraint' (Hahn [9] p. 418). Individuals may be rationed with regard to the consumption of particular commodities, as with public goods, to consumption at particular dates, or to the supply of labour. In principle, these cases, and those of differing prices, could be treated by an appropriate definition of 'equivalent income', but the implementation of such an approach poses a number of difficulties, not least the informational requirements. (This is illustrated by the literature on the valuation of public goods.)

The third reason for a multi-dimensioned treatment is that we may wish to depart from the 'welfarism' (Sen [25]) assumption that the social valuation is based solely on individual utilities and to allow other information. This interpretation can be given to the income/life expectancy example described above, and the same may apply to public goods. When the variables include consumption at future dates, the government may wish to act as the custodian of the interests of future generations, entering their consumption as a separate argument. (The implications for the measurement of social mobility between generations are examined in Chapter 3.) A further example is provided by the concept of horizontal equity in public finance (see Chapter 5 and King [14]), when the pre-government distribution also enters the social decision.

We concentrate in this chapter on the third of these cases, in that we assume that the social criterion makes no use of information on individual i's relative valuation of the different elements of x^i. In other words, we consider a social welfare function defined over the named vectors x^i, and investigate the implications of different assumptions about the form of this social welfare function.

The analysis of the multi-dimensioned case is the subject of two papers by Kolm [15] [17]. He notes that, as in the one-dimensioned case, one can exploit the parallel with choice under uncertainty. Kolm provides a number of interesting extensions of the one-dimension results. These do not, however, bear directly on the situation where the marginal distributions are identical but there are differing degrees of inter-dependence between the elements of x. It is the latter situation which introduces crucial new issues into the problem, and it is to this that we pay especial attention. In section 2, we summarise the relevant results from the literature on uncertainty, and provide an extension to the condition for second-degree stochastic dominance. In section 3, we describe the application to the measurement of bi-variate inequality, and the implications of different assumptions about the welfare function. There is, as in the one variable case, a trade-off between the strength of the conditions on the distribution and the strength of the assumptions about the form of the social welfare function. In section 4, we examine the interpretation of the conditions for stochastic dominance, and their relation to the incomplete second moment (analogous to the Lorenz curve in one-dimension). The use of the results is illustrated in section 5 by an application to the international distribution of income and life expectancy. Section 6 contains concluding comments.

2   Multi-variate Results for Choice under Uncertainty

We are interested in comparing two multi-variate distributions, represented by the (continuous) cumulative distribution functions $F(x)$ and $F^*(x)$, where x is a vector of random variables. It is assumed that the comparison is based on the difference in expected utility:

$$\Delta W = \int U(x)\, dF - \int U(x)\, dF^*$$ (1)

where expected utility is assumed to be well-defined. One distribution, F, is said to stochastically dominate the other, F^*, for a specified class of utility functions ($U \in \mathcal{U}$) when ΔW is non-negative for all $U \in \mathcal{U}$ and is strictly positive for some U. The conditions for F to dominate F^* become progressively weaker as one strengthens the conditions on the class $\mathcal{U}$. In the literature on the one-dimension case, there is a sequence of theorems on first-degree dominance (for the set of increasing utility functions), for second-degree dominance (when the utility function is in addition assumed to be concave), and so on.

The results on stochastic dominance for the multi-variate case have tended to concentrate on first-degree dominance, and we begin with this. In summarising the results, our aim is to provide the essentials of the argument rather than to obtain the greatest possible generality. To this end, we consider the case of two dimensions (although a number of the results can be extended to n dimensions), restricted to a finite range. We also assume that the function

U is continuously differentiable to the required degree.[1] Writing the density function explicitly as $f(x_1, x_2)$, and defining the range to be $[0, a_i]$, the difference in expected utility is:

$$\Delta W = \int_0^{a_1} \int_0^{a_2} U(x_1, x_2) \Delta f(x_1, x_2) dx_2 dx_1 \tag{1'}$$

where Δf denotes $f - f^*$ (and ΔF denotes $F - F^*$).

As in the one-dimensional case (see, for example, Hadar and Russell [8]), the argument proceeds by integration by parts. Taking first the inner integral with respect to x_2:

$$\Delta W = \int_0^{a_1} \left[U(x_1, a_2) \int_0^{a_2} \Delta f(x_1, x_2) dx_2 \right.$$

$$\left. - \int_0^{a_2} U_2(x_1, x_2) \int_0^{x_2} \Delta f(x_1, t) \, dt \, dx_2 \right] dx_1 \tag{2}$$

In performing the second integration, it is convenient to define:

$$F_1(x_1) = \int_0^{x_1} \int_0^{a_2} f(s, x_2) \, dx_2 \, ds \tag{3}$$

with a corresponding definition for $F_2(x_2)$. This is the marginal distribution (and is equal to $F(x_1, a_2)$). We now integrate the right-hand side of (2) again by parts, this time with respect to x_1 (in integrating the second term, the order of integration is reversed):

$$\Delta W = U(a_1, a_2) \int_0^{a_1} \int_0^{a_1} \Delta f(x_1, x_2) dx_2 \, dx_1$$

$$- \underbrace{\int_0^{a_1} U_1(x_1, a_2) \, \Delta F_1(x_1) \, dx_1}_{(\equiv I_1)} - \underbrace{\int_0^{a_2} U_2(a_1, x_2) \Delta F_2(x_2) dx_2}_{(\equiv I_2)}$$

$$+ \underbrace{\int_0^{a_1} \int_0^{a_2} U_{12}(x_1, x_2) \Delta F(x_1, x_2) dx_2 \, dx_1.}_{(\equiv I_3)} \tag{4}$$

The first term is proportional to $\Delta F(a_1, a_2)$, which is zero by the definition of a distribution function.

We now define the class of utility functions, $\mathscr{U}^-$, such that U is increasing in both x_1 and x_2 and that $U_{12} \leq 0$. (The different classes of utility function considered in the chapter are summarised in Table 1.) It is apparent from (4)

Table 1 *Definition of classes of function U*

First-degree dominance results

Class $\mathscr{U}^-$:	$U_1, U_2 \geq 0;\ U_{12} \leq 0$	for all x_1, x_2
Class $\mathscr{U}^+$:	$U_1, U_2 \geq 0,\ U_{12} \geq 0$	for all x_1, x_2
Class $\mathscr{U}$	Union of $\mathscr{U}^-$ and $\mathscr{U}^+$	

Second-degree dominance results

Class $\mathscr{U}^{--}$:	Conditions for $\mathscr{U}^-$ and $U_{11}, U_{22} \leq 0$;
	$U_{112}, U_{122} \geq 0;\ U_{1122} \leq 0$ for all x_1, x_2
Class $\mathscr{U}^{++}$:	Conditions for $\mathscr{U}^+$ and $U_{11}, U_{22} \leq 0$;
	$U_{112}, U_{122} \leq 0;\ U_{1122} \geq 0$ for all x_1, x_2

that a sufficient condition for expected utility to be not lower for all $U \in \mathscr{U}^-$ is that:[2]

$$\Delta F(x_1, x_2) \leq 0 \qquad \text{for all } x_1, x_2 \tag{5a}$$

which implies as a special case $\Delta F_1(x_1) \leq 0$ for all x_1, $\Delta F_2(x_2) \leq 0$ for all x_2. This is theorem 5.7 of Hadar and Russell [8], and they show that it can be extended to n-dimensions (theorem 5.8), when the conditions on the utility function involve cross-derivatives up to $_{12\ldots n}$. A further result for the two-dimension case by Levy and Paroush ([20], theorem 2) gives conditions for the class $\mathscr{U}^+$ (where $U_1, U_2 \geq 0$ and $U_{12} \geq 0$). This result may be obtained from (4) by writing I_1 as:

$$I_1 = \int_0^{a_1} U_1(x_1, 0) \Delta F_1(x_1) dx_1 + \int_0^{a_1} \int_0^{a_2} U_{12}(x_1, x_2) \Delta F_1(x_1) dx_2 dx_1 \tag{6}$$

with a similar expression for I_2, so that:

$$\Delta W = \int_0^{a_1} \int_0^{a_2} U_{12}(x_1, x_2) [\Delta F(x_1, x_2) - \Delta F_1(x_1) - \Delta F_2(x_2)] dx_2 dx_1$$

$$- \int_0^{a_1} U_1(x_1, 0) \Delta F_1(x_1) dx_1 - \int_0^{a_2} U_2(0, x_2) \Delta F_2(x_2) dx_2. \tag{7}$$

Let us define

$$K(x_1, x_2) \equiv -[F(x_1, x_2) - F_1(x_1) - F_2(x_2)] \tag{8}$$

so that (noting that $\Delta K(x_1, 0) = \Delta F_1(x_1)$):

$$\Delta W = -\int_0^{a_1}\int_0^{a_2} U_{12}(x_1,x_2)\Delta K(x_1,x_2)dx_2\,dx_1$$

$$-\int_0^{a_1} U_1(x_1,0)\Delta K(x_1,0)dx_1 - \int_0^{a_2} U_2(0,x_2)\Delta K(0,x_2)dx_2. \qquad (9)$$

It follows that when $U \in \mathscr{U}^-$ a sufficient condition for expected utility to be no lower is that:

$$\Delta K(x_1,x_2) \leqq 0 \quad \text{for all } x_1,x_2. \qquad (5b)$$

Where U belongs to the union, $\mathscr{U}$, of $\mathscr{U}^+$ and $\mathscr{U}^-$ (i.e. we know that $U_1, U_2 \geqq 0$ and that U_{12} is either everywhere positive or everywhere negative) then (5a) and (5b) together are sufficient. (The necessity of the conditions can be demonstrated by an argument similar to that for the one-dimension case.)

It should be noted that if the marginal distributions are identical, then (5a) and (5b) can only be satisfied simultaneously if $\Delta F(x_1,x_2)=0$ for all x_1,x_2. In order to compare two distinct distributions (i.e. with $\Delta F \neq 0$ for some x_1,x_2) with identical margins, we need more information about U_{12} than that it is one-signed (in itself a considerable restriction).

It is in the nature of first-degree stochastic dominance results that they impose strong requirements on the distributions. The dominance condition (5a) requires that the cumulative distribution, taken over the rectangle $(0, x_1; 0, x_2)$ is everywhere less, or no greater, for F than for F^*, and (5b) requires that the cumulative distribution taken over the rectangle $(x_1,a_1; x_2,a_2)$ is everywhere greater, or no smaller. The latter interpretation may be seen from Figure 1. The condition on ΔF corresponds to the rectangle A; the condition on ΔK corresponds to $A + B + C$, since $F_1(x_1)$ corresponds to $A + B$ and $F_2(x_2)$ to $A + C$. Hence the condition on ΔK is equivalent to the reverse condition on the cumulative distribution taken over the area D.[3]

The fact that the conditions on ΔF and ΔK are rather demanding suggests that we should seek to extend the results to second-degree stochastic dominance, by imposing further conditions on the function U. Russell and Seo [22] also present a second-degree dominance result, but the condition they derive on the distribution function is not easy to apply in practice. First, we may note that the integral I_3 in equation (4) has the same form as ΔW in equation (1'), with U_{12} replacing U, and ΔF replacing Δf. It follows that integrating twice by parts yields (using (4)):

$$I_3 = U_{12}(a_1,a_2)\,\Delta H(a_1,a_2) - \int_0^{a_1} U_{112}(x_1,a_2)\Delta H(x_1,a_2)dx_1$$

$$-\int_0^{a_2} U_{122}(a_1,x_2)\Delta H(a_1,x_2)dx_2 + \int_0^{a_1}\int_0^{a_2} U_{1122}(x_1,x_2)\Delta H(x_1,x_2)dx_2\,dx_1$$

$$(10)$$

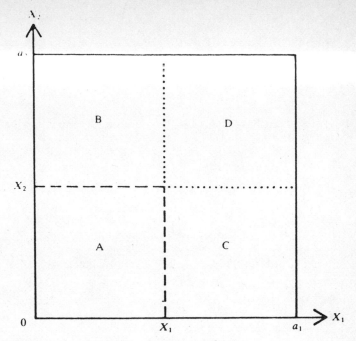

Figure 1 *Interpretation of first-degree dominance conditions*

where

$$H(x_1, x_2) \equiv \int_0^{x_1} \int_0^{x_2} F(s,t)\,dt\,ds. \tag{11a}$$

The integrals I_1 and I_2 can be evaluated by parts:

$$-I_1 = -U_1(a_1, a_2)\Delta H_1(a_1) + \int_0^{a_1} U_{11}(x_1, a_2)\Delta H_1(x_1)\,dx_1. \tag{12}$$

with a corresponding expression for I_2; where

$$H_1(x_1) \equiv \int_0^{x_1} F_1(s)\,ds \tag{13}$$

and $H_2(x_2)$ is defined similarly. This gives, from $-I_1 - I_2 + I_3$:

$$\Delta W = -U_1(a_1, a_2)\Delta H_1(a_1) - U_2(a_1, a_2)\Delta H_2(a_2)$$

$$+ \int_0^{a_1} U_{11}(x_1\, a_2)\Delta H_1(x_1)\,dx_1 + \int_0^{a_2} U_{22}(a_1, x_2)\Delta H_2(x_2)\,dx_2$$

$$+ U_{12}(a_1,a_2)\,\Delta H(a_1,a_2)$$

$$- \int_0^{a_1} U_{112}(x_1,a_2)\,\Delta H(x_1,a_2)\,dx_1 - \int_0^{a_2} U_{122}(a_1,x_2)\,\Delta H(a_1,x_2)\,dx_2$$

$$+ \int_0^{a_1}\!\int_0^{a_2} U_{1122}(x_1,x_2)\,\Delta H(x_1,x_2)\,dx_2\,dx_1. \tag{14a}$$

Alternatively, we could have started from equation (9), and defined

$$L(x_1,x_2) = \int_0^{x_1}\!\int_0^{x_2} K(s,t)\,dt\,ds. \tag{11b}$$

From this, we obtain:

$$\Delta W = - U_1(a_1,0)\,\Delta H_1(a_1) - U_2(0,a_2)\,\Delta H_2(a_2)$$

$$+ \int_0^{a_1} U_{11}(x_1,0)\Delta H_1(x_1)\,dx_1 + \int_0^{a_1} U_{22}(0,x_2)\Delta H_2(x_2)\,dx_2$$

$$- U_{12}(a_1,a_2)\,\Delta L(a_1,a_2)$$

$$+ \int_0^{a_1} U_{112}(x_1,a_2)\Delta L(x_1,a_2)\,dx_1$$

$$+ \int_0^{a_2} U_{122}(a_1,x_2)\Delta L(a_1,x_2)\,dx_2$$

$$- \int_0^{a_1}\!\int_0^{a_2} U_{1122}(x_1,x_2)\Delta L(x_1,x_2)\,dx_2\,dx_1 \tag{14b}$$

We now define, by analogy with the earlier results, the classes of utility functions, $\mathscr{U}^{--}$ and $\mathscr{U}^{++}$ (see Table 1), where in both cases $U_1, U_2 \geqq 0$ and $U_{11}, U_{22} \leqq 0$, but for $\mathscr{U}^{--}$

$$U_{12} \leqq 0 \qquad U_{112}, U_{122} \geqq 0 \qquad U_{1122} \leqq 0$$

and for $\mathscr{U}^{++}$ these signs are reversed. (The reasonableness, or otherwise, of these assumptions is discussed in the next section.) We can then see from (14a) that sufficient conditions for expected utility to be no lower for all $U \in \mathscr{U}^{--}$ are:

$$\Delta H_1(x_1) = \int_0^{x_1} \Delta F_1(s)\,ds \leqq 0 \qquad \text{all } x_1 \tag{15a}$$

$$\Delta H_2(x_2) = \int_0^{x_2} \Delta F_2(s)\,ds \leqq 0 \qquad \text{all } x_2 \tag{15b}$$

$$\Delta H(x_1,x_2) \leqq 0 \qquad \text{all } x_1, x_2 \tag{15c}$$

and corresponding conditions for all $U \in \mathscr{U}^{++}$ are (15a), (15b) and

$$\Delta L(x_1,x_2) \leqq 0 \qquad \text{all } x_1, x_2. \tag{15d}$$

For the distribution to dominate for all U belonging to the union of U^{--} and $\mathscr{U}^{++}$, the four conditions are sufficient. (Necessity can again be shown applying the same kind of approach as in the first-degree dominance case, replacing U by U_{12}.)

The first two requirements, (15a) and (15b), correspond to the one-dimension conditions for the marginal distributions (see, for example, Hadar and Russell [8] p. 135). These conditions are given, for the case of discrete income distributions, in the results of Kolm ([15], [17]). It is the conditions (15c) and (15d) which are new and of particular interest, since they involve the joint distribution of the two variables. The application of the conditions to the comparison of distributions of economic indicators, and their interpretation, are discussed in the next sections. The extension of the conditions to n dimensions is straightforward in principle, but complicated in that it involves derivatives up to the order $2n$.

The families $\mathscr{U}^{++}$ and $\mathscr{U}^{--}$ may be considered as straightforward extensions of the families $\mathscr{U}^{+}$ and $\mathscr{U}^{-}$ used for first-degree dominance. The alternating signs they impose on second, third and fourth cross-derivatives may seem unduly restrictive, however, and one may want to be able to make welfare comparisons under alternative conditions about the sign of those derivatives. This may be done by applying the general property where V is an arbitrary, differentiable function:

$$\int_0^{a_1} V(x_1,a_2) G(x_1,a_2) dx_1$$

$$= \int_0^{a_1} V(x_1,0) G(x_1,a_2) dx_1 + \int_0^{a_1} \int_0^{a_2} V_2(x_1,x_2) G(x_1,a_2) dx_2 dx_1$$

or, the corresponding one for x_2, to the various terms on the right-hand side of (14a). For instance, modifying the two third-derivative terms yields the following dominance criterion in addition to (15a) and (15b):

$$\left. \begin{array}{c} \Delta H(x_1,x_2) - \Delta H(x_1,a_2) - \Delta H(a_1,x_2) \geqq 0 \\[2mm] \\ \Delta H(x_1,a_2), \ \Delta H(a_1,x_2) \leqq 0 \end{array} \right\} \quad \text{for all } x_1, x_2 \tag{15e}$$

and

for the class of utility functions such that:

$$U_{12} \leqq 0 \qquad U_{112}, U_{122} \geqq 0 \qquad U_{1122} \geqq 0.$$

It is clear that it is possible to derive dominance criteria corresponding to different combinations of assumptions about the derivatives U_{12}, U_{112}, U_{122} and U_{1122}. Also, as in the first-degree dominance case, we may derive conditions for the union of different classes. For example, if $U_{12} \leq 0$; U_{112}, $U_{122} \geq 0$ and U_{1122} is one-signed (either positive or negative), then sufficient conditions are (15c) and (15e), in addition to (15a) and (15b).

3 Comparison of Distributions of Economic Status and Properties of the Social Welfare Function

In applying the results on stochastic dominance, we assume that the social welfare function is additively separable and symmetric with respect to individuals. Additive separability can be relaxed, as in the literature on the one-dimension case (see, for example, Sen [23]), but we do not pursue this here. The assumption is convenient in that it allows a direct interpretation of equation (1) as the difference in social welfare, where W is taken as the additive form of the social welfare function (which is only defined up to an increasing monotonic transformation). The properties of the social welfare function then depend on $U(x_1, x_2)$, which is treated here as a subject for social decision. We are making no use of information on individual relative valuation of x_1 and x_2 (although the implications of different properties of, for example, the indirect utility function may be seen from our results).

In order to provide some intuitive feeling for the new issues introduced in the multi-variate case, it may be helpful to consider two distributions which differ only in the following transformation (suggested by Hamada [10]):

$$T_i(x_1,x_2) \equiv \left\{ \begin{array}{ccc} & x_1 & x_1+h \\ & \text{density reduced} & \text{density increased} \\ x_1 & \text{by } \varepsilon & \text{by } \varepsilon \\ \\ & \text{density increased} & \text{density reduced} \\ x_2+k & \text{by } \varepsilon & \text{by } \varepsilon \end{array} \right\} \text{where } h,k > 0 \quad (16)$$

This transformation leaves the marginal distributions unchanged, but reduces the correlation between x_1 and x_2. It is this type of transformation which renders the two-dimension case intrinsically different from the one-dimension case, and makes assumptions on the sign of U_{12} necessary. We have seen that, with identical margins, we need more information than that U_{12} is one-signed. Put another way, assumptions on the concavity of U, as in Kolm [15], [17] or Russell and Seo [22], which are the analogue of those in the one-dimension case, do not allow us to compare two distributions with identical margins but distinct degrees of correlation.

In making assumptions about U_{12}, the natural starting point is the case where $U_{12} = 0$. In this situation, it is only the marginal distributions which are relevant, and the interdependence between x_1 and x_2 does not enter the picture. There are certain circumstances in which the assumption of additivity may be considered appropriate. For example, in the analysis of intertemporal allocation it is commonly assumed that the welfare function is additive. In this example, it is only the distributions within time periods which are relevant. On the other hand, it seems unlikely that we would be willing to restrict attention to the additive case. In the simplest situation, we may wish to consider the family of concave transformations of additive functions, $\mathcal{U}^*$, such that:

$$U = V[\Phi(x_1) + \Psi(x_2)]$$

where Φ', $\Psi' > 0$, Φ'', $\Psi'' \leq 0$, $V' > 0$, and $V'' < 0$. These conditions imply that $U_{12} < 0$. This provides an example satisfying the conditions for the class $\mathcal{U}^-$.

The example just given suggests that we may wish to distinguish between the ordinal preferences embedded in the function and the particular cardinal representation. For this purpose, it is useful to consider the class of least concave functions corresponding to a given preference ordering (Debreu [4]): i.e. $u(x_1, x_2)$ such that every concave function $v(x_1, x_2)$ representing the same preferences is given by:

$$v(x_1, x_2) = \Omega[u(x_1, x_2)]$$

where Ω is a strictly monotone and concave function. (Least concave functions are unique up to translations and multiplications by positive constants.) It follows that:

$$v_1 = \Omega' \cdot u_1; \qquad v_2 = \Omega' \cdot u_2; \qquad v_{12} = \Omega' \cdot u_{12} + \Omega'' \cdot u_1 u_2$$

and hence:

$$\frac{v_{12} \cdot v}{v_1 v_2} = \left[\frac{u_{12} \cdot u}{u_1 u_2} - \left(\frac{-u\Omega''}{\Omega'} \right) \right] \left(\frac{\Omega}{u\Omega'} \right). \tag{17}$$

The two terms in the square bracket allow us to separate two influences on the sign of v_{12}. The second term is readily recognisable as the standard measure of relative risk aversion (this approach is suggested by Kihlstrom and Mirman [13]). If $u_{12} = 0$, this risk aversion towards u is the sole determinant of v_{12}. On the other hand, if we were to take the least concave representation ($\Omega'' = 0$), then the sign of v_{12} depends solely on the preferences. Where these are homothetic, the first term in the square bracket equals to $1/\sigma$, where σ is the usual definition of the elasticity of substitution. (The family of functions corresponding to homothetic preferences and $\Omega'' = 0$ is referred to below as $\mathcal{U}^{**}$.) Where the preferences are homothetic, but we allow concave transformations, then the sign of v_{12} depends on whether the degree of relative risk aversion is greater or less than $1/\sigma$.

When the social welfare function belongs to the class $\mathcal{U}^-$, as with the family $\mathcal{U}^*$, the condition for first-degree stochastic dominance is given by (5a). The significance of the interdependence via U_{12} is that we require F to be lower (or no higher) at all points interior to the rectangle $(0, a_1; 0, a_2)$, not just at the margins. The interpretation of this condition may be seen in terms of the transformation (16). The effect is to reduce F over the rectangle $(x_1, x_2: x_1 + h, x_2 + k)$, except at the outer boundary, and to leave it otherwise unchanged. If the distribution F can be reached from another, F^*, by a sequence of such transformations, then the first-degree stochastic dominance condition is satisfied. Conversely, it requires only that F and F^* differ by two such transformations in opposite directions, at different points, for no unambiguous ranking to be possible for all social welfare functions in the class $\mathcal{U}^-$. (The equivalence is demonstrated by Epstein and Tanny [6].) When the social welfare function belongs to $\mathcal{U}^+$, as with the family $\mathcal{U}^{**}$, the condition for first-degree dominance is (5b), requiring that K be lower (or no higher) at all points. The effect of the transformation (16) is to raise K and hence is considered in this case undesirable. This reflects the different attitude to the distribution embodied in $\mathcal{U}^+$. For example the covariance belongs to this class, so that, other things equal, a higher correlation is preferred.

An illustration may be helpful at this stage. In Figure 2 we have shown the distribution of *per capita* income and life expectancy for eight countries, comparing the position in 1960 with that in 1970 (data drawn from the World

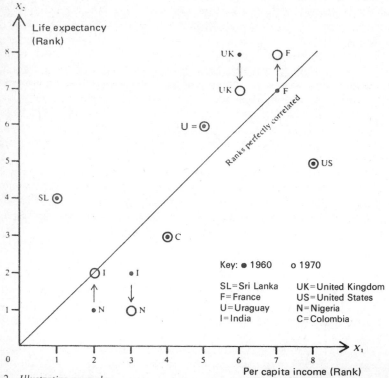

Figure 2   *Illustrative example*

Bank Tables [11], but with some approximate adjustments). The figures are shown simply as ranks, so that the marginal distributions are identical in the two years. The dots refer to 1960 and the circles to 1970, and $\odot$ implies that the points coincide. The differences lie in the position of (I, N) and of (UK, F). In the former case, the 1970 distribution can be reached from that for 1960 by a transformation of the type (16), which reduces the correlation. If this were the only difference, then the 1970 distribution would dominate that for 1960 for $\mathscr{U}^-$. However, the transformation of UK and F is in the opposite direction, increasing the correlation and the conditions (5a) and (5b) are not satisfied. We cannot therefore rank the two distributions for all social welfare functions belonging to the class $\mathscr{U}^-$, nor for all those belonging to the class $\mathscr{U}^+$. (With identical marginal distributions, $\Delta K = -\Delta F$, so that if one cannot rank for one of the classes, $\mathscr{U}^-$ and $\mathscr{U}^+$, then no ranking is possible for the other.)

The illustration given above serves to bring out why the second-degree dominance results may be of interest. Suppose that we consider the case where $U_{12} < 0$. Now we may be willing to attach more weight to transformations (of a given 'size') at low levels of x_1 or x_2. In that case we may regard the 'improvement' for (I, N) as outweighing the 'worsening' for (UK, F). This intuitive notion is captured in the second-degree dominance conditions. If we are willing to restrict attention to the narrower class of functions, $\mathscr{U}^{--}$, then the dominance condition is the weaker (15a–15c). In the illustration of Figure 2, the conditions (15a) and (15b) are satisfied automatically, since there are identical marginal distributions, and it can be checked that the condition (15c) is satisfied.[4] We are therefore able to reach an unambiguous conclusion that 1970 is ranked above 1960 for the more restricted class of utility functions $\mathscr{U}^{--}$. Indeed in this illustration the conditions (15e) are also satisfied, so that we require only that U_{112}, U_{122} be positive, and U_{1122} one-signed. (A geometric interpretation of the conditions may be given in terms of Figure 1. In this example, the integral of F taken over $A+B+C+D$ is zero, and (15e) implies that the integral taken over D be non-negative, whereas (15c) requires that the integral over A be non-positive.) The same argument applies in reverse when we consider the case $U_{12} > 0$.

This illustration shows how it is possible to rank distributions if one can specify further properties of the welfare function. These properties are essentially concerned with the relative effects of transformation (16) in different locations of the plane (x_1, x_2). In this example, the transformations were of the pattern:

$$\begin{pmatrix} & T_{-\varepsilon} \\ T_{\varepsilon} & \end{pmatrix}$$

and the required properties were those of the third derivative. If the transformations had been of the pattern:

$$\begin{pmatrix} T_{-\varepsilon} & T_{\varepsilon} \\ T_{\varepsilon} & T_{-\varepsilon} \end{pmatrix}$$

(not possible in the case of ranks), then the sign of the fourth derivative would have entered the picture. The parallel in the one-dimensioned case is with the principle of diminishing transfers (Kolm [16]).

The appearance in the definition of the class $\mathcal{U}^{--}$ of conditions on the third and fourth derivatives of the function U is a natural result of the extension to second-degree dominance (in the bi-variate case), but it is difficult to form a judgement about the strength of the conditions. It may be helpful to note first that the family, $\mathcal{U}^*$, of concave transformations of additive functions yields:

$$U_{112} = V'''(\Phi')^2\Psi' + V''\Phi''\Psi'$$

$$U_{1122} = V''''(\Phi'\Psi')^2 + V'''((\Phi')^2\Psi'' + (\Psi')^2\Phi'') + V''\Phi''\Psi''.$$

This family of functions belongs therefore to the class $\mathcal{U}^{--}$ where $V''' > 0$ and $V'''' < 0$. Suppose now we consider the constant elasticity case. If U is linearly homogeneous (i.e. the family $\mathcal{U}^{**}$)[5] and has constant elasticity of substitution, σ, then we know from the earlier results that U belongs to $\mathcal{U}^+$. On the other hand, we may take the following iso-elastic transformation ($v \neq 1$):

$$U_v = \frac{1}{1-v}[(\alpha_1 x_1^{1-1/\theta} + \alpha_2 x_2^{1-1/\theta})^{1/(1-1/\theta)}]^{1-v}: \tag{18}$$

If $v > 1/\sigma$, then U_V belongs to $\mathcal{U}^-$, and it may similarly be shown that the signs of higher derivatives depend on the relation between the degree of 'inequality-aversion' (v) and the degree of substitution (σ). It should also be noted that (18) may be used to generate a quantitative index, e.g. an equally distributed equivalent where x_1 and x_2 are in proportion to the mean values.

Next we may consider the effect on the derivatives of transformations of the variables. Suppose x_i is replaced by $\delta_i(x_i)$, where $\delta_i' > 0$, $\delta_i'' < 0$:

$$U = V[\delta_1(x_1), \delta_2(x_2)]. \tag{19}$$

Then:

$$U_{12} = V_{12}\delta_1'\delta_2' \tag{19a}$$

$$U_{112} = V_{112}(\delta_1')^2\delta_2' + V_{12}(\delta_1''\delta_2') \tag{19b}$$

$$U_{1122} = V_{1122}(\delta_1'\delta_2')^2 + V_{112}\delta_2''(\delta_1')^2 + V_{122}\delta_1''(\delta_2')^2 + V_{12}\delta_1''\delta_2''. \tag{19c}$$

It follows that:

$$V_{12} < 0, \qquad V_{112}, V_{122} > 0, \qquad V_{1122} < 0$$

implies:

$$U_{12} < 0, \qquad U_{112}, U_{122} > 0, \qquad U_{1122} < 0$$

and the same result follows with all signs reversed. We can see therefore that V belonging to $\mathcal{U}^{--}$ (or $\mathcal{U}^{++}$) implies that U also belongs. The transformation does not affect the properties required in the earlier results, which is reassuring since the variables may not be truly cardinal. Certainly we would not want to rule out linear transformations.

Finally, we may relate the properties of the function U to the properties of the implied 'demand' functions – as in the single-variable case. The cross-derivative, U_{12}, which defines the classes $\mathcal{U}^-$ and $\mathcal{U}^+$, plays some role even if we consider only the ordinal properties of the function. When $U_{12} > 0$, for example, neither x_1 nor x_2 can be inferior: the expansion path, at fixed 'prices', must slope upwards (Chipman [3]). As noted by Kanai [12], $U_{12} > 0$ implies $u_{12} > 0$ where u is the least concave representation; and the latter can be related to the degree of substitutability, as was brought out explicitly for the linearly homogeneous case. The cardinal properties become relevant when U is interpreted in terms of attitudes towards risk. In the literature on multivariate risk aversion, the measures proposed typically depend on U_{ij}/U_i (see, for example, Duncan [5]). By the same token, the derivatives entering the definition of $\mathcal{U}^{--}, \mathcal{U}^{++}$ may be interpreted as influencing the variation of risk aversion with the scale of the portfolio (as with increasing/decreasing risk aversion in the single-variable case).

4   Interpretation of Dominance Conditions

We turn now to the interpretation of the conditions on the distributions, to see in more detail the meaning of the second-degree dominance conditions (15), concentrating on the classes $\mathcal{U}^{--}$ and $\mathcal{U}^{++}$. The purpose of imposing stronger conditions on the social welfare function is to weaken the requirements on the distributions, and we need to consider how these may be checked.

The first point to note is that when the variables are independent, the conditions reduce to those for dominance at the margins. The class of cases for which this is true is however wider than that of independent distributions. To see this, let us follow Levy and Paroush [20] and define the 'dependency cumulative function', $D(x_1, x_2)$ of a distribution by[6]:

$$D(x_1, x_2) \equiv -F(x_1, x_2) + F_1(x_1)F_2(x_2) \tag{20}$$

The conditions (15c) and (15d) may then be shown to be equivalent to:

$$\int_0^{x_1} \int_0^{x_2} \Delta[F_1(s)F_2(t)]\, dt\, ds \leq \int_0^{x_1} \int_0^{x_2} \Delta D(s,t)\, dt\, ds \tag{21}$$

$$\leq \int_0^{x_1} \int_0^{x_2} \Delta[(1 - F_1(s))(1 - F_2(t))]\, dt\, ds$$

When the distributions are independent $D(x_1, x_2) = 0$, and the condition (21) is implied by the marginal dominance conditions (15a) and (15b).[7] The middle integral is however zero more generally, since we require only that $\Delta D(x_1, x_2)$ $= 0$ all x_1, x_2. This condition of identical dependency functions may apply, for example, when one considers redistributions of income independent of other variables. This can be seen by defining the conditional distribution, C_2, of x_2 for values of the first variable below x_1:

$$C_2(x_2|x_1) = \frac{F(x_1, x_2)}{F_1(x_1)} \tag{22}$$

so that:

$$D = F_1(x_1)(F_2(x_2) - C_2(x_2|x_1)). \tag{23}$$

Suppose that the government redistributes income (x_2), leaving x_1 unchanged, in such a way that it affects the conditional distribution for a given x_2 equally at all values of x_1, i.e.:

$$C_2^*(x_2|x_1) - C_2(x_2|x_1) \text{ constant all } x_1. \tag{24}$$

Then the $\Delta D = 0$ condition is satisfied.

When this situation does not apply, we have to consider the conditions (15c) and (15d). In the single variable case we know that the dominance conditions have a simple interpretation in terms of the incomplete mean (Lorenz curve). By rearranging the earlier results we can show that they have a parallel interpretation in terms of the incomplete covariance.

We consider first (15c), applicable when the social welfare function belongs to $\mathcal{U}^{--}$. This requires that:

$$\Delta H = \int_0^{x_1} \int_0^{x_2} \Delta F(s, t) \, dt \, ds \leq 0 \qquad \text{all } x_1, x_2. \tag{15c}$$

Integrating by parts:

$$H = \int_0^{x_1} \left[x_2 F(s, x_2) - \int_0^{x_2} t \frac{\partial F}{\partial t} \, dt \right] ds \tag{25}$$

and again:

$$= x_1 x_2 F(x_1, x_2) - \int_0^{x_1} x_2 s \frac{\partial F}{\partial s}(s, x_2) \, ds$$

$$- \int_0^{x_2} x_1 t \frac{\partial F}{\partial t}(x_1, t) \, dt + \int_0^{x_1} \int_0^{x_2} st f(s, t) \, dt \, ds$$

$$= \int_0^{x_1} \int_0^{x_2} (x_1 - s)(x_2 - t) f(s, t) \, dt \, ds \tag{26}$$

or:

$$= F(x_1, x_2)[\overline{\text{cov}}(x_1, x_2) + (x_1 - \bar{x}_1(x_1, x_2))(x_2 - \bar{x}_2(x_1, x_2))]$$
$$= F(x_1, x_2)R(x_1, x_2)$$

(27)

where $\bar{x}_i(x_1, x_2)$ is the incomplete mean taken over the range $(0, x_1; 0, x_2)$:

$$\bar{x}_1(x_1, x_2) \equiv \frac{1}{F(x_1, x_2)} \int_0^{x_1} \int_0^{x_2} sf(s, t) \, dt \, ds$$

(28)

and cov denotes the incomplete covariance taken over the same range:

$$\text{cov}(x_1, x_2) \equiv \frac{1}{F(x_1, x_2)} \int_0^{x_1} \int_0^{x_2} [st - \bar{x}_1(x_1, x_2)\bar{x}_2(x_1, x_2)] f(s, t) \, dt \, ds.$$

(29)

These transformations of the dominance condition provide additional insight. From (26) we can see that, for $\mathcal{U}^{--}$, it requires that the incomplete cross-product, taken about the point (x_1, x_2) be everywhere smaller (or identical). This is the two-dimensional analogue of the corresponding expression for the one-dimensional case, which may be written in terms of the marginal distributions:

$$\int_0^{x_1} (x_1 - s) \, dF_1(s)$$

(30)

(and similarly for x_2). The covariance now plays explicitly the role which one would intuitively expect. At interior points, we require:

$$F(x_1, x_2)R(x_1, x_2) \leq F^*(x_1, x_2)R^*(x_1, x_2).$$

(31)

Comparing this with condition (5a) we can see that it weakens the first-order dominance result by allowing F to be greater than F^*, when this is offset by a lower value for R. Evaluating (27) at (a_1, a_2) we can see that the condition requires

$$\text{cov} + (a_1 - \mu_1)(a_2 - \mu_2) < \text{cov}^* + (a_1 - \mu_1^*)(a_2 - \mu_2^*)$$

(32)

where μ_i, μ_i^* denote the overall means. For two distributions with the same means, that with the higher covariance cannot dominate the other. When the means differ, then the marginal conditions (15a) and (15b) imply that only a distribution with higher (or no smaller) means can dominate. Suppose that $\mu_i \geq \mu_i^*$, then cov $<$ cov* is sufficient for (32) but not necessary.[8]

Turning to the condition (15d), this may be rearranged in a similar fashion:

$$L = x_1 x_2 \left[F_1(x_1) \left(1 - \frac{\bar{x}_1(x_1, a_2)}{x_1} \right) + F_2(x_2) \left(1 - \frac{\bar{x}_2(a_1, x_2)}{x_2} \right) \right]$$
$$- F(x_1, x_2) R(x_1, x_2) \tag{33}$$

In the first two terms, we may see the incomplete means as modifying the earlier first-order dominance conditions ($\Delta F_1 < 0$). In the last term, the covariance now enters negatively, and evaluating at (a_1, a_2):

$$L(a_1, a_2) = (a_1 a_2 - \mu_1 \mu_2) - \text{cov}. \tag{34}$$

It follows that when distributions have the same means, that with the lower covariance cannot dominate (the reverse of the implication of (15c)). When $\mu_i \geq \mu_i^*$, then $\text{cov} > \text{cov}^*$ is sufficient, but not necessary.

5 Application: International Distribution of Income and Life Expectancy

To illustrate some of the results described above, we have taken the distribution of *per capita* incomes (x_1) and of life expectancy (x_2) across sixty-one countries. The comparisons made are across time, comparing 1970 with 1960, in one case taking the actual distribution in 1970 and in the other taking a hypothetical redistribution of income. It should be emphasised that the purpose of the analysis is to illustrate the analytical results, not to arrive at definitive conclusions.

The data on annual *per capita* incomes are taken from the 1976 World Tables [11] and are expressed in US dollars, converted using the purchasing power parities estimated by Kravis, Heston and Summers [18]. The range in 1970 is from $114 to $4900. The life-expectancy data are from the 1976 World Tables and range in 1970 from 35·0 to 74·5 years. The two variables are positively correlated across countries, the correlation coefficient for 1970 being 0·82, but the rankings are by no means identical.

We discuss first the comparisons of 1960 and 1970. As in the one-variable case, we have to consider the issue of normalisation. It is conventional in the literature on income inequality to abstract from differences in the level of incomes, it being assumed, either implicitly or explicitly, that the measure of inequality is invariant with respect to proportional shifts in the distribution ('scale independence'). This is, for example, implicit in the use of Lorenz curves to make comparisons of distributions with different mean incomes. Here we have followed the same procedure for incomes, normalising the distribution for 1970 by a constant proportional factor to give the same mean as in 1960. In the case of life expectancy, the arguments for scale independence are much less compelling,[9] and in the first example we work with the absolute levels. Given the improvement in life expectancy over the decade, this means that 1960 cannot dominate 1970 (the mean of x_2 increased from 54·8 years to 59·1 years).

The issue is therefore whether 1970 can dominate 1960 for all social welfare functions in one of the classes identified earlier. First, we consider the conditions for first-degree dominance. For this purpose, we evaluate ΔF (i.e.

Table 2 *Income* (x_1) *and life expectancy* (x_2): *comparison of 1960 and 1970*

Dominance map H and L

$\Delta H_1(x_1)$																
15	1	11	11	11	11	11	11	11	11	11	11	11	11	11	11	11
14	1	11	11	11	11	11	11	11	11	11	11	11	11	11	11	11
13	1	11	11	11	11	11	11	11	11	11	11	11	11	11	11	11
12	1	11	11	11	11	11	11	11	11	11	11	11	11	11	11	11
11	1	11	11	11	11	11	11	11	11	11	11	11	11	11	11	11
10	1	11	11	11	11	11	11	11	11	11	11	11	11	11	11	11
9	1	12	12	12	12	11	11	11	11	11	11	11	11	11	11	11
8	1	12	12	12	12	12	12	12	12	12	11	11	11	11	11	11
7	1	12	12	12	12	12	12	12	12	12	12	11	11	11	11	11
6	1	12	12	12	12	12	12	12	11	11	11	11	11	11	11	11
5	1	12	12	12	12	12	12	11	11	11	11	11	11	11	11	11
4	1	12	12	12	12	12	12	11	11	11	11	11	11	11	21	21
3	1	12	12	12	12	12	12	11	21	21	21	21	21	21	21	21
2	1	12	12	22	22	21	21	21	21	21	21	21	21	21	21	21
1	1	12	22	21	21	21	21	21	21	21	21	21	21	21	21	21
$\Delta H_2(x_2)$		2	2	2	2	2	2	2	2	2	1	1	1	1	1	1
		1	2	3	4	5	6	7	8	9	10	11	12	13	14	15

x_2

Dominance map F and K

$\Delta F_1(x_1)$	x_1															
15	0	10	10	10	10	10	10	10	10	10	10	20	10	10	10	00
14	0	10	10	10	10	10	12	12	10	10	10	20	11	10	10	00
13	2	12	12	12	12	12	12	12	12	12	12	22	11	12	20	20
12	2	12	12	12	12	12	12	12	12	12	12	22	11	11	21	20
11	1	11	11	11	11	11	11	11	11	11	11	21	11	11	11	10
10	1	11	11	11	11	11	11	11	11	11	11	21	11	11	11	10
9	1	11	11	11	11	11	11	11	11	11	11	21	11	11	11	10
8	1	11	11	11	11	11	11	11	11	11	11	21	11	11	11	10
7	2	12	12	12	12	12	12	12	12	12	12	22	21	21	21	20
6	2	12	12	12	12	12	21	21	11	21	21	22	21	21	21	20
5	1	11	11	11	11	11	21	11	11	11	11	12	11	11	11	10
4	2	12	12	11	12	12	21	21	11	21	21	22	21	21	21	20
3	2	12	11	11	12	12	21	21	21	21	21	22	21	21	21	20
2	2	12	12	21	22	21	21	21	21	21	21	22	21	21	21	20
1	2	21	11	11	21	21	21	21	21	21	21	22	21	21	21	20
$\Delta F_2(x_2)$		1	1	1	1	1	1	1	1	1	1	2	1	1	1	0
		1	2	3	4	5	6	7	8	9	10	11	12	13	14	15

x_2

Note. $\Delta K(x_2, 0) = \Delta F_i(x_i)$.

$F_{70} - F_{60}$) and ΔK at a grid defined by 15 brackets.[10] In the lower part of Table 2, we show the sign at each point first for ΔF (1 denoting negative, so $F_{60} > F_{70}$, 2 denoting positive, so $F_{60} < F_{70}$, and 0 denoting identical values), and then for ΔK. It may be seen that the condition for dominance of 1970 in terms of ΔF (i.e. for class $\mathscr{U}^-$) is satisfied on neither margin, and that ΔF changes sign on a number of occasions. In the case of ΔK, this too changes sign at a number of points. The first-degree dominance conditions cannot therefore be applied. The upper part of Table 2 shows the conditions for second-degree dominance, with ΔH being given first and ΔL second. The marginal condition for variable $x_1 (\Delta H_1(x_1) \leqq 0)$ is in this case satisfied, so that the marginal dominance condition holds for the 1970 distribution. On the other hand, the marginal condition for x_2 is not satisfied, and at interior points ΔH and ΔL both change sign. There is therefore no unambiguous conclusion that can be reached for either class $\mathscr{U}^{--}$ or class $\mathscr{U}^{++}$. At the same time, there is a more systematic pattern. In the case of ΔH, for example, the 'wrong' signs (from the standpoint of 1970) are confined to the bottom right-hand corner. It is also interesting to note the number of points at which ΔH and ΔL have opposite signs.

The second example, given in Table 3, concerns a hypothetical distribution in 1970 obtained from 1960 by assuming a 5% annual rate of growth for countries below \$500, 4% for those in the range \$500–\$2000, and 3% above \$2000. Again income is normalised to give a mean at the 1960 level, and in this case we also normalise life expectancy applying a proportionate adjustment to give the same mean as in 1960. Once again the first-degree results cannot be applied, there being numerous changes of sign. On the other hand, the second-degree dominance conditions, on ΔH_1, ΔH_2 and ΔH, are satisfied – see the upper part of Table 3. It is therefore the case that the 1970 distribution dominates that for 1960 for all functions belonging to $\mathscr{U}^{--}$. At the same time, the condition on ΔL is not satisfied in the upper right-hand region. No unambiguous conclusion can be reached therefore for the class $\mathscr{U}^{--}$.

6 Concluding Comments

The aim of this chapter has been to investigate some of the issues which arise with multi-variate inequality, assessed in terms of its implications for social welfare. We have tried in particular to demonstrate that there are crucial new factors, not present in the one-dimension case and not covered by a straightforward extension of the one-dimension results. These are illustrated clearly by the situation where the marginal distributions are identical but there are differing degrees of correlation. In such situations, the comparison of distributions involves a substantial increase in the information required about the properties of the social welfare function. It is not easy to provide an intuitive explanation of the conditions, but it is clear that judgements about higher derivatives have to be made if any substantial progress is to be made in ranking distributions.

There are many issues which warrant closer attention and we have not attempted to give an exhaustive treatment. We have concentrated on criteria for dominance, analogous to the non-intersection of Lorenz curves in the single-variable case. In subsequent work, we explore some of the properties of summary measures, including those associated with the iso-elastic form (18), and consider the special case where one margin is identical (e.g. where there is a fixed distribution of preferences in the population).

Table 3   *Income* (x_1) *and life expectancy* (x_2)*: comparison of 1960 and hypothetical distribution in 1970*

Dominance map H and L

$\Delta H_1(x_1)$																
15	x_1 1	11	11	11	11	11	11	11	11	11	12	12	12	12	12	12
14	1	11	11	11	11	11	11	11	11	11	12	12	12	12	12	12
13	1	11	11	11	11	11	11	11	11	11	11	12	12	12	12	12
12	1	11	11	11	11	11	11	11	11	11	11	11	12	12	12	12
11	1	11	11	11	11	11	11	11	11	11	11	11	12	12	12	12
10	1	11	11	11	11	11	11	11	11	11	11	11	12	12	12	12
9	1	11	11	11	11	11	11	11	11	11	11	11	11	12	12	12
8	1	11	11	11	11	11	11	11	11	11	11	11	11	11	11	11
7	1	11	11	11	11	11	11	11	11	11	11	11	11	11	11	11
6	1	11	11	11	11	11	11	11	11	11	11	11	11	11	11	11
5	1	11	11	11	11	11	11	11	11	11	11	11	11	11	11	11
4	1	11	11	11	11	11	11	11	11	11	11	11	11	11	11	11
3	1	11	11	11	11	11	11	11	11	11	11	11	11	11	11	11
2	1	11	11	11	11	11	11	11	11	11	11	11	11	11	11	11
1	1	11	11	11	11	11	11	11	11	11	11	11	11	11	11	11
$\Delta H_2(x_2)$		1	1	1	1	1	1	1	1	1	1	1	1	1	1	1 x_2
		1	2	3	4	5	6	7	8	9	10	11	12	13	14	15

Dominance map F and K

$\Delta F_1(x_1)$																
15	x_1 0	10	10	10	10	20	10	10	10	10	20	20	20	20	00	00
14	0	10	10	10	10	22	12	10	10	10	20	20	21	22	00	00
13	2	12	12	12	12	22	12	12	12	12	22	21	20	20	20	20
12	2	12	12	12	12	22	12	12	12	12	22	22	21	20	20	20
11	2	12	12	12	12	22	12	12	12	12	22	22	22	22	20	20
10	2	12	12	12	12	22	12	12	12	12	22	22	22	22	20	20
9	1	11	11	11	11	21	11	11	11	11	21	21	12	12	10	10
8	1	11	11	11	11	21	11	11	11	11	21	21	12	12	10	10
7	1	11	11	11	11	21	11	11	12	12	22	12	12	12	10	10
6	2	12	12	12	12	22	21	21	21	22	22	22	22	22	20	20
5	1	11	11	11	11	22	21	11	11	11	12	12	12	12	10	10
4	1	11	11	11	11	22	21	11	11	12	22	12	12	12	10	10
3	1	11	11	11	11	12	11	11	11	11	12	12	12	12	10	10
2	1	11	11	11	11	12	11	11	11	11	12	12	12	12	12	10
1	1	11	11	11	11	12	11	11	11	11	12	12	12	12	10	10
$\Delta F_2(x_2)$		1	1	1	1	2	1	1	1	1	2	2	2	2	0	0 x_2
		1	2	3	4	5	6	7	8	9	10	11	12	13	14	15

Acknowledgements

We wish to acknowledge the helpful comments of M. A. King, A. Sen, N. H. Stern and two anonymous referees. We would like to thank the CNRS and the SSRC for their support.

Notes

1 As in the one-dimension case, this requirement can be dropped, although care is necessary in the statement of the more general results – see Testfatsion [28].
2 The result is stated in the weak form ('no lower'); the strong condition can be obtained by appropriate modification of the conditions.
3 Levhari, Paroush and Peleg [19] discuss the conjecture that the conditions are sufficient for the general class of non-decreasing continuous utility functions, and present a counter-example. This brings out the crucial role played by the additional condition imposed on U_{12}.
4 The sum of F is less for 1970 for $(2 \leqq x_1; 1 \leqq x_2 \leqq 6)$ and for $(2 \leqq x_1 \leqq 5; x_2 \geqq 7)$; it is otherwise equal to that for 1960.
5 The least concave representation of homothetic preferences may be written in linear homogeneous form (Kihlstrom and Mirman [13]).
6 We take the reverse sign from that of Levy and Paroush.
7 The left-hand side follows from writing

$$\Delta(F_1 F_2) = F_1 \Delta F_2 + F_2 \Delta F_1 - \Delta F_1 \Delta F_2$$

the right-hand side from writing

$$\Delta[(1 - F_1)(1 - F_2)] = -(1 - F_1) \Delta F_2 - (1 - F_2^*) \Delta F_1$$

8 It may be noted that a_1, a_2 may be increased arbitrarily without affecting the welfare comparison; the condition $\mu_i > \mu_i^*$ ensures that (32) continues to hold.
9 In the case of income, too, the assumption of scale independence may be questioned – see Kolm [15].
10 It may be noted that the calculations are straightforward, involving only the evaluation of incomplete means and covariances, and that in principle there is no problem in extending them to more than two dimensions.

References

[1] Atkinson, A. B. (1980), 'Horizontal equity and the distribution of the tax burden', Chapter 5 in this volume.
[2] Atkinson, A. B. (1981), 'The measurement of economic mobility', Chapter 3 in this volume.
[3] Chipman, J. S. (1977). 'An empirical implication of Auspitz–Lieben–Edgeworth–Pareto complementarity', *Journal of Economic Theory*, **14**, 228–31.
[4] Debreu, G. (1976), 'Least concave utility functions', *Journal of Mathematical Economics*, **3**, 121–9.
[5] Duncan, G. T. (1977), 'A matrix measure of multivariate local risk aversion', *Econometrica*, **45**, 895–903.
[6] Epstein, L. G. and Tanny, S. M. (1980), 'Increasing generalized correlation: a definition and some economic consequences', *Canadian Journal of Economics*, **13**, 16–34.
[7] Fisher, F. M. (1956), 'Income distribution, value judgments and welfare', *Quarterly Journal of Economics*, **70**, 380–424.
[8] Hadar, J. and Russell, W. R. (1974), 'Stochastic dominance in choice under uncertainty', in M. S. Balch, D. L. McFadden and S. Y. Wu (eds.), *Essays on Economic Behavior Under Uncertainty*, Amsterdam, North-Holland.
[9] Hahn, F. H. (1971), 'Equilibrium with transaction costs', *Econometrica*, **39**, 417–40.
[10] Hamada, K. (1974), 'Comment' on Hadar and Russell (1974).

[11] IBRD (1976), *World Tables 1976*, Johns Hopkins University Press.

[12] Kannai, Y. (1980), 'The ALEP definition of complementarity and least concave utility functions', *Journal of Economic Theory*, 22, 115–17.

[13] Kihlstrom, R. E. and Mirman, L. J. (1981), 'Constant increasing and decreasing risk aversion with many commodities', *Review of Economic Studies*, 48, 271–80.

[14] King, M. A. (1980), 'An index of inequality with applications to horizontal equity and social mobility', *Econometrica* (forthcoming).

[15] Kolm, S.-Ch. (1973), 'More equal distributions of bundles of commodities', CEPREMAP, Paris.

[16] Kolm, S.-Ch. (1976), 'Unequal inequalities', *Journal of Economic Theory*, 12 and 13, 416–42 and 82–111.

[17] Kolm, S.-Ch. (1977), 'Multidimensional egalitarianisms', *Quarterly Journal of Economics*, 91, 1–13.

[18] Kravis, I., Heston, A. and Summers, R. (1978), 'Real GDP estimates for more than one hundred countries, *Economic Journal*, 88, 215–43.

[19] Levhari, D., Paroush, J. and Peleg, B. (1975), 'Efficiency analysis for multivariate distributions', *Review of Economic Studies*, 42, 87–91.

[20] Levy, H. and Paroush, J. (1974), 'Toward multivariate efficiency criteria', *Journal of Economic Theory*, 7, 129–42.

[21] Roberts, K. W. S. (1980), 'Price-independent welfare prescriptions', *Journal of Public Economics*, 13, 277–98.

[22] Russell, W. R. and Seo, T. K. (1978), 'Ordering uncertain prospects: the multivariate utility functions case', *Review of Economic Studies*, 45, 605–10.

[23] Sen, A. K. (1973), *On Economic Inequality*, London, Oxford University Press.

[24] Sen, A. K. (1976), 'Real national income', *Review of Economic Studies*, 43, 19–40.

[25] Sen, A. K. (1977), 'On weights and measures', *Econometrica*, 45, 1539–72.

[26] Sen, A. K. (1979), 'Ethical measurement of inequality: some difficulties', in W. Krelle and A. F. Shorrocks (eds.), *Personal Income Distribution*, Amsterdam, North-Holland.

[27] Stiglitz, J. E. (1976), 'Simple formulae for optimal income taxation and the measurement of inequality', mimeo, Oxford University.

[28] Testfatsion, L. (1976), 'Stochastic dominance and the maximization of expected utility', *Review of Economic Studies*, 43, 301–15.

[29] Ulph, D. T. (1978), 'On labour supply and the measurement of inequality', *Journal of Economic Theory*, 19, 492–512.

3 The Measurement of Economic Mobility*

1 Introduction

In his volume on *Income Distribution*, Professor Pen [10] noted that 'There is no bridge between the figures on vertical mobility and income distribution ... Not a single textbook on economics, as far as I know, points out that for an understanding of personal income distribution it is necessary to have an insight into vertical mobility' (pp. 264–5). He goes on to ask, for example, 'if the vertical mobility (measured by this or that index) is increased by 1 %, what will the personal distribution (measured by, for instance, the Gini Concentration Ratio, the share of the top 10 %, or another criterion) do then?' (p. 265). The aim of this chapter is to contribute towards building this bridge. In particular, it examines the relationship between the measurement of mobility and the measure of inequality which have been employed in the field of income distribution.

A great deal has been written by sociologists on the subject of social mobility, and a wide variety of summary measures have been proposed. Bartholomew [5] and Boudon [6], among others, have reviewed this literature and discussed the properties of different indicators, Shorrocks [13] has discussed the issue from the perspective of an economist. The approach adopted here is rather different in two respects. First, the measurement of mobility is related to the properties of a social welfare function defined over incomes at different dates. This may be contrasted with the approach based directly on assumptions about the mobility indicator (as in the axiomatisation by Shorrocks). Secondly, the focus is not on the derivation of particular indices of mobility, but rather on obtaining conditions under which one can rank degrees of mobility (e.g. comparing different countries) for a class of different indicators. The approach is parallel in this respect to that in the field of income inequality, where the condition that the Lorenz curves do not intersect allows one to give an unambiguous ranking for a wide range of inequality measures.

In section 2, different approaches to the measurement of mobility are outlined briefly, and the social welfare function approach is described in more detail. The relationship between the comparison of mobility and the properties

* Reprinted from *Essays in Honour of Jan Pen*, 1981.

of the welfare function is introduced in section 3. As in the literature on the measurement of inequality, there is a theoretical similarity to the problem of choice under uncertainty, in this case multi- rather than single-dimensioned. Some of the key results from the analysis of uncertainty are set out in section 4 (with further details in the Appendix). These results are used in section 5 to derive conditions under which unambiguous rankings of mobility processes can be made, and these are shown to correspond to straightforward tests, analogous to the comparison of Lorenz curves.

2   Approaches to the Measurement of Mobility

The measurement of mobility can be approached in a number of different ways.[1] Mobility may, first of all, be viewed as an objective in its own right. Society may attach a positive weight to fluidity as such. Such a standpoint appears to underlie some discussions of the topic, although it is not typically made explicit; and it may be seen as providing a basis for the direct axiomatisation of measures of mobility. A second approach views mobility as desirable in that it is *instrumental* in leading to greater efficiency: for example, where control of production is determined by ability rather than inherited wealth. In this context, a measure of the implications of mobility requires a detailed analysis of the effects on production. A third approach views mobility similarly as instrumental, but as ensuring less inequality of opportunity. This accords with a long tradition, but the precise interpretation of inequality of opportunity is open to debate, and the relation with mobility depends on the social and economic mechanisms at work (see Chapter 4).

A fourth approach, and the one which we examine in this chapter, sees mobility as influencing the overall level of social welfare, defined over the distribution of income, taken over different generations. It is this viewpoint which appears to lie behind Pen's reference to the impact of increased vertical mobility on the Gini Ratio. We need in effect to extend the measure of inequality to two or more generations and to consider how this measure is affected by different degrees of mobility. For mobility within a generation, this approach has been studied by Shorrocks [14], but he takes a rather different direction, concentrating on the implications for measures of lifetime income and of changes in the accounting period.

In order to explore further the social welfare approach to the measurement of mobility, we consider the case where there are two generations and where their lifetime economic status can be measured by indicators y_1 and y_2, respectively, for the successive generations. The extension to several generations can be carried out, but complicates the exposition. By assuming a single index of economic status, we are leaving on one side the issues which arise in the measurement of lifetime income (and intra-generational mobility). Any dependence of y_2 on y_1, or vice versa, is also being ignored.[2] The social welfare function, W, is assumed to be defined over y_1 and y_2, and to be additively separable and symmetric with respect to individuals (or families, if they are the unit of analysis). This can be given a utilitarian interpretation, with W being the sum of the utilities of individuals or of dynastic utility functions, but this is not the only possible interpretation and it is not one we follow here. The joint distribution of y_1 and y_2 is given by the bi-variate density function $f(y_1, y_2)$ and these variables are assumed to have the finite range $0 \leqslant y_i \leqslant a_i$. The social welfare function may therefore be written:

$$W \equiv \int_0^{a_1} \int_0^{a_2} U(y_1, y_2) f y_1, y_2) dy_2 dy_1 \tag{1}$$

The function $U(y_1, y_2)$ is assumed to be increasing; further assumptions about U are discussed below (we take U to be continuously differentiable to the required degree). If two distributions are being compared, $f(y_1, y_2)$ and $f^*(y_1, y_2)$, then we denote the difference by:

$$\Delta f = f(y_1, y_2) - f^*(y_1, y_2) \tag{2}$$

and the difference in social welfare by

$$\Delta W = \int_0^{a_1} \int_0^{a_2} U(y_1, y_2) \Delta f(y_1, y_2) \, dy_2 \, dy_1 \tag{3}$$

In comparing the distributions, $f(y_1, y_2)$ and $f^*(y_1, y_2)$, there may be differences in the marginal distributions for the two generations taken individually: e.g. the distribution of y_1 may be less unequal for f than for f^* and/or the distribution of y_2 may be less unequal for f than for f^*. Alternatively, the marginal distributions may be identical, but there may be differences in the relation between y_1 and y_2 for the two distributions. Much of the literature on social mobility has been concerned with separating the latter differences (in 'exchange' mobility) from the former differences (in 'structural' change). Here, in order to focus on the pure mobility effect, we consider the case where the distributions of y_1 and y_2 taken separately – the marginal distributions – are identical for f and f^*. This assumption is intended to separate the issues rather than to be realistic, but the underlying mathematical results can be extended to the case where this does not hold (with additional complexity). The marginal density of y_1 is denoted by:

$$m_1(y_1) \equiv \int_0^{a_2} f(y_1, y_2) dy_2 \tag{4}$$

and the assumption we are making is that:

$$\left. \begin{array}{l} m_1(y_1) = m_1^*(y_1) \text{ all } y_1 \\ m_2(y_2) = m_2^*(y_2) \text{ all } y_2 \end{array} \right\} \tag{5}$$

The distribution has been represented in continuous form, but in a number of empirical applications the distribution is assumed to be discrete. This applies particularly to occupational status, but income data may be presented in terms of ranges or quantile groups. Suppose that there are n ranges, with income y^j in range j, and that the number in range j in generation i is m_i^j (these are the marginal frequencies). The pattern of mobility may then be represented by the transition matrix, A, where:

$$\underline{m}_2 = \underline{m}_1 A \tag{6}$$

and $\underline{m}_i$ denotes the vector $(m_i^1, m_i^2, \ldots, m_i^n)$, and a_{ij} is the proportion of those in range i whose children are in range j. Given that the marginal distribution, m_1, is assumed to be the same, we are concerned with the comparison of the transition matrix A with, say, A*. The criterion is again the level of social welfare:

$$W = \sum_{j=1}^{n} \sum_{k=1}^{n} U(y_1^j, y_2^k) a_{jk} \, m_i^j \tag{7}$$

3   Comparing Mobility and the Social Welfare Function

Much of the literature on social mobility has been concerned with deriving summary measures, reducing, in the discrete case, the transition matrix, A, to a single number, which can be compared with that for an alternative matrix, A*. In contrast, our concern here is with the conditions under which we can rank A and A* without necessarily agreeing on a particular measure of mobility. Put in terms of the social welfare function, do there exist conditions on A and A* which ensure that one matrix is considered to exhibit greater mobility for all social welfare functions in a specified class? This will not in general allow a complete ranking of all transition matrices – there will be some cases where we cannot make an unambiguous comparison – but there are obvious advantages in allowing for a range of different social values (within the specified class). As noted earlier, there is a parallel with the case of a single variable where Lorenz curves do not intersect, and we obtain the same ranking for all S-concave welfare functions (Sen, [12]).

An example may be helpful. Suppose that we consider the income range divided into quartiles, ranked in order of increasing income, and:

$$A = \begin{pmatrix} \frac{1}{2} & \frac{1}{4} & \frac{1}{4} & 0 \\ \frac{1}{4} & \frac{1}{2} & \frac{1}{8} & \frac{1}{8} \\ \frac{1}{4} & \frac{1}{8} & \frac{1}{2} & \frac{1}{8} \\ 0 & \frac{1}{8} & \frac{1}{8} & \frac{3}{4} \end{pmatrix} \qquad A^* = \begin{pmatrix} \frac{5}{8} & \frac{1}{8} & \frac{1}{4} & 0 \\ \frac{1}{8} & \frac{5}{8} & \frac{1}{8} & \frac{1}{8} \\ \frac{1}{4} & \frac{1}{8} & \frac{1}{2} & \frac{1}{8} \\ 0 & \frac{1}{8} & \frac{1}{8} & \frac{3}{4} \end{pmatrix} \tag{8}$$

(which differ in the underlined elements). In that the diagonal elements in A* are larger (or no smaller), and the off-diagonal elements are smaller (or no larger), it seems reasonable to conclude that A* exhibits less mobility than A. What we would like to know is how this 'reasonable' conclusion relates to the properties of the social welfare function, and how widely it can be applied.

The crucial role played by the properties of the social welfare function may be seen from the case where U is additive:

$$U(y_1, y_2) = \phi(y_1) + \psi(y_2)$$ (9)

where ϕ', $\psi' > 0$ and ϕ'', $\psi'' \leq 0$.
Substituting in (7)[3]:

$$W = \sum_{j=1}^{n} \phi(y_1^j) m_1^j + \sum_{k=1}^{n} \psi(y_2^k) m_2^k$$ (10)

so that, where the marginal distributions are identical, the level of social welfare is the same, irrespective of the other properties of the transition matrix, A. (The same applies for continuous distributions.) In this additive case, the degree of mobility does not influence the level of social welfare (Markandya, [9]), and the two matrices A and A* are ranked the same. This may appear counter-intuitive, since it appears quite obvious that A exhibits greater mobility, but it must be remembered that we are concerned here not with mobility as such but with its implications for social welfare. With a social welfare function of the form (9), mobility is irrelevant. From some standpoints, the adoption of an additive function may appear quite acceptable. It may be argued, for example, that we should only be concerned with the distribution at each date and not worry about the movement between income ranges. On this view, the important feature is that x% of the population in each generation are poor, not that a disproportionate number of poor children had poor parents. Alternatively, the function (9) may be justified on strict utilitarian grounds. On the other hand, we should clearly consider other forms of the function, and at the very least it seems unlikely that we would exclude concave transformations:

$$U = \Omega(\phi(y_1) + \psi(y_2))$$ (11)

where $\Omega' > 0$, $\Omega'' \leq 0$. It may be noted that, in contrast to (9), where $U_{12} = 0$,

$$U_{12} = \Omega'' \cdot \phi' \cdot \psi' \leq 0$$ (12)

Where $U_{12} \neq 0$, the level of social welfare is no longer independent of the degree of mobility. Where $U_{12} < 0$, we would expect intuitively that social welfare is lower, the more highly correlated are y_1 and y_2, since an increase in y_2 lowers the social valuation of a marginal increase in y_1. On this basis, A* would be ranked inferior to A. This intuitive idea may be demonstrated formally using results from the literature on uncertainty described in the next section.

4   Results on Stochastic Dominance

The results from the literature on uncertainty which are of particular assistance are those concerned with *stochastic dominance*. A probability distribution is said to stochastically dominate another if the level of expected utility is at least as high for all utility functions belonging to a specified class U. The interest of conditions for stochastic dominance is that they allow us to rank certain distributions without knowing the precise form of the utility function, only that it belongs to U. The parallel between the results on uncertainty and those for the distribution of income may be seen if we replace 'probability distribution' by 'income distribution', replace 'expected utility' by 'social welfare', and 'utility functions' by U. Alternatively, we may interpret W in equation (1) as expected utility.[4] The formal parallel between the two problems will be exploited in the next section; first, we present some of the main results on stochastic dominance.

The stochastic dominance results involve in essence a trade-off between the assumptions about the class of functions, U, and the strength of the conditions on the distributions. If we can only make weak assumptions about the class U, then we are only able to conclude that one distribution dominates another in rather special circumstances. In this situation we are only likely to be able to make a small number of definite comparisons, and in most cases no ranking may be possible (f is preferred for some utility functions belonging to U, but f^* is preferred for others). On the other hand, if we make stronger assumptions about U, reducing the class of possible utility functions, then we can rank more cases.

Much of the literature on stochastic dominance has concentrated on the single variable case; here, however, we are concerned with the bivariate case, where results are more limited. The most straightforward of these (given by Hadar and Russell [7]) is based on the fact that, in the case of identical marginal distributions:

$$\Delta W = \int_0^{a_1} \int_0^{a_2} U_{12}(y_1, y_2) \Delta F(y_1, y_2) dy_2 \, dy_1 \tag{13}$$

where F is the cumulative distribution. We have therefore *Result A* where:

$$F(y_1, y_2) \leqslant F^*(y_1, y_2) \text{ for all } y_1, y_2 \tag{14}$$

then F stochastically dominates F^* for all

$$U \in U^- \text{ such that } U_{12} \leqslant 0 \tag{15}$$

(The derivation of this result is sketched in the Appendix.) As is shown by Levy and Paroush [8], the reverse condition holds for the class U^+ (where $U_{12} \geqslant 0$).[5]

The Result A bears out the earlier intuitive discussion. Where $U_{12} = 0$, $\Delta W = 0$. Where $U_{12} \neq 0$, then the condition depends on the sign of the cross-derivative. It is conceivable that social values are such that $U_{12} > 0$, but, as we have seen, where the social welfare function is a concave transformation of an additive function (equation (11)), then $U_{12} \leqslant 0$. In this case, condition (14) allows us to rank all distributions such that the cumulative distribution is at all points no greater. This is a strong condition on the distributions and reflects the relatively weak assumptions made about the class of utility functions.

The result given above corresponds to 'first-degree' stochastic dominance, and by imposing further conditions on the class of functions, U, we may be able to rank more cases. Second-degree dominance results are given for the multi-variate case by Russell and Seo [11], but here we make use of a rather different result derived in Chapter 2. This is based on the following indicator (see Appendix):

$$H(y_1, y_2) \equiv \int_0^{y_1} \int_0^{y_2} F(s,t) \, dt \, ds \qquad (16)$$

From this, we can, in the case of identical marginal distributions, obtain *Result B* where:

$$H(y_1, y_2) \leqslant H^*(y_1, y_2) \text{ for all } y_1, y_2 \qquad (17)$$

then F stochastically dominates F* (to the second degree) for all $U \in U^{--}$ such that:

$$U_{12} < 0; \qquad U_{112}, U_{122} \geqslant 0; \qquad U_{1122} \leqslant 0 \qquad (18)$$

The condition (17) is weaker than (14) of Result A in that it allows the cumulative distribution F to be greater than F* at some point, providing that the integral of F remains less than the corresponding integral for F*. We can therefore obtain a more complete ranking of distributions, if we are willing to restrict attention to the class of functions, U^{--}. The appearance of conditions on the third and fourth derivatives of the function, U, is a natural result of the extension to second-degree dominance, but the reader may have difficulty in forming a judgement on the reasonableness – or otherwise – of the conditions. Returning to the case of equation (11), where the social welfare function is a concave transformation of an additive function, we can see that:

$$U_{112} = \Omega'''(\phi')^2 \psi' + \Omega'' \phi'' \psi' \qquad (19a)$$

$$U_{1122} = \Omega''''(\phi' \psi')^2 + \Omega'''((\phi')^2 \psi'' + (\psi')^2 \phi'') + \Omega'' \phi'' \psi'' \qquad (19b)$$

It follows that, where $\Omega'' \leqslant 0$, $\Omega''' \geqslant 0$ and $\Omega'''' \leqslant 0$, the function belongs to the class U^{--}. There is therefore at least one interesting class of cases for which the dominance condition (17) is relevant.

5 The Comparison of Mobility

As indicated in the previous section, the results on stochastic dominance can be reinterpreted to provide insights into the measurement of mobility.

We begin with Result A and consider the case where the social welfare function is assumed to belong to class U^-. Where $U_{12} < 0$, a higher level of social welfare is associated with a distribution which has a lower cumulative density at all y_1, y_2. As remarked earlier, this is a fairly restrictive condition. The interpretation may be seen in terms of the following operation:

$$
\begin{array}{ccc}
 & y_1 & y_1 + h \\
y_2 & \text{density reduced by} & \text{density increased by} \\
 & \varepsilon & \varepsilon \\
y_2 + k & \text{density increased by} & \text{density reduced by} \\
 & \varepsilon & \varepsilon
\end{array}
\tag{20}
$$

(This operation leaves the marginal distributions unchanged.) The operation reduces $F(y_1, y_2)$, and leaves F everywhere else either lower or unchanged, so that the distribution after such an operation dominates that before the operation. This operation in effect shifts weight away from the diagonal of the joint distribution. Where one distribution can be reached from another by a sequence of such operations, then it is stochastically dominant. On the other hand, it only requires distributions to differ by two such operations in opposite directions, at different points, for us to be unable to compare the degree of mobility.

The application may be illustrated by a simple example with a discrete distribution. Suppose that we consider four quartiles, ranked in order of increasing income, with a transition matrix:

$$
A = \begin{pmatrix}
a_{11} & a_{12} & a_{13} & a_{14} \\
a_{21} & & & \cdot \\
a_{31} & & & \cdot \\
a_{41} & \cdot & \cdot & a_{44}
\end{pmatrix}
\tag{21}
$$

The cumulative distribution (i.e. the sum of the densities up to y_1^j, y_2^k) is given by[6]:

$$
\alpha \equiv \begin{pmatrix}
\dfrac{a_{11}}{4} & \dfrac{a_{11}+a_{12}}{4} & \dfrac{a_{11}+a_{12}+a_{13}}{4} & \tfrac{1}{4} \\[2ex]
\dfrac{a_{11}+a_{21}}{4} & \dfrac{a_{11}+a_{12}+a_{21}+a_{22}}{4} & \dfrac{a_{11}+a_{12}+a_{21}+a_{22}+a_{13}+a_{23}}{4} & \tfrac{1}{2} \\[2ex]
\dfrac{a_{11}+a_{21}+a_{31}}{4} & \cdots & \cdots & \tfrac{3}{4} \\[2ex]
\tfrac{1}{4} & \tfrac{1}{2} & \tfrac{3}{4} & 1
\end{pmatrix}
\tag{22}
$$

For the level of social welfare to be higher for a matrix A, compared with A*, we require α to be smaller for some element, and not larger for any element, than α^*. Thus, taking the earlier example (8):

$$A = \begin{pmatrix} \frac{1}{2} & \frac{1}{4} & \frac{1}{4} & 0 \\ \frac{1}{4} & \frac{1}{2} & \frac{1}{8} & \frac{1}{8} \\ \frac{1}{4} & \frac{1}{8} & \frac{1}{2} & \frac{1}{8} \\ 0 & \frac{1}{8} & \frac{1}{8} & \frac{3}{4} \end{pmatrix} \qquad A^* = \begin{pmatrix} \frac{5}{8} & \frac{1}{8} & \frac{1}{4} & 0 \\ \frac{1}{8} & \frac{5}{8} & \frac{1}{8} & \frac{1}{8} \\ \frac{1}{4} & \frac{1}{8} & \frac{1}{2} & \frac{1}{8} \\ 0 & \frac{1}{8} & \frac{1}{8} & \frac{3}{4} \end{pmatrix} \qquad (8)$$

then:

$$\alpha - \alpha^* = \begin{pmatrix} -1/32 & 0 & 0 & 0 \\ 0 & 0 & 0 & 0 \\ 0 & 0 & 0 & 0 \\ 0 & 0 & 0 & 0 \end{pmatrix} \qquad (23)$$

So it follows that A gives a higher level of social welfare for all $U \in U^-$.

The technique described above provides a simple method of comparing degrees of mobility, since α is readily calculated (where the densities in the initial ranges are not identical, then n – in our case, 4 – is replaced by the relevant frequency). Moreover, it appears to coincide with an intuitive notion of shifting weight away from the diagonal. The matrix A in the example is in fact obtained from A* by a single operation of type (20), applied to the first and second rows and columns. At the same time, we can only rank in certain cases. Suppose:

$$A^{**} = \begin{pmatrix} \frac{5}{8} & \frac{1}{8} & \frac{1}{4} & 0 \\ \frac{1}{8} & \frac{5}{8} & \frac{1}{8} & \frac{1}{8} \\ \frac{1}{4} & \frac{1}{8} & \frac{3}{8} & \frac{1}{4} \\ 0 & \frac{1}{8} & \frac{1}{4} & \frac{5}{8} \end{pmatrix} \qquad (24)$$

This is again obtained from A* by a single operation of type (20), and we can rank A** relative to A*, but not relative to A (for all $U \in U^-$):

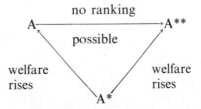

In other words, there are functions U, belonging to U^-, which rank A and A**

differently, and without further restrictions on the class of functions we cannot draw definite conclusions.

Further restrictions on the class of social welfare functions are introduced in Result B. If we are willing to restrict attention to the class U^{--}, which imposes conditions on higher cross-derivatives, then the condition for dominance is weakened to one on the cumulative sum of F (in the discrete case). If α_{ij} denote the elements of the matrix α in equation (22), then we require that:

$$A_{ij} \equiv \sum_i^k \sum_j^l \alpha_{ij} \leqslant \sum_i^k \sum_j^l \alpha_{ij}^* \tag{25}$$

In the case of A and A**, we have:

$$\alpha - \alpha^{**} = \begin{pmatrix} -1/32 & 0 & 0 & 0 \\ 0 & 0 & 0 & 0 \\ 0 & 0 & 1/32 & 0 \\ 0 & 0 & 0 & 0 \end{pmatrix} \tag{26}$$

and the cumulative matrix with elements A_{ij}:

$$A - A^{**} = \begin{pmatrix} -1/32 & -1/32 & -1/32 & -1/32 \\ -1/32 & -1/32 & -1/32 & -1/32 \\ -1/32 & -1/32 & 0 & 0 \\ -1/32 & -1/32 & 0 & 0 \end{pmatrix} \tag{27}$$

So, with the additional restriction of U to the class U^{--}, we can now conclude that A gives a higher level of social welfare. In effect, the functions belonging to this class attach a higher weight to the greater mobility at the lower income ranges.

The interpretation of the second-degree stochastic dominance condition is not particularly obvious, and may be aided by the transformation, derived in Atkinson and Bourguignon [3], of $H(y_1, y_2)$ to (see Appendix):

$$H(y_1, y_2) = \int_0^{y_1} \int_0^{y_2} (y_1 - s)(y_2 - t) f(s,t) dt ds \tag{28}$$

From this, we can obtain:
Result C. The second-degree stochastic dominance condition (17) requires that the *incomplete* cross-product about (y_1, y_2) be no greater for all (y_1, y_2).

This result relates the incomplete moment (i.e. integrating over the range 0 to y_i) to the stochastic dominance condition, in just the same way as the result for the Lorenz curve in the one dimension problem.[7] It requires in effect that the distribution be more concentrated in the direction of the boundaries joining (y_1, y_2) to the axes. Again this can be calculated quite readily. We may also note that, given the assumption of identical marginal distributions, a necessary condition is that the correlation of y_1 and y_2 be lower.[8]

B   Conclusions

In this chapter we have not derived specific summary measures of mobility. The analysis does not allow us to provide a precise quantitative answer to the question proved by Professor Pen and quoted in the Introduction. In order to do this, we would need, following the approach adopted here, to specify fully the form of the social welfare function.

The task attempted in this chapter is a related, but rather different, one. The aim has been to derive 'dominance' conditions under which we can rank mobility processes for a class of social welfare functions satisfying certain general properties. This does not allow a complete ranking; we may be able to rank one process as leading to a higher level of social welfare than some, but not all, other processes. The conditions are comparable to those for Lorenz dominance in the comparison of income distributions, in that we can only compare distributions with non-intersecting Lorenz curves. As in the case of Lorenz dominance, such conditions are of considerable value, since we may be able to agree on certain properties of the social welfare function even if we cannot agree on its precise form. Alternatively, where the dominance conditions are satisfied, we may be able to deduce that the same conclusions will be drawn from a wide variety of summary measures of mobility.

The dominance results described in this chapter lead to two straightforward tests which can be applied to mobility processes. The first concerns the cumulative distribution and involves, in the case of a transition matrix, adding the elements cumulatively (weighted by the appropriate frequencies). If the elements of this cumulative matrix are everywhere smaller, or identical, for one process, A, then it ensures a higher or identical level of social welfare for all social welfare functions such that the cross-derivative is non-positive. Such a restriction on the welfare function involves in effect a preference for mobility in terms of transformations of type (20). The second applies the same summation operation to the cumulative distribution, requiring that the elements of the new matrix formed in this way be everywhere smaller, or identical. This is a weaker condition on the distribution, in that the cumulative may be lower at some points, but it ensures dominance for a narrower class of welfare functions (involving restrictions on the first and second derivatives of U_{12}). The restrictions are however satisfied for the class of concave transformations of an additive function, given by (11), with the further conditions that $\Omega''' \geqslant 0$, Ω'''' $\leqslant 0$, which seems a class of particular interest.[9]

As emphasised at the outset, the approach to the measurement of mobility adopted here is only one of several possible. Mobility is seen in terms of its implications for social welfare, and the ranking of processes is derived from these implications rather than from a direct consideration of what is meant by mobility. This approach does however seem a promising way – and one capable of further development – of building the bridge with the measurement of income inequality which Professor Pen saw to be necessary.

Appendix

The purpose of this appendix is to provide a heuristic account of the steps leading to Results A, B and C used in the text. No attempt is made to provide a full account, and the reader is referred to Chapter 2 for further details and results.

The results can be seen most easily by integrating by parts the expression for ΔW (equation (3)). Taking first the inner integral, with respect to y_2:

$$U(y_1,a_2)\int_0^{a_2}\Delta f dy_2 - \int_0^{a_2}U_2\left(\int_0^{y_2}\Delta f(y_1,t)dt\right)dy_2 \tag{A1}$$

Integrating the first term by parts with respect to y_1, we obtain:

$$U(a_1,a_2)\int_0^{a_1}\int_0^{a_2}\Delta f dy_2 dy_1 - \int_0^{a_1}U_1\int_0^{y_1}\int_0^{a_2}\Delta f(s,y_2)dy_2 ds dy_1 \tag{A2}$$

Now:

$$\int_0^{y_1}\int_0^{a_2}\Delta f(s,y_2)dy_2 ds = \int_0^{y_1}\Delta m_1(s)ds \tag{A3}$$

is the difference in the cumulative marginal distributions. We are assuming identical marginal distributions, so that this is zero. Also the first term in (A2) is zero by the definition of a distribution function (i.e. the integral of f over the whole range is unity). The first term in (A1) therefore vanishes. Integrating the second term with respect to y_1, again by parts, yields[10]:

$$-\int_0^{a_2}U_2(a_1,y_2)\left(\int_0^{a_1}\int_0^{y_2}\Delta f(y_1,t)dt dy_1\right)dy_2$$
$$+\int_0^{a_2}\int_0^{a_2}U_{12}(y_1,y_2)\left[\int_0^{y_1}\int_0^{y_2}\Delta f(s,t)dt ds\right]dy_1 dy_2 \tag{A4}$$

In the first term, the difference between the distributions again appears via the marginal distribution (in this case m_2), and the assumption of identical marginals again implies that it is zero.

It follows that ΔW reduces to the second term in (A4), and this gives equation (13) in the text. The inner integral, in the square bracket, is the difference in the cumulative distribution, ΔF. Where $U_{12}\leqslant 0$, $\Delta F\leqslant 0$ ensures that $\Delta W\geqslant 0$ (Result A).

The derivation of the second-degree result follows by a similar process. Integrating by parts the expression for ΔW in equation (13), and taking first the inner integral with respect to y_2:

$$U_{12}(y_1,a_2)\int_0^{a_2}\Delta F dy_2 - \int_0^{a_2}U_{122}\left(\int_0^{y_2}\Delta F(y_1,t)dt\right)dy_2 \tag{A5}$$

Integrating the first term by parts with respect to y_1, we obtain:

$$U_{1\,9}(u_1,u_2)\int_0^{a_1}\int_0^{a_2} \Delta H(y,\ldots)\,dy_1 = \int_0^{a_1}\int_0^{a_2} \Delta\Gamma\,dy\,/\,da\,dy_1 \tag{A6}$$

Integrating the second term by parts with respect to y_1, we obtain (reversing the order of integration):

$$-\int_0^{a_2} U_{122}\left(\int_0^{a_1}\int_0^{y_2}\Delta F(y,t)\,dt\,dy_1\right)dy_2$$

$$+\int_0^{a_2}\int_0^{a_1} U_{1122}(y_1,y_2)\left[\int_0^{y_1}\int_0^{y_2}\Delta F(s,t)\,dt\,ds\right]dy_1\,dy_2 \tag{A7}$$

As in the text, we define:

$$H(y_1,y_2)\equiv\int_0^{y_1}\int_0^{y_2} F(s,t)\,dt\,ds \tag{16}$$

with the condition (17) giving:

$$\Delta H(y_1,y_2)\leqslant 0 \text{ for all } y_1,\ y_2 \tag{A8}$$

Combining (A6) and (A7), we can see that (A8) ensures $\Delta W\geqslant 0$ where $U_{12}\leqslant 0$, $U_{112},U_{122}\geqslant 0$, $U_{1122}\leqslant 0$, which are the conditions for Result B.

To obtain Result C, we integrate the right-hand side of (16) by parts, first with respect to t:

$$H=\int_0^{y_1}\left[y_2 F(s,y_2)-\int_0^{y_2} t\frac{\partial F}{\partial t}\right]ds \tag{A9}$$

Integrating again with respect to s,

$$H=y_1 y_2 F(y_1,y_2)-y_2\int_0^{y_1} s\frac{\partial F(s,y_2)}{\partial s}ds$$

$$-\int_0^{y_2} t\frac{\partial F(y_1,t)}{\partial s}dt+\int_0^{y_1}\int_0^{y_2} st\frac{\partial^2 F}{\partial s\partial t}dt\,ds \tag{A10}$$

$$=\int_0^{y_1}\int_0^{y_2}(y_1-s)(y_2-t)f(s,t)\,dt\,ds \tag{29}$$

Notes

1 Some aspects are discussed further in Atkinson [1] and Chapter 2 of Atkinson, Maynard and Trinder [4]. The latter contains empirical evidence on intergenerational income mobility in the United Kingdom.
2 Thus, if y_i denotes consumption, this depends on the pattern of transfer of wealth between generations. If y_1 is high, then this may be associated with substantial bequests, and hence high y_2; conversely, where the parents expect the children to enjoy high consumption levels, they may leave smaller bequests (or the children may support their parents).
3 And using the fact that:

$$\sum_j a_{jk} m_1^j = m_2^k$$

4 It is assumed that the distribution is normalised such that:

$$\int_0^{a_1} \int_0^{a_2} f(y_1, y_2) dy_2 dy_1 = 1$$

5 The conditions have been stated in terms of weak inequalities. For strict dominance, it is necessary that $F < F^*$ for some (y_1, y_2).
6 The initial frequencies, m_1^j, are $\frac{1}{4}$, since the matrix is defined in terms of quartiles.
7 The one dimension condition is in terms of

$$\int_0^{y_1} (y_1 - s) f(s) ds$$

8 This may be seen from $H(a_1, a_2) = (a_1 - a_2)(\bar{y}_1 - \bar{y}_2) + \text{cov}(y_1, y_2)$, where $\bar{y}_i$ denotes the mean, and cov denotes the covariance. Alternatively, we may note that $-y_1 y_2$ belongs to the class U^{--}.
9 More general results are given in Atkinson and Bourguignon [3], which deals with the general problem of multivariate comparisons.
10 Integrating by parts, after reversing the order of integration, i.e.:

$$\int_0^{a_2} \left[\int_0^{a_1} U_2(y_1, y_2) \left\{ \int_0^{y_2} f(y_1, t) dt \right\} dy_1 \right] dy_2$$

References

[1] Atkinson, A. B. (1979), 'Intergenerational income mobility', *IHS-Journal*, vol. 3, Series A, pp. 61–73.
[2] Atkinson, A. B. (1980), 'Income distribution and inequality of opportunity', Chapter 4 in this volume.
[3] Atkinson, A. B. and Bourguignon, F. (1980), 'The comparison of multi-dimensioned distributions of economic status', Chapter 2 in this volume.
[4] Atkinson, A. B., Maynard, A. K. and Trinder, C. G. (1981), Report on the Rowntree Study, London School of Economics.
[5] Bartholomew, D. J. (1973), *Stochastic Models for Social Processes*, 2nd edn, Wiley, London.
[6] Boudon, R. (1973), *Mathematical Structures of Social Mobility*, Elsevier, Amsterdam.
[7] Hadar, J. and Russell, W. R. (1974), 'Stochastic dominance in choice under uncertainty', in Balch, M. S., McFadden, D. L. and Wu, S. Y. (eds.), *Essays on Economic Behaviour under Uncertainty*, North-Holland, Amsterdam.
[8] Levy, H. and Paroush, J. (1974), 'Toward multivariate efficiency criteria', *Journal of Economic Theory*, vol. 7, pp. 129–42.
[9] Markandya, A. (1980), 'Towards a theory of intergenerational economic mobility', University College London, Discussion Paper in Public Economics 13.

[10] Pen, J. (1971), *Income Distribution*, Allen Lane, London.
[11] Russell, W. R. and Seo, T. K. (1978), 'Ordering uncertain prospects: the multivariate utility functions case', *Review of Economic Studies*, vol. 45, pp. 605–10.
[12] Sen, A. K. (1973). On Economic Inequality Oxford University Press, London.
[13] Shorrocks, A. F. (1978a), 'The measurement of mobility', Econometrica, vol. 46, pp. 1013–24.
[14] Shorrocks, A. F. (1978b), 'Income inequality and income mobility', *Journal of Economic Theory*, vol. 19, pp. 376–93.

4 Income Distribution and Inequality of Opportunity*

1 Introduction

'Equality of opportunity' is a phrase which occurs frequently in public debate, appearing in party manifestos, political speeches, and tracts on educational and social reform. It has been widely accepted as a goal of government policy, and many writers treat it as of self-evident merit. Recently it has indeed been argued – at least in Britain – that equality of opportunity should be the sole principle of justice guiding social decisions. On this 'new' view the government should cease to concern itself with the distribution of income or wealth – that is, with inequality of outcome or results – and consider only the barriers to equality of opportunity. This position is well illustrated by Joseph and Sumption [22], who first deny that equality of results is a proper objective of government policy, claiming that it is 'morally indefensible, misconceived in theory and repellant in practice' (p. 19), and then contrast it with equality of opportunity, which is 'a commanding rally cry ... an attack on privilege in the name of liberty' (p. 29).

In the light of this, it seems timely to examine once again the concept of inequality of opportunity. There are several questions which need to be explored:

What exactly is meant by inequality of opportunity?
How can it be related to the mechanisms determining the distribution of income?
Can we give a quantitative measure of the extent of inequality of opportunity?
What is the relation between inequality of opportunity and inequality of outcome?

It is these questions that are the subject of this chapter. As we shall see, they are more complex than may at first sight appear; and no pretence is made to deal with them exhaustively. It is hoped however that the analysis illuminates some of the issues and the problems which remain to be resolved.

* This is revised version of a lecture given at the Institute of Advanced Studies, Vienna, in September 1979 and is reprinted from *IHS Journal*, vol. 4, 1980, © Physica Verlag, Wien.

2   The Definition of Inequality of Opportunity

There have been a variety of definitions of equality of opportunity, but the following may serve to illustrate the general concept.[1] According to the classic essay by Tawney ([35] pp. 103–4), equality of opportunity obtains in so far as, and only in so far as, each member of a community, whatever his birth, or occupation, or social position, possesses in fact, and not merely in form, equal chances of using to the full his natural endowments of physique, of character, and of intelligence. For the Oxford philosopher Plamenatz [29], 'Man, as a worker, has equality of opportunity with other men when he is free to choose any occupation he is fit for, and when his chance of acquiring that fitness is limited only by defects of nature and morals and not by lack of education or wealth or social prestige' (p. 93). Finally, a recent statement by an economist is that of Taubman [33], for whom equality of opportunity eliminates: 'all the barriers that prevent individuals from obtaining the training necessary to convert the potential talents implicit in their genetic endowments into capabilities' (p. 6).

In these definitions there is a core of agreement, but their implications are not easily understood in abstract. In order to investigate them more fully, a simple model of the determination of earnings is employed.[2] This model is not intended to be realistic; its function is rather to serve as a laboratory within which we can explore the concept of inequality of opportunity. (Such inequality also arises of course with investment income, and it is necessary to consider the role of inheritance, preferential investment or borrowing opportunities, differential information, etc.; here for simplicity attention is focused on earnings.)

In all three definitions quoted there is a notion of inborn abilities or fitness of individuals which are relevant to earning power. These may relate to intellectual capacities, to physical skills, to personality, or to other aspects. They may influence earnings directly or may work indirectly via facilitating schooling and training. These relationships are shown in Figure 1, supplemented by a chance or stochastic factor at each stage.

If the earnings relationship holds in identical form for everyone with the same distribution of the chance variable, then the conditions for equality of opportunity are satisfied in the sense that the *ex ante* distribution of earnings is the same for all people with identical innate abilities. What then generates

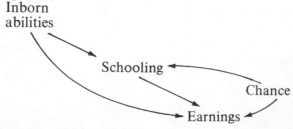

Figure 1   *Model of determination of earnings.*

inequality of opportunity? First, the earnings relationship may not be the same for everyone. There may, for example, be systematically higher earnings for people of one race or sex or religious group, and this may persist even in a perfectly competitive economy. This is referred to here as 'discrimination', although it may encompass a variety of phenomena, including possibly some factors which might otherwise have been treated as part of the stochastic term. Second, there may be a systematic link with family background: the privileges enjoyed by the children of higher income parents.

These sources of inequality of opportunity are introduced in Figure 2, where

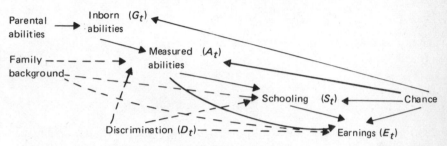

Figure 2   *Sources of inequality of opportunity.*

they are indicated by the dashed lines. The influence of family background may operate at several levels. It may be reflected in the performance of children in tests of ability, such as IQ tests, and to indicate this, controversial, link a distinction is drawn between inborn abilities and 'measured' abilities.[3] (A link is also drawn between discrimination and measured ability.) The advantages of family background may be revealed in terms of access to education or superior quality of education. This has been incorporated into the human capital approach to earnings determination (e.g. Becker [5]) as well as in the radical literature (e.g. Bowles [8]). Finally, the latter – but not the human capital school – would emphasise the direct link between family background and earnings. Well-off families may be able to secure good openings for their children; or the recruitment policies of firms may favour those from a superior social background (e.g. Bowles [9]).

3   A Formal Model

The model just described may be set out algebraically, on the assumptions that the variables enter linearly,[4] that for present purposes we can concentrate on the male line, and that family background may be represented by father's earnings. The subscript t indicates the generation, and u_t^x denotes in each case the stochastic term (which has constant mean and diagonal covariance matrix – see the Appendix). The approach follows that of Conlisk [12 and 13].

The first equation represents the genetic relation across generations, where g measures the extent of heritability:[5]

$$G_t = gG_{t-1} + u_t^G. \tag{3.1}$$

The second equation allows for the possibility that discrimination may be correlated across generations (as with race):

$$D_t = dD_{t-1} + u_t^D \tag{3.2}$$

The measured ability variable reflects genetic endowment, family background, and, possibly, discrimination (defined to enter positively):

$$A_t = a_1 G_t + a_2 E_{t-1} + a_3 D_t + u_t^A \tag{3.3}$$

The remaining structure follows the recursive pattern:

$$S_t = s_1 A_t + s_2 E_{t-1} + s_3 D_t + u_t^S \tag{3.4}$$

$$E_t = e_1 A_t + e_2 S_t + e_3 E_{t-1} + e_4 D_t + u_t^E. \tag{3.5}$$

The variable E_t is taken to be the logarithm of earnings. Equation (3.5) may then be seen as a generalisation of the equation typically estimated in the human capital literature. The endogeneity of schooling and measured ability is, however, recognised explicitly, and from (3.3)–(3.5) we can derive the reduced form:

$$E_t = \alpha G_t + \beta E_{t-1} + \gamma D_t + u_t^e. \tag{3.6}$$

The coefficients α, β, γ include both direct and indirect effects, so that, for example:

$$\beta = e_3 + e_1 a_2 + e_2(s_2 + s_1 a_2) \tag{3.7}$$

If this earnings relationship is assumed to hold for all individuals, if the stochastic terms satisfy certain conditions (see Appendix), and if the population is sufficiently large that we can replace sample moments by the corresponding population moments,[6] then the equilibrium distribution of earnings may be obtained in a straightforward manner. From equations (3.1), (3.2) and (3.6) we can derive a set of difference equations in the first and second moments of G_t, D_t and E_t, and under the conditions $0 < g, d, \beta < 1$ convergence to a steady state is ensured. (See Appendix.)

In this steady state, the variance of the logarithm of earnings (E_t) is given by:

$$\sigma_E^2 = \frac{1}{1 - \beta^2} \left[\alpha^2 \left(\frac{1 + \beta g}{1 - \beta g} \right) + \gamma^2 \frac{1 + \beta d}{1 - \beta d} + \Sigma_e^2 \right] \tag{3.8}$$

where Σ_e^2 denotes the variance of u_t^e. Since the units of G_t and D_t have not been defined, we may normalise by setting $\sigma_G = \sigma_D = 1$, and this has been done in

(3.8). (It may also be noted that Σ_e^2 depends on the parameters e_1, e_2, s_1 of the structural equations.)

From Equation (3.8) we can see how the mechanisms identified as causing inequality of opportunity – those shown by dashed lines in Figure 2 contribute to the inequality of outcome. If $\beta = \gamma = 0$, then the variance of E_t would be reduced to:

$$\tilde{\sigma}_E^2 = \alpha^2 + \sigma_e^2. \tag{3.9}$$

It has been suggested by Taubman [33, 34] that the extent of inequality of opportunity may be measured in terms of the variation in inequality of earnings attributable to these mechanisms:

$$I = 1 - \tilde{\sigma}_E^2/\sigma_E^2 \tag{3.10}$$

Taubman goes on to argue that inequality of opportunity, measured in this kind of way, is relatively unimportant: 'much of the current inequality of outcome is not due to inequality of opportunity, but is largely due to variation in individual genetic endowments'. In quantitative terms, inequality of opportunity is estimated by him to account for less than 20% of the variance in outcomes. The relationship to the parameters of the model may be illustrated by the following hypothetical examples. Suppose that we set $g = 2/3$ (which implies an 'intermediate' degree of heritability), $d = 0$ (no heritability of discrimination) and $\Sigma_e^2 = 0.16$. Then values of $\alpha = 0.3$, $\beta = \gamma = 0.1$, imply $I = 9\%$. In contrast, if we switch the values, so that $\alpha = 0.1$, $\beta = \gamma = 0.3$, the value of I rises to 42%.

4 Assessment

So far we appear to have made progress in applying the concept of inequality of opportunity to the determination of earnings. A definition has been given, and it has been related to the underlying mechanisms posited in the simple model of section 3. There is a clear-cut correspondence between inequality of opportunity and inequality of results. The latter, measured by the variance of logarithms, is a declining function of β and γ (holding Σ_e^2 constant) so that measures to reduce inequality of opportunity will, on these assumptions, reduce inequality of outcome. Finally, an index of the extent of inequality of opportunity has been defined, along the lines suggested by Taubman.

In the remainder of this chapter, it is argued that this progress is to a considerable extent illusory, and that there are serious problems in the interpretation and application of the concept of inequality of opportunity.

These problems arise at several levels. First, there are well-known ethical objections to the principle as defined earlier. Although some writers regard the merits of equality of opportunity as self-evident (for example Joseph and Sumption ([22], p. 28) claim that 'No one would overtly deny that it is just'), it has long been recognised that there are difficulties in justifying the sharp distinction drawn between genetic and material endowment. Knight ([24], p. 151), for instance, argued that 'there is no visible reason why anyone is more or less entitled to the earnings [resulting from] inherited personal capacities than to those of inherited property in any other form'.[7] The same point is made by Johnson ([21], p. 60), who also notes the vested interest of intellectuals in drawing the distinction.

If the sharp distinction cannot be drawn, then one may decide to include the variance of genetic endowments as a source of inequality of opportunity, so that the measure I becomes:

$$I' = 1 - \frac{\Sigma_e^2}{\sigma_E^2} \tag{4.1}$$

In this case, the difference between equality of opportunity and equality of outcome reduces simply to the distinction between *ex ante* and *ex post*. This is a valid distinction, but quite different from what many people seem to have in mind. Alternatively, some writers have been led in the opposite direction – to question whether even the redistribution of material property can be justified. Nozick ([27], p. 235), for example, argues that 'holdings to which ... people are entitled may not be seized, even to provide equality of opportunity to others'. Put another way, the dynamic aspect of inheritance inevitably involves a tension between the liberty of the donors and the unequal advantage provided to the recipients. The principles of equality of opportunity and of liberty are in conflict. A similar argument is made by Lloyd Thomas [26], who refers to 'an inevitable conflict between the pursuit of competitive equality of opportunity and the exercise of autonomous choice'.

It appears then that one must attempt to provide a rationale for the distinction drawn between genetic and material advantage,[8] or else risk seeing the concept slip from one's fingers – in the direction either of *ex ante* equality of outcome or of its repudiation along Nozick lines.

The second class of difficulties are those concerned with the relationship between inequality of opportunity and different economic mechanisms. We have identified inequality of opportunity with the family background and discrimination variables, but it is clear that the effects of these – and of their removal – can operate in several different ways. Consider, for example, the effect of discrimination on access to education (the family background effect being ignored for the moment). This aspect of inequality of opportunity could be eliminated by providing all those discriminated against (i.e. $D < D^{max}$) with sufficient education to bring them up to the same level (subject to the stochastic term) as those who were most favoured and had the same level of measured ability (where $s_3 > 0$):

$$S_t = s_1 A_t + s_3 D^{max} + u_t^s \tag{4.2}$$

In contrast, this aspect of inequality of opportunity could alternatively be eliminated by *redistributing a given distribution of schooling*. Okun ([28],

p. 81n, his italics), considers explicitly the 'redistribution of a *given* amount of higher education', which involves a more 'efficient' allocation according to abilities,

$$S_t = s_1^1 A_t + \tilde{u}_t^S \tag{4.3}$$

where the new coefficient s_1^1 ($> s_1$), and stochastic variable, are such as to hold constant the mean and variance of S_t. This would have rather different implications, and illustrates the general point that quite disparate policies may be put forward under the general banner of 'equalising opportunity'.

Thirdly, the quantitative index of inequality of opportunity may be questioned. At one level it may appear inconsistent that the measure is based on the effect on *outcomes*, when the principle has been put forward by some proponents as an alternative to equality of outcome. Indeed, by focusing on outcomes, the index disregards the process by which the inequality is generated, which may be an important reason for concern about inequality of opportunity. At another level, the use of the variance of logarithms as a measure of inequality may be debated. As has become clear in other contexts, statements about the extent of inequality, and its decomposition into causal factors, may depend crucially on the choice of indicator (see, for example, Davies and Shorrocks [15]). The variance of logarithms has obvious attractions, but there is no reason to suppose that the implied weights on incomes at different levels are appropriate (we may for example be particularly concerned with inequality of opportunity for the lowest groups).

These problems suggest that the concept of inequality of opportunity, and empirical measures of its extent, may need to be treated with considerable caution. This is reinforced by examination of two further important questions: the extent to which equality of opportunity and equality of outcome are indeed complementary, and the difficulties in empirical implementation. These are taken up in turn.

5   The Trade-off with Equality of Results

In the model described in section 3, a measure which decreased inequality of opportunity by reducing β or γ, with no other effects, would reduce the inequality of outcome. In this respect, it embodies the expectations of many authors. Okun [28], for example, recognises that there is no logical necessity, but is 'confident that greater equality of opportunity would produce greater equality of income. [This is] one trade-off that is not seriously vexing in the real world' (pp. 83–4).

In contrast, Joseph and Sumption (p. 30) criticise the view that reduced inequality of opportunity will contribute to equality of outcome, claiming that 'perfect equality of opportunity will give rise to very striking inequalities of results'. Similarly, Hernstein ([20], p. 151) argues that: 'Greater wealth, health, freedom, fairness, and educational opportunity are *not* going to give us automatically the egalitarian society of our philosophical heritage. They will instead give us a society sharply graduated, with even greater innate separation between the top and the bottom.'

Finally, Rawls ([31], p. 84) argues that, although he attaches a condition of equal opportunity to the difference principle, it might conflict with securing the greatest benefit for the least advantaged: 'It may be possible to improve everyone's situation by assigning certain powers and benefits to positions despite the fact that certain groups are excluded from them.'

There is therefore a marked divergence of opinion about the relationship between inequality of opportunity and of results. This divergence lies in part in the measures for equalisation which are contemplated. As noted above, these may have quite different implications. The levelling-up indicated by equation (4.2), where the other relationships are unchanged, implies a reduction in γ and hence in the variance of E_t. On the other hand, the redistribution of a given distribution of schooling, as in (4.3), where the coefficient s_1 is increased to maintain the variance of schooling, may work in the opposite direction. In terms of the reduced form equation (3.6) for earnings, the difference is between those who view the reduction of inequality of opportunity in terms of a reduction in β or γ – the elimination of privilege or discrimination – and those who see it as allowing superior abilities to be more fully reflected in earnings (removing barriers to the able) leading to a rise in α. Other things equal, the former reduces the variance of E_t; the latter increases it. It is also conceivable that the removal of barriers will increase the variance of the stochastic component (e.g. as a result of a rise in s_1).[9]

From this we may go on to a second important source of differences about the trade-off – the modelling of the labour market. To this point we have interpreted the earnings equation (3.5) in essentially the same way as the typical human capital approach. Earnings are assumed to reflect personal characteristics, and an increment in individual capacities affects only the earnings of the person concerned. There is in effect assumed to be a perfectly elastic demand for the characteristics, A_t, S_t and D_t. This assumption is far from satisfactory, and we need to consider in more detail the other side of the market, and the general equilibrium determination of earnings.

The implications of alternative assumptions about the labour market may be seen clearly from the polar opposite case where there is a fixed structure of jobs, and associated wages. The distribution of earnings is then determined solely from the demand side, and the equation (3.5) should be interpreted as governing the allocation of individuals to this fixed structure of jobs. In the terminology of Lloyd Thomas [26], we have to consider 'competitive', as opposed to 'non-competitive', equality of opportunity.[10] In this situation, the hope of Okun that reduced inequality of opportunity would diminish income inequality, and the prediction of Joseph and Sumption that it would have the reverse effect, are both precluded by assumption. The pursuit of equality of opportunity must be as a good in its own right. Moreover, it is the case that the effective fall in inequality of opportunity may be considerably different from the first round impact.[11] Suppose, for example, that a quite revolutionary educational policy reduces the variance of schooling to zero. This immediate source of inequality in earnings then disappears. On the other hand, suppose employers now attach more weight to other criteria when recruiting. These must involve tests of ability, so that the coefficient e_1 in equation (3.5) is effectively increased. In this situation, all three assumptions of β must, in the reduced form equation may be affected (as may the variance of the chance term, Σ_e^2). Where the employers attach more weight to family background when recruiting, then it is quite possible that the coefficient β is increased, and that the ultimate effect on inequality of opportunity, measured according to an index such as I, is the reverse of the initial effect.[12]

6 Empirical Implementation

The claim that there is relatively little inequality of opportunity in modern societies is sometimes supported by examples of successful entrepreneurs who have started from nothing (e.g. Joseph and Sumption cite the case of William Morris, founder of the car firm that has become British Leyland). Here however attention is focused on statistical evidence of the kind advanced by Taubman [33 and 34] rather than on the biography of entrepreneurship.

Drawing inferences from statistical data about the extent of income inequality is a difficult exercise. A central problem is that the variables with which we are working are either not measured or only measured with considerable error in the available sets of data. Thus parental earnings are rarely recorded in studies of economic success (the available evidence is reviewed in Atkinson [1]), and investigators have had to employ a variety of proxy indicators, such as parental education or occupation. For example, of the eight studies listed in Corcoran, Jencks and Olneck [14] of the effects of family background on earnings, only one – that by Sewell and Hauser [32] – contains data on parental income. The collection of such information can clearly be set in hand (one study in the UK is that by Atkinson, Maynard and Trinder [3]); and there are likely to be richer data sets in the future. The problems will not however be totally eliminated. Thus, for instance, E_{t-1} measures parental income, not the advantage derived by a particular child. This depends on decisions within the family, of the kind discussed by Becker and Lewis [6], Liebowitz [25], Griliches [19], and others. Even accurately measured parental income may only be an indicator of the extent of advantage. Other variables involve similar difficulties. The effect of discrimination may be represented by dummy variables such as those for race or location, but these are again only imperfect indicators. The genetic contribution, G_t, is inherently unobservable.

Some of the ways in which this problem has been tackled may be seen from a consideration of the reduced form (3.6), where at least one, and possibly all, of the right-hand side variables (G_t, E_{t-1} and D_t) are not observed. One approach has been to consider observations where E_{t-1} is not observed, but it is known to have common value. This applies to data on brothers used by Chamberlain and Griliches [10 and 11], and on male twins, used by Taubman *et al.* (for example Behrman, Taubman, Wales and Hrubec [7]). If we assume that the moments of the distribution are constant across generations (an assumption which need not, of course, be satisfied), then the predicted correlation of the earnings of two brothers, i and j, would be:

$$\beta^2 + \frac{\alpha^2}{\sigma_E^2} r(G^i, G^j) + \frac{\gamma^2}{\sigma_E^2} r(D^i, D^j)$$

$$+ \frac{2\alpha\beta\sigma_{EG}}{\sigma_E^2} r(G_t, G_{t-1})$$

$$+ \frac{2\gamma\beta\sigma_{DE}}{\sigma_E^2} r(D_t, D_{t-1}) \tag{6.1}$$

where $r(X, Y)$ denotes the correlation, and σ_{XY} the co-variance. The introduction of such paired data does not solve the problem, since we have the unknown parameters ($r(G^i, G^j)$, $r(D^i, D^j)$, $r(G_t, G_{t-1})$ and $r(D_t, D_{t-1})$). It may however be possible to bring outside theoretical considerations to bear. For example, for monozygotic (MZ) identical twins, $r(G^i, G^j) = 1$, and the model of genetic determination implies that for dizygotic (DZ), or fraternal, twins or for brothers $r(G^i, G^j) = g^2$ and $r(G_t, G_{t-1}) = g$. We can also use the theoretical model of section 3, and the steady state assumption, to relate the covariance terms to the parameters. This allows us to write the predicted correlations as:

Brothers/dizygotic twins (DZ)

$$r_{DZ} = \beta^2 + g^2 \left(\frac{\alpha}{\sigma_E}\right)^2 + r_{DZ}(D^i, D^j)\left(\frac{\gamma}{\sigma_E}\right)^2$$

$$+ \frac{2\beta g}{1 - \beta g}\left(\frac{\alpha}{\sigma_E}\right)^2 + \frac{2\beta d}{1 - \beta d}\left(\frac{\gamma}{\sigma_E}\right)^2 \tag{6.2}$$

Monozygotic twins (MZ)

$$r_{MZ} = \beta^2 + \left(\frac{\alpha}{\sigma_E}\right)^2 + r_{MZ}(D^i, D^j)\left(\frac{\gamma}{\sigma_E}\right)^2$$

$$+ \frac{2\beta g}{1 - \beta g}\left(\frac{\alpha}{\sigma_E}\right)^2 + \frac{2\beta d}{1 - \beta d}\left(\frac{\gamma}{\sigma_E}\right)^2 \tag{6.3}$$

From a comparison of (6.2) and (6.3), it can be seen that taking the difference between r_{DZ} and r_{MZ} gives a relation between the contribution of the two unobservable components:

$$r_{MZ} - r_{DZ} = \left(\frac{\alpha}{\sigma_E}\right)^2 (1 - g^2) + \left(\frac{\gamma}{\sigma_E}\right)^2 [r_{MZ}(D^i, D^j) - r_{DZ}(D^i, D^j)] \tag{6.4}$$

This is in essence the method employed in the most straightforward analysis of the twin data by Taubman (see Goldberger [16]). Making the assumption that both kinds of twins have the same degree of correlation of the unobserved ʜɪ⧸ᴄʀɪᴍɪɴᴀᴛɪᴏɴ ᴠᴀʀɪᴀʙʟᴇ, ᴀɴᴅ ᴛᴀᴋɪɴɢ $g^2 = 1/2$, ᴛʜᴇ ᴠᴀʟᴜᴇ ᴏꜰ $(\alpha/\sigma_E)^2$ ᴍᴀʏ ʙᴇ estimated as 0.48, since the correlations observed by Taubman are $r_{MZ} = 0.54$ and $r_{DZ} = 0.30$. This high estimated value for the contribution of the genetic factor implies a low value for the coefficient β. Taking the discrimination effect to be zero gives an upper bound on β, which may be calculated (with $g^2 = 1/2$) to be some 0.075.

It is on the basis of this, and more elaborate, analysis of the evidence for male twins that Taubman ([33], p. 69) concludes that 'programs of equality of opportunity will have little effect on reducing inequality in income'. One has however to be extremely cautious in drawing such inferences. First, it is clear that the estimates of β are highly sensitive to the observed correlations. This is illustrated in Figure 3 for the case where there is no discrimination effect ($\gamma = 0$).

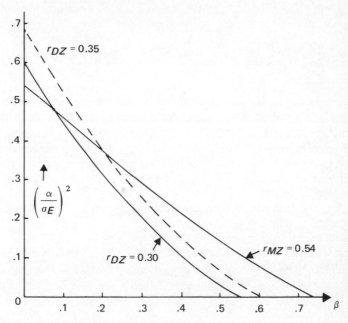

Figure 3   *Estimation of genetic contribution $(\alpha/\sigma_E)^2$ and β.*

The two solid lines show the relationships (6.2) and (6.3) with the observed values of r_{DZ} and r_{MZ} and the assumed value for g ($= \sqrt{1/2}$). The intersection gives the estimated value for β of 0.075 (where $\gamma = 0$). Suppose however that the correlation for dizygotic twins was 0.35, rather than 0.3. This yields the dashed line in Figure 3, and it may be seen that the estimated value of β is now close to 0.2. The sensitivity of the results is demonstrated at greater length in Goldberger [16].

Secondly, it is clear that in order to draw inferences from the observed correlations, it is necessary to impose identifying restrictions. In some cases these may have some inherent rationale; in others they may be highly debatable. In the case of (6.4), it was assumed that the square bracket was zero: i.e. that both types of twin had the same degree of correlation of the unobserved discrimination variable. Even interpreted literally in terms of 'discrimination', this assumption appears doubtful; if D_t is taken more broadly to represent characteristics of the environment, it seems even less plausible.

Thirdly, there are reasons to believe that the results from identical twin data may be rather special,[13] and we need to consider what can be learned from other types of evidence. Suppose, for example, that we consider the correlation across generations. From (3.6):

$$r(E_t, E_{t-1}) = \beta + \frac{\alpha \sigma_{EG}}{\sigma_E^2} r(G_t, G_{t-1}) + \frac{\gamma \sigma_{DE}}{\sigma_E^2} r(D_t, D_{t-1}) \tag{6.5}$$

Using the theoretical model and the steady state assumption, this parent-child correlation may be written:

$$r_{PC} = \beta + \frac{g}{1 - \beta g} \left(\frac{\alpha}{\sigma_E}\right)^2 + \frac{d}{1 - \beta d} \left(\frac{\gamma}{\sigma_E}\right)^2 \tag{6.6}$$

Again, by making assumptions about the unobserved variables one can obtain estimates from the parent–child correlation. For example, suppose we set $g = \sqrt{1/2}$, $\gamma = 0$, then $r_{DZ} = 0.30$, $r_{PC} = 0.47$ would imply $\beta = 0.25$ and a genetic contribution of only 26% (compared with 48%). On the other hand, it is clear both that the assumptions are equally arbitrary in this case and that the results are highly sensitive to the value of r_{PC}. Another approach would be to consider observations where the discrimination variable is likely to take on a common value: for example, those who are neighbours (where local labour market experience is a relevant factor).

This review of the empirical literature has been selective. We have not, for example, considered the additional information which can be obtained where the unobservable influences more than one variable (as where the full system (3.3)–(3.5) is estimated). It should however be clear that there are substantial difficulties in drawing straightforward conclusions from the statistical analysis of earnings data.

7 Concluding Comments

This chapter has taken a notion widely current in public discussion and tried to see what it implies and how it can be applied to the distribution of earnings. The principal conclusion is that inequality of opportunity is a considerably more complex concept than appears at first sight. There are ethical difficulties in its formulation; the relationship with the underlying mechanisms needs to be further investigated; there is no straightforward link between inequality of opportunity and inequality of results; and the measurement of inequality poses both theoretical and empirical problems. It does not appear correct to view the concept of inequality of opportunity as necessarily more self-evident and more straightforwardly applicable than that of inequality of outcome.

Appendix: Model of the Distribution of Earnings[14]

The basic equations of the model are:

$$G_t = gG_{t-1} + u_t^G \tag{3.1}$$

$$D_t = dD_{t-1} + u_t^D \tag{3.2}$$

$$A_t = a_1 G_t + a_2 E_{t-1} + a_3 D_t + u_t^A \tag{3.3}$$

$$S_t = s_1 A_t + s_2 E_{t-1} + s_3 D_t + u_t^S \tag{3.4}$$

$$E_t = e_1 A_t + e_2 S_t + e_3 E_{t-1} + e_4 D_t + u_t^E \tag{3.5}$$

From (3.3)–(3.5), one can obtain the reduced form

$$E_t = \alpha G_t + \beta E_{t-1} + \gamma D_t + u_t^e \tag{3.6}$$

These relationships are assumed to be identical for all members of the population. The stochastic vector (u_t^G, u_t^D, u_t^e) is assumed to be distributed independently of the state variables, to be independent across individuals and across generations, and to have constant mean and variance-covariance matrix (the latter being taken for simplicity as diagonal). Finally, it is assumed that we can replace sample moments by the corresponding population moments. With these assumptions the behaviour of the first and second moments may be described. The mean of G_t, denoted by $\bar{G}_t$, satisfies the difference equation:

$$\bar{G}_t = g\bar{G}_{t-1} + \mu_G \tag{A.1}$$

where μ_G denotes the mean of u_t^G, and converges where $0 < g < 1$. The variance, σ_G^2, satisfies:

$$\sigma_G^2(t) = g^2 \sigma_G^2(t-1) + \Sigma_G^2 \tag{A.2}$$

where Σ_G^2 denotes the variance of u_t^G, and again convergence is ensured. (The normalisation $\sigma_G^2 = 1$ in steady state determines Σ_G^2.) The same analysis applies to D_t, given the assumption $0 < d < 1$.

In the case of E_t, we are interested in the variance, σ_E^2, and the covariance with G_t ($\equiv \sigma_{EG}$) and D_t ($\equiv \sigma_{DE}$). These are governed by the difference equations (where we have used (3.1) and (3.2)):

$$\sigma_E^2(t) = \alpha^2 \sigma_G^2(t) + \beta^2 \sigma_E^2(t-1)$$
$$+ \gamma^2 \sigma_D^2(t) + 2\alpha\beta g \sigma_{EG}(t-1)$$
$$+ 2\beta\gamma d \sigma_{DE}(t-1) + \Sigma_e^2 \tag{A.3}$$

$$\sigma_{EG}(t) = \alpha \sigma_G^2(t) + \beta g \sigma_{EG}(t-1) \tag{A.4}$$

$$\sigma_{DE}(t) = \gamma \sigma_D^2(t) + \beta d \sigma_{DE}(t-1) \tag{A.5}$$

The steady state is described by (with the normalisation $\sigma_G^2 = \sigma_D^2 = 1$):

$$\sigma_{EG} = \frac{\alpha}{1 - \beta g} \qquad \sigma_{DE} = \frac{\gamma}{1 - \beta d} \tag{A.6}$$

and

$$(1 - \beta^2)\sigma_E^2 = \alpha^2 + 2\alpha\beta g \sigma_{EG} + \gamma^2 + 2\beta\gamma d \sigma_{DE} + \Sigma_e^2 \tag{A.7}$$

From these equations, (3.8) in the text may be derived. Moreover, convergence to the equilibrium is assured by the assumption that d, g, β lie strictly between 0 and 1.

Acknowledgement

I am most grateful to Mervyn King, Anil Markandya and Michael Wagner for their helpful comments in the preparation of this chapter.

Notes

1 Here, and elsewhere, I have drawn on the valuable discussion by Klappholz [23], which contains extensive references to the literature.
2 A similar approach has been followed by Psacharopoulos [30] who is particularly concerned with the role played by education.
3 It may be debated which is the relevant concept of 'abilities' for the purposes of defining inequality of opportunity, but the statement by Tawney explicitly concerns 'natural' endowments, and Taubman refers similarly to 'genetic' endowments, and that is the interpretation adopted here.
4 This means, for example, that we do not consider interactions such as that between the discrimination variable and the coefficient on education.
5 More completely,

$$G_t = g_1(G_t^m + G_t^f) + u_t^G \tag{3.1'}$$

where G^m, G^f denote the genetic contribution of mother and father respectively. Assuming that marriage takes place assortatively according to abilities, and that the correlation is ρ, this implies $g = g_1(1 + \rho)$. The degree of heritability indicated by (3.1') is $(h \equiv) \, 2g_1^2(1 + \rho)$. Thus, $g_1 = 1/2$, $\rho = 1/2$ implies $g = h = 0.75$; $g_1 = 0.4$, $\rho = 1/2$ implies $g = 0.6$ and $h = 0.48$.
6 We are thereby moving from a stochastic to a distributional model. See Atkinson and Harrison ([2], ch. 8).
7 This quotation is taken from Klappholz ([23], p. 254) who discusses the issue further.
8 The justification provided by Taubman [34] for distinguishing between genetic and other

causes of inequality of opportunity is that this focuses attention on the 'big trade-off' between equality and efficiency: i.e. those factors are included whose elimination/counterbalancing would contribute to increasing efficiency. However it does not seem to me particularly helpful to rest the justification on empirical assertions about the nature of trade-offs, which may change as new sources of evidence become available.

9 It may be noted that this interpretation of reduced inequality of opportunity is the reverse of that given by Conlisk ([12], p. 84), who sees the random term as reflecting unequal opportunity.

10 The difference may be illustrated by one of the athletic analogies so popular in writing on inequality of opportunity. The fixed job structure corresponds to the usual notion of a race, with a pre-specified structure of prizes; the human capital approach corresponds to swimming certificates, where the award to one child (e.g. for swimming 100 metres) is independent of the number of other qualified swimmers.

11 The measure of inequality of opportunity must of course now be re-interpreted.

12 Suppose e_3 rises to keep σ_E^2 unchanged, but e_1 is unchanged. This means that α falls (since $s_1 = 0$), and that Σ_e^2 is smaller (via s_1 and the variance of u_i^S); in the absence of discrimination this implies a rise in the index I.

13 The sensitivity of estimates of heritability in the case of IQ to the observations for twins is brought out in Goldberger [16].

14 The model, without the discrimination variable, but with capital income, is discussed more extensively in Atkinson and Stiglitz ([4], ch. 9) and Chapter 9.

References

[1] Atkinson, A. B. (1980), 'Intergenerational income mobility', *IHS Journal*, **3**, Series A, 61–73.

[2] Atkinson, A. B. and Harrison, A. J. (1978), *The Distribution of Personal Wealth in Britain*, Cambridge.

[3] Atkinson, A. B., Maynard, A. K. and Trinder, C. G. (1981), *Report on the Rowntree Study*, London School of Economics.

[4] Atkinson, A. B. and Stiglitz, J. E. (1980), *Lectures on Public Economics*, Maidenhead and New York.

[5] Becker, G. S. (1975), *Human Capital*. 2nd edn, New York.

[6] Becker, G. S. and Lewis, H. G. (1973), 'On the interaction between quantity and quality of children', *Journal of Political Economy*, **81**, S279–S288.

[7] Behrman, J., Hrubec, Z., Taubman, P. and Wales, T. (1980), *Socioeconomic Success*, Amsterdam, North-Holland.

[8] Bowles, S. (1972), 'Schooling and inequality from generation to generation', *Journal of Political Economy*, **80**(3), part II, S219–S251.

[9] Bowles, S. (1973), 'Understanding unequal economic opportunity', *American Economic Review*, Papers and Proceedings, **63**, 346–56.

[10] Chamberlain, G. and Griliches, Z. (1975), 'Unobservables with a variance-components structure: ability, schooling and the economic success of brothers', *International Economic Review*, **16**, 422–49.

[11] Chamberlain, G. and Griliches, Z. (1977), 'More on brothers', *Kinometrics*, Taubman, P. (ed.), Amsterdam.

[12] Conlisk, J. (1974), 'Can equalisation of opportunity reduce social mobility?', *American Economic Review*, **64**, 80–90.

[13] Conlisk, J. (1977), 'An exploratory model of the size distribution of income', *Economic Inquiry*, **15**, 345–66.

[14] Corcoran, M., Jencks, C. and Olneck, M. (1976), 'The effects of family background on earnings', *American Economic Review*, *Papers and Proceedings*, **66**, 430–5.

[15] Davies, J. B. and Shorrocks, A. F. (1978), 'Assessing the quantitative importance of inheritance in the distribution of wealth', *Economica*, **30**, 138–49.

[16] Goldberger, A. S. (1978a), 'The genetic determination of income: a comment', *American Economic Review*, **68**, 960–9.

[17] Goldberger, A. S. (1978b), *Models and Methods in the IQ Debate*, part I, SSRI Workshop Series 7801, University of Wisconsin.
[18] Goldberger, A. S. (1979), 'Heritability', *Economica*, **46**, 327–47.
[19] Griliches, Z. (1979), 'Sibling models and data in economics', *Journal of Political Economy*, **87**, S37–S64.
[20] Hernstein, R. (1973), *IQ in the Meritocracy*, Boston.
[21] Johnson, H. G. (1973), *Some Micro-Economic Reflections on Income and Wealth Inequalities*, Annals of the American Academy of Political and Social Science, September, 53–60.
[22] Joseph, K. and Sumption, J. (1979), *Equality*, London.
[23] Klappholz, K. (1972), 'Equality of opportunity, fairness and efficiency, *Essays in Honour of Lord Robbins*, Peston, M. and Corry, B. (eds.), London.
[24] Knight, F. H. (1947), *Freedom and Reform*, New York.
[25] Liebowitz, A. (1974), 'Home investments in children', *Journal of Political Economy*, **82**, S111–S131.
[26] Lloyd Thomas, D. A. (1977), 'Competitive equality of opportunity', *Mind*, **86**, 388–404.
[27] Nozick, R. (1974), *Anarchy, State and Utopia*, Oxford.
[28] Okun, A. M. (1975), *Equality and Efficiency: The Big Trade-off*, Washington, DC.
[29] Plamenatz, J. P. (1957), *Equality of Opportunity. Aspects of Human Equality*, Bryson, L. *et al.* (eds.), New York.
[30] Psacharopoulos, G. (1976), *Investment in Education and Equality of Opportunity, Educational Need in the Public Economy*, Alexander, K. (ed.), Florida.
[31] Rawls, J. (1971), *A Theory of Justice*, Cambridge, Mass.
[32] Sewell, W. H. and Hauser, R. M. (1975), *Education, Occupation and Earnings*, New York.
[33] Taubman, P. (1978), *Income Distribution and Redistribution*, Reading, Mass.
[34] Taubman, P. (1979), 'Equality of opportunity and equality of outcome: lessons from studies of twins', *IHS-Journal*.
[35] Tawney, R. H. (1964), *Equality*, 4th edn, London.

5 Horizontal Equity and the Distribution of the Tax Burden*

Joseph Pechman and Benjamin Okner's *Who Bears the Tax Burden?* already is a modern classic and follows a distinguished tradition of studies of the distributional impact of taxation.[1] The Pechman and Okner study represented a departure from earlier work in two major respects. First, the authors carried out a more detailed analysis of the sensitivity of the results to the assumptions made about the incidence of different taxes. Second, their use of a micro-data file allowed them to examine the variation in individual tax burdens. In contrast to studies in which taxes are allocated to broad income classes,[2] Pechman and Okner calculated individual tax burdens and did not rely on the assumption that these burdens are uniform within an income class. Somewhat surprisingly this latter aspect has received relatively little attention. The authors themselves devoted only one paragraph of their summary chapter to it, and reviewers have tended to concentrate on the treatment of different incidence assumptions.

The neglect of this feature of the Pechman and Okner monograph is unfortunate since it bears on the concept of horizontal equity, which is widely held to be a major objective of the tax system. Individuals with identical incomes and family circumstances may face different tax burdens because their incomes come from different sources, because they consume different goods, because they live in rural rather than urban areas, and so on. As a result, taxation may change the ranking between the pre- and post-tax distributions of income. The extent of such re-ranking is a question of considerable interest. Pechman and Okner were able to investigate the degree of variation in tax rates by using the Brookings MERGE data file and calculating the individual tax burdens of the 72,000 families represented.

In this chapter I shall pursue this issue further, focusing in particular on the conceptual problems that arise. The first section describes the analytical framework within which the 'mobility' induced by taxation may be examined. The second section reviews the concept of horizontal equity, the various ways it may be interpreted, and possible measures of it.

The Redistributive Impact of Taxation

The standard approach to measuring the redistributive impact of taxation is to compare the distribution after tax with that assumed to hold in the absence of taxation (on the basis of specified assumptions about incidence). Before the introduction of taxes, individual i has income Y_i, and this is converted into a post-tax income Y_i^N. The standard procedure considers the distribution Y_i (ranked in increasing order $i=1,\ldots,n$) and compares it with the distribution Y_i^N (ranked in the same way $i=1,\ldots,n$). Commonly, in empirical applications the data are grouped. The standard procedure then is to consider the distribution ranked according to average income before tax in each group, constructing, for example, the Lorenz curve, and to compare this with the distribution obtained for the same groups ranked in the same way.

This approach, however, ignores the fact that taxation may change the ranking of individuals in the distribution. The person or group at the top of the pre-tax distribution may be lower down the post-tax distribution. The people who were in the same range of pre-tax income may be in different post-tax ranges. As a result, measures calculated according to the pre-tax ranking, as in the standard approach, typically understate the inequality of post-tax incomes. The Gini coefficient, for example, calculated from the pre-tax ranks, can be shown to be less than or equal to that calculated using the correct post-tax rankings. It is therefore an important distinguishing feature of the Pechman and Okner study that estimation of the tax burden for individual units permits the authors to draw the Lorenz curve corresponding to the re-ranked distribution and to calculate more accurately the various summary measures derived from it.[3]

The process of re-ranking is of interest in its own right as well as in obtaining an accurate measure of redistribution. We are concerned not only with the position of the Lorenz curves but also with how much 'mobility' is induced by taxation. Where do the people at the lower quartile of the before-tax distribution end up in the distribution of the after-tax incomes? How much variation is there in the post-tax incomes of individuals who are identically situated before tax? These questions, discussed below, are related to the concept of horizontal equity.

Before turning to a more formal analysis, a simple example may help illustrate the effects of changes in rankings. Assume the following distribution of incomes before and after tax:

| | | *Income* | |
Taxpayer	*Class*	*Before tax*	*After tax*
1	Top 40%	1000	800
2		1000	640
3	Next 40%	800	800
4		800	512
5	Bottom 20%	640	640

Analysis of the data on an individual basis and calculation of the Gini coefficient indicates a fall (from 0.087 to 0.053) on the basis of the pre-tax rankings, whereas it is clear that a correct calculation based on the re-ranked data would show no change (the Lorenz curves are identical). What happens if one groups the data? The three income classes shown in the second column indicate a progressive rate structure (average tax rates from the bottom up of 18% and 28%), and the grouped Lorenz curve moves toward the diagonal.[1] The individual data show, however, that the fact that the tax on the average is progressive is offset by the differential treatment of people with the same before-tax income – by the mobility induced by the tax system.

Differences between the taxes paid by people with the same pre-tax income may arise for a number of reasons.[5] First, on equity grounds the government may recognise certain characteristics as warranting differential treatment. The most obvious examples are allowances for different family sizes or special provisions for the elderly or disabled. Second, the government may deliberately treat differently certain types of income or taxpayer for efficiency reasons; for example, it may want to encourage owner-occupation or discourage people from consuming certain products. Third, some horizontal inequities not desired by the government may be inherent in the tax system – an unavoidable by-product. For example, where there is less than 100% checking of income tax returns, one person may be caught but another, identically situated, may successfully evade. Another example is that some people may have a stronger preference for goods the government cannot tax (for example, leisure).

The discussion that follows concentrates on the second and third categories. In other words, it is concerned with differential treatment that has no equity justification. The income, Y_i^N, of individual i should, for example, be interpreted as having been expressed in per adult equivalent terms, using an appropriate equivalence scale.

Tax mobility matrices

Starting with the case of individual taxpayers, the effect of taxation on the Lorenz curve may be decomposed into two stages. The first gives the after-tax income Y_i^N corresponding to pre-tax income Y_i for a fixed ranking i. The second is the permutation to give the ranking according to Y_i^N. Denoting this latter ranking by k, one can write $k = iP$, where P is a permutation matrix. A tax that causes no change in ranking is associated with the identity matrix; a tax that completely reverses rankings has the opposite diagonal permutation matrix.

In any actual application the individual data are likely to be treated in groups. For convenience I take equal size groups, each containing a proportion, $1/n$, of the population. The generalisation of the permutation matrix is then the transition matrix A where a_{ij} denotes the proportion of those in pre-tax group i entering post-tax group j. This matrix is bistochastic (each row and each column add to 1), and the extent of mobility depends on the off-diagonal elements $(j \neq i)$. The standard assumption described earlier is that these are zero, A being the identity matrix. The study of tax mobility means in effect supplementing the measures defined over the n pre- and post-tax groups by the $n \times n$ matrix mapping the movement of individuals between these groups.

There is a clear parallel with the measurement of social mobility across generations. In the extensive literature on this subject many attempts have been made to reduce the transition matrix A to a single measure of the extent of mobility; for example, Bartholomew suggests the following measure of social mobility:

$$B = \frac{1}{n} \sum_i \sum_j a_{ij} |i - j|, \tag{1}$$

which is zero when A is the identity matrix.[6]

It is possibly more natural in the present case to relate the measure to conventional indices of inequality. These, of course, do not depend intrinsically on the ranking, but in some cases the ranking is an intermediate step in the calculation. The Gini coefficient is a good illustration, since it is often related to the area between the diagonal and the Lorenz curve (hence depending on the ranking).

The mobility matrix can readily be calculated from micro-unit data. For present purposes an illustrative matrix has been constructed using the data on the distribution of tax rates contained in chapter 5 of *Who Bears the Tax Burden?* A number of assumptions were made in the calculations (see notes to Table 1) and it is not claimed that the results closely approximate those that would be obtained from the original MERGE file. It should also be stressed that there are several reasons why the degree of mobility may be inaccurately

Table 1   *Illustrative tax mobility matrix*

Pre-tax decile group in order of increasing income	Post-tax decile groups in order of increasing income (per cent)									
	1	2	3	4	5	6	7	8	9	10
1	94	6								
2	6	85	9							
3		9	75	1414	3					
5				19	67	13	1			
6					17	66	16	1		
7						18	62	19	1	
8							20	66	14	
9							1	14	72	13
10									13	87

Sources and notes: Calculated from the information on median-quartile tax rates by decile (Pechman J. A. and Okner, B., *Who Bears the Tax Burden?* Brookings Institution, 1974, table 5-1, p. 67) and on pre-tax ranges (interpolated from the same source, table 4-5, p. 53). The calculations were adjusted to impose the row and column sum conditions (items less than 1% being neglected). The figures all relate to the 'most progressive' set of incidence assumptions (Variant 1c). The calculations are intended only to be illustrative and should be read in conjunction with the qualifications in the text.

measured, even if the original file is used. For example, because the data are not adjusted for family size, differences in tax rates may reflect the intended unequal treatment of families with the same income but different needs. The data are derived from surveys, and part of the variation may be due to recording errors. Working in the opposite direction is the fact that in the MERGE file consumption is based on averages for income classes and demographic groups and hence would not capture all the variability in consumption patterns (for example, the different tax burdens of smokers and non-smokers). Moreover, because the population is divided into only ten groups, each covering a wide range of income, a substantial amount of mobility is not reflected in the table. Finally, the results depend on the assumptions about incidence.

For these reasons, the matrix shown in Table 1 should not be regarded as more than illustrative; and no attempt has been made to carry out accurate calculations. Inspection of the table suggests that the diagonal entries are dominant; at the same time, some of the elements adjacent to the diagonal are quite large. The matrix is approximately tridiagonal, with the elements bordering the diagonal of the order of 10–20% for decile groups 2–10, and the other off-diagonal elements close to zero. In other words, it appears from the table that variability in the tax rate tends to shift people but not typically further than one decile group.

Mobility and inequality

Changes in the ranking of observations as a result of taxation do not in themselves affect the degree of inequality in the post-tax distribution. They do, however, influence certain ways of representing the distribution and of calculating summary measures of inequality. In this section I consider the effect of rank changes on the Lorenz curve and the Gini coefficient, both widely used in the analysis of the incidence of taxation.

In order to see the effect of changes in ranking, I define the concentration curve, which gives the cumulative percentage of a particular variable, X_i, where observations are ranked according to a variable Z_i; that is:

$$C(m, X, r(Z)) \tag{2}$$

denotes the cumulative total (expressed as a proportion of the overall total) for m observations of variable X_i, ranked in increasing order of Z_i. This gives as a special case the Lorenz curve $C(m, X, r(X))$.[7]

The first result that is readily proved is that if a ranking j is obtained by a permutation of the ranking $r(X)$, then the resulting concentration curve lies inside the Lorenz curve (or is coincident with it); that is:

$$j = r(X)P \tag{3}$$

where P is a permutation matrix, implies:

$$C(m, X, j) \geqslant C(m, X, r(X)) \tag{4}$$

for all m.

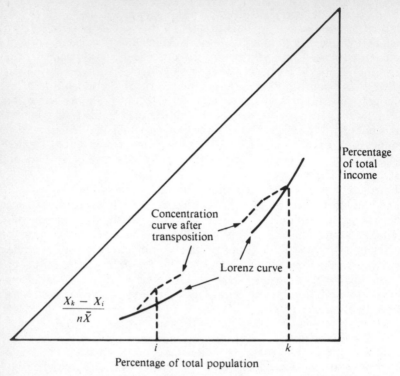

Figure 1   *Effect of transposition of individuals i and k on the Lorenz curve.*

The proof may be seen by considering a sequence of transpositions in which the ranks of X_i and X_k ($k > i$, $X_k > X_i$) are reversed (see Figure 1).

This result shows that calculating the shares in post-tax total income according to the rankings by pre-tax income gives too high a figure if there is any substantive change in ranking (that is, for persons with different post-tax incomes). There is indeed no reason why the concentration curve need be below the diagonal, as may be seen from the example where the first person ($X_1 < \bar{X}$, where $\bar{X}$ denotes the mean) and the last person ($X_n > \bar{X}$) are interchanged. The Lorenz curve then starts off above the diagonal and ends above it.

The direction of the effect of re-ranking is readily apparent; of more interest is its possible magnitude. Figure 1 shows that the transposition of i and k raises the curves for $i < m < k$ by an amount $(X_k - X_i)/n\bar{X}$. Thus in a population of 100 people switching the person at the lower quartile, with an income of, say, three-quarters of the mean, with the person at the upper quartile, with an income of one and one-half times the mean, raises the cumulative shares in the range 25–49% by 0.75%. It is also possible to calculate the effect on the Gini coefficient, which is reduced as a result of the re-ranking by:

$$\frac{2(k-i)}{n^2}\left(\frac{X_k - X_i}{\bar{X}}\right) \tag{5}$$

With the example of the interquartile range used above, this turns out to be the same as the change in the cumulative shares, that is, 0.75%.

The effect of a general re-ranking may be built up from a sequence of such transpositions. In order to get some feeling for the overall effect, consider the case where the data are grouped into ranges with equal frequencies and the transition matrix is tridiagonal:

$$
\begin{bmatrix}
1 - \alpha_1 & \alpha_1 & 0 & \cdots & 0 \\
\alpha_1 & (1 - \alpha_1 - \alpha_2) & \alpha_2 & \cdots & 0 \\
0 & \alpha_2 & (1 - \alpha_2 - \alpha_3) & \cdots & 0 \\
0 & 0 & \alpha_3 & \cdots & 0 \\
\cdot & \cdot & \cdot & \cdots & \cdot \\
\cdot & \cdot & \cdot & \cdots & \cdot \\
\cdot & \cdot & \cdot & \cdots & \cdot \\
0 & 0 & 0 & \cdots & 0 \\
0 & 0 & 0 & \cdots & \alpha_{n-1} \\
0 & 0 & 0 & \cdots & 1 - \alpha_{n-1}
\end{bmatrix}
\tag{6}
$$

The reduction in the Gini coefficient is then the sum of the individual transpositions and may be shown to equal:

$$\frac{2}{n^2}\sum_{i=1}^{n-1} \alpha_i^2 \left(\frac{X_{i+1} - X_i}{\bar{X}}\right) \tag{7}$$

(this may be seen geometrically from the Lorenz curve, where a fraction α_i is moved to the adjacent group). Suppose that the groups are by deciles and that the value of α_i is taken as 0.15. The reduction in the Gini coefficient is then in percentage points $0.045 \times (X_n - X_i)/(\bar{X})$. If, for example, the top income exceeds the bottom by six times the mean, then the Gini coefficient falls by 0.27%; if the relationship is 12:1, the fall is 0.54%. If the value of α_i is taken as 0.1, then the figures become 0.12 and 0.24, respectively; if α were 0.2, then the figures are four times larger.

This kind of difference may appear reassuringly small when compared with the absolute value of the coefficient (around 42% for the Pechman-Okner data); on the other hand, it is quite large when viewed in relation to the difference between before-tax and after-tax distributions. Thus Pechman and Okner report the following Gini coefficients for different assumptions about incidence, given here in percentages:[8]

Variant	Before-tax income	After-tax income (families re-ranked)	Difference
1a	43.21	41.56	− 1.65
1b	43.29	41.56	− 1.73
1c	43.67	41.58	− 2.09
2a	43.63	41.92	− 1.71
2b	43.75	42.17	− 1.58
3a	42.77	42.03	− 0.74
3b	42.52	42.40	− 0.12
3c	43.40	41.71	− 1.69

If the figures for the possible effect of re-ranking are at all realistic, they suggest that it might be quite significant in relation to the redistributive impact of taxation.

Finally, I make a comparison with the effects of interpolating grouped observations.[9] Unless the number of groups is very limited, the effect of re-ranking may warrant at least as much attention in empirical studies as that of grouping.

Horizontal Equity and the Assessment of Tax Systems

In the previous section I set out a simple framework within which to examine the re-ranking induced by the tax system and suggested that it may be of some empirical significance. If one leaves to one side differences justified on equity grounds, such as those related to age and family size, the fact that people with identical pre-tax income pay different amounts of tax leads to horizontal inequity. Such inequity is frequently taken to be an undesirable feature of a tax system; however, relatively little consideration seems to have been given to the status of horizontal equity as a principle of tax design. The concept of horizontal equity is open to several different interpretations.

Horizontal equity and the social welfare function
The first view is that horizontal equity is simply an implication of the more general principle of welfare maximisation. Pigou stated this view explicitly: 'Tax arrangements that conform to the principle of least sacrifice always and necessarily conform also to the principle of equal sacrifice among similar and similarly situated persons.'[10] A more recent example is provided by Musgrave and Musgrave: 'Both equity rules [horizontal and vertical]... follow from the same principle of equal treatment.'[11]

The reasoning underlying this view has been set out clearly by Feldstein:

With the assumption that individuals all have the same utility function, the principle of horizontal equity requires nothing more than that individuals with the same consumption bundle (including leisure) should pay the same tax. ... *Since violation of this condition would reduce aggregate social welfare*, the equal taxation of equals is implied directly by utilitarianism and does not require a separate principle of horizontal equity.[12]

Feldstein goes on to argue that this condition does not hold when there is diversity of tastes, but without introducing this complication the argument may be shown to be incorrect. Even if tastes are identical, the equal treatment of equals is not necessarily implied by welfare maximisation – the italicised statement in the quotation above does not always hold. In particular, where the feasible set is non convex, treating otherwise identical individuals differently may increase social welfare.[13] If the feasible set has the (symmetric) shape drawn and the social welfare contour is as indicated (again symmetric), then differential treatment raises aggregate social welfare (see Figure 2).

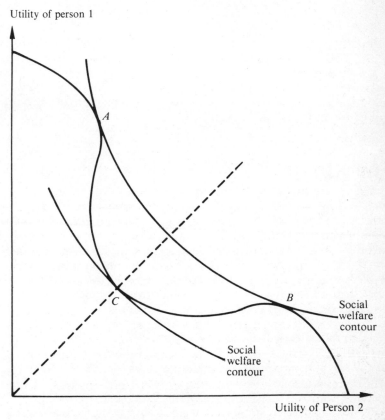

Figure 2   *Illustrative non-convex, symmetric feasible set showing that social welfare is maximised at either A or B and that C is a minimum.*

Horizontal equity as an independent principle

This brings me to the second view of horizontal equity – that it is an independent principle that has to be balanced with maximisation of welfare. Although not usually made explicit, this interpretation appears to be what lies behind some treatments of the subject. The translation of the principle into an explicit measure has not, however, been widely attempted. The ideal of zero inequity is straightforward to define, but how can one compare the degrees of horizontal inequity in states that fall short of the ideal?

In a paper that has received relatively little attention, Johnson and Mayer discuss a number of ways in which an index of horizontal inequity might be constructed.[14] They consider in effect persons with identical pre-tax incomes and suggest that the index might be a function of the number of inequities between people or of the differences in taxation. In the present context the former would lead to an index for pre-tax class i (with a transition matrix A):

$$J_i = 1 - \sum_j a_{ij}^2 \qquad (8)$$

This reaches a maximum where $a_{ij} = 1/n$ and a minimum for $a_{ij} = 1$ for some j (not necessarily i, a feature discussed later). Feldstein makes a number of interesting suggestions, among them that one could take the after-tax variance of utilities of people with equal before-tax utility.[15] Thus, if the welfare of individuals in post-tax class j is denoted by U_j, the measure of horizontal inequity for pre-tax class i would be:

$$F_i = \sum_j a_{ij}(U_j - \bar{U}_i)^2, \qquad (9)$$

where $\bar{U}_i$ is the mean for those in pre-tax class i.

One possible rationalisation of these approaches follows a parallel with the Rawlsian 'original position'.[16] Rawls supposes that principles of justice are chosen as from behind a 'veil of ignorance', with people unaware of their income. Suppose instead that individuals know their pre-tax income but are uncertain about the impact of taxation, knowing only the distribution of post-tax incomes conditional on gross income. The measure of horizontal equity may then be derived from the attitudes of individuals toward risk, given their ignorance about the impact of taxation. This characterisation does not of course apply to certain factors that may lead to differential taxation and are known to the individual, but it is relevant to a number of aspects (including differences arising from successful and unsuccessful tax evasion,[17] and the 'random' taxation considered by Stiglitz).[18]

The representation of the horizontal equity objective in terms of individual uncertainty captures some elements of the problem but is open to objections. First, it may be held to attach undue status to the pre-tax distribution. (The next section deals with this problem.) Second, even if one accepts the basic framework, there is the question as to how the 'risk' associated with taxation should be measured. The related literature on portfolio theory indicates that one cannot expect to define a complete ranking without specification of the individual utility function, but it is possible to define the concept analogous to a mean-preserving spread.[19] Thus if the third row in the transition matrix is changed from $(0, 0.2, 0.6, 0.2, 0)$ to $(0, 0.1, 0.8, 0.1, 0)$, this matrix can be said to exhibit less horizontal inequity. This example also serves, however, to bring out a further shortcoming of this line of approach. Suppose that the third row had become $(0, 0, 0.1, 0.8, 0.1)$. This is less dispersed, but the weight has shifted away from the pivotal a_{33}. In effect this treatment ignores the ranking of i vis-à-vis other pre-tax groups, as noted by Feldstein: '[The variance] would be sensitive to unequal treatment of equals but would not reflect the utility reversals as such.'[20] For the indices J_i and I_i to take the value zero it is necessary only that *some* $a_{ij} = 1$; it is not required that $a_{ii} = 1$.

This fact suggests that the measurement of horizontal equity should take explicit account of the distance moved from the pre-tax ranking.[21] Such a measure can be reduced to a single number, as with the example of the Bartholomew index B given earlier, but any such summary statistic involves assumptions that may be little more than arbitrary. It may therefore be preferable to present the whole permutation or transition matrix; use of this matrix (or of the Lorenz curve) avoids the need to choose from the summary measures of inequality. In the same way, such a matrix can only provide a partial ordering of degrees of horizontal inequity; a comparison can be made where one ranking can be obtained from another by a sequence of rank-reversing transpositions.

Status of horizontal equity
The ethical significance of horizontal equity may be seen as depending on the status of the pre-tax distribution (that is, the distribution in the absence of the state). On an entitlement view of justice, of the kind advanced by Nozick, the pre-tax position has a particular claim on our attention,[22] and horizontal inequity is of central concern. In contrast, moral arguments based on end-result principles, such as utilitarian or Rawlsian theories, see the distribution of post-tax income as the sole matter for concern; no equity significance is attached to the degree of mobility induced by taxation.[23] A similar line has been taken in radical critiques of traditional normative tax theory that argue that the pre-tax income has no equity significance and that it is wrong to place 'normative emphasis on the preservation of the ordinal ranking of individual labour incomes as one moves from the market to the post-tax-and-transfer distribution'.[24]

There is, however, a third position: that horizontal equity is concerned, not with outcomes or with changes in position, but with the means by which they are achieved. In this view, horizontal equity is 'a safeguard against capricious discrimination'.[25] It may require, for instance, that the tax rate should not vary, *ceteris paribus*, with a person's race or religion. It is a restriction on the class of tax instruments the government may use. Thus in the case of indirect taxes the government may be constrained from varying the tax rate on commodities between which differences in consumption are mainly matters of taste (for example, taxing different brands of beer at different rates).[26]

The status of horizontal equity and the relationship of tax-induced mobility to social justice depend therefore on the position adopted. Even if one attaches no significance to mobility from an ethical point of view, however, this does not mean that the study of such mobility is redundant. The magnitude of changes in ranking induced by taxation is an interesting feature in its own right. Most important, it helps explain why the tax system is less progressive in effect than it nominally appears – the theme that runs through so much of Joseph Pechman's work.

Acknowledgement

This paper is part of work on a programme of research on Taxation, Incentives, and the Distribution of Income financed by the Social Science Research Council. I am grateful to Michael J. Boskin, Harvey Brazer and Mervyn King for helpful comments on an earlier version.

Notes

1 Pechman, J. A. and Okner, B. A., *Who Bears the Tax Burden?* (Brookings Institution, 1974). For other major investigations carried out in the United States, see Tarasov, H., *Who Pays the Taxes? (Allocation of Federal, State, and Local Taxes to Consumer Income Brackets)*, Monograph 3, Temporary National Economic Committee: *Investigation of Concentration of Economic Power*, 76 Congress 2 sessions (Government Printing Office, 1940); Musgrave, R. A., 'Distribution of tax payments by income groups: a case study for 1948', *National Tax Journal*, vol. 4, March 1951, pp. 1–53; Conrad, A. H., 'Redistribution through Government budgets in the United States, 1950', in Peacock, A. T. (ed.), *Income Redistribution and Social Policy*, London, Jonathan Cape, 1954, pp. 178–267; and others. In the United Kingdom, calculations of the incidence of taxation by income class had been made by S. Jevons in 1869 (see Roseveare, H., *The Treasury, 1660–1870*, London, Allen & Unwin, 1973), and later contributions include Lord Samuel, 'The taxation of the various casses of the people', *Journal of the Royal Statistical Society*, vol. 82, March 1919, pp. 143–82; Barna, T., *Redistribution of Income through Public Finance in 1937*, Oxford University Press, 1945; Cartter, A. M., *The Redistribution of Income in Postwar Britain: A Study of the Effects of the Central Government Fiscal Program in 1948–49*, Yale University Press, 1955, Port Washington, NY, and London, Kennikat Press, 1973; and Nicholson, J. L., *Redistribution of Income in the United Kingdom in 1959, 1957 and 1953*, London, Bowes & Bowes, 1964.
2 See, for example, Musgrave, R. A., Case, K. E. and Leonard, H. 'The distribution of fiscal burdens and benefits', *Public Finance Quarterly*, vol. 2, July 1974, pp. 259–311.
3 For an earlier discussion of the movements from one income range to another, see Nicholson, *Redistribution of Income in the United Kingdom*, (*op. cit.*).
4 It should be noted that methods of putting bounds on the Lorenz curves of grouped data, as suggested by Gastwirth, J. L. 'The estimation of the Lorenz curve and Gini index', *Review of Economics and Statistics*, vol. 54, August 1972, pp. 306–16, would not apply in this case, since the curve (ranked by pre-tax income) is non-convex.
5 The term 'taxes paid' should be taken to include all sources of differences between income in the absence of the fiscal system, and the after-tax position with the fiscal system in operation. Thus, for example, in the case of tax-exempt bonds adjustment should be made for the interest differential. Moreover, although the issue is discussed with reference to taxation, the same questions arise with government spending.
6 Bartholomew, D. J. *Stochastic Models for Social Processes*, 2nd edn, Wiley, 1973, p. 24. For a discussion of this index, see Shorrocks, A. F., 'The measurement of mobility', *Econometrica*, vol. 46, September 1978, pp. 1013–24.
7 For a discussion of the relation between concentration and Lorenz curves, see, for example, Kakwani, N. C., 'Applications of Lorenz curves in economic analysis', *Econometrica*, vol. 45, April 1977, pp. 719–27.
8 Pechman and Okner, *Who Bears the Tax Burden?* (*op. cit.*) Tables 4–7, p. 56. The incidence assumptions of the variants are as follows: All variants distribute individual income tax payments among tax payers and sales taxes among consumers in proportion to estimated consumption of taxed commodities. The corporation income tax is distributed among taxpayers according to estimated dividends received in Variants 2a and 2b, according to

estimated property income in general in Variants 1a and 1b; under Variants 1c and 3c, half on the basis of dividends received and half on the basis of property income in general; under Variant 1a half to dividends, one-fourth on the basis of consumption, and one-fourth on the basis of earnings, under Variant 1b, half on the basis of property income in general and half on the basis of consumption. The property tax is distributed on the basis of property income in general in Variants 1b and 1c and on the basis of land ownership in all other variants. The payroll tax on employees is distributed on the basis of employee compensation in all variants. The payroll tax on employers is distributed half on the basis of employee compensation and half on the basis of consumption under Variants 2b and 3b; under all other variants it is distributed on the basis of employee compensation. See *ibid.*, pp. 35–9.

9 The results of Gastwirth based on census of population data give bounds, using his refined method, of 40.055% and 40.175% (the true value was 40.14%) for the case of twenty-eight groups. See 'The estimation of the Lorentz curve and Gini index', pp. 310–11.
10 Pigou, A. C., *A Study in Public Finance*, 3rd rev. edn, Macmillan, 1947, p. 45.
11 Musgrave, R. A. and Musgrave, P. B., *Public Finance in Theory and Practice*, 2nd edn, McGraw-Hill, 1976, p. 216n.
12 Feldstein, M. 'On the theory of tax reform', *Journal of Public Economics*, vol. 6, July–August 1976, p. 82 (emphasis added).
13 Atkinson, A. B. and Stiglitz, J. E., 'The design of tax structure: direct versus indirect taxation', Chapter 11 in this volume; and Stiglitz, J. E., 'Utilitarianism and horizontal equity: the case for random taxation', *Journal of Public Economics* (forthcoming).
14 Johnson, S. B. and Mayer, T., 'An extension of Sidgwick's equity principle', *Quarterly Journal of Economics*, vol. 76, August 1962, pp. 454–63.
15 Feldstein (*op. cit.*), p. 83. See also White, M. and White, A., 'Horizontal inequality in the federal income tax treatment of home owners and tenants', *National Tax Journal*, vol. 18, September 1965, pp. 225–39.
16 Rawls, J., *A Theory of Justice*, Harvard University Press, 1971.
17 To consider tax evasion in terms of expected income (as, for example, Kakwani, N. C. does in 'Income tax evasion and income distribution', in Toye, J. F. J. (ed.), *Taxation and Economic Development*, Frank Cass, 1978, pp. 161–73) obscures this issue and seems particularly unsatisfactory.
18 Stiglitz, *op. cit.*
19 See Rothschild, M. and Stiglitz, J. E. 'Increasing risk: I, a definition', *Journal of Economic Theory*, vol. 2, September 1970, pp. 225–43.
20 Feldstein, *op. cit.*
21 Note the affinity with Pyatt's 'statistical game' interpretation of the Gini coefficient: 'For each individual [i] we conduct an experiment. First, some income ... is selected at random from the population of incomes. ... If the income selected is greater than the actual income of the individual then he can retain the value selected: otherwise he retains his actual income. ... If we now average these expected gains over all individuals, i, we obtain [the numerator of the Gini coefficient].' See Pyatt, G., 'On the interpretation and disaggregation of Gini coefficients', *Economic Journal*, vol. 86, June 1976, p. 244.
22 See Nozick, R., *Anarchy, State and Utopia*, Basic Books, 1974.
23 This may need to be modified where individuals are concerned about their *relative* position. It is possible, for example, that the 'reference group' is defined with respect to pre-tax income.
24 Gordon, D. M., 'Taxation of the poor and the normative theory of tax incidence', *American Economic Review*, vol. 62, May 1972, *Papers and Proceedings*, p. 321.
25 Musgrave, R. A., *The Theory of Public Finance: A Study in Public Economics*, McGraw-Hill, 1959, p. 160.
26 See Atkinson and Stiglitz, *op. cit.*

PART II
WEALTH AND REDISTRIBUTION

Introduction to Part II

Chapter 6   The Distribution of Wealth in Britain

The essays in Part I are concerned with conceptual issues in the measurement of inequality and mobility. The first chapters of Part II turn to the twin problems of securing adequate data to implement the concepts empirically, and of interpreting the evidence in the light of differences between that available and the ideal for the purpose. These problems are all too often ignored. Economists, and other social scientists, can frequently be criticised for the cavalier, or uncritical, way in which they use data. Elaborate models are commonly constructed, and complex inferences drawn, on the basis of data which are seriously deficient and where the deficiencies may dominate the conclusions drawn. To take one example, the statistics from the New Earnings Survey in Britain (carried out by the Department of Employment) are widely used for the analysis of changes in wages without regard to the substantial element of non-response, to variation over time in the method by which the survey is conducted, to the effects of back-dating settlements, etc. (These issues are well discussed by Micklewright and Trinder [17].)

The activity of assembling and assessing data is not typically regarded as an important function of the economist. Times have changed since Bowley wrote

just as a theoretical chemist will have little or no power unless he fully appreciates experimental methods and difficulties ... so no student of political economy can pretend to complete equipment unless he is master of the methods of statistics, knows its difficulties, can see when accurate figures are possible, can criticise the statistical evidence, and has an almost instinctive perception of the reliance that he may place on the estimates given him ([4], p. 9).

In part, times have changed in that the government statistical service has taken over the provision of many of the statistics developed in the first half of the century by Bowley and others. There have, in particular, been great improvements over the 1960s and 1970s in official statistics in Britain in the area of the distribution of income and wealth; but this does not mean that they should cease to be the subject of academic study. The interpretation and development of official published statistics can add considerably to their value, and help avoid misunderstanding. Moreover, many of the advances in official statistics on distribution have been reversed since the Conservative government of Mrs Thatcher took office. In 1981, the report on the Central Statistical Office as part of the Raymer Review revealed that:

Work on estimates of the distribution of wealth...is being stopped. Estimates of the distribution of income [have in the past been published annually]. Faced with the costs, officials in the Treasury – the main government users – indicated less frequency estimates would be sufficient. We noted a sizeable part of the annual cycle of work in CSO was devoted to methodological improvement. It is not clear to us that this is needed.

A depressing commentary for those concerned about this field!

The distribution of wealth, the subject of Chapter 6, written jointly with Alan Harrison, provides a good illustration of the way in which distributional statistics have evolved in Britain. More than a century ago, Baxter [3] made estimates of total personal wealth by applying multipliers to the revenue from probate duties, and the method was refined by Mallet [14] in the early 1900s. The application to the distribution of wealth was pioneered by Clay [5] in 1925, and then developed in significant respects by Daniels and Campion [6], Langley [12] and Lydall and Tipping [13]. When, therefore, the Inland Revenue began to publish 'official' estimates of the size distribution in 1961, they could build on extensive foundations. The government statisticians have since added considerably, and their research effort was substantially increased in response to the requests made by the Royal Commission on the Distribution of Income and Wealth. The Commission was established by the Labour government in 1974, and was dissolved by the Conservatives in 1979. (I was a member from 1978 to 1979.) When announcing the dissolution, the Secretary of State for Employment stated that 'As a consequence of the Commission's recommendations the Government's own regular statistics on income and wealth are now providing more and better information. There is therefore no continuing need for a standing Commission' (House of Commons, 11 June 1979). Within two years, work on wealth estimates had been dropped and information about the distribution of income seriously curtailed.

The main focus of Chapter 6 is on the trends over time in the degree of concentration of wealth, and it presents a series for the period 1923–72 for England and Wales, and 1938–72 for Great Britain, derived by multiplying up the estate statistics. This series is constructed as far as possible on a consistent basis, and does not incorporate all the refinements which can be made for the more recent years (see Atkinson and Harrison [2]). For instance, an allowance is made for the wealth of those not covered by the basic estate returns, but not for wealth missing from those covered (e.g. that held in discretionary trusts). This should be borne in mind when comparing the estimates with those published by the Inland Revenue for the latter part of the 1970s. Figure 1 shows the estimates for Chapter 6, Table 2 (Great Britain) and the Inland Revenue estimates (Inland Revenue Statistics 1981, Table 4.8) series C for the United Kingdom up to 1979. Taking the Inland Revenue estimates as consistently measuring the trend over the 1970s, there was a fall of seven percentage points in the share of the top 1% between 1971 and 1979. This may be viewed in the light of the regression equations estimated in Chapter 6 for the period 1923–72. According to the simple regression model (equation 2) there was a downward trend of some 0.4 percentage points per annum, which would imply a fall of 3.2 percentage points over the period 1971–9. There appears therefore to have been other factors in operation; moreover, from the graph we

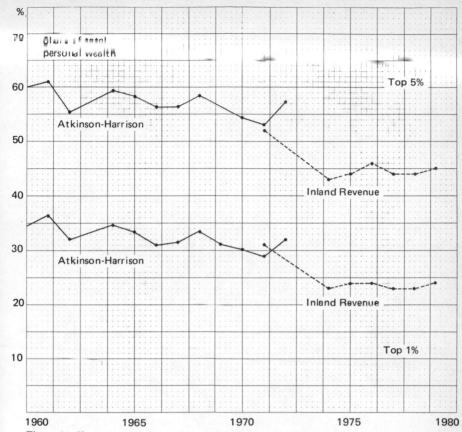

Figure 1   *Shares in total personal wealth in Britain. 1960–79.*

can see that the bulk of the fall took place between 1971 and 1974. This brings us to the movement of stock exchange prices, referred to at the end of Chapter 6, where we suggest that the 1973–4 fall in these prices could have been associated with a decline in the share of the top 1% of some 3–4 percentage points. Since 1974 the series has remained more or less constant, and the experience of the 1970s illustrates the dangers of extrapolating trends into the future without investigation of their causes.

In using the Inland Revenue series, linked to our estimates, assumptions are being made about the consistency of the estimates for different years. One of the aims of Chapter 6 is to stress the difficulty in ensuring such consistency. This is illustrated by the changes in the tax system which have taken place since 1972. In the Finance Act 1975, Estate Duty was replaced by Capital Transfer Tax. This involved major changes in the form of the tax and its treatment of different types of property, notable examples being the provisions for gifts, for transfers between spouses, and for discretionary trusts. There have been, moreover, a number of subsequent amendments. These changes may well have affected the form, and the interpretation, of the wealth statistics, and are an example of the need for continual development of statistical information in this area.

Chapter 7   Wealth and the Life-cycle

Chapter 7 was written before I embarked on the investigation of wealth statistics with Alan Harrison, and more recent empirical findings are contained in Atkinson and Harrison [2]. The essay is included because of the importance of the issues raised, and because it provides a link with the theoretical analyses in Chapters 8 and 9.

In discussing the concentration of wealth in Chapter 6 we are dealing with the current distribution among the entire population, considering people of all ages. Part of the observed differences may, however, be attributable to systematic variation of wealth with age – the life-cycle effect. From the standpoint of equity this may be of less concern to us than the differences which arise among people of the same age. If, for example, we are concerned about inequality of opportunity (Chapter 4), then we may want to focus on the inequality of *inherited* wealth. The aim of Chapter 7 is to bring out this point, and to provide some insight into its likely quantitative significance. (A similar observation was later made by Paglin [19] in connection with income inequality.)

Since Chapter 7 was written there have been several developments. There have been a number of studies constructing more elaborate models to assess the probable impact of the life-cycle factor, including Kessler and Masson [11], Davies and Shorrocks [7], Jones [10], Masson and Strauss-Kahn [15], Oulton [18] and Wolfson [24]. The empirical evidence on the wealth with age in Britain has been examined by Astin [1], the Royal Commission on the Distribution of Income and Wealth [21] and Shorrocks [22]. Particular reference should be made to two points. The first is that the estimates based on estate data tend to be over-value life assurance policies (Dunn and Hoffman [8]) and the overstatement varies systematically with age. Shorrocks [23] has shown that correction for over-valuation has noticeable impact on the age profile of wealth. Secondly, Chapter 7 contains estimates of the value of pension rights, an aspect subsequently taken up with enthusiasm by Polanyi and Wood [20] in Britain, Feldstein [9] in the United States, and others. I draw attention to the discussion in Chapter 7 since the qualifications made there about these estimates have not always been heeded. In my view the assumptions implicit in calculations of 'state pension wealth' are such as to render their value highly dubious.

Chapter 8   The Life-cycle and Individual Savings

Life-cycle savings are also the subject of Chapter 8, which applies a concept of lifetime equity identical to that in Chapter 7. The emphasis here, however, is on the theoretical analysis of the impact of taxation on individual saving and bequest behaviour.

The central concern of Chapter 8 is with the choice between different forms of wealth taxation. At the time it was written, Britain operated an Estate Duty with only limited taxation of gifts *inter vivos*, and there was no wealth tax. Since then, Estate Duty has been replaced by Capital Transfer Tax; and there has been a Select Committee on a Wealth Tax reporting in 1977. Despite these events, the analysis remains of interest since it cannot be claimed that capital taxation has reached its final state.

In order to capture the essential features of the different wealth taxes it is necessary to incorporate the bequest motive for savings. Chapter 8 shows how, in a partial equilibrium context, the long-run development of wealth-holding may depend on the bequest relationship. The model is based on the assumption that individuals derive utility from the size of bequest. The case where utility depends on the circumstances of succeeding generations has been developed by Meade, Becker and others (see the references in Chapter 9). It is, of course, open to question how far bequests are an important motive for saving and, to the extent that they are, whether they are well represented in terms of utility-maximisation. Capitalists may just accumulate.

Chapter 9   Inheritance and Redistribution

The approach to wealth accumulation in Chapter 9 is more flexible than in Chapter 8 in that the basic bequest relationship (equation 8) allows of a life-cycle interpretation and of a 'class' saving interpretation. The latter refers back to the equation used in the empirical analysis of Chapter 6 (equation 5), inspired by the work of Meade [16], where there is a fixed tendency of capital to reproduce itself.

The aim of Chapter 9, written for a volume in honour of James Meade, is to provide a more general formulation of the inter-generational process. It develops the analyses of Chapter 8 in the treatment of savings, in the incorporation of different assumptions about the division of estates (and marriage), and in the general equilbrium setting. The last, by introducing the determinants of earnings, brings us close to the model used in Chapter 4 (compare Figure 2 with Figure 3 in Chapter 9). Although purely theoretical, the model is designed with a view to empirical implementation. This may take the form of an analysis of properties of the overall distribution, as in Chapter 6 where we examine the determinants of the share of the top 1%, or it may involve the use of micro-economic data. In either form the econometric analysis of distributional behaviour is likely to be an important area for future research.

References

[1] Astin, J. A. (1975), 'The distribution of wealth and the relevance of age', *Statistical News*, pp. 1–28.

[2] Atkinson, A. B. and Harrison, A. J. (1978), *Distribution of Personal Wealth in Britain*, Cambridge, Cambridge University Press.

[3] Baxter, R. D. (1869), *The Taxation of the United Kingdom*, London, Macmillan.

[4] Bowley, A. L. (1937), *Elements of Statistics*, London, P. S. King.

[5] Clay, H. (1925), 'The distribution of capital in England and Wales', *Transactions of Manchester Statistical Society*.

[6]   Daniels, G. W. and Campion, H. (1936), *The Distribution of National Capital*, Manchester, Manchester University Press.

[7]   Davies, J. B. and Shorrocks, A. F. (1978), 'Assessing the quantitative importance of inheritance in the distribution of wealth', *Oxford Economic Papers*, vol. 30, pp. 138–49.

[8]   Dunn, A. T. and Hoffman, P. D. R. B. (1978), 'The distribution of personal wealth', *Economic Trends*, issue 301, pp. 101–18.

[9]   Feldstein, M. S. (1976), 'Social security and the distribution of wealth', *Journal of the American Statistical Association*, vol. 71, pp. 800–7.

[10] Jones, E. (1978), 'Estimation of the magnitude of accumulated and inherited wealth', *Journal of the Institute of Actuaries*, vol. 105, pp. 131–75.

[11] Kessler, D. and Masson, A. (1979), 'Transmission, accumulation et immobilité', *Consommation*, pp. 77–105.

[12] Langley, K. M. (1950, 1951), 'The distribution of capital in private hands in 1936–38 and in 1946–47', *Bulletin of the Oxford University Institute of Statistics*, vol. 12, pp. 339–59, and vol. 13, pp. 34–54.

[13] Lydall, H. F. and Tipping, D. G. (1961), 'The distribution of personal wealth in Britain', *Bulletin of the Oxford University Institute of Economics and Statistics*, vol. 23, pp. 83–104.

[14] Mallet, B. (1908), 'A method of estimating capital wealth from the estate duty statistics', *Journal of the Royal Statistical Society*, vol. 71.

[15] Masson, A. and Strauss-Kahn, D. (1979), Facteurs de l'inègalitè des patrimonies', *Annales de l'Insée*, vols. 33–4, pp. 59–87.

[16] Meade, J. E. (1964), *Efficiency, Equality and the Ownership of Property*, London, Allen & Unwin.

[17] Micklewright, J. and Trinder, C. (1981), 'New Earnings Surveys 1968–80: Sampling methods and non-response', *Taxation, Incentives and Distribution of Income Research Programme*, Discussion Paper 31, London School of Economics.

[18] Oulton, N. (1976), 'Inheritance and the distribution of wealth', *Oxford Economic Papers*, vol. 28, pp. 86–101.

[19] Paglin, M. (1975), 'The measurement and trend of inequality', *American Economic Review*, vol. 65, pp. 598–609.

[20] Polanyi, G. and Wood, J. B. (1974), *How Much Inequality?*, London, Institute of Economic Affairs.

[21] Royal Commission on the Distribution of Income and Wealth (1977), *Report No. 5*, London, HMSO.

[22] Shorrocks, A. F. (1975), 'The age-wealth relationship', *Review of Economics and Statistics*, vol. 57, pp. 155–63.

[23] Shorrocks, A. F. (1981), 'Life insurance and asset holding in the United Kingdom', in D. Currie, D. Peel and W. Peters (eds.), *Microeconomic Analysis*, London, Croom Helm.

[24] Wolfson, M. C. (1980), 'The bequest process and the causes of inequality in the distribution in wealth', in J. D. Smith (ed.), *Modeling the Distribution and Intergenerational Transmission of Wealth*, Chicago, University of Chicago Press.

6 The Analysis of Trends over Time in the Distribution of Personal Wealth in Britain*

Introduction

The trends over time in the distribution of personal wealth in Britain have been one of the most widely studied aspects of the subject. A number of investigators have used estimates of the distribution derived from application of the estate multiplier method to British estate data to measure trends in the shares of top wealth-holders, for example the Royal Commission on the Distribution of Income and Wealth [8], referred to below as the *Royal Commission* and the conclusions drawn from this analysis have been widely quoted. Additionally, others have drawn inferences from such an analysis on such questions as the impact of a slump in the stock market or land prices on the distribution. These issues are the subject of this chapter.

A major problem when examining the trends in the distribution is that of securing a series which is consistent over time. This is recognised explicitly by the *Royal Commission* ([8], p. 97), although it must be said that others who have used estate estimates to assess trends in the distribution have frequently overlooked this important point. Only when it has been firmly established that the basic estimates are reasonably reliable can one proceed to an analysis of influences on the trends over time in the distribution, and we therefore begin this chapter with a discussion of how we attempt to overcome the difficulties of the basic estate data and the methodological problems encountered when estimating the distribution from these data. Section 2 presents new estimates covering the period 1923–72, and compares these with those used in earlier studies. Then, in section 3, we present the results of an econometric investigation of the different forces influencing the degree of concentration in the distribution of wealth.

1 Problems in Securing a Consistent Series

Problems which arise when attempts are made to estimate a consistent set of estimates of the distribution of wealth for the period we are considering fall

* Reprinted from *Annales de l'Insée*, 1979.
A. B. Atkinson and A. J. Harrison.

into three categories. First, there are difficulties associated with the *source statistics*, the basic estate data. These have been published for many years but their form and coverage have changed on a number of occasions. These changes have occurred because of new estate duty legislation, changes in estate duty practice, or variation in the methods by which the statistics are collected or tabulated. The second source of difficulty is in the application of consistent *mortality multipliers*. Our analysis of multipliers elsewhere (Atkinson and Harrison [1], ch. 3) suggests that differences would not lead to dramatic changes in the results, but that the estimates could change by one or two percentage points. Thirdly, there are problems regarding the *adjustments to the estate estimates*. Not only has the need for such adjustments varied with changes in the coverage of the estate figures, but also the raw data necessary to make the adjustments are available with varying degrees of accuracy. In what follows, we describe each of the problems in greater detail, before describing the steps we have taken to secure a more consistent set of estimates.

(i) Source statistics

The first point to make when considering the source statistics is that it is these which determine the years for which estimates of the distribution of wealth can be prepared. More precisely, we require estate statistics classified by sex, age, country and estate size. Thus no estimates are possible for years prior to 1923 since this was the first year that the estate statistics were disaggregated by sex.[1] Similarly, the 1963 estate statistics relate to Great Britain, rather than to individual countries, and are therefore not able to be used in our work. The full list of years for which suitable estate data are available is 1923–30, 1936, 1938, 1950–62, 1964–present,[2] although even here, as we have mentioned, there exist problems of comparability over time.

First, for much of the period the data do not cover estates below the estate duty exemption level. Only since 1960 have the data included details of estates below the exemption level which come to the notice of the Inland Revenue, thereby extending their coverage considerably. Secondly, in the period before 1960 the exemption level increased from £100 in 1923 to £3000 by 1959 so that a much smaller proportion of total deaths was covered by the statistics in the late 1950s than had been covered in the 1920s. A major part of this jump in the exemption level occurred between 1938 (the last pre-war figures) and 1950 (the first post-war figures), a point to which we return below. The third problem associated with the estate statistics is that up to and including 1936 they refer to England and Wales only, whereas for 1938 and subsequent years statistics are published for Scotland also.[3]

As a consequence of these problems in sections 2 and 3 we break the period 1923–72 into three sub-periods: 1923–38, 1950–59 and 1960–72. This allows for the possible breaks in the series between 1938 and 1950, when the substantial increase in the estate duty threshold reduced the coverage of the data, and between 1959 and 1960, when data on estates below the threshold were first published. Also we present two separate series, one for England and Wales and one for Great Britain dating respectively from 1923 and 1938. This allows us to examine the differences in the two series during the period of overlap.

(ii) Mortality multipliers

One of the primary adjustments to the mortality multipliers is that made to accommodate the assumed correlation between wealth and social class, and the observed one between social class and longevity. This is usually achieved by applying a social class differential to the basic multiplier, where the latter is the simple result of dividing the population in a particular age/sex group by the number of deaths recorded for the group.[4] The differentials used here are given below in Table 1, and their derivation is discussed in detail in Atkinson and Harrison ([1], especially Appendix VI). The basic sources from which they are taken are the Decennial Supplements to the censuses of 1921, 1931, 1951 and 1961, which contain information on mortality by social class. Again, however, it is the case that a number of adjustments have to be made to the published figures.

Table 1 *Social class differentials used here (England and Wales)*

Age range	1921 Male	1921 Female	1931 Male	1931 Female	1951 Male	1951 Female	1961 Male	1961 Female
20–24	1.21	–	1.12	1.37	1.04	1.50	1.18	1.05
25–34	1.25	–	1.33	1.34	1.32	1.38	1.40	1.29
35–44	1'25	–	1.31	1.24	1.35	1.18	1.43	1.27
45–54	1.18	–	1.19	1.18	1.24	1.12	1.35	1.20
55–64	1.13	–	1.10	1.13	1.19	1.08	1.26	1.16
65–74	1.11	–	1.05	1.10	1.14	1.09	1.11	1.05
75–84	1.07	–	1.00	1.08	1.10	1.09	1.07	1.02
85 and over	1.04	–	1.00	1.04	1.04	1.05	1.04	1.01

The basic approach involves finding the ratio of the mortality multiplier for social classes I and II[5] to the general mortality multiplier. The former is typically higher than the latter so that the ratio, the social class differential, is greater than one. The first problem occurs because of discrepancies between census declarations of occupation and those made on behalf of deceased persons on the death certificate. The latter tends on occasions to be somewhat exaggerated, and in consequence the recorded deaths in the highest social classes are artificially swollen and the social class differential correspondingly understated. This is adjusted for in the figures given in Table 1, and the adjustment partly explains the differences between our figures for 1921 and 1931 and those used by Daniels and Campion [4] for 1924–30, which were based on the Decennial Supplements of 1921 and 1931.

No Decennial Supplement was published between 1931 and 1951 and during this time, or indeed even in the normal ten-year period between Supplements, quite large changes in social class differentials can occur. In reality, of course, the differential changes much more smoothly over time than these discrete jumps suggest, so that the second problem associated with mortality multipliers is finding the appropriate social class differentials for years between censuses. The simplest procedure, and the one we adopt here, is to estimate the differentials for these years as linear interpolations of those for census years.[6]

Finally there remains the question of what differentials should be applied to the non-dutiable estates which appear in the statistics after 1960. The approach adopted here is to use a differential of one, that is to apply the general mortality multiplier without any adjustment for social class. It should be added that the cut-off point below which this practice is adopted is not always the exemption level for estate duty; rather, we prefer to use the exemption level in 1960 of £3000 for that year and then to increase the cut-off in stages to £10,000 by 1972 so as to keep broadly constant the proportion of estates above the cut-off.

(iii) Adjustments to the estate estimates

Once the mortality multipliers, suitably adjusted for social class, are applied to the estate data, estimates are obtained of the numbers of people and amounts of wealth in different ranges of the distribution of wealth. When the numbers and amounts are aggregated across ranges, both differ from the true figures, the former because all deaths do not come to the notice of the estate duty office, the latter for the same reason, and also because, even in estates which are reported, some assets can be transferred without duty being paid and without their value appearing in the statistics.

It might be thought that the true population figure is easily found, but this begs the question of the definition of adult (presuming, of course, that it is accepted that the adult population, rather than the total population, is what we should be interested in). Neither is it simply a matter of securing a standard definition, since social changes over the period may mean that the definition should vary over time. What is really required is a definition of economic independence allowing us to exclude those young people who are still financially dependent on their parents. It seems clear that there has been a downward trend in the average age of economic independence, for although some factors may have worked in the opposite direction, such as the expansion of higher education, this has surely been more than offset by the trend toward earlier marriage and the acquisition of wealth by young earners. We take the age of majority (eighteen) as the basis in 1973, and the age of twenty, following Lydall and Tipping, as appropriate in 1953. Extrapolating linearly gives twenty-three as the cut-off in 1923, with in-between years obtained by graduation at the rate of 1/10th per annum.

Turning to the aggregate wealth figure, the full list of possible adjustments is extremely lengthy. However, over the period under consideration here, the information necessary for these is not available, so that the only one we attempt is that for the wealth of those excluded from the estate estimate of the total population. The extent of the adjustment in this case cannot, of course, be specified precisely, and we prefer to provide estimates on a variety of assumptions B2–B4, (described in more detail in Atkinson and Harrison [1], pp. 299–305), where B2 is an upper estimate of the wealth of the excluded population and hence a lower estimate of the shares of the top 1%, 5% etc., B4 is the reverse, and B3 is a central figure and our preferred estimate.

In brief, the series presented here is specified as follows:

(i) Geographical coverage: separate estimates for England and Wales and for Great Britain as a whole.
     Period: 1923–72 for England and Wales.
              1938–72 for Great Britain.
(ii) Mortality multipliers: based on social class differentials obtained from the Registrar General's Decennial Supplement adjusted for errors in occupational statements and for the unoccupied.
(iii) Total population: equals those economically independent, taken as those above an age threshold reduced linearly from 23 in 1923 to 18 in 1973.
(iv) Total wealth: equals unadjusted wealth as estimated from the estate statistics plus the wealth of the excluded population. The latter is based on a range of assumptions (B2–B4) with a central figure (B3).

2   Towards a Consistent Series

The estimates obtained on the basis of the assumptions outlined at the end of section 1 are set out in Tables 2 and 3. The former shows estimates using the central figure (B3) for the wealth of the excluded population, covering both England and Wales and Great Britain. The latter shows the estimates for England and Wales only, with the range of variation resulting from assumptions B2 and B4. The range of variation B2–B4 changes over time, depending on the accuracy of the underlying data. In particular, it is considerably greater in the 1950s. Thus, the range for 1959 of 60–74% for the share of the top 5% is sufficiently wide for us to be considerably less sure about the central B3 figure than for 1969 when the range is 54–8%.

It should be noted that, following the standard practice, we have obtained the shares by log-linear interpolation. This does, however, introduce a source of error, particularly where, as in many of the earlier years, the data are grouped in broad ranges (in 1950, for example, the share of the top 5% is interpolated from figures for the top 3.5 and 8.5%). Moreover, unlike some earlier authors, we have not attempted to interpolate outside the range of the estate data.

We believe that the series presented here is closer to being consistent over time than the estimates usually quoted. At the same time, we should like to emphasise that it falls short of being ideal in a number of important respects. First, we have drawn attention to the changes which took place over the period in the form and coverage of the estate statistics, which may have affected their comparability; the most serious of these possible breaks in the series – between 1938 and 1950, and between 1959 and 1960 – have been indicated in the tables by horizontal lines. Secondly, we have made no adjustments to the series for the problems of valuation or of wealth missing from the estate returns.

Taking first the question of valuation, the estimates are closest to a realisation basis,[7] with the one important exception of life policies which are valued for estate duty purposes in terms of the sums assured. Analysis of this problem in Atkinson and Harrison ([1], ch. 4) suggests that an adjustment for

Wealth and Redistribution

Table 2   *Shares in total wealth 1923–72 (assumption B3)*

	England and Wales				Great Britain			
	Top 1%	Top 5%	Top 10%	Top 20%	Top 1%	Top 5%	Top 10%	Top 20%
1923	60.9	82.0	89.1	94.2				
1924	59.9	81.5	88.1	93.8				
1925	61.0	82.1	88.4	93.8				
1926	57.3	79.9	87.4	93.2				
1927	59.8	81.3	88.3	93.8		not available		
1928	57.0	79.6	87.2	93.1				
1929	55.5	78.9	86.3	92.6				
1930	57.9	79.2	86.6	92.6				
1936	54.2	77.4	85.7	92.0				
1938	55.0	76.9	85.0	91.2	55.0	77.2	85.4	91.6
1950	47.2	74.3	–	–	47.2	74.4	–	–
1951	45.8	73.6	–	–	45.9	73.8	–	–
1952	43.0	70.2	–	–	42.9	70.3	–	–
1953	43.6	71.1	–	–	43.5	71.2	–	–
1954	45.3	71.8	–	–	45.3	72.0	–	–
1955	44.5	71.1	–	–	43.8	70.8	–	–
1956	44.5	71.3	–	–	44.0	71.1	–	–
1957	43.4	68.7	–	–	42.9	68.6	–	–
1958	41.4	67.8	–	–	40.9	67.7	–	–
1959	41.4	67.6	–	–	41.8	67.9	–	–
1960	33.9	59.4	71.5	83.1	34.4	60.0	72.1	83.6
1961	36.5	60.6	71.7	83.3	36.5	60.8	72.1	83.6
1962	31.4	54.8	67.3	80.2	31.9	55.4	67.9	80.7
1963		not available*				not available*		
1964	34.5	58.6	71.4	84.3	34.7	59.2	72.0	85.2
1965	33.0	58.1	71.7	85.5	33.3	58.7	72.3	85.8
1966	30.6	55.5	69.2	83.8	31.0	56.1	69.9	84.2
1967	31.4	56.0	70.0	84.5	31.5	56.4	70.5	84.9
1968	33.6	58.3	71.6	85.1	33.6	58.6	72.0	85.4
1969	31.1	56.1	67.7	83.3	31.3	56.6	68.6	84.1
1970	29.7	53.6	68.7	84.5	30.1	54.3	69.4	84.9
1971	28.4	52.3	67.6	84.2	28.8	53.0	68.3	84.0
1972	31.7	56.0	70.4	84.9	32.0	57.2	71.7	85.3

Notes: Dashes denote that the information is outside the range of estate data.

* The estate data were not available by country for 1963: this means that we could not calculate a figure for Great Britain comparable with those for other years.

this would tend to increase the relative shares of the top groups. Turning to the question of missing wealth, our inability to make allowance here for missing items may significantly influence the estimate of the degree of concentration at a point in time. Moreover, it may also affect the trends over time, and in particular we need to take account of the changes which have taken place in estate taxation over the course of this century and of the changing pattern of response of those who wish to avoid tax.

It is not possible for us to discuss in any detail the modifications to legislation over the fifty years, of which there were a large number.[8] Some of

Table 3 *Sensitivity of shares to assumptions about wealth of excluded population (England and Wales 1923–72)*

| | Top 1% | | Top 5% | | Top 10% | | Top 20% | |
	B2	B4	D2	B4	D2	B4	B2	D1
1923	60.1	61.7	80.9	83.0	88.0	90.3	93.0	95.4
1924	59.1	60.8	80.4	82.7	86.9	89.4	92.6	95.2
1925	60.2	61.9	81.0	83.2	87.3	89.7	92.6	95.1
1926	56.6	58.1	78.8	81.0	86.2	88.6	92.0	94.5
1927	59.0	60.6	80.3	82.4	87.2	89.5	92.6	95.0
1928	56.2	57.7	78.5	80.7	85.9	88.3	91.8	94.4
1929	54.7	56.4	77.7	80.1	85.0	87.6	91.2	94.0
1930	57.1	58.7	78.0	80.3	85.4	87.8	91.3	93.8
1936	53.5	54.9	76.3	78.4	84.6	86.9	90.7	93.2
1938	54.3	55.6	75.9	77.8	84.0	86.1	90.1	92.3
1950	43.7	50.0	68.8	78.7	–	–	–	–
1951	42.1	48.8	67.6	78.5	–	–	–	–
1952	39.6	45.7	64.7	74.6	–	–	–	–
1953	39.7	46.9	64.6	76.4	–	–	–	–
1954	41.3	48.5	65.5	76.9	–	–	–	–
1955	39.1	49.2	62.5	78.6	–	–	–	–
1956	39.0	49.3	62.4	79.0	–	–	–	–
1957	38.2	48.0	60.4	75.9	–	–	–	–
1958	36.7	45.4	60.1	74.5	–	–	–	–
1959	36.6	45.4	59.9	74.3	–	–	–	–
1960	32.8	34.6	57.5	60.7	69.3	73.1	80.6	84.9
1961	35.3	37.3	58.7	61.9	69.6	73.4	80.8	85.2
1962	30.6	32.0	53.4	56.0	65.5	68.7	78.0	81.8
1963				not available*				
1964	33.5	35.2	56.8	59.9	69.3	73.0	82.3	86.7
1965	31.9	33.8	56.2	59.6	69.3	73.4	82.7	87.6
1966	29.6	31.3	53.6	56.8	67.0	70.9	81.1	85.8
1967	30.3	32.1	54.0	57.3	67.5	71.7	81.5	86.5
1968	32.2	34.6	55.8	60.0	68.6	73.7	81.5	87.6
1969	29.8	32.1	53.8	57.9	64.9	69.9	79.8	86.0
1970	28.2	30.6	51.0	55.3	65.4	70.9	80.4	87.2
1971	27.2	29.2	50.2	53.7	64.8	69.4	80.8	86.5
1972	30.2	32.7	53.3	57.7	62.7	72.6	80.8	87.5

See Notes to Table 2.

these extended the scope of wealth covered by the statistics, and in so far as much of this property would have been owned by those in the higher wealth ranges the changes would have led to an apparent increase in concentration. To this extent, therefore, the downward trend in the top shares would be understated. Working in the opposite direction has been the growth of certain forms of tax avoidance. Not all forms of avoidance lead to wealth being missing from the statistics, but where it does, this is likely to cause an understatement of the degree of concentration. For example, the effect of rising rates of duty, and the closing of other loopholes, undoubtedly led to a growth in non-dutiable trusts.

Wealth and Redistribution

(i) A comparison of the estimated trend

Having presented our estimates, and the qualifications which must accompany them, it is interesting to examine to what extent the trends over time implied by our estimates differ from the figures conventionally used. To this end, Table 4 presents a series of estimates brought together by Polanyi and

Table 4   *Comparison of our estimates with those of earlier studies*

| | England and Wales | | | Great Britain | | |
	1924–30	1936	1951–56	1960	1965	1970
Earlier studies						
Top 1%	60	56	42	39	34	31
Top 5%	83	81	68	64	62	56
Top 10%	90	83	79	76	75	70
Top 20%	96	94	89	91	89	87
Our estimates (B3)						
Top 1%	58	54	44	34	33	30
Top 5%	80	77	72	60	59	54
Top 10%	87	86	–	72	72	69
Top 20%	93	92	–	84	86	85

Sources: Polanyi and Wood ([7], Tables 3 and 4) and Table 2.
Note: Dashes denote that the information is outside the range of estate data.

Wood [7] with, below it, our figures presented in the same form. The estimates for 1970 are relatively close, our figures being some 1–2% lower than those in the top half of Table 4 (reflecting the fact that we have made an allowance for the wealth of the excluded population). For certain other years, however, the differences are more marked; for example, our estimate for 1960 shows the share of the top 1% as 5% lower, and that of the top 20% as 7% lower. Such differences may not seem especially important, but again this illustrates the fact that the measurement of the trends may be more problematic than determining the degree of concentration at a point in time. Both sets of estimates could be said, for example, to be consistent with the view that the share of the top 5% was 80% in the 1920s and 70% in the 1950s. However, in one case the estimated annual downward (arithmetic) trend is 0.6%, whereas in the other it is 0.3%. In the same way, the estimates agree that the share of the top 20% in the 1960s was 85–90%, but in one case the share fell at a rate of 0.4% per annum and in the other the share rose very slightly.

If we turn now to the questions raised earlier, the first step is to examine the effect of introducing Scotland into the analysis in 1938. In fact, it is clear that the figures for England and Wales are the dominant influence on those for Great Britain,[9] and in view of this we base our subsequent discussion on the longer series for England and Wales. This does not necessarily provide a reliable guide to what has happened in Scotland, but closely approximates the position for Britain as a whole; moreover the series for England and Wales is less likely to be subject to sampling fluctuations that that for Scotland.

The second step is to consider the sub-periods for which the estimates may be regarded as comparable. Our earlier discussion of the possible discontinuities, marked by lines in the tables, suggests that it may be best to consider three sub-periods. This, however, seriously limits the conclusions which can be drawn from Table 4, since we have only three observations on the trends over time: 1924–30 to 1936, 1960 to 1965 and 1965 to 1970. In fact, this approach to the measurement of the trends – via estimates averaged over a number of years – involves a significant loss of information. For this reason we prefer a regression approach which initially attempts only to give some indication of the trend in the figures, while allowing for the possible discontinuities by the use of shift dummies. Then, in section 3 below, we elaborate on this approach and attempt to assess which variables are important as influences on the trend.

(ii) The regression approach
Consider the simple model:

$$W^*_{x,t} = a + bT + cD_1 + dD_2 \qquad (1)$$

where $W^*_{x,t}$ is the true share of the top $x\%$, T is a time trend and D_1 (0 until 1938, 1 thereafter) and D_2 (0 until 1959, 1 thereafter) are dummy variables. Using the full set of observations for England and Wales (data based on assumption B3 and similar to those in Table 2, but given to 2 decimal places) we obtained the following estimates for the share of the top 1%, and the top 5%, measured in percentage points:

$$\hat{W}_{1,t} = 60.6 - 0.42T - 2.91D_1 - 6.90D_2 \qquad \bar{R}^2 = 0.98 \qquad (2)$$
$$\phantom{\hat{W}_{1,t} = 60.6} (6.5) \quad (1.6) \qquad (7.1)$$

$$\hat{W}_{5,t} = 82.7 - 0.42T + 1.88D_1 - 9.16D_2 \qquad \bar{R}^2 = 0.98 \qquad (3)$$
$$\phantom{\hat{W}_{5,t} = 82.7} (6.6) \quad (1.1) \qquad (9.5)$$

where the figures in brackets are t-statistics.

The Durbin-Watson statistic indicates that in both cases we cannot reject the hypothesis of zero first-order correlation at the 5% level. In the case of the top 1%, the statistic exceeds 2.0, but it is less than the critical value $(4 - d_u = 2.35)$.

Equations (2) and (3) have a number of interesting implications. First, they suggest a substantial shift between 1959 and 1960 (around 7% for the top 1%). When allowance has been made for this, the trend in the share of the top 1% is approximately 0.4% per annum. Secondly, the annual decline in the share of the top 5% is precisely the same so that the group just below the top 1% appears to be maintaining its share.

A further question to which an extension of our analysis allows us to offer an answer is whether the trend in the share of the top 1% is accelerating over time. This is a popular view[10] but not one which can be substantiated. Adding T^2 to our simple regression model we find:

$$\hat{W}_{1,t} = 60.8 - 0.45T + 0.0006T^2 - 2.72D_1 - 7.10D_2 \qquad \bar{R}^2 = 0.98 \qquad (4)$$
$$\quad\quad\;\; (3.7) \quad (0.3) \quad\quad (1.4) \quad\quad (6.0)$$

so that the coefficient on T^2 is both insignificant and wrongly signed.
   The main features of our analysis so far are therefore:

(i) a downward trend of some 0.4% per annum in the share of the top 1%;
(ii) no apparent acceleration in the arithmetic rate of decline in the share of the top 1%; and
(iii) no apparent downward trend in the share of the next 4% below the top 1%.

   We turn next to an assessment of how much of this can be explained in terms of the factors we would expect to impinge on the share of the top 1%.

3   Determinants of the Share of the Top 1 per cent

(i) The basic model
In order to investigate the impact of factors influencing the distribution of wealth, we first need to identify those factors which are most likely to be important. The approach we adopt here is to begin with the Meade [6] theory of wealth accumulation, expressed in continuous time as:

$$\dot{K} = SE + (Sr - \theta)K \qquad (5)$$

where K is wealth, S is the savings propensity, E is earnings, r is the rate of interest, and θ represents the assumption that for a given income $y (= E + rK)$, the amount saved will be lower the higher is K. The composite variable $(Sr - \theta)$ can also be seen as the 'internal rate of accumulation', or the tendency of capital to reproduce itself. We assume that this process applies both to total wealth (K), and, with different parameters, to the wealth of the top 1% (K_1).[11]
   We begin with total wealth. Integrating equation (5), we obtain:

$$K(t) = K(0)e^{(Sr-\theta)t}\left[1 + \frac{\int_0^t SEe^{-(Sr-\theta)(u-t)}\,du}{K(0)e^{(Sr-\theta)t}}\right] \qquad (6)$$

The second term in the square brackets reflects the saving out of earned income, and we assume that it can be represented by $a_5 PW$ where PW is the ratio of popular assets to other wealth (the coefficient a_5 takes account of the fact that it is only a proxy for this form of saving).
   For the top 1%, we assume that saving out of earned income is relatively unimportant.[12] The main driving forces are taken to be the internal rate of accumulation and 'entrepreneurial profits' although the latter cannot be represented directly in this deterministic model. In the former case we feel it is desirable to treat saving out of capital gains as a separate component. Where Π denotes the index of capital values, the formulation:

$$\dot{K}_1 = (S_1 r - \theta_1)K_1 + S_2(\dot{\Pi}/\Pi)K_1 \qquad (7)$$

allows for a different rate of response of K_1 (the capital of the top 1% to different types of income). If $S_2 > S_1$, then consumption adjusts more slowly to capital gains than to dividend and interest income (r) – see Feldstein [5] – and this seems a reasonable assumption to make. Integrating equation (7), we derive:

$$K_1(t) = K_1(0)e^{(S_1 r - \theta_1)t}\Pi^{S_2} \tag{8}$$

where $\Pi(0) = 1$. Entrepreneurial profits can be introduced in an *ad hoc* fashion as a source of 'new' wealth in the same way as saving out of earned income (SE). The modification to the equation for $K_1(t)$ may be seen by analogy with equation (6), and we assume that the effect can be represented by a term $(1 + a_4\Pi)$. In other words the accumulated capital gains are taken as a proxy for this form of saving. In both this formulation and that in equation (8) we take capital gains on shares as the most important class of assets owned by the top 1%.

Combining equations (6) and (8), we obtain the share of the top 1% (K_1/K).[13] Denoting its true, as opposed to its observed value by W_1^*, and taking logarithms (to base e), we have:

$$\log(W_1^*) = a_0 + a_1 T + a_4 \log \Pi + \log(1 + a_5 PW) \tag{9}$$

where $a_1 = (S_1 r - \theta_1) - (Sr - \theta)$, i.e. the difference between the internal rates of accumulation, and $a_4 = S_2$. In order to estimate a_5 without recourse to a non-linear procedure, we approximated the last term by $a_5 PW$ (the accuracy of this is discussed below). The formulation described above is based on equation (8); if instead we had taken account of saving out of 'entrepreneurial profits', then $a_4 \log \Pi$ is replaced by $\log(1 + a_4\Pi)$ which is approximated by $a_4\Pi$.

To this point we have assumed that the internal rates of accumulation are constant over time. The first modification to this which should be considered is that there may have been a shift as a result of the Second World War. (This may affect savings behaviour, as suggested by Sargan [10], or it may affect the way in which estates are divided.) For this reason we feel it is necessary to add the dummy variable D_1 to equation (9). The second modification is to allow for variation in the rate of return, and for taxation. Where Sr varies over time, and is subject to income tax, the appropriate term in the equation for $\log(W_1^*)$ is:

$$\int_0^t [S_1 r(1 - I_1) - Sr(1 - I)]\, du \tag{10}$$

where I_1 is the rate of income tax for the top 1% and I the rate for the population as a whole. In the absence of suitable evidence on S_1 and S, it is difficult to decide on an appropriate specification. As one variation, we include RR (real net dividend yield), although this is not a fully satisfactory procedure. The treatment of transfer taxes is more straightforward. The equation for $\log(W_1^*)$ is modified by the term:

$$a_7 \int_0^t (\tau_1 - \tau) \, du \tag{11}$$

where a_7 is the fraction of the tax paid out of reducing saving, τ_1 is the tax rate (as a percentage of capital) for the top 1% and τ is the average tax rate on all capital. This variable is referred to as ED.

The basic equation in which we are interested is therefore:

$$\log W_1^* = a_0 + a_1 T + a_2 D1 + a_4 \Pi \text{ (or } \log \Pi) + a_5 PW \tag{12}$$

with variations where the terms $a_6 RR$ and $a_7 ED$ are added. The variables are T (time trend), D1 (dummy variable 0 until 1938, 1 from 1950), Π (index of share prices), PW ('popular' wealth as a percentage of the remainder of personal wealth), RR (dividend yield after tax and inflation), and ED (estate duty paid by top 1% as proportion of capital). Equation (12) however relates to W_1^*, so that in order to relate it instead to observed values, we need to allow for discontinuities in the data and for the error process.[14] This leads to the following equation to be estimated:

$$\log W_1 = a_0 + a_1 T + a_2 D1 + a_3 D2 + a_4 \Pi \text{ (or } \log \Pi) + a_5 PW + \varepsilon \tag{13}$$

where ε is a normally and independently distributed random variable with zero mean and constant variance (the question of serial correlation is taken up below).

(ii) The estimates

In order to relate the results obtained with equation (13) to those in section 2, we begin with a logarithmic form of the main equation discussed there. This is equation A in Table 5. The results are similar to those in the linear form (which is given for reference at the top of the table). The time trend, for example, is 1% per annum, or 0.43 percentage points at the mean value (compared with 0.42 percentage points); the shift between 1959 and 1960 (dummy variable D2) is 7.5% (compared with 6.9%); and the variable D1 is not significant.

The results obtained with equation (13) are shown in lines B and C of Table 5, the former relating to the specification with Π and the latter to that with $\log \Pi$. Equation B appears to be superior: the $\bar{R}^2$ is higher and the standard error of the regression is smaller. Our discussion relates therefore to this equation.

Comparing equations A and B, we can see that the latter provides a better fit, with the standard error of the regression being reduced from 0.038 to 0.034. The coefficients of the variables added (Π and PW) are of the expected sign, and are significant at the 5% and 1% levels, respectively. A rise in the share price index of 20 points from its 1972 level of 211 would lead to an increase in the share of the top 1% of nearly 1% (in 1972). The coefficient of PW means that a rise in the value of owner-occupied houses and consumer durables from 40–50% of other wealth would reduce the share of the top group

Table 5 *Regression equation for the share of the top 1%*

Equation	Constant	Dummy variables		Time T	Share price		'Popular' wealth PW	Net return RR	Estate Duty ED	$\bar{R}^2$	SE	DW four (gaps)
		$D1$	$D2$		Π	$Log\,\Pi$						
	60.6	−2.91	−6.90	−0.42	—	—	—	—	—	0.983	1.42	2.26
		(1.6)	(7.1)	(6.5)								
A	4.12	−0.002	−0.201	−0.0097	—	—	—	—	—	0.977	0.0381	2.23
		(0.5)	(7.7)	(5.6)								
B	4.10	−0.017	−0.235	−0.0089	0.0014	—	−0.151	—	—	0.982	0.0344	2.19
		(0.3)	(5.4)	(4.2)	(2.6)		(2.8)					
C	4.12	−0.035	−0.223	−0.0097	—	0.057	−0.066	—	—	0.978	0.0377	2.22
		(0.6)	(6.4)	(3.5)		(1.1)	(1.6)					
D	4.10	−0.017	−0.237	−0.0088	0.0014	—	−0.149	—	—	0.981	0.0350	2.18
		(0.3)	(8.0)	(4.0)	(2.6)		(2.7)					
E	4.08	−0.025	−0.200	−0.0022	0.0016	—	0.064	0.042	−0.024	0.982	0.0339	2.13
		(0.5)	(5.1)	(0.4)	(2.9)		(0.7)	(0.2)	(1.3)			
F	4.07	−0.034	−0.192	—	0.0016	—	0.041	—	−0.030	0.983	0.0334	2.09
		(0.8)	(6.1)		(3.0)		(0.7)		(4.5)			

Note: The dependent variable is log W_1, log (to base e) of share of top 1% as shown in Table 2, but to 2 decimal places, except in the equation from section 2 where it is W_1. The figures in parentheses are t-statistics.

Sources:

Share price: Π is the price index for industrial ordinary shares published in *Key Statistics 1900–1970* by the London and Cambridge Economic Service (Table M), extended to 1972.

Popular wealth: PW is estimated from national balance sheet data, information on owner-occupation and the number of dwellings derived from *Housing Statistics*, Censuses of Population and a variety of other sources, and the house price index published in *Key Statistics* (Table I), again extended to 1972.

Net return: RR is dividend yield based on index published by de Zoete and Bevan (*Equity and Fixed Interest Investment*, annual), less the standard rate of income tax on investment income and the rate of inflation (increase in retail prices).

Estate Duty: ED is revenue from death duties (from annual reports of the Inland Revenue) expressed as a percentage of total capital, multiplied by $(X_1/W_1 − 1)$ where X_1 is the share of duties paid by the top 1% (estimated from information in the Inland Revenue annual reports about net receipts by ranges), and cumulated since 1923.

by about $\frac{1}{2}\%$ (in 1972). (It may also be noted that the terms $a_4\Pi$ and a_5PW both have mean values of around 0.09; this suggests that the approximation $\log(1+ax) \simeq ax$ may not be unreasonable, since the terms in $(ax)^2$ and higher powers are likely to be small.)

The dummy variable for the impact of the Second World War is not significant; this does not however necessarily mean that there is no such effect. This depends on the interpretation of the discontinuities in the data. In Atkinson and Harrison ([1], p. 167) we show that, to some extent, the data shift applies only during the 1950s, reflecting the much reduced coverage in that period and the possibility that we may have understated the wealth of the excluded population. If this is so, then the data discontinuities would cause an apparent upward jump between 1938 and 1950, and the insignificance of D1 may result from this cancelling with a genuine downward shift as a result of the war. The existence of such an effect would be consistent with the evidence about the trend in the distribution of income, although it is difficult to reach any firmer conclusion. This clearly warrants further consideration.

The model is extended to include the rate of return (RR) and estate duty variables (ED) in equations D–F. The rate of return is the dividend yield after allowing for tax at the standard rate and for the effect of inflation. From equation D it may be seen that the coefficient is nowhere near being significant. This may reflect the wrong choice of variable or be interpreted as saying that the rate of return does not contribute to the explanation of the *differential* rate of accumulation. In the case of Estate Duty we should expect the differential impact to be greater. In equations E and F, we have taken the difference between the death duties estimated to have been paid by the top 1% as a percentage of their capital and the average rate of death duties on all capital. The amount is cumulated from 1923 onwards. The results in equation E are rather mixed. The overall fit is (marginally) improved but none of the explanatory variables apart from D2 and the share price index is significant. The remaining variables, particularly T, PW and ED are highly collinear; moreover, it is possible that the time trend in earlier equations has been standing as a proxy for other factors, including the progressive impact of Estate Duty. In view of this, we have omitted T from the final equation. The fit appears more satisfactory (the standard error of the regression is the smallest of all six equations), although the coefficient of PW is not significantly different from zero. The coefficients of Π and ED are significant at the 1% level, and the latter implies that if the top 1% pay $2\frac{1}{2}$ times their 'share' of death duties and the revenue is 0.3% of total wealth, then the share of the top 1% would be reduced by 4% in ten years.

Because of the way in which our estimates of the share of the top 1% are derived, it is quite possible that the errors, ε, might be negatively serially correlated, since a bunching of estates in one year might well be followed by an error in the opposite direction in the next year. In support of this it is interesting to note that all the equations in Table 5 have Durbin-Watson statistics in excess of two; however, the critical value for five explanatory variables, apart from the constant, at the $2\frac{1}{2}\%$ level is 2.26, so that the results do not lead us to reject the hypothesis of zero serial correlation.[15]

Conclusion

To summarize, we have two equations which provide a reasonable fit to the data, but which embody rather different explanations of the decline in the share of the top 1%. According to equation B, the decline has been associated with the spread of 'popular' wealth, coupled with an exogenous downward trend (possibly reflecting differential rates of accumulation or changes in marriage and inheritance customs), with the upward movement in share prices working in the opposite direction. In equation F there is no exogenous downward trend, and the effect of popular wealth is insignificant. According to this, the main forces have been Estate Duty, either directly through transferring money to the Treasury or indirectly via family rearrangements of wealth, and – in the opposite direction – the rise in share prices. In both cases, there may or may not have been a shift between 1938 and 1950 reflecting the impact of social changes in the war-time period; this depends on the way in which the discontinuities in the data are interpreted.

The results are not, therefore, conclusive. They do nonetheless provide some insight into the processes at work, as may be illustrated by considering the 1973–4 fall in share prices. Some commentators suggested that this had caused a dramatic decline in the share of the top 1%. Day, for example, writing in the *Observer* (22 September 1974) estimated that the top 1% had lost between a quarter and a third of their share of total wealth between 1973 and 1974. During this period, share prices fell by about 40%, equivalent to a fall of around 85 points in the index Π. Both equations B and F have similar coefficients for this variable (0.0014 to 0.0016), implying a fall of about an eighth in the share of the top 1%. On this basis, the 1973 figure for the share of the top 1% estimated by the *Royal Commission* ([8], Table 49) of 27.6% would have fallen, *ceteris paribus*, to 24.5% in 1974.[16]

To conclude, then, it should be clear both from the nature of our analysis, and from the many qualifications we have expressed, that a full-scale testing of different models requires further developments both in terms of theory and the econometric methods applied. The models, and the restrictions they embody, need to be cast in a form such that we can relate them to the observed evidence. The econometric treatment, to be sure, needs to be refined. For example, it is possible that alternative assumptions about the error process may be more appropriate; the study of these is, however, limited by gaps in the data, and this is a subject we leave to a later occasion. In the same way it would be interesting to extend the analysis of the share of groups below the top 1% (e.g. the next 4%), where the explanatory variables are likely to be rather different, and to make use of the fact that the error terms are likely to be correlated across equations (applying the technique of seemingly unrelated regressions). We hope however that we have shown that this rather neglected subject – the time-series analysis of distributional data – would repay further attention.

Notes

1 Clay [3], Daniels and Campion [4] and Campion [2] have made estimates for 1911–13 by making assumptions about the proportion of female deaths in the statistics, but our feeling is that this introduces too strong an element of uncertainty into the analysis.

2 These data actually relate to tax years ending 31 March so that for example 1936 is more precisely 1936–7. We however follow the normal practice of assuming that, because of lags between deaths and payment of duty, the data in fact refer to calendar years.

3 For a few years statistics are available for England and Wales separately, but for most years these countries are combined.

4 In other words, the basic multiplier is the reciprocal of an age- and sex-specific mortality rate.

5 These classes broadly comprise managerial and professional workers.

6 In the case of women, we use the 1931 differentials for the period 1923–30.

7 In Atkinson and Harrison [1], we distinguish between valuation on a realisation basis, and valuation as a going concern. The former refers to a value determined by a sale in an open market, the latter to a value assuming the asset is retained.

8 Wheatcroft [11] lists thirty-nine Finance Acts which altered the provisions in that period.

9 The coefficient of correlation between the figures for the share of the top 1% for the two series is 0.99.

10 'The erosion of the share of personal wealth held by the richest [has been] gradual during the first half of the twentieth century, but gathering momentum since the Second World War.' *Sunday Times*, 3 August 1975.

11 This should not be taken to imply that the composition of the top 1% does not change over time, but rather that the behaviour of those who comprise the top 1% does not change.

12 To the extent that this is incorrect, it will be reflected in a lower value of a_5 (see below).

13 An alternative approach would be to treat K as the wealth of the bottom 99%. This leads to rather similar results.

14 In Atkinson and Harrison ([1], ch. 5) we spend some time on a discussion of the error process. In particular it is possible that there will be negative serial correlation if a bunching of estates occurs in one year, followed by an error in the opposite direction in the following year.

15 This is for a one-tailed test against the alternative of negative serial correlation; for a two-tailed test the significance level is 5%.

16 The actual Royal Commission estimate for 1974 is in fact 23.9%, which re-emphasises that Day's predictions were appreciably excessive.

References

[1] Atkinson, A. B. and Harrison, A. J. (1978), *The Distribution of Personal Wealth in Britain*, Cambridge University Press.

[2] Campion, H. (1939), *Public and Private Property in Great Britain*, Oxford University Press.

[3] Clay, H. (1925), 'The distribution of capital in England and Wales', *Transactions of the Manchester Statistical Society*.

[4] Daniels, G. W. and Campion, H. (1936), *The Distribution of National Capital*, Manchester University Press.

[5] Feldstein, M. S. (1973), 'Tax incentives, corporate saving and capital accumulation in the United States', *Journal of Public Economics*, vol. 2, pp. 159–71.

[6] Meade, J. E. (1964), *Efficiency, Equality and the Ownership of Property*, Allen & Unwin.

[7] Polanyi, G. and Wood, J. B. (1974), *How Much Inequality?* Institute of Economic Affairs.

[8] Royal Commission on the Distribution of Income and Wealth (1975), *Initial Report on the Standing Reference*, Cmnd. 6171, HMSO.

[9] Royal Commission on the Distribution of Income and Wealth (1977), *Third Report on the Standing Reference*, Cmnd. 6999, HMSO.

[10] Sargan, J. D. (1957), 'The distribution of wealth', *Econometrica*, vol. 25, pp. 568–90.

[11] Wheatcroft, G. S. A. (1972), *Guide to the Estate Duty Statutes*, Sweet & Maxwell.

7 The Distribution of Wealth and the Individual Life-Cycle*

The distribution of wealth in Britain has been the subject of considerable discussion, and many people have drawn attention to the apparent degree of concentration. On the basis of the distribution derived from the estate returns, it can be estimated that the top 1% of the adult population own between $\frac{1}{4}-\frac{1}{3}$ of the total personal wealth, and the top 10% own more than half. In interpreting this evidence it must be borne in mind, however, that it relates to the distribution of *current wealth* among all people alive at a particular date, and that this includes the wealth that people have accumulated for life-cycle purposes (particularly saving for retirement). It may therefore exhibit inequality simply because people are at different stages of the life-cycle: the top 10% may own more than their share because they are older and have saved more for old age. If this were the case, we should be less concerned about inequality, and there are strong grounds for arguing that our primary concern should be with the distribution of *inherited wealth* rather than the current distribution. We should assess inequality in terms of the value of wealth that a person receives over the course of his life in the form of bequests, gifts, and other capital receipts, and not in terms of his wealth-holding at some arbitrary date. This lifetime view of equity is clearly more appropriate if our concern is with unequal 'life chances', and has the merit of treating an individual's lifetime as a whole rather than considering each year in isolation.

If this viewpoint is accepted, we have to consider the importance of life-cycle factors and the inferences that can be drawn from the observed current distribution regarding inequality in inherited wealth, and it is with this problem that the present chapter is concerned. In considering the importance of life-cycle factors, the natural reference standard is the case of a *perfectly egalitarian* society where everyone has the same inherited wealth (and is identical in all other relevant respects). In such a society there is still likely to be inequality in the current distribution of wealth as a result of differences in wealth-holding according to age – a point that was made very clearly in an editorial in *The Times*, 28 September 1968:

Quite obviously in the most egalitarian of societies one would not expect the newborn baby and the man on the point of retirement to have identical savings, or even the fifty year old and the sixty year old, and there must therefore be a concentration of wealth in a minority of hands in any society one can conceive of.

* Reprinted from *Oxford Economic Papers*, vol. 23, **2**, July 1971.

This effect is more marked than most people would suppose. If one calculates the probable pattern of savings in a hypothetical society with total equality of male incomes and a total prohibition on inheritance, and if one assumes that the savings will belong to men as the main earners, then in that most egalitarian society over 80% of the total private wealth would be in the hands of men over fifty who would comprise less than 15% of the population. Where inheritance is not allowed, only the old can be rich.

It is not obvious, however, that the quantitative importance attached by *The Times* to life-cycle differences is correct, and the first section of this chapter examines in more detail the likely degree of inequality in a hypothetical egalitarian society of this type. Section 2 adopts a rather different approach and discusses the evidence that can be derived by breaking down the estate statistics by age groups. By examining the distribution of wealth among people of the same age, we can hope to eliminate the major life-cycle differences and this provides an alternative way of assessing their importance.

1 Life-Cycle Differences in a Hypothetical Egalitarian Society

Suppose everyone was identical in every respect apart from age (having the same market opportunities and the same tastes) and inheritance and gifts were prohibited. How much inequality would there still be in the current distribution of wealth as a result of differences in age? This section attempts to answer this question in the context of a number of explicit (although inevitably rather stylised) models of individual savings behaviour.

Let us consider first a model where all individuals live for a fixed period (T years). They spend the first N years of their lives working for a wage $w(t)$, and during this period they save for their retirement. They can borrow or lend freely at a constant interest rate r. They are assumed to know for certain that they will live for T years and to plan for their consumption to grow at a constant exponential rate g. (This would be the optimal consumption policy for a person maximising an additively separable, iso-elastic utility function.) They leave no bequests and make no gifts. Everyone faces the same r and $w(t)$ and chooses the same g. Simplifying still further and setting $r = 0$, $g = 0$, and $w(t)$ constant all t gives the Modigliani–Brumberg model [4]. If in this case we set $T = 50$, $N = 40$ (assuming that life begins at twenty-five) and assume a constant population, the pattern of wealth-holding has the particularly straightforward form shown in Figure 1. From this it can readily be calculated that the wealthiest 10% of the population (those aged 62–6) account for 19% of the total wealth, which is considerably less than the figures estimated for Britain.

Even within the context of the models discussed here, the Modigliani–Brumberg case is a very special one and it is interesting to examine the effect of allowing positive interest rates (as well as for the growth over time of consumption, earnings, and population). The upper part of Table 1 shows the results obtained from the model described earlier for different values of r and g (on the assumption that both population and real earnings grow at the rate of 2%). In general the shares are broadly similar to those suggested by the very simple model: the share of the top 10% ranges from 17–27% of total wealth. The degree of concentration tends to rise with the rate of interest, but a *real*

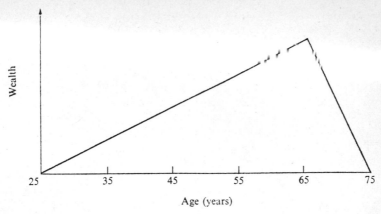

Figure 1

Table 1   *Inequality in a hypothetical egalitarian society*

Rate of growth of consumption		Real rate of interest r		
		3%	4½%	6%
2%	Share of top 1%	2.4	2.8	3.1
	Share of top 5%	11.7	13.1	14.6
	Share of top 10%	22.5	24.7	27.4
3%	Share of top 1%	1.9	2.1	2.2
	Share of top 5%	9.4	10.1	10.8
	Share of top 10%	18.4	19.6	20.9
4%	Share of top 1%	1.7	1.8	2.0
	Share of top 5%	8.6	9.1	9.7
	Share of top 10%	17.1	18.0	19.0

Rate of growth of consumption 3%, real rate of interest 4½%

Rate of growth of population		Rate of growth of real earnings		
		1%	2%	3%
0%	Share of top 1%	1.7	1.8	2.2
	Share of top 5%	8.5	9.1	10.6
	Share of top 10%	16.9	17.8	20.6
2%	Share of top 1%	1.9	2.1	2.5
	Share of top 5%	9.5	10.1	12.1
	Share of top 10%	18.7	19.6	23.2
4%	Share of top 1%	2.2	2.4	3.0
	Share of top 5%	10.8	11.4	14.1
	Share of top 10%	21.1	22.0	26.4

In all cases $T = 55$, $N = 45$.
Rate of population growth = 2%, real earnings growth = 2%.

(after-tax) rate of 6% would be quite high. Concentration also tends to increase as we take lower rates of growth of consumption; it seems reasonable, however, to suppose that consumption would grow at least as fast as earnings. It might be expected that a faster rate of population growth would lead to more concentration, since there would be proportionately fewer old (and therefore rich) people. The results given in the lower part of Table 1, however, suggest that variations in the rate of growth of population do not have a particularly marked effect. They also show that a higher rate of growth of earnings increases concentration but that again the effect is fairly small.

The demographic assumptions made so far are simplistic to an extreme, and it might be thought that more realistic assumptions would give rather different results. To see whether this is so, further calculations on the basis of the actual survival rates observed in England and Wales are shown in Table 2.[1] Since it is

Table 2   *Inequality with realistic survival rates and earnings profile*

Rate of growth of consumption		Real rate of interest r		
		3%	$4\frac{1}{2}$%	6%
2%	Share of top 1%	2.6	3.0	3.5
	Share of top 5%	12.4	14.2	16.4
	Share of top 10%	24.0	27.1	30.9
3%	Share of top 1%	2.0	2.2	2.3
	Share of top 5%	10.0	10.7	11.6
	Share of top 10%	19.8	21.2	22.7
4%	Share of top 1%	1.9	1.9	2.0
	Share of top 5%	9.2	9.7	10.1
	Share of top 10%	18.4	19.2	20.0

Rate of population growth = 2%, earnings growth = 2%.

no longer reasonable to assume that individuals expect to live for a fixed period, it is assumed instead that they plan for their consumption to grow at a constant rate subject to the condition that their expected wealth at death must be zero (the conditions under which this behaviour can be derived from utility maximisation are described in the Appendix, which also discusses the treatment of cases where people die in debt). These calculations also allow for a more realistic lifetime earnings profile reflecting the tendency for earnings to rise and then fall with age.[2] Comparing the results with those from Table 1, it is clear that there is no major difference: the share of the top 10% is on average higher but only.a few per cent.

The effect of introducing equal inheritance
The hypothetical egalitarian society considered so far ruled out inheritance and gifts altogether; however, a more general case of a perfectly egalitarian society is one where wealth *is* transmitted from generation to generation, but in such a way that everyone receives the same amount. If, as seems likely, this

inheritance is not received until middle age or later, this would tend to increase the degree of 'apparent' concentration, since it would increase still further the wealth of the old relative to that of the young. It is interesting, therefore, to examine the effect of equal inheritance on the degree of inequality in the current distribution.

Let us consider first the effect on the simple Modigliani–Brumberg model (with constant population). At the age of fifty everyone inherits I from their fathers; they hold this intact until they die, when it passes to the next generation (since the population is assumed not to be growing, the estate does not have to be divided). The effect of this on the share of the top 10% (those aged 62–6) can be calculated quite simply, and becomes:

$$\frac{38w + 5I}{200w + 25I} = 0.19 + 0.01 \left[\frac{I}{8w + I} \right]$$

In other words, their share goes up by less than 1% however large is I. This results from the fact that the share of the top 10% in inherited wealth is only very slightly larger than their share in total wealth. The degree of concentration of inherited wealth is clearly largest when it is held for the shortest possible period. However, if each generation passes on its wealth at the same age, this period equals the difference between the ages of the father and the son and is not likely to be less than twenty years. In that case (where the son inherits at the age of fifty-five) the share of the top 10% could rise at most by 6% — so that it was 25% in all.[3]

The results derived from this simple model suggest that the introduction of equal inheritance does not lead to a large increase in the degree of apparent inequality. This model takes no account, however, of the fact that even if inheritance is equal, everyone does not necessarily inherit at the same date. Those whose fathers die young will inherit early and those whose fathers are octogenarians (and hang on to their estate) may not inherit until they are well into their sixties. For this reason, it may be interesting to examine the effect of equal inheritance in the context of the model based on actual survival rates (assuming that the fathers were subject to the same mortality pattern). Table 3 shows the results obtained from this model with different amounts of inherited wealth. In each case the value of the inheritance discounted to age twenty-five is expressed as a multiple of earnings at that age (if we take earnings at twenty-five as £1500, then with an interest rate of 3% $I = 5$ is approximately equivalent to £20,000 inherited at the age of fifty-five).[4] As I increases, the distribution approaches that of inherited wealth taken by itself (which depends on the mortality of the fathers) and there is little change as I rises above twenty-five. The results show that the introduction of equal inheritance increases the degree of inequality, but even where the inheritance is substantial the share of the top 10% is only some 30%.

Women and the distribution of wealth
So far no explicit account has been taken of the role played by women in the distribution of wealth. At one extreme, we could assume that women own no

Table 3   *Equal inheritance in a hypothetical egalitarian society*

Present value of inheritance at age twenty-five expressed as multiple of annual earnings	Share in total wealth of top		
	1%	5%	10%
$I = 0$	2.4	11.5	22.4
1	2.6	12.8	24.9
5	3.1	15.2	29.6
25	3.1	15.4	30.0
50	3.1	15.4	30.0

Real rate of interest $= 3\%$, rate of population growth $= 2\%$, earnings $= 3\%$, consumption $= 3\%$.

property at all. It is clear, however, that this is not the case: in 1967, 38% of the personal wealth in Britain recorded in the Inland Revenue estimates was owned by women. At the same time, it is not obvious that in their effect on wealth-holding they can be regarded in the same way as men. Revell has commented as follows [5]:

In any distribution of wealth owned by individuals women have a rather peculiar role. They have some savings before they marry, but most of the wealth which accrues to a married couple (except perhaps direct gifts and bequests to the wife) will go into the husband's name and appear in his estate when he dies. ... Once the husband dies, however, what is left of her husband's estate after the payment of estate duty partly or wholly falls to the widow.

If the pattern described by Revell is broadly correct, it may not be seriously inaccurate to regard married women as having no wealth while their husbands are alive but inheriting their estates when they die. Since married women account for about one-third of the adult population, we ought to allow for approximately one property-less person per two propertied adults, so that what was referred to earlier as the share of the top $x\%$ becomes the share of the top $2x/3\%$.

Conclusions – The Times' *view*

In *The Times* editorial quoted earlier, it was claimed that in a perfectly egalitarian society with no inheritance there would be substantial apparent concentration of wealth: 80% of the total wealth would be in the hands of men over fifty who would comprise less than 15% of the population. The results reached here, however, are rather different. Even stacking the cards in one direction by taking a high interest rate (6% in real terms), a low rate of growth of consumption over the individual's lifetime (2% in real terms), and assuming that married women are property-less, the share of the top 15% is 53% – or considerably less than 80%. For other values of the parameters it is typically around 40%. There are two main reasons for the discrepancy between our results and the view of *The Times*. First, *The Times* assumed that no women held wealth, an assumption which we have seen not to be justified. Secondly, it expressed the number of men over fifty as a percentage of the total *population* rather than as a percentage of total *adults*, which is the base generally used in the estimates of inequality in Britain. The importance of this can be seen from the following figures for the United Kingdom in June 1969:[5]

Men over fifty as % of total population	11%
Men over fifty as % of population over twenty-five	22%

2 Evidence From the Estate Statistics

In the introduction to the chapter it was argued that our primary concern should be with the distribution of inherited wealth – or the total that a person receives over his life in the form of bequests, gifts, or other capital receipts. The information required to measure directly the concentration of inherited wealth is not available, but it is possible to make estimates from the estate statistics of the distribution of wealth within age (and sex) groups. By standardising for age in this way, we should be able to eliminate the major life-cycle differences, and hence throw some light on the distribution of inherited wealth and the importance of life-cycle factors in giving rise to 'apparent' inequality in the current distribution.[6]

Inequality by age groups

The approach used to estimate the distribution of wealth within each age group is basically the same as that adopted in estimating the overall distribution. The method, which dates back to the work of Mallet and others at the beginning of the century, has been described in detail by a number of writers.[7] Essentially it is assumed that those dying in a particular year are a representative sample of the living, so that we can blow up the estate figures by a 'mortality multiplier' to give an estimate of the total wealth of the living. The mortality multiplier is in general the inverse of the mortality rate for a particular age group (adjusted for differences by social class): so that if the mortality rate for a particular group is 0.05 we assume that their total wealth is twenty times that recorded in the estate statistics. When considering individual age groups, the application of the method is particularly straightforward, since the only differences in the multipliers are those reflecting the adjustment for social class.[8]

The deficiencies of this method of estimating the distribution of wealth have been well documented. The most important are:

(i) The statistics cover only those estates for which probate is granted, so that there is only limited coverage of estates below the exemption limit (£5000 from 1963–4 to 1968–9).[9]

(ii) The small numbers in certain cells mean that the results are subject to large sampling errors – particularly in the case of the youngest age groups: in 1967–8 only one person died between the ages of twenty-five and thirty-four with an estate of over £200,000.

(iii) Certain kinds of property disappear at death and therefore do not appear in the statistics. The most important of these are pensions and annuities. Other kinds of property are also excluded from the statistics: for example, property settled on the spouse and passing on his/her death, and property held under discretionary trusts (for the period considered here).

There is also the problem of wealth avoiding taxation through gifts *inter vivos*, but this is more a question of interpretation than a deficiency of the figures as such.

The importance of the incomplete coverage of the estate figures can be seen from the fact that in 1967 the returns accounted for only 44% of all deaths in that year. We have, therefore, to decide what allowance should be made for the wealth of those not covered. In its estimate of total personal wealth the Inland Revenue ignores this group, and since this is the simplest approach it is adopted initially here (the effect of alternative assumptions is discussed below). The importance of the second problem (the small numbers in certain cells) can be reduced by averaging over a number of years, and the five-year period 1963–7 is taken as a basis for the estimates. This also serves to reduce the error introduced by the fact that the estate statistics do not relate precisely to deaths occurring in one year,[10] and by short-term fluctuations in the prices of assets such as shares and real property. The third of the problems (wealth not appearing the statistics) is discussed below.

Using the method and the assumptions described above, we obtain the estimates of the inequality in the distribution of wealth by age (and sex) groups for 1963–7 shown in Table 4. These estimates suggest that wealth within age

Table 4   *Inequality by age and sex group – Great Britain, 1963–7*

| | Male | | | Female | | |
| | Proportion of wealth in that class owned by top | | | | | |
Age	1%	5%	10%	1%	5%	10%
25–34	31.2	50.5	64.1	54.8	80.6	92.7
35–44	27.5	49.3	63.1	43.9	74.6	88.5
45–54	28.3	52.7	66.8	38.2	66.4	81.2
55–64	26.8	51.2	66.0	29.0	56.9	71.5
65–74	27.5	52.8	68.1	26.8	54.1	69.3
75–84	28.9	57.1	72.4	26.4	53.6	68.8
85+	30.4	60.1	74.7	27.5	56.8	72.2
Whole population over age twenty-five (male and female combined)	31.5	58.3	72.7	31.5	58.3	72.7

groups is still very unequally distributed. In no case do the top 10% of a group own less than 60% of the group's total wealth; and the share of the top 1% ranges from 26 to 55%. It is interesting to note that the degree of inequality is very similar for all groups except that of women aged 25–54, where the share of the top 10% is over 80% (this presumably reflects the tendency of married women to have little property in their own name).

To put these figures in perspective, we may compare them with the degree of inequality in the overall distribution. Applying the same method of estimation, we arrive at the figures for the whole adult population (male and female combined) shown at the bottom of Table 4, and we can see that the inequality within age and sex classes is not substantially less than that for the population as a whole.[11] In four out of fourteen groups the share of the top 10% is actually greater than the share of the top 10% in the wealth of the entire adult population. In the most egalitarian age group, the share of the top 10% is 63.1% – which is not a great deal less than the figure of 72.7% for the entire population. These results suggest therefore that if we standardise for age and sex, the degree of inequality is not substantially reduced.

It is also interesting to examine the age distribution of total wealth-holding. If the life-cycle phenomenon were important, we should expect to find that those aged over (say) fifty-five would own nearly all of the total personal wealth. As *The Times* said: 'Where inheritance is not allowed only the old can be rich.' Table 5 shows, however, that the over fifty-fives owned only slightly over half of the total personal wealth of the adult population in 1963–7, and those over sixty-five only slightly over one-quarter. Moreover, if we look at the top wealth-holders, they are far from exclusively old; of those with wealth over £200,000 only a half were over fifty-five and only one-quarter over sixty-five.

Table 5 *Wealth and age, Great Britain, 1963–7*

| Age | Distribution of total wealth by age groups | | | Proportion of total adults with wealth over £200,000 | | |
	Male	Female	All	Male	Female	All
25–34	9.4	2.4	11.8	13.1	2.5	15.6
35–44	11.6	4.3	15.9	13.0	2.2	15.2
45–54	12.9	7.3	20.2	15.4	3.8	19.2
55–64	14.5	10.3	24.8	16.4	8.5	24.9
65–74	8.2	8.4	16.6	8.4	5.4	13.8
75–84	3.7	5.1	8.8	4.8	4.1	8.9
85–	0.7	1.2	1.9	1.4	1.0	2.4
Total	61.0	39.0	100.0	72.5	27.5	100.0

Interpretation of the results
The figures presented above show that there is considerable inequality even among people of the same age, and this in turn suggests that there must be significant inequality in the distribution of inherited wealth. However, before we can draw any such conclusion, we must consider the role of two factors which may influence the interpretation of the results: the pattern of transmission of wealth between generations, and the importance of wealth not included in the estimates.

It is possible that some of the inequality within age groups can be explained by the way in which wealth is transmitted between generations. If it is passed on at death, inequality may simply reflect differences in the dates of death of the preceding generation. Those whose fathers died young would initially make up the top 1% and would own a large share of the wealth of their age group. As they got older, they would find their share falling as successively

more and more of their contemporaries inherited. The evidence presented in
the earlier sections does not, however, suggest any clear tendency for
inequality to decline with age – at least in the case of men. It is of course
possible that the tendency for inequality to fall on this account is offset by
certain families choosing to pass on their wealth well before death. However,
this argument depends on the two factors cancelling more or less exactly, and
it seems unlikely that this could explain a major part of the observed
inequality. Wedgwood [9] argued that inequality in the age group 55–64
might provide a reasonable guide to the degree of inequality of inherited
wealth on the grounds that they would in general have already inherited, but
not yet made substantial gifts *inter vivos*. Unfortunately, our knowledge of the
processes by which wealth is transmitted is so limited that it is hard to assess
the validity of this argument. It is interesting to note, however, that the
inequality among this group is not significantly lower than that for other age
groups.

The estimates given above followed the method used by the Inland Revenue
and as such excluded certain types of wealth 'missing' from the estate statistics:
'small' wealth-holdings, the value of pension rights and annuities, and
property settled on the spouse or held in discretionary trusts. This procedure
was justified on the grounds that we were *comparing* inequality within sub-
groups with that in the population as a whole; and it does allow us to say that
life-cycle differences are not an important explanation of the inequality shown
by the estimates of the Inland Revenue. If, however, we are going to draw
conclusions about the *absolute* degree of inequality within age groups, we
clearly have to make allowance for the 'missing' wealth.

There are good grounds for expecting that the effect of such adjustments
would be to reduce the degree of inequality. This is obviously true of those
estates excluded because probate was not required, although the amount
involved is likely to be small.[12] More important in quantitative terms is the
value of rights to state pensions (and other National Insurance benefits). Their
value is likely to be broadly the same for all those of the same age,[13] and their
inclusion will definitely reduce inequality. In addition, there is the value of
occupational pension rights and annuities. The estimates of Revell for 1961
suggested that the value of life and occupational pension funds (including an
allowance for the actuarial value of non-funded rights) 'missing' from the
figures was of the order of £10,000 million – or 13% of total personal wealth.
Unlike the state pensions, these are not distributed equally between people of
the same age, and the same is true of property held in discretionary trusts or
settled on a surviving spouse (it seems quite possible that this wealth would be
at least as unequally distributed as that included in the statistics).

To give some indication of the importance of allowing for 'missing' wealth,
alternative estimates have been made of the degree of concentration based on
the following assumptions:

(i)   An average allowance is made of £750 per man and £250 per woman
      excluded from the estate statistics. These are essentially arbitrary figures,
      but give some idea of the sensitivity of the results.

(ii) It is assumed that the value of occupational pension rights and settled property is equal to 15% of the wealth included in the estate statistics for ᵃⁿᵒᵗ ᵗᵗᵗᵉ ᵧᵢᵢᵢᵢᵢᵢ ᵃⁿᵈ ⁱᵒ ᵈⁱᵒᵗᵗⁱᵇᵘᵗᵉᵈ in the same way.

(iii) An allowance is made for the ᵃᵈᵈⁱᵗⁱᵒⁿᵃˡ ᵥᵃˡᵘₑ ᵒᶠ ᵗⁱᵍʰᵗᵒ ⁱⁿ ᴺᵃᵗⁱᵒⁿᵃˡ Insurance retirement pensions. The detailed assumptions underlying this estimate are described in the notes to Table 6, but the most important are the choice of interest rate and the fact that benefits are valued in terms of prospective benefits rather than contributions paid. The value of the

Table 6 *Inequality adjusted for 'missing' wealth – Great Britain, 1963–7*

| | Adjusted for 'missing' wealth | | | Unadjusted | | |
| | Proportion of total wealth owned by top | | | | | |
Male wealth-holders aged	1%	5%	10%	1%	5%	10%
25–34	25.1	40.9	52.3	31.2	50.5	64.1
35–44	20.9	37.7	48.9	27.5	49.3	63.1
45–54	20.2	38.4	49.4	28.3	52.7	66.8
55–64	18.8	36.4	48.0	26.8	51.2	66.0
65–74	18.7	36.4	48.2	27.5	52.8	68.1
75–84	22.8	45.4	58.4	28.9	57.1	72.4
85+	26.3	52.4	65.4	30.4	60.1	74.7
Distribution as a whole (male + female)	21.7	41.0	52.3	31.5	58.3	72.7

Notes on method of valuing rights to National Insurance pensions
 (i) The present discounted value of the rights is calculated using an interest rate of 5% (in money terms).
 (ii) The pension is based on the average rate in force over the period 1963–7 (basic pension only, with no allowance being made for the graduated pension or other additions). It is assumed that both pensions and contributions rise at a steady rate of 5% (in money terms), which has been approximately the long-run trend in the past.
(iii) The pension rights of a person aged 25–64 are valued in terms of expected benefits (calculated on the basis of the person's current life expectancy). A person is assumed to have earned a proportion of the benefit equal to the proportion paid to date of the present value of contributions over his life (assuming that contributions are paid from the age of twenty to the age of sixty-four). The life expectancies used are those for the general population, and were taken from the Registrar-General's Decennial Supplement, *Life Tables for England and Wales*, 1961.

rights would be higher if a lower interest rate were used, but it does not seem reasonable to suppose that it should be much lower than the figure of 5% (in money terms) used in Table 6. Since the present value of benefits exceeds that of contributions at an interest rate of 5% (see [1]), valuation in terms of contributions paid would tend to reduce the importance of pension rights.

Table 6 shows the results obtained in the case of male wealth-holders in different age groups. As is to be expected, the effect of allowing for 'missing' wealth is most marked among those aged 45–74, since these have the most valuable pension rights. For these age groups, the share of the top 1% is reduced by around 8%, and the share of the top 10% by some 15–20%. However, even with these allowances, the degree of inequality within age groups is still very striking: the share of the top 1% is in no case less than 18% nor that of the top 5% less than 36% of the total wealth. If we compare the degree of inequality within age groups with that in the overall distribution, the differences are smaller than in the 'unadjusted' case. In the most egalitarian age group, the share of the top 1% is only 3% lower than the corresponding figure for the distribution as a whole. These results do nothing, therefore, to alter the conclusion that life-cycle differences are not an important factor in explaining the observed concentration.

3 Concluding Comments

It is clear from the analysis of the last section that life-cycle factors cannot explain the upper tail of the current distribution of wealth in Britain, and there are good reasons for believing that there is a high degree of concentration in the distribution of wealth inherited by people over their lives. It might be asked, however, whether we can reasonably regard inherited wealth as explaining the share of the top 1% or 5%, but life-cycle factors as explaining the rest of the distribution. If we were to take out the top 5%, the distribution (allowing for 'missing' wealth) among the remainder would be as follows:

$$
\begin{aligned}
\text{First} \quad 1\% &= 3.9\% \\
\text{First} \quad 5\% &= 18.3\% \\
\text{First} \quad 10\% &= 30.6\%
\end{aligned}
$$

These figures are not too different from some of the more unequal distributions generated in the hypothetical egalitarian society considered in section 1. However, it should be emphasised that life-cycle factors cannot be expected to explain even this amount of inequality in the Inland Revenue distribution, since this excludes a large component of wealth acquired for life-cycle reasons.[14]

In the last part of section 2, I have presented an alternative estimate of the overall distribution of wealth allowing for wealth 'missing' from the Inland Revenue figures. This estimate departs from earlier work in allowing for the value of rights to state pensions; and it is interesting to see that even with this allowance the degree of concentration remains very substantial: the top 1% own more than 20% of total wealth and the top 10% more than half. The distribution of wealth is still much more unequal than the distribution of before-tax income. There are, however, two points that should be borne in mind with regard to this estimate. First, the assumptions made (particularly the choice of interest rate, and the valuation of rights in terms of benefits) mean that it is likely to over-state the importance of pension rights and hence to *understate* the degree of inequality. The 'true' degree of inequality probably lies, therefore, between these figures and those derived from the Inland Revenue estimates. Secondly, there are a number of important questions not discussed in this chapter regarding the meaing of 'ownership'. Pension rights can be said to represent claims on future consumption; however, they are not assets over which the individual has current command (he cannot even borrow on the strength of them as with life insurance policies), and they are not relevant to assessing the distribution of control over wealth.

Appendix

Suppose that the consumer plans his lifetime consumption to maximise:

$$\int_0^T U(c_t)e^{-\alpha t}f(t)\,dt$$

where $f(t)$ is the probability of his being alive at time t and $U'(c)=c^{-\varepsilon}$. Suppose further that his budget constraint is of the form:

$$\int_0^T (w_t-c_t)e^{-rt}f(t)\,dt=0$$

i.e. the present discounted value of expected consumption must equal the present discounted value of his expected wage income.

The solution to this maximisation problem is obtained by introducing a Lagrange multiplier λ and maximising:

$$\int_0^T [U(c_t)e^{-\alpha t}+\lambda(w_t-c_t)e^{-rt}]f(t)\,dt$$

which gives as a necessary condition:

$$U'(c_t)=\lambda e^{-(r-\alpha)t} \quad \text{or} \quad c=c_0 e^{(r-\alpha)t/\varepsilon}$$

so that the optimal policy involves consumption growing at a steady rate as assumed in the text. The rate of growth depends on the rate of interest, but also on α and ε and any combination of r and $g=(r-\alpha)/\varepsilon$ is possible.

With the budget constraint assumed above, there is nothing to prevent a person planning to have negative net worth in a period when there is a non-zero probability of his dying, and we must consider under what institutional circumstances this is possible. The assumption made here is that borrowing is always secured by life insurance – as discussed by Yaari [10]. This raises the question of how negative net worth should be treated in estimating the degree of inequality. In the calculations given in Tables 2 and 3, it is assumed that those with negative net worth would be treated as though they owned nothing, on the grounds that debts would not appear in estate-duty based estimates (in this respect assets and liabilities are treated asymmetrically – it being assumed that assets are included even though held in the form of annuities or pensions).

For further discussion of this model see Tobin [8] and Yaari [10].

Acknowledgement

I am grateful to J. E. Meade, J. R. S. Revell, and A. Shorrocks for their comments on an earlier draft of this chapter.

Notes

1 *Annual Abstract of Statistics*, 1967, Life Tables for England and Wales. The rates used are those for the male population and relate to 1964–6.
2 *Ministry of Social Security Annual Report*, 1967. It is assumed that an individual now aged u expects to earn at age t the current average earnings of people now aged t increased by the general growth of earnings (i.e. by a factor of $e^{g(t-u)}$).
3 The effect of inheritance on the distribution of wealth depends on the point at which it is transferred. It is largest when inherited wealth is held during that part of the person's lifetime when his 'accumulated' wealth is at its peak – as is the case with the example given here.
4 The index of inter-generational equity used here is the ratio of inherited wealth to the present value of earnings. If inherited wealth accumulates at a rate r and this is equal to the rate of growth of earnings (as in the example given in Table 3), then inter-generational equality (in this sense) is preserved.
5 Most of the earlier studies of wealth-holding in Britain have defined the adult population as those over the age of twenty-five.
6 A similar study for the years 1911–14 and 1923–5 was made by Wedgwood [9], Chapter VII.
7 Cf. Langley [2].
8 For estates under £3000 the mortality multipliers were those for the general population (Source: *Annual Abstract of Statistics*); for estates over £3000, the mortality rate was adjusted using the figures given by Revell [6], Table 5.4 (the same adjustment is made for males and females).
9 The deficiency became more important after the Small Payments Act 1965, which raised the limit below which probate was not necessary.
10 For this reason the general practice is followed of treating the estate returns for the year ending in March as relating to deaths in the preceding calendar year.
11 The overall distribution of wealth differs from that given in the Inland Revenue Annual Reports, since different multipliers are used and the estates of those aged under twenty-five, and where age is not stated, are not included here.
12 It seems very unlikely that the average wealth of those not appearing in the estate statistics would exceed £1000. For a person not to appear means either that no property was left or that the assets were of a kind where small amounts could be transferred without probate (principally National Savings and deposits in building and friendly societies). Lydall and Tipping [3] estimated that in 1954 those excluded from the Estate Duty Statistics had average wealth of under £300.
13 Their value would tend to be higher for the wealthier, on account of their higher survival rates and of the differential pension under the graduated scheme (although this would have been extremely small for the period considered).
14 The Inland Revenue distribution does show substantial variation in average wealth between age groups, but it increases steadily with age rather than exhibiting the inverse U-shape predicted by the life-cycle savings theories discussed in section 1.

References

[1] Atkinson, A. B. (1970), 'National superannuation: redistribution and value for money', *Bulletin of the Oxford Institute of Economics and Statistics*, August.
[2] Langley, K. M. (1950), 'The distribution of capital in private hands in 1936–1938 and 1946–1947', *Bulletin of the Oxford University Institute of Statistics*, December.
[3] Lydall, H. F. and Tipping, D. G. (1961), 'The distribution of personal wealth in Britain', *Bulletin of the Oxford University Institute of Statistics*, February.
[4] Modigliani, F. and Brumberg, R. (1954), 'Utility analysis and the consumption function: an

interpretation of cross section data', in K. K. Kurihara (ed.), *Post Keynesian Economics*, Rutgers University Press.

[5] Revell, J. R. S. (1965), 'Changes in the social distribution of property in Britain during the [illegible] Congr. d. International d'Histoire Economique, vol. i, Munich.

[6] Revell, J. R. S. (1967), *The Wealth of the Nation*, Cambridge University Press.

[7] Strotz, R. H. (1955–6), 'Myopia and inconsistency in dynamic utility maximisation', *Review of Economic Studies*.

[8] Tobin, J. (1967), 'Life cycle saving and balanced growth', in *Ten Economic Studies in the Tradition of Irving Fisher*, Wiley.

[9] Wedgwood, J. (1929), *The Economics of Inheritance*.

[10] Yaari, M. E. (1965), 'Uncertain lifetime, life insurance and the theory of the consumer', *Review of Economic Studies*, April.

8 Capital Taxes, the Redistribution of Wealth and Individual Savings*[1,2]

Taxes on wealth-holding or on wealth transfers are used in many advanced countries as a means of achieving a more equitable distribution of wealth. In Britain, bequests and gifts are taxed under Capital Transfer Tax (previously Estate Duty). The United States has both federal estate and gift taxes. The Scandinavian countries have an annual tax on wealth; and many countries have resorted at some time to a capital levy. However, despite the wide variety of capital taxes in use, only limited attention has been given to examining the effects of these different types of taxation. The aim of this chapter is to begin to provide an analysis of three different types of capital taxation: a capital levy, a comprehensive tax on all wealth transfers, and an annual wealth tax.

One of the principal deficiencies of the existing literature on capital taxes is that little of it has been based on any very satisfactory analysis of the factors underlying the development of wealth-holding. The assumptions about individual behaviour are often far from explicit, and where they are made explicit, they are generally of an *ad hoc* nature (such as the assumption that a person saves a constant proportion of his income). In this chapter, I have tried therefore to provide a rigorous discussion of the effects of the different capital taxes in the context of a fully explicit model of individual savings and bequest behaviour. While this model involves a number of strong assumptions and is essentially partial in nature, it does, I think, capture some important features of reality which would otherwise be lost.

Section 1 sets out the underlying model of individual behaviour. This model is of the 'life-cycle' type that has been discussed a great deal, but incorporates in addition the bequest motive for saving. The bequest motive has in fact been treated in the same way by Yaari,[3] to whose work I owe a considerable debt; however, he did not develop its implications for the dynamics of wealth-holding over generations. Since this is clearly central to the problem discussed, I have extended his analysis in this direction. In section 2 this extended life-cycle model is then used to examine the effect of the three capital taxes on wealth-holding, the transmission of wealth from generation to generation, and on the level of personal savings. Section 3 is concerned with comparing the effects of the different taxes, and deals in particular with the underlying concept of equity and the problem of determining a satisfactory basis for tax comparisons in a dynamic model.

* Reprinted from *The Review of Economic Studies*, vol. 38, **2**, April 1971.

1   The Model of Individual Savings and Bequest Behaviour

The basic assumption of the model is that the individual plans his consumption over his lifetime of T years so as to maximise:

$$\int_0^T U(c_t)e^{-\alpha t}\,dt + e^{-\alpha T}\phi(S_T), \tag{1}$$

where c_t denotes consumption, S_t his assets, at time t, and it is assumed that the functions U and ϕ are increasing, strictly concave and differentiable.[4] In other words, he maximises the integral of instantaneous utility from consumption discounted at rate α plus the utility from bequests made at death, where it is assumed that he acts as though he knows T with certainty. These assumptions are clearly strong. The additive separability of the utility function is unfortunately restrictive – as is the assumption that the utility derived from bequests is independent of the circumstances of the recipients.[5]

It is assumed that the consumer faces a perfect capital market on which he can borrow or lend at a constant interest rate r,[6] and that he earns a wage w, which is assumed to be constant (although more realistic patterns of lifetime earnings could be easily incorporated). During his life he receives bequests, the value of which discounted back to his birth is denoted by S_0. He makes no gifts while he is alive.

As a result of these assumptions, his budget equation is:

$$\dot{S}_t = rS_t + w - c_t, \tag{2}$$

and his assets at time t (including anticipated bequests):

$$S_t e^{-rt} = S_0 + \int_0^t (w - c_u)e^{-ru}\,du. \tag{3}$$

The solution to the consumer's problem of maximising (1) subject to (2) is straightforward. Applying the calculus of variations, we obtain the following Euler equation:

$$d[U'e^{-\alpha t}]/dt = -rU'e^{-\alpha t}$$

which may be re-written as:

$$\varepsilon(c_t)\dot{c}_t = (r - \alpha)c_t, \tag{4}$$

where $\varepsilon(c_t) = (-U'')c_t/U'$ (the elasticity of the marginal utility of consumption). Throughout I shall assume that $r > \alpha$ so that consumption will be increasing over his lifetime. In addition to (4), there is also the terminal condition:

$$U'[c_T] = \phi'[S_T] \tag{5}$$

i.e. the marginal utility of £1 bequeathed must be equal to the marginal utility of consuming it on his deathbed.

Armed with this information, we can draw the phase diagram shown in Figure 1. The optimal path is that which starts from S_0 and terminates after T years on the dashed line $U'[c_T] = \phi'[S_T]$.[7] As shown, S_t rises and then falls as he gets older; however, the optimal path need not be of this form and may

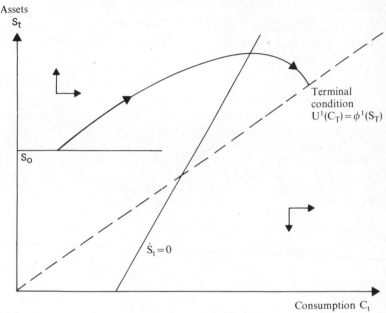

Figure 1.

involve either a steady rise or a steady fall in his asset level. None the less, it is clear that where $r > \alpha$ we do not need the strong assumption of a perfect capital market; we simply require that a person be able to borrow against anticipated bequests.[8]

At times it is convenient to work with the more restrictive class of constant elasticity utility functions:

$$U'(c) = c^{-\varepsilon}, \qquad \phi'(S_T) = A S_T^{-\mu}, \qquad \varepsilon, \mu \geqslant 0.$$

The optimal path then involves consumption rising exponentially:

$$c_t = c_0 e^{\gamma t} \tag{6}$$

where $\gamma \equiv (r - \alpha)/\varepsilon$.
From (5):

$$c_0 = B S_T^{\mu/\varepsilon} e^{-\gamma T} \quad \text{(where } B \text{ is a constant)}, \tag{7}$$

and from the budget equation:

$$S_T e^{-rT} = S_0 + w\theta(r) - c_0\theta(\delta), \tag{8}$$

where $\delta \equiv r - \gamma$ and:

$$\theta(x) \equiv \int_0^T e^{-xt} \, dt.$$

So far we have characterised the optimal consumption path for a given level of bequests received. In particular, we can express the bequests *left* by the consumer as a function of the bequests *received*:

$$S_T^i = F[S_0^i]$$

where the superscript relates to the generation: i.e. S_0^i is the discounted value of bequests received or expected by generation i. It is clear that $F' > 0$, and that $F(0) > 0$. If we confine our attention to the case of constant elasticity functions, then by eliminating c_0 from (7) and (8) we can see that F is defined implicitly by:

$$S_T e^{-rT} = S_0 + w\theta(r) - \theta(\delta)S_T^{\mu/\varepsilon} B e^{-\gamma T}, \tag{9}$$

so that:

$$\frac{\partial S_T}{\partial S_0} = 1 \Big/ \left[e^{-rT} + B\frac{\mu}{\varepsilon}\theta(\delta)S_T^{(\mu-\varepsilon)/\varepsilon} e^{-\gamma T} \right] \equiv 1/\Delta. \tag{10}$$

From this it follows that F is convex where $\mu < \varepsilon$ and concave where $\mu > \varepsilon$.

In order to examine the development of wealth-holding over time, we need to introduce some demographic and institutional assumptions. Suppose that when each individual is aged H he/she (no distinction is made) has e^{nH} children, and that when he dies $T - H$ years later his estate is shared equally among his children. This means that the bequests received by a person in generation $i + 1$ are:

$$S_0^{i+1} = S_T^i e^{-r(T-H)} e^{-nH} = G[S_T^i] \tag{11}$$

On the assumption that all generations are alike in their preferences, family-size and market opportunities, we may look for an equilibrium level of bequests S_0^* per person such that:

$$S_0^* = G[F[S_0^*]].$$

In Figure 2, I have shown the situation where the utility functions have constant elasticity. There are three cases:

A. *Single, globally stable equilibrium.* This occurs when $\mu > \varepsilon$ (as shown in Figure 2a) or when $\mu < \varepsilon$ and $r < n$.[9]

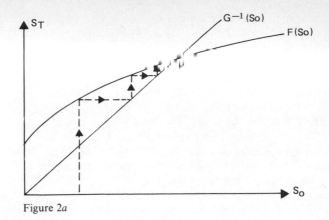

Figure 2a

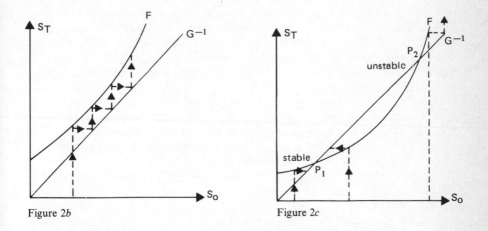

Figure 2b

Figure 2c

B. No equilibrium – as shown in Figure 2b. This can only occur with $\mu < \varepsilon$ and $r > n$.

C. Two equilibria – as shown in Figure 2c. This again can only occur with $\mu < \varepsilon$ and $r > n$. The lower equilibrium (P_1) is locally stable, the upper equilibrium (P_2) is unstable.

It may be interesting to draw out some of the implications of this analysis for the distribution of wealth between families. Suppose that we consider two families with the same preferences with regard to consumption and bequests, the same family-size and facing the same market opportunities, but which started off with different levels of inherited wealth. Where there is a globally stable equilibrium level of bequests (Case A), the gap between the families will be narrowing all the time. Even where bequests are increasing in both cases, the initially poorer family will always have the faster proportional rate of growth so that the gap is narrowing in relative terms. In this case, any observed tendency for inequality to increase must be attributed to differences in preferences, market opportunities or family-size. On the other hand, in Cases B and C we can observe increasing inequality even when families are identical in these respects. This is most obvious in Case C, where a family initially between P_1 and P_2 will experience a fall in the level of bequests, but one initially above P_2 will have successively larger and larger bequests. (This case resembles the low-level equilibrium trap models of underdeveloped countries.) In Case B, all families will have an increasing level of bequests, but it is quite possible for the gap to widen in relative terms.[10] It is not, of course, suggested that factors such as differences in family-size are unimportant;[11] however, it is interesting that even without introducing these factors we may still get increasing concentration in the distribution of bequests.

We have seen that the existence of a stable equilibrium level of wealth for the family depends on the form of the utility functions and on whether or not the rate of interest exceeds the rate of growth of the number of members. The conditions have a straightforward interpretation. First, $\mu < \varepsilon$ implies that the proportion of lifetime wealth spent on bequests rises with the level of wealth – i.e. bequests are a 'luxury' good and consumption is a 'necessity'. As a result rich families save more for posterity and they get richer still, so that if we do not allow for population growth there will be no tendency towards a stable level of bequests. If, however, they have large families, then under our assumptions the estate will be equally divided and this tends to dampen the growth of wealth-holding. As a result, where $n > r$, there is a stable equilibrium level of wealth even through $\mu < \varepsilon$. It seems more likely, if anything, that bequests are in fact a luxury good, but there is no firm evidence on which to draw. As a result, it seems best to examine both possibilities, even though this means that the analysis becomes regrettably taxonomic.

At this point, the assumption of constant r and w and the relationship between consumer asset formation and the rest of the economy should clearly be discussed. Where $\mu > \varepsilon$, and consumers are identical apart from their initial wealth, we have seen that for any given r and w there is an equilibrium level of bequests to which all families converge. In this case, the total stock of assets per person is constant and can be written as a function of r and w. The supply of assets to the personal sector can then be introduced and this will determine the long-run behaviour.[12] On the other hand, where $\mu < \varepsilon$ and $r > n$, there are families whose wealth is growing at a rate faster than n and the total stock of assets per person will be rising. If as a result of this r is driven down, then eventually the economy enters Case A and there is a long-run equilibrium with $r < n$.[13] However, while we can say something about the long-run behaviour of the economy where r and w depend on consumer asset formation, the short-run behaviour seems to be completely intractable. Since my purpose is not to discuss the working of the whole economy, but rather to examine the effects of taxation on the personal sector, I shall therefore make the very simplest assumption – that we are concerned with a small country that faces an internationally given interest rate. Under this assumption, Cases B and C could endure for ever, with the increasing wealth of the rich being channelled into overseas investment.

2 The Effect of Capital Taxes

In this section I examine in turn the effects of three different kinds of capital taxation:

(a) Capital levy – an unanticipated once-for-all tax on net worth levied at time 0.
(b) Wealth transfer tax – a tax on all wealth transfers (bequests and gifts *inter vivos*) introduced at time 0 and assumed not to have been anticipated.
(c) Wealth tax – a continuing tax on net worth introduced at time 0 and assumed not to have been anticipated.

For simplicity, I concentrate on the case of proportional taxes, but the results can in general be extended to cover the progressive tax schedules which are more likely in practice. It is assumed that the revenue from the taxes is used to redeem government debt, and that this has no further repercussions.

(a) Capital levy

The effect of the levy is to reduce the assets of all those alive at that data. In the case of a person aged A at time 0 (where $T-H \leq A \leq T$: i.e. he has already received his inheritance), the levy reduces his assets at time 0 by $t_c S_A$, where t_c is the rate of levy. He then replans his consumption – a process exactly the same as that described above, except that the planning period is $T-A$ rather than T years. This gives the same optimality conditions as before (equations (4) and (5)). Differentiating (4) with respect to t_c, we have:[14]

$$\frac{\partial}{\partial t_c}\left(\frac{\partial c}{\partial t}\right) = \frac{\partial}{\partial t}\left(\frac{\partial c}{\partial t_c}\right) = \gamma\left[1 - \frac{\varepsilon' c}{\varepsilon}\right]\frac{\partial c}{\partial t_c} \tag{12}$$

For simplicity, it is assumed that the square bracket is positive: i.e. that the elasticity of marginal utility does not change too rapidly with increasing consumption. From equation (12) it follows that $\partial c_t/\partial t_c$ cannot change sign. Moreover, from (5), $\partial c_T/\partial t_c$ and $\partial S_T/\partial t_c$ must have the same sign, and hence from the budget constraint both bequests and consumption at every point are reduced by the capital levy: under our assumptions, bequests and consumption are normal goods and a reduction in the person's lifetime wealth reduces both of them.

For a person aged A where $0 \leq A \leq T-H$, the capital levy falls on $\max[S_A - S_0 e^{rA}, 0]$: he is taxed solely on the assets which he has saved for himself and not on bequests anticipated but not received. However, as we have just seen, the levy reduces the size of the bequest that he will receive, so that his assets are reduced indirectly in this way. For individuals as yet unborn the whole effect is through reduced bequests received.

In the short run the capital levy reduces the level of bequests. Whether it has any enduring effect depends on the factors governing the development of wealth-holding. If there is a unique, stable equilibrium level of bequests, as in Case A, this is not affected by the capital levy and in the long run the effect of the levy dies away. On the other hand, if there is no globally stable equilibrium level of bequests, as in Cases B and C, the levy may well have a lasting effect. Suppose that before the levy a family was to the right of P_2 in Figure 2c, so that the level of bequests was steadily increasing. If the levy is sufficiently large, it shifts the family to the left of P_2 and thus drags it down towards the low-level equilibrium trap at P_1. In this way, a capital levy might have quite dramatic effects on the distribution of bequests.

The effect of the capital levy on savings is slightly more difficult to determine. Differentiating the budget constraint with respect to t_c:

$$\frac{\partial}{\partial t_c}\left(\frac{\partial S}{\partial t}\right)=\frac{\partial}{\partial t}\left(\frac{\partial S}{\partial t_c}\right)=r\frac{\partial S}{\partial t_c}-\frac{\partial c}{\partial t_c} \tag{13}$$

Together with (12) this gives us a pair of differential equations in $\partial c_t/\partial t_c$ and $\partial S/\partial t_c$, from which we can draw the phase diagrams shown in Figure 3. As an initial condition we have:

$$\partial S_A/\partial t_c = -S_A.$$

Moreover, differentiating the terminal condition (5) with respect to t_c:

$$U''(\partial c_T/\partial t_c)=\phi''(\partial S_T/\partial t_c)$$

which is shown in Figure 3 by the dashed line. Figure 3a shows the case where this curve is steeper than $\frac{\partial}{\partial t}\left(\frac{\partial S}{\partial t_c}\right)=0$: i.e.:

$$U''[c_T]/\phi''[S_T]>1/r, \tag{14}$$

and Figure 3b the case where the condition is reversed. We have already seen that $\partial c_t/\partial t_c \leqq 0$. Moreover, if we were to begin to the left of the point A, we should obviously never approach the terminal condition. This means that we must follow a path beginning between the points A and B on the initial condition line. In the case of Figure 3a (where condition (14) holds) it can be deduced that both $\partial S/\partial t_c$ and $\partial \dot{S}/\partial t_c$ are everywhere negative, so that the capital levy reduces the person's assets and his savings at every point in his life. Although he reduces his consumption, this is not sufficient to offset the fall in his interest income. On the other hand, where condition (14) is reversed, then his assets are still reduced at every point of his life, but his savings may rise for all or part of his life (and they are certainly higher at the end of his life).

In the case of constant elasticity functions, condition (14) becomes:

$$\mu c_T < \varepsilon r S_T;$$

in other words, it depends on the relative importance of consumption and bequests. Where bequests are a luxury good ($\mu<\varepsilon$), S_T/c_T increases with a person's wealth, and we can deduce that there is a certain level of wealth such

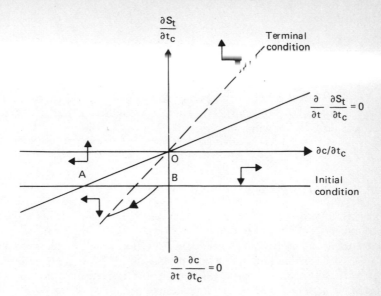

Figure 3a

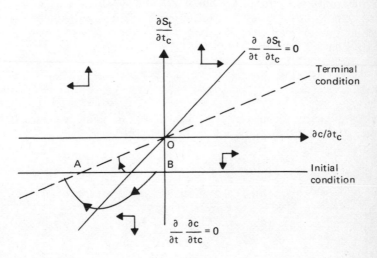

Figure 3b

that persons above this level definitely reduce their saving and persons below increase their saving for part (possibly all) of their lives. Where $\mu > \varepsilon$ this condition is reversed: poorer families reduce their saving, and the rich increase their saving for part or all of their lives.

(b) Wealth transfer tax

The allocation problem for a consumer aged $A(>T-H)$ at time 0 now becomes (assuming that he derives his utility from bequests *net of tax*):

maximise:

$$\int_A^T U(c)e^{-\alpha t}\,dt + e^{-\alpha T}\phi[S_T(1-t_i)]$$

subject to the budget constraint and his assets at time 0 (where t_i denotes the rate of tax on wealth transfers). The only condition that is affected is the terminal condition, which becomes:

$$U'(c_T) = \phi'[S_T(1-t_i)](1-t_i) \tag{15}$$

From this it is straightforward to show that the effect of the wealth transfer tax depends on whether the elasticity of ϕ' at S_T is greater than or less than 1. If the elasticity of ϕ' is greater than 1, then the right-hand side of (15) rises with t_i for constant S_T. From the budget equation, S_T and c_T must move in opposite directions, and clearly we can rule out S_T falling and c_T rising since this would not satisfy (15). It follows that where the elasticity of ϕ' is greater than 1, before-tax bequests are increased as a result of the tax and consumption at every point in his life reduced. Moreover, since consumption at every point is reduced, savings must be increased. On the other hand, where the elasticity of ϕ' at S_T is less than 1, all these results are reversed: before-tax bequests are reduced, consumption is increased and savings fall. In both cases, however, the net-of-tax bequest is reduced i.e.:

$$\frac{\partial}{\partial t_i}[S_T(1-t_i)] < 0.$$

For the case of constant elasticity utility functions, we can calculate the precise effect of the tax. From the budget constraint:

$$e^{-rT}(\partial S_T/\partial t_i) = -\theta_A(\delta)(\partial c_A/\partial t_i),$$

where $\theta_A(x) = \int_A^T e^{-xt}\,dt$. Differentiating (15) with respect to t_i:

$$\frac{\mu}{S_T}\frac{\partial S_T}{\partial t_i} = \frac{(\mu-1)}{(1-t_i)} + \frac{\varepsilon}{c_A}\frac{\partial c_A}{\partial t_i}. \tag{16}$$

Combining these:

$$\Delta_A\frac{\partial S_T}{\partial t_i} = \frac{(\mu-1)c_A\theta_A(\delta)}{\varepsilon(1-t_i)} \tag{17}$$

where Δ_A is defined as Δ, except that θc_0 is replaced by $\theta_A c_A$. Moreover, for net bequests we have:

$$\Delta_A\frac{\partial[S_T(1-t_i)]}{\partial t_i} = -\left[S_T e^{-rT} + \frac{c_A\theta_A(\delta)}{\varepsilon}\right]. \tag{18}$$

This analysis applies to those older than $T - H$ when the tax is introduced. For those younger, or not yet born, the bequests received are also reduced as a result of the tax. The long run effect of the wealth transfer tax on bequest levels is illustrated in Figure 4. Where there is a globally stable equilibrium level of bequests, the long-run effect is greater than the immediate effect (see Figure 4a). Figure 4b shows the case where there are two equilibria. The bottom equilibrium is reduced as a result of the tax, but the upper (unstable) equilibrium is increased. This means that those at the bottom are worse off, but also that the catchment area for the two-level equilibrium trap is widened; thus a family previously above P_2 may now be dragged down into the trap.

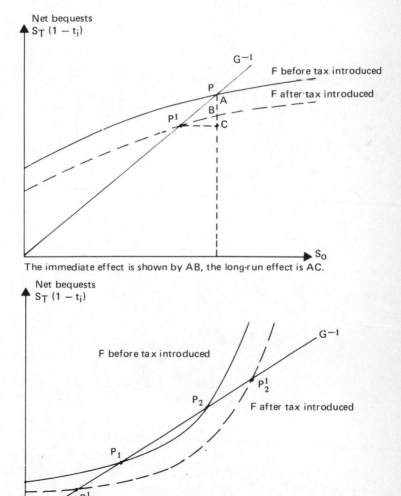

Figure 4a   The immediate effect is shown by AB, the long-run effect is AC.

Figure 4b

(c) A wealth tax

As far as those with positive net worth are concerned, a proportional wealth tax is equivalent in this one asset model to a reduction in the rate of interest – the return on saving falls from r to $r - t_w$ (where t_w is the rate of wealth tax).[15] The effect of the rate of interest on the level of savings is, however, a question to which no definite answer can be given. In this life-cycle model, just as in simple two-period models, savings may rise or fall as a result of a reduction in the rate of interest. Nonetheless, there are some definite conclusions that we can reach regarding the effect of a wealth tax on asset-holding.

The effect of the wealth tax for a person aged between $T - H$ and T can be seen by differentiating equations (2) and (4) with respect to t_w (and writing $r' = r - t_w$):

$$\frac{\partial}{\partial t}\left(\frac{\partial S}{\partial t_w}\right) = r'\frac{\partial S}{\partial t_w} - S - \frac{\partial c_t}{\partial t_w}, \tag{19}$$

$$\varepsilon(c)\frac{\partial}{\partial t}\left(\frac{\partial c}{\partial t_w}\right) = -c + \left[1 - \frac{\varepsilon' c}{\varepsilon}\right]\frac{\partial c}{\partial t_w}(r' - \alpha). \tag{20}$$

Moreover, from the terminal condition it follows that:

$$\frac{\mu}{S_T}\frac{\partial S_T}{\partial t_w} = \frac{\varepsilon}{c_T}\frac{\partial c_T}{\partial t_w}. \tag{21}$$

As in the case of the capital levy, we can draw a phase diagram in $(\partial S/\partial t_w, \partial c/\partial t_w)$ space – see Figure 5 (again assuming $\varepsilon' c/\varepsilon < 1$). However, the

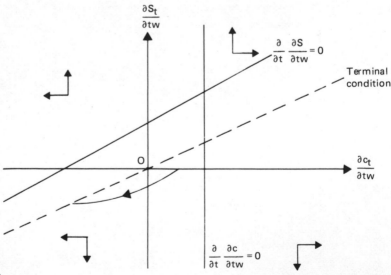

Figure 5

problem is more complicated than before, since the equations are non-autonomous and the lines $\frac{\partial}{\partial t}\left(\frac{\partial S}{\partial t}\right)=0$ and $\frac{\partial}{\partial t}\left(\frac{\partial c_t}{\partial t_w}\right)=0$ are shifting over time.

All the same, we can deduce that the line $\frac{\partial}{\partial t}\left(\frac{\partial c}{\partial t_w}\right)=0$ always lies to the right of the origin. Moreover, if we assume that $t_w<r-\alpha$, then S_t is positive for all t, so that the line $\frac{\partial}{\partial t}\left(\frac{\partial S}{\partial t}\right)=0$ always cuts the horizontal axis to the left of the origin.

Since we must begin with $\frac{\partial S}{\partial t_w}=0$ and end at a point satisfying condition (21), it follows that the level of bequests is always reduced by the wealth tax. For if we start to the left of the origin $\partial c/\partial t_w$ is always negative and we must end at a point satisfying the terminal condition in the bottom left-hand quadrant. Beginning to the right of the origin, we can again only approach the terminal condition line in the bottom left-hand quadrant, since we cannot leave the bottom right-hand quadrant going upwards. From this we can deduce that a wealth tax leads to a reduction in the bequests passed on to the next generation by those aged between $T-H$ and T when it is introduced. Similarly, c_T is lower than it would have been without the tax. If we look at consumption at earlier points in the person's life (when he is aged t), then:

$$U'[c_t]=e^{(r'-\alpha)(T-t)}\phi'[S_T].$$

From this it follows that:

$$\frac{\varepsilon(c)}{c_t}\frac{\partial c_t}{\partial t_w}=(T-t)+\frac{\mu(S)}{S_T}\frac{\partial S_T}{\partial t_w} \tag{22}$$

where $\mu(S)=-\phi''S/\phi'$. In the case of ε constant, it follows that the proportionate reduction in consumption increases over a person's life, and it is quite possible that consumption may initially be increased as a result of the wealth tax. If consumption does in fact rise at the outset, then savings are decreased, since:

$$\frac{\partial \dot{S}_A}{\partial t_w}=-S_A-\frac{\partial c_A}{\partial t_w}.$$

However, in general the effect on saving cannot be determined: it may rise or fall at any stage.

In the case of constant elasticity functions, we can calculate the precise effect on bequests. Differentiating the budget constraint with respect to t_w:

$$\frac{\partial}{\partial t}\left(\frac{\partial S}{\partial t_w}\right)=r'\frac{\partial S}{\partial t_w}-S-\frac{\partial c}{\partial t_w},$$

and then integrating this differential equation in $\partial S/\partial t_w$:

$$e^{-rT}\frac{\partial S_T}{\partial t_w} = -\int_A^T Se^{-rt}\,dt - \int_A^T \frac{\partial c}{\partial t_w}e^{rt}\,dt. \tag{23}$$

Combining this with (22), we obtain:

$$\Delta'_A\frac{\partial S_T}{\partial t_w} = -\int_A^T Se^{-rt}\,dt - \frac{1}{\varepsilon}\int_A^T c_t(T-t)e^{-rt}\,dt, \tag{24}$$

where:

$$\Delta'_A \equiv e^{-rT} + \frac{\mu}{\varepsilon S_T}\int_A^T c_t e^{-rt}\,dt.$$

If we look at the effect on the *initial* level of savings, it can be calculated that:

$$\frac{\partial \dot{S}_A}{\partial t_w} = -S_A + \frac{c_A}{\varepsilon S_T \Delta'_A}\left[(\mu-1)(T-A)S_T e^{-rT} - \frac{\mu}{\varepsilon}\int_A^T (t-A)\left\{\varepsilon\left(\frac{w}{c}-1\right)+1\right\}ce^{-rt}\,dt.\right] \tag{25}$$

It is interesting to compare this expression with the corresponding result for the two period case (with no bequests). Then savings are reduced if (see, for example, Feldstein and Tsiang [3]):

$$1 + \varepsilon\left(\frac{w}{c_2}-1\right) > 0, \tag{26}$$

which clearly corresponds to the last term in equation (25). From this Feldstein and Tsiang conclude that an increase in the interest rate (fall in the tax rate) increases saving among those income groups where there is little or no saving ($w \geqq c_2$). However, in the present model it is clearly not sufficient that $c_t \leqq w$ for $t > A$. Although the first and last terms would then be negative, the second term would be positive where $\mu > 1$.

So far we have discussed the effect of the wealth tax on a person aged over $T-H$ when the tax is introduced. For those who are younger, or not yet born, we must take account of the fact that the wealth tax would only be levied on those people with positive net worth (i.e. net borrowers would not be subsidised). We have seen that $S_t \geqq 0$, all $0 \leqq t \leqq T$; however, for $0 \leqq t \leqq T-H$ this includes bequests which are anticipated but have not yet been received, so that the true net worth for this period is $S_t - S_0 e^{rt}$. The condition for this to be positive for all $0 \leqslant t \leqslant T-H$ is that:

$$\int_0^{T-H} (w - c_t)e^{-rt}\,dt > 0. \tag{27}$$

For simplicity, let us concentrate on the case where this holds, i.e. where people do not in fact borrow against their anticipated inheritance.[16] If the tax is imposed when generation i is aged A, then:

$$S_0^{i+1} = S_T^i e^{-r'(T-A-H)-rA-nH}$$

so that:

$$\frac{1}{S_0^{i+1}} \frac{\partial S_0^{i+1}}{\partial t_w} = \frac{1}{S_T^i} \left[\frac{\partial S_T^i}{\partial t_w} + (T - A - H) \right].$$

As we have seen, the wealth tax reduces the estate left by generation i so that the first term is negative. But since the tax lowers the effective interest rate for those who are net lenders, the value of a given bequest discounted back to the beginning of the recipient's life has gone up. So the second term is positive, and the net effect on the initial assets of generation $i+1$ indeterminate. Where condition (27) holds, we can show, however, that in Case A the long-run level of *bequests* is reduced and that in Case C the catchment area of the low-level trap is widened.

Summary
The results of this section have shown that the *immediate* effect of all three taxes is to lead those alive when the tax is introduced to reduce the net bequest passed on to the next generation. In the case of capital levy, its *long-run* effect depends on the conditions governing the development of wealth-holding. Where there is a globally-stable equilibrium, its effect dies away. On the other hand, where bequests are a luxury good and the rate of interest exceeds the rate of population growth, the levy has a permanent effect on the distribution of wealth. In contrast to this, the wealth transfer tax quite definitely leads to a reduction in the long-run level of bequests, and our results suggest that this is also the case with the annual wealth tax (although they do not cover those who dissave in early life). Finally, if we consider the immediate effect on consumption, we have shown that the capital levy leads to a reduction, as does the wealth transfer tax where the elasticity of the marginal utility of bequests is greater than 1, but the effect of the wealth tax is indeterminate.

3   Comparing Capital Taxes – Redistribution and Savings

So far I have discussed each of the capital taxes in isolation; in this section I consider how the results given earlier can be used to compare the relative merits and demerits of the different taxes. This comparison is clearly of great importance for policy purposes; however, it also involves a number of problems of considerable complexity. As a result, the conclusions reached in this section are only very limited in scope. Indeed, the primary aim of the section is not so much to present results as to bring out the problems of comparing taxes in a dynamic model of this type – problems which have received virtually no attention in the literature.

(a) The concept of lifetime equity

The principal argument for taxing capital is that of achieving a more equitable distribution of wealth and this is clearly the first standard by which we should judge the different taxes. However, this criterion is not as straightforward as may appear at first sight and in particular we need to examine precisely what is meant by 'a more equitable distribution of wealth'.

The evidence regarding inequality in the distribution of wealth is usually presented in terms of the current distribution of wealth between all individuals alive at a particular date. However, in terms of the life-cycle savings model discussed here, this approach means that there would be inequality in the distribution of wealth even if everyone received the same bequests and faced the same market opportunities. There would be inequality in the instantaneous distribution of wealth because the pattern of asset-holding varies over a person's lifetime and people of different ages would have different wealth levels. (This aspect is discussed in Chapter 7.)

For this reason, I feel that the instantaneous concept of equity is not appropriate for our purpose, and that the analysis should be based primarily on a concept of lifetime equity. Equality or inequality should be measured in terms of the distribution of *lifetime* and not just *current* wealth. In this way, we should regard as perfectly egalitarian a society in which everyone received the same total discounted value of wealth transfers over their life (and *w* is equally distributed), even though this may still involve considerable inequality in the distribution of wealth at a particular date. On these grounds, I have compared the redistributional effects of the different capital taxes in terms of their impact on bequests – or on the transfer of wealth between generations.

It should be emphasised that this approach will give rather different results from those reached if we look at the effect on the instantaneous distribution of wealth. We may, for example, have a situation in which a particular tax reduces inequality in the distribution of bequests, but by changing the lifetime pattern of asset-holding it leads to greater inequality in the instantaneous distribution. Moreover, we should bear in mind that in adopting this lifetime approach we are taking a longer term view of the problem. Even if we were to bring about complete equality of bequests as a result of introducing a capital tax, this would not affect in the same way those who had already received their inheritance: for one generation there would still be inequality in the lifetime distribution. Finally, it should be noted that the lifetime *utility* derived from a given inheritance S_0 will be affected by the introduction of capital taxes, so that we should really be concerned with the distribution of:

$$V(S_0) = \int_0^T U(c_t^*) e^{-\alpha t}\, dt + e^{-\alpha T} \phi[S_T^*]$$

where c_t^*, S_t^* represent the consumption plan chosen by the individual to maximise V subject to S_0 and the ruling tax rates. Adopting this criterion would allow for the possible excess burden of taxation,[17] and the possibility that a reduction in bequests passed on by the rich may be accompanied by an increase in their consumption. While for simplicity I shall concentrate at present on the distribution of bequests, this qualification should clearly be borne in mind.

(b) Equal yield comparisons

The conventional basis for comparing taxes in a static model is that of equal revenue yield and although this is far from fully satisfactory even in a static context, it provides a convenient starting point. In extending this equal revenue yield concept to a dynamic model, the usual approach is to compare taxes such that a 'representative individual' pays the same present discounted value of taxes over his lifetime.[18] This would mean, for example, comparing a capital levy at rate t_c when the individual was aged A with a wealth transfer tax at rate $t_c S_A/[S_T e^{-r(T-A)}]$. As I shall argue below, this conventional approach is far from ideal, but it may none the less be useful to summarise briefly the results that it would give in the present model.

From the results of section 2, we can see that the effect on the net bequests left by a person aged A ($> T-H$) when the tax is introduced is given in the constant elasticity case by:

$$\frac{\partial S_T}{\partial t} = -S_A e^{-rA}/\Delta_A, \tag{28}$$

$$\frac{\partial [S_T(1-t_i)]}{\partial t_i} = -\left[S_T e^{-rT} + \frac{c_A}{\varepsilon}\theta_A(\delta)\right]/\Delta_A, \tag{18}$$

$$\frac{\partial S_T}{\partial t_w} = -\left[\int_A^T Se^{-rt}\,dt + \frac{1}{\varepsilon}\int_A^T (T-t)c_t e^{-rt}\,dt\right]/\Delta_A, \tag{24}$$

where in each case the derivative of the net bequest level with respect to the tax rate is evaluated at a zero tax level, i.e. the results apply to infinitesimal taxes. These expressions may be interpreted as follows: in each case the first term is of the form $(\partial R/\partial t_x)/\Delta_A$ where R denotes the present value of tax payments over the person's life *discounted at the interest rate r*. If we assume that the government applies the same discount rate as the individual, the difference between equal yield taxes is represented by the second term. As we should expect, both the wealth transfer and wealth taxes have a greater effect than the capital levy. With the capital levy, we only have a 'wealth' effect, whereas with the other two taxes there is also a 'substitution' effect against bequests. If we compare the wealth transfer tax and the wealth tax, the condition for the transfer tax to have a larger impact on bequests can be reduced to:

$$\int_A^T \left[c_t - w + S^T e^{-rT}\frac{c_t}{c_A\theta_A}\right](t-A)e^{-rt}\,dt > 0.$$

If we consider families identical apart from their initial wealth, it is clear that there is a critical level of wealth above which the wealth transfer tax is more effective. It is interesting to note that a sufficient condition for the wealth transfer tax to be more effective is that consumption is always greater than earned income.

So far we have considered only the possibility of reducing inequality in the distribution of bequests by reducing the transfer of wealth by the rich. But the government may also want to improve the distribution by *increasing* the bequests left by those at the lower end of the scale. To do this we could turn the different taxes on their heads: the wealth tax would become an interest subsidy, and the capital levy a once-for-all capital bounty. From the preceding analysis, we can see that the interest subsidy would be more effective per pound sterling of present discounted value of benefit received by the individual.[19]

(c) Objections to the conventional approach

There are two major objections that can be raised against the conventional equal yield approach described above:

 (i) that revenue is not the appropriate basis for comparison,
 (ii) that the concept of a 'representative individual' has little meaning in a dynamic model.

In what follows I shall discuss these objections in turn.

The argument for comparing taxes on the basis of the present discounted value of revenue is not usually made explicit, but presumably rests on the assumption that the government can borrow or lend at a fixed interest rate and is concerned with comparing taxes with the same ultimate effect on the level of government debt. However, even though this assumption might be more applicable to the small open economy considered here than to a closed economy, it is not at all clear that it is the kind of 'equal repercussions' assumption that is relevant to government policy. In particular, the government is likely to be more concerned with the impact of taxes on the level of consumption and personal saving than with the effect on the national debt. Certainly the arguments regarding the introduction of new capital taxes have centred round the effect on consumption. In view of this, a more relevant question may be to examine the effect on consumption of taxes having the same redistributional impact (for a 'representative individual').

From the results given earlier, we can obtain the following 'equal-effect' tax rates for an individual aged A when the tax is introduced $(A > T - H)$:

$$\frac{dt_c}{\partial t_w} = (T - A) + \frac{\int_A^T (T - t)\left[w - c_t + \frac{c_t}{\varepsilon}\right] e^{-rt}\, dt}{S_A e^{-rA}}, \tag{29}$$

$$\frac{dt\cdot}{\delta t_w} = (1-A)\cdot\frac{\int_A^T (t-A)\left[w - c_t + \frac{c_t}{\varepsilon}\right]e^{-rt}\,dt}{\left[S_T e^{-m} + \frac{c_n H_n(A)}{\varepsilon}\right]} \tag{30}$$

The appearance of the term $T-A$ is intriguing because it corresponds to the figure one would naturally try first in a 'back of the envelope' calculation of the equivalent tax rate (using some 'average' age for $T-A$): a 1% wealth tax would be equivalent, say, to a 30% wealth transfer tax.[20] In general, however, the second term will come into the calculation, and it may take either sign. It is interesting to note that the numerator of the second term is in both cases closely related to the 'two period savings condition' – condition (26). In particular, where $c_t < w\frac{\varepsilon}{(\varepsilon-1)}$ the equivalent wealth transfer tax rate is less, and the equivalent capital levy greater, than $T-A$ times the annual wealth tax.

(d) Effect on savings and consumption

The major argument made against capital taxation is that it would lead to a reduction in personal savings. We have seen, however, that this is not necessarily the case. Where $\mu > 1$, the wealth transfer tax leads to an increase in saving: the knowledge that his bequest will be taxed leads the donor to save more while alive in order to offset part of the tax burden. In the case of a capital levy, we have seen that where bequests are a luxury good people with wealth below a certain level increase their saving for part or all of their lives. Finally, it is quite possible for a wealth tax to lead to a rise in savings – for those with positive net worth it is equivalent to a fall in the interest rate, and as is well known this may cause savings to rise or fall.

Moreover, even if the capital taxes do lead to a reduction in personal saving, it is not clear that this is a compelling argument against them – since the government can save. Any fall in personal saving can be offset by an increase in public saving. But while this is so, there may be constraints on the government's freedom of action which limit the possibilities for an offsetting increase in public saving. Suppose, for example, that a tax not merely reduces saving but leads to an increase in consumption, as may be the case with an annual wealth tax or with a wealth transfer tax (where $\mu < 1$). In order to maintain the overall level of saving (private + public), the government would then have to raise other taxes, but for various reasons this may not be possible. In this situation, the government may well be interested in the effects of the different taxes on the level of *consumption*.

Collecting together the results of the earlier analysis, we can see that for an individual aged A $(\geq T-H)$ when the tax is introduced the effect on his consumption at time t is given by:

$$\frac{\varepsilon}{c_t}\frac{\partial c_t}{\partial t_c}=\frac{\mu}{S_T}\frac{\partial S_T}{\partial t_c},$$

$$\frac{\varepsilon}{c_t}\frac{\partial c_t}{\partial t_i}=\frac{1}{(1-t_i)}\left[\frac{\mu}{S_T}\frac{\partial[S_T(1-t_i)]}{\partial t_i}+1\right]\quad\text{(derived from (16)),}$$

$$\frac{\varepsilon}{c_t}\frac{\partial c_t}{\partial t_w}=\frac{\mu}{S_T}\frac{\partial S_T}{\partial t_w}+(T-t). \tag{22}$$

It is obvious that for a given redistributional effect the wealth transfer tax and the wealth tax both reduce consumption less than a capital levy. The wealth transfer tax makes consumption more attractive relative to bequests and the wealth tax leads people to re-arrange their consumption pattern in favour of present consumption. If we compare the wealth transfer tax and the wealth tax, it is clear that consumption under the former is higher towards the end of a person's lifetime (as $t \to T$). If we compare their initial effects on consumption, then it is lower under the wealth transfer tax (for infinitesimal taxes) where:

$$\int_A^T (t-A)\left[w-c_t+\frac{c_t}{\varepsilon}\right]e^{-rt}\,dt>0, \tag{31}$$

A sufficient condition for this to be satisfied is that $\varepsilon<1$; where $\varepsilon>1$, there is a certain wealth level above which the wealth transfer tax reduces initial consumption less (raises it more) than the equivalent annual wealth tax.

Condition (31) is again analogous to the condition for savings to rise with the interest rate in the simple two period model (condition (26)). It is interesting to see that while this condition is not sufficient for savings to rise with the interest rate in the present model, it does guarantee that a reduction in the wealth tax rate (rise in the interest rate) increases consumption less than an equivalent reduction in the wealth transfer tax rate. From the results of the previous section, we can also deduce that a wealth transfer tax reduces consumption more when the equivalent tax rate is less than $T-A$ times the wealth tax rate.

The results obtained can be summarised as follows. Consumption is always higher at the end of the person's life under the wealth transfer tax; moreover, it is higher *at all points* of his life where $\varepsilon>1$ and his wealth exceeds some critical level. These findings are of some interest in view of the common belief that a wealth transfer tax would have less of an effect on saving than a wealth tax, because it falls only on saving for bequests and not on saving for retirement.[21] However, in the present model no such simple statement seems possible. Finally, if we consider the objective of increasing wealth-holding at the bottom of the scale, then the results for the capital levy and the wealth tax can be reversed, and we can deduce that for any given effect on bequests an interest subsidy adds less to consumption than a capital bounty.

(e) A more general approach

The second objection to the conventional approach (which applies equally to the previous section) is that the concept of a 'representative individual' has little meaning in the type of model discussed here. First of all, people differ in their initial assets - if they did not, then we should not be concerned with redistributing wealth. Secondly, even if there were an equal distribution of bequests, there would still be differences according to age, and as can be seen from the earlier analysis the equivalent tax rate (whether in terms of revenue or of the effect on bequests) depends on the age of the person when the tax is introduced.

It might be thought that these problems could be avoided by considering the effect on the long-run equilibrium. There are, however, a number of reasons why this is not a very promising approach. First, it assumes the existence of a globally stable long-run equilibrium, which, as we have seen, is not necessarily guaranteed. Secondly, even if there is a long-run equilibrium, it does not allow us to make any comparison in the case of the capital levy. Finally, it implies a very long-term view of the problem: it would be analogous to choosing the savings rate according to the Golden Rule.

There is no alternative, therefore, to taking explicit account of the timepath of effects and of inequality in the distribution of initial assets. Suppose that the government's views about the distribution of initial wealth can be represented by an additively separable, symmetric social welfare function in the individual lifetime utilities:

$$W = \int_0^\infty e^{-\eta t} \, dt \int_0^\infty V(S_0) f(S_0, t) \, dS_0,$$

where $f(S_0, t)$ is the density function of initial assets S_0 inherited by those born at t and η is the social rate of time discount. From this we can compare the effects on (say) savings of taxes giving the same increase in aggregate social welfare.[22] It should be clear, however, that obtaining analytic results from the comparison of taxes on this basis is going to be extremely difficult – even with strong simplifying assumptions about the initial distribution of bequests.

4   Concluding Comments

The primary aim of this chapter has been to explore the effects of three different types of capital taxation in the context of a life-cycle model of individual savings. The conclusions reached are only very limited in scope – both the model involves a number of strong assumptions and because even with these assumptions it appears difficult to obtain clearcut results. They are sufficient, however, to cast doubt on certain commonly held beliefs – such as that capital taxes necessarily lead to a reduction in savings and that a capital levy can have only a temporary impact on the distribution of wealth. Unfortunately, no clear answer emerges to the question as to the best way of taxing wealth. If we confine our attention to the case of a 'representative individual' alive when the tax is introduced, and are concerned with achieving a given redistributional impact with the least adverse effect on savings, then the capital levy comes out best. If the capital levy is ruled out – either because it does not guarantee a permanent effect on bequests or on grounds of political feasibility – then we have seen that (where $\varepsilon > 1$) there is a certain critical lifetime wealth level above which the wealth tax reduces consumption more at all points of his life than the wealth transfer tax. Although the results are only limited, I hope that the analysis has also served to demonstrate the importance of the concept of lifetime (as opposed to instantaneous) equity and to bring out some of the conceptual problems involved in the comparison of taxes in a dynamic model.

The need for further work in this area should be quite obvious. First, the results of this chapter need to be extended to allow more general assumptions about individual preferences and the production side of the economy. Secondly, the three taxes considered here far from exhaust the possibilities of capital taxation. There are a large number of variations on the wealth transfer tax: the rate of tax could, for example, be related to the wealth of the recipient or to the amount inherited by the donor as proposed by Rignano [7].[23] Finally, there are the very interesting problems involved in determining the *optimal structure* of a particular tax.

Notes

1 This chapter has benefited from comments at seminars at Cambridge, the London School of Economics and Nuffield College, Oxford.
2 I am very grateful to P. A. Diamond, F. H. Hahn, J. E. Stiglitz and the referees for valuable criticism.
3 Cf. [11]. See also the paper by Meade [4] and Tobin [10].
4 It is also assumed that $U'(x)$, $\phi'(x)$ tend to ∞ as x tends to 0, and tend to 0 as x tends to ∞.
5 For alternative assumptions about the utility derived from bequests, see Meade [4].
6 This is in fact a stronger assumption than is needed where $r > \alpha$ (see below). In any case, more realistic assumptions such as differing borrowing and lending rates could easily be incorporated.
7 Assuming that there is a consumption plan satisfying the necessary conditions (4) and (5), then it is unique and differentiable. See [11].
8 At this point it may be noted that the consumer's plans are consistent in the Strotz sense under the assumption that the utility from bequests is discounted at the same rate α as utility from consumption. In other words, when he reaches the age u he will consume the amount c_u that he planned to at time 0.
9 In the latter case, $1/\Delta$ tends to a limit e^{rT} as S_T tends to ∞, which is less than the slope of G^{-1}.
10 This can occur where the poorer family is below the point of tangency of F with a ray through the origin and the richer family is above this point.
11 For an interesting discussion of these factors, see Stiglitz [9].
12 No allowance has been made so far for technical progress. In view of the non-homotheticity of consumer preferences, this would preclude a steady state solution; however, it may be reasonable to assume that a relative income effect is operative and that tastes shift from generation to generation with rising *per capita* incomes.
13 And hence is inefficient in the Phelps-Koopmans sense.
14 The reversal of the order of differentiation is legitimate since the variables c_t and S_t are continuous in S_0 and hence in t_c.
15 This is only true, however, where a person has positive net worth. See below.
16 A more general treatment requires explicit recognition of the differing net of tax borrowing and lending rates, which affect the form of the optimal consumption policy.
17 It should be noted that since bequests represent an externality in consumption (providing benefit to both donor and recipient), if there were no distributional considerations we should want to subsidise bequests relative to consumption.

18 See, for example, Musgrave [5], pp. 260–4.
19 Sandford [8] has suggested a recurring capital bounty paid to each generation when it comes of age which would be equivalent in this model to a rise in w_0.
20 This is in fact similar to the method used by Sir Henry Primrose and others at the turn of the century to calculate the income burden of capital taxes. See Barna [1].
21 See, for example, Prest [6] p. 89. 'The substitution of death duties for annual investment income taxation would add one powerful incentive to save: all that class of saving ("hump" saving) destined to be spent before death would not be subject to tax in the death duty case, whereas the annual income from it would be taxable in the investment income case.' (Although it should be noted that Prest is here concerned with an equal revenue comparison and that the British death duties were rather different from the wealth transfer tax considered here.)
22 The existence of tax rates satisfying this condition is not, of course, guaranteed. It should be noted, however, that there is no reason why the tax rates should be proportional or constant over time. Ideally, one would want to design an optimal tax *structure* – both across individuals in one generation and across generations.
23 Moreover, in a number of countries transfers at death (or within a certain number of years of death) are taxed more heavily than transfers earlier in life – the extreme case being that of the British death duties.

References

[1] Barna, T. (1941), 'Death duties in terms of an annual tax', *Review of Economic Studies*, November.
[2] Cass, D. and Yaari, M. E. (1967), 'Individual saving, aggregate capital accumulation and efficient growth', in K. Shell (ed.), *Essays on the Theory of Optimal Economic Growth*, M.I.T. Press.
[3] Feldstein, M. S. and Tsiang, S. C. (1968), 'The interest rate, taxation and the personal savings incentive', *Quarterly Journal of Economics*, August.
[4] Meade, J. E. (1966), 'Life-cycle savings, inheritance and economic growth', *Review of Economic Studies*, January.
[5] Musgrave, R. A. (1959), *The Theory of Public Finance*, McGraw-Hill.
[6] Prest, A. R. (1967), *Public Finance in Theory and Practice*, 3rd edn, Weidenfeld & Nicolson.
[7] Rignano, E. and Stamp, J. C., *The Social Significance of Death Duties*, Noel Douglas.
[8] Sandford, C. T. (1969), *Economics of Public Finance*, Pergamon Press.
[9] Stiglitz, J. E. (1969), 'Distribution of income and wealth among individuals', *Econometrica*, July.
[10] Tobin, J. (1967), 'Life cycle saving and balanced growth', in *Ten Economic Studies in The Tradition of Irving Fisher*, Wiley.
[11] Yaari, M. E. (1964), 'On the consumer's lifetime allocation process', *International Economic Review*, September.
[12] Yaari, M. E. (1965), 'Uncertain lifetime, life insurance and the theory of the consumer', *Review of Economic Studies*, April.

9 Inheritance and the Redistribution of Wealth*

1 Introduction

In his writing James Meade has been very much concerned with the relationship between economic analysis and economic policy. He has always emphasised the development of economic models not for their own sake but for the light that they cast on the solution of economic problems; at the same time he has remained deeply convinced of the value of economic analysis as an aid to the formation of policy. The choice of topic for this chapter has been greatly influenced by the important contributions that he has made. The taxation of inheritance – and, more generally, the redistribution of income and wealth – is a subject on which he has written extensively and persuasively. His *Economic Analysis and Policy* [20] contains a substantial discussion of the distribution of income among persons and of the effects of taxation. In *Planning and the Price Mechanism* [21], and more recently in *The Intelligent Radical's Guide to Economic Policy* [25], he has elaborated the case for reform, and this reaches its culmination in the Meade Report on *The Structure and Reform of Direct Taxation* [27]. Alongside this discussion of policy he has pioneered the development of models of wealth distribution, notably in *Efficiency, Equality and the Ownership of Property* [22], which contains a rich account of the factors influencing the distribution. This essay has stimulated much of the subsequent research in this area, and Meade himself has taken the subject further in his Keynes Lecture of 1973 (*The Inheritance of Inequalities* [24]) and in *The Just Economy* [26].

The aims of this chapter are to survey the literature on inheritance, to bring out its relationship to the distribution of wealth, and to assemble some of the building blocks necessary for an analysis of redistributive policies. Section 2 is concerned with the bequest motive for saving. It describes several different formulations and discusses some of the implications for the taxation of inheritance. (Throughout, the term 'inheritance' is used to refer to all transmission of material wealth, whether through bequest or gift.) Section 3 takes up the division of estates. It first examines the treatment of sons and daughters and the role played by marriage. It then considers situations where wealth is unequally divided between sons or daughters. Stress is placed on the

* Reprinted from *Public Policy and the Tax System, Essays in Honour of James Meade.*

inter-relationship between different aspects of the inheritance process, and it is shown that the conclusions drawn concerning the impact of taxation may critically depend on the pattern of inheritance. The analysis to this point is in partial equilibrium terms and focuses on unearned incomes. In section 4 the model is set in a general equilibrium context, and the inter-relation with earned incomes is discussed. The main conclusions, and some of the directions for further research, are summarised in section 5.

Meade once described his work as that not 'of a tool-maker nor a tool-user, but of a tool-setter'. This chapter is written in a similar spirit. It is not the intention to develop basic theoretical ideas, nor to examine in detail particular policy proposals; rather, it attempts to provide an analytical framework within which policy can be discussed. It is concerned with the relation between the formulation of economic models and the nature of the policy conclusions drawn. This is illustrated by reference to inheritance taxation, and numerical examples are given in sections 3 and 4, but it is not the purpose here to argue for particular reforms of the tax system or to assess the relative contribution of fiscal and other measures to redistribute wealth.

2   The Bequest Motive and the Taxation of Inheritance

A simple bequest model
As a starting point for the discussion of different treatments of the bequest motive we may take the straightforward extension of the Fisherian lifetime consumption model to allow for utility derived from wealth transfers. In its simplest form, where the person expects confidently to live for a fixed lifetime, the lifetime utility function may be written (Yaari [36] and [37]):

$$\int_0^1 U(c_v)\, dv + \phi(B) \tag{1}$$

where the unit of time is taken as the lifetime and there is assumed to be no discounting of utility. (This can readily be introduced, however.) Consumption c_v, at time v, and bequests B at death, are related by the intertemporal budget constraint. In a perfect capital market, where the individual can borrow or lend freely at a rate of interest r, and where r is assumed constant over time, this constraint is of the form:

$$\int_0^1 c_v e^{-rv}\, dv + B e^{-r} = \int_0^1 w_v e^{-rv}\, dv + I \equiv Z \tag{2}$$

where w_v denotes the wage income received at time v and I the present value of inheritances received. The present value of wages plus I, denoted by Z, is referred to as 'lifetime wealth'. (It is assumed that wealth transfers are only made at death, via B, but other transfers can be incorporated.) In this and the next section we shall take a partial equilibrium approach, assuming that the wage and rate of interest are exogenously determined (and constant); the general equilibrium aspects are taken up in section 4.

The essence of the model is that the individual chooses his consumption stream and bequests to maximise lifetime utility, subject to the lifetime budget constraint (2). From this formulation one can derive the bequest behaviour as a function of r and Z and examine the implications of wealth transfer taxes (as in Chapter 8). These clearly depend on the form of the utility functions $U(c)$ and $\phi(B)$. One special, and not necessarily realistic, case is that where the elasticities of the marginal utility of consumption, and of bequests, are constant and equal. Bequests are then proportional to lifetime wealth; that is:

$$B = s_1(r)Z = s_1(r)\left(I + \int_0^1 w_v e^{-rv}\, dv \right) \qquad (3)$$

Where the wage is constant ($w_v = w$), this may be rewritten as:

$$B = s_1(r)I + s_2(r)w \qquad (4)$$

This brings us close to the savings model applied by Meade [22] to the distribution of wealth. The main difference is that the process is here given an explicit inter-generational setting, and we can consider the evolution of wealth-holding across generations.

The savings model provides a relationship between the present value of wealth inherited by one generation, say t, at the beginning of its life, denoted by I_t, and the amount bequeathed at death to the next generation $(t+1)$, denoted by B_t. The second link in the process is that between B_t and I_{t+1}. At this point we need to introduce assumptions about the division of estates. For the present it is assumed that each family has h children and that the wealth is divided equally among them, so that the *per capita* inheritance is:

$$I_{t+1} = \frac{B_t}{h} \qquad (5)$$

The h children are assumed to be of the same sex and to reproduce themselves unaided. (The division between sons and daughters and the role of marriage are discussed in the next section.)

Combining the savings relationship (4) and the division of bequests equation (5), we can trace out the dynamics of wealth-holding across generations. The case where the savings relationship is of the form shown in equation (4) is depicted in Figure 1. In Figure 1a there is stable equilibrium at point E, and the equilibrium level of wealth is given by:

$$I^* = \frac{s_2 w}{h - s_1} \qquad (6)$$

Thus starting, for example, from inherited wealth I_0, the level of bequests is determined by B_0 (see dotted lines). Divided among h heirs, this provides in turn I_1 each in the next generation. As the dynamic path is traced out, E is

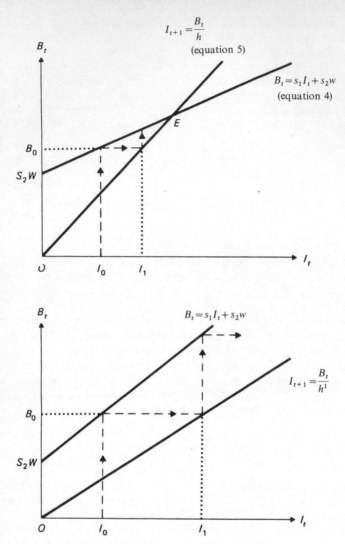

Figure 1 *Alternative time paths for bequests and inheritances.*

approached. In Figure 1*b* the bequest levels tend to diverge. (The more general case where bequests are not necessarily proportional to lifetime wealth is discussed in Chapter 8.)

The condition for Figure 1*a* to apply, rather than Figure 1*b*, is that $s_1(r) < h$. This condition illustrates a key feature, namely that the distribution of wealth depends on the balance between those forces leading to the accumulation of capital (s_1) and those leading to the division of capital (h). Where the latter are more powerful, individual wealth tends across generations to an equilibrium level; where the 'internal' growth of capital is larger ($s_1 > h$), individual wealth increases without limit. (The relation with the aggregate equilibrium is discussed below.)

Alternative treatments of the bequest motive

This treatment of bequests may be criticised from two different directions. First, it can be argued that the formulation in terms of the function $\phi(B)$ is *ad hoc* and that the bequest motive should be derived from more basic assumptions about preferences. Thus, $\phi(B)$ may adequately capture the utility obtained by a person concerned solely with the size of his estate (e.g. with the thought of the prospective entry in the newspaper Wills column), but it does not allow for the case where bequests are merely the instrument for achieving other objectives (e.g. increasing the welfare of the children). Meade himself [23] has formulated the problem in terms of concern for the consumption level of the children, with parents making a transfer sufficient to allow the children's consumption to attain a specified ratio of their own. Since the children's own plans will be influenced by concern for their children, this involves an indirect concern for the grandchildren, and so on to succeeding generations. More recently, Barro [5] has used a closely related model of overlapping generations, where the attainable utility of generation $(t+1)$ enters the lifetime utility function of generation t, and such interdependencies have been discussed more generally by Becker [6] and others.

The main feature introduced by this refinement of the bequest motive is that the utility derived from wealth transfers depends on the circumstances of succeeding generations. One argument commonly used in discussion of the moral justification of inherited wealth is that parents seek to make provision for children whose earning capacity is expected to be low (e.g. the disabled). Conversely, parents may feel less need to make bequests where the general level of earnings is increasing secularly. This aspect has been brought out by Shorrocks [33], who has assumed that individuals maximise the sum of lifetime utilities over the next M generations and shown that (with an isoelastic utility function and a single heir):

$$B = [1 - \omega(r, M)]Z - \omega(r, M)e^{-r}X(r, M) \tag{7}$$

where X denotes the discounted value of the expected earnings of the next M generations. The marginal propensity to consume lifetime wealth, ω, depends on the rate of return, on the time horizon (which is a measure of the degree of altruism), on taxation (not explicitly included) and on the parameters of the utility function. On the other hand, bequests are reduced by a proportion ωe^{-r} of expected future income. As Shorrocks has noted, it is quite possible for transfers to be negative, with high earning children supporting their parents in old age.

The second direction of criticism is that bequests are not in fact determined by individual utility-maximising calculus but reflect instead a combination of class expectations and chance. We may, for example, go back to the class savings model of Kaldor [18] and Pasinetti [29]. If there are fixed propensities to save out of wage and capital income, and the model is interpreted in intergenerational terms, we obtain a bequest relationship such as that in equation (4), with a different interpretation to s_1 and s_2.

We can, however, go further and argue that for those primarily dependent on wage income the bequest motive is unimportant (Atkinson [3]; Marglin [19]). To the extent that workers do leave bequests it is the result of chance; for example, in an imperfect annuity market people may leave substantial estates 'by mistake' if they die young. On the other hand, those who have inherited significant wealth are likely to have inherited at the same time 'tastes' that lead them to pass on wealth. The notion that one's inheritance should be passed on, suitably augmented, is endogenously implanted. Finally, there is a third group, namely, those who have acquired substantial wealth through 'entrepreneurship' (broadly interpreted to include, for example, those benefiting from capital gains without active business participation). The members of this group do pass on wealth, but the origin of their fortunes is not to be found in wage income. This source of new capital accumulation may indeed be seen more as the product of random chance.

In elaborating the model to take account of these different views a course has to be steered between realism and tractability. Thus, the extension of the model to include explicit intergenerational altruism along the lines of Shorrocks means that we have to consider the expected future income for M generations to come. In order to illustrate the different approaches we bring them together in a formulation that is simpler but includes elements of both intergenerational altruism and the alternative class model just outlined thus:

$$B_t = s_1(r)I_t + s_2(r)w_t - s_3(r)w_{t+1} + s_4(r)u_B \qquad (8)$$

where u_B is a stochastic variable. The model of equation (4) is the case where $s_3 = s_4 = 0$. The intergenerational altruism model is that where there is the term in s_3 (>0) looking forward to the earnings prospects of the next generation (and $s_4 = 0$). It is simpler than equation (7) in that it depends on the earned income of only the next generation; that is, $M = 1$. The class model is the special case where $s_2 = s_3 = 0$, and bequests are determined by the amount inherited and the random term, the latter including both chance bequests by wage earners and bequests made out of entrepreneurial income.

The formulation in (8) allows one to assess the impact of different views of the bequest process and how they influence the conclusions drawn regarding the effect of inheritance on the distribution of wealth. Suppose, for example, that we have the class model ($s_2 = s_3 = 0$), which is used considerably in what follows. From (8), the mean and variance of bequests are respectively given by:

$$\bar{B}_t = s_1\bar{I}_t + s_4\mu_B \qquad (9a)$$

$$\sigma_B^2(t) = s_1^2\sigma_I^2(t) + s_4^2\Sigma_B^2 \qquad (9b)$$

where $\bar{X}_t$ and $\sigma_X^2(t)$ are respectively the mean and variance of variable X at time t, and μ_B and Σ_B^2 are respectively the mean and variance of the stochastic term (which is assumed to be independent of I_t). If we now combine this with the assumption of equal division of the estate (using equation (5)), equation (91) yields:

$$\sigma_I^2(t+1) = \left(\frac{1}{h}\right)^2 \left[s_1^2\sigma_I^2(t) + s_4^2\Sigma_B^2\right] \tag{10}$$

Assuming that the variance of the stochastic term is constant over time, we can solve for the behaviour of the variance of bequests. As before, this depends on whether $s_1 \gtrless h$. If $s_1 > h$, the variance grows without limit; if $s_1 < h$, the variance of inherited wealth tends to an equilibrium level at:

$$\sigma_I^2 = \frac{(s_4/h)^2\Sigma_B^2}{1 - (s_1/h)^2} \tag{11}$$

In other words, where the internal rate of accumulation (s_1) is less than the growth of the population (h), the variance converges to a finite level, which is given by the variance of 'new' wealth $(s_4/h)^2\Sigma_B^2$, magnified by the effects of saving out of inheritance $[1 - (s_1/h)^2]^{-1}$. Where $s_1 < h$, the mean level of inherited wealth also converges to an equilibrium value, obtained by combining equation (9a) with the equal division relationship (equation (5)):

$$\bar{I} = \frac{s_4\mu_B}{h - s_1} \tag{12}$$

It follows that the equilibrium coefficient of variation, which may be taken as an indicator of *relative* inequality, is given by:

$$V_I^2 \equiv \frac{\sigma_I^2}{\bar{I}^2} = \frac{\Sigma_B^2}{\mu_B^2}\left(\frac{h - s_1}{h + s_1}\right) \tag{13}$$

Taxation and bequests
This framework may be used to examine the effects of fiscal measures to redistribute wealth. Suppose, for example, that on account of taxation the propensity to save out of stochastic income (s_4) is reduced; this could come about as a result of more effective legislation on capital gains tax, for instance. If we interpret B_t as relating to bequests net of taxation and consider the class model ($s_2 = s_3 = 0$), where the stability condition $s_1 < h$ is assumed to be satisfied, then the effect of the reduction in s_4 is to bring about a fall in the equilibrium variance of inherited wealth (see equation (11)). At the same time there is also a fall in the mean level of inherited wealth, and the coefficient of variation (equation (13)) is unchanged. Relative inequality of inherited wealth is not therefore directly affected by the reduction in s_4 in this model.

Inheritance taxation, however, may influence the different propensities (s_i) in rather different ways. The consequences of changes in s_2 and s_3 depend on the inter-relation between capital and earned income, discussed in section 4. The effects on s_1 can be seen to be particularly crucial. First, a reduction in s_1, where s_1 was previously below h, would have the apparently paradoxical effect of *increasing* the coefficient of variation. As can be seen from equation (13), V_I^2 is a *decreasing* function of s_1. For example, if the inheritance tax reduced s_1 from $\frac{1}{2}h$ to zero, the coefficient of variation would rise by a factor of 3. The reason for this is that inherited wealth, being divided at each death, tends to moderate the inequality generated by 'new' wealth.

The possibility that inheritance taxation may have the reverse effect of that intended (i.e. magnifying rather than reducing inequality) has been given prominence by some writers (e.g. Stiglitz [35]). The conclusions do, however, depend on the assumption made concerning the division of estates, and this is investigated further in section 3. In the present context we may note that, if s_1 is originally above h, the effect of inheritance taxation may be to reduce s_1 below h and hence change the qualitative behaviour of the distribution. In terms of Figure 1, we may be switched from a situation like that in Figure 1b, where inherited wealth grows without limit, to one like that in Figure 1a, where there is a stable equilibrium. In this case it *does* have the intended effect.

To this point we have simply assumed that taxation affects the net propensities to make bequests. In the case of the class savings model it is hard to go further, since the propensities are simply parameters of the model. In contrast, the utility-maximising framework allows the response to different types of taxation to be deduced. Suppose, for example, that there is a proportional tax, at rate τ, on bequests. If the Fisherian model is defined in terms of net bequests, so that $\phi(B)$ is replaced by $\phi[B(1-\tau)]$, it can be shown that, although the net bequest is always reduced, the impact on the gross bequest depends on the parameters of the utility function (see Chapter 8).

The influence of taxation also depends on the nature of the tax system, and Meade [22] has discussed the merits of different types of wealth transfer taxation. He has attached particular weight to the effect on the division of estates, and we shall turn now to a closer examination of this aspect.

3 Division of Estates and Marriage

Sons and daughters

In the analysis so far we have not considered the role played by marriage in the inheritance process. There have been no wealthy heiresses pursued by penniless adventurers or, more probably, by wealthy heirs. How far does marriage permit the consolidation of large holdings? This in turn raises the question of the division of estates between sons and daughters. Obviously, if sons (respectively, daughters) inherit everything, the pattern of marriage is not relevant.

In order to see some of the implications we begin with the case considered by Blinder [9], where each family has only two children: one boy and one girl. The population is therefore constant in size. Blinder has assumed that the total estate left by husband and wife, denoted by B_t, is divided so that the son receives a fraction λ $(0 \leqslant \lambda \leqslant 1)$. The children are all assumed to marry. The total inherited wealth of a couple in the next generation is given by:

$$I_{t+1} = \lambda B_t^h + (1-\lambda)B_t^w \tag{14}$$

where B^h and B^w denote the estates left by the husband's and wife's parents respectively. The variance of inherited wealth is therefore:

$$\sigma_I^2(t+1) = [\lambda^2 + (1-\lambda)^2]\sigma_B^2(t) + 2\lambda(1-\lambda)[\text{cov}(B_t^h, B_t^w)] \tag{15}$$

where $\text{cov}(X, Y)$ denotes the covariance. Defining ρ to be the correlation between the inheritances of husbands and wives, we have:

$$\sigma_I^2(t+1) = [\lambda^2 + (1-\lambda)^2 + 2\lambda(1-\lambda)\rho]\sigma_B^2(t) \tag{16}$$

$$= [1 - 2\lambda(1-\lambda)(1-\rho)]\sigma_B^2(t) \tag{17}$$

Blinder has in effect assumed that there is no net accumulation over a generation, so that $\sigma_B^2(t) = \sigma_I^2(t)$, and this equation then governs the development of the inherited wealth distribution over time.

From equation (17) we can see some of the factors influencing the distribution of wealth. No equalisation takes place where $\lambda = 1$ (i.e. all wealth goes to sons) or $\lambda = 0$ (i.e. all wealth goes to daughters). It estates are divided $(0 < \lambda < 1)$, the variance will decline (since the square bracket in (17) is less than 1) where $\rho > 1$. Put another way, assortative marriage $(\rho > 0)$ tends to offset the effects of the division of estates, and where $\rho = 1$ this offset is complete, the variance remaining unchanged across generations. This last case is that of 'class' marriage and is equivalent, in this respect, to everyone's marrying his/her own sister/brother.

The influence of wealth transfer taxation via the division of estates may be seen from equation (17). If the structure of taxation is such as to induce a less unequal division between sons and daughters, and if $\rho < 1$, the decline of the variance of inherited wealth is faster. (The term $\lambda(1-\lambda)$ reaches a maximum where estates are equally divided.) The division may also be affected by other instruments of government policy, including legislation, as with the law of *legitim*, where division of the estate is statutorily prescribed. Moreover, it is conceivable that the degree of assortative marriage may itself be influenced by policy. Meade [26] has noted, for example, the possible link with education reform:

A system of higher education which was less structured according to social class would tend to bring boys and girls together according to their intellectual ability ... Only the able children of gentlefolk would get to the university where, for the first time, they would meet the selected able children of the working class. (p. 167)

(This would also have implications for the correlation of earned incomes.)

Unequal division
The treatment by Blinder illustrates clearly the interaction between the pattern

of marriage and the division of estates between sons and daughters, but his analysis is limited in that he has considered only a static population. Since each family has only one son or daughter, it is not possible to explore the consequence of unequal division of property between children of the same sex. There is, for instance, no difference in his model between primogeniture and equal division among sons. (An early analysis of the consequences of unequal division is that in Champernowne [12].)

Suppose first that we consider the case of equal division among sons ($\lambda = 1$), where the pattern of marriage is irrelevant. With a stationary population and no net saving ($B_t = I_t$) the variance and the mean of lifetime wealth are unchanged across generations. If we now modify this by allowing each family to have h (>1) sons, the variance of total (family) inherited wealth is:

$$\sigma^2(t+1) = \left(\frac{1}{h}\right)^2 \sigma_B^2(t) = \left(\frac{1}{h}\right)^2 \sigma_I^2(t) \tag{18a}$$

and:

$$\bar{I}_{t+1} = \frac{\bar{I}_t}{h} \tag{18b}$$

It follows that the coefficient of variation is unchanged across generations, since both mean and standard deviation are reduced by a factor $1/h$. In this sense population growth makes no difference.

Suppose now that we consider primogeniture, where this is interpreted to mean that all property is left to the eldest son. Where $h = 1$, the outcome is the same; that is, the coefficient of variation is constant across generations. However, where $h > 1$, there are penniless younger children. The variance of inherited wealth is then given by:

$$\sigma_I^2(t+1) = \left[\sum_i (I_{t+1}^i - \bar{I}_{t+1})^2 + (h-1)P_t \bar{I}_{t+1}^2 \right] \frac{1}{P_{t+1}} \tag{19}$$

where P_t is the number of males in the generation and I_{t+1}^i is the inherited wealth of the eldest sons. The first term in this expression is the sum over those in generation $(t+1)$ who have inherited (P_t in all); the second is the contribution to the variance of the younger sons. (Again, we are concerned with family wealth, so that husbands and wives are treated as a single unit.) The right-hand side of (19) can be rearranged thus:

$$\sigma_I^2(t+1) = \left\{ \sum_i [(I_{t+1}^i - \bar{I}_t) + \bar{I}_t - \bar{I}_{t+1}]^2 \right\} \frac{1}{P_{t+1}} + \left(\frac{h-1}{h}\right)\bar{I}_{t+1}^2 \tag{20}$$

Since I_{t+1}^i is distributed in the same way as I_t^i and:

$$\bar{I}_{t+1} = \frac{\bar{I}_t}{h} \qquad P_{t+1} = hP_t \tag{21}$$

we can derive:

$$u_I^2(t+1) - \frac{1}{h}\sigma_I^2(t) + (h-1)\bar{I}_{t+1}^2,\qquad(??)$$

The behaviour of the coefficient of variation is given by:

$$V_I^2(t+1)=\frac{\sigma_I^2(t+1)}{\bar{I}_{t+1}^2}=hV_I^2(t)+(h-1)\qquad(23)$$

If $h>1$, the coefficient of variation grows without limit. Without the damping influence of new accumulation of wealth, primogeniture leads to ever-increasing relative inequality (Atkinson [2]; Meade [24]).

Primogeniture may also be interpreted as meaning that the property is left to the eldest child, whether boy or girl. In order to see the implications let us suppose that in θ cases a son inherits and in $(1-\theta)$ a daughter. If the distribution of wealth is identical in both cases, then by an argument analogous to that in the previous paragraph we can write the variances of wealth inherited by sons (I^s) and daughters (I^d) respectively as:

$$\sigma_s^2(t+1)=\theta\left(\frac{1}{h}\sigma_I^2(t)+(h-\theta)\bar{I}_{t+1}^2\right)\qquad(24a)$$

$$\sigma_d^2(t+1)=(1-\theta)\left(\frac{1}{h}\sigma_I^2(t)+(h-1+\theta)\bar{I}_{t+1}^2\right)\qquad(24b)$$

Let us denote by ρ the correlation between the inherited wealth of sons and daughters. (We ignore the complications caused by the fact that brothers and sisters cannot marry.) The variance of (I^s+I^d) is then:

$$\sigma_I^2(t+1)=\sigma_s^2(t+1)+\sigma_d^2(t+1)+2\rho\sqrt{[\sigma_s^2(t+1)\sigma_d^2(t+1)]}\qquad(25)$$

In the special case where $\theta=\frac{1}{2}$, the variances of I^s and I^d are equal, and the coefficient of variation may be written:

$$V_I^2(t+1)=h(1+\rho)V_I^2(t)+(h-\tfrac{1}{2})(1+\rho)\qquad(26)$$

If $\rho>0$, then, even where $h=1$, the coefficient of variation is increasing over time; the speed of divergence depends on the pattern of marriage and can be rapid where ρ is close to 1. Where $h=2.0$ and $\rho=1$, the sequence of values for V_I^2 in successive generations is 1.0, 2.6, 5.6, which may be compared with 1.0, 1.7, 2.6 in the case where primogeniture means inheritance by the eldest son (from equation (23)). (It may be noted that the permissible range of values taken by ρ depends on the structure of wealth-holding, it being bounded below by the case where no heirs marry heiresses, which gives the previous results.)

Table 1   *Interaction of pattern of bequests, marriage and population growth*

Pattern of bequests	With class marriage ($\rho=1$) and constant population ($h=1$)	Implications of marriage and population growth
Property left to all sons (or all daughters)	Constant coefficient of variation	Population growth and marriage make no difference
Property left to eldest son (or eldest daughter)	Constant coefficient of variation	Marriage makes no difference. With population growth ($h>1$) the coefficient of variation increases over time
Property left to eldest child (whether son or daughter)	Coefficient of variation increasing over time	Speed of divergence increases with population growth and is lower where some degree of randomness in marriage exists ($0 \leqslant \rho < 1$)

These results, summarised in Table 1, bring out once more the inter-dependence of different mechanisms. The impact of changes in one social institution, such as the division of bequests, depends on other features of the process, such as the marriage pattern and the family size. We can clearly go further in the direction of incorporating further inter-relations. We have, for example, assumed that family size is uniform, whereas differential fertility may be a significant factor. We have not allowed for the facts that the sex of children is stochastic and that some people do not marry. However, rather than pursue these aspects here we shall turn to examine the relationship between the division of estates and the accumulation of wealth, as discussed in section 2.

Accumulation and the pattern of bequests
In the Blinder model, and its generalisation in the preceding section, there is assumed to be no net accumulation. The relationship between the rate of accumulation and the pattern of bequests is, however, a further example of the interdependence between different mechanisms. In order to see this let us replace the assumption that $B_t^i = I_t^i$ by the class savings relationship:

$$B_t^i = s_1 I_t^i + s_4 u_B^i \qquad (27)$$

Suppose that estates are divided into λB_t^i, shared equally by h sons, and $(1-\lambda)B_{t+1}^i$, shared equally by h daughters. Where all children marry, the wealth inherited by a couple in the next generation is:

$$I_{t+1}^i = [\lambda B_t^h + (1-\lambda)B_t^w]\frac{1}{h} \qquad (28)$$

This is of the same form as equation (14) except for the factor h. Combining (27) and (28), the mean inherited wealth is governed by:

$$\bar{I}_{t+1} = \frac{\bar{u}_t}{h} = \frac{s_1}{h} I_t + \frac{s_4}{h} \mu_B \tag{29}$$

where μ_B is the mean of u_B. As before, the condition for stability is that $s_1 < h$. If that is satisfied, mean inherited wealth tends to an equilibrium value at:

$$\bar{I} = \frac{s_4 \mu_B}{h - s_1} \tag{30}$$

The variance of inherited wealth is governed as before by (parallel to equation (17)):

$$\sigma_I^2(t+1) = [1 - 2\lambda(1-\lambda)(1-\rho)]\sigma_B^2(t)\frac{1}{h^2} \equiv \alpha\sigma_B^2(t)\frac{1}{h^2} \tag{31}$$

Using (27), we get:

$$\sigma_I^2(t+1) = \alpha\left[\left(\frac{s_1}{h}\right)^2\sigma_I^2(t) + \left(\frac{s_4}{h}\right)^2\Sigma_B^2\right] \tag{32}$$

where u_B is assumed to be independent of I. If the stability condition $s_1 < h$ is satisfied, the variance converges to:

$$\sigma_I^2 = \frac{s_4^2\Sigma_B^2}{(h^2/\alpha) - s_1^2} \tag{33}$$

and the equilibrium coefficient of variation is:

$$V_I^2 = \frac{\Sigma_B^2}{\mu_B^2}\left(\frac{(h-s_1)^2}{(h^2/\alpha) - s_1^2}\right) \tag{34}$$

In this model, where the stability condition holds, the equilibrium level of concentration of inherited wealth depends on the inequality in the stochastic term (the first term in (34) is the square of the coefficient of variation of u_B) modified by the effects of inheritance. As before, the impact of random marriage ($\rho < 1$) is to reduce α where $\lambda(1-\lambda) > 0$. A lesser degree of assortative marriage works to reduce concentration. Where $\alpha = 1$, the level of concentration is the same as that found in section 2 (see equation 13)). As there, the coefficient of variation is a declining function of s_1, and an inheritance tax that reduces s_1 will have the effect of increasing relative inequality. This finding, which holds true for all α ($0 < \alpha \leqslant 1$), depends on the stability condition's being satisfied (the internal rate of accumulation being less than the rate of population growth) and on the distribution's being sufficiently close to the equilibrium for the steady state properties to be relevant. (On this, see Shorrocks [32].)

The conclusions reached concerning the impact of inheritance taxation may, however, be highly sensitive to the assumptions about the pattern of bequest. To demonstrate this, let us take the extreme case of primogeniture, where all wealth is left to the eldest son. The behaviour of $\bar{I}_t$ is unaffected, but:

$$\sigma_I^2(t+1) = \frac{1}{h}\sigma_B^2(t) + (h-1)\bar{I}_{t+1}^2 \tag{35}$$

(Cf. equation (22).) Using (27), we get:

$$\sigma_I^2(t+1) = \frac{s_1^2}{h}\sigma_I^2(t) + \frac{s_4^2}{h}\Sigma_B^2 + (h-1)\bar{I}_{t+1}^2 \tag{36}$$

Where $s_1 > 1$, the condition $s_1 < h$ is no longer sufficient to ensure convergence of the second moment. For this we require $s_1^2 < h$. If this holds, then in steady state:

$$\sigma_I^2 = \left[\frac{s_4^2}{h}\Sigma_B^2 + \left(\frac{(h-1)s_4^2}{(h-s_1)^2}\right)\mu_B^2\right]\frac{1}{1-(s_1^2/h)} \tag{37}$$

Using (30), the coefficient of variation is given by:

$$V_I^2 = \frac{h(h-1)}{h-s_1^2} + \frac{\Sigma_B^2}{\mu_B^2}\left(\frac{(h-s_1)^2}{h-s_1^2}\right) \tag{38}$$

Comparing this with equation (34), we can see that, if h were equal to unity, the coefficient of variation would be the same as in equation (34) with $\alpha = 1$. The consequences of primogeniture are that h^2 is replaced by h in the denominator of the second term and that the first term is now positive. We may contrast the result with that obtained where there is no net accumulation. In that situation the mean inherited wealth falls with the rising population, and the *relative* position of the wealthy improves, so that the coefficient of variation increases over time (see equation (23)). Here there is new accumulation, which, where $s_1^2 < h$, dampens the effect of primogeniture.

With primogeniture the effect of an inheritance tax may be quite different. In equation (38) the first term is unambiguously increasing in s_1, and the second term is increasing where $s_1 > 1$. An inheritance tax that reduces s_1 will definitely reduce the coefficient of variation where $s_1 > 1$. Policy will work in the expected direction. Moreover, it is quite possible that the variance does not converge to an equilibrium value. Suppose that $s_1 < h < s_1^2$, so that the mean inheritance converges but the variances does not. Taking $\bar{I}_t = \bar{I}_{t+1} = \bar{I}$, the coefficient of variation is governed by:

$$V_I^2(t+1) = \frac{s_1^2}{h} V_I^2(t) + \frac{\Sigma_B^2}{\mu_B^2}\left(\frac{(h-s_1)^2}{h}\right) + (h-1) \qquad (39)$$

The variance grows without limit, and a rise in s_1 speeds the rate of increase where:

$$V_I^2 > \left(\frac{h}{s_1} - 1\right)\frac{\Sigma_B^2}{\mu_B^2} \qquad (40)$$

In other words, beyond a certain point an inheritance tax that reduces s_1 will slow down the rate of increase in inequality.

A numerical example

A simple numerical example may help to pull together the threads of this discussion. As we have seen, there are several different factors at work, and it is their interaction that influences the development of inherited wealth across generations.

The first consideration is how wealth is divided between sons and daughters (λ) and how this wealth is then recombined through marriage (ρ). These two parameters together determine α. For purposes of illustration we take three values. The first assumes equal division between sons and daughters ($\lambda = \frac{1}{2}$) and random marriage ($\rho = 0$), so that $\alpha = \frac{1}{2}$; in this case the pattern is that most favourable to the division of estates, and there is no offsetting assortative marriage. The second case assumes that sons receive the lion's share ($\lambda = \frac{3}{4}$) and that there is a correlation ($\rho = \frac{2}{3}$); this means that $\alpha = \frac{7}{8}$ and that the equalising forces are considerably less strong. The third case is the extreme one where $\alpha = 1.0$.

The second consideration is how wealth is divided among sons or daughters. We consider two cases: equal division and primogeniture (to the eldest son). In this context the family size h is relevant, since with $h = 1$ there is no difference between equal division among sons and primogeniture (eldest son). We assume that $h = 2.0$, which with a generation of thirty years implies a population growth rate of 2.3% per annum.

The third set of factors are those governing accumulation. Here we have assumed the class savings model ($s_2 = s_3 = 0$). In this context the key role is played by the internal rate of accumulation (s_1). We assume in the example that the stability condition $s_1 < h$ is satisfied, but we take a range of values $1 \leqslant s_1 < h$.

The numerical example is given in Table 2, which shows the equilibrium value of the coefficient of variation of inherited wealth (squared). The value of Σ_B^2/μ_B^2 is taken as 4.0. If the distribution were log-normal, this would imply that the top percentile of u_B was some twenty times the median. The first three lines in the table are calculated from equation (34), the fourth line from equation (38). The differing values of s_1 indicate what may be achieved by inheritance taxation. The results bring out quite clearly how the conclusions drawn for policy depend on the assumptions of the model. Where there is equal division,

Table 2 *Numerical example: rate of accumulation, pattern of bequests and equilibrium value of coefficient of variation of inherited wealth (squared)*

Pattern of bequests	Rate of accumulation (s_1)				
	1.0	1.2	1.4	1.6	1.8
Equal division (among sons and daughters respectively):					
$\alpha = \frac{1}{2}$	0.57	0.39	0.24	0.12	0.03
$\alpha = \frac{7}{8}$	1.12	0.82	0.55	0.32	0.12
$\alpha = 1$	1.33	1.00	0.71	0.44	0.21
Primogeniture (eldest son)	6.00	8.14	86.00	Does not converge to finite value	

Note: $h = 2.0$, $\Sigma_B^2 / \mu_B^2 = 4.0$.

an inheritance tax that reduces s_1 from, say, 1.4 to 1.2 leads to an increase in the steady state coefficient of variation. Where there is unequal division (the extreme being that of primogeniture, as shown in the table), the tax leads to a substantial reduction in the coefficient of variation. Put another way, policy measures that influence the *pattern* of bequests may lead to a qualitative change in behaviour.

4 Bequests in a Broader Framework

The discussion so far has concentrated on individual bequest behaviour without considering the wider context and the possible interactions with the economic system. In this section we shall consider in turn a general equilibrium formulation and the inter-relation between earned and unearned incomes. Both of these may significantly affect the conclusions drawn. In the previous sections we have noted that the condition for the convergence of mean wealth is related to the general equilibrium of the economy as a whole. We shall next discuss the connection between the stability condition ($s_1 < h$) and the behaviour of aggregate economy. We have also discussed policy measures on the assumption that they do not affect earned incomes; it is possible, however, that parents make transfers in the form of increased earning power. A tax on the transmission of material capital may lead to increased transfers via human capital. This aspect is discussed below.

General equilibrium of the economy
Much of the analysis of bequest behaviour has, like the preceding sections, been explicitly partial equilibrium in nature, taking the rate of interest and the wage rate as fixed exogenously (and typically constant). The accumulation of capital for bequest purposes may influence the rate of return, however, and this general equilibrium effect needs to be taken into account. On the other hand, the construction of a full-scale general-equilibrium model involves a great deal of complexity. For this reason a number of writers (e.g. Stiglitz [34]; Conlisk

[13]) have adopted a more limited approach. This is based on the assumption that the microrelationships are linear in the variables that differ across individuals, so that the aggregate behaviour is determined independently of the distribution. Thus, shifts in bequests may affect r and w, but only through their effect on mean capital. This approach is restrictive and does not allow for any feedback from the distribution to factor returns; on the other hand, it allows the model to be solved recursively. One first calculates w and r, as determined by the aggregate variables, and then uses these values when solving for the distribution. This means that one can introduce at least one aspect of the general equilibrium effects into the distributional model, and as such it represents a definite step forward.

To illustrate the approach we take the savings model of equation (8) with $s_3 = 0$ (i.e. without the forward-looking element). We assume that in generation t output per person (Y_t) is a function of mean inherited capital per person ($\bar{I}_t$), that is:

$$Y_t = f(\bar{I}_t) \tag{41}$$

where $f' > 0$, $f'' < 0$, $f(0) = 0$, $f'(0) = \infty$ and $f'(\infty) = 0$. Given that the population grows by a factor h in each generation, the behaviour of $\bar{I}_t$ is governed by:

$$\bar{I}_{t+1} = \frac{\bar{B}_t}{h} = (s_1 \bar{I}_t + s_2 \bar{w}_t + s_4 \mu_B) \frac{1}{h} \tag{42}$$

Suppose first that:

$$s_1 = 1 + s_2 r$$

where s_2 is constant and r is the rate of return per generation ($\bar{w}_t$ being interpreted similarly), and that $s_4 = s_2$. Equation (42) can then be rewritten:

$$\bar{I}_{t+1} - \bar{I}_t = \frac{s_2}{h}(r\bar{I}_t + \bar{w}_t + \mu_B) - \left(\frac{h-1}{h}\right)\bar{I}_t$$

$$= \frac{s_2}{h} f(\bar{I}_t) - \left(\frac{h-1}{h}\right)\bar{I}_t \tag{43}$$

(The payments to capital, labour and 'entrepreneurship', via u_B, are assumed to add up to total output.)

Assuming that $h > 1$, we may depict the aggregate equilibrium in this case as in Figure 2. Given the assumptions about the production function, there is a unique steady state at point P, and it is globally stable. If $\bar{I}_t$ is strictly less than $\bar{I}^*$, then $\bar{I}_{t+1} > \bar{I}_t$; conversely, if $\bar{I}_t$ is strictly greater than $\bar{I}^*$, then $\bar{I}_{t+1} < \bar{I}_t$. Point P is the standard Solow equilibrium of neoclassical growth theory, since

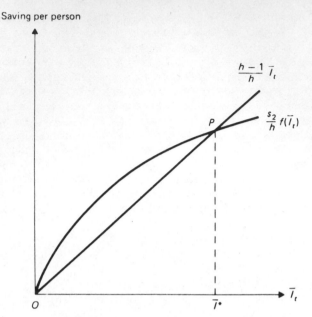

Figure 2   *Aggregate equilibrium.*

with proportional savings we have $s_2 f = (h-1)\bar{I}_t$, where $(h-1)$ is the growth in the population. It has, however, implications for the distribution of wealth. From the definition of s_1, in steady state:

$$s_1 \bar{I} = (1 + s_2 r)\bar{I}$$
$$= \bar{I} + s_2[f(\bar{I}) - \bar{w} - \mu_B]$$
$$= h\bar{I} - s_2(\bar{w} + \mu_B) \tag{44}$$

where the last step uses the steady state condition $s_2 f = (h-1)\bar{I}$. It follows that in steady state $s_1 < h$. The stability condition assumed earlier is an implication of the aggregate steady state. (This result has been given in a continuous time model by Stiglitz [34], although it should be noted that here we have not assumed perfect competition.)

This aggregate analysis shows how the determination of $(\bar{w} + \mu_B)$ and r may be made endogenous to the model and how the aggregate properties may have implications for the distribution. At the same time the assumptions are strong and need to be relaxed. For example, we need to explore the consequences of non-proportional savings, as with the class savings model, and we need to allow for the dependence of s_1, s_2 and s_4 on the rate of return. The introduction of these considerations can change the conclusions drawn regarding the stability condition.

Special reference should be made to the relationship between current aggregate variables and the lifetime wealth that has been the focus of the distributional model. In the treatment so far we have equated $\bar{I}_t$ with the capital available for production, but this ignores the contribution of life-cycle savings. If we consider a continuous lifetime process embedded within the discrete generational model, as we have indeed done in section 2, the 'average' capital relevant to the aggregate analysis is not the same as average inherited wealth. (This aspect has been discussed by Conlisk [13].) It means in particular that there is not necessarily a direct link between the conditions for the convergence of aggregate capital and the behaviour of inherited wealth.

Inheritance and earnings
The discussion so far has concentrated on the transmission of material wealth, but parents may also provide advantages to their children through enhanced earnings potential. This includes the provision of private schooling, the financing of higher education, the role of 'contacts' and of the parental social network in securing entry to jobs, nepotism and selective recruiting. The role of the parents in financing education, for example, and its relation to financial transfers have been examined in a life-cycle context by Ishikawa [17]. Such mechanisms may be important in the persistence of economic status from generation to generation, and inheritance taxation is itself likely to provide an incentive for transmission to take the form of human rather than non-human capital.

Some of the different factors at work are brought out here in a simple recursive model for the determination of earnings (as used, for example, by Bowles and Nelson [10]). This is depicted in Figure 3 and set out algebraically below. Person i in generation t starts life with a genetic endowment of ability

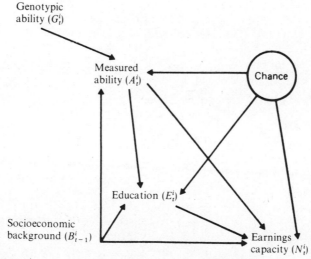

Figure 3 *Influences on earnings.*

(G_t^i) and family background, represented by the bequest level (B_{t-1}^i). The joint influence of these factors is reflected first in measured ability (A_t^i). (In the case of IQ the contribution of the two factors is, of course, highly controversial.) This affects, together with family background, access to education (E_t^i); and education, measured ability and family background in turn are assumed to determine earnings capacity (N_t^i). In addition, at each stage there is an additive stochastic component (i.e. 'chance'). This may be set out algebraically as follows:

$$G_t^i = gG_{t-1}^i + u_G^i \tag{45a}$$

$$A_t^i = a_1 G_t^i + a_2(B_{t-1}^i - \bar{B}_{t-1}) + u_A^i \tag{45b}$$

$$E_t^i = a_3 A_t^i + a_4(B_{t-1}^i - \bar{B}_{t-1}) + u_E^i \tag{45c}$$

$$N_t^i = a_5 A_t^i + a_6(B_{t-1}^i - \bar{B}_{t-1}) + a_7 E_t^i + \bar{u}_N^i \tag{45d}$$

(The impact of family background is defined as advantage relative to the mean.) From the last three equations we can obtain the reduced form:

$$N_t^i = (a_5 + a_3 a_7)a_1 G_t^i + [a_6 + a_4 a_7 + a_2(a_5 + a_3 a_7)]$$
$$\times (B_{t-1}^i - \bar{B}_{t-1}) + \tilde{u}_N^i + a_7 u_E^i + (a_5 + a_3 a_7)u_A^i$$
$$\equiv cG_t^i + b(B_{t-1}^i - \bar{B}_{t-1}) + u_N^i \tag{46}$$

so that earnings are governed by equations (45a) and (46), where the coefficients c and b reflect both direct and indirect effects, the latter being those via measured ability and education.

In order to illustrate the inter-relation between earned incomes and inherited wealth, let us assume that all property is held by men (alternatively, all held by women) and that men (alternatively, women) are the only earners. Moreover, let us take the class accumulation relationship:

$$B_t^i = s_1 I_t^i + s_4 u_B^i \tag{27}$$

If, in addition, estates are equally divided, then:

$$I_t^i = \frac{B_{t-1}^i}{h} \tag{47}$$

We can therefore summarise the model in terms of the stochastic difference equations thus:

$$G_t^i = gG_{t-1}^i + u_G^i \tag{45a}$$

$$B_t^i = \frac{s_1}{h} B_{t-1}^i + s_4 u_B^i \tag{48}$$

$$N_t^i = cG_t^i + b(B_{t-1}^i - \bar{B}_{t-1}) + u_N^i \tag{46}$$

From these cumulative we can derive the time path of lifetime income, which we take here to be defined as:

$$Y_t^i = wN_t^i + rI_t^i + u_B^i \tag{49}$$

Finally, we need to specify the assumptions concerning the random vector (u_G^i, u_N^i, u_B^i). This is assumed to be distributed independently of the state variables and to have mean and diagonal variance-covariance matrix that are constant over time and across individuals. The vector is assumed to be independent over individuals i and across generations. It is also assumed that the population is sufficiently large that we can replace sample moments by the corresponding population moments, in this way moving from a stochastic to a distributional model (Atkinson and Harrison [4], ch. 8).

For simplicity we assume that the factor prices (w and r) are constant (i.e. that the economy is in aggregate equilibrium). We then characterise the behaviour of the distribution in terms of the first and second moments, where the former satisfy the following equations:

$$\bar{G}_t = g\bar{G}_{t-1} + \mu_G \tag{50a}$$

$$\bar{B}_t = \frac{s_1}{h}\bar{B}_{t-1} + s_4\mu_B \tag{50b}$$

$$\bar{N}_t = c\bar{G}_t + \mu_N \tag{50c}$$

where μ_X denotes the mean of u_X^i. It is assumed that $0 \leqslant g < 1$, which ensures the convergence of $\bar{G}_t$ and hence $\bar{N}_t$. The stability condition $s_1 < h$ ensures the convergence of $\bar{B}_t$. The variances (σ_X^2) and covariances (σ_{XY}) are governed by:

$$\sigma_G^2(t) = g^2\sigma_G^2(t-1) + \Sigma_G^2 \tag{51a}$$

$$\sigma_B^2(t) = \left(\frac{s_1}{h}\right)^2 \sigma_B^2(t-1) + s_4^2\Sigma_B^2 \tag{51b}$$

$$\sigma_N^2(t) = c^2\sigma_G^2(t) + b^2\sigma_B^2(t-1) + \Sigma_N^2 + 2bcg\sigma_{BG}(t-1) \tag{51c}$$

$$\sigma_{BG}(t) = \frac{gs_1}{h}\sigma_{BG}(t-1) \tag{51d}$$

$$\sigma_{GN}(t) = c\sigma_G^2(t) + bg\sigma_{BG}(t-1) \tag{51e}$$

$$\sigma_{BN}(t) = c\sigma_{BG}(t) + \frac{bs_1}{h}\sigma_B^2(t-1) \tag{51f}$$

Note that in obtaining some of these results we have substituted for G_t^i in equation (46) and that equation (51b) is obtained from equation (32) with $\alpha = 1.0$. The earlier assumptions ensure convergence to the following steady-state values:

$$\sigma_G^2 = \frac{\Sigma_G^2}{1-g^2} \tag{52a}$$

$$\sigma_B^2 = \frac{s_4^2 \Sigma_B^2}{1-(s_1/h)^2} \tag{52b}$$

$$\sigma_{BG} = 0 \tag{52c}$$

$$\sigma_{GN} = c\sigma_G^2 \tag{52d}$$

$$\sigma_{BN} = \frac{bs_1}{h}\sigma_B^2 \tag{52e}$$

$$\sigma_N^2 = c^2\sigma_G^2 + \Sigma_N^2 + b^2\sigma_B^2 \tag{52f}$$

and we may deduce that the steady-state variance of lifetime income is:

$$\sigma_Y^2 = w^2\sigma_N^2 + \left(\frac{r}{h}\right)^2\left(1+\frac{2bs_1w}{r}\right)\sigma_B^2 + \Sigma_B^2 \tag{53}$$

$$= w^2(c^2\sigma_G^2 + \Sigma_N^2) +$$

$$\Sigma_B^2\left(1+\frac{(s_4/h)^2}{1-(s_1/h)^2}(b^2h^2w^2 + 2bws_1r + r^2)\right) \tag{54}$$

This model provides a framework within which one can analyse the implications of changes in policy parameters. Consider first the impact of a capital gains tax that reduces saving out of 'entrepreneurial' income (i.e. s_4 is reduced). From equation (54) we may see how this reduces the variance of lifetime income. The effect depends on the return to capital and the interaction with earned income via the parameter b, which captures the effect of family background on earnings. It is also magnified by the factor $1/[1-(s_1/h)^2]$, which represents the effects of inheritance. (Note that we are considering here the variance, not the coefficient of variation). Similarly, we can see the impact of an inheritance tax that works to reduce s_1. Again, this interacts with the family background effect.

Moreover, we can see how the effect may be reversed if parents switch their transfers from material to human capital, so that s_1 falls but b rises. To take an extreme case, suppose (1) that before the introduction of the tax there is no family background effect ($b=0$), and (2) that the effect of the tax is to eliminate accumulation out of inherited wealth ($s_1=0$) but for parents to make transfers of human capital ($b>0$). From equation (54) we can see that the condition for the variance of lifetime wealth to decline is:

$$\frac{r^2}{1-(s_1/h)^2} > r^2 + b^2h^2w^2 \tag{55}$$

This may be rearranged as:

$$\frac{s_1^2/h^2}{1-(s_1/h)^a} \gtrless \frac{b^2 w^2}{(r/h)^2} - ?$$

(56)

The right-hand side has the following interpretation. The increment in lifetime wealth per £1 of B_{t-1} via earnings is bw; the increment via inheritance is r/h. The value of γ is therefore greater (less) than unity as the earnings (inheritance) effect is larger. If, for example, they are equally matched, the variance of lifetime income is decreased where the saving out of inherited wealth is greater than $\sqrt{\frac{1}{2}h}$.

A numerical example

As in the preceding section, a numerical example may be helpful. For this purpose we take over the earlier assumptions that $h=2.0$ and $\Sigma_B^2/\mu_B^2=4.0$. Moreover, it is assumed that the aggregate production and distribution relations are such that the shares of wages, capital and entrepreneurial income are constant and equal to 0.7, 0.2 and 0.1 respectively.

Dividing equation (53) by $\bar{Y}^2$, the coefficient of variation of lifetime income in steady state is given by:

$$V_Y^2=\left(\frac{w\bar{N}}{\bar{Y}}\right)^2 V_N^2+\left(\frac{r\bar{I}}{\bar{Y}}\right)^2\left(1+\frac{2s_1}{h}\gamma\right)V_B^2+\left(\frac{\mu_B}{\bar{Y}}\right)^2\frac{\Sigma_B^2}{\mu_B^2}$$

(57)

where (using the definition of γ):

$$V_N^2=\frac{c^2\sigma_G^2+\Sigma_N^2}{\bar{N}^2}+\gamma^2\left(\frac{r\bar{I}}{w\bar{N}}\right)V_B^2$$

(58)

The term $(c^2\sigma_G^2+\Sigma_N^2)/\bar{N}^2$ is the value taken by the coefficient of variation (squared) if there is no family background effect. Let us assume that this is 0.15, which means, with a log–normal distribution of earnings, that the Gini coefficient is around 0.2. Using (50b), we get:

$$V_B^2=\frac{\Sigma_B^2}{\mu_B^2}\left(\frac{h-s_1}{h+s_1}\right)$$

(59)

This corresponds to equation (34), with $\alpha=1$, and we can read off the values of V_B from the line $\alpha=1$ in Table 2.

Table 3 shows the results obtained from different values of s_1 and γ. These may be taken as representing the possible influence of inheritance taxation, namely reducing s_1 and increasing b (which enters γ). Suppose, for example, that $s_1=1.6$, so that $V_B^2=0.44$. If $\gamma=0.8$, this means that $V_N^2=0.17$ (using the value of $r\bar{I}/w\bar{N}=0.2/0.7$). Substituting in turn into V_Y^2, we obtain a value of:

Table 3   *Coefficient of variation (squared) of lifetime income (V_y^2), the rate of accumulation, and the inter-relation with earned incomes*

	Rate of accumulation (s_1)				
	1.0	1.2	1.4	1.6	1.8
$\gamma=0.5$					
V_B^2	1.33	1.00	0.71	0.44	0.21
V_N^2	0.18	0.17	0.16	0.16	0.15
V_y^2	0.21	0.19	0.17	0.15	0.13
$\gamma=0.8$					
V_B^2	1.33	1.00	0.71	0.44	0.21
V_N^2	0.22	0.20	0.19	0.17	0.16
V_y^2	0.24	0.22	0.19	0.16	0.14
$\gamma=1.0$					
V_B^2	1.33	1.00	0.71	0.44	0.21
V_N^2	0.26	0.23	0.21	0.19	0.17
V_y^2	0.27	0.24	0.21	0.18	0.15

Note: $h=2.0$, $\Sigma_B^2/\mu_B^2=4.0$.

$$(0.7)^2(0.17)+(0.2)^2[1+(1.6)(0.8)](0.44)+(0.1)^2(4.0)=0.16$$

This calculation and those given in the table provide some indication of the sensitivity to the parameters, although it must be borne in mind that they relate to one special set of assumptions about the accumulation relationship (class savings), about the division of estates (equal division among sons) and about the sources of earnings (only men work).

Concluding Comments

One of the principal points of this chapter has been to bring out the inter-relation between different factors influencing the distribution of wealth. The influence of marriage patterns depends on how estates are divided; the impact of the division of estates depends on the process of accumulation; the conditions of aggregate equilibrium have implications for the behaviour of the distribution; the inheritance of wealth may facilitate the enhancement of earnings potential; the accumulation of capital may in turn depend on earnings and expected earnings in the next generation. In view of this it is clear that one should be cautious in drawing conclusions about the impact of policy instruments without a complete model of the distribution.

Some of the building blocks for such a complete model have been examined in this chapter. In section 2 a formulation of the bequest relationship (equation (8)) that allows for several different interpretations of the motives for passing on wealth to the next generation has been given. Section 3 has discussed different patterns of inheritance, allowing for variation in the division of estates and for the role of marriage. The model can be put in a general equilibrium context along the lines described in section 4, with the distinction being drawn between lifetime and current wealth. The determinants of earnings can be introduced via the recursive structure, described above.

At the same time a great deal remains to be done. First, each of these building blocks can at best be described as a stylisation, and individual elements of the model are in need of considerable development. For example, there is the nexus of family decisions concerning fertility and the allocation of resources to children (whether child care, education or inheritance). The work of Becker and others on child 'quality' and intergenerational transmission (see, for example, Becker and Lewis [7]; Becker and Tomes [8]) rests on strong assumptions about family behaviour but raises important questions about the advantage derived from family background and interfamily allocation. To take another example, we have not modelled explicitly the risk-taking behaviour that lies behind the accumulation of wealth (see, for example, Stiglitz [35]; Pestieau and Possen [30]).

Secondly, the assembly of the blocks is not necessarily an easy operation. What we are doing may be seen as formalising relationships typically presented in words (or in ingenious diagrams such as Meade's [24], p. 8). This formalisation has the merit that one can characterise the equilibrium of the process and examine the dynamic development of the distribution. The balance between equalising and disequalising factors can be assessed and comparative static properties derived. However, these advantages can typically only be realised at the cost of considerable simplification. Analytical tractability can often involve sacrificing some of the richness of the analysis. Simulation methods (as in Pryor [31]) appear to be an attractive alternative, but interpretation of the results may nonetheless require considerable understanding of the analytical structure.

Finally, the empirical implementation of the model poses serious problems. Certain relationships have been extensively examined, such as the links between earnings, education and ability (see, for example, Griliches [14]), but even here there remains controversy (e.g. about the effect of parental wealth, i.e. the coefficient b). In other areas, such as that of bequest behaviour, the evidence is much more fragmentary. (For the United Kingdom, see Harbury and Hitchens [15]. For the United States, see Brittain [11], Menchik [28].) While it may be possible to make plausible guesses about the likely ranges of coefficients, the micro-econometrics of the distribution of income and wealth is an underdeveloped field.

References

[1] Atkinson, A. B. (1971), 'Capital taxes, the redistribution of wealth and individual savings', Chapter 8 in this volume.

[2] Atkinson, A. B. (1972), *Unequal Shares*, London, Allen Lane.

[3] Atkinson, A. B. (1974), 'A model of the distribution of wealth', MIT Discussion Paper.

[4] Atkinson, A. B. and Harrison, A. J. (1978), *Distribution of Personal Wealth in Britain*, Cambridge, Cambridge University Press.

[5] Barro, R. J. (1974), 'Are government bonds net wealth?', *Journal of Political Economy*, vol. 82, pp. 1095–118.

[6] Becker, G. S. (1974). 'A theory of social interactions', *Journal of Political Economy*, vol. 82, pp. 1063–94.

[7] Becker, G. S. and Lewis, H. G. (1973), 'On the interaction between quantity and quality of children', *Journal of Political Economy*, vol. 82, pp. S279–S288.

[8]   Becker, G. and Tomes, N. (1976), 'Child endowments and the quantity and quality of children', *Journal of Political Economy*, vol. 84, pp. S143–S162.
[9]   Blinder, A. S. (1973), 'A model of inherited wealth', *Quarterly Journal of Economics*, vol. 87, pp. 608–26.
[10] Bowles, S. and Nelson, V. (1974), 'The "inheritance of IQ" and the intergenerational reproduction of economic inequality', *Review of Economics and Statistics*, vol. 56, pp. 39–51.
[11] Brittain, J. A. (1978), *Inheritance and the Inequality of Material Wealth*, Washington, DC, Brookings Institution.
[12] Champernowne, D. G. (1973), *The Distribution of Income between Persons*, Cambridge, Cambridge University Press.
[13] Conlisk, J. (1977), 'An exploratory model of the size distribution of income', *Economic Inquiry*, vol. 15, pp. 345–66.
[14] Griliches, Z. (1977), 'Estimating the returns to schooling: some econometric problems', *Econometrica*, vol. 45, pp. 1–22.
[15] Harbury, C. D. and Hitchens, D. M. W. N. (1979), *Inheritance and Inequality in Britain*, London, Allen & Unwin.
[16] Institute for Fiscal Studies (1978). *The Structure and Reform of Direct Taxation*, report of a committee chaired by Professor J. E. Meade, London, Allen & Unwin.
[17] Ishikawa, T. (1975), 'Family structures and family values in the theory of income distribution', *Journal of Political Economy*, vol. 83, pp. 987–1008.
[18] Kaldor, N. (1955–6), 'Alternative theories of distribution', *Review of Economic Studies*, vol. 23, pp. 83–100.
[19] Marglin, S. A. (1975), 'What do bosses do? – part II', *Review of Radical Political Economics*, vol. 7, pp. 20–37.
[20] Meade, J. E. (1936), *Economic Analysis and Policy*, London, Oxford University Press.
[21] Meade, J. E. (1948), *Planning and the Price Mechanism*, London, Allen & Unwin.
[22] Meade, J. E. (1964), *Efficiency, Equality and the Ownership of Property*, London, Allen & Unwin.
[23] Meade, J. E. (1966), 'Life-cycle savings, inheritance and economic growth', *Review of Economic Studies*, vol. 33, pp. 61–78.
[24] Meade, J. E. (1973), *The Inheritance of Inequalities*, London, Oxford University Press.
[25] Meade, J. E. (1975), *The Intelligent Radical's Guide to Economic Policy*, London, Allen & Unwin.
[26] Meade, J. E. (1976), *The Just Economy*, London, Allen & Unwin.
[27] Meade, J. E. (1978), see Institute for Fiscal Studies, 1978.
[28] Menchik, P. L. (1977), 'Primogeniture, equal sharing and the US distribution of wealth', *Quarterly Journal of Economy*, vol. 14, pp. 299–316.
[29] Pasinetti, L. (1962), 'Rate of profit and income distribution in relation to the rate of economic growth', *Review of Economic Studies*, vol. 29, pp. 267–79.
[30] Pestieau, P. and Possen, U. M. (1979), 'A model of wealth distribution', *Econometrica*, vol. 47, pp. 761–72.
[31] Pryor, F. L. (1973), 'Simulation of the impact of social and economic institutions on the size distribution of income and wealth', *American Economic Review*, vol. 63, pp. 50–72.
[32] Shorrocks, A. F. (1975), 'On stochastic models of size distributions', *Review of Economic Studies*, vol. 42, pp. 631–41.
[33] Shorrocks, A. F. (1979), 'On the structure of intergenerational transfers between families', *Economica*, vol. 20, pp. 415–25.
[34] Stiglitz, J. E. (1969), 'Distribution of income and wealth among individuals', *Econometrica*, vol. 37, pp. 382–97.
[35] Stiglitz, J. E. (1978), 'Equality, taxation and inheritance', in W. Krelle and A. F. Shorrocks (eds.), *Personal Income Distribution*, Amsterdam, North-Holland.
[36] Yaari, M. E. (1964), 'On the consumer's lifetime allocation process', *International Economic Review*, vol. 5, pp. 304–17.
[37] Yaari, M. E. (1965), 'Uncertain lifetime, life insurance and the theory of the consumer', *Review of Economic Studies*, vol. 32, pp. 137–50.

PART III

DESIGN OF TAXATION

Introduction to Part III

Chapters 10–12   Optimum Taxation

The normative theory of public finance – the design of taxation and expenditure policies – has enjoyed a revivial of interest in the past 10–15 years. The pioneering studies of Ramsey [15] and Samuelson [16] have been rediscovered and, following the influential contribution of Diamond and Mirrlees [6], there has developed a large literature on optimum taxation. The questions posed in this literature are, however, those which have concerned public finance writers since the subject began. What goods should be taxed? What should be the balance between direct and indirect taxation? What is a just allocation of the burden of income taxation? Should savings be exempt from taxation?

It is with issues of these kinds that Part III is concerned. Before embarking on a summary of the results obtained, it is important to make clear the objectives of this kind of analysis. It should be stressed that it is not intended to produce definitive answers, but rather to illuminate the structure of the arguments which could lead to a particular answer. The end result is not typically a recommendation that the optimum sales tax on wind-surfers is 45%, but an understanding of the kind of arguments which could be advanced for a high indirect tax on commodities with certain characteristics. As it is put by Hahn, the concern of this literature is 'the grammar of arguments about policy' ([7], p. 106) not with the advocacy of policies themselves.

Chapters 10–12 form a group in that all are concerned with the central 'Ramsey' tax problem. The problem posed by Pigou to Ramsey is described by the latter as follows:

a given revenue is to be raised by proportionate taxes on some or all uses of income, the taxes on different uses being possibly at different rates; how should these rates be adjusted in order that the decrement of utility may be a minimum? ([15], p. 47)

The framework within which he set out to answer the question is highly simplified; none the less, the answer is not self-evident. As Ramsey observed 'we shall find that the obvious solution that there should be no differentiation is entirely erroneous' (ibid.). The solution obtained by Ramsey in the general case is indeed far from transparent. The conditions are reinterpreted by Samuelson [16], but do not yield any simple propositions about the optimum tax structure. For this reason, Ramsey considered the special case, equivalent to partial equilibrium analysis, where the conditions can be written in terms of the elasticity of demand ε_i (and supply), but this has been dismissed as too restrictive.

In Chapter 10, published in the first issue of the *Journal of Public Economics*, Joseph Stiglitz and I attempted to provide results mid-way in generality between these two approaches, offering additional insight into the way in which the pattern of consumer preferences influences the optimum tax structure. The essay also offered some illustrative empirical calculations based on estimated demand systems. (More recent attempts at empirical implementation include Deaton [5], and Harris and MacKinnon [8].)

Ramsey is quite explicit that he is ignoring the distribution between consumers. However, it is argued in Chapter 11, also written jointly with Joseph Stiglitz, that the choice of indirect tax structure is of little policy relevance unless there are distributional considerations. If the government can levy a poll tax, and this is effectively lump-sum, then this is the most efficient way of raising revenue and indirect taxes are not utilised. The first aim of Chapter 11 is to analyse the optimum tax structure where individuals differ, building on the work of Diamond and Mirrlees [6]. We show, for example, that the analogue of Ramsey's partial equilibrium condition is that the tax on good i, t_i, satisfies equation (7):

$$\frac{t_i}{1+t_i} = \frac{1 - \overline{b}r_i}{\varepsilon_i} \tag{1}$$

where r_i is the distributional characteristic of good i, and $\overline{b}$ the average net social marginal valuation of income. Where there is an optimally chosen poll tax on subsidy, $\overline{b}=1$ and the case for differentiation depends on the distributional characteristic and the elasticity of demand (which may be related).

The second purpose of Chapter 11 is to bring out the dependence of the optimum tax structure on the range of instruments assumed to be at the disposal of the government. We have already seen the implications of introducing a poll tax into the Ramsey problem. A less immediately intuitive result is that where the government can levy a *non-linear* income tax, and where individuals differ only in the wage rates they face, then if the individual utility function is weakly separable between labour and all goods, then no indirect taxation is necessary to achieve the optimum. This result (also contained in Chapter 16) has been further discussed by Mirrlees [11] and [12], Seade [17], and others.

Finally, Chapter 11 examines the relation between the optimum tax formulation and the principle of horizontal equity, raising some of the issues examined in Chapter 5.

The analysis of the optimum tax problem is often quite complex and the results tend to be inaccessible to the policy-maker. The intention of Chapter 12, delivered as the W. A. Mackintosh Lecture at Queen's University, Canada, is to elicit the implications of the recent literature for the age-old problem of direct versus indirect taxation, drawing on the results of Chapter 11. It may be less colourful than Gladstone's speech to the House of Commons, but it may provide more insight.

Chapter 13   Optimum Taxation and Public Goods

Many of the issues discussed in the recent research on optimum taxation are to be found in Pigou's *A Study in Public Finance* [14]. In this remarkable book, he recognises the new considerations which arise when governments have to rely on distortionary taxation – as in the problem he posed to Ramsey. At the same time, his intuitive reasoning was on occasion misleading; indeed one of the lessons from the recent literature is that, once we leave the familiar terrain of the first-best, intuition may be a treacherous guide.

This is illustrated in Chapter 13, written jointly with Nicholas Stern, where we consider the optimum provision of public goods if they have to be financed by distortionary taxation. In this context, Pigou had argued that 'in general, expenditure ought not to be carried so far as to make the real yield of the last unit of resources expended by the government equal to the real yield of the last unit left in the hands of the representative citizen' ([4], p. 34). As we suggest, this can be given two interpretations. The first is that the standard first-order condition for the provision of public goods should be modified to:

$$\sum \frac{\text{marginal rates of}}{\text{substitution}} = \frac{\text{marginal rate of}}{\text{transformation}} + \frac{\text{cost of distortionary}}{\text{taxation}} \quad (2)$$

The second interpretation is that the optimum level of public goods is lower where use has to be made of distortionary taxation. These are quite different statements – a point which should be emphasised, since it apparently frequently gives rise to misunderstanding. One cannot, in general, draw conclusions about the optimum quantities directly from first-order conditions such as (2). Suppose, for example, there were no additional term on the right-hand side of equation (2) above, this would not mean that the optimum levels were necessarily the same under different methods of finance.

Chapter 13 highlights an issue which recurs in the design of policy in a situation where individuals' decisions are affected at the margin by government actions. The resulting optimisation problem, even with strong simplifying assumptions, has a quite complex structure. Economists, accustomed to maximisation as a routine matter, have (with a few notable exceptions) been slow to recognise the complexity of these problems and the difficulties in drawing conclusions about the properties of optimum policies.

Chapter 14   Optimum Taxation in a Dynamic Economy

Chapters 10 and 11 discuss briefly the application of the optimum tax results to the treatment of saving. When, however, I came to consider the issue of income versus consumption taxation, as a result of the support given to the latter by the members of the Meade Committee on *The Structure and Reform of Direct Taxation*, it became clear that the results could only be applied directly in a limited set of circumstances.

The aim of Chapter 14, written with Agnar Sandmo, is to show how the optimum taxation of savings depends on the range of instruments available to the government and its capacity to secure a desired intertemporal allocation. The vehicle employed is a two-period life-cycle overlapping generations model, representing a simplified version of that considered in Chapters 7 and 8, but set in a general equilibrium context. The model has been widely discussed in the recent literature, and an extensive treatment is given by Balasko and Shell [3], [4] and in conjunction with Cass [2]. The properties of the model are also discussed in the papers in Kareken and Wallace [9].

For the person seeking an easy answer to the income versus expenditure tax question Chapter 14 will not be rewarding reading. Even where the standard optimum tax results can be applied, the solution depends on parameters, such as the interest elasticity of labour supply about which we have little firm evidence. This situation frequently arises: e.g. weak separability, critical to the results of Chapter 11, is typically imposed as a precondition in econometric estimation of commodity demand-labour supply systems. But, as stressed at the outset, what we are seeking at this stage are insights rather than definitive answers. Here the analysis of Chapter 14, and of the other essays, may be of more assistance.

Chapter 15   The Structure of Income Taxation

The design of the income tax structure enters into several of the essays, but Chapter 15 is devoted exclusively to this topic, ignoring the possibility of differentiated indirect terms. The paper was written shortly after the publication of the seminal, but very difficult, article on the optimum income tax by Mirrlees [10]. The intention of Chapter 15 is to bring out some of the essential features in a less complicated framework – one which permits an explicit solution for the optimum tax rate.

The 'simple model' of Chapter 15 may indeed be seen as comparable with the simplified results in Chapter 11. A constant marginal tax on wage income at rate $(1-\beta)$ may be seen as equivalent to a tax on goods at rate τ, where $(1-\beta)=\tau/(1+\tau)$. The choice of α in Chapter 15 is equivalent to setting $\bar{b}=1$ in equation (1) above. We have therefore:

$$1-\beta=\frac{1-r}{\varepsilon} \tag{3}$$

Individuals are assumed to differ only in the ability variable, n, and the social welfare function is assumed to be utilitarian. With these assumptions, and the particular utility function used in Chapter 15, $\varepsilon=1$ and r is equal to the ratio of the harmonic mean, n^H, to the arithmetic mean, $\bar{n}$. Equation (3) therefore yields:

$$\beta=\frac{n^H}{\bar{n}} \tag{4}$$

which is equation (22) in Chapter 15. This holds for all distributions, not just the Pareto, such that people of all ability levels are working (case A in Chapter 15).

The principal conclusions of Chapter 15 concern the role of different formulations of the government's objective. The discussion here may be read in conjunction with that in Part I. It illustrates, for example, the importance of distinguishing between a Rawlsian approach to social justice and a principle based on egalitarianism. This is discussed further by Phelps [13], and Atkinson and Stiglitz [1], among others.

References

[1.] Atkinson, A. B. and Stiglitz, J. E. (1980), *Lectures on Public Economics*, London and New York, McGraw-Hill.

[2] Balasko, Y., Cass, D. and Shell, K. (1980), 'Existence of competitive equilibrium in a general overlapping generations model', *Journal of Economic Theory*, vol. 23, pp. 307–22.

[3] Balasko, Y. and Shell, K. (1980), 'The overlapping generations model I', *Journal of Economic Theory*, vol. 23, pp. 281–306.

[4] Balasko, Y. and Shell, K. (1981), 'The overlapping generations model III', *Journal of Economic Theory*, vol. 24, pp. 143–52.

[5] Deaton, A. S. (1977), 'Equity, efficiency and the structure of indirect taxation', *Journal of Public Economics*, vol. 8, pp. 299–312.

[6] Diamond, P. A. and Mirrlees, J. A. (1971), 'Optimal taxation and public production', *American Economic Review*, vol. 61, pp. 8–27, 261–78.

[7] Hahn, F. H. (1973), 'On optimum taxation', *Journal of Economic Theory*, vol. 6, pp. 96–106.

[8] Harris, R. G. and MacKinnon, J. G. (1979), 'Computing optimal tax equilibria', *Journal of Public Economics*, vol. 11, pp. 197–212.

[9] Kareken, J. and Wallace, N. (eds.) (1980), *Models of Monetary Economics*, Minneapolis, Federal Reserve Bank.

[10] Mirrlees, J. A. (1971), 'An exploration in the theory of optimum income taxation', *Review of Economic Studies*, vol. 38, pp. 175–208.

[11] Mirrlees, J. A. (1976), 'Optimal tax theory: a synthesis', *Journal of Public Economics*, vol. 6, pp. 327–58.

[12] Mirrlees, J. A. (forthcoming), 'The theory of optimal taxation', in K. J. Arrow and M. D. Intriligator (eds.), *Handbook of Mathematical Economics*, Amsterdam, North-Holland.

[13] Phelps, E. S. (1973), 'The taxation of wage income for economic justice', *Quarterly Journal of Economics*, vol. 87, pp. 331–54.

[14] Pigou, A. C. (1947), *A Study in Public Finance*, (3rd edn), London, Macmillan.

[15] Ramsey, F. P. (1927), 'A contribution to the theory of taxation', *Economic Journal*, vol. 37, pp. 47–61.

[16] Samuelson, P. A. (1951), Unpublished memorandum, US Treasury.

[17] Seade, J. K. (1977), 'On the shape of optimal tax schedules', *Journal of Public Economics*, vol. 7, pp. 203–36.

10 The Structure of Indirect Taxation and Economic Efficiency*

The literature on indirect taxation has been characterised by two disjoint strands. On the one hand, there are the advocates of the replacement of differentiated indirect taxes by a uniform tax on all commodities (such as a value added tax). Their case is based in part on administrative simplicity, but rests largely on the belief that a uniform tax is more conducive to economic efficiency. On the other hand, there is the literature on 'optimal commodity taxation' arguing that different commodities ought to be taxed at different rates, since this reduces the dead weight loss. This line of argument, which was first put forward by Ramsey [14] and later extended by Samuelson [15], has been the subject of a number of papers.[1] Although both advocates and critics of differentiated indirect taxes have been primarily concerned with economic efficiency, the debate has never really been joined: each side has discussed the issue as though the other did not exist. The results of Ramsey have been ignored or dismissed as being of little practical significance (cf. Prest [13]; Musgrave [12]). On the other hand, the recent studies in optimal taxation have made little attempt to relate their findings to the conventional views – to show to what extent they are simply alternative forms of conventional maxims for the design of the tax system and to what extent they are in fact contradictory.

The purpose of this chapter is to present a new formulation of the optimal tax problem which gives more insight into the structure of the solution and provides more easily interpreted results. Using this formulation, we try to clarify the relationship between the results on optimal taxation and the conventional wisdom, making clear where and under what conditions they are in agreement. Moreover, using this new approach it is possible to calculate the optimal tax structure corresponding to empirically estimated demand functions, and some numerical results are presented.

1 The Conventional Wisdom

A number of criteria for evaluating alternative tax structures have been proposed: (a) efficiency, (b) equity, (c) administrative simplicity, and (d)

* Reprinted from *Journal of Public Economics*, **1**, 1972.
A. B. Atkinson and J. E. Stiglitz.

flexibility (usefulness for stabilisation policies). This chapter focuses primarily on the first of these considerations, since it is the efficiency aspects that have received most attention. The analysis does, however, have important implications for the conflict between efficiency and equity and these are discussed briefly in the final section. (In Chapter 11 the distributional arguments and the relationship between direct and indirect taxation are examined in more detail.) The last two considerations – administrative simplicity and flexibility – are not discussed, but it should be emphasised that this does not imply that in our judgement these other effects are not of importance. Against any gains from differentiation on the first two accounts must be set some judgement of the political[2] and economic benefits to be had from the simpler administrative structure associated with uniform taxes.

The conventional analysis of the efficiency arguments presented in most textbooks is based on a partial equilibrium model of a single market (see Figure 1). As a result of the tax at rate t, the supply curve shifts up from SS to $S'S'$. The tax revenue is $AP'CB$. The excess loss of consumer surplus is $PP'F$ and of producer surplus is PCF. The total dead weight loss for a given revenue (R) may be approximated for small taxes by (see Bishop [1], p. 211):

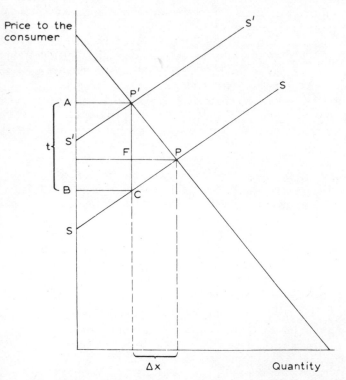

Figure 1

$$\frac{R^2}{2ax\left(\frac{1}{\varepsilon_d} + \frac{1}{\varepsilon_s}\right)}$$

where ε_d and ε_s denote the elasticities of demand and supply, and qx denotes expenditure on the commodity. From this are derived the following maxims: to minimise distortion we should tax those goods which (i) have a low price elasticity of demand, (ii) have a low price elasticity of supply, (iii) form an important part of people's budgets.[3]

This geometric analysis gives somewhat similar results to those reached by Ramsey in one of the special cases he considered. The relationship between them has, however, been obscured by the confusion in much of the literature of two different questions:

(a) If taxes can only be imposed on one commodity (or a subset of commodities), which should be chosen? This is in effect the question considered by Hicks.
(b) If there is more than one taxable commodity, what should be the relative tax rates on different commodities? This is the question considered by Ramsey.

In the former case, we wish to tax the commodity for which the dead weight loss is lowest for a given revenue, and here maxims (i)–(iii) apply. In the Ramsey case, we wish to minimise the total dead weight loss over all taxable commodities, so that for each commodity the marginal dead weight loss associated with raising a marginal dollar of tax revenue must be the same. In the case of a perfectly elastic supply this requires (for small taxes):

$$\frac{t_i}{q_i} \varepsilon_d^i = \text{constant for all commodities } i = 1,\ldots,n,$$

or that the (*ad valorem*) tax rates be inversely proportional to the elasticity of demand in each industry. (Note that in this case the importance of the good in consumers' budgets is not relevant.) It is on the Ramsey question that we focus in this chapter.

This partial equilibrium analysis is clearly unsatisfactory in view of the restrictive assumptions on which it is based. In particular, it requires (a) the absence of income effects, and (b) the independence of demand functions. There has therefore been considerable scepticism about its applicability. Prest [13], for example, dismisses the Ramsey results with the comment that 'such restrictive assumptions have to be made in order to derive a solution, that they appear to have little practical significance' (although he offers nothing in its place). In contrast to the restrictive partial equilibrium analysis, the results of Ramsey [14], Samuelson [15], Boiteux [2] (and more recently Diamond and Mirrlees [5]) are in many respects more general. In particular, they have led to the important finding that the optimal tax structure requires that (for infinitesimal taxes) the compensated demand for each good be reduced by the same proportion.[4] However, while this provides considerable insight into the form of the solution, it does not yield any simple qualitative propositions about the optimal tax structure. It does not, for example, suggest which goods should be taxed more heavily – or indeed whether a differentiated tax structure is in fact optimal. Moreover, it does not readily permit the calculation of optimal rates of taxation on the basis of empirically estimated demand functions.

The aim of this chapter is to derive results midway in generality between those obtained from partial equilibrium analysis and the Ramsey–Samuelson results. The results we derive allow straightforward statements to be made in the case where all consumers are identical about the effect of efficiency considerations on the structure of indirect taxation and facilitate the estimation of the optimal tax structure. The basic model is described in section 2; the central results are set out in section 3; and the implications are discussed in the remainder of the chapter.

2 The Model

(i) Assumptions about production
We shall focus on the role of demand factors in determining the optimal structure of indirect taxation, and therefore make the simplest possible assumptions about production. Most importantly, we assume constant returns to scale, which precludes any discussion of the role of supply elasticities.[5] For ease of exposition, it is also assumed that producer prices are fixed for all commodities and labour (the only factor supplied by households), although the results in no way depend on this assumption. Writing q_i for the consumer price of good i, p_i for the producer price, we have $q_i = p_i + t_i$.[6] We assume without loss of generality that one good (leisure) is not taxed and that the wage is unity.

(ii) Assumptions about consumption
A consumer is assumed to maximise a function $U(x, L)$ subject to the budget constraint:

$$\sum_{i=1}^{n} q_i x_i = L, \tag{1}$$

where L is the amount of labour supplied and x_i is the amount of the consumption good purchased. Writing α for the marginal utility of income, this gives the first-order conditions:

$$U_i = \alpha q_i \qquad i = 1, \ldots, n \tag{2a}$$

$$-U_L = \alpha. \tag{2b}$$

(iii) Social-welfare function
The general assumption made is that the government maximises a

social welfare function which is individualistic and impersonal: $W[U^1,$ $U^2, U^3, \ldots, U^m]$ where U^k is the utility of the kth man. However, in order to focus on the efficiency aspects, we assume here that all consumers are identical, which means that we can consider the welfare of a representative individual:

$$U(x, L).$$

(iv) Government budget constraint
It is assumed that the purpose of commodity taxation is to raise a certain revenue R (which will purchase a fixed quantity of any of the goods at producer prices):

$$R = \sum_{i=1}^{n} t_i x_i = \sum_{i=1}^{n} (q_i - p_i) x_i = L - \sum_{i=1}^{n} p_i x_i. \tag{3}$$

3   Derivation of Optimal Tax Formula

The problem faced by the government is to choose t_i $(i = 1, \ldots, n)$ to maximise $U(x, L)$ subject to (3) and the conditions for individual utility maximisation (1) and (2). Following the approach of Ramsey we can regard the t_i and α as functions of x_i and L from equations (2) and frame the problem in terms of choosing (x_i, L) to maximise the Lagrangian:[7]

$$U(x, L) + \mu \left[\sum_{i=1}^{n} q_i x_i - L \right] - \lambda \left[R + \sum_{i=1}^{n} p_i x_i - L \right].$$

This formulation differs from that of Diamond and Mirrlees [5], who worked with the indirect utility function and the tax rates as control variables.
   If we define $-L$ as good 0, we may write the Lagrangian in vector notation:

$$U + \frac{\mu}{\alpha} U'x - \lambda(R + px), \tag{4}$$

where U' denotes the vector U_i $(i = 0, \ldots, n)$ and the q_i have been eliminated using conditions (2). The first-order conditions are:

$$\left(1 + \frac{\mu}{\alpha} \right) U' + \frac{\mu}{\alpha} U''x = \lambda p, \tag{5}$$

where U'' denotes the matrix U_{ij} $(i, j = 0, \ldots, n)$. Let us define:

$$H^k = \sum_{i=0}^{n} \frac{(-U_{ik}) x_i}{U_k},$$

i.e. H^k is the sum of the elasticities of the marginal utility of x_k with respect to each of the commodities. Then the first-order condition can be written as:

$$q_k[\alpha + \mu(1 - H^k)] = \lambda p_k \qquad k = 0, \ldots, n .\tag{6}$$

But from the normalisation $t_0 = 0$:

$$\mu = \frac{\lambda - \alpha}{1 - H^0}\tag{7}$$

so that the optimal tax rates t_k^* as a percentage of consumer prices are characterised by[8]:

$$\frac{t_k^*}{p_k + t_k^*} = \frac{\lambda - \alpha}{\lambda} \frac{H^k - H^0}{1 - H^0}\tag{8}$$

While this equation does not in general provide an explicit formula for the optimal tax rate (since the H^k depend on the tax rates), it does allow us to draw a number of conclusions about the optimal structure of taxation. The implications of equation (8) will be the subject of the remainder of the chapter.[9]

4   Implications of Basic Optimal Tax Formula – Uniform taxation?

One of the main questions of policy importance is whether or not a uniform structure of taxation would be desirable.[10]

Let us consider first the case where the marginal utility of leisure is independent of the consumption of every commodity. Then $t_k^* = t_j^*$ all $k, j \geqslant 1$ implies *either* $-H^0 = \infty$ or that $H^k = H^j$. The first condition means that:

$$\frac{-U_{00}L}{U_0} = \infty ,$$

or that the elasticity of marginal utility of labour is infinite, which implies a completely inelastic supply of labour. The implications of the second condition can be seen as follows: differentiate the first-order conditions and budget constraint (1) and (2), to obtain:

$$
\begin{bmatrix}
U_{11} & U_{12} & \cdots & -q_1 \\
U_{21} & U_{22} & \cdots & -q_2 \\
\cdots & \cdots & \cdots & \\
-q_1 & -q_2 & \cdots & 0
\end{bmatrix}
\begin{bmatrix}
dx_1 \\
dx_2 \\
\cdots \\
d\alpha
\end{bmatrix}
=
\begin{bmatrix}
0 \\
0 \\
\cdots \\
-dE
\end{bmatrix}
$$

where $E = \sum_{i=1}^{n} q_i x_i =$ total expenditure; defining $H_{ki} = \dfrac{-U_{ki} x_i}{U_k}$ we obtain (by appropriate normalisation):

$$\begin{bmatrix} H_{11} & H_{12} & \cdots & 1 \\ H_{21} & H_{22} & \cdots & 1 \\ \cdots & \cdots & & \\ q_1 x_1 & q_2 x_2 & \cdots & 0 \end{bmatrix} \begin{bmatrix} d \ln x_1 \\ d \ln x_2 \\ \cdots \\ d \ln \alpha \end{bmatrix} = \begin{bmatrix} 0 \\ 0 \\ \cdots \\ dE \end{bmatrix} \tag{9}$$

Denote by D the determinant of the matrix of coefficients of the left-hand side of (9). Then:

$$D\left[\frac{d \ln x_1}{dE} - \frac{d \ln x_2}{dE}\right] = \begin{vmatrix} 0 & H_{12} & H_{13} & \cdots & 1 \\ 0 & H_{22} & H_{23} & \cdots & 1 \\ 1 & q_2 x_2 & \cdots & \cdots & 0 \end{vmatrix} - \begin{vmatrix} H_{11} & 0 & H_{12} & \cdots & 1 \\ H_{21} & 0 & H_{23} & \cdots & 1 \\ q_1 x_1 & 1 & \cdots & \cdots & 0 \end{vmatrix}$$

$$= (-1)^n \left\{ \begin{vmatrix} H_{12} & H_{13} & \cdots & 1 \\ H_{22} & H_{23} & \cdots & 1 \\ \cdots & \cdots & \cdots & \cdots \end{vmatrix} + \begin{vmatrix} H_{11} & H_{13} & \cdots & 1 \\ H_{22} & H_{23} & \cdots & 1 \\ \cdots & \cdots & \cdots & \cdots \end{vmatrix} \right\}$$

$$\sim (-1)^n \begin{vmatrix} H_{12} + H_{11} & H_{13} & \cdots & 1 \\ H_{22} + H_{21} & H_{23} & \cdots & 1 \end{vmatrix}$$

$$= (-1)^n \begin{vmatrix} H_{12} + H_{11} & H_{13} & \cdots & \Sigma_i H_{1i} & 1 \\ H_{22} + H_{21} & H_{23} & \cdots & \Sigma_i H_{2i} & 1 \end{vmatrix} = 0,$$

(since $H^k = \Sigma_i H_{ki}$), i.e. we require equal, and hence unitary, *expenditure* elasticities of all commodities. If $U_{i0} \neq 0$ for some i, then t_i may equal t_j even without unitary expenditure elasticities. The effects of the interactions among the commodities directly may just be offset by the interactions between the commodities and leisure. (This is illustrated in a three-commodity example given in section 8.)

In this section we have examined the conditions under which the optimal tax structure will be uniform. It is clear that there is no presumption that these conditions are likely to obtain and in the following sections we examine how the optimal tax rates depend on the characteristics of different commodities.

5 Implications of Optimal Tax Formula – Two Polar Cases

We now show how the results of Ramsey and others can be obtained as polar cases of formula (8). Assume first that there is constant marginal disutility of labour. Then $H^0 = 0$ and the optimal tax is given by:

$$\frac{t_k^*}{1 + t_k^*} = \frac{\lambda - \alpha}{\lambda} H^k. \tag{10}$$

If in addition we assume that $U_{ij} = 0$ ($i \neq j$), we can see that H^k is inversely proportional to the elasticity of demand.[11] We have, therefore, obtained the

Ramsey result that the optimal taxes should be inversely proportional to the price elasticity of demand.

On the other hand, if we suppose that $(-H^0)$ tends to infinity, which corresponds to the case of a completely inelastic supply of labour, then:

$$\frac{t_k^*/(1+t_k^*)}{t_1^*/(1+t_1^*)} = \frac{H^k/(-H^0)+1}{H^1/(-H^0)+1} \to 1,$$

i.e. uniform rate of tax on all goods. Since a uniform rate of tax on all goods is equivalent to a tax on labour alone, this corresponds to the conventional prescription that where there is a factor which is completely inelastically supplied, this should bear all the tax.

Our formula (8) can be seen therefore as the kind of 'weighted average' that Lerner [11] has suggested might exist. There are two 'extreme' optimal tax systems: the uniform tax and taxes proportional to H^k. Where between these two extremes the optimal tax system lies will depend on $(-H^0)$.

6   Implications of Optimal Tax Formulae – Direct Additivity and Strong Separability

The formulation of the optimal tax in equation (8) suggests a special case which allows easily interpreted results to be obtained: direct additivity of the utility function. This implies that there exists some monotonic transformation of the utility function such that $U_{ij}=0$ for $i \neq j$: i.e. H^k may be written:

$$H^k = \left(\frac{-U_{kk}x_k}{U_k} \right),$$

(which is invariant with respect to monotonic transformations of the utility function).[12]

By differentiating equations (2), we can see that this is inversely proportional to the income elasticity of demand for good k (see Houthakker [10]):

$$\left(\frac{-U_{kk}x_k}{U_k} \right) \frac{1}{x_k} \frac{\partial x_k}{\partial m} = \frac{-1}{\alpha} \frac{\partial \alpha}{\partial m}.$$

Moreover, if we assume that $U_{ii}<0$ for all $i=0,\ldots,n$, it follows that $\lambda > \alpha$ if a positive revenue is to be raised.[13] We have therefore the useful result that *when the utility function is directly additive, the optimal tax rate depends inversely on the income elasticity of demand*. This clearly has important implications for the conflict between equity and efficiency which are discussed further below.

Examples of the solution for directly additive functions are (i) the direct addilog function:

$$U(x,L) = (\bar{L}-L)^{\beta_0} + \frac{1}{1-\beta_i} \sum_{i=1}^{n} x^{1-\beta_i},$$

$$\beta_i > 0, \qquad i=1,\ldots,n .$$

In the case $\beta_i = \beta$, $i = 1, \ldots, n$ this has unitary expenditure elasticities, and we can deduce that the optimal tax system is proportional. In the more general case where the β_i are different, the tax rate will increase with β_i. (ii) Stone–Geary utility function:

$$V(L) + \sum_{i=1}^{n} \beta_i \log(x_i - c_i). \qquad \Sigma_i \beta_i = 1.$$

This function was considered by Diamond and Mirrlees [5], but they were unable to say more than that the optimal tax would not be uniform. Using the approach adopted here, we can see that:

$$H^k = \frac{x_k}{(x_k - c_k)} = \frac{\text{total expenditure on good } k}{\text{`luxury' expenditure on good } k}.$$

This suggests that the optimal tax will be high on those goods which are basically necessities and low on luxury goods.

Direct additivity is a restrictive assumption. It is, however, considerably less restrictive than the assumptions required for partial equilibrium analysis to be valid (for $H^0 \neq 0$, direct additivity does not imply zero cross-price effects). In view of the fact that additivity is undoubtedly more appealing at the level of broad commodity groups than of individual commodities, it is perhaps best to interpret our results in this way. Suppose that the utility function is strongly separable:

$$U(x) = F[U^1(x^1) + U^2(x_2) + \ldots],$$

where x^i denotes a subset of commodities $x_{i1}, x_{i2}, \ldots$. Then the optimal tax rates taking the commodity groups as a whole (regarding them as a composite commodity) are given by (8). It seems likely for administrative or other reasons that commodities would in fact have to be grouped for tax purposes, although the groups would not necessarily coincide with the subgroups x^i. Where this does not apply, we can regard the determination of the optimal tax structure as a two-stage process: what should be the relative taxes within a group, and what should be the average tax rates between groups? We may note that where there are only two goods in a subgroup x^i, the relative tax rates depend simply on the relative expenditure elasticities: from the first-order conditions:

$$\begin{bmatrix} H_{11} & H_{12} & 1 \\ H_{21} & H_{22} & 1 \\ q_{11}x_{11} & q_2 x_{21} & 0 \end{bmatrix} \begin{bmatrix} d\ln x_{11} \\ d\ln x_{21} \\ d\ln \alpha \end{bmatrix} = \begin{bmatrix} 0 \\ 0 \\ dE_1 \end{bmatrix},$$

where E_1 is the total expenditure on the group of commodities. Thus:

$$D\left[\frac{d \ln x_{11}}{dE_1} - \frac{d \ln x_{21}}{dE_1}\right] = H_{12} - H_{22} + H_{11} - H_{21}$$

$$= H^1 - H^2,$$

(since $H^1 = H_{11} + H_{12}$, etc.).

7 Applications of Additivity and Separability: Savings and Risk-taking

In this section we discuss briefly two cases where the direct additivity results seem particularly applicable.

(i) Taxation of savings

Suppose that lifetime utility for the representative individual is given by the sum of instantaneous utility from consumption x_i in period i (regarded as a composite good) and the disutility of effort from working in period 0:

$$V(L_0) + \sum_{i=1}^{n} U(x_i).$$

We can deduce that when the elasticity of marginal utility is constant, the optimal tax is a uniform tax on consumption in all periods. If the elasticity of marginal utility rises as consumption rises, and if the optimal plan involves a rising level of consumption (as it will if there is a positive interest rate and no time discounting), the optimal tax rate will be higher on consumption at later dates – a uniform consumption tax would need to be supplemented by a tax on interest. (This case is one in which consumption today is a luxury good and savings a necessity.) If, on the other hand, the elasticity of marginal utility falls with rising consumption, a uniform consumption tax should be supplemented by a subsidy on interest. If further we add a term in bequests, then the optimal tax will be higher on bequests than on consumption only if bequests are a necessity (i.e. the proportion of wealth allocated to bequests falls as wealth increases). (See Chapter 14 for further discussion.)

(ii) Risk-taking

Suppose that a person earns L in period 0, and saves this for consumption in the next period. He allocates an amount z_1 to a safe asset (yielding r with certainty) and z_2 to a risky asset yielding an uncertain pattern of returns $\tilde{R}$. His income in state θ is:

$$Y(\theta) = (1 + \tilde{R})z_2 + (1 + r)z_1.$$

His expected utility is:

$$V(L) + EU(Y).$$

Although the utility function is additive in Y, it is not additive in z_1 and z_2. It is, however, separable between z_1 and z_2 on the one hand and L on the other, and we can apply the result given in the previous section. Thus we obtain the interesting result that optimal taxation requires that the risky industry be taxed at a higher or lower rate than the safe as the expenditure elasticity of demand for the risky industry is less than or greater than unity. This result may be reinterpreted in terms of properties of the utility function: the risky industry should be taxed at a higher or lower rate than the safe as there is increasing or decreasing relative risk aversion. If and only if there is constant relative risk aversion ought we to tax both industries at the same rate.[14]

8 Complementarity with Leisure and the Optimal Tax Structure

While direct additivity may seem reasonable for broad commodity groups, it may be less appealing to assume that the marginal utility of leisure is independent of the consumption of different goods. Moreover, it has commonly been suggested that the degree of complementarity with leisure is one determinant of the optimal tax structure. Prest [13], for example, says that:

Indirect taxes on commodities which do not soak up a large fraction of the expenditure from marginal earnings (i.e. commodities not highly competitive with leisure ...) earn higher marks than those which do. Ideally, one would like to tax those goods which are in joint demand with leisure, i.e. where the elasticity of demand for leisure is negative with respect to their price. (p. 376)

In order to explore the dependence of the optimal tax rate on the degree of complementarity with leisure we consider a model with three goods – two consumption goods and the (untaxed) factor labour. This model has earlier been discussed by Corlett and Hague [4] and Harberger [8]; however, they carried out their analysis in terms of the properties of the demand functions rather than of the utility function. Following the same procedure in section 4, we can write (where I denotes unearned income and good zero is taken as leisure $(-L)$):

$$D\left[\frac{d\log x_1}{dI} - \frac{d\log x_2}{dI}\right] = \begin{vmatrix} H_{00} & H_{02} & 1 \\ H_{10} & H_{12} & 1 \\ H_{20} & H_{22} & 1 \end{vmatrix} + \begin{vmatrix} H_{00} & H_{01} & 1 \\ H_{10} & H_{11} & 1 \\ H_{20} & H_{21} & 1 \end{vmatrix}$$

$$= \begin{vmatrix} H_{00} & H^0 & 1 \\ H_{10} & H^1 & 1 \\ H_{20} & H^2 & 1 \end{vmatrix},$$

where $D>0$ from second-order conditions. From this it follows that:

$$(H^1 - H^0) = (H^2 - H^0)\left[\frac{H_{10} - H_{00}}{H_{20} - H_{00}}\right] -$$
$$- \frac{D}{[H_{20} - H_{00}]}\left[\frac{d\log x_1}{dI} - \frac{d\log x_2}{dI}\right]. \tag{11}$$

From (8) we can see that the relative optimal tax rates depend on $H^k - H^0$, so that (11) allows us to deduce the conditions under which the tax rates will be higher on one good than on another.

Equation (11) tells us that when we relax the assumption of direct additivity the optimal tax rate depends not only on the difference in the income elasticities but also on whether $H_{10} \gtrless H_{20}$. This can be interpreted as follows: H_{i0} is the elasticity of the marginal utility of good i with respect to an increase in leisure. If this is high, the good can be said to be complementary with leisure, and according to (11) to tax rate on this good should, *ceteris paribus*, be high. If the marginal utility of tennis racquets increases proportionately more with a rise in leisure than the marginal utility of food, then the former should be taxed more heavily.[15]

The notion of complementarity introduced in the previous paragraph follows that of Edgeworth and Pareto and differs from the more usual Hicksian definition, which is framed in terms of the compensated elasticity of demand.[16] In the present three good model, we can see that (defining $\eta_{ij} = q_j S_{ij}/x_i$ where S_{ij} is the Slutsky term):

$$\frac{1}{D}[\eta_{20} - \eta_{10}] = \begin{vmatrix} H_{10} & H_{11} & 1 \\ H_{20} & H_{21} & 1 \\ (-x_0 U_0) & -x_1 U_1 & 0 \end{vmatrix} + \begin{vmatrix} H_{10} & H_{12} & 1 \\ H_{20} & H_{22} & 1 \\ (-x_0 U_0) & -x_2 U_2 & 0 \end{vmatrix}$$

$$\sim \begin{vmatrix} H_{01} & H^1 & 1 \\ H_{02} & H^2 & 1 \\ (-x_0 U_0) & 0 & 0 \end{vmatrix} = (-U_0 x_0)(H^1 - H^2).$$

This gives the result reached by Corlett and Hague, Harberger and others, that the good with the highest cross elasticity with labour will be taxed less heavily; i.e. we should tax more heavily goods which are complementary with leisure. It is important, however, to emphasise that it has nothing to do with leisure *per se*. The general principle is that if we have one untaxed good, we should tax more heavily that good most complementary with it, since it is a way of indirectly 'taxing' the untaxed good. It just happens that we are here assuming that leisure is untaxed.

9 Numerical Illustration of Optimal Tax Calculations

One of the advantages of the approach adopted here is that it readily allows us to calculate the optimal structure of indirect taxes from empirically estimated demand functions. In particular, the assumption of direct additivity is made in much of the empirical work on consumer demand and a number of studies employ the special functional forms examined in section 6. There is, however, the difficulty in using such estimates that we require for our analysis a simultaneous estimation of the labour supply function together with the commodity demand functions, and this is not in general available. For this reason, estimates have to be based on assumed values for the elasticity of the supply of labour and we concentrate here on the case $H^0 = 0$ (where the supply of labour is completely slanting slack, as have seen that in this case the divergences from uniform tax rates are greatest (in the other polar case, $H' \rightarrow -\infty$, a uniform tax is optimal).

The optimal structure of taxation depends on the terms H^k and in general these will be functions of the tax rates – we have to allow for the fact that changing the tax rates will affect the income elasticities of demand. In the special case of the direct addilog utility function, however, the terms H^k are constant and we can calculate the optimal tax rates directly. In Table 1 we present the optimal tax rates derived from the estimates given of direct addilog demand functions by Houthakker [10]. In each case the tax rates are

Table 1   *Optimal tax structure: direct addilog function*

	Ad valorem tax rates (%)		
	Sweden	Canada	OEEC
Food	29.6	21.4	26.9
Clothing	25.6	5.5	18.8
Rent	27.8	30.9	40.0
Durables	10.0	10.0	10.0
Other goods	29.6	31.3	24.4

Source: Calculations based on weighted mean estimates given in Houthakker [10], Table 2.

normalised so that the tax rate for durables is 10%. The differences between the tax rates on different commodities are quite substantial: the range between the rate for the most heavily taxed commodity and that for the lowest is 3:1 in Sweden, 6:1 in Canada, and 4:1 for the OEEC. As one would expect from the earlier results, it is the 'necessities' – food and rent – that are taxed heavily, whereas durable goods with a high income elasticity are taxed at a low rate. At least as far as food is concerned, the pattern is very different from that actually in force in most counrries.

In Table 2 we present results based on the linear expenditure system, using the estimates of Stone [18] for the United Kingdom for 1920–38. In this case the H^k are functions of the tax rates, since the demand functions are given by:

$$q_k x_k = q_k c_k + \beta_k / \alpha .$$

However, in the case where $H^0 = 0$, α is independent of the tax rate and equation (8) reduces to the quadratic:

$$\left(\frac{q_k}{p_k}\right)^2 \frac{(\alpha p_k c_k)}{\beta_k}(\lambda - \alpha) - \frac{q_k \alpha}{p_k} + \lambda = 0 .$$

This determines the optimal *ad valorem* tax rates $t_k^* (= 1 - (p_k/q_k))$, and sample

Table 2   *Optimal tax structure: linear expenditure system*

		Ad valorem tax rates (%)	
$\lambda/\alpha =$	1.025	1.05	1.075
Commodity groups:			
Meat, fish, dairy products and fats	11.1	27.8	63.2
Fruits and vegetables	8.2	18.6	33.4
Drink and tobacco	10.1	24.1	48.5
Household running expenses	5.3	11.4	18.2
Durable goods	5.6	11.8	19.0
Other goods and services	6.2	13.4	22.0

Notes:
(a) Based on estimates given by Stone [18], Table 1 of c_k, β_k and $1/\alpha$ (= total expenditure minus 'committed' expenditure).
(b) Relationship between producer and consumer prices based on that for 1938 as obtained from National Income and Expenditure [12a]. Groups (1) and (2) were combined for this purpose.
(c) Group (4) includes rent, fuel and light, non-durable household goods and domestic service. Group (5) includes clothing, household durables, vehicles, transport and communication services.

calculations are given in Table 2 for a range of values of λ/α (reflecting different levels of revenue). (The sources of the estimates of c_k, β_k, p_k and $1/\alpha$ are described in the notes to Table 2.) Again the range of tax rates is wide and food (although not in this case housing) is taxed much more heavily than durables.

It should be emphasised that these calculations are presented only to illustrate the application of the theoretical approach developed in the earlier sections. The use of alternative specifications of the demand equations, or of alternative estimates of the same forms, may well give rather different results.

10   Concluding Comments

The principal conclusion we have reached is that if direct additivity is a reasonable assumption for broad commodity groups, then the optimal structure of taxation from an efficiency viewpoint is one that taxes more heavily goods which have a low income elasticity of demand. This result generalises the conventional wisdom based on partial equilibrium analysis, which can be obtained as a special case where the supply of labour becomes completely elastic. Moreover, in terms of the debate about the introduction of a uniform system of indirect taxes referred to at the beginning of the chapter, we have seen that there is no general presumption in favour of uniform taxation on grounds of allocative efficiency.

The analysis suggests two important areas for further research. First, although we have shown that uniform taxation cannot be justified by appeal to considerations of allocative efficiency, it may still be true that the welfare loss involved in using uniform rather than optimal taxes may be small. Secondly, the conclusion that goods with a low income elasticity should be taxed heavily brings out very sharply the conflict between equity and efficiency considerations. The recognition of equity objectives would be expected to lead to important modifications of the conclusions.[17]

Appendix

Equation (8) can be written:

$$t_k^* = \alpha q_k C_1 H^h + C_2 U_k,$$

where $C_1 = \dfrac{\lambda - \alpha}{\alpha \lambda} \dfrac{1}{1 - H^0}$, $C_2 = \dfrac{-H^0}{1 - H^0} \dfrac{\lambda - \alpha}{\lambda} \dfrac{1}{\alpha}$,

so:

$$t_k^* = -C_1 \Sigma_i U_{ik} x_i + C_2 U_k$$

and:

$$0 = -C_1 \Sigma_i U_i x_i .$$

These equations can be written:

$$(t^*, 0) = V(-C_1 x, C_2)',$$

where ' denotes the transposition and:

$$V = \begin{bmatrix} U_{ij} & U_i \\ U_j & 0 \end{bmatrix}.$$

Hence $(-C_1 x, C_2) = V^{-1}(t^*, 0)$. But:

$$V^{-1} = C_3 \begin{bmatrix} S_{ij} & \partial x_i / \partial I \\ \partial x_j / \partial I & 0 \end{bmatrix},$$

where S_{ij} denote the Slutsky terms. We thus obtain by inverting (8) the familiar result:

$$\Sigma_i S_{ik} t_i = -C_1 / C_3 x_k$$

obtained by Samuelson [15]: the compensated demand for each good should be reduced by the same proportion (for infinitesimal taxes).

Acknowledgements

The authors are grateful to J. A. Mirrlees for his very helpful comments on an earlier version of this paper. It has also benefitted a great deal from comments made at seminars at the universities of Essex, Kent, Southampton, York, University College, London and Nuffield College, Oxford. Stiglitz's research was supported under grants from the Ford Foundation and the National Science Foundation.

Notes

1 The revival of interest in this area owes much to the paper by Diamond and Mirrlees [5], see also Stiglitz and Dasgupta [16], Dixit [6], and Lerner [11].

2 In particular, once the principle of differentiation is accepted, the tax system may be subjected to the pressures of special interest groups; each group would argue that special considerations dictate that the tax on its commodity (its factor use) be lowered. The tax structure eventually emerging might well be based as much on relative strengths of these pressure groups as on relative dead weight losses.

3 The following passage from Hicks [9] perhaps comes closest to giving a fair representation of the conventional wisdom. 'For a given revenue the loss of surplus will be larger, the larger is the elasticity of demand or supply; if either is completely inelastic the loss of surplus falls to zero, and there is no tendency to substitute any other good for the taxed commodity, the outlay tax becomes equivalent to a lump sum taken from the taxpayer ... in all ordinary circumstances, however, there will be some loss of surplus. This loss will also vary (this time inversely) with the amount spent on the article, i.e. its importance in consumption. For to raise a given revenue from an "unimportant" commodity, very high rates of tax may be required; with any normal elasticity of demand or supply the loss of surplus will be severe' (p. 149).

4 From what it would have been had producer prices been charged. This result is still dependent on certain restrictive assumptions, e.g. constant returns to scale in the private sector.

5 For a discussion of the role of supply considerations, see Stiglitz and Dasgupta [16].

6 We shall assume that these producer prices correctly reflect social costs, i.e. there are no externalities or 'imperfections of competition'.

7 The budget constraint has to be introduced separately as it does not appear in equations (2).

8 It can be seen that the assumption of fixed producer prices does not affect this result: if the government revenue constraint were replaced by a production constraint $F(x) = 0$, the analysis would go through as before with F_i replacing p_i. Since F_i is homogeneous of degree zero, equation (2) is unaffected.

9 Equation (8) can also be obtained from the results of Samuelson, Diamond and Mirrlees by inverting their formulae (see Appendix).

10 From this point we set $p_i = 1$ all i (without loss of generality), so that uniform taxation implies $t_k^* = t_j^*$, $k, j \geq 1$.

11 From differentiating the first-order conditions, we obtain $U_{ii}(\partial x_i / \partial q_i) = \alpha$ (since α is constant), so $H^k = (1/\varepsilon_d^k)$.

12 In the general case, replace U by $V(U)$, so that $V_i = V'U_i$ and $V_{ij} = V'U_{ij} + V''U_iU_j$, then:

$$\sum_i \frac{(-V_{ik})x_i}{V_k} = \sum_i \frac{(-U_{ik})x_i}{U_k} - \frac{V''}{V'}\sum_i U_i x_i,$$

but the second term disappears (using the budget constraint), establishing that H^k is invariant.

13 Since $H^k > 0$ and $H^0 < 0$, so that the tax rates are all positive if $\lambda > \alpha$, negative if $\lambda < \alpha$. For discussion of these restrictions, see Green [7].

14 For a more extensive discussion of the taxation of safe and risky industries, see Stiglitz [17]. Unfortunately, these appealing results carry over to cases with more than one risky asset only in those situations where the portfolio separation theorem obtains (see Cass and Stiglitz [3]).

15 Thus, for example, it is a sufficient condition for the optimal tax to be uniform for the income elasticities to be identical and for $H_{10} = H_{20}$. However, this is not necessary and we may have $t_1^* = t_2^*$ when the income elasticity of 1 is higher than that of 2, but H_{10} is greater than H_{20}. As we noted earlier, homotheticity is not required for taxes to be uniform.

16 Although it should be noted that in the form used here ($H_{01} \gtrless H_{02}$), it is invariant with respect to monotonic transformations of U.

17 One important contribution of Diamond and Mirrlees [5] is to extend the Ramsey–Samuelson analysis to the many-consumer case: however, like the analysis for the single consumer, it does not readily allow conclusions to be drawn about which goods should be taxed more heavily.

References

[1] Dmhón, A. J. (1960), 'The effects of specific and *ad valorem* taxes', *Quarterly Journal of Economics*, 82, pp. 109–118.

[2] Boiteux, M. (1951), 'Le "revenue distribuable" et les pertes économiques, *Econometrica*, 19 pp. 112–33.

[3] Cass, D. and Stiglitz, J. E. (1972), 'The structure of investor preferences and asset returns, and separability in portfolio allocation', *Journal of Economic Theory*, vol. 2, pp. 122–60.

[4] Corlett, W. J. and Hague, D. C. (1953), 'Complementarity and the excess burden of taxation', *Review of Economic Studies*, 21, pp. 21–30.

[5] Diamond, P. A. and Mirrlees, J. A. (1971), 'Optimal taxation and public production', *American Economic Review*, 61, pp. 8–27 and 261–78.

[6] Dixit, A. K. (1970), 'On the optimum structure of commodity taxes', *American Economic Review*, 60, pp. 295–301.

[7] Green, H. A. J. (1961), 'Direct additivity and consumers' behaviour', *Oxford Economic Papers*, 13, pp. 132–6.

[8] Harberger, A. C. (1964), 'Taxation, resource allocation, and welfare', in *The Role of Direct and Indirect Taxes in the Federal Revenue System*, Princeton University Press.

[9] Hicks, U. K. (1968), *Public Finance* (3rd edn), London and New York, Cambridge University Press.

[10] Houthakker, H. S. (1960), 'Additive preferences', *Econometrica*, 28, pp. 244–57.

[11] Lerner, A. P. (1970), 'On optimal taxes with an untaxable sector', *American Economic Review*, 60, pp. 284–94.

[12] Musgrave, R. A. (1959), *The Theory of Public Finance*, New York, McGraw-Hill.

[12a] *National Income and Expenditure of the United Kingdom 1938 to 1946* (1947), HMSO, Cmnd. 7099.

[13] Prest, A. R. (1967), *Public Finance in Theory and Practice* (3rd edn), Weidenfeld & Nicolson.

[14] Ramsey, F. P. (1927), 'A contribution to the theory of taxation', *Economic Journal*, 37, pp. 47–61.

[15] Samuelson, P. A. (1951), *Memorandum for US Treasury*, unpublished.

[16] Stiglitz, J. E. and Dasgupta, P. S. (1971), 'Differential taxation, public goods, and economic efficiency', *Review of Economic Studies*, 38, pp. 151–74.

[17] Stiglitz, J. E. (1970), 'Taxation, risk taking, and the allocation of investment in a competitive economy', in Jensen, M. (ed.), *Studies in the Theory of Capital Markets*.

[18] Stone, R. (1954), 'Linear expenditure systems and demand analysis: an application to the pattern of British demand', *Economic Journal*, 64, pp. 511–27.

11 The Design of Tax Structure: Direct Versus Indirect Taxation*

1 Introduction

The recent literature on optimal taxation may be seen as attempting to clarify the structure of the arguments advanced to support changes in the tax system, tracing the implications of taxes and quantifying (analytically) the trade-offs between the various objectives of tax policy. This literature has examined the optimal structure for particular types of taxation taken in isolation, such as the optimal rates of excise tax and the optimal income tax schedule. Our purpose, on the other hand, is to provide a broader framework and to consider the interaction between different kinds of taxation. To illustrate this, we re-examine the age-old question of direct versus indirect taxation and the relationship of these taxes to the goals of efficiency, vertical equity and horizontal equity.

After describing, in section 2, the general framework of the analysis, and arguing that any treatment of the choice of tax structures must be centrally concerned with distributional considerations, we begin in section 3 with the extension of the classic Ramsey formula for optimal excise taxation to include vertical equity objectives. This was considered by Diamond and Mirrlees [8], but the results given here are in a rather different form.[1] The rest of the chapter is concerned with the case where the government can employ both income and excise taxes. In section 4 it is shown that the existence of an optimal linear income tax may lead to quite different results. Section 5 introduces the possibility of a general nonlinear income tax, and argues that under a relatively wide class of conditions – separability between leisure and consumption – the optimal tax system can rely solely on income taxation. This brings out clearly the importance of considering simultaneously the whole range of tax instruments open to the government. Finally, section 6 examines the relationship between vertical and horizontal equity, and the implications of differences in tastes.

2 The Basic Framework for Taxation

The general problem of taxation of individuals may be posed as follows. There are a large number of people in any economy who differ with respect to a

* Reprinted from *Journal of Public Economics*, **6**, 1976.
A. B. Atkinson and J. E. Stiglitz.

number of characteristics, in particular their endowments and tastes. On the basis of certain ethical premises, it is decided that individuals with different characteristics should pay varying amounts of tax. If we could observe these characteristics costlessly and perfectly, that would be the end of the analysis: we would simply impose a lump-sum tax on individuals, with the amount differing according to their characteristics. The theory of optimal taxation would then be concerned simply with deriving, on the basis of the specified ethical premises, what the functional relationship between characteristics and taxes 'ought to be'.[2]

It is the difficulties associated with observing characteristics which make the theory of taxation an interesting and difficult problem. The theory may be seen as being concerned with the choice of certain easily observable characteristics which are related systematically to the unobservable characteristics in which we are really interested. It is thus part of what has come to be called the 'theory of screening'. The use of these surrogate characteristics gives rise to a number of problems similar to those discussed in the screening literature (see, for example, Spence [18] and Stiglitz [25]).

(1) Many of the characteristics which may be used for screening are, at least to some extent, under the control of the individual, and basing a tax on these is inevitably distortionary.

(2) Almost all characteristics which may be used for screening are imperfect; that is, the surrogate characteristics employed to determine tax liability are not perfectly correlated with the characteristics with which we are really concerned.

(3) There are costs (e.g. of administration) associated with even non-distortionary screening systems.

This general view of taxation shows that the analysis of tax systems must be inherently concerned with individual differences. As a consequence, the treatment of, say, optimal excise taxation in a world where individuals are assumed to be identical is at best of limited relevance. In what follows we assume that people differ with respect to their abilities (earning power) and their tastes, although for the main part of the chapter (sections 3–5) we concentrate on differences in ability. For simplicity we assume that this can be measured by a single parameter, n, so that an individual of ability n_1 can do in $1/n_1$ hours what an individual of ability n_2 can perform in $1/n_2$ hours. We assume, however, that ability is not observable directly. What one can identify depends on the nature of the employment relationship. The following are three of the most important possibilities, where L is the number of labour hours worked, e is the level of effort, and income is given by $Y = neL$.

(i) Income is observable, but effort and labour time are not. This makes sense for unincorporated businesses, although not necessarily for employees.

(ii) Wages per hour ($w \equiv ne$) are observable, but not labour hours and hence not income. This applies where individuals may have several jobs and it may be difficult to keep track of them. It should be noted that where effort is unobservable, one cannot infer ability, even when one can observe the wage rate.

(iii) Both wages and hours are observable, but since effort is not, ability cannot
be inferred.

Case (i) corresponds to that where income taxation is employed (Y is the
surrogate characteristic), case (ii) to that where there is a wage tax (w is the
surrogate characteristic), and in case (iii) there is a choice of screening devices.

In addition to income and wages, other economic variables on which
taxation might be based are purchases by different individuals of different
commodities. In a world where income and wages are unobservable, but
purchases of certain luxuries are observable, the latter may provide the best
screening device. Whether such purchases remain good screening devices
when income and wages *are* observable is one of the question to which we
address ourselves in this chapter. Still other economic variables that may be
useful as screening devices are the sources of income, e.g. the government could
distinguish between salaried and wage workers, between earned and unearned
income, or, within unearned income, between dividends and capital gains. For
the purposes of this chapter, however, we consider only labour income and do
not distinguish among types of jobs, except in terms of the wages they pay.
There are certain other distinctions, such as the sex, age, and marital status of
the worker, which are relatively costless to observe. An argument can be made
for differentiation on this basis (see Boskin [5]), but again, for present
purposes, we ignore these distinctions.

Thus, if x_i are the individual's purchases of commodity i, we can describe a
general tax system as a relationship between potentially observable characteristics, x_i, Y and w, and his tax payments: $T = T(x, Y, w)$. In practice, almost all
tax systems possess a high degree of separability, and indeed are often linear in
some or all of the arguments. There are good reasons why this is so. Not only
are there greater costs of calculating tax liabilities when non-separable and
non-linear tax systems are employed, but also there are significantly higher
costs of record-keeping and enforcement (with linear commodity taxes, for
example, no record of the number of units purchased by a given person need be
kept). Thus although separability and linearity have great analytical advantages, and will be assumed in much of what follows, there are also strong
economic grounds for making these assumptions.

Within this framework, we can consider the following taxes.

Excise tax: $T = \sum_i t_i x_i = t \cdot x$

Where $t \cdot x$ denotes the inner product of the two vectors. In the simplest case
the tax rates t_i are constant, but in certain situations (e.g. housing subsidies) the
tax may be non-proportional. Taxes may also be income-related, $t_i(x_i, Y)$, or
wage-related $t_i(x_i, w)$, the latter applying, for example, to job-related subsidies.

Income tax: $T = T(Y)$

In certain cases the tax base may depend on the consumption of commodities
(e.g. medical care), so that $T = T(Y, x_i)$; it may be constrained to be linear
(constant marginal tax rate) or allowed to vary freely.

Wage tax: $T = \tau(w)L$

Again the tax schedule may be constrained to be linear. (The problem of the optimal wage structure in a socialist country may be viewed as determining the function τ.)

Thus the theory of optimal taxation must be concerned with the choice of tax base as well as the structure of taxes imposed. A full analysis would, of course, begin with the general function $T(x, Y, w)$ and examine its properties. The difficulty with such a completely general approach is that it does not appear – at least at this juncture – to lead to any simple or clear prescriptions. In this chapter we attempt a less ambitious task and focus primarily on the relationship between excise and income taxation. This piecemeal approach has obvious limitations, but we hope that it is sufficient to demonstrate the importance of a unified treatment of the choice of tax base and the optimal design of tax rates. As a preliminary to this, we review in the next section the main results regarding excise taxes viewed in isolation; then, in sections 4–6, we examine the interaction with income tax.

3   Excise Taxes and Distribution

The optimal structure of indirect taxation, and particularly whether there should be differential rates of tax, is an old issue which has recently be re-examined in a series of papers. Much of this literature has ignored differences in endowments and has concentrated on efficiency aspects. At the same time, it has been recognised that the policy prescriptions would need to be modified when distributional considerations were introduced. This aspect of the problem was first discussed by Diamond and Mirrlees [8], their treatment was, however, somewhat different from that given below.

We assume that there are N individuals, denoted by a superscript h. Each individual has a well-behaved utility function defined over the n commodities and labour:[3]

$$U^h = U^h(x, L).\tag{1}$$

The individual maximises utility subject to the budget constraint:

$$q \cdot x = w^h L^h,\tag{2}$$

where q is the price of the commodity to the consumer, and w^h is his after-tax wage. The solution leads to individual demand and labour supply functions. Substituting these back into the utility function gives the indirect utility function $V^h(q, w^h)$. There is no loss of generality (with the assumptions made below) in letting labour be the numeraire and in assuming it to be untaxed (a proportional tax on labour income is simply equivalent to a uniform commodity tax). This will be done throughout the analysis. Finally, we denote by X_i the total demand for good i summed over all individuals ($\Sigma_h x_i^h$).

At this stage it is assumed that the only taxes open to the government are proportional excise taxes at the rate t_i on commodity i, and that no lump-sum taxes or subsidies are allowed.[4] For simplicity, we take producer prices as fixed and normalise them at unity, so that $q_i = 1 + t_i$. We assume that the government wishes to raise a given amount of revenue:

$$R \equiv \sum_h t \cdot x^h \geqslant \bar{R}, \tag{3}$$

and that subject to this constraint it aims to maximise a social welfare function of the Bergson form $G(U^1, \ldots, U^N)$, where G is increasing in all its arguments. Forming the Lagrangian:

$$\mathscr{L} = G(V^h) + \lambda \left[\sum_h t \cdot x^h - \bar{R} \right], \tag{4}$$

straightforward manipulation yields the result that the first-order conditions imply:[5]

$$\left[\sum_k t_k^{(S_{ik}^h)} \right] = - \left[1 - \sum_h b^h \left(\frac{x_i^h}{X_i} \right) \right], \quad i = 1, \ldots, n, \tag{5}$$

where:

$$S_{ik}^h = \left(\frac{\partial x_i^h}{\partial p_k} \right)_{\bar{U}},$$

the compensated price derivative:

$$b^h = \frac{\beta^h}{\lambda} + \frac{\partial R}{\partial I^h},$$

the *net* social marginal utility of income for household h, using government income as numeraire:

$$\beta^h = \frac{\partial G}{\partial V^h} \frac{\partial V^h}{\partial I^h},$$

the gross social marginal utility of income (consumption) accruing to household h; and:

$$\frac{\partial R}{\partial I^h} = \sum_k t_k \frac{\partial x_k^h}{\partial I^h},$$

the marginal tax paid by household h on receiving an extra dollar of income. In interpreting b^h, note that there are two effects of transferring a dollar to the hth household: the direct effect, which is just β^h/λ measured in government revenue, plus an indirect effect – the effect of the transfer on government income. It may also be noted that the mean ($\bar{b}$) is the net value of giving an equal lump-sum payment to everyone. Thus, if uniform lump-sum payments or taxes were allowed, the government would set them at a level such that $\bar{b}=1$. The implications of this are explored in the next section.

The left-hand side of (5) has the usual interpretation of the proportional reduction of the consumption of the *i*th commodity along the compensated demand schedules. We can immediately see that this is no longer necessarily the same for all commodities. Sufficient conditions for it to be independent of *i* are *either* that b^h be the same for all *h* *or* that x_i^h/X_i be the same for all commodities (there are no goods which are consumed disproportionately by rich or poor). In general, where these are not satisfied, the compensated reduction in demand with the optimal tax structure is smaller:[6] (1) the more the good is consumed by individuals with a high net social marginal utility of income, (2) the more the good is consumed by households with a high marginal propensity to consume taxed goods.

Equation (5) can be rewritten in two ways which will prove useful in the subsequent discussion:

$$\sum_h \sum_k t_k S_{ik}^h = -X_i(1-\bar{b}r_i), \qquad i=1,\ldots,n, \tag{5'}$$

where:

$$r_i = \sum_h \left(\frac{x_i^h}{X_i}\right)\left(\frac{b^h}{\bar{b}}\right), \tag{6}$$

and:

$$\sum_h \sum_k t_k S_{ik}^h = -X_i[(1-\bar{b})-\bar{b}\phi_i], \qquad i=1,\ldots,n, \tag{5''}$$

where $\phi_i \equiv r_i - 1$ is the normalised covariance between the consumption of the *i*th commodity and the net social marginal utility of income (a result derived independently by Diamond [7]). In the first of these formulae, r_i is a generalisation of the 'distributional characteristic' of Feldstein [10 and 11]. It shows that if $\bar{b}$ is large, i.e. if there would be large gains from a uniform lump-sum payment, then distributional considerations are to be weighed more heavily.

The extension of the Ramsey formula given above is relatively general. In particular, it allows individuals to differ with respect to both tastes and endowments; other taxes (e.g. a lump-sum tax) may be imposed; and not all commodities need be taxed. (As in the earlier Ramsey analysis, the result does, however, depend on there being either constant returns to scale in production or 100% profits taxes – see Stiglitz and Dasgupta [24].) However, to obtain detailed results on the optimal tax structure, we need to make more specific assumptions about the nature of differences between individuals and the form of the utility function. Here, and until section 6, we assume that everyone has the same tastes, that effort is not a variable, and that individuals differ solely with respect to their ability (wage rate). For ease of analysis, we assume a continuum of individuals, and replace the summation signs in the previously derived formulae by integrals. We let F represent the distribution function of abilities, where we normalise such that $F(\infty) = 1$. The special case of the utility function we consider for purposes of illustration is that where all individuals have independent compensated demand schedules. Equations (5′) and (5″) then give:

$$\frac{t_i}{1+t_i} = \frac{1 - \bar{b}r_i}{\bar{\varepsilon}_i} = \frac{(1-\bar{b}) - \bar{b}\phi_i}{\bar{\varepsilon}_i}, \tag{7}$$

where $\bar{\varepsilon}_i$ is the weighted average compensated price elasticity, the weights being the consumption of the different individuals.[7]

In the case where everyone is identical, (7) reduces to the familiar formula that taxes should be inversely proportional to demand elasticities. Equation (7) provides a simple adjustment to this formula for distributional considerations. The value of r_i depends now solely on the social marginal valuation of income received by different households and on the proportion of total consumption which goes to them. In particular, it depends on the degree of aversion to inequality. If β is constant, i.e. society is indifferent with regard to the distribution, then the optimal tax formula is the familiar one. But if the social marginal valuation of income falls with w, this tends to increase the tax rate on goods which are primarily consumed by those at the top of the scale.[8]

A formula similar to (7) was given by Feldstein [10 and 11], but he did not bring out the inherent conflict between equity and efficiency considerations. With an additively separable utility function and constant marginal utility of leisure, demands depend on the ratio of commodity price to wage. This means that a commodity with a low elasticity of demand appears from an efficiency standpoint to be a good candidate for taxation, but that since the consumption of such a commodity rises only slowly with w, this points to low tax rates for equity reasons. Which of these factors will predominate depends on the form of the social welfare function and on the shape of the distribution of abilities.

One especially simple case to examine is that where the government maximises the sum of utilities – the classical utilitarian case – and where the compensated demand curves have constant elasticity. In Table 1, we present the value of ϕ_i and the associated form of equation (7) for the Pareto and lognormal distributions. For the Pareto distribution, it follows that where the government would like to make a uniform lump-sum transfer to every one ($\bar{b} > 1$), the tax rate rises with the elasticity of demand; this is therefore a sufficient condition for equity to outweigh efficiency considerations and for goods with a high price elasticity to be taxed more heavily. It may also be noted that the magnitude of the distributional term falls with δ, or as the distribution of abilities becomes less unequal (for the same mean, see Chipman [6]). For the lognormal distribution, if $\bar{b} > 1$ and σ is small, then again the distributional considerations dominate; but if σ is not small, then as the

Table 1   *Values of distributional characteristics: Pareto and lognormal distributions*

(a) Pareto distribution: $f = \delta \tilde{w}^\delta w^{-(1+\delta)}$ (where it is required that $\delta > \varepsilon_i$):

$$\phi_i = \frac{-\varepsilon_i}{\delta(1+\delta-\varepsilon_i)}, \qquad \frac{t_i}{1+t_i} = -\frac{(\bar{b}-1)}{\varepsilon_i} + \frac{\bar{b}}{\delta(1+\delta-\varepsilon_i)}.$$

(b) Lognormal distribution (where $(e^{\sigma^2}-1)^{1/2}$ is the coefficient of variation):

$$\phi_i = e^{-\varepsilon_i \sigma^2} - 1, \qquad \frac{t_i}{1+t_i} = -\frac{(\bar{b}-1)}{\varepsilon_i} + \frac{\bar{b}(1-e^{-\varepsilon_i \sigma^2})}{\varepsilon_i}.$$

elasticity of demand increases, the tax rate may at first increase (for low elasticities, distributional considerations are more important) and then decrease (for high elasticities, efficiency dominates).[9]

4   Excise Taxes with an Optimal Linear Income Tax

Thus far we have considered indirect taxation in isolation from the rest of the tax system, and in particular we have not examined how the possibility of employing *direct* taxes affects the optimal structure of *indirect* taxation. How does the existence of a progressive income tax affect the balance between equity and efficiency considerations in determining the optimal rates of excise taxation?

A first step towards considering the interaction between direct and indirect taxation may be taken by a relatively straightforward modification of the analysis of the previous section. The simplest progressive income tax is that where there is an exemption level and a proportional rate of tax both above and below this level (the tax below the exemption level being a negative income tax, so that the taxpayer receives a supplement from the revenue). Such a linear income tax schedule can readily be incorporated into the model we have been discussing, since wages are the only source of income and a uniform tax on all commodities is equivalent to a proportional tax on wages. The only difference therefore is in the exemption level, which can be introduced by supposing that the government provides a lump-sum payment identical in amount (E) to all individuals (if E is negative, it is a lump-sum tax). We assume an additive, symmetric, social welfare function and write the Lagrangian:

$$\mathscr{L} = \int_0^\infty [G\{V(t,E)\} + \lambda\{t \cdot x - E - \bar{R}\}] \, dF. \tag{8}$$

The indirect utility function now depends on E, where $\partial V/\partial E = \alpha$, the marginal utility of income. The first-order conditions give:

$$\frac{\partial \mathscr{L}}{\partial t_i} = \int_0^\infty \left[(\lambda - G'\alpha)x_i + \lambda \sum_k t_k \frac{\partial x_k}{\partial t_i} \right] dF = 0, \qquad i = 1, \ldots, n, \tag{9}$$

$$-\frac{\partial \mathscr{L}}{\partial H} - \int_A^\infty \left[(\lambda - G'\alpha) - \lambda \sum_k t_k \frac{\partial x_k}{\partial I} \right] dF = 0 . \tag{10}$$

Since $\beta = G'\alpha$, (10) is equivalent to $\bar{b} = 1$, as the previous section indicated. Thus, with an optimal linear income tax, the percentage reduction of consumption along the compensated demand schedule is simply *equal* to the normalised covariance between consumption of the commodity and the net marginal social utility of income (equation (5″) with $\bar{b} = 1$).

If β were constant, that is, if society were indifferent regarding the distribution, then $\{t_i = 0, \text{ all } i\}$ would provide a solution to the first-order conditions, and if there were a positive revenue requirement, it would all be raised by a poll tax $(E < 0)$. This is a quite intuitive result, since we should expect that efficiency considerations taken on their own would dictate using solely a lump-sum tax. Where the government is concerned with the distribution of income, i.e. β is a decreasing function of w, then indirect taxes would in general be employed. The question, however, is whether they would be employed with differential rates, since, as we have seen, a uniform indirect tax is equivalent – in this model – to a proportional income tax.

The point at issue may be illustrated by one very special example. Suppose that the utility function is quadratic (an example used by Ramsey), that the cross-terms are zero, and that the marginal utility of leisure is constant:

$$U = \sum_i \left(a_i x_i - \frac{c_i}{2} x_i^2 \right) - vL . \tag{11}$$

In the absence of the income tax, it may be shown that the optimal tax rates vary according to $a_i(1 - \bar{b})$, and would in general differ across commodities. However, the introduction of an income tax with the exemption level E means that $\bar{b} = 1$, and that the optimal tax structure is uniform. It follows that no indirect taxation need be employed, and that the optimum may be achieved simply through a linear income tax. (Another example is the linear expenditure system – see Chapter 12.)

Where the utility function is more general, but the compensated demands are still independent, we can see from equation (7) that $t_i/(1 + t_i) = -\phi_i/\bar{\varepsilon}_i$. We may note two features of this result. First, it implies that there is no case for subsidising normal goods; an increase in the lump-sum subsidy is always superior. Secondly, the tax rates depend on the level of revenue to be raised only through the dependence on the covariance of x_i with net marginal social utility of income. With a constant marginal utility of leisure and $G' = 1$, ϕ_i is independent of the level of revenue to be raised – any increase in $\bar{R}$ is met by a reduction in E. Hence for sufficiently large $\bar{R}$, the tax system is regressive.

From Table 1 we can derive the optimal tax rates in the constant elasticity case. For the Pareto distribution, the tax is higher on goods with a higher price elasticity (which is also the elasticity with respect to w). With $\delta = 3.0$, the tax rates vary from 9.5% with $\varepsilon = 0.5$, to 16.7% with $\varepsilon = 2.0$. In the case of the lognormal, it is quite possible for the tax rate to fall with ε: for example, if $(\sigma^2 \varepsilon)$

is sufficiently less than 1 for third and higher powers to be neglected, then the tax rate may be approximated by $\sigma^2 - \varepsilon\sigma^4/2$, which gives the following results (where all individuals work).

σ^2	ε		
	0.5	1.0	2.0
0.16	15%	15%	13%
0.24	23%	21%	18%

The fact that the tax structure may be regressive (i.e. the rates fall with ε) may appear to conflict with the intuitive notion discussed above that efficiency considerations would point to the use of a poll tax and that it is concern for the distribution which leads to the use of commodity taxes. However, when distributional objectives are relevant, indirect taxes play two roles. First, by taxing luxuries at a higher rate they may increase the progressitivity of the tax system; secondly, they provide an alternative source of revenue, allowing the regressive poll tax to be reduced or converted into a lump-sum payment. In the latter case, the revenue would be raised in the distortion-minimising way, and the final tax structure would balance the two sets of considerations.

Going back to the general formulation (5″), we can see that:

$$\int_0^\infty \left(\sum_k S_{ik} t_k \right) dF = \int_0^\infty (x_i - X_i)(b - \bar{b}) \, dF, \tag{12}$$

so that the reduction of consumption along the compensated demand curve is simply equal to the covariance between the consumption of that good and the net marginal social utility of income. For small variance, the tax structure may be approximated by taking a Taylor series expansion of the RHS of (12):

$$x_i \phi_i \approx \frac{dx_i}{dw} \frac{\partial b}{\partial w} \sigma_w^2,$$

where σ_w^2 is the variance of wages (abilities). Thus, the percentage reduction (along the compensated demand curve) in consumption is exactly proportional to the uncompensated derivative of the commodity with respect to the wage. If there is constant marginal utility of leisure and separable demand functions, we obtain:

$$x_i \phi_i \approx q_i \left(\frac{\partial x_i}{\partial q_i} \right)_U \frac{\partial b}{\partial w} \sigma_w^2,$$

so:

$$\frac{t_i}{1+t_i} \approx \frac{\partial\phi}{\partial w} U_w^{l_i}$$

independent of i: i.e. to the first order of approximation, there should be uniform taxation.

Expanding ϕ_i further shows that to the second order of approximation, differences in tax rates depend on the concavity or convexity of the demand functions $(\partial^2 x_1/\partial q_i^2)$ and the third moment of the ability distribution, parameters for which we are unlikely to obtain robust estimates.

The examples given above show that the results described in the previous section may need significant modification where the government is able to employ income taxation, even where this is restricted to a simple linear schedule. In the next section we examine the relationship between direct and indirect taxation where the income tax schedule may be freely varied.

5   Excise Taxes and Optimal Income Taxation

We assume that the income tax schedule is differentiable,[10] but apart from that may be of any form. We also allow for the possibility that the tax rate on commodities may be a function of the level of consumption.[11] The individual with wage w faces a budget constraint:

$$\sum_i (x_i + t_i(x_i)) = wL - T(wL), \tag{13}$$

and the first-order conditions for utility maximisation are[12]:

$$U_i = \frac{(1+t_i')(-U_L)}{w(1-T')}, \qquad i = 1, \ldots, n. \tag{14}$$

The government maximises the social welfare function subject to:

$$\int_0^\infty \left[\sum_i t_i(x_i) + T(wL) \right] dF = \bar{R},$$

or:

$$\int_0^\infty \left[wL - \sum_i x_i - \bar{R} \right] dF = 0. \tag{15}$$

This problem may be treated in a number of different ways. In the heuristic argument which follows, we take $x_2, \ldots, x_n$ and L as the control variables, treating U as a state variable, and making use of the fact that x_1 depends on U, $x_2, \ldots, x_n$ and L. Moreover:

$$\frac{dU}{dw} = \frac{-U_L L}{w} \equiv -U_L \theta(w, L). \tag{16}$$

The Hamiltonian may then be written:

$$H = \left[G(U) + \lambda(wL - \sum_i x_i - \bar{R}) \right] f - \mu \phi U_L, \tag{17}$$

where f is the density function. Maximising H with respect to x_i, we obtain as necessary conditions:

$$-\lambda \left[\left(\frac{\partial x_1}{\partial x_i} \right)_U + 1 \right] - \frac{\mu}{f} \left[U_{L1} \left(\frac{\partial x_1}{\partial x_i} \right)_{\bar{U}} + U_{Li} \right] \theta = 0. \tag{18}$$

From (14) it is immediate that:

$$\left[\frac{\partial x_1}{\partial x_i} \right]_U = -\frac{U_i}{U_1} = -\frac{(1 - t_i')}{(1 + t_1')}. \tag{19}$$

Thus we can rewrite (18) as:

$$\lambda \left[\frac{1 + t_i'}{1 + t_1'} - 1 \right] = \frac{\mu \theta U_i}{f} \frac{d \log \left(\dfrac{U_i}{U_1} \right)}{dL}. \tag{20}$$

Without loss of generality, we set $t_1' = 0$. Hence:

$$\frac{t_i'}{1 + t_i'} = \frac{\mu \theta \alpha}{\lambda f} \frac{d \log \left(\dfrac{U_i}{U_1} \right)}{dL}. \tag{21}$$

Tax rates are simply proportional to the rate at which the marginal rate of substitution between commodity i and commodity 1 changes with a change in the consumption of leisure.

From this analysis we obtain at once an interesting result. If the utility function is weakly separable between labour and all consumption goods (taken together), then no commodity taxation need be employed ($t_i = 0$). It is immediate that we could have allowed U to depend on n as well, as long as we maintain our separability hypothesis: $U = U(V(x_1, \ldots, x_n), L, n)$. With the greater flexibility provided by the non-linear income tax schedule, the result found for special cases in the previous section now holds for much more general utility functions. The assumption of separability between consumption and labour may well be regarded as a reasonable first approximation for our purpose; and even if it is in fact empirically rejected, it is a useful benchmark case.[13] From the results given above, it follows that goods which are complementary (in the Edgeworth, not the more usual Hicksian, sense) with leisure ($U_{iL} < 0$) will face lower tax rates, whereas substitutes face higher tax rates. Finally, it is interesting to note that relative tax rates are independent of the social welfare function, so that they may be viewed as conditions for constrained Pareto optimality.[14]

There are three interesting applications of the results given above which should be mentioned briefly (see also Chapter 16). First, if the goods are interpreted as consumption at different dates, then the analysis shows that the conventional presumption in favour of consumption rather than income taxation may be interpreted as assuming separability between leisure and consumption. Perhaps a more reasonable structure of preferences in this context is:

$$U = U_1(c_1, L) + U_2(c_2),$$

in which case whether there should be an interest income tax or subsidy depends on the complementarity or substitutability (in the Edgeworth sense) between the first-period consumption and labour (but see Chapter 14). The second application is to the question of the differential treatment of safe and risky assets: x_i is then treated as purchases of the ith security. Our theorem then says that where the individual maximises $V(L) + EU(Y)$, there should be no differential treatment of risk assets (Stiglitz [20] and Chapter 10).

The third application is to the use of quotas of specific allocations for distributing certain goods. Some economists (e.g. Tobin [25]) have argued that there exist certain inelastically supplied commodities (medical care, at least in the short run) where quotas might be desirable. Such quota systems can be viewed as an extreme non-linear commodity tax-subsidy scheme: below the quota the price is zero, above the quota, infinite. Viewed this way, the question of the desirability of quotas is equivalent simply to the question of whether it is optimal to have such an extreme form of progression for some particular commodity. The import of our theorem is that, provided the separability assumption is satisfied, not only should no quota be employed for such commodities, but not even a tax should be imposed. The result does not depend on the supply elasticities for the commodities in question.[15]

The basic intuition behind the argument that quotas might be desirable for inelastic commodities was that, if commodities are elastically supplied, then individuals should be allowed to trade off consumption of one good against the other: an individual's increased consumption of vanilla ice-cream cones does not deprive someone else of his consumption of vanilla ice-cream cones. When commodities are inelastically supplied, then there is no production inefficiency introduced by quotas. But prices serve as signals not only for the production of goods but also for the allocation of goods among individuals (the conventional exchange model). So long as tastes differ, the use of quotas will result in exchange inefficiency.

But, it might be argued, if we had a separable utility function, a first-best solution would entail allocating the same amount of the given good to everyone (if they had the same utility function) and hence we could achieve a first-best allocation of this particular good, with no loss of production efficiency. Such an argument, though plausible at first sight, fails to recognise the second-best nature of the problem we are considering: satisfying one of the first-best conditions (equating marginal utilities of consuming this particular good) does not necessarily represent an improvement when the other conditions are not satisfied.

A more plausible argument is that if we are able to discriminate among those with higher incomes by charging them a higher price (e.g. by having price an increasing function of quantity consumed) we would improve welfare, since such a differential price imposes a higher cost on those with lower marginal utilities of income. But there is a cost in dead weight loss from such differential pricing, and the import of our theorem is that in the central case examined, the cost outweighs the gains.[16]

6   Differences in Tastes and Horizontal Equity

The existence of differences in tastes among individuals of the same ability raises issues in the design of the tax structure which we have not yet taken into account. In the conventional treatment, the principle of horizontal equity – that people who are in all relevant senses identical ought to be treated identically – plays an important role. In this section, we discuss, necessarily briefly, the nature of this principle as well as its implications for the design of tax policy. We first point out that the principle of horizontal equity may be in direct conflict with the utilitarian maximum even when tastes are identical; next we examine the case where tastes differ and show that the principle does not imply, as some have suggested, uniform taxation; finally, we consider more generally the status of horizontal equity as an objective of government policy.

The literature on optimal taxation has typically assumed that the re-distributive goals of the government may be represented by maximising a Bergsonian social welfare function, such as $G(U)$ defined above, and has not discussed the relationship between this and the concept of horizontal equity. Some earlier authors have taken the view that there is no conflict: 'the requirements of horizontal and vertical equity are but different sides of the same coin' (Musgrave [15], p. 160). However, this need not be so. It is quite possible that the maximisation of a Bergsonian social welfare function may indicate that individuals with identical tastes and endowments should be taxed at different rates (if this is feasible), thus violating conventional notions of horizontal equity (see Chapter 5 and Atkinson and Stiglitz [4]).[17]

The point is that if the feasible set of allocations is not convex (as it may be when only indirect taxes are employed), optimality may entail treating otherwise identical individuals differently.[18] An even stronger conflict has been noted by Stiglitz [22], where horizontal equity may conflict with the principle of Pareto optimality. Even before we introduce taste differences, therefore, there is a possible conflict between horizontal equity and the maximisation of a social welfare function of the type usually assumed.

If we now introduce differences in tastes, the immediate consequence is that we must confront the interpersonal comparability question, which we have ignored thus far. When individuals have the same indifference curves, it is natural simply to use the same cardinal number of the indifference curves for different individuals. But when tastes differ, this is no longer so. Even if everyone had the same homothetic indifference maps, we must still decide which indifference curve for individual 1 corresponds to a given curve for individual 2.

The point is that the utilitarian system evaluates taxes in terms of the individual's ability to derive utility from goods and leisure, and in this respect may be contrasted with the alternative criterion of 'ability to pay,' that is, of basing taxation on opportunity sets. When the only differences are those in the ability to produce, then a utilitarian ethic leads to redistribution from those with 'better' opportunity sets to those with 'poorer'. There is no conflict between it and the ability-to-pay approach. But this may arise as soon as tastes differ. Suppose individual 1 has a higher productivity, so that his budget constraint lies outside that of individual 2. The ability-to-pay criterion would indicate that individual 1 paid more tax, but there are obviously numberings of their indifference curves which lead to the opposite result with the utilitarian objective.

In order to contrast these two approaches, let us suppose that tastes may be represented by a single parameter, γ, so that the indirect utility function may be written as $V(q, w, \gamma)$. The utilitarian principle recognises such taste differences as a legitimate basis for discrimination, and the government maximises $G[V(q, w, \gamma)]$. On the other hand, if we introduce the concept of horizontal equity and interpret this as meaning that differences in tastes are not 'relevant' characteristics on which discrimination ought to be based, then this has two implications. First, it introduces a cardinalisation $V(1, w, \gamma) = \tilde{V}(1, w)$, so that only endowments, w, and consumer prices (normalised at unity before tax) are relevant. Secondly, it constrains the government in levying taxes ($q \neq 1$) to maintain:

$$V(q, w, \gamma) = \tilde{V}(q, w). \tag{22}$$

Suppose that the government were to adopt this version of horizontal equity; what would be the implications for the optimal tax structure? It is popularly believed that it would require uniform taxation. If two individuals are identical in all respects except that one likes chocolate ice-cream and the other likes vanilla, a system which taxes chocolate ice-cream at a higher rate is felt to be horizontally inequitable.[19] This is not however necessarily correct, as may be seen from the following example:

$$U = \sum_i (A_i(\gamma))^{(1/\varepsilon_i)} \frac{x_i^{1-(1/\varepsilon_i)}}{1-(1/\varepsilon_i)} - vL.$$

(It should be noted that we are assuming that there are no differences between people in the marginal utility of leisure, and that ε_i is independent of γ.) Let us further assume that A_i is independent of γ, for $i = 3, \ldots, n$, and that $A_1 = \gamma$. The requirement of normalisation is then that $A_2(\gamma)$ is such that $V(1, w, \gamma) = V(1, w)$: i.e. that all those with the same w have the same pre-tax utility. Using this, it can be shown that the horizontal equity condition (22) requires that:[20]

$$q_1^{1 - \varepsilon_1} = q_2^{1 - \varepsilon_2}. \tag{23}$$

The condition for horizontal equity is not, therefore, uniform taxation; only if the price elasticity is the same – as it may well be in the chocolate/vanilla ice-cream case – would uniform tax rates be horizontally equitable. This may be related to the argument made by Pigou [17]:

Suppose that there are two persons of equal income and general economic status, that in the aggregate of their tastes they are similar, in the sense that they would get equal satisfactions from equal incomes if they were permitted to spend them as they chose, but that one likes and purchases commodity A and not commodity B, the other commodity B and not commodity A. Suppose, further, that taxes are imposed upon commodities A and B in such ways that both these persons pay the same amount of tax. It will not necessarily follow that they suffer equal real burdens. If the demand of one for his commodity is more elastic than the demand of the other for his, the former will suffer the larger hurt (p. 77).

The model just described is a very simple one, but it brings out clearly the conflict between horizontal equity and the maximisation of a social welfare function of the Bergson type. For example, where $G' = 1$ (the classical utilitarian case), the latter leads to the first-order condition:

$$1 - \frac{1}{q_i} = \frac{1 - \bar{b}r_i}{\varepsilon_i},$$

as before. This is not in general consistent with the requirement of horizontal equity, equation (23).

This raises the important issue of the status of the horizontal equity principle. It is often suggested that horizontal equity is in some sense prior to vertical equity: 'it is sometimes said that the horizontal aspect is more basic and less controversial' (Musgrave and Musgrave [16], p. 199). Most authors, including Musgrave and Musgrave, go on to argue that neither is more basic than the other; however, this ignores the conflict which we have seen to arise between the two principles, at least in the form presented here. Faced with this potential conflict, it might seem more reasonable to view the social welfare function as lexicographic. For certain classes of goods, probably those marked by considerable diversity of tastes, the horizontal equity requirement is imposed, and the government then maximises a Bergsonian social welfare function subject to this constraint. As Pigou (p. 51) put it, 'the ideal of least sacrifice has to be pursued subject to a handicap'. The optimal structure of taxation, and the choice between direct and indirect taxes, will depend on how wide is the range of goods covered by constraints such as (23).

7 Concluding Comments

In this chapter, we have attempted to present a framework within which we can evaluate the appropriateness of different tax bases and to apply this framework to the classical question of the use of direct versus indirect taxation.

The general framework employed may be summarised as follows. The necessity for any form of taxation other than a uniform lump-sum tax arises from the fact that individuals have differing characteristics (endowments or tastes). If we could observe all relevant characteristics costlessly and perfectly, we should be able to achieve a first-best solution. However, in practice we have to make use of surrogate characteristics, which are related systematically to the characteristics on which we would like to differentiate individuals, but which are not perfectly correlated and which are, to some extent, under the control of the individual. Certain ethical principles, notably those which fall under the rubric of horizontal equity, limit further the set of surrogates which may be used. Having established an admissible class of characteristics, the problem then becomes one of determining which are to be employed (the choice of tax base) and the structure of the tax schedule.

The application of this framework to the direct/indirect tax problem led to the following results. First, if the government had no distributional objectives and was concerned solely with efficiency, it may employ only direct taxation and this would take the form of a poll tax. This is a very straightforward prescription, but it has the implication, which runs counter to much popular belief, that the use of indirect taxation stems from a pursuit of distributional objectives. The extent to which indirect taxes are employed to this purpose – that is, purchases of different commodities are used as a screening device – depends on the form of consumer preferences and on the restrictions (if any) on the type of income taxation employed. If a general income tax function may be chosen by the government, we have shown that, where the utility function is separable between labour and all commodities, no indirect taxes need be employed. In this case, the use of consumption of particular commodities as a screening device offers no benefit. Finally, we have seen that horizontal equity considerations may impose constraints on the structure of taxes which may be levied.

Throughout the chapter, we have stressed the importance of the interactions between different taxes, and the fact that a piecemeal approach may be misleading. In section 4, for example, it was shown that in the quadratic case considered by Ramsey (plus constant marginal utility of leisure and independence) the introduction of an optimal linear income tax meant that indirect taxation was no longer necessary. The Ramsey-style results would, therefore, only be relevant where there were constraints on the use of income taxation. Such interactions are equally a warning that the results given in this paper should be treated with considerable caution. For this and other reasons, such as the failure to incorporate the costs of administration,[21] the theory may be more useful in illuminating the structure of the argument than in providing definite answers to policy issues.

Acknowledgement

This is a revised and condensed version of the paper given at the ISPE meeting under the title 'Alternative approaches to the distribution of income'. Parts of the paper have been presented by the first author at seminars at the Universities of Essex, Harvard and Namur, and by the second author at Chicago, National Bureau of Economic Research–West and Stanford, and they are grateful to participants in these seminars for their helpful comments. This work was supported in part by National Science Foundation Grant SOC73-22182 at the Institute of Mathematical Studies in the Social Sciences at Stanford University, and in part by the Guggenheim and Ford Foundations.

Notes

1 This section includes the distributional results referred to in Chapter 10.
2 Another potentially important function of the tax system – to provide signals concerning the demand for public goods – is not discussed here.
3 The labour variable may be treated more generally as a vector, including elements such as hours, effort, etc.
4 Such a restriction makes sense in the context of the general approach taken in this chapter only if 'individuals' are not directly observable as individuals, e.g. with a lump-sum subsidy, they could collect twice under different 'names' or with a lump-sum tax they disappear into the bush.
5 This by making use of the fact that $\partial V/\partial q_i = - x_i^h \alpha^h$, where α^h is the private marginal utility of income of individual h, and of the Slutsky equation:

$$\frac{\partial x_k}{\partial q_i} = S_{ki} - x_i \frac{\partial x_k}{\partial I},$$

where $\partial x_k/\partial I$ is the derivative with respect to income (evaluated at $I = 0$ in this case) and S_{ki} is the compensated price term.
6 Diamond and Mirrlees [8] derived the analogous expression for the uncompensated changes. Since the uncompensated reductions in demand with the optimal tax structure are not the same even without distributional considerations, to make comparisons with the Ramsey results more direct, we have employed compensated derivatives. In the uncompensated form, Diamond and Mirrlees have identified a third factor determining the percentage reduction in demand: it will be greater the more the demand for the commodity is concentrated among individuals for whom the product of the income derivative of demand for that good and total taxes paid is large.
7 The first-order conditions need careful interpretation since they may not lead to a unique solution. Where the price elasticity varies with q_i there may be multiple solutions, and the optimal tax structure may involve taxing at different rates two goods with identical demand curves.
8 That is, letting r_i be a function of p, some measure of inequality aversion with $p = 0$ corresponding to no inequality aversion, then $r_i(0) = 1$, for all i, and:

$$r_i(p) - r_i(0) = \frac{\sum (x_i^h - \bar{x}_i)(b^h - \bar{b})}{\bar{b} X_i} \gtrless 0 \quad \text{as} \quad \frac{\partial x^h}{\partial b^h} \gtrless 0,$$

i.e. households which consume more of x_i (relative to mean consumption $\bar{x}_i$) have a higher or lower valued net marginal social utility of income. (For the meaning of inequality aversion, see Chapter 1; and Diamond and Stiglitz [9].) Because of our normalisation, $\bar{x}_i = X_i$.

9 This may be seen by expanding the term $\exp(-\varepsilon_i\sigma^2)$ and first considering terms of order σ^2, and then of order σ^4 (it is assumed that $\sigma^2\varepsilon_i<1$).

10 See Mirrlees [13]. In general this need not be the case. For an analysis of such non-differentiabilities within the context of this class of 'screening' problems, see Stiglitz [21].

11 Actually we could have considered a general tax function of the form $T(x, L, w)$. In fact, for this particular problem, the results for the more restrictive, but practically more important, tax structure involving separability assumed here are identical to those in which the separability is dropped. This may be seen most easily by observing that nowhere in the analysis is the separability restriction on the tax function actually used.

12 For an interior solution; we do not consider the case where labour supply is zero, although the analysis could easily be modified.

13 Where a subset of commodities is separable from labour, then the commodities in this group should all be taxed at the same rate.

14 We are indebted to J. A. Mirrlees for pointing this out in his discussion of the paper at the Paris conference.

15 In our proof, we assume an elastic supply of all commodities, but it is easy to establish that, provided profits (rents) are fully taxed, the results are true for any production technology (including the limiting case of a perfect inelastically supplied commodity).

16 Spence [19] and Weitzman [26] have discussed this issue in a partial equilibrium context. The fact that their results differ from those given here is attributable to the fact that the presence of the optimal income tax has important implications for the role to be played by other distributive mechanisms, as we have emphasised throughout this chapter.

17 Consider the simplest possible case of labour and a single consumption good (C), with two identical individuals. We assume that lump-sum taxes (poll taxes) are not admissible. The utilitarian problem may be formulated as:

$$\max V(q_1)+V(q_2),$$

subject to:

$$\tau_1 C_1 + \tau_2 C_2 = \bar{R},$$

with first-order conditions:

$$V_{q_i}(q_i) = -\lambda\left(C_i + \tau_i\frac{\partial C_i}{\partial q_i}\right),$$

where λ is the Lagrange multiplier associated with the constraint. It is obvious that:

$$q_i = q_2 = q^* = 1 + \tau^*$$

where:

$$2\tau^* C(q^*) = \bar{R},$$

satisfies the first-order conditions. But:

$$V_{qq} + \lambda\left(\tau_i\frac{\partial^2 C_i}{\partial q_i^2} + \frac{2\partial C_i}{\partial q_i}\right)$$

may well be positive at $q_i = q^*$, which would mean that this represents a local minimum.

18 Analogous results in different contexts have been noted by Stiglitz [22] and Mirrlees [14].

19 Pigou [17] gives a nice example: 'When England and Ireland were united under the same taxing authority, it was strongly argued that, owing to the divergent tastes of Englishmen and Irishmen, it was improper to subject them to the same tax formulae in respect of beer and whiskey.' The tax on spirits, more generaly consumed in Ireland, was more than two-thirds of the price, whereas the tax rate on beer was only about one-sixth of the price.

20 It may be noted that (for $\varepsilon_i \neq 1$):

$$V(q, w, \gamma) = \sum_i \frac{A_i(\gamma)}{(\varepsilon_i - 1)} \left[\frac{(vq_i)}{w} \right]^{1 - \varepsilon_i}$$

21 See Heller and Shell [12] for an attempt to introduce administration costs into the analysis of optimal taxation.

References

[1] Atkinson, A. B. (1970), 'On the measurement of inequality', Chapter 1 in this volume.

[2] Atkinson, A. B. (1974), 'Housing allowances, income maintenance and income taxation', Chapter 16 in this volume.

[3] Atkinson, A. B. and J. E. Stiglitz (1972), 'The structure of indirect taxation and economic efficiency', Chapter 10 in this volume.

[4] Atkinson, A. B. and Stiglitz, J. E. (1980), *Lectures on Public Economics*, Maidenhead and New York, McGraw-Hill.

[5] Boskin, M. J. (1973), *Optimal Tax Treatment of the Family*, Memorandum 143, Center for Research in Economic Growth, Stanford University, Stanford, Ca.

[6] Chipman, J. S. (1974), 'The welfare ranking of Pareto distributions', *Journal of Economic Theory*, **9**, 275–82.

[7] Diamond, P. A. (1975), 'A many-person Ramsey tax rule', *Journal of Public Economics*, **4**, 335–43.

[8] Diamond, P. A. and Mirrlees, J. A. (1971), 'Optimal taxation and public production', *American Economic Review*, **61**, 8–27 and 261–78.

[9] Diamond, P. A. and Stiglitz, J. E. (1974), 'Increases in risk and in risk aversion', *Journal of Economic Theory*, **9**, 337–60.

[10] Feldstein, M. S. (1972a), 'Distributional equity and the optimal structure of public prices', *American Economic Review*, **62**, 32–6.

[11] Feldstein, M. S. (1972b), 'Equity and efficiency in public pricing', *Quarterly Journal of Economics*, **86**, 175–87.

[12] Heller, W. P. and Shell, K. (1974), 'On optimal taxation with costly administration', *American Economic Review*, **74**, papers and proceedings, 338–45.

[13] Mirrlees, J. A. (1971), 'An exploration in the theory of optimum income taxation', *Review of Economic Studies*, **38**, 175–208.

[14] Mirrlees, J. A. (1972), 'Population policy and the taxation of family size', *Journal of Public Economics*, **1**, 169–98.

[15] Musgrave, R. A. (1959), *The Theory of Public Finance*, McGraw-Hill, New York.

[16] Musgrave, R. A. and Musgrave, P. B. (1973), *Public Finance in Theory and Practice*, McGraw-Hill, New York.

[17] Pigou, A. C. (1947), *A Study in Public Finance*, Macmillan, London.

[18] Spence, M. (1973), 'Job market signalling', *Quarterly Journal of Economics*, **87**, 355–79.

[19] Spence, M. (1977), 'Nonlinear prices and welfare', *Journal of Public Economics*, **8**, 1–18.

[20] Stiglitz, J. E. (1970), 'Taxation, risk-taking and the allocation of investment in a competitive economy', in M. Jensen (ed.), *Studies in the Theory of Capital Markets*.

[21] Stiglitz, J. E. (1974a), *Monopoly and Imperfect Information*, Oxford and Stanford University, mimeo.

[22] Stiglitz, J. E. (1974b), 'The efficiency wage hypothesis, surplus labor and the distribution of income in LDCs', *Technical Report 152*, IMSSS, Stanford University, Stanford, Ca.

[23] Stiglitz, J. E. (1975), 'The theory of "screening", education and the distribution of income', *American Economic Review*, **65**, 283–300.

[24] Stiglitz, J. E. and Dasgupta, P. S. (1971), 'Differential taxation, public goods, and economic efficiency', *Review of Economic Studies*, **38**, 151–74.

[25] Tobin, J. (1970), 'On limiting the domain of inequality', *Journal of Law and Economics*, **13**, 263–78.

[26] Weitzman, M. L. (1977), 'Is the price system or rationing more effective in getting a commodity to those who need it most?', *Bell Journal of Economics*, **8**, 517–24.

12 Optimal Taxation and the Direct Versus Indirect Tax Controversy*

This chapter is concerned with one of the oldest issues of taxation policy – the choice between direct and indirect taxation. It is also intended to illustrate a broader theme – that of the relation between economic theory and the advice which economists can give to practical men such as ministers of finance and chancellors of the exchequer.

Public finance is a subject where such concern is particularly relevant. There has been a great increase in interest in theoretical aspects of tax and expenditure policy, particularly in the field of optimal taxation. Following pioneering work by Diamond, Mirrlees, and others, it has become a very active area of research. At the same time it has not been well integrated within the mainstream of traditional public finance. Optimal taxation has attracted many people whose background is in economic theory rather than in public finance, and public finance economists have tended to question whether the recent flurry of articles has done any more than formalise what was known already.

For this reason the present chapter takes one major issue of taxation policy with the aim of examining what the public finance literature in both its traditional and its modern varieties has to say which may guide the government in taking decisions. In order to do this, we first need to define the problem, and the first section sets out a schema of different types of taxation. The next section describes the two main views which appear to be held on this issue, at least in the public finance textbooks. We then survey in three sections the theoretical literature of the past forty years, beginning with the debate in the 1930s and 1940s on the 'direct-indirect tax problem', and then going in greater depth into the optimal taxation results. In this survey there is no attempt to present rigorous derivations, and the aim is to concentrate on the interpretation of results and on their relevance to the choice between direct and indirect taxation. The last section summarises the main conclusions.

Definition of the Problem

The basic question is that of the choice of tax base. What should be the weight of the two different types of taxation in the government budget? In order to

* Reprinted from *Canadian Journal of Economics*, **4**, November 1977.

answer this we need to define more precisely what is meant by direct and indirect taxation. In the literature, and in common usage, there are a variety of definitions. Historically, the distinction no doubt arose from the method of administration, in that the taxpayer handed over income tax directly to the revenue authorities, but only paid sales taxes indirectly via the purchase of goods. As Hicks [22] has noted, the phrase 'assise directement' was apparently in use for personal taxes in France in the sixteenth century, and these were contrasted with excise taxes, or 'tarifs'. There is, however, no reason to expect any such administrative classification to have economic significance. The development, for example, of withholding at source is unlikely in itself to have affected the economic impact of income taxation. Similarly, definitions of direct and indirect taxes based on legal powers are probably of limited relevance to economic analysis. For example, the United States Constitution at one time restricted the use of direct taxes by the federal government, and as a result the Supreme Court obligingly declared income tax to be an indirect tax. This kind of definition, described by Dalton [7] as 'the economics of clever lawyers in a tight place' (p. 24), is clearly not what we have in mind.

Turning to a definition related to the economic effects of different types of taxation, that most commonly found in the public finance literature is based on some presumption about the ultimate incidence of the tax. For example, according to Buchanan [4], 'Direct taxation is defined as taxation imposed upon the person who is intended to be the final bearer of the burden of payment. Indirect taxation is defined as taxation imposed upon others than the person who is intended to bear the final burden' (p. 141). According to Due and Friedlaender [11], 'Some taxes – often called *direct* taxes – reduce the real incomes of the persons who pay them to the government ... Other taxes may be shifted from some persons to others ... Taxes believed to be shifted in this fashion are called *indirect* taxes' (p. 229). Such a definition may, however, lead to difficulties where the degree of shifting is neither zero, as assumed for direct taxes, nor 100%, as assumed for indirect taxes. Moreover, it seems unsatisfactory to relate the classification of taxes to assumptions about shifting which may not in the event be realised (for example, income tax may be shifted via wage bargaining).

In view of this, attention is focused here on what seems to be the essential aspect of the distinction: the fact that direct taxes may be adjusted to the individual characteristics of the taxpayer, whereas indirect taxes are levied on transactions irrespective of the circumstances of buyer or seller. Such a definition makes no assumption about shifting and in my view corresponds to the feature which most people have in mind when discussing the choice between direct and indirect taxation. It coincides with the definition of 'means-test devices' used by Rolph [28], which is the class of taxes 'whose base is systematically related to some relevant index of the taxpayer's economic position' (p. 522). Or, as it was put by Shoup [30], 'the most useful distinction to make between direct and indirect taxes is that direct taxes can be "personalised" or tailored to the particular economic and social characteristics of the household being taxed, whereas indirect taxes cannot be so tailored' (p. 301). The only way in which sales taxes can be related to circumstances is *indirectly* via the differences in consumption patterns.

In order to see how this definition works in terms of actual taxes, the following typology of taxes may be helpful:

Indirect:	1	Differentiated sales tax,
	2	⎰ Uniform sales tax (same percentage on all
Transitional:		⎱ commodities),
	3	Proportional expenditure tax,
Direct:	4	⎰ Linear direct tax (constant marginal tax rate),
	5	⎱ Non-linear direct tax (varying marginal tax rate).

This begins with what is clearly an indirect tax: a differentiated sales tax with varying rates for different goods and services. From there one moves to a uniform sales tax, which is on the borderline between direct and indirect. It is on the borderline since in the present context it is equivalent to a proportional tax on personal expenditure, as indicated in the schema above. (In practice, such general sales taxes are relatively rare, since even taxes with a single rate typically allow certain goods to be tax-free, so that there are in effect two rates.) The addition of a personal allowance or exemption to the proportional tax converts it into the linear direct tax shown in the fourth line, where the marginal, but not the average, tax rate is constant.[1] Finally, we have the general direct tax, with varying marginal rates of tax. In its sharpest form, the choice between direct and indirect taxation may be seen, therefore, as the choice between, on the one hand a direct tax on total income or expenditure, with varying marginal rates of tax, and on the other hand a sales tax with differentiated rates for the various commodity groups. In comparing these two types of taxation it is illuminating, however, to proceed via the transitional cases, and this will be the approach adopted below.

Before examining the arguments which can be made for the different types of tax outlined above, three qualifications should be entered. The first is that there is no discussion of short-run issues of macro-policy. There are clearly considerations such as the effect of indirect taxes on the retail price index and of direct taxes on wage negotiations which in the short run are likely to be very much in the mind of a minister of finance. What this chapter is concerned with, however, is the long-run direction in which the minister should move, in so far as the short-run constraints (such as anti-inflationary policy) allow him any room for manoeuvre. The second qualification is that there is no consideration of the tax treatment of savings. This is an important issue but there is not space to do it justice here.[2] In order to simplify the discussion it will therefore be assumed that there are no savings, and the direct tax will be treated interchangeably as a tax on income or a tax on total expenditure (a Mill-Fisher-Kaldor expenditure tax). Thirdly, it will be assumed, again for simplicity, that there are constant returns to scale in production, so that there are no pure profits.

Prevailing Views on Direct Versus Indirect Taxation

It is clearly impossible to provide an adequate summary of all the views which have been expressed on this controversial subject over the course of several centuries. However, there are two 'conflicting' opinions which seem to have attracted considerable support over the years, and these two views provide a useful basis for the subsequent analysis.

View A – Desirable balance
The first view is that there should be a broad balance between direct and indirect taxation, a view which appears to find favour with many politicians, as is illustrated by the following piece of Gladstonian rhetoric:

> I never can think of direct and indirect taxation except as I should think of two attractive sisters each with an ample fortune, both having the same parentage (for the parents of both I believe to be Necessity and Invention), differing only as sisters may differ. I cannot conceive any reason why there should be unfriendly rivalry between the admirers of these two damsels. I have always thought it not only allowable, but even an act of duty, to pay my addresses to them both. I am, therefore, as between direct and indirect taxation, perfectly impartial (House of Commons, 1861).

The reasons why Gladstone held such a view are not apparent, but in much popular discussion one can discern a Mundell-type assignment of instruments to targets. Suppose that one views the long-run goals of taxation policy as being, in general terms, efficiency and equity. Many people tend to assign direct taxation to the equity objective and indirect taxation to the goal of raising revenue efficiently. The rationale for the first assignment is easy to see. It lies in the view that indirect taxation, even differentiated according to luxuries and necessities, is a poor redistributive instrument. This is well illustrated by the Carter Commission [5], who felt 'no doubt that, from an equity point of view, income taxes are superior to sales taxes ... If we could be reasonably certain that there would be no adverse economic effects ... we would recommend that sales taxes be replaced by higher federal income taxes.' The case for the second assignment (of the indirect tax instrument to the efficiency target) is suggested by the latter part of this quotation – that sales taxation is a method of raising revenue with less adverse economic effects. Thus it is felt that indirect taxation is an effective method of raising revenue, or at very least that it would be unwise to rely solely on direct taxation for this purpose, so that 'No unqualified argument can be made for the superiority of the practically feasible kinds of direct taxation, and ... in the post-war era the direct-indirect mix of our tax structure has been slanted too strongly toward direct taxation. [The] various kinds of inevitable inefficiency and equity need to be mixed' (Fellner, [13], pp. 79–80).

View B – Superiority of direct taxes
The alternative view is that direct taxation is superior on both counts and should be employed to meet both equity and efficiency objectives. This view was stated forcefully in Britain in the Minority Report of the Colwyn Committee in 1927 [6]: 'We are ourselves of the opinion that taxes upon commodities ... are objectionable in principle, and that the important place which they occupy in our tax system can only be defended on the ground that they are survivals from a period when the administration of direct taxation was much more difficult than it is today' (p. 372). That this view is held today among public finance economists is illustrated by the quite unambiguous

conclusion reached in the recent textbook by Fromm and Taubman [15]: 'Direct taxes are judged to meet the equity, efficiency and administrative cost criteria better than indirect taxes. Hence a direct tax system is "better" from an economic viewpoint' (p. 139).

The aim of the subsequent analysis is to throw some light on the support which can be provided for these two conflicting views.

The Efficiency Objective in an Economy of Identical Individuals

The main emphasis will be on recent developments, but it is none the less useful to begin with the lengthy debate on the issue of direct versus indirect taxation which took place between 1938 and the early 1950s. This debate has been well summarised by Walker [32]. The controversy arose from the attempt by Hicks [21] and, in a more circumspect manner, by Hotelling [23] to demonstrate the superiority of direct taxes for efficiency purposes, or in other words to justify the second of the two views outlined above (View B). Thus Hicks argued[3] that 'A tax on commodities lays a greater burden on consumers than an income tax. If the price of [taxed commodities falls] as the result of a reduction in taxation, then [there is a reduction in tax receipts]. If this is taken from him by an income tax, he is still left better off, and the government no worse off' (p. 41). This argument, although misleading, provides a convenient point of entry into the analytical literature.

In this discussion Hicks concentrated on the case of a single individual or, alternatively, an economy where everyone is identical. This means that both the consumer's decision-making, and the determination of the social optimum, may be seen in terms of maximising the utility of a representative individual,[4] written as:

$$U(x_1, \ldots, x_n, L),\tag{1}$$

where x_i denotes the consumption of the ith commodity $(i = 1, \ldots, n)$ and L the supply of labour. The choice of taxes with which Hicks was concerned may be seen by writing the consumer's budget constraint as (with the price of the ith commodity denoted by p_i and the wage by w):

$$\sum_{i=1}^{n} p_i(1 + t_i)x_i = wL,\tag{2}$$

where t_i denotes the *ad valorem* tax rate on good i, and, as noted earlier, it is assumed that there are no savings and labour is the only source of income. In this context a proportional income tax T reduces the right-hand side of (2) by $(1 - T)$, and this can be seen as equivalent to increasing all indirect taxes by a factor $1/(1 - T)$. The choice considered by Hicks was therefore, in effect, the choice between a differentiated tax on commodities t_k and a uniform tax on all commodities (at rate $1/(1 - T)$). Or, to put it another way, the government faces the problem of choosing t_k to raise revenue in the most efficient manner, or so as to maximise the social welfare function $G(U)$. See column 1, Table 1.

Table 1 *Summary of optimal tax models*

	Indirect taxation and identical individuals	*Indirect taxation and redistribution*	*Indirect taxation and a linear income tax*	*Indirect taxation and a general income tax*
1. Individual	All individuals identical maximum U subject to $$\sum_i p_i(1+t_i)x_i = wL$$	Individuals differ in w maximum U subject to $$\sum_i p_i(1+t_i)x_i = wL(w)$$	Individuals differ in w maximum U subject to $$\sum_i p_i(1+t_i)x_i = wL + Z$$	Individuals differ in w maximum U subject to $$\sum_i p_i(1+t_i)x_i = wL - T(wL)$$
2. Government	Maximum social welfare function $G(U)$ subject to revenue requirement $$\sum_i t_i p_i x_i = R^*$$	maximum $\int G(U)dF$ subject to $$\int\left(\sum_i t_i p_i x_i\right)dF = R^*$$	maximum $\int G(U)dF$ subject to $$\int\left(\sum_i t_i p_i x_i - Z\right)dF = R^*$$	maximum $\int G(U)dF$ subject to $$\int\left(T(wL) + \sum_i t_i p_i x_i\right)dF = R^*$$
3. First-order conditions for optimality	$$\sum_i t_i p_i S_{ki} = -(1-b)x_k$$ for $k = 1,\ldots,n$ where $$b = \frac{G\alpha}{\lambda} + \sum_i t_i p_i \frac{\partial x_i}{\partial I}$$	$$\int\left(\sum_i t_i p_i S_{ki}\right)dF = -\bar{X}_k[(1-b) - b\varphi_k]$$ for $k = 1,\ldots,n$ where $$b\bar{X}_k\varphi_k = \int(x_k - \bar{X}_k)(b-\bar{b})dF$$ $$\bar{X}_k = \int x_k dF$$	$$\int\left(\sum_i t_i p_i S_{ki}\right)dF = \bar{X}_k\varphi_k$$ for $k = 1,\ldots,n$	$$\frac{t_k}{1+t_k} = \frac{\mu\alpha x}{\lambda fw}\frac{d\log(U_k/U_1)}{d\log L}$$ for $k = 1,\ldots,n$ where normalised such that $t_1 = 0$ and μ is a Lagrange multiplier

Note: α is the private marginal utility of income and λ the multiplier associated with the revenue constraint, $\int dF = 1$.

Now there are two surprising aspects of this problem as formulated. The first is that it is precisely the question set by Pigou to Ramsey and solved by the latter in 1927. The solution is set out in the third line, where it has been put in the slightly different form given by Samuelson [29] in 'a pearl now before the US Treasury' (p. 95). What this shows is that the taxes are related to the compensated elasticities of demand S_{ik} (as one would expect, the distortion caused depends on the substitution terms) and on the factor b. The latter is the benefit, measured in terms of revenue, of transferring $1 to the representative individual ($G'\alpha/\lambda$, where α is the private marginal utility of income and λ is the shadow price associated with the numeraire (revenue)), allowing for the fact that this has an income effect and may lead him to buy some taxed goods, some of the $1 finding its way back to the Treasury ($\sum t_i p_i \partial x_i/\partial I$).[5] The factor b is referred to here as the social marginal valuation of income.

The choice between a uniform and a differentiated tax depends therefore on the compensated elasticities of the demand for goods and of the supply of labour. In the case which Hicks implicitly assumed – that the supply of labour was totally inelastic – efficiency does imply that uniform taxes are optimal. However, in general this is not necessarily the case, and where labour is supplied elastically a differentiated tax structure may be required in order to minimise the excess burden. As Little [24], Friedman [14], and others pointed out, there is no presumption in favour of uniform taxation.[6]

The second surprising feature of the Hicks treatment is that the 'direct' tax examined is not a direct tax at all according to our classification. He considered in effect a uniform tax on all expenditure, which on the typology given is only 'transitional'. It does not in itself incorporate any element which is tailored to individual circumstances. This is surprising because a very simple element of direct taxation could be brought in which would lead to dramatic changes in the conclusions. This is the poll tax or subsidy. With identical individuals this is in fact all that is necessary to take us from line 3 to line 4 in the classification given earlier. The only difference between a proportional tax on all spending and a linear tax is that the latter has an exemption such that the tax payable is:

$$T(wL - E) \qquad (3)$$

(if $wL < E$ then there is a 'negative' tax repayment). The consumer's budget constraint becomes:

$$\sum_i p_i(1 + t_i)x_i = wL(1 - T) + TE. \qquad (4)$$

If, as before, we normalise by dividing by $(1 - T)$, then the required modification is simply the addition of a term Z ($= TE/(1 - T)$) to the right-hand side of the budget constraint. This term Z is clearly an aspect of direct taxation, since each tax unit only gets one exemption or allowance.

The introduction of Z takes us outside the Ramsey framework, but it is immediately clear what the implications are. The government chooses to set

$t_k = 0$ and to raise all the revenue through a poll tax ($Z < 0$). It can always reduce Z and reduce the distortionary commodity taxes in such a way as to be welfare-improving. In terms of the first-order conditions, $b = 1$, and the cost of raising revenue λ equals the social marginal utility of income $G'\alpha$, that is, the poll tax is non-distortionary.

This observation is quite simple and intuitive. It does, however, have two important implications. First, it casts serious doubt on the standard formulation of the Ramsey problem with identical individuals. In effect this problem only arises because the constraint of no poll taxation is imposed, and there seems no clear rationale for ruling out this simple lump-sum tax – indeed it is implied by virtually any direct tax. Secondly, it suggests that there is something wrong with the target/instrument View A described earlier. If one is concerned solely with efficiency, as one is in an economy with identical consumers, then only the simplest of direct taxes should be used, and indirect taxes should not be employed. On reflection this is obvious, and was recognised by Smith: 'In countries where the ease, comfort and security of the inferior ranks of people are little attended to, capitation taxes are very common' [31], p. 690).

The final feature of the Hicks formulation which should be noted is that his conclusion was framed in terms of a comparison of two equilibria separated by a discrete change in tax rates. In the formulation here we have given the first-order conditions for an optimum. This latter approach avoids the difficulty arising from the prior existence of distortionary taxes stressed by a number of writers (see Walker [32]), since they are subsumed in t_k. On the other hand the first-order conditions are not sufficient, and one has to be careful in interpreting them. The standard convexity properties do not apply to the Ramsey problem.[7] It is quite possible that the first-order conditions may not lead to a unique solution, and that it is necessary to compare directly the level of social welfare at each solution. Such cases may lead to results which have not been sufficiently appreciated in the literature. For example, one may have utility functions, such as:

$$U = \sqrt{x_1} + \beta \log(\sqrt{x_1} - \beta) + \sqrt{x_2} + \beta \log(\sqrt{x_2} - \beta) - vL, \qquad (5)$$

where, even though x_1 and x_2 have identical demand functions, it may be desirable to tax them at different rates. This is certainly counter-intuitive. Similarly, if we were to interpret x_1 and x_2 as the consumption of the same goods by different (but identical) people, and if the government wanted to maximise the sum of utilities (which is given by U where $L = L_1 + L_2$), then if it could tax different (but identical) people at different rates it would in certain circumstances want to do so. This discriminatory tax treatment would clearly lead to conflict with the principle of horizontal equity, since consumption of a particular good by person j would bear a different tax from consumption by person i (see Chapter 11).

Redistribution and a Linear Direct Tax

We have seen that the simplest of direct taxes is superior to indirect taxation from the standpoint of minimising excess burden in an economy with identical individuals. How is this conclusion modified when we bring in differences between people and distributional objectives? In order to simplify the discussion it will be assumed that the differences between people take the form of varying wage rates w and that their tastes are assumed identical.[8]

The modifications to the Ramsey problem (due originally to Diamond and Mirrlees [10]) are shown in the second column of Table 1. The government now maximises the integral of $G(U)$ over the distribution $F(w)$, and in the first-order conditions the changes typically involve replacing terms by the appropriate averages, e.g. $\bar{b}$ is the social marginal valuation of income averaged over all individuals. However, there is an important additional term ϕ_k which is in essence the co-variance between x_k and b. Just as one would expect, the optimal tax structure depends on which goods are consumed by people for whom the social marginal valuation of income is high, where this may be high either because they are considered 'deserving' ($G'\alpha$ is large) or because they have a high propensity to consumed taxed goods ($\sum_i t_i p_i \partial x_i/\partial I$ is high).

In an economy with identical individuals, no redistributional considerations come into play, and the optimal tax structure may be seen as solely by the efficiency objective. Where individuals differ, both equity and efficiency are relevant. The precise definition of such objectives is far from unambiguous however; and indeed it may be argued that no distinction is necessary, both being subsumed under the maximisation of social welfare. None the less, the two concepts do feature prominently in public discussions of policy, and many people appear to find the distinction a meaningful one. It is therefore worthwhile trying to bring out its application in the present context.

The pursuit of the efficiency objective is typically seen in terms of the government being indifferent as to who receives benefits or pays taxes. This could be interpreted as meaning that the social welfare function is such that $G'\alpha$ is the same for all individuals. However, a more natural interpretation in the present context is that b is the same for all individuals (equality of the social marginal valuation of income), i.e. that the government takes account of the income effect on revenue. If b were the same for all w, then $\phi_k = 0$, and we should be left with the first term on the right-hand side of the first-order conditions (third line of column 2). In this way, we can interpret the term $(1 - \bar{b})$ as corresponding to 'efficiency' considerations in a many-person economy and $\bar{b}\phi_k$ as corresponding to 'equity' considerations.

This identification of equity and efficiency considerations is relevant when we introduce the linear direct tax (column 3, Table 1), where it is assumed that the exemption level is the same for everyone (in practice it will vary with family-size, etc.). As before, it is equivalent to adding a poll subsidy Z, and the first-order condition is the simple extension of $b=1$, that is, $\bar{b}=1$. Again it has dramatic effects. The efficiency component of the first-order conditions vanishes, and we are left with the equity term. This means that indirect taxes are associated with the equity objective, and the conventional view of targets and instruments is turned precisely on its head. For efficiency, the government employs the poll tax element of direct taxation ($b = \bar{b}$ for all w implies that only a poll tax will be employed), and if this is felt to be unjust then indirect taxes are brought into play to redistribute. With this insight, view A appears scarcely sustainable, and on reflection this is not surprising, since historically the role of indirect taxes has often been precisely this. Thus in seventeenth-century England, taxes on silks, coffee and newspapers, which were luxuries, were seen as more progressive than a one shilling a head poll tax.

The results described above are quite intuitive and do not rely on any elaborate formal analysis (indeed one could argue that it was Hicks' indifference curve formalisation of the problem that led him to overlook the crucial role played by the implicit assumption of fixed pre-tax income). Intuition can, however, be a treacherous guide to second-best policy problems, as may be illustrated by the model considered here. If we argue along the lines of the preceding paragraph that the introduction of a poll tax/subsidy element Z leaves only a redistributional role for indirect taxation, then it might appear, intuitively, that it would involve heavier taxes on luxury goods (those with a high income elasticity).

Such an intuitive argument is not correct, however, as is shown, for example, by the linear expenditure system. This allows goods to be luxuries or necessities, depending on the parameter values, but substitution into the first-order conditions shows (see Appendix) that the only solutions which satisfy the first-order conditions involve $t_k = t$ for all k. Where there is a lump-sum element to the direct tax, then whether or not certain goods are luxuries the optimal indirect tax structure is a uniform tax – in other words no indirect taxation need be employed. This is counter-intuitive; however, when distributional objectives are relevant, indirect taxes play two roles. First, by taxing luxuries at a higher rate they may increase the progressivity of the tax system; secondly, they provide an alternative source of revenue, allowing the regressive poll tax to be reduced or converted into a lump-sum payment. In the latter case the government would want to raise the revenue in the distortion-minimising way, and the final tax structure would balance the two sets of considerations. In the case of the linear expenditure system we have seen that they exactly offset each other, and the optimal tax structure is uniform.

Redistribution and Optimal Direct Taxation

The linear expenditure example of the previous section provides an example where View B – the superiority of direct taxes – appears to be justified. We now consider how generally this is likely to be true. In doing so it is important to bear in mind that the restriction of the direct tax schedule to being linear may be seen as loading the dice against direct taxation. In this section we consider therefore the more general case where the marginal tax rate may vary with income.

This more general problem is set out in the fourth column of Table 1. In effect it combines the Ramsey problem with the treatment by Mirrlees of the optimum income tax [25]. The first-order conditions for optimality given in line 3 are those derived by Atkinson and Stiglitz (see Chapter 11). In interpreting these, it should be noted that they have been normalised so that $t_1 = 0$; if any t_k is non-zero this will mean that there is a differentiated indirect tax structure. In fact it is clear that there is a wide class of cases where no indirect taxation need be employed, and we have the following proposition:

Proposition. Where the utility function is weakly separable between labour and all goods taken together, then there is no need to employ indirect taxation in the optimum solution.

In other words, if the marginal rate of substitution between any two goods is independent of labour supplied, then $t_k = 0$ for all k.[9] Where a subset of commodities is separable from labour, then they should be taxed at the same rate.

This result provides some support for View B. Not just in the case of the linear expenditure system, but in a much wider class of demand systems, there is no need to employ indirect taxation to achieve an optimum (and if indirect taxation is employed then it should be uniform). There is no need for separability between goods, just weak separability between labour and all goods. At the same time it does not provide a blanket justification for the view that direct taxes are superior, and one can well imagine that even this limited separability requirement may not in practice be met: for example in the case of leisure goods. For this reason no such categorical assertion can be made as that by Fromm and Taubman [15] quoted above.

The proposition described above is not one which could readily have been reached without a mathematical formulation. One can however see intuitively that there is a parallel with the second-best literature. We have a situation where there are differences in endowments w which we should ideally like to correct through first-best taxation linked directly with w. In practice, however, we are constrained to employ income taxation, and the problem becomes a second-best one.[10] As a result, the optimum involves in general a wedge between before- and after-tax returns to labour at the margin, but this leaves open the question whether we want to have the first-best conditions satisfied elsewhere. As it was put by Davis and Whinston [8]: 'The second-best is concerned with the usefulness of the usual Pareto conditions in a situation in which there are imperfections in areas of the economic system which are not the particular ones of immediate concern. When and under what conditions does the existence of imperfections in these "other areas" cause it to be undesirable (from the point of view of efficiency) to design policies for the achievement of the Pareto conditions in the area of immediate concern?' (p. 330).

Where the government is concerned with redistribution, the same kind of question arises. What the proposition given earlier does is to make precise the separability required in order for no indirect taxation to be needed (i.e. for the Pareto conditions for the allocation between *goods* not to be disturbed).

Lessons to be Drawn

The starting point for this chapter was the relationship between economic theory and the advice which can be given to policy makers. They themselves tend to be rather dubious. Gladstone, for example, prefaced the quotation given earlier with the statement that: 'I have always thought it idle for a person holding the position of finance minister to trouble himself with what to him is necessarily an abstract question.' More recently, a Canadian Treasury Board president asked in the first issue of *Canadian Public Policy* what all this mathematics means to the 'sheriff who does not know an optimum from an integral'.

The reasons for such scepticism are clear. There is much that has been left out of the analysis described above. We have not considered the administration of the two types of taxation, and the possibility that one may be more difficult to avoid or evade. Such considerations would undoubtedly weigh heavily with policy makers. The discussion of equity was concerned solely with vertical equity and did not consider horizontal equity, which some people regard as grounds for preferring direct to indirect taxation. The analysis took no account of the supposed preference of taxpayers for indirect taxation on the grounds that it offers them choice, or that it is less visible.[11] All these matters may well seem to the minister of finance more pressing than the balancing of efficiency and vertical equity on which the optimum tax literature has focused.

These seem fair strictures; however, they do not necessarily suggest that the exercise is in vain. What they indicate is that the treatment needs to be enriched, and there are clearly ways in which it can be developed. The existence of administrative costs could well be treated within the framework of the growing literature on transaction costs in general equilibrium (see Heller and Shell [20]). In the same way, optimum tax theory could draw on the work on incentive mechanisms and the revelation of preferences in the field of public goods (see, for example, Groves and Loeb [17]). In the case of horizontal equity, the concept needs to be clarified and its status in relation to other objectives established (see Chapters 5 and 11). Finally, one needs to consider more generally the notion of the 'burden' of taxation, and the question of taxpayers' preferences for one form of tax rather than another.

Moreover, one has to ask what alternatives there are to analysis of the kind described here. The minister of finance or chancellor of the exchequer may rely on conventional wisdom. However, we have seen that in the present case the views which seem to be most widely held need to be qualified in important respects. The assignment of direct taxation to achieving equity and of indirect taxation to efficiency (View A) may, if anything, be the reverse of that required. The view that direct taxes are superior on both equity and efficiency grounds (View B) has to be qualified in the way described in the previous section.[12]

On the part of economists it may be felt that such conclusions could have been reached by an intuitive argument without the need for a formal mathematical treatment. It certainly is true that the superiority on efficiency grounds of the poll tax/subsidy element of direct taxation can be seen without any elaborate demonstration. However, this instrument allows us to attain a first-best solution (in the case of identical individuals), and once we leave the first-best, intuition becomes a much less reliable guide. In this chapter this has been illustrated by the optimal pattern of indirect taxation, where intuition might lead one to expect the structure to tax luxuries more heavily, and by the counter-intuitive results which may arise as a result of non-convexity. Moreover, it is unrealistic to suppose that the separability conditions of the previous section could be derived without a formal treatment. The recent literature, although in need of development, may therefore have something to offer.

Appendix: Example of Linear Expenditure System

All individuals are assumed to have identical utility functions:

$$U = \sum_{i=1}^{n} \beta_i \log(x_i - \gamma_i) + \beta_0 \log(\gamma_0 - L), \tag{A1}$$

where:

$$\sum_{i=0}^{n} \beta_i = 1.$$

They differ in w, and face budget constraints:

$$\sum_{i=1}^{n} p_i(1 + t_i)x_i = wL + Z, \tag{A2}$$

where t_i and Z are identical for all and it is assumed that all work ($L > 0$). The relevant characteristics of the demand equations are that (where $q_k = p_k(1 + t_k)$):

$$S_{ik} = \frac{1}{\alpha} \frac{\beta_i \beta_k}{q_i q_k} (i \neq k), \qquad S_{kk} = \frac{\beta_k(\beta_k - 1)}{\alpha q_k^2},$$

$$\frac{\partial x_k}{\partial I} = \beta_k / q_k.$$

The left-hand side of the first-order conditions (line 3, column 3, Table 1) reduces therefore to:

$$\frac{\beta_k}{q_k} \left(\int \left(\frac{1}{\alpha}\right) dF \right) [H - t_k p_k / q_k], \tag{A3}$$

where $H \equiv \sum \beta_i t_i p_i / q_i$. In evaluating the right-hand side of the first-order conditions we may note that $\bar{b} = 1$ implies (with $G' = 1$):

$$\int \left(\frac{\alpha}{\lambda}\right) dF = 1 - H.$$
(A4)

The right-hand side $(\phi_k \bar{X}_k)$ equals (where $G' = 1$):

$$\frac{\beta_k}{q_k} \int \left[\frac{1}{\alpha} - \int \frac{1}{\alpha} dF\right]\left[\frac{\alpha}{\lambda} + H\right] dF = \frac{\beta_k}{q_k}\left[\frac{1}{\lambda} - (1-H) \int \left(\frac{1}{\alpha}\right) dF\right]$$
(A5)

(using A4). Equating A3 and A5:

$$\frac{t_k}{1+t_k} = 1 - \frac{1}{\int \left(\frac{\lambda}{\alpha}\right) dF}$$
(A6)

which gives the result referred to in the text.

Acknowledgement

This is a revised version of the W. A. Mackintosh Lecture delivered at Queen's University, Canada, March 1976. I am grateful to the referees for very helpful comments and to the members of the Department of Economics at Queen's for their hospitality during my visit.

Notes

1 It is assumed that below the exemption a negative tax operates.
2 The application of the optimal tax results to the tax treatment of savings is discussed in Chapter 14.
3 Considerably earlier Edgeworth [12] had argued that taxes on commodities were 'more burdensome than direct taxation', since they cause 'a loss of consumer rent, which does not occur when the amount is directly subtracted from income' (p. 568). A similar argument had also been made by Barone. See Walker [32].
4 This assumes that fiscal policy is non-discriminatory (i.e. all individuals face the same tax schedule); see below.
5 The term $\partial x_i/\partial I$ denotes the marginal propensity to consume out of lump-sum income I; this is well defined even though we are assuming $I = 0$ at present.
6 The case for differentiation does of course depend on there being different demand characteristics for the various commodity groups, but in practice this is likely to be the case.
7 After giving this lecture I discovered the elegant treatment of this problem by Harris [19].
8 This is not necessary for much of the analysis. See Chapter 11.
9 As noted by a referee, the result may be seen from the fact that the weak separability condition implies that we may treat goods as an aggregate, and, since one normalisation is possible, this may be taken as the untaxed good.
10 As Hahn [18] has argued, the reasons why the range of instruments should be constrained in this way have not been adequately explained in the literature. On the other hand, his contention that lump-sum taxes (varying with w) could be employed is highly questionable. His appeal to the English poll tax of 1660 as evidence overlooks the fact that it was not in fact lump-sum: as indicated, for example, by the tax of 2% on land, money or stock, the provision that the payment by clergy was subject to a minimum-income qualification, and the fact that hackney-coach keepers were to pay a fixed contribution in respect of each coach and pair. The

poll taxes of the seventeenth century should not be seen as a first-best fiscal Garden of Eden from which legislators have banished themselves, but rather as rudimentary and inefficient ~~forerunners of the modern income tax~~

11 As It is rather nicely ~~put by the Marquis Garnier [16] in his Introduction to the French~~ translation of *The Wealth of Nations*: 'C'est au milieu de la profusion des repaux que se paient les taxes sur le vin, la bière, le sucre, le sel, et les articles de ce genre, et le trésor public trouve un source de gain dans les provocations à la dépense qui sont excitées par l'abandon et la gaieté des fêtes' (p. 1xv).

12 The fact that the relationship between direct/indirect taxation and the goals of equity/efficiency is less straightforward than sometimes supposed means that one would need to exercise care in testing a 'socio-political' explanation of the changes in tax shares. This aspect is discussed by Musgrave [26], pp. 132–4).

References

[1] Atkinson, A. B. and Sandmo, A. (1980), 'The welfare implications of personal income and consumption taxes', Chapter 14 in this volume.

[2] Atkinson, A. B. and Stiglitz, J. E. (1976), 'The design of tax structure', Chapter 11 in this volume.

[3] Atkinson, A. B. and Stiglitz, J. E. (1980), *Lectures on Public Economics*, Maidenhead and New York, McGraw-Hill.

[4] Buchanan, J. M. (1970), *The Public Finances*, Irwin.

[5] Carter, K. le M. (1966–7), *Royal Commission on Taxation, Chairman's Report*, Ottawa, Queen's Printer.

[6] Committee on National Debt and Taxation (1927), *Report*, HMSO.

[7] Dalton, H. (1954), *Principles of Public Finance*, Routledge.

[8] Davis, O. A. and Whinston, A. B. (1967), 'Piecemeal policy in the theory of second best', *Review of Economic Studies*, **34**, 323–31.

[9] Diamond, P. A. (1975), 'A many-person Ramsey tax rule', *Journal of Public Economics*, **4**, 335–42.

[10] Diamond, P. A. and Mirrlees, J. A. (1971), 'Optimal taxation and public production', *American Economic Review*, **61**, 8–27, 261–78.

[11] Due, J. and Friedlaender, A. F. (1973), *Government Finance*, Irwin.

[12] Edgeworth, F. Y. (1897), 'The pure theory of taxation', *Economic Journal*, 7, 46–70, 226–38, 550–71.

[13] Fellner, W. (1964), 'Comment', in *The Role of Direct and Indirect Taxes in the Federal Revenue System*, National Bureau of Economic Research.

[14] Friedman, M. (1952), 'The welfare effects of an income tax and an excise tax', *Journal of Political Economy*, **60**, 25–33.

[15] Fromm, G. and Taubman, P. (1973), *Public Economic Theory and Policy*, Macmillan.

[16] Garnier, le Marquis (ed.) (1822), *Recherches sur le nature et les causes de la richesse des nations*, Paris.

[17] Groves, T. and Loeb, M. (1975), 'Incentives and public inputs', *Journal of Public Economics*, **4**, 211–26.

[18] Hahn, F. H. (1973), 'On optimum taxation', *Journal of Economic Theory*, **6**, 96–106.

[19] Harris, R. (1975), 'A note on convex-concave demand systems with an application to the theory of optimal taxation', Discussion Paper No. 197, Kingston, Queen's University.

[20] Heller, W. P. and Shell, K. (1974), 'On optimal taxation with costly administration', *American Economic Review*, Papers and Proceedings, **64**, 338–45.

[21] Hicks, J. R. (1939), *Value and Capital*, Oxford University Press.

[22] Hicks, U. K. (1946), 'The terminology of tax analysis', *Economic Journal*, **56**, 38–50.

[23] Hotelling, H. (1938), 'The general welfare in relation to problems of taxation and of railway and utility rates', *Econometrica*, **6**, 242–69.

[24] Little, I. M. D. (1951), 'Direct versus indirect taxes', *Economic Journal*, **61**, 577–84.

[25] Mirrlees, J. A. (1971), 'An exploration in the theory of optimum income taxation', *Review of Economic Studies*, **38**, 175–200.

[26] Musgrave, R. A. (1969), *Fiscal Systems*, Yale University Press.
[27] Ramsey, F. P. (1927), 'A contribution to the theory of taxation', *Economic Journal*, **37**, 47–61.
[28] Rolph, E. (1968), 'Taxation', in *International Encyclopedia of the Social Sciences*, Macmillan.
[29] Samuelson, P. A. (1964), 'Discussion', *American Economic Review*, Papers and Proceedings, **54**, 93–6.
[30] Shoup, C. (1964), *Role of Direct and Indirect Taxes in the Federal Revenue System*, National Bureau of Economic Research.
[31] Smith, Adam, 1892, *Wealth of Nations*.
[32] Walker, D. (1955), 'The direct/indirect tax problem: fifteen years of controversy', *Public Finance*, **10**, 153–76.

13 Pigou, Taxation and Public Goods[1]

1 Introduction

The results of Samuelson [5–7] in the theory of public goods have provided the basis for most subsequent discussion of the optimum provision of public goods. Samuelson showed that a necessary condition for Pareto optimality (and hence for maximising a social welfare function which responds positively to individual utilities) is that the sum of the marginal rates of substitution (Σ MRS) between a public good and a private good be equal to the marginal rate of transformation (MRT). The sole constraint is that production is in the aggregate production set. This optimum can be achieved as a competitive equilibrium with the government supplying the public good up to the point where Σ MRS = MRT and financing its production by lump-sum taxation. Lump-sum transfers may also be employed to achieve the appropriate income distribution.

The achievement of the 'full' optimum described above depends on lump-sum taxes and transfers being feasible. If the taxation tools available exclude lump-sum taxation, then the optimisation problem must be modified to include explicitly the means by which government revenue is raised. The importance of this point was clearly recognised by Pigou [3], who argued that the cost to consumers of the public good would be larger than just the necessary resources on account of the 'indirect' damage caused by taxation:

Where there is indirect damage, it ought to be added to the direct loss of satisfaction involved in the withdrawal of the marginal unit of resources by taxation, before this is balanced against the satisfaction yielded by the marginal expenditure. It follows that, in general, expenditure ought not to be carried so far as to make the real yield of the last unit of resources expended by the government equal to the real yield of the last unit left in the hands of the representative citizen. ([3], p. 34)

This problem has received more formal attention from Diamond and Mirrlees [2] and Stiglitz and Dasgupta [8]. In particular, the latter authors have challenged Pigou's conclusion, and have argued that in certain circumstances it may not be correct. The economics of their argument and the circumstances in which Pigou's reasoning breaks down was, however, obscure and they failed to distinguish between a number of different interpretations of Pigou's statement. The purpose of this chapter is to clarify the meaning of the results obtained by Stiglitz and Dasgupta, and to elucidate how Pigou's intuitively appealing (if informal) argument goes wrong.

A. B. Atkinson and N. H. Stern.

2 The Problem

In examining the effect of the means of finance on the optimum provision of public goods, it is important to distinguish two questions which have tended to be confused in the literature:

(i)   the appropriate benefit measure for incremental output of the public good (e.g. for use in benefit-cost analysis),
(ii) the appropriate output level for public goods.

(i) Benefit measures and the Conventional Rule
The first of these questions, which is the one to which we give most attention in this chapter, may best be approached through consideration of the methods of benefit-cost analysis. This analysis proceeds by dividing the net effect of an increment in expenditure into costs and benefits. This division can in principle be carried out in many ways, but here we shall assume that the cost side is represented by the marginal rate of transformation and concentrate on the value to which this should be equated (or the *benefit measure*). The rationale for this procedure is that the cost-benefit analyst will usually work out the cost of producing a public good at some set of accounting prices and this will correspond to the marginal cost (or MRT). He will then want to know the benefit measure with which this cost should be compared. Traditional practice in cost-benefit analysis has been to use Σ MRS as the benefit measure (Prest and Turvey [4]): e.g. a road project where the benefits are measured by the sum of the value of possible savings to the users. In what follows the practice of using Σ MRS as a benefit measure will be referred to as the Conventional Rule.

The rationale for the Conventional Rule clearly derives from the first-order conditions for a full optimum, and where the expenditure has to be financed by distortionary taxation the benefit measure has to be modified.[2] The question with which we are concerned here is whether this modified benefit measure will be less than or greater than that indicated by the Conventional Rule. Pigou's intuition was that the Conventional Rule would overstate the true benefits because it ignored the 'indirect damage' caused by raising revenue. Stiglitz and Dasgupta, on the other hand, argue that the condition for the Conventional Rule to overstate the benefits is that 'the share of tax revenue from the ith commodity is ... greater than the elasticity of tax revenue from an increase in the tax rate on the ith commodity: or equivalently, as the marginal revenue from raising the tax on the ith commodity by a unit is ... less than C_i [consumption of good i]' ([8], p. 189). Unfortunately, no adequate interpretation of this result is given by Stiglitz-Dasupta, and we have no means of telling from the above result whether the case where the Conventional Rule understates the benefits is a likely one or merely an abnormality. Moreover, Stiglitz and Dasgupta overlook the important consideration that their result depends on the choice of which goods are taxed. These questions are taken up in section 3.

(ii) Output of public goods and over- and under-supply
The second question concerns the level of output of public goods. The

statements by Stiglitz and Dasgupta that the Conventional Rule would lead to an 'under- or over-supply' (p. 159) suggest that they have thrown light on this question, but they do not in fact specify what they mean by under- and over-supply. There are a number of possible interpretations which could be given. It could mean that the solution to the problem where public goods are financed by distortionary taxation but where Σ MRS = MRT is imposed as a constraint leads to output levels which are larger or smaller than the output levels where the constraint is removed. Alternatively, it could mean that the optimum output levels where public goods are financed by distortionary taxation are larger or smaller than the levels in the full optimum (financed by lump-sum taxation). The latter interpretation[3] is perhaps the more interesting and it is the one on which we focus – see section 4. The approach adopted is to examine the changes in optimum output levels as the availability of lump-sum finance increases (from zero to the level of the full optimum). This raises slightly more general questions of the welfare effects of changes from commodity taxation to lump-sum taxation. These questions are discussed further in the Appendix.

3 Benefit Measures and Commodity Taxation

A wide range of taxes could be used to finance expenditure on public goods, but in this chapter it is assumed that *ad valorem* commodity and factor taxes are employed. In this we are following Diamond and Mirrlees and Stiglitz and Dasgupta, and the model described below is based on their work (the notation is that of Diamond and Mirrlees).

Assumptions
Households. There are assumed to be h identical households[4] maximising utility functions $U(x, e)$ subject to $q.x = 0$, where x denotes the net consumption of the n private goods by the household (factors supplied being treated as negative demands), q denotes the prices faced by consumers and e denotes the supply of public goods. The indirect utility function is denoted by $V(q, e)$. It is assumed that the utility function is such that x is a well-defined function of q and e.
Production. The production constraint is written as $G(X, e) = 0$, where $X = hx$ is the total net consumption and it is assumed that there are constant returns to scale. Private producers are price-makers and the first-order conditions for profit maximisation mean that G_k is proportional to p_k where p_k is the producer price of the kth good.[5] The tax rate on the kth good is $t_k = q_k - p_k$.
Government. The government is assumed to maximise a social welfare function $hV(q, e)$ subject to the production constraint. (The requirement of market clearing ensures that the government budget is balanced.) The controls at the government's disposal are the tax rates t_k and the expenditure on the public good e (for simplicity attention is focused on the case where there is a single public good, but the analysis can readily be extended). It may also be noted that we may assume without loss of generality that one good is not taxed (given that there are no lump-sum transfers, net consumer expenditure is zero, so that a proportional tax on all commodities raises no revenue). It is assumed that the

untaxed good is good one, and that this is taken as the numeraire ($p_1 = q_1 = 1$). If we further assume that G is defined such that $G_1 = 1$, this implies that $G_k = p_k$.

The government's maximisation problem may be formulated in terms of the Lagrangian: $\mathscr{L} = hV(q, e) - \lambda G[X(q, e), e]$. The first-order condition[6] for e is given by (where $G_i = \partial G/\partial X_i$, $G_e = \partial G/\partial e$):

$$h\frac{\partial V}{\partial e} - \lambda\left[\sum_{i=1}^{n} G_i\frac{\partial X_i}{\partial e} + G_e\right] = 0,$$

(1)

which may be written as:

$$h\frac{\partial V/\partial e}{\alpha q_k} = \frac{p_k}{q_k}\frac{\lambda}{\alpha}\frac{G_e}{G_k} + \frac{\lambda}{\alpha q_k}\sum_{i=1}^{n} p_i\frac{\partial X_i}{\partial e},$$

(2)

where α denotes the individual marginal utility of income.

The left-hand side of equation (2) is the sum of the marginal rates of substitution between the public good and the private good k. In order to proceed from this equation to discussion of the Conventional Rule ($\Sigma\,\mathrm{MRS} = \mathrm{MRT}$), we need to specify the good k used in the comparison. As usually presented (see, for example, Aaron and McGuire [1], p. 909) the Conventional Rule takes the marginal rate of substitution between the public good and the private good selected as numeraire, and in the present case this corresponds to the untaxed good ($k = 1$). Equation (2) may then be rewritten:

$$\frac{G_e}{G_1} = \frac{\alpha}{\lambda}\frac{h\dfrac{\partial V}{\partial e}}{\alpha} - \sum_{i=1}^{n} (q_i - t_i)\frac{\partial X_i}{\partial e}$$

or:

(3)

$$\mathrm{MRT} = \frac{\alpha}{\lambda}\Sigma\,\mathrm{MRS} + \frac{\partial}{\partial e}\left[\sum_{i=1}^{n} t_i X_i\right],$$

where we have used the fact that $\sum_{i=1}^{n} q_i\partial X_i/\partial e = 0$ (from the budget constraint of the consumer).

Equation (3) allows us to see whether the benefit measure with commodity taxation is greater than or less than that with the Conventional Rule. Beginning with the second term on the right-hand side, we can see that this represents a factor overlooked by Pigou – the effect on tax revenue resulting from complementarity and substitutability between private and public goods. If increased government expenditure leads to a greater consumption of taxed private goods, this reduces the revenue which has to be raised and hence increases the benefit measure. An example of this would be if the provision of a further television channel increased demand for television sets and these were subject to an indirect tax. This point, which was brought out by Diamond and

Mirrlees, is however a straightforward one and is not central to this chapter, and in what follows it will be assumed that $\partial X_i/\partial e = 0$ for $i = 1,\ldots,n$.

If the second term vanishes, the right-hand side of equation (3) becomes $(\alpha/\lambda)\Sigma$ MRS and the departure of the benefit measure from the Conventional Rule depends simply on whether $\alpha \gtrless \lambda$. Since α is the marginal utility of income to the consumer and λ is the social marginal cost of raising revenue, Pigou's argument leads one to expect that where taxes are distortionary $\lambda > \alpha$ and hence that the true benefit is less than Σ MRS. In order to see where this breaks down, we need to look at the optimal tax structure. The first-order conditions are:

$$h\frac{\partial V}{\partial q_k} = \lambda\left(\sum_{i=1}^{n} G_i\frac{\partial X_i}{\partial q_k}\right) = \lambda\frac{\partial}{\partial t_k}\left(\sum_{i-1}^{n} p_iX_i\right).$$

Since $V_k = -\alpha x_k$ and $\partial(\Sigma p_iX_i)/\partial t_k + \partial(\Sigma t_iX_i)/\partial t_k = 0$ (from differentiating the consumer budget constraint), we can write this as:

$$\frac{\alpha}{\lambda} = \frac{\dfrac{\partial}{\partial t_k}\left(\displaystyle\sum_{i=1}^{n} t_iX_i\right)}{X_k}. \tag{4}$$

on which the Stiglitz-Dasgupta condition is based (see p. 120). However, this condition is not framed in terms of readily recognisable parameters (neither of the demand functions nor of the utility function) and does not provide much insight into whether or not it is in fact likely that $\alpha > \lambda$.

Using the Slutsky relationship, equation (4) may be rewritten as:

$$\frac{\alpha}{\lambda} = 1 - \sum_{i=1}^{n} t_i\frac{\partial X_i}{\partial I} + \sum_{i=1}^{n} t_i(S_{ik}/X_k), \tag{5}$$

where S_{ik} denotes the Slutsky term and $\partial X_i/\partial I$ denotes the income term:

(i.e. $\partial X_i/\partial q_k = S_{ik} - X_k(\partial X_i/\partial I)$).

From this we can see that whether $\alpha \gtrless \lambda$ depends on two factors.

(i) A '*distortionary effect*', represented by the third term on the right-hand side. If we multiply by t_kX_k and sum, we obtain:

$$\left(\frac{\alpha}{\lambda} - 1 + \sum_{i=1}^{n} t_i\frac{\partial X_i}{\partial I}\right) = \left(\sum_{i=1}^{n}\sum_{k=1}^{n} t_iS_{ik}t_k\right)\bigg/R, \tag{6}$$

where $R = \sum_{k=1}^{n} t_kX_k$, from which it can be deduced (following Diamond and Mirrlees) that where the revenue is positive (as it will be for positive government expenditure) then:

$$\sum_{i=1}^{n} t_i(S_{ik}/X_k) \lessgtr 0 \tag{7}$$

using the negative semi-definiteness of the Slutsky matrix. This term works in the direction of $\alpha < \lambda$, and may be interpreted as representing the distortionary effect with which Pigou was concerned – the excess burden (at the margin of tax revenue) associated with commodity as opposed to lump-sum taxation. (This may be demonstrated by examining the effect of allowing the government to use lump-sum taxation up to an amount T – see Appendix.) To this extent Pigou's excess burden argument is, therefore, correct; however, he overlooked the second term in equation (5).

(ii) A *'revenue' effect*, represented by the second term on the right-hand side of (5) or the marginal rate of tax as income I increases. If this were always positive, then it would be guaranteed that $\alpha < \lambda$ and hence (where $\partial X_i/\partial e = 0$) that the benefit measure is less than Σ MRS. However, this condition cannot be guaranteed and the term may well be negative. Moreover, the sign of the term depends on the choice of which goods are taxed. This may be illustrated by the case where there is one private consumption good, and one factor supplied by the household. If public expenditure is positive, revenue must be positive, so that if the factor is untaxed the consumption good must be taxed at a positive rate. The marginal tax rate will then be positive where the consumption good is a normal good, which is clearly a rather weak requirement. If, on the other hand, the consumption good is untaxed, we have to subsidise leisure (a negative tax rate on leisure raising a positive revenue) and the marginal tax rate will only be positive where leisure is an inferior good.[7] The reason for the dependence of the sign on the choice of the taxed good is fairly clear: the 'income' effect of taxation *reduces* the revenue from a consumption tax given normality but *increases* the revenue from a factor tax given normality of leisure.

In their paper, Stiglitz and Dasgupta give the impression that Pigou's intuitive argument was quite wrong. From the more detailed analysis given in this section it appears that – if interpreted carefully – the excess burden argument has some relevance; however, Pigou overlooked the other aspects of distortionary taxation described under (ii) which may reverse his conclusion that the Conventional Rule overestimates the benefits.

4 Output Levels and Distortionary Taxation – an Example

The second question outlined above – the relationship between the optimum level of public good output under distortionary taxation and that in the full optimum – may be approached by supposing that the government levies a lump sum tax T per household, with the balance of the revenue required to finance public expenditure being raised by commodity taxation. We may then examine the relationship between T and the output of public goods, and in particular compare e_{CT} with e_{LS} where the subscript CT denotes the commodity tax optimum (where $T=0$) and LS the lump-sum optimum (where $t=0$). To keep things simple, we consider the special case where there is one private good and one factor, and where producer prices are taken as constant (at unity). It may be noted that the comparison of e_{CT} with e_{LS} is not affected by the choice of untaxed good, since the physical quantities in the two optima do not depend on the normalisation. We assume for the details of our analysis that the factor (L) is taxed at rate t (so that the wage faced is $(1-t)$) and the commodity (X) is taken as the untaxed good. We also assume that the utility function is separable in public and private goods: $U(X,L)+H(e)$.

The government's maximisation problem may be written in terms of the Lagrangian:

$$hV(t,T,e)+\lambda[hT+thL-e]$$

and the first-order conditions are:

$$V_t+\lambda\left[L+t\frac{\partial L}{\partial t}\right]=0 \tag{8}$$

$$hV_e-\lambda=0 \tag{9}$$

$$hT+htL-e=0. \tag{10}$$

In the maximisation described above, T is taken as a parameter; we are interested in the way in which t and e change as T is allowed to vary. Differentiating the first-order conditions with respect to T[8]:

$$
\begin{bmatrix}
V_{tt}+\lambda\left(2\dfrac{\partial L}{\partial t}+t\dfrac{\partial^2 L}{\partial t^2}\right) & 0 & L+t\dfrac{\partial L}{\partial t} \\[3ex]
0 & hV_{ee} & -1 \\[3ex]
h\left(L+t\dfrac{\partial L}{\partial t}\right) & -1 & 0
\end{bmatrix}
\begin{bmatrix}
\dfrac{dt}{\partial T} \\[3ex]
\dfrac{de}{\partial T} \\[3ex]
\dfrac{d\lambda}{dT}
\end{bmatrix}
=-
\begin{bmatrix}
V_{tT}+\lambda\left(\dfrac{\partial L}{\partial T}+t\dfrac{\partial^2 L}{\partial t\,\partial T}\right) \\[3ex]
0 \\[3ex]
h\left(1+t\dfrac{\partial L}{\partial T}\right)
\end{bmatrix}
\tag{11}
$$

Evaluating at the full optimum ($t=0$, $\alpha=\lambda$), and denoting the matrix of coefficients by A, we obtain:

$$\frac{1}{h}|A|\frac{de}{dT}=\left(V_{tT}+\alpha\frac{\partial L}{\partial T}\right)L-V_{tt}-2\frac{\alpha\,\partial L}{\partial t}.$$

Since:

$$V_{tT}=-\alpha_t\,,\qquad V_{tt}=-\alpha_t L-\alpha\frac{\partial L}{\partial t}$$

this gives:

$$\frac{1}{h}|A|\frac{de}{dT}=\alpha L\frac{\partial L}{\partial T}-\alpha\frac{\partial L}{\partial t}=\alpha S,$$

where S denotes the compensated change in L in response to a rise in the wage rate. The second-order conditions require $|A|\gtreqless 0$, and since $S>0$, it follows that a small reduction in the possibilities for lump-sum taxation from the full optimum would lead to a fall in the optimum quantity of the public good.

The establishment of global results is more difficult, but the points at issue are brought out in Figure 1. From equation (9) we can draw the 'demand'

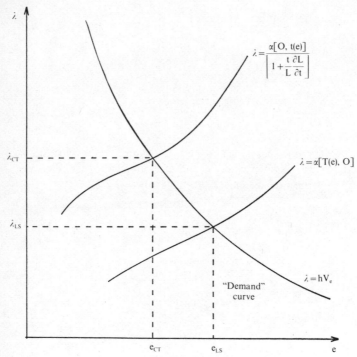

Figure 1

Note: It is assumed that $H_{ee}<0$ so that the demand curve is downward sloping, and the second-order conditions ensure that the supply curve cuts the demand curve from below.

schedule for public goods $\lambda=hV_e$; and we can use equations (8) and (10) to define a social 'supply' curve for the commodity tax optimum. From (8), and using the fact that $V_t=-\alpha L$:

$$\lambda=\alpha\left/\left(1+\frac{t}{L}\frac{\partial L}{\partial t}\right)\right.,\tag{12}$$

where t is a function of e from (10). Similarly, we may derive a 'supply curve' $\lambda = \lambda$ for the case where the revenue is raised solely by lump-sum taxation. It should be noted that α is a function of T and t, so that in the first case we may write $\alpha[0, t(e)]$ and in the second $\alpha[T(e), 0]$. For $e_{CT} < e_{LS}$ (as shown in the diagram), we require:

$$\lambda_{CT} > \lambda_{LS}(=\alpha_{LS}).$$

The condition given by Stiglitz and Dasgupta (in this case that the supply curve of labour be upward sloping) ensures that:

$$\lambda_{CT} > \alpha_{CT},$$

but it is clear that this condition is not by itself sufficient for $e_{CT} < e_{LS}$. It has still to be demonstrated that $\alpha_{CT} > \alpha_{LS}$.

The case of the Cobb–Douglas utility function:

$$U(X, L, e) = \alpha \log x + (1-a) \log (1-L) + H(e)$$

(where $0 < a < 1$) illustrates the inadequacy of the Stiglitz and Dasgupta condition since the condition is exactly satisfied at the commodity tax optimum,[9] and according to their analysis we should expect the Conventional Rule to give the right answer. However, it is clear (see Figure 1) that:

$$e_{CT} \gtrless e_{LS} \quad \text{as} \quad \alpha_{CT} \lessgtr \alpha_{LS}.$$

From the first-order conditions and the individual budget constraint,

$$1/\alpha = (1-t) - T.$$

From the government budget constraint:

$$hT + ht\left(a + \frac{(1-a)T}{1-t}\right) = e$$

so that:

$$1/\alpha_{CT} = 1 - e_{CT}/ah$$

$$1/\alpha_{LS} = 1 - e_{LS}/ah$$

Since $e_{CT} > e_{LS}$ and $\alpha_{CT} < \alpha_{LS}$ is inconsistent with this pair of equations, it follows that the level of public good provision is lower in the commodity tax optimum than in the lump-sum optimum.

5 Conclusions

The analysis of this chapter supports the criticism made by Stiglitz and Dasgupta of Pigou in the sense that the Conventional Rule as defined above may be an over- or under-estimate of the incremental benefits of a public good. The correct benefit measure with distortionary taxation may exceed the sum of the marginal rates of substitution:

(a) where the public good is complementary with taxed private goods,
(b) where a rise in exogenous income would lead to a fall in the net tax paid:

$$\partial(\Sigma t_i X_i)/\partial I < 0.$$

This is likely to occur where taxed goods are inferior or normally supplied factors are subsidised. In such cases, substitution away from the taxed good is not as large as it would otherwise be, and the change in taxation needed to raise an extra £1 is smaller.

On the other hand, Stiglitz and Dasgupta failed to point out that whether the Conventional Rule provides an under- or over-estimate depends on the choice of taxed goods (as is clear from (b) above). We have also seen that the question of the appropriate output level for public goods is a rather different one – a point not made clear by Stiglitz-Dasgupta – and that their analysis throws no light on whether output levels in the full optimum are greater or less than the optimum output level when expenditure is financed by distortionary taxation.

Appendix

It was asserted that the term $\sum_{i=1}^{n} t_i(S_{ik}/X_k)$ corresponded to the excess burden associated with the use of (optimum) commodity taxes as opposed to lump-sum taxes. This may be demonstrated by examining the effect of allowing the government to use lump-sum taxation at level T. The government's maximisation problem may then be formulated in terms of the Lagrangian (where $h = 1$):

$$\mathscr{L} = V(q, e, T) - \lambda G[X(q, e, T), e] \tag{A1}$$

giving the same first-order conditions for the choice of t_k as before (equation (5)):

$$\sum_{i=1}^{n} t_i(S_{ik}/X_k) = \alpha/\lambda - 1 + \sum_{i=1}^{n} t_i \frac{\partial X_i}{\partial I}. \tag{A2}$$

Let us examine the effect of allowing the government to make a small increase dT in the lump-sum tax (moving away from the optimum described above), where adjustments are made in the commodity tax rates to hold e constant and ensure that the production constraint holds. Since $\partial \mathscr{L}/\partial t = 0$ it follows that $d\mathscr{L}/dT = \partial \mathscr{L}/\partial T$. Moreover, given that the production constraint continues to hold $d\mathscr{L} = dV$, which is the change in welfare brought about by the adjustment.[10] From (A1):

$$\frac{\partial \mathscr{L}}{\partial T} = -\alpha - \lambda \sum_{i=1}^{n} G_i \frac{\partial X_i}{\partial T} = -\alpha - \lambda \sum_{i=1}^{n} (q_i - t_i) \frac{\partial X_i}{\partial T}$$

(since $V_T = -\alpha$). From the consumer budget constraint we may note that:

$$\sum_{i=1}^{n} q_i \frac{\partial X_i}{\partial T} = 1$$

Moreover, $\partial X_i/\partial T = -\partial X_i/\partial I$, so that:

$$\frac{\partial \mathscr{L}}{\partial T} = -\alpha + \lambda\left(1 - \sum_{i=1}^{n} t_i \frac{\partial X_i}{\partial I}\right)$$

which from (A2):

$$= -\lambda \sum_{i=1}^{n} t_i(S_{ik}/X_k) \tag{A3}$$

In the text it has been shown that the right-hand side of this expression is positive, so that there is a welfare gain to the increased use of lump-sum taxes. It should, however, be emphasised that this result only holds where *optimum* commodity taxes are employed. In the case where the tax rates are selected arbitrarily, there is no guarantee that a switch to lump-sum taxation will raise the level of welfare.

A similar argument shows that there is a 'route' from the commodity tax optimum to the lump-sum optimum such that welfare increases all the way. For each level of T choose the optimum $e(T)$ and $t(T)$, so that along the path $\partial \mathscr{L}/\partial e = \partial \mathscr{L}/\partial t = 0$. Then at each point on the path we have $dV/dT = d\mathscr{L}/dT = \partial \mathscr{L}/\partial T > 0$.

Acknowledgement

The authors are grateful to P. A. Diamond, A. K. Dixit, A. K. Klevorick, J. A. Mirrlees and A. Sandmo for their comments on earlier versions of this chapter.

Notes

1 Reprinted from *The Review of Economic Studies*, vol. 41, **1**, January 1974.
2 With the procedure followed here (which is that adopted by Diamond and Mirrlees), the costs of raising revenue are subtracted from the benefit side. The same results could equally well be described as adding the costs of raising revenue to the cost side – as is done by Pigou and Stiglitz and Dasgupta.
3 The last sentence in the quotation from Pigou given above suggests that it was the comparison of output levels which he had in mind.
4 This assumption is made for simplicity; for discussion of the case where consumers are not identical, see Diamond and Mirrlees [2].
5 The production side is discussed further in Diamond and Mirrlees. If non-constant returns permit positive profits the results carry through, in the case of identical consumers, if 100% profits taxes are allowed (see e.g. [8]).
6 We assume in this chapter that functions are differentiable to the relevant order.
7 In this case, the condition for $\alpha > \lambda$ (combining (i) and (ii)) is that the supply curve of labour be backward-bending, which is not implausible. This result is given by Stiglitz and Dasgupta

(p. 159), but they do not appear to appreciate its dependence on the choice of untaxed good.

8 It should be noted that the assumption of constant producer prices is important at this point.

9 The supply curve of labour is given by $L = a + T(1-a)/(1-t)$, so that $\partial L/\partial t = 0$ at $T = 0$.

10 An identical change in welfare would be brought about by increasing lump-sum taxation by dT and spending all the revenue on the public good (keeping commodity taxation unchanged).

References

[1] Aaron, H. and McGuire, M. C. (1970), 'Public goods and income distribution', *Econometrica*.

[2] Diamond, P. A. and Mirrlees, J. A. (1971), 'Optimal taxation and public production', *American Economic Review*, March and June.

[3] Pigou, A. C. (1947), *A Study in Public Finance*, 3rd edn, Macmillan.

[4] Prest, A. R. and Turvey, R. (1965), 'Cost-benefit analysis – A survey', *Economic Journal*, December.

[5] Samuelson, P. A. (1954), 'The pure theory of public expenditure', *Review of Economics and Statistics*, **36**.

[6] Samuelson, P. A. (1955), 'Diagrammatic exposition of a theory of public expenditure', *Review of Economics and Statistics*, **37**.

[7] Samuelson, P. A. (1958), 'Aspects of public expenditure theories',/*Review of Economics and Statistics*, **40**.

[8] Stiglitz, J. E. and Dasgupta, P. (1971), 'Differential taxation, public goods and economic efficiency', *Review of Economic Studies*, **38**, April.

14 Welfare Implications of the Taxation of Savings*

Historically, the welfare aspects of the taxation of savings have mainly been discussed in the context of the relative merits of income and consumption (expenditure) taxation. These have long been the subject of debate, with the book by Kaldor [19] being probably the best known contribution. In this chapter, we examine the role of the two types of taxation in the context of a model that draws both on modern analysis of optimal taxation and on the theory of economic growth. In so doing, we feel that the issues involved can be discussed in greater depth, but the cost is that some important matters have to be left out. Thus, we do not discuss the implications of alternative tax structures for short-run stabilisation policy, nor do we consider the costs of tax administration.[1] Moreover, we neglect problems of distributive justice within a given generation of individuals. Instead, we concentrate on the implications of taxation for the efficiency of resource utilisation and for the intertemporal allocation of consumption.

In popular expositions one often encounters the following efficiency argument in favour of expenditure taxation. An income tax applies to both labour earnings and interest on savings. The imposition of such a tax introduces (into an otherwise first-best world) distortions in both the labour market and the capital market. By comparison, the expenditure tax, while affecting the labour–leisure choice, is 'neutral' with respect to savings decisions, and thus appears to dominate the income tax in terms of efficiency considerations. Although still current,[2] this view is not very convincing. The theory of the second-best has taught us that one cannot evaluate alternative tax systems by simply comparing the *number* of distortions involved; it is essential to consider the magnitude of the various distortions as well as their interaction. Among other aspects, the conventional argument ignores the possibility that a tax on interest income might be desirable in order to offset the distortions introduced by a tax on labour earnings.

A more sophisticated argument, taking account of this objection, is that developed by Feldstein [16] and others based on the theory of optimum taxation. Since the static general equilibrium model used in this literature (see, for example, Diamond and Mirrlees [13], Atkinson and Stiglitz (Chapter 10 in

* Reprinted from *The Economic Journal*, **90**, September 1980.
A. B. Atkinson and A. Sandmo.

this volume) and Sandmo [35] can easily – although perhaps somewhat artificially – be given an intertemporal interpretation, it might seem that it would be a straightforward task to apply optimum tax theory to the problem at hand.[3] Thus Feldstein [16] makes use of the results given in Atkinson and Stiglitz (Chapter 11 in this volume). He notes that the conditions for the pure consumption tax to be optimal are unlikely to be satisfied, but suggests that 'the efficiency gain from switching completely to a progressive consumption tax may ... be large even if a consumption tax is not itself the optimum optimorum' ([16], p. 49). Similarly, Bradford and Rosen [7] refer to this result and argue that this 'illustrates the challenge implicit in the optimal tax approach to the widespread acceptance of taxation on the basis of Haig-Simons income' (p. 96).

This straightforward application of the optimum tax literature may, however, be misleading, and one of the main purposes of this chapter is to show that it neglects important features of the problem. One can only apply the standard results to a dynamic model under certain conditions. In particular, it depends on the other instruments which can be employed by the government and its ability to achieve a desired intertemporal allocation. In order to bring this out, we have adopted an explicitly intertemporal model of growth with overlapping generations, a topic first investigated by Samuelson [31] and later extended to an economy with production by Diamond [11]. This framework is described in section 1 where particular attention is paid to the range of fiscal instruments at the disposal of the government.

Section 2 formulates the problem faced by the government in designing the structure of taxation to maximise a social welfare function defined as the discounted sum of individual lifetime welfares. This social welfare function is open to question, but is the natural analogue of that employed in static treatments of optimum taxation. Although the full dynamic path is considered, the interpretation of the results focuses on the steady state of the economy.[4] Section 3 discusses the case where the government can use lump-sum taxes, or debt policy, to achieve a desired intertemporal allocation. It is shown that, in this situation, the standard optimum tax results can be employed, and we discuss the implications for the choice between income and expenditure taxation. Where, however, the government is constrained, and cannot achieve a first-best level of the capital–labour ratio, the standard analysis can no longer be directly applied. Section 4 describes the necessary modifications to the conditions for optimality, and illustrates with a simple Cobb–Douglas example.

The choice between tax bases depends also on the objectives pursued by the government. In particular, we need to consider the treatment of different generations – the issue of intertemporal distribution – and the extent to which the government respects the valuations placed by individuals on consumption at different dates. Section 5 considers alternative formulations of the social welfare function and the implications of non-Paretian objectives.

In examining these questions, we have built on earlier work by a number of writers. Particular reference should be made to the treatment of optimum taxation in an intertemporal setting by Diamond [12], on whose analysis we have drawn in several respects. As in Diamond [11], the model is one where individuals live for two periods, working in the first and being retired in the second and there are no bequests. This framework is also adopted by Hamada [17], who studies a model with individuals of differing abilities in an economy where there is a linear tax on wage income (but no tax on capital income); he is then able to analyse the trade-off between equity and dynamic efficiency. Pestieau [29] introduces taxes on both labour and interest income, but he focuses primarily on the interaction between the tax structure and public investment criteria. Of the articles by Ordover and Phelps [27] and Ordover [26], the former is closer to our approach, but both differ from the contributions previously mentioned in adopting a Rawlsian rather than a utilitarian welfare function. Moreover, Ordover [26] makes special assumptions about the supply of labour which in fact cause it to be independent of the rate of interest. Mitra [25] provides a unified treatment of a range of tax policies in a dynamic context, and considers the implications of different objectives. His paper is not, however, explicitly directed to the choice between income and expenditure taxation which is our main concern here.[5]

1 The Framework

As noted at the outset, we rule out any consideration of redistribution within a generation, which is taken to consist of identical individuals. The preference of a particular generation are represented by the utility function of a representative member of the generation born at time i (referred to as generation i):

$$U = U(C_1^i, C_2^{i+1}, L^i), \tag{1}$$

where C_1^i, C_2^{i+1} are consumption in the first and second periods, respectively, of the individual's life and L^i is labour hours per worker supplied in period i. In the second period, individuals are retired and their consumption is constrained by savings carried over from the first period. The number of individuals in each generation is $(1+n)$ times that in the previous one, so there are $N_0(1+n)^i$ ($\equiv N^i$) workers at time i. In the absence of taxes the budget constraint of a representative member of the generation starting life at i would be:

$$C_1^i + \frac{1}{1+r^{i+1}} C_2^{i+1} = w^i L^i, \tag{2}$$

where w^i is the wage rate at time i and r^{i+1} is the next-period rate of interest. The individual is assumed to have perfect foresight regarding r^{i+1} (and regarding taxes).[6]

The economy is assumed to be perfectly competitive, with firms maximising profits:

$$Y^i - w^i L^i N^i - r^i K^i, \tag{3}$$

where Y^i, K^i denote output and capital, respectively, subject to a constant returns to scale production function (assumed unchanging over time, although Harrod–neutral technical progress could readily be introduced):

$$Y^i = L^i N^i f(k^i/L^i) \qquad \text{where } f' > 0, \ f'' < 0. \tag{4}$$

The capital stock per worker is denoted by k^i, so that k^i/L^i is the capital per worker hour. We assume for convenience that there is no depreciation of capital. In the absence of taxation, and government debt, the supply of capital is determined by the level of savings for retirement of the preceding generation:

$$K^{i+1} = (w^i L^i - C_1^i) N^i \tag{5}$$

or:

$$k^{i+1} = \frac{w^i L^i - C_1^i}{1+n}. \tag{6}$$

We now introduce taxation, and begin with a full statement of the range of policy instruments considered. The literature on optimum taxation has demonstrated how the results may be very sensitive to the assumptions made about the types of taxation which are possible (Atkinson and Stiglitz, Chapter 11 in this volume). We confine our attention to linear taxes, but otherwise allow for a tax on labour income (t_w), a tax on interest income (t_r), a tax on consumption (t_C) and lump-sum taxes in periods 1 and 2 $(T_1$ and $T_2)$. Each of these may be varied at each date, so that a superscript i should be added. In addition, the government issues one period debt D^i per worker, which bears the same interest as other capital.

The individual budget constraint now becomes:

$$C_1^i(1+t_C^i) + \frac{C_2^{i+1}(1+t_C^{i+1}) + T_2^{i+1}}{1+r^{i+1}(1-t_r^{i+1})} = w^i(1-t_w^i)L^i - T_1^i. \tag{7}$$

It may be noted that we are assuming that all those alive at a particular date pay the same indirect tax, but that the lump-sum taxes may be differentiated by generation (as where there is a state pension scheme). The *per capita* level of savings by generation i is now:

$$w^i(1-t_w^i)L^i - T_1^i - C_1^i(1+t_C^i) \equiv A^i. \tag{8}$$

The interest income tax paid (in period $i+1$) is therefore per worker in period $i+1$:

$$t_r^{i+1} r^{i+1} A^i/(1+n). \tag{9}$$

The government is assumed to have a revenue constraint which requires it to raise an amount G per worker in each period, expressed in units of consumption, in addition to financing the repayment of existing debt, net of the issue of new debt. At time i this may be written:

$$t_w^i w^i L^i + t_C^i \left(C_1^i + \frac{C_2^i}{1+n} \right) + t_r^i r^i \frac{A^{i-1}}{1+n} + T_1^i + \frac{T_2^i}{1+n} = G + \left(\frac{1+r^i}{1+n} \right) D^{i-1} - D^i. \tag{10}$$

The government may be seen as choosing the tax rates, and debt policy, subject to this revenue constraint and the capital market equilibrium condition, which now becomes:

$$(1+n)k^{i+1} = A^i - D^i, \tag{11}$$

where the right-hand side is private saving net of the holding of government debt. It is, however, more straightforward to work with the aggregate production constraint:

$$Y^i = L^i N^i f(k^i/L^i) = N^i C_1^i + N^{i-1} C_2^i + N^i G + K^{i+1} - K^i \tag{12}$$

or, dividing by N^i:

$$L^i f(k^i/L^i) = C_1^i + \frac{C_2^i}{1+n} + G + (1+n)k^{i+1} - k^i. \tag{13}$$

(It may be checked that (13) and (11), together with the individual budget constraint, imply the revenue constraint (10).)

This formulation allows for a wide range of tax and debt policies, but not all of them are independent. In particular, debt policy can be shown to be equivalent in this model to use of the lump-sum taxes T_1 and T_2, as has been noted by Diamond ([12], p. 222) and Bierwag, Grove and Khang [6]. This may be seen by considering a unit rise in T_1^i, coupled with a fall in T_2^{i+1} equal to:

$$\frac{1}{1+r^{i+1}(1-t_r^{i+1})}.$$

This leaves unchanged the present value of lump-sum tax payments by the individual in generation i (see the budget constraint (7)). If at the same time D^i is reduced by 1 unit, this leaves the capital market condition unchanged (see equations (8) and (11)). If we now turn to the government revenue constraint, the one unit changes in T_1^i and D^i ensure that it is unchanged in period i; and the change in T_2^{i+1} is similarly offset in period $(i+1)$ by the fall in D^i (allowing for the effect via A^i). From this point on, we therefore drop any explicit reference in the model to government debt ($D^i = 0$ for all i). It should, however, be noted that when we refer to restrictions on the use of lump-sum taxes, these also apply to debt policy.

Finally, we may simplify the representation of the impact of taxation by introducing the new variables:

$$\omega^i \equiv w^i(1-t_w^i), \tag{14a}$$

which is the net of tax wage rate:

$$Z^i \equiv T_1^i + \frac{T_2^i}{1+r^{i+1}(1-t_r^{i+1})}, \tag{14b}$$

which is the present value of lump-sum tax payments made by generation i, and:

$$p^{i+1} \equiv \frac{1}{1+r^{i+1}(1-t_r^{i+1})}\left(\frac{1+t_C^{i+1}}{1+t_C^i}\right), \tag{14c}$$

which is the 'price' to generation i of second period consumption relative to that in the first. The individual budget constraint for generation t is then:

$$(1+t_C^i)(C_1^i+p^{i+1}C_2^{i+1})=\omega^i L^i - Z^i. \tag{15}$$

The behaviour of generation i (C_1^i, C_2^{i+1}, L) may therefore be treated as a function of t_C^i, p^{i+1}, ω^i and Z^i. Moreover, it is invariant with respect to (positive) proportional changes in $(1+t_C^i)$, ω^i and Z^i. The aggregate duction constraint is unaffected, since the policy variables do not enter directly.

With this reformulation, the choice between income and expenditure taxation may be seen in terms of the choice of p^{i+1}. If p^{i+1} is greater than $1/(1+r^{i+1})$, then the tax system departs from a pure expenditure tax in the direction of taxing second period consumption more heavily. This may be achieved either by a rising rate of indirect taxation over time or by the taxation of interest income $(t_r^{i+1}>0)$. For a pure income tax, $t_r^{i+1}=t_w^{i+1}$ (and t_c zero). In what follows, particular attention is paid to the relationship between p^{i+1} and $1/(1+r^{i+1})$.

2 Formulation of the Government's Problem

At this stage we assume that the government's objective is to maximise the discounted sum of individual lifetime welfares. The choice of discount factor allows some flexibility in the formulation, but the assumption that governments respect individual lifetime valuations is a restrictive one, and in section 5 we consider an alternative treatment.

In order to formalise this we introduce the indirect utility function giving lifetime welfare for generation i as a function of ω^i, t_C^i, p^{i+1} and Z^i. This is denoted by:

$$V^i=V^i(\omega^i,t_C^i,p^{i+1},Z^i). \tag{16}$$

If α^i is the private marginal utility of income, then the derivatives of V^i are given by:

$$\frac{\partial V^i}{\partial \omega^i} = \alpha^i L^i, \qquad \frac{\partial V^i}{\partial t_1^i} = -\alpha^i (C_1^i + p^{i+1} C_2^{i+1}),$$

$$\left. \begin{array}{l} \\ \\ \end{array} \right\} \tag{17}$$

$$\frac{\partial V^i}{\partial p^{i+1}} = -\alpha^i (1 + t_C^i) C_2^{i+1}, \qquad \frac{\partial V^i}{\partial Z^i} = -\alpha^i.$$

The government's objective at time j may be written as maximising:

$$\sum_{i=j}^{\infty} (\gamma)^i V^i, \tag{18}$$

where we assume $0 < \gamma < 1$. (The welfare of generation $j-1$, in the second period of their lives at j, is taken as given.) This objective may be interpreted in several ways. If the government is concerned with discounted *total* utility, then $\gamma = (1+n)/(1+\delta)$, n being the rate of population growth and δ the discount factor, with $\delta > n$. If, as in much of the optimum growth literature, the objective is the discounted sum of *average* utility, then $\gamma = 1/(1+\delta)$.[7]

The government is assumed to have inherited at time j a capital stock per worker, k^j, and the policy parameters set in the preceding period $(\omega^{j-1}, t_C^{j-1}, p^j, Z^{j-1}, T_1^{j-1})$. (It may be noted that these determine the welfare of generation $j-1$.) We can then introduce the state valuation function $\Gamma(k^j, \omega^{j-1}, t_C^{j-1}, p^j, Z^{j-1}, T_1^{j-1})$ to represent the maximal level of social welfare (discounted to time j) obtainable given these initial conditions. The government maximises by choosing k^{j+1}, ω^j, t_C^j, p^{j+1}, Z^j and T_1^j subject to the constraints. The latter may be written in the form:

$$k^j + L^j f(k^j/L^j) = C_1^j + \frac{C_2^j}{1+n} + G + A^j \tag{19}$$

(eliminating k^{j+1} from (11) and (13)) or:

$$k^j + L^j [f(k^j/L^j) - \omega^j] = \frac{C_2^j}{1+n} + G - T_1^j - t_C^j C_1^j \tag{20}$$

(using the definition of A^j from equation (8)), and:

$$k^{j+1} = L^j \left[f(k^j/L^j) - C_1^j - \frac{C_2^j}{1+n} - G + k^j \right] / (1+n) \tag{21}$$

(rearranging (13)). If we now introduce the multiplier λ^j for the constraint (20), we can apply the principle of optimality of dynamic programming (this is the same method as employed by Diamond [12]). In view of the stationarity of the problem:

$$\Gamma(j) \equiv \Gamma(k^j, \omega^{j-1}, t_C^{j-1}, p^j, Z^{j-1}, T_1^{j-1})$$

$$= \max \left\{ V^j + \lambda^j \left[k^j + L^j(f - \omega^j) - \frac{C_2^j}{1+n} - G + T_1^j + t_C^j C_1^j \right] + \gamma \Gamma(j+1) \right\},$$

(22)

where k^{j+1} in $\Gamma(j+1)$ is given by equation (21).

The simplest case to consider is that where there is no restriction on lump-sum taxation, so that T_1^j can be varied freely (or equivalently the government can employ debt policy). Since T_1^j does not affect the maximum attainable level of welfare, for a given k^{j+1}, the derivative $(\partial\Gamma(j+1)/\partial T_1^j)$ of the valuation function is zero, and the necessary condition for optimality is simply that $\lambda^j = 0$. This accords with intuition in that the government now has sufficient instruments to achieve the desired intertemporal allocation. Where this is the case, by varying T_1^j the government can ensure that a level of k^{j+1} which is feasible according to the production constraint can be achieved by individual savings decisions.[8]

Where $\lambda^j = 0$, the problem may be simplified by setting $t_C^j = 0$ all j. We have earlier noted that consumer behaviour was invariant with respect to (positive) proportional changes in $(1 + t_C^j)$, ω^j and Z^j; and from (21) it is clear that k^{j+1} is unaffected. We therefore adopt this normalisation. The necessary conditions for optimality may be set out in terms of the choice of ω^j, t_C^j, p^{j+1} and Z^j (k^{j+1} is eliminated using equation (21)). The first-order conditions for maximisation are:

$$-V_\omega^j = \gamma \Gamma_2(j+1) + \frac{\gamma}{1+n} \Gamma_1(j+1) \left[\left(f - \frac{f'k^j}{L^j} \right) L_\omega^j - C_{1\omega}^j \right],$$

(23a)

where Γ_i denotes the derivatives with respect to the ith argument, and L_x^j, C_{1x}^j denote the derivative with respect to x,

$$-V_p^j = \gamma \Gamma_4(j+1) + \frac{\gamma}{1+n} \Gamma_1(j+1) \left[\left(f - \frac{f'k^j}{L^j} \right) L_p^j - C_{1p}^j \right]$$

(23b)

and:

$$-V_Z^j = \gamma \Gamma_5(j+1) + \frac{\gamma}{1+n} \Gamma_1(j+1) \left[\left(f - \frac{f'k^j}{L^j} \right) L_Z^j - C_{1Z}^j \right].$$

(23c)

The second set of equations are those obtained by differentiating the recursion relation (22) with respect to the state variables k^j, ω^{j-1}, p^j and Z^{j-1}:

$$\Gamma_1(j) = \frac{\gamma}{1+n} \Gamma_1(j+1)(1+f'),$$

(24a)

$$\Gamma_2(j) = \frac{\gamma}{1+n} \Gamma_1(j+1) \left(-\frac{c_{2\omega}^j}{1+n} \right),$$

(24b)

$$\Gamma_4(j) = \frac{\gamma}{1+n}\Gamma_1(j+1)\left(-\frac{C_{2p}^j}{1+n}\right), \tag{24c}$$

$$\Gamma_5(j) = \frac{\gamma}{1+n}\Gamma_1(j+1)\left(-\frac{U_{l_2}^j}{1+n}\right). \tag{24d}$$

In the next section we turn to the interpretation of these results. Throughout this discussion we assume both that an optimum policy exists and that it converges to a steady state.[9]

3   Interpretation of the Results: First-best Intertemporal Allocation

This section examines the interpretation of the results obtained where T_1 is freely variable (so that $\lambda^j = 0$ all j), focusing on the steady-state properties. (The properties of the approach to steady state can readily be deduced.) In this steady state, the condition (24a) yields $\Gamma_1(j) = \Gamma_1(j+1)$ or:

$$1 + f' = \frac{1+n}{\gamma}. \tag{25}$$

Where the objective function takes the total utility form (i.e. $\gamma = (1+n)/(1+\delta)$), this means that $f' = \delta$. The intertemporal allocation is such that the rate of return equals the rate of discount applied to different generations (as in Diamond [12] and Pestieau [29]). Where the objective is of the average utility form (i.e. $\gamma = 1/(1+\delta)$), this means that $1 + f' = (1+n)(1+\delta)$, which is often referred to as the 'modified golden rule' (e.g. Cass and Shell [8] and Dixit [14]).

In the steady state, the values of Γ_i/Γ_1 are given by (24b–d). Substituting first into (23c), we obtain, dropping the time superscript and using the properties of the indirect utility function (17):

$$\left(\frac{\alpha}{\Gamma_1}\right)\left(\frac{1+n}{\gamma}\right) = \frac{\gamma}{1+n}(-C_{2Z}) + (wL_Z - C_{1Z}). \tag{26c}$$

From the individual budget constraint (differentiating with respect to Z):

$$C_{1Z} + pC_{2Z} = w(1 - t_w)L_Z - 1. \tag{27}$$

Hence (26c) yields the condition:

$$\mu \equiv \left(\frac{1+n}{\gamma}\right)\left(\frac{\alpha}{\Gamma_1}\right) - t_w wL_Z - rC_{2Z} = 1, \tag{28}$$

where:

$$\tau \equiv p - \frac{1}{1+f'} = \frac{1}{1+r(1-t_r)} - \frac{1}{1+f'} = \frac{pf't_r}{1+f'}, \tag{29}$$

and we have used the steady-state condition (25).

The condition (28) has a straightforward interpretation. The left-hand side (μ) measures the benefit, denominated in terms of government revenue, of a unit increase in lump-sum income, or equivalently a unit reduction in the lump-sum tax. The second and third terms are the change in revenue arising from the income effect; the first term is the private marginal utility of income divided by the 'shadow' price of revenue (i.e. the effect of an easing of the revenue target). This has been referred to in the optimum tax literature as the 'net social marginal valuation of income' (Atkinson and Stiglitz [5]). Where the government can employ lump-sum taxes, then the necessary condition is that $\mu = 1$; moreover, as in the standard literature, this implies that there is no recourse to distortionary income or expenditure taxes. This may be seen from (23a) and (23b). Making use of the steady-state conditions for Γ_2/Γ_1 and Γ_4/Γ_1, and the properties of the indirect utility function:

$$-\left(\frac{\alpha}{\Gamma_1}\right)\left(\frac{1+n}{\gamma}\right)L = \left(\frac{-C_{2\omega}}{1+f'}\right) + (wL_\omega - C_{1\omega}), \tag{26a}$$

$$\left(\frac{\alpha}{\Gamma_1}\right)\left(\frac{1+n}{\gamma}\right)C_2 = \left(\frac{-C_{2p}}{1+f'}\right) + (wL_p - C_{1p}). \tag{26b}$$

Using the budget constraint, and the Slutsky relationships,[10] these may be rewritten:

$$-t_w w S_{LL} - \tau S_{2L} = (\mu - 1)L, \tag{30a}$$

$$t_w w S_{L2} + \tau S_{22} = (\mu - 1)C_2. \tag{30b}$$

Thus if the government can use lump-sum taxes freely ($\mu = 1$), the right-hand side of both equations is zero.

In the model as formulated, there is no apparent reason why lump-sum taxes cannot be employed. As argued in Atkinson and Stiglitz (Chapter 11 in this volume), ideally one should build into the analysis the reasons why in reality governments are not happy to rely principally on lump-sum taxes, particularly on account of distributional objectives. Our purpose here is to focus on the relative merits of income and expenditure taxation, and in view of this we simply assume that there is a limit to the use of lump-sum taxation – for example because of its adverse intratemporal distributional consequences.

Where the government cannot employ lump-sum taxation, we have the standard Ramsey results. We are therefore in a situation where the argument of Feldstein and others applies. If we define the compensated elasticities:

$$\left.\begin{array}{cc} \sigma_{LL} = \dfrac{\omega}{L} S_{LL}, & \sigma_{2L} = \dfrac{\omega}{C_2} S_{2L}, \\[4mm] \sigma_{L2} = \dfrac{p}{L} S_{L2}, & \sigma_{22} = \dfrac{p}{C_2} S_{22}, \end{array}\right\} \tag{31}$$

and eliminate μ from (30a) and (30b), we obtain (using the fact that $S_{2L} = -S_{L2}$):

$$\frac{t_w}{1-t_w}(\sigma_{LL} - \sigma_{-L}) = \frac{\tau}{p}(\sigma_{\tau_1} - \sigma_{\tau_1}) \tag{32}$$

As noted by Diamond [12] and Pestieau [29], this is the application to the dynamic case of the results obtained by Corlett and Hague [9].

In seeking to use this analysis to make an efficiency argument for expenditure taxation, people have adopted two approaches. First, one can seek qualitative statements. This is illustrated by the results of Atkinson and Stiglitz (Chapter 10 in this volume) for the case where U is directly additive. In that situation, unitary expenditure elasticities imply that the optimal tax rate τ is zero, hence there should be no taxation of savings. This can be shown from equation (32) by noting that direct additivity implies that the substitution terms can be expressed in terms of income derivatives (see, for example, Houthakker [18], p. 248) and then making use of the unitary elasticity condition $(1/C_1)(dC_1/dI) = (1/C_2)(dC_2/dI)$.[11] This assumption of unitary expenditure elasticities would therefore justify the expenditure tax, but there is no strong reason to believe that it is valid.

The second approach is to make use of empirical estimates of the parameters σ_{ij}. This faces the difficulty that there is considerable disagreement about key parameters, and that in some cases there is virtually no empirical evidence at all. This applies particularly to the cross-elasticities, σ_{L2} and σ_{2L}, very little being known, for example, about the elasticity of labour supply with respect to the interest rate.[12]

Moreover, experimentation with possible values shows that the results may be highly sensitive. If we start with $\sigma_{L2} = \sigma_{2L} = 0$, then $\sigma_{LL} = 0.3$ and $\sigma_{22} = -1.5$ would imply a positive tax on savings. There is, however, no reason why it should equal the income tax rate: e.g. with $t_w = \frac{1}{3}$, $r = 1$, it is less than the equivalent income tax.[13] On the other hand, if the elasticity of labour supply were larger,[14] and that of savings lower, this could imply a higher rate of tax on capital income – a surcharge on investment income – for all likely values of the tax rates. For example, if $\sigma_{LL} = 1.5$ and $\sigma_{22} = -0.5$, savings would be taxed more heavily where t_w is less than $\frac{2}{3}$. At the same time, there is no reason to suppose that the cross-elasticities are zero, and the conclusions reached can depend sensitively on their value. If σ_{2L} were 0.3, τ would fall to zero, whereas $\sigma_{2L} = -0.3$ would double the optimum tax rate on investment income. It is unfortunate that the conclusions appear to rest on the values of elasticities which have typically been ignored in empirical work. Even if we could agree on estimates of the own-elasticities, there would remain a considerable range of estimates of the tax rates.

It should be clear from the foregoing that it is difficult to make a strong case *either* for the expenditure tax *or* for taxing interest income at the same rate as wage income. It is in fact expecting too much to hope that one could derive such concrete conclusions. What the optimum tax literature can do is to indicate some of the factors influencing the design of tax structure. For example, the condition (32) depends on the direct compensated elasticities in the way intuition suggests: the tax on savings is more likely to raise welfare, the larger is the compensated elasticity of labour supply (σ_{LL}) relative to that of future consumption ($-\sigma_{22}$). It may also suggest some qualitative propositions. For example, the fact that σ_{2L} and σ_{L2} are of opposite signs means that a sufficient condition for an increase in τ above zero to be optimal is that $\sigma_{2L} \leqslant 0$ (the compensated supply of labour must decrease with the interest rate).[15] However, it is in our view a misapplication of the optimum taxation literature to suggest that it provides a clear-cut answer to the choice between income and consumption bases. This is even more true when there are restrictions on the government's ability to achieve a desired intertemporal allocation – a case to which we now turn.

4 Constraints on Intertemporal Allocation

In the previous section it was assumed that the government could use the timing of lump-sum taxation (i.e. vary T_1 for a given Z), or debt policy, to achieve the desired intertemporal allocation. Thus, with the total utility formulation of the objective, the steady state capital stock satisfies the 'first-best' condition $f' = \delta$. On the other hand, the assumption that the government possesses this degree of control is crucial to the results. In particular, if the government cannot achieve the desired level of capital by varying lump-sum taxes, then the standard optimum tax results no longer necessarily apply.

The introduction of such constraints raises a number of questions. What is it that prevents the government from levying differential lump-sum taxes? If there are constraints on using the income tax for this purpose (e.g. that the tax exemption must be identical for all), what is to stop the generations from being treated differently under a social security scheme (e.g. Samuelson [32])? If tax policy cannot be used, what are the limitations on the use of debt policy? In a full treatment, these issues need to be addressed. Our purpose here, however, is not to explore these questions, but rather to draw attention to some of the possible implications of such constraints. *If the government is constrained in this way, how do the results need to be modified?*

In order to illustrate the effects of constraints on the intertemporal allocation, we assume that there is no lump-sum taxation ($T_1^i = T_2^i = Z^i = 0$ all i), no debt ($D^i = 0$ all i) and no indirect taxation ($t_C^i = 0$ all i).[16] The maximisation problem may be reformulated as (using Ω in place of Γ):

$$\Omega(j) = \Omega(k^j, \omega^{j-1}, p^j)$$

$$= \max \left\{ V^j + \lambda^j \left[k^j + L^j(f - \omega^j) - \frac{C_2^j}{1+n} - G \right] + \gamma \Omega(j+1) \right\}. \tag{33}$$

The necessary conditions are:

$$(-V_\omega^j) = \lambda^j [(f - \omega^j - f'k^j/L^j)L_\omega^j - L^j] + \gamma \Omega_2(j+1)$$

$$+ \left(\frac{\gamma}{1+n} \right) \Omega_1(j+1)(w^j L_\omega^j - C_{1\omega}^j) \tag{34a}$$

and:

$$(\quad V_p^j) - \lambda^j [(f - \omega^j - f'k^j/l^j)l_p^j] + \gamma\Omega_1(j+1)$$
$$+ \left(\frac{\gamma}{1+n}\right)\Omega_1(j+1)(w^j L_p^j - C_{1p}^j). \tag{34b}$$

The recursion equation yields:

$$\Omega_1(j) = [1 + f'(k^j)]\left[\lambda^j + \frac{\gamma}{1+n}\Omega_1(j+1)\right], \tag{35a}$$

$$\Omega_2(j) = \left(-\frac{C_{2\omega}^j}{1+n}\right)\left[\lambda^j + \frac{\gamma}{1+n}\Omega_1(j+1)\right], \tag{35b}$$

$$\Omega_3(j) = \left(-\frac{C_{2p}^j}{1+n}\right)\left[\lambda^j + \frac{\gamma}{1+n}\Omega_1(j+1)\right]. \tag{35c}$$

In steady state, equation (35a) gives (dropping the time superscript):

$$\frac{\lambda}{\Omega_1} = \frac{1}{1+f'} - \frac{\gamma}{1+n} \tag{36}$$

and from (35b) and (35c) we can solve for Ω_2/Ω_1 and Ω_3/Ω_1 as functions of λ/Ω_1. Substituting into (34a) and (34b), and using the Slutsky equations, yields:

$$-t_w w S_{LL} - \frac{\gamma(1+f')}{1+n}r S_{2L} = (\mu^* - 1)L, \tag{37a}$$

$$t_w w S_{L2} + \frac{\gamma(1+f')}{1+n}r S_{22} = \left[\mu^* - 1 + (1+f')\frac{\lambda}{\Omega_1}\right]C_2, \tag{37b}$$

where:

$$\mu^* \equiv \frac{\alpha(1+f')}{\Omega_1} - t_w w L_z - \frac{\gamma(1+f')}{1+n}\tau C_{2z}. \tag{37c}$$

If $(1+f')$ were equal to $(1+n)/\gamma$, as in the 'first-best' condition (25), then these equations would reduce to the standard Ramsey formula. In order to see what happens where the first-best cannot be attained, let us consider first the case where the objective is of the total utility form, so that $\gamma/(1+n) = 1/(1+\delta)$. If we then define:

$$\theta \equiv -\frac{\lambda}{\Omega_1}(1+f') = \frac{1+f'}{1+\delta} - 1, \tag{38}$$

this will be positive (negative) where the capital stock is less than (greater than) the 'first-best' level: i.e. as f' is greater (less) than δ. Substituting into (37a) and (37b), and eliminating μ^*, we obtain:

$$\frac{t_w}{1-t_w}(\sigma_{LL}-\sigma_{2L})=\frac{\tau}{p}(\sigma_{L2}-\sigma_{22})(1+\theta)-\theta. \qquad (39)$$

This is the analogue of condition (32), and reduces to this when $\theta=0$.[17] If instead the objective is formulated in terms of average utility, with $\gamma=1/(1+\delta)$, then θ is positive where $(1+f')>(1+n)(1+\delta)$. Where $\delta\to0$, this gives the 'golden rule' condition: θ is positive (negative) where the capital stock is below (above) the golden rule. (Here, since $\gamma=1$, a different argument is necessary to characterise the optimum.)

The equation (39) does not allow us to draw direct conclusions about the effect of constraints, since θ is itself a variable of the problem. To get a better understanding of the nature of the solution, it is useful to work out a specific example. Suppose that the individual utility functions are Cobb–Douglas:

$$U=a_1\log C_1+a_2\log C_2+a_3\log(1-L), \qquad (40)$$

where $a_1+a_2+a_3=1$. This example is chosen because it is simple and because we know that in this case the standard optimal taxation framework would involve $\tau=0$, since the expenditure elasticities with respect to labour income are all equal to one. The compensated elasticities in the Cobb–Douglas case are:[18]

$$\left.\begin{array}{c}\sigma_{LL}=\sigma_{2L}=a_3, \qquad \sigma_{22}=a_2-1, \\[2mm] \sigma_{L2}=-a_2a_3/(1-a_3).\end{array}\right\} \qquad (41)$$

Substituting these values into (39), we obtain:

$$\frac{\tau}{p}=\left(\frac{\theta}{1+\theta}\right)\left(1+\frac{a_2}{a_1}\right). \qquad (42)$$

(This confirms that where $\theta=0$ there should be no tax on savings.) Suppose that the objective function is of the total utility form. From the capital market equation (8) and the production constraint (20), and assuming that the production function is also Cobb–Douglas $(f=B(k/L)^\eta)$, we can then calculate that:

$$\left(1/\eta+\frac{a_2}{a_1}\right)(f'-\delta)=\left(\frac{1-\eta}{\eta}\right)(f_0'-\delta)+\frac{G}{k}, \qquad (43)$$

where f_0' denotes the return to capital at the no-tax equilibrium.[19] We may also note that the after-tax interest rate at the optimum is (using (38) and (42)):

$$r(1-t_r) = r - (1+r)\frac{\tau}{p} = \delta - (f' - \delta)\frac{a_2}{a_1}. \qquad (44)$$

From this we may conclude that if in the absence of taxation the capital stock is less than its 'first-best' level, and if $G \geqslant 0$, then at the optimum $f' > \delta$ and hence $\theta > 0$. In other words, the gap between f' and δ may be reduced by the optimum choice of tax policy but not totally eliminated. This in turn implies that there will be a positive level of taxation on savings. Suppose, for example, that in the no-tax situation, $f' = 2.0$, $\delta = 1.2$, and that $a_1 = a_2$, $\eta = \frac{1}{3}$. Then with zero revenue requirement, the optimum f' may be seen from equation (43) to be 1.6. This implies $\theta = 0.18$ and an optimum tax rate on capital income of 50%. The after-tax interest rate faced by the individual is 0.4 of the no-tax value.

The Cobb–Douglas case is illustrated in Figure 1, where we have plotted the levels of C_1 and C_2 (L being a constant). In the absence of taxation, the feasible

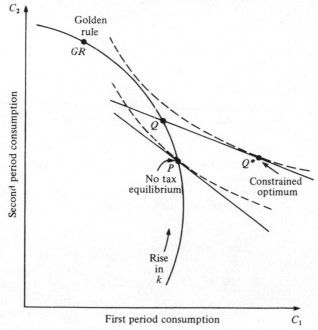

Figure 1 *Cobb–Douglas example: steady states.*

frontier follows the curve through P and GR. Each point on the curve is associated with a particular level of k, and k rises, f' falls, as we move up the curve. The point GR is that where $f' = n$, or the golden rule, but there is no reason to expect the competitive equilibrium to be at this point (Diamond [11]). In Figure 1, we have shown the no-tax competitive equilibrium as occurring at P, where $f'_0 > n$. On the assumption that $f'_0 > \delta > n$, the optimal steady state solution involves a rise in k (to point Q) and a reallocation between generations (to point Q^*).

It may appear paradoxical that where the no-tax capital stock falls short of the 'first-best' level there should be a positive tax rate on capital (in the Cobb–Douglas example). The reason for intervention is, however, the level of capital formation and – with the particular savings function – private savings are increased by a switch from t_w to τ.[20] This is a special feature of the particular example, but the important point is that, where the government is constrained in achieving the desired intertemporal allocation, it is the absolute effect on savings which is relevant. The essential element is the *uncompensated* response, rather than the *compensated* effects which have received most attention in the optimum tax literature.

5　Alternative Formulations of the Government Objective

In the previous section we have seen that the standard optimum tax formulae need to be modified where the government does not have sufficient instruments to ensure the intertemporal allocation condition:

$$1+f'=\frac{1+n}{\gamma}\equiv1+\varepsilon.\qquad(45)$$

Thus the nature of the solution, and the desirability of income or expenditure taxation, depends on the instruments at the disposal of the government. It also depends on the objective pursued by the government, and in this section we explore some of the implications of alternative goals.

The first aspect considered is the effect of variation in γ. This may be illustrated by the Cobb–Douglas example used in the previous section. Defining ε as in equation (45), the optimum steady state value of f' can be obtained from equation (43) by replacing δ by ε. The optimum tax rate on capital income may in turn be obtained (see (44)):

$$t_r=\left(1+\frac{a_2}{a_1}\right)\left(\frac{r-\varepsilon}{\varepsilon}\right)=\frac{(a_1+a_2)[(1-\eta)(r_0-\varepsilon)+\eta(G/k)]}{\varepsilon(a_1+\eta a_2)}.\qquad(46)$$

It follows that the tax rate is lower, the larger is ε. A rise in the discout rate, reducing γ and hence raising ε, leads to lower taxation on capital income. (As noted before, this is a product of the particular savings function implied by the Cobb–Douglas utility function.)

The consequences of the replacement of the total utility objective by that of average utility may therefore be seen directly. The latter implies that:

$$\varepsilon=(1+n)(1+\delta)-1,$$

which exceeds δ where $n>0$, and the tax rate on capital income is lower with the average utility objective. On the other hand, if we reduce δ, while maintaining the average utility assumption, then the tax rate rises; and in the limiting 'golden rule' case, with $\delta = 0$, the value of ε is lower (we assumed $\delta > n$ in the earlier discussion). The 'golden rule' solution involves a higher level of taxation, and of capital formation.

Secondly, we may relate our analysis to the debate between Samuelson [31], Lerner [21] and others concerning the formulation of government objectives and intertemporal allocation. In order to see some of the issues involved, let us consider the case where the utility function may be written:

$$u_1(C_1, L) + u_2(C_2). \tag{47}$$

The debate has largely been carried out in terms of comparing steady state paths. In this context, Samuelson took as the social utility function the welfare of a representative generation, i.e. (47). In our terms, this is equivalent to the case where $\gamma = 1$, and it leads, as Diamond [11] has shown for a production economy, to the golden rule solution. Alternatively, one can consider the welfare of those alive at a representative instant, weighted by their numbers and discounted according to their generations i.e.:

$$u_1(C_1, L) + \left(\frac{1+n}{1+\delta}\right) u_2(C_2). \tag{48}$$

This may be seen as corresponding to the Lerner alternative formulation (see also Asimakopoulos [2]), although Lerner himself took $\delta = 0$. This alternative is given in our case by $\gamma = (1+n)/(1+\delta)$, and hence leads to a lower level of taxation on capital income where $\delta > n$.

To this point we have assumed that the discounting applies to generations; it can, however, be argued that the discounting should apply to calendar time. The distinction between these is discussed by Mitra [25] who refers to the former as discounting for the remoteness of future generations in time and the latter as allowing for the probability of extinction. With the latter approach, there is the distinct possibility that private and social judgements will differ. In order to explore this, let us suppose that the government attaches a weight h to the second period component of the utility function (u_2). Where the government applies a value of h greater than 1, it is in effect attaching a higher probability to survival than the individual. Alternatively, it may be seen as acting less myopically.[21]

The implications of $h \neq 1$ may be seen in the case where the government is unconstrained in its intertemporal allocation (as in section 3), but is constrained not to employ Z^i. We need to replace the derivatives of the indirect utility function by:

$$\frac{\partial V}{\partial \omega} = +\alpha L + \alpha(h-1)p\frac{\partial C_2}{\partial \omega}, \tag{49a}$$

$$\frac{\partial V}{\partial p} = -\alpha C_2 + \alpha(h-1)p\frac{\partial C_2}{\partial p}. \tag{49b}$$

Using the Slutsky equations and definitions of the elasticities in equations (31), the first-order condition can be shown to be:

$$\frac{\tau}{p} + (h-1)\left(\frac{\alpha}{\Gamma_1}\right)\left(\frac{1+n}{\gamma}\right) = \left(\frac{t_w}{1-t_w}\right)\frac{\sigma_{LL} - \sigma_{2L}}{\sigma_{L2} - \sigma_{22}}. \tag{50}$$

If, for example, the right-hand side is zero (as in the Cobb–Douglas case), then $h > 1$ implies that the optimum tax on savings is now negative. Where the government attaches more weight than the individual to future consumption, savings are subsidised rather than exempt (as they would be if $h=1$). The magnitude of the corrective subsidy depends on the extent of the difference between private and social valuations, and on the 'cost' of raising revenue, as measured by the ratio of the private marginal utility of income (α) to the 'shadow' price of revenue ($\gamma\Gamma_1/(1+n)$).

The consequences may be illustrated by the Cobb–Douglas example. In that case it may be shown that the optimum tax is given by:

$$\frac{\tau}{p} = 1 - h. \tag{51}$$

From this simple result, we may see that a 20% difference in the weight attached by the government implies a 20% subsidy on capital income.

The non-Paretian objective function, where the government does not respect individual preferences, provides a further departure from the standard optimum tax formulae, although in this case the modification takes a quite intuitive form.

6 Conclusions

In the course of this chapter we have examined how the standard optimum tax results may need to be modified when applied to intertemporal problems, particularly the choice between income and expenditure taxation. The main results are summarised in Table 1 which shows the conditions for optimality and the results in the special Cobb–Douglas case.

The main lesson is that it is difficult to argue on the basis of existing results for the welfare superiority of either an expenditure tax or a pure income tax. Even in the case where the standard optimum tax results may be directly applied (section 3), there is no strong reason to suppose that the exemption of saving is desirable on efficiency grounds. There are situations, including the Cobb–Douglas example (more generally, where there are unitary expenditure elasticities), such that $t_r = 0$ satisfies the first-order conditions, but the existing empirical evidence does not allow us to draw firm conclusions. It is indeed the case that the calculated tax results may depend crucially on parameters, such as the interest elasticity of labour supply, which have typically been disregarded in empirical studies.

When the government is constrained in the instruments it can employ to achieve a desired intertemporal allocation, the results need to be modified. As

Table 1 *Summary of main results*

First-order conditions	*Cobb–Douglas utility and production functions (where G = 0)*

First-best intertemporal allocation (*section 3*)

$$\frac{t_w}{1-t_w}(\sigma_{LL}-\sigma_{2L})=\frac{\tau}{p}(\sigma_{L2}-\sigma_{22})$$

$$t_r=0$$

equation (32)

Constraints on intertemporal allocation
(*sections 4 and 5*)

$$\frac{t_w}{1-t_w}(\sigma_{LL}-\sigma_{2L})=\frac{\tau}{p}(\sigma_{L2}-\sigma_{22})(1+\theta)-\theta$$

$$\frac{\tau}{p}=\left(\frac{\theta}{1+\theta}\right)\left(\frac{a_1+a_2}{a_1}\right)$$

equation (39)   equation (42)

where objective sum of utilities

$$\theta=\frac{r-\delta}{1+\delta},$$

$$t_r=(1-\eta)\frac{(r_0-\delta)}{\delta}\left(\frac{a_1+a_2}{a_1+\eta a_2}\right)$$

where objective is 'average' utility

$$\theta=\frac{r-n-\delta-n\delta}{(1+n)(1+\delta)}$$

$$t_r=(1-\eta)\frac{(r_0-\varepsilon)}{\varepsilon}\left(\frac{a_1+a_2}{a_1+\eta a_2}\right)$$

where $\varepsilon=(1+n)(1+\delta)-1$
equation (46)

Non-Paretian objective (*section 5*)
(where first-best intertemporal allocation)

$$\frac{t_w}{1-t_w}(\sigma_{LL}-\sigma_{2L})$$

$$=\left[\frac{\tau}{p}+(h-1)\frac{\alpha}{\Gamma_1}\left(\frac{1+n}{\gamma}\right)\right](\sigma_{L2}-\sigma_{22})$$

$$\frac{\tau}{p}=1-h$$

equation (50)   equation (51)

is illustrated by the Cobb–Douglas example, if the non-intervention capital stock differs from its 'first-best' level there may be a case for taxing or subsidising capital income. In that example, if the capital stock is below the 'first-best', a tax on capital income raises welfare, bringing the capital closer to the full optimum but not closing the gap entirely. The optimum tax on capital depends on the response of savings and on the nature of government objectives. For example, in the Cobb–Douglas case, the optimum tax on capital income is a declining function of the social discount rate. Moreover, where the government's valuation departs from that of the individual – as may quite easily happen in a dynamic context – this provides a further modification of the results.

The analysis does not therefore lead to clear-cut policy conclusions; rather the lessons to be drawn are about the *nature* of the arguments which can be made in this field. We have for example tried to bring out the interdependence between different policy instruments, and the way in which the case for different tax bases depends on the range of measures at the disposal of the government to achieve a desired intertemporal allocation. We have shown how the results may need to be modified where these are constrained, and how they are affected by different formulations of the social welfare function. In part these conclusions are quite intuitive: for example, the correction for divergences between private and social valuations (equation (50)). Others are less obvious: for example, the fact that it is the uncompensated rather than compensated response of savings which is relevant) in section 4).

The analysis has been limited in several important respects. In particular, we have been concerned with intertemporal allocation, which is essentially a question of intergenerational equity, but we have not addressed the issue of intragenerational redistribution. This is important both in its own right and also because of its implications for the policy instruments which can be employed (particularly the limitations on the use of poll taxes). A natural extension of the model is to assume that individuals have the same preferences, but differ in their earning abilities; this is the formulation of Mirrlees [24], taken over in an intertemporal context by Hamada [17], Ordover and Phelps [27] and Ordover [26]. These authors allow in effect for differences in wage rates; we should also take account of differences in rates of return which may arise in an 'imperfect' capital market. This can be modelled in a number of different ways,[22] but is an important phenomenon which should be incorporated, along with uncertainty, into the intertemporal treatment of the design of taxation.

Acknowledgement

Previous versions of this chapter were presented to the Franco-Swedish seminar in public economics at Sarlat, France in March 1976, and to the University of Aarhus conference on public economics at Sandberg, Denmark in April 1978. These versions, the latter of which was also circulated as a discussion paper, were entitled 'The Welfare Implications of Personal Income and Consumption Taxes'. We are indebted to many seminar participants, to John Kay, Mervyn King, Joe Stiglitz, the Editor and a referee for a number of helpful comments and suggestions.

Notes

1 For a good discussion of these and other matters with a view to practical implementation, see Andrews [1] and Kay and King [20].
2 Recent examples are Meade [23]: 'the intelligent radical would welcome [the replacement of]

the progressive taxation of income by a progressive taxation of expenditure. ... A tax on income discriminates against private savings, whereas a tax on consumption does not do so' (pp. 93–4), and Feldstein: 'income tax lowers the rate of return on savings and thus distorts everyone's choice between consuming today and saving for a higher level of consumption in the future... The consumption tax would eliminate this wasteful distortion' ([15], p. 16) (To be fair, Feldstein [16] has given a clear account of why this argument is unconvincing.)

3 Interestingly, little reference has been made to the discussion of the tax treatment of savings in Ramsey's original paper [30]. On the basis of an assumed infinite elasticity of demand for saving and a finite supply elasticity, he argues 'that income-tax should be partially but not wholly remitted on savings' (p. 59).

4 In earlier versions of this chapter, we confined the analysis to a choice between steady states, as in the articles by Hamada [17], Ordover and Phelps [27], and Ordover [26].

5 The reader is also referred to Ordover and Phelps [27], which we received after the analysis of this chapter was essentially completed.

6 Here, and on the production side, we are abstracting from the problems introduced by uncertainty. The effects of income and expenditure taxes on risk-taking need further investigation.

7 Although this formulation has been the more popular, its rationale may be questioned (see, for example, Dasgupta [10]).

8 There may be constraints on the range within which T_i^j may be varied. Here, as elsewhere, we are not attempting to give a full characterisation of the optimum policy.

9 For discussion of a fully-controlled economy, and references to the literature, see for example Cass and Shell [8].

10 I.e. where I denotes lump-sum income:

$$\frac{\partial L}{\partial \omega} = L \frac{\partial L}{\partial I} + S_{LL}, \quad \frac{\partial L}{\partial p} = -C_2 \frac{\partial L}{\partial I} + S_{L2}, \quad \frac{\partial C_2}{\partial \omega} = L \frac{\partial C_2}{\partial I} + S_{2L}, \quad \frac{\partial C_2}{\partial p} = -C_2 \frac{\partial C_2}{\partial I} + S_{22}.$$

11 The term $\sigma_{LL} - \sigma_{2L}$ is proportional to:

$$\chi \equiv \frac{1}{L} \frac{dL}{dI} + \frac{1}{\omega L} - \frac{1}{C_2} \frac{dC_2}{dI}.$$

From the budget constraint:

$$C_1(1/C_1)(dC_1/dI) + pC_2(1/C_2)(dC_2/dI) = 1 + \omega L(1/L)(dL/dI).$$

Hence the unitary elasticity condition (and $I=0$, $Z=0$) implies $\chi=0$. See also Sandmo [33] for a similar analysis.

12 As noted earlier, in Ordover's [26] model this cross-elasticity is identically zero. The reason is that variations in effective labour supply in his model come about through the choice of how much of the first period to devote to education, and since there is no labour supply in the second period of an individual's life, the interest rate becomes irrelevant to the educational decision. While the model is perfectly logical, this implication may seem somewhat paradoxical, because one might have expected the introduction of investment in education to be the most interesting way of introducing a relationship between labour supply and the rate of interest.

13 It should be noted that the relevant time period is a generation. With other values of t_w and r, the rate may exceed the equivalent income tax.

14 The labour supply decision should be interpreted broadly to include participation, retirement, emigration, etc.

15 This is the analogue, in terms of compensated demand functions, of what Ordover and Phelps [27] call the anti-Hicks–Lucas case. (Their failure to refer to it as the anti-Hicks–Lucas–*Rapping* case is particularly strange in a paper on justice.)

16 In this case the normalisation of tax rates is not an arbitrary matter. From the individual

budget constraint (15), an equal proportionate rise in $(1 + t_C^i)$ and ω^i leaves the individual unaffected (with $Z^i = 0$), but the level of private savings is changed, and hence affects (19). Put another way, the government is no longer indifferent about the timing of receipts.

17 One interpretation of the relationship between (39) and (32) is that the former contains an additive term to correct for the 'externality' arising from the change in savings when the economy is not at the 'first-best'. For a general analysis of the additivity property of optimal taxes when there are externalities, see Sandmo [34].

18 The maximisation of U subject to the individual budget constraint yields:

$$L = a_1 + a_2; \qquad C_1 = a_1 \omega; \qquad p C_2 = a_2 \omega.$$

19 The no tax equilibrium has $r = \eta(1 - a_3)(1 + n)/[a_2(1 - \eta)]$. This is the same as the example given by Diamond ([11], p. 1135) except that he does not allow for any labour response.

20 The level of private savings is:

$$A = w(1 - t_w)L - C_1 = a_2 w(1 - t_w)$$

and hence rises if r is increased and t_w reduced.

21 This is related to the concept of Allais optimality (see Malinvaud [22], ch. 10), in that individual preferences *within* a period are respected.

22 There are two approaches that seem to be worth pursuing. In the first, the rate of interest r_i is simply individual i's marginal productivity of capital as derived from his personal production function. Thus, there is really no capital market at all, and each individual's future consumption is constrained by the return on his real investment undertaken in the first period. In the second interpretation there is a capital market, but because of imperfect information, transactions costs etc. consumers do not have the same degree of access and therefore receive different rates of return.

References

[1] Andrews, W. D. (1974), 'A consumption-type or cash flow personal income tax', *Harvard Law Review*, vol. 87, pp. 1113–88.

[2] Asimakopoulos, A. (1968), 'Optimal economic growth and distribution and the social utility function', *Canadian Journal of Economics*, vol. 1, pp. 540–50.

[3] Atkinson, A. B. and Stiglitz, J. E. (1972), 'The structure of indirect taxation and economic efficiency', Chapter 10 in this volume.

[4] Atkinson, A. B. and Stiglitz, J. E. (1976), 'The design of tax structure: direct versus indirect taxation', Chapter 11 in this volume.

[5] Atkinson, A. B. and Stiglitz, J. E. (1980), *Lectures on Public Economics*, Maidenhead and New York, McGraw-Hill.

[6] Bierwag, G. O., Grove, M. A. and Khang, C. (1969), 'National debt in a neoclassical growth model: comment', *American Economic Review*, vol. 59, pp. 205–10.

[7] Bradford, D. F. and Rosen, H. S. (1976), 'The optimal taxation of commodities and income', *American Economic Review*, vol. 66, Papers and Proceedings, pp. 94–101.

[8] Cass, D. and Shell, K. (1976), 'The structure and stability of competitive dynamical systems', *Journal of Economic Theory*, vol. 12, pp. 31–70.

[9] Corlett, W. J. and Hague, D. C. (1953), 'Complementarity and the excess burden of taxation', *Review of Economic Studies*, vol. 21, pp. 21–30.

[10] Dasgupta, P. S. (1969), 'On the concept of optimum population', *Review of Economic Studies*, vol. 36, pp. 295–318.

[11] Diamond, P. A. (1965), 'National debt in a neoclassical growth model', *American Economic Review*, vol. 55, pp. 1125–50.

[12] Diamond, P. A. (1973), 'Taxation and public production in a growth setting', In *Models of Economic Growth*, J. A. Mirrlees and N. H. Stern (eds.), pp. 215–35, London, Macmillan.

[13] Diamond, P. A. and Mirrlees, J. A. (1971), 'Optimal taxation and public production', *American Economic Review*, vol. 61, pp. 8–27, 261–78.

[14] Dixit, A. K. (1976), *The Theory of Equilibrium Growth*, London, Oxford University Press.

[15] Feldstein, M. S. (1976), 'Taxing consumption', *The New Republic*, 28 February.

[16] Feldstein, M. S. (1978), 'The welfare cost of capital income taxation', *Journal of Political Economy*, vol. 86 (supplement) pp. S29–S51.

[17] Hamada, K. (1977), 'Lifetime equity and dynamic efficiency on the balanced growth path' *Journal of Public Economics*, vol. 1, pp. 379–96.

[18] Houthakker, H. S. (1960), 'Additive preferences', *Econometrica*, vol. 28, pp. 244–57.

[19] Kaldor, N. (1955), *An Expenditure Tax*, London, Allen & Unwin.

[20] Kay, J. A. and King, M. A. (1978), *The British Tax System*, London, Oxford University Press.

[21] Lerner, A. P. (1959), 'Consumption loan interest and money', *Journal of Political Economy*, vol. 67, pp. 523–5.

[22] Malinvaud, E. (1972), *Lectures on Microeconomic Theory*, Amsterdam, North-Holland.

[23] Meade, J. E. (1975), *The Intelligent Radical's Guide to Economic Policy*, London, Allen & Unwin.

[24] Mirrlees, J. A. (1971), 'An exploration in the theory of optimum income taxation', *Review of Economic Studies*, vol. 38, pp. 175–208.

[25] Mitra, P. K. (1975), 'Taxation and intergenerational equity', Mimeographed, University College, London.

[26] Ordover, J. A. (1976), 'Distributive justice and optimal taxation of wages and interest in a growing economy', *Journal of Public Economics*, vol. 5, pp. 139–60.

[27] Ordover, J. A. and Phelps, E. S. (1975), 'Linear taxation of wealth and wages for intragenerational lifetime justice: some steady-state cases', *American Economic Review*, vol. 65, pp. 660–73.

[28] Ordover, J. A. and Phelps, E. S. (1979), 'The concept of optimal capital taxation in the overlapping-generations model of capital and wealth', *Journal of Public Economics*, vol. 12, pp. 1–26.

[29] Pestieau, P. M. (1974), 'Optimal taxation and discount rate for public investment in a growth setting', *Journal of Public Economics*, vol. 3, pp. 217–35.

[30] Ramsey, F. P. (1927), 'A contribution to the theory of taxation', *Economic Journal*, vol. 37, pp. 47–61.

[31] Samuelson, P. A. (1958), 'An exact consumption-loan model of interest with or without the social contrivance of money', *Journal of Political Economy*, vol. 66, pp. 467–82.

[32] Samuelson, P. A. (1975), 'Optimum social security in a life-cycle growth model', *International Economic Review*, vol. 16, pp. 539–44.

[33] Sandmo, A. (1974), 'A note on the structure of optimal taxation', *American Economic Review*, vol. 64, pp. 701–6.

[34] Sandmo, A. (1975), 'Optimal taxation in the presence of externalities', *Swedish Journal of Economics*, vol. 77, pp. 86–98.

[35] Sandmo, A. (1976), 'Optimal taxation: an introduction to the literature', *Journal of Public Economics*, vol. 6, pp. 37–54.

15 How Progressive Should Income Tax Be?*

> The moment you abandon ... the cardinal principle of
> exacting from all individuals the same proportion of their
> income or their property, you are at sea without rudder or
> compass, and there is no amount of injustice or folly you may
> not commit. ... Graduation is not an evil to be paltered with.
> Adopt it and you will effectively paralyse industry. ... The
> savages described by Montesquieu, who to get at the fruit cut
> down the tree, are about as good financiers as the advocates
> of this sort of taxes. (J. R. McCulloch, 1845)

1 Introduction

In Britain the marginal rate of income tax on earned income is zero initially,
then at a constant rate for a wide range of incomes and finally increases quite
sharply for higher rate taxpayers. Is this structure too progressive or
insufficiently so? The aim of this chapter is to explore some of the arguments
that could be applied in the unlikely event of the Chancellor of the Exchequer
asking economists for guidance on this question, and to see just what can be
said about how progressive the income tax should be. The first half of the
chapter surveys the current state of knowledge: the traditional sacrifice
theories and the more recent extensions of these by Mirrlees and others. The
second half introduces a simple model designed to throw light on the way in
which the aims of the government influence the optimal degree of progression
and to bring out considerations which have been obscured in the earlier
literature.

It should be made clear at the outset we make no attempt to provide a
definite answer to the question posed in the title. Indeed one of the main
conclusions is that such an answer cannot be given without further clarifi-
cation of social objectives. Instead we attempt to illuminate the basic structure
of the problem and to provide insight into the kind of argument required to
justify positions which are commonly taken on this question. Two other
qualifications should also be entered. The chapter is concerned only with the
taxation of earned income, and not with the taxation of investment income

* Reprinted from *Essays in Modern Economics*, Longman, 1973.

which introduces quite different considerations. Second, the chapter deals only with income taxes and does not consider the possibility that other forms of taxation (such as a wage tax) might be employed.

2 The Minimum Sacrifice Theory

Those textbooks which discuss the question of the optimal degree of progression usually begin by referring to the theories of equal sacrifice. The statements by Adam Smith that subjects should 'contribute in proportion to their respective abilities', and by John Stuart Mill that 'whatever sacrifices [the government] requires... should be made to bear as nearly as possible with the same pressure upon all' were translated by later writers into more precise principles of equal sacrifice. These took a number of different forms, but the principle of equal marginal sacrifice put forward by Edgeworth, Pigou and others had the clearest rationale, being derived from the utilitarian objective of the maximisation of the sum of individual utilities.

Let us suppose that individuals differ in their earning ability and that this is denoted by n. The before-tax earnings of a person of type n are denoted by $z(n)$ and the tax paid by $T(n)$. The utility derived from the after-tax income is given by $U_n[z(n) - T(n)]$, so that if $f(n)$ is the frequency distribution of people of type n the sum of individual utilities is denoted by:

$$W = \int_0^\infty U_n[z(n) - T(n)] f(n) \, dn \qquad (1)$$

The government is assumed to choose the tax rates to maximise W subject to the revenue constraint:

$$\int_0^\infty T(n) f(n) \, dn = \bar{R} \qquad (2)$$

(where $\bar{R}$ denotes the net revenue to be raised and $T(n)$ may be negative). The solution is straightforward (on the assumption that U is concave):

$$U_n'[z(n) - T(n)] \text{ equal all } n \qquad (3)$$

and if an identical marginal utility of income schedule is assumed, the tax structure is such that after-tax incomes are equalised:[1] 'A system of equi-marginal sacrifice fully carried out would involve lopping off the tops of all incomes above the minimum income and leaving everybody, after taxation, with equal incomes' (Pigou [18], pp. 57–8).

The minimum sacrifice theory has come under a great deal of attack and is dismissed by most authors. Two main lines of criticism may be distinguished:

(a) that the minimum sacrifice theory takes no account of the possible disincentive effect of taxation ($z(n)$ may be influenced by the tax structure),
(b) that the underlying utilitarian framework is inadequate.

The next section examines the contribution made by the recent work of Mirrlees and others to overcoming the first of these objections. The second line of criticism is taken up later.

3   Income Tax Progression and Work Incentives

The importance of the possible disincentive effect of taxation was clearly recognised in the discussion by Sidgwick: 'It is conceivable that a greater equality in the distribution of produce would lead ultimately to a reduction in the total amount to be distributed in consequence of a general preference of leisure to the results of labour' (see [6], p. 104). The proponents of the minimum sacrifice approach did not, however, make any attempt to arrive at a tax formula incorporating these considerations. One of the main contributions of the recent papers in this area has been to fill this gap and to derive optimal tax schedules taking account of the effects of taxation on work effort. This section describes the formulation of the problem and the principal results obtained.

The recent revival of interest in this area is largely attributable to the important paper by Mirrlees [14], where he considers the influence of taxation on the work/leisure choice. A person of type n determines the proportion of the day he spends at work ($y(n)$) so as to maximise his utility $U[x(n), y(n)]$ where $x(n)$ denotes his after-tax income and is given by:

$$x(n) = z(n) - T[z(n)] \qquad (4)$$

and:

$$z(n) = n y(n) \qquad (5)$$

(i.e. the parameter of earning ability, n, represents the wage per unit of time for a man of type n). Otherwise, the formulation is identical to that described in section 2. The government chooses the income tax function $T(z)$ to maximise the sum of individual utilities (where it is assumed that all individuals have identical utility functions):[2]

$$W = \int_0^\infty U[x(n), y(n)] f(n) \, dn \qquad (6)$$

subject to the revenue constraint (2).

With the introduction of the work/leisure choice, the problem becomes a considerably more difficult one than the simple minimum sacrifice theory. The first part of Mirrlees' paper is concerned with the derivation of general properties of the optimal tax function $T(z)$, but the results he obtains are limited to establishing that:

(a) the optimal marginal tax rate lies between zero and one,
(b) it will be optimal (in most interesting cases) for some of the population to remain idle (i.e. $y(n) = 0$).

More than this cannot be said: 'The optimum tax schedule depends upon the distribution of skills within the population ... in such a complicated way that it is not possible to say in general whether marginal tax rates should be higher for high-income, low-income, or intermediate income groups' ([14], p. 186).

In the later part of his paper, Mirrlees goes on, therefore, to consider the special case where:

$$U = \log_e \left[x^a (1 - y) \right]$$

and $f(n)$ is either the lognormal or the Pareto distribution. This special case is considered analytically in section 8, and for a range of numerical calculations (with $a = 1$ and $f(n)$ lognormal) in section 9.

On the basis of his analysis, and in particular of the numerical calculations, Mirrlees draws a number of (qualified) conclusions. Two of the most important for policy purposes are that: (a) the optimal tax structure is approximately linear, i.e. a constant marginal tax rate, with an exemption level below which negative tax supplements are payable; (b) the marginal tax rates are rather low and tend to fall rather than rise with the level of income. (See Table 1 for two illustrative cases.) The second conclusion is an unexpected one. Mirrlees comments that 'I had expected the rigorous analysis of income taxation in the utilitarian manner to provide an argument for high tax rates', and expresses surprise that it has not done so.

Table 1　*Optimal tax rates – Mirrlees Cases I and II*

	Case I		Case II	
	Average tax rate %	*Marginal tax rate %*	*Average tax rate %*	*Marginal tax rate %*
Bottom decile	− 5	24	− 38	20
Median	5	22	− 12	19
Top decile	13	19	2	17
Top percentile	14	17	7	16

Source: Interpolated from [14], Tables I–IV. In Case I the revenue requirement is positive, in Case II it is negative (the government is disposing of the profits of public sector production).

It is clear that the conclusions drawn by Mirrlees rest heavily on the particular assumptions made. In his concluding section he draws attention to the fact that 'the shape of the optimum earned-income tax schedule is rather sensitive to the distribution of skills within the population and to the income – leisure preferences postulated'. The latter assumption is, as he says, 'heroic' and may well overstate the sensitivity of labour supply to changes in the marginal rate of income tax. There is, however, an aspect of the special cases taken by Mirrlees to which he does not draw adequate attention – the effect of the choice of a particular functional form to represent given income/leisure preferences.

In the minimum sacrifice theory, the particular cardinalisation selected did not affect the tax structure (providing it was the same for all). If we replace U by $G[U]$ where $G' > 0$, $G'' < 0$ the first-order condition is:

$$G'\{U'[z(n)-T(n)]\} \qquad \text{equal all } n$$

giving the same solution. In the present case, however, this is no longer true. In order to clarify this point, let us consider the particular transformations of the utility function:

$$\frac{(V^{1-\rho}-1)}{1-\rho} \tag{7}$$

where V is normalised so that for $\rho=0$ it just satisfies the concavity requirement, which in the present case means that:

$$V=x^A(1-y)^{1-A} \tag{8}$$

The case taken in Table 1 corresponds to $\log_e V$ or to $\rho=1$.[3] If, however, we were to take a higher value of ρ, this would lead to the optimal tax structure being more progressive. As ρ rises, the marginaly utility of income diminishes more rapidly and the 'cost' of inequality (in terms of the loss of aggregate utility) increases.

The effect of changes in ρ may be illustrated by the numerical examples given by Mirrlees where:

$$G=-e^{-U} \tag{9}$$

which corresponds to the case $\rho=2$. His results are not presented in such a way as to facilitate the comparison, since the amount of revenue to be raised is not held constant in the different cases. However, the optimal marginal tax rate tends to fall as the revenue to be collected falls, so that the comparisons shown in Table 2 will tend to understate the rise in the optimal tax rate as ρ increases. It is clear in fact that the increase in ρ leads to definitely higher marginal tax rates.

Table 2   *Effect of increase in ρ on optimal marginal tax rates*

	$\rho=1$ Revenue 7% of income Marginal tax rate %	$\rho=2$ Revenue 2% of income Marginal tax rate %
Bottom decile	24	33
Median	22	30
Top decile	19	26
Top percentile	17	21
	Revenue 10% of income Marginal tax rate %	Revenue 20% of income Marginal tax rate %
Bottom decile	20	28
Median	19	26
Top decile	17	24
Top percentile	16	21

Source: Interpolated from [14], Tables I–VIII.

This conclusion leads one to ask how Mirrlees' results would be affected by taking still larger values of ρ. Is it possible that he would have found optimal tax rates of the order of 50% or more if he had chosen higher values of ρ? One way in which we can test this is by taking the limit as $\rho \to \infty$:

$$\min V(n) \tag{10}$$

i.e. we can obtain an upper bound on the effect of increasing ρ by examining the tax structure which maximises the utility of the worst-off person.

A second important contribution is that by Fair [8]. The model considered by him differs from that of Mirrlees in two important respects:

(a) hourly earnings are assumed to be a function not only of ability but also of the level of education. If we denote the proportion of working hours spent in education by E, earnings are:

$$z(n) = y(1 - E)g(n, E) \tag{11}$$

where $g(n, E)$ is the wage rate per working hour.

The individual utility function is the same as before – education is purely an investment and does not provide consumption benefits – and E is chosen to maximise $z(n)$.

(b) the range of tax schedules under consideration is restricted to:

$$T'(z) = \alpha_0 \log_e [1 + z]$$

or:

$$T(z) = \alpha_0 [(z + 1) \log_e [1 + z]] - \alpha - \alpha_0 z \tag{12}$$

where α represents a guaranteed minimum income (if $z = 0$).

The results obtained by Fair are numerical ones only, and are based on a normal distribution of abilities and an approximated relationship $g(n, E)$. The conclusions are primarily summarised in terms of the Gini coefficient of concentration, but it is possible to calculate the average and marginal tax rates for two of his nine earnings functions for people at different points on the ability range.

Table 3   *Optimal tax rates – results of Fair*

	Earnings function 5		Earnings function 8	
	Average tax rate %	Marginal tax rate %	Average tax rate %	Marginal tax rate %
Individual's position in ability range				
1% from bottom	17	29	<0	29
Median	23	32	19	41
1% from top	32	38	40	49

Source: Calculated from [8], Table VI (case where a constant).

The optimal rates of tax are rather higher than in the case of the results reached by Mirrlees. At the same time, the top rates (those on the man 1% from the top of the ability range) are still a long way below those indicated by the Edgeworth–Pigou analysis. Again, the form of the utility function adopted is important. The results given all relate to a case where $\rho = 1$, and it may be expected that higher values of ρ would have led to a more progressive tax structure.[4]

4   Recent Work – Conclusions

The contributions by Mirrlees and Fair suggest that the introduction of efficiency considerations may lead to a considerably less progressive tax structure than that indicated by the minimum sacrifice theory. At the same time they do not adequately consider the sensitivity of their results to the specification of the government objectives. In particular, the precise cardinalisation adopted, which was not important in the Edgeworth–Pigou analysis, may significantly affect the optimal tax structure.

The work of these authors has demonstrated that the introduction of the work/leisure choice adds considerably to the complexity of the solution and that analytic results are very difficult to obtain. This means that we have to choose between strongly simplified models for which analytic solutions can be obtained and more realistic models solved numerically. While the latter will undoubtedly be necessary for the formulation of actual policy prescriptions, at the present time it seems more useful to concentrate on identifying the considerations which are likely to have a significant influence on the solution. In the remainder of this chapter a model is developed which, while highly stylised, does serve this purpose.

5   A Simple Model

The model developed in this section is considerably simpler than that considered by Mirrlees and Fair, and in particular assumes:

(a)   that attention is restricted to the case of linear tax schedules:

$$T(z) = (1 - \beta)z - \alpha \tag{13}$$

i.e. a guaranteed minimum income α combined with a proportional tax on all income at rate $(1 - \beta)$ (see Figure 1). This is the simplest form of progressive tax to consider; and corresponds quite closely to the kind of tax schedule actually in force.[6]

(b)   that the distribution of abilities is assumed to be Pareto in form:

$$f(n) = \mu \mathbf{n}^{\mu} n^{-\mu - 1} \tag{14}$$

where $\mathbf{n}$ represents the lowest value of n (see Figure 2). (The exponent μ is assumed to be greater than or equal to 2.) This assumption is made primarily for its analytical convenience, and is one of the least satisfactory aspects of the model.[7]

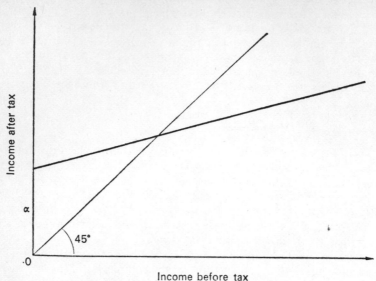

Figure 1   *Income tax schedule.*

(c)   that the individual's earnings are assumed to depend only on ability (n) and on the number of years of education received (S), i.e. hours of work (effort) are assumed to be fixed. While undergoing education the individual has zero earnings and is not eligible for the guaranteed minimum. He earns $z(n, S)$ when at work and retires after R years of work. He maximises the present value (at interest rate i) of his lifetime income:

$$I = \int_{S}^{R+S} [z - T(z)] e^{-it} \, dt$$

$$I = A[z - T(z)] e^{-iS} \tag{15}$$

where:

$$A = \frac{(1 - e^{-iR})}{i}.$$

Finally we suppose (modifying a suggestion of Becker [3]), that $z(n, S) = nS$.[8]

Combining the different elements of the model, we can see that the individual's choice of S will be determined by maximising:

$$(\alpha + \beta nS) e^{-iS}$$

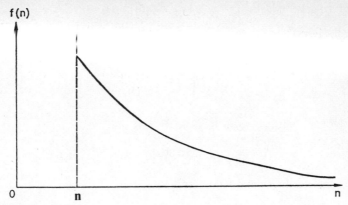

Figure 2   *Pareto distribution.*

which gives:

$$S = \frac{1}{i} - \frac{\alpha}{\beta n}$$

for $n \geqslant i\alpha/\beta \equiv n_0$:

$$S = 0 \qquad \text{for } n \leqslant n_0 \qquad\qquad (16)$$

The resulting level of I is given by:

$$I = A\left(\frac{\beta n}{i}\right)e^{(\alpha i/\beta n - 1)} \qquad\qquad (17)$$

for $n \geqslant n_0$. For $n \leqslant n_0$, $I = A\alpha$.

It may be noted that in the absence of taxation everyone would choose the same level of S; the effect of taxation is to widen pre-tax income differentials while narrowing after-tax differentials.

From the individual supply functions we can derive the possibilities open to the government, as determined by the revenue constraint:

$$\int_0^\infty T(z)f(n)\,\mathrm{d}n = 0 \qquad\qquad (18)$$

where it is assumed that the population is constant in size (so that there are the same number of taxpayers for each n) and that no net revenue is required ($\bar{R} = 0$). With the particular distribution chosen, the constraint may take one of two forms:

Case (A) $n_0 \leqslant \mathbf{n}$

Case (B) $n_0 > \mathbf{n}$

Attention is focused here on case (A) where the revenue constraint is:

$$\left(\text{since } \int_n^\infty f(n)\mathrm{d}n = 1 \right)$$

$$\alpha = (1 - \beta) \int_n^\infty \left(\frac{n}{i} - \frac{\alpha}{\beta} \right) f(n) \; \mathrm{d}n$$

Using the fact that $n_0 = i\alpha/\beta$, this can be written:

$$n_0 \beta/(1 - \beta) = \bar{n} - n_0$$

where $\bar{n}$ denotes the mean value, and this gives:

$$\beta = 1 - \frac{n_0}{\bar{n}} \qquad (19)$$

Equation (19) gives the combination of β and n_0 (which together determine the optimal tax structure) satisfying the revenue constraint (subject to $n_0 \leqslant \mathbf{n}$).[9]

As a background to the problem faced by the government, it is interesting to examine the choice that would be made by an individual aiming to maximise $I(n)$, where we denote by $n_0^*(n)$ the value of n_0 satisfying (19) chosen by a man of type n. Given that $n_0^*(n) \leqslant n$, the person maximises $\beta e^{n_0^*/n}$, or (from 19):

$$\frac{n_0^*}{n} + \log_e \left[1 - \frac{n_0^*}{\bar{n}} \right]$$

The first-order condition is given by:

$$\frac{\bar{n}}{n} = \frac{1}{\left(1 - \dfrac{n_0^*}{\bar{n}} \right)}$$

reducing to:

$$1 - \beta = \frac{n_0^*}{\bar{n}} = 1 - \frac{n}{\bar{n}}$$

Since:

$$\bar{n} = \left(\frac{\mu}{\mu - 1} \right) \mathbf{n}$$

the tax rate chosen falls from $1/\mu$ to zero at $n = \bar{n}$. Those with above average n would choose a lump-sum tax and subsidy on earnings ($\alpha < 0$, $\beta > 1$) if that were possible (see Figure 3).[10]

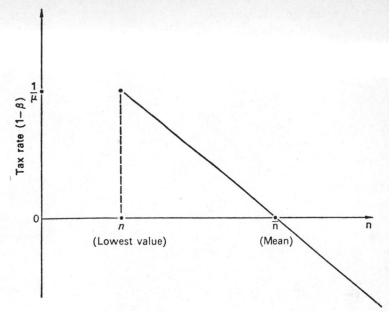

Figure 3   *Tax rate chosen by person of type n.*

The presentation in terms of individual choice about taxation allows us to consider the possibility of majority voting. Although it is unlikely that the precise details of the tax structure would be subject to voting, issues of broad policy regarding the degree of progression may well be settled by appeal to the electorate. This question has been discussed by Foley [10], who considers the stability of different tax structures against majority rule (i.e. whether there is a tax schedule for which there will always be a majority in favour versus any alternative). As he points out, where the class of tax schedules under consideration is unrestricted, no element is stable against majority rule, but if attention is restricted to the class of linear tax schedules (for example), this will contain a stable element. Foley does not allow for the effect of taxation on the earnings of the individual, but his results can readily be extended to that case. In terms of the model set out above, an increase in n_0 ($= i\alpha/\beta$) will always be preferred by those for whom $n_0^* > n_0$ and opposed by those for whom $n_0^* < n_0$. It follows that the tax rate reached as a result of majority voting will be that given by $n_0^*(n_m)$ where n_m is the median, which can be calculated to be:

$$1 - \beta = 1 - 2^{1/\mu}(1 - 1/\mu)$$

so that for $\mu = 2$ we obtain 29% and for $\mu = 3$ we obtain 16%. (Since the distribution is skew, $n_m < \bar{n}$, so this would always give a positive tax rate.)

6   Utilitarian and Other Objectives

Let us examine first the optimal tax structure where the government pursues
the utilitarian objective of maximising the sum of individual utilities:[11]

$$W = \int_{\mathrm{n}}^{\infty} U[I(n)] f(n)\, dn \tag{20}$$

As we have seen in section 3, the solution depends on the precise form of the
function $U(I)$. In order to explore this further, let us suppose that U can be
written in the iso-elastic form:

$$U = \frac{I^{1-\rho}}{1-\rho}$$

The case $\rho = 1$ corresponds to that taken by Mirrlees in the first of his examples
and means that the maximand becomes:

$$\log W = \int_{\mathrm{n}}^{\infty} \log[I(n)] f(n)\, dn$$

$$= \log \beta + \int_{\mathrm{n}}^{\infty} \log(An/i) f(n)\, dn$$

$$+ \int_{\mathrm{n}}^{\infty} \left(\frac{n_0}{n} - 1 \right) f(n)\, dn \tag{21}$$

Substituting from the revenue constraint and differentiating, we obtain the
first-order condition:

$$\int_{\mathrm{n}}^{\infty} n^{-1} f(n)\, dn = \frac{1}{\beta \bar{n}} \tag{22}$$

From this it follows that:

$$\beta = \frac{1 + \mu \mathbf{n}}{\mu} \frac{1}{\bar{n}} = 1 - \frac{1}{\mu^2}$$

i.e. the optimal tax rate is $1/\mu^2$. If $\mu = 2$, this indicates a tax rate of 25%; if $\mu = 4$,
the tax rate is as low as 6.25%.[12]

  As ρ increases, the optimal rate of tax rises. This can be seen as follows. In
the case where $\rho \neq 1$, we have:

$$\frac{W^{1-\rho}}{1-\rho} = \left(\frac{\beta^{1-\rho}}{1-\rho} \right) \left(\frac{Ae^{-1}}{i} \right)^{1-\rho} \int_{\mathrm{n}}^{\infty} n^{1-\rho} e^{n_0(1-\rho)/n} f(n)\, dn \tag{23}$$

Using the revenue constraint (19):

$$\frac{1}{W}\frac{\partial W}{\partial n_0} = \frac{1}{\beta}\frac{\partial \beta}{\partial n_0} = \frac{\int_n^\infty n^{-\rho}e^{n_0(1-\rho)/n}f(n)\,dn}{\int_n^\infty n^{-\rho}e^{n_0(1-\rho)/n}f(n)\,dn} \tag{24}$$

giving a first-order condition:

$$\beta = \frac{\int_n^\infty n^{1-\rho}e^{n_0(1-\rho)/n}f(n)\,dn}{\int_n^\infty \frac{\bar{n}}{n}b^{1-\rho}e^{n_0(1-\rho)/n}f(n)\,dn}$$

Writing:

$$K(\mu,\rho) = [n_0(\rho-1)]^{\rho+\mu-1}\int_n^\infty n^{-(\rho+\mu)}e^{n_0(1-\rho)/n}\,dn$$

this gives an equation for n_0:

$$1 - \frac{n_0}{\bar{n}} = \frac{n_0(\rho-1)}{\bar{n}}\frac{K(\mu,\rho)}{K(\mu+1,\rho)} \tag{25}$$

Table 4 *Optimal tax rates obtained from equation (25)*

	Value of μ		
	2.0	3.0	4.0
Values of ρ	%	%	%
1.0	25	11	6
2.0	33	18	9
4.0	36	21	14
6.0	39	24	15
8.0	40	25	18
16.0	43	28	21
Limit	50	33	25

The solution to this equation for different values of ρ and μ is given in Table 4.[13] As ρ increases above 1, the optimal tax rate rises quite significantly. For $\rho = 2$ (the second case considered by Mirrlees), the tax rate is 33% rather than 25% (where $\mu = 2$). Joreover, the limit as $\rho \to \infty$ can be derived from the earlier analysis: as $\rho \to \infty$ the social welfare function tends to the maxi-min form:

$$\max I(n)$$

and from the analysis of page 304 we can see that the optimal rate is $1/\mu$. As ρ increases, the optimal tax rate moves up along the line shown in Figure 4. At the extreme point the optimal tax is considerably larger (by a factor of μ) than at $\rho = 1$.

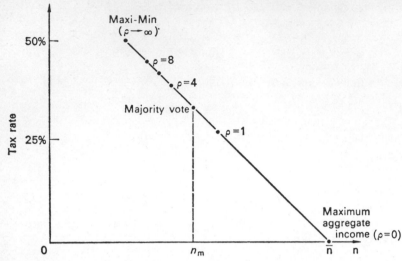

Figure 4   *Different solutions (for $\mu = 2$).*

The results given in Table 4 suggest that the optimal rate of income taxation may depend quite sensitively on the particular cardinalisation adopted. At the same time it is not clear that we can obtain any firm estimate from individual behaviour of the value that is likely to be taken by ρ (the elasticity of the marginal utility of income). Moreover, we have to consider the possibility that ρ may reflect social values as well as individual utility. Mirrlees' formulation, for example, allows for the possibility that the objective function is:

$$\int G[U] f(n) \, dn$$

where G is a social welfare function defined on individual utilities. In this case ρ represents the elasticity of the *social* marginal utility of income, which may be expected to be higher than the private elasticity. For these reasons there is no clear *a priori* expectation that the value of ρ would lie between 1 and 2 (the values taken by Mirrlees) and we should entertain the possibility that it may be considerably higher.

To this point the basic utilitarian framework has not been discussed. This framework does however suffer from well-known disadvantages, and these have led many authors to draw the conclusion that the equi-marginal or other sacrifice principles cannot provide a useful guide to policy. Prest, for example, writes that: 'It seems reasonable to conclude that sacrifice is not only unmeasurable and incapable of quantification for any one individual but also not comparable as between individuals. With such fundamental objections it would seem to be impossible to accept the conclusions derived from the theories of sacrifice' ([19], pp. 117–18).

In the same way, Johansen concludes that 'On the whole ... the ability principle, in so far as attempts have been made to define and elaborate it with the aid of the theory of utility function, is mainly of abstract theoretical interest, and will not be able to play any significant role in the actual formulation of income taxation' ([12], p. 217).

If the utilitarian approach underlying the minimum sacrifice theories, and the recent extensions of these, is to be rejected, it is reasonable to ask what can be offered in its place. As Fisher commented, 'philosophic doubt is right and proper, but the problems of life cannot and do not wait' ([9], p. 180). There are in fact two main alternative approaches which can be identified: (*a*) maximisation of the welfare of the worst-off individual; (*b*) considerations of income inequality.

(*a*) *Fairness and 'maxi-min'*

The first of these lines of argument has been developed by Rawls from considerations of the nature of the social contract. The foundation of this approach are the two basic principles of justice put forward by Rawls: 'First, each person engaged in an institution ... has an equal right to the most extensive liberty compatible with a like liberty for all; and second, inequalities ... are arbitrary unless it is reasonable to expect that they will work out to everyone's advantage' ([20], p. 61).

The second of these principles is interpreted by Rawls to mean the maximisation of the welfare of the worst-off individual (a 'maxi-min' criterion): 'The basic structure is just throughout when the advantages of the more fortunate promote the well-being of the least fortunate, that is, when a decrease in their advantages would make the least fortunate even worse off than they are' ([20], p. 66).

This formulation does not, of course, avoid all the difficulties of utilitarianism; at the same time the requirements are rather different (to apply the 'maxi-min' criterion, we require comparability of welfare levels, but not cardinality. See Sen [21]). Moreover, the maxi-min criterion does seem to capture some of the notions of 'fairness' which are current in public discussion and it is interesting to examine its implications.

If we can assume that individual utility is related to income in such a way that the worst-off individual is the man with the lowest n, the solution with this objective can be seen from the preceding analysis to be $1/\mu$. This tax rate may well seem surprisingly low. Although not much weight should be attached to the actual numerical values, it would indicate a tax rate of between 30–45% using the values of μ estimated by Lydall [13]. These rates are considerably higher than those given by Mirrlees, but none the less lower than one could expect from such an apparently egalitarian objective function. It is interesting to compare the maxi-min case with the egalitarian prescriptions of Pigou and Edgeworth, which led to 100% marginal rate of tax. In the present case this does not happen because of the effects on the work decisions of the better-off groups. It is in the interests of the worst-off person to reduce the rate below 100% to increase the revenue raised from those higher up the scale.[14]

(b) Income inequality
The second alternative approach is well described by Simons:

Taxation must affect the distribution of income ... and it is only sensible to face the question as to what kinds of effects are desirable. To do this is to reduce the discussion frankly to the level of ethics or aesthetics. Such procedure, however, is certainly preferable to the traditional one of 'describing' the attributes of the good life in terms which simply are not descriptive. The case for drastic progression in taxation must be rested in the case against inequality – on the ethical or aesthetic judgement that the prevailing distribution of wealth and income reveals a degree (and/or kind) of inequality which is distinctly evil or unlovely ([24], pp. 18–19).

If, however, considerations of income inequality are to provide a guide to the rate of income taxation, they have to be more precisely formulated. A natural way in which this can be done is through one of the summary measures of inequality which are commonly employed in empirical studies of tax progression; we would, for example, choose the optimal income tax so as to minimise the Gini coefficient. This kind of procedure suffers, however, from two disadvantages:

(a) as I have argued elsewhere [Chapter 1], the conventional summary measures have no inherent rationale and little interpretation can be given to them,
(b) the use of such measures implicitly involves a trade-off between inequality and some measure of the average level of incomes, and this trade-off has to be specified.[15]

One way of overcoming these difficulties is to follow the approach examined in Chapter 1 which assumes that we rank income distributions according to a social welfare function:

$$J = \int_{n}^{\infty} H[I(n)]f(n)\,dn \tag{26}$$

where $H(I)$ denotes the social valuation of income accruing to an individual. The particular functional form explored is:

$$H = \frac{I^{1-\rho}}{1-\rho} \qquad \rho \geqslant 0$$

It appears at first sight that this is identical to the utilitarian approach discussed earlier. It is important to emphasise, however, that H represents the *social* valuation of income,[16] and that the choice of ρ is based on social values about inequality. The parameter ρ reflects in fact the degree of aversion to inequality in the society: $\rho = 0$ corresponds to maximising the sum of incomes, and increasing values of ρ mean that the society is more averse to inequality. The solutions obtained using this approach can be read off from Table 4. For $\rho = 0$ (zero inequality aversion), the optimal solution is a zero tax rate, and for higher values of ρ the optimal tax rate increases until it reaches the limiting case of maxi-min ($\rho \to \infty$).

The fact that the maxi-min solution represents the limiting case, and that, as we have seen, this does not necessarily lead to very high rates of taxation, may lead us to question whether the formulation (26) adequately captures our ⲛⲟⲧⲓⲟⲛ ⲟⲃⲟⲩⲧ ⲓⲛⲉⲩⲁⲗⲓⲧⲩ Ⲧⲟ ⲡⲁⲧⲓⲛⲩⲗⲁⲣ ⲓⲧ ⲙⲁⲩ ⲛⲟⲧ ⲛⲉⲥⲉⲥⲥⲁⲣⲓⲗⲩ ⲁⲅⲣⲉⲉ ⲧⲃⲁⲧ ⲧⲃⲉ ⲥⲟⲥⲓⲁⲗ welfare function is increasing in all its arguments: it is quite conceivable that a gift of £1.00 from Mars to the richest person in Britain may be considered to lower the level of social welfare. It is possible that we may attach particular weight to the distance between the top and the bottom. Fair [8] refers to the belief of Plato that no one in a society should be more than four times richer than the poorest member of society. If this is so, we may well choose tax rates higher than the maxi-min solution. Although this would reduce the lifetime income of the poorest man it would narrow the gap between him and those at the top. In the present model the after-tax income of the lowest man as a percentage of the average is (for $n_0 < \mathbf{n}$):

$$(1 - 1/\mu)e^{t/\mu - 1}$$

The value of this ratio for different values of t (where $\mu = 3$) is given:

$t = 0$	Ratio $= 66\%$
$t = 33\frac{1}{3}\%$ (maxi-min solution)	Ratio $= 79\%$
$t = 50\%$	Ratio $= 86\%$
$t = 66\frac{2}{3}\%$	Ratio $= 94\%$

It is possible, therefore, that concern for income inequality may lead to the choice of a tax rate above that indicated by the maxi-min criterion. This would involve the government selecting a policy which in terms of individual lifetime incomes was Pareto-inferior.[17] If the tax rate is above $1/\mu$, all individuals would favour a tax reduction. The reason the government might choose such a policy is that the loss to the highest income groups is larger than to the lowest, and hence the gap between them would be narrowed.

7 Conclusions

The value of a model such as that discussed in this chapter does not lie in the precise solutions obtained. It should indeed be obvious that the specification of the model is inadequate to provide any detailed prescriptions as to what the rate of income tax should be. The labour supply assumptions, for example, are highly stylised and leave out many important factors. The analysis may however have served to provide some insight into the structure of the arguments and to bring out the significance of considerations not discussed adequately in earlier contributions. In particular, I have tried to emphasise the role played by the formulation of the objectives of the government. This has been shown to be important at two levels. First, within the utilitarian framework underlying the minimum sacrifice theories and the work by Mirrlees and others, the results may depend sensitively on the particular cardinalisation adopted. Second, alternative approaches based on considerations of 'fairness' or 'inequality' may lead to very different results.

One point which emerges clearly as significant is the importance of the maxi-min solution. Not only does it have considerable intuitive appeal, but also it provides a limiting case for the utilitarian approach and an interesting watershed for those concerned about inequality.

Acknowledgement

I am very grateful to C. J. Bliss, J. A. Mirrlees and J. M. Parkin for their comments on earlier versions of this chapter.

Notes

1   This will only, of course, ensure an equal level of utility where the origins of the utility functions are identical (they are fully comparable. See Sen [21]).

     If $T(n)$ were constrained to be non-negative, we would have the solution described by Dalton: 'Taxing only the largest incomes, cutting down all above a certain level to that level, and exempting all below that level' ([5], p. 59).

2   No account is taken here of differing needs, and this problem clearly requires further analysis. For discussion of the variation of taxation with family size, see Mirrlees [15].

3   Writing the social welfare function:

$$\frac{1}{\varepsilon}W^{\varepsilon} = \int\left(\frac{1}{\varepsilon}\right)(V^{\varepsilon} - 1)f(n)\,dn$$

(where $\varepsilon = 1 - \rho$), in the limit as $\varepsilon \to 0$, $\log W \to \int \log Vf(n)\,dn$. See Hardy, Littlewood and Polya [11], Chapter 2.

4   Fair does report briefly on the results obtained when $\rho = 0$ (p. 574) and comments that 'the results did not change much'. However, the results are given in terms of the after-tax Gini coefficient and it is hard to see what is implied for the marginal rates of taxation.

6   The linear tax case is examined by Sheshinski [22], Wesson [26] and Atkinson [2]. It should be noted that Blum and Kalven [4] regard such a tax as being basically different from a general progressive tax with increasing marginal rates of tax, and that it does not allow us to consider the desirability of a 'surtax' or of a negative income tax rate different from that for the positive tax schedule.

7   Lydall [13], Chapter 3 produces evidence that the upper tail of the earnings distribution approximately follows the Pareto law. It is also well known that the distribution of the number of scientific papers published per author is approximately Pareto in form (Simon [25])!

8   This model owes a great deal to that of Sheshinski [23]. His formulation is, however, different:

$$I = z - T(z) - g(S)$$

and is rather more difficult to interpret.

9   In case (B) the revenue constraint is:

$$\alpha = (1 - \beta)\int_{n_0}^{\infty}\left[\frac{n}{i} - \frac{\alpha}{\beta}\right]f(n)\,dn$$

using the fact that $n_0 = i\alpha/\beta$:

$$n_0\frac{\beta}{1-\beta} = \mu\int_{n_0}^{\infty}\left(\frac{n}{\mathbf{n}}\right)^{-\mu}dn - n_0\left(\frac{n_0}{\mathbf{n}}\right)^{-\mu}$$

or:

$$\frac{\beta}{|1 \quad \beta|} = \frac{1}{(\mu \quad 1)}\left(\frac{n_0}{m}\right)^{-\mu}$$

10   The solution for $n_0^*(\mathbf{n})$ is given by $\mathbf{n}/(\mu-1)$, which is less than or equal to $\mathbf{n}$ for $\mu \geqslant 2$, so that the revenue constraint is of type A.

11   It is assumed here, as earlier, than an individual's utility depends only on his own income.

12   The data given by Lydall [13] for Britain, France, Germany and the United States suggest values of μ between 2.27 and 3.5.

13   Substituting:

$$m = n_0 \frac{(\rho-1)}{n}$$

gives the incomplete gamma function:

$$K(\mu, \rho) = \int_0^{\mathbf{m}} e^{-m} m^{\rho+\mu-2} \, dm$$

where $\mathbf{m} = n_0(\rho-1)/\mathbf{n}$. The equation to be solved may be written as:

$$\frac{K(\mu, \rho)}{K(\mu+1, \rho)} = \frac{1}{\mathbf{m}}\left(\frac{\mu}{\mu-1}\right) - \frac{1}{(\rho-1)}$$

The left-hand side is evaluated using the tables published by Pearson [17].

14   The extent to which this is worth while depends, of course, on the elasticity of the supply function. In this context it should be noted that the earnings function assumed here may well over-emphasise the effect of taxation on work incentives. The earnings function is in fact identical with that obtained from the utility function:

$$U(x, y) = \log x - iy$$

where x denotes consumption and y hours of work. The fact that this corresponds to a perfectly elastic supply of effort suggests that the simple model used here may understate the optimal tax rate.

15   The Gini coefficient would be minimised, for example, if all incomes were zero.

16   This formulation is in effect that proposed by Musgrave: 'The concept of subjective utility is translated into one of social income utility. We may then postulate a marginal-utility schedule that seems proper as a matter of social policy. ... If we proceed along these lines, the principle of ability to pay ceases to be the subjective matter that J. S. Mill had thought it to be. It becomes a question of social value' ([16], p. 109).

17   It is important to emphasise at this point that no account has been taken of inter-dependencies (the possibility that a person's welfare may depend on the incomes of others). If such interdependencies exist, raising the tax rate above $1/\mu$ may still be Pareto-optimal in terms of individual utilities.

References

[1]   Atkinson, A. B. (1970), 'On the measurement of inequality', Chapter 1 in this volume.

[2]   Atkinson, A. B. (1972), '"Maxi-min" and optimal income taxation', mimeo.

[3]   Becker, G. S. (1964), *Human Capital*, Columbia University Press.

[4]   Blum, W. J. and Kalven, H. (1963), *The Uneasy Case for Progressive Taxation*, Phoenix edition, University of Chicago Press.

[5]   Dalton, H. (1954), *Principles of Public Finance*, Routledge & Kegan Paul.

[6] Edgeworth, F. Y. (1925), 'Papers relating to political economy', vol. ii, *Royal Economic Society*, London.
[7] Fagan, E. (1938), 'Recent and contemporary theories of progressive taxation', *Journal of Political Economy*, pp. 457–9, August.
[8] Fair, R. C. (1971), 'The optimal distribution of income', *Quarterly Journal of Economics*, pp. 551–79, November.
[9] Fisher, I. (1927), 'A statistical method for measuring "marginal utility" and testing the justice of a progressive income tax', in *Economic Essays Contributed in Honour of John Bates Clark*, New York.
[10] Foley, D. (1967), 'Resource allocation and the public sector', *Yale Economic Essays*, vol. 7, pp. 45–98, Spring.
[11] Hardy, G. H., Littlewood, J. R. and Polya, G. (1952), *Inequalities*, 2nd edn, Cambridge University Press.
[12] Johansen, L. (1965), *Public Economics*, North-Holland.
[13] Lydall, H. F. (1968), *The Structure of Earnings*, Oxford University Press, London.
[14] Mirrlees, J. A. (1971), 'An exploration in the theory of optimum income taxation', *Review of Economic Studies*, pp. 175–208, April.
[15] Mirrlees, J. A. (1972), 'Population policy and the taxation of family size', *Journal of Public Economics*, pp. 169–98, August.
[16] Musgrave, R. A. (1959), *The Theory of Public Finance*, McGraw-Hill.
[17] Pearson, K. (ed.) (1965), *Tables of the Incomplete Γ-Function*, Cambridge University Press.
[18] Pigou, A. C. (1947), *A Study in Public Finance*, 3rd edn, Macmillan.
[19] Prest, A. R. (1967), *Public Finance in Theory and Practice*, 3rd edn, Weidenfeld & Nicolson.
[20] Rawls, J. 'Distributive justice', in P. Laslett and W. G. Runciman, *Philosophy, Politics and Society*, Third Series, Blackwell.
[21] Sen, A. K. (1970), *Collective Choice and Social Welfare*, Oliver & Boyd.
[22] Sheshinski, E. (1972), 'The optimal linear income tax', *Review of Economic Studies*, vol. 39, pp. 297–302.
[23] Sheshinski, E. 'On the theory of optimal income taxation', mimeo.
[24] Simons, H. (1938), *Personal Income Taxation*, University of Chicago Press.
[25] Simon, H. A. (1955), 'On a class of skew distribution functions', *Biometrika*, **42**, pp. 425–40.
[26] Wesson, J. (1972), 'On the distribution of personal incomes', *Review of Economic Studies*, vol. 29, pp. 7786.

PART IV

ISSUES OF PUBLIC POLICY

Introduction to Part IV

Chapters 16 and 17   Housing Policy

The essays in Part IV are concerned with the application of economic analysis to particular areas of policy, drawing on the more theoretical treatment of Part III. My interest in these areas arises from policy discussions in Britain, and Chapter 17 (like Chapters 21 and 22) is expressly about Britain. However, the problems considered are not unique to Britain, and I hope that the discussion will be found of value in other countries as well.

The subject of housing is an important and wide-ranging one. The level of house-building, the condition of the housing stock, and the problem of homelessness all raise major questions about the adequacy of housing provision. The ramifications of housing extend from the construction industry on one side, through the tangled web of central–local government relations, to the operations of financial intermediaries, such as building societies and banks. Chapters 16 and 17 are concerned with only one of these many aspects: housing finance and its relation to income taxation and to income maintenance.

The finance of housing has never been simple, but its complexity has increased significantly in recent years. For local authority (council) tenants, the extension of rent rebate schemes to a national basis since 1972 means that net rent now depends on income, where such rebates are received, a position which is complicated for some people by the interaction with supplementary benefits (although this will be changed by the introduction of a new unified housing benefit). For private tenants the same provisions were introduced by the 1972 Housing Finance Act. For owner-occupiers, the fall in the income tax threshold means that many more now benefit from the deductibility of mortgage interest and from the fact that imputed rent is not taxed. Consequently, the cost of these 'tax expenditures' has risen substantially. In 1980–1, the estimated cost of the mortgage deduction is some £2 billion, or 7% of the revenue from income tax. It may also be noted that the estimated cost of relief from capital gains taxation for owner-occupiers is £2.4 billion. These sums receive less attention than the more obvious costs of subsidising local authority housing.

As is observed in Chapter 17, this system of housing finance 'leads both to patent inequities and to a bizarre pattern of incentives'. For some families paying for accommodation imposes a severe financial strain; for others inflation has reduced their mortgage payments to a small fraction of their earnings. For some families, the tax system means that owner-occupation is a most attractive form of investment; for others, the means-tested rent rebates are an important element in the 'poverty trap'. A complete re-examination of housing finance is sorely needed – an opportunity which was missed in the Housing Policy Review of 1977. Without such an overall perspective, piecemeal policy, such as the sale of council houses, or a new housing benefit, is likely to make little sense.

In such a reassessment three major factors have to be determined. The first is the degree of subsidy, if any, to be provided to housing as a whole; the second concerns the relative treatment of different types of tenure; the third is the relationship between housing costs and income. Chapter 16 deals with the first and third of these elements. It examines the arguments which can be advanced for a general subsidy on housing, and for the particular subsidy which is provided by the tax-deductibility of housing expenditures (whether by owner-occupiers or by tenants). The theoretical framework in the main part of the chapter is similar to that used in Part III, and the weak separability result of Chapter 11 is employed in the case of non-linear income tax schedules. The last part of the chapter, however, points to the dependence of the results on the assumption that there are no intrinsic inequalities in access to housing. To introduce such inequalities in a general analysis, together with differences in earning power, is a problem of considerable difficulty (see Mirrlees [14] and Seade [16]).

Chapter 17, written jointly with Mervyn King, emphasises the importance in reality of differences in the circumstances of individual families, and the need for such diversity to be taken into account in any analysis of policy. This chapter draws on research carried out by King and myself, in conjunction with Nicholas Stern, as part of the SSRC Programme on Taxation, Incentives and the Distribution of Income. One of the aims of this programme has been to show that examination of micro-data on individual households, such as those covered by the Family Expenditure Survey, is essential in judging the impact of taxation and government expenditure. This is illustrated in the case of housing by King [13].

Chapter 17 is concerned with all three of the factors listed above, giving especial attention to the implications of inflation. Here, we discuss different proposals for reform. The merits of these can be debated, and will doubtless change with changing circumstances, but whatever happens we remain of the view that 'reform of housing finance will be successful only if the problem is viewed as a whole, and a consistent set of principles applied to each major sector'.

Chapter 18   Charitable Contributions

In his *Agenda for Progressive Taxation* (1947), William Vickrey presented a systematic and penetrating analysis of the United States income tax. When the book was reprinted in 1970, he remarked rather sadly that 'of the specific proposals outlined ... only one was ever adopted in full' ([19], p. 5). This, however, considerably understates the extent of his contribution, which has significantly influenced thinking in this area of public finance. Moreover, a number of his specific proposals have come back onto the agenda in recent years, as is illustrated by Chapter 18, written for a volume in his honour.

The proposal made by Vickrey for the income tax treatment of charitable contributions was that tax deductibility should be replaced by a flat-rate tax credit. In Chapter 18, I examine the arguments which can be made for such a reform. The issue has similarity with that discussed in Chapter 16, and like that chapter draws on the optimum tax formulation. But it is evident that the non-linearity of the income tax is crucial in the present case (with a constant marginal tax rate, the only issue is the choice of the rate of tax credit). The model has also to be extended to incorporate the motives for charitable giving. Here the model of Chapter 18 is a very special one, and, as noted in a perceptive review by Small [17], the assumption that G_0 equals zero in the second interpretation of equation (9) is not a very satisfactory one. More generally, the model is concerned with redistributive charitable activities rather than those concerned with the provision of educational, medical or other facilities. For a model more directed at the latter, see Feldstein [8].

Chapter 19   The Welfare Economics of Smoking

Chapter 18 is concerned with positive interdependencies between people arising from charitable giving; Chapter 19 deals with a subject where the interdependencies are more likely to be negative – the welfare economics of smoking. It is not however the external diseconomies of smoking that are the principal topic of the chapter. Rather, the aim is to see what *other* considerations may enter the calculation of the 'cost' of smoking, and in particular the role of habit formation and imperfect information. Both aspects have been the subject of considerable recent research. Habit formation and endogenous change of tastes are discussed by Pollak [15] and Hammond [9]; for rather different views, see Elster [7] and Stigler and Becker [18]. Welfare economics with changing tastes is well reviewed in Hammond [10], who goes on to the question of imperfect information. As he notes, one of the aims of Chapter 19 is to raise the problem that policy-makers may be able to control the information available to people. Is it always right to inform smokers of the health risks? Hammond quite fairly comments that the analysis of Chapter 19 provides little in the way of conclusions, but at least it recognises that there is a question to be answered.

Chapter 19 was the outcome of research carried out in conjunction with Thomas Meade and Joy Skegg on the economics of smoking. Articles dealing with the empirical aspects in Britain include Atkinson and Meade [2], and Atkinson and Skegg [4] and [5]. (For references to research in the United States, see Harris [11] and [12].)

Chapter 20   Capital-Sharing

The essays in Part II describe some of my research on the concentration of wealth in Britain and the implications of capital taxation. In Chapter 20 I examine an alternative approach to the redistribution of wealth, via schemes for capital-sharing. As is observed in the introduction, such schemes have received little attention in Britain. There are however two reasons why they may warrant closer investigation. First, experience with the reform of capital transfer taxation, and with the abortive proposals for a wealth tax, has led some people to doubt the effectiveness of fiscal measures. Second, if there is to be any successful long-term incomes policy, then there must be provisions for the treatment of profit incomes. (Here again I am dubious about the proposals for reliance on taxation.)

The aim of Chapter 20 is to explore the implications of a capital-growth–sharing scheme in the context of a simple, stylised model of the growth of the firm. As is noted, the traditional theory is not adequate for this purpose, but it should be pointed out that, since the essay was written, there have been significant advances in the theory of the firm. Most importantly, there has been analysis of the nature of the contract between firm and employee, particularly in the presence of uncertainty about employment. This literature on 'implicit' contracts is surveyed by Azariadis [6]. (Some of the implications of uncertainty for profit-sharing are discussed in Atkinson [1].)

Chapters 21 and 22

Any discussion of capital-sharing in the 1980s is likely to be heavily influenced by consideration of the impact on employment, and unemployment is the subject of the last two chapters in the volume. Chapters 21 and 22 are not, however, concerned with the availability of jobs as much as with the position of the unemployed and the operation of unemployment insurance.

Chapter 21, written jointly with John Flemming, appeared in Autumn 1978. It opens with the statement that 'unemployment is likely to remain a major social and economic problem for several years'. Unfortunately, this has proved to be correct; indeed the situation in 1982 is considerably worse. Measured in terms of recorded unemployment, the line has gone right off the scale of Figure 1 in Chapter 21. Perhaps more significantly, there are more than 3/4 million people who have been out of work for more than a year – which is more than ten times the number of twenty years ago.

The first aim of Chapter 21 is to set out the evidence about income maintenance provisions for unemployment and their relation to the differing circumstances of the unemployed. Much of public discussion about social security is based not on the actual income received, but on hypothetical calculations for a representative family. The reason is quite simple. It is about hypothetical families that MPs ask questions in the House of Commons and these provide a convenient source of information. But such hypothetical calculations do not necessarily measure the benefit actually received. For example, the standard assumptions are that an unemployed man receives national insurance benefit for fifty-two weeks and that he claims supplementary benefit when entitled. But eligibility for national insurance may be affected by past unemployment or by an incomplete contribution record; a person may be disqualified; he may not claim supplementary benefit. As in the case of housing, the answer is to look at actual information for individual households, and in recent research with John Micklewright [3] I have used the Family Expenditure Survey for this purpose. This shows that in the period 1972–7, only about a third of unemployed men had the pattern of benefits assumed in the hypothetical calculations.

The reality of benefit receipt is relevant to the question of incentives, which is discussed in Chapter 21 and developed further in Chapter 22. Here we review evidence derived both from time-series and from cross-section studies. The time-series treatment of unemployment insurance is important in the light of the increasing use of benefit variables in macro-economic models. Typically, however, these variables are based on hypothetical calculations of the type we have just described and are of dubious relevance. Even if regarded as an indicator of the general level of benefits, they fail to recognise that the identity of the 'marginal' unemployed may change with varying labour market conditions. The impact of the changing state of the labour-market is also relevant when considering the cross-section investigations of Lancaster, relating to 1973, and Nickell, relating to 1972 (both discussed in Chapter 22). Their findings concerning the relation between duration of unemployment and the level of benefits may not be applicable to a situation where the overall level of unemployment is very considerably higher.

In Chapter 21, Flemming and I discussed a number of possible reforms of the income maintenance provisions. Two of these have since been introduced: the earnings-related supplement has been abolished from 1982 and unemployment benefit subjected to income tax. In the House of Commons debate on the latter, our article was quoted in support by the government spokesman, Mr Nigel Lawson (Hansard, 11 May 1981). However, as Mr Robin Cook was quick to point out, Mr Lawson was ignoring the second part of our recommendations, that 'the taxation of benefits would provide additional revenue and we would strongly urge that this be used for the improvement of benefits'. This has not happened.

References

[1] Atkinson, A. B. (1977), 'Profit-sharing, collective bargaining and "employment risk"', *Zeitschrift fur die Gesamte Staatswissenschaft*, pp. 43–52.

[2] Atkinson, A. B. and Meade, T. W. (1974), 'Methods and preliminary findings in assessing the economic and health services consequences of smoking', *Journal of the Royal Statistical Society*, series A, vol. 137, pp. 297–312.

[3] Atkinson, A. B. and Micklewright, J. (1980), 'Unemployment Project Working Notes 2 and 3', *SSRC Programme on Taxation, Incentives and the Distribution of Income*, London School of Economics.

[4] Atkinson, A. B. and Skegg, J. L. (1973), 'Anti-smoking publicity and the demand for tobacco in the UK', *Manchester School*, vol. 41, pp. 265–82.

[5] Atkinson, A. B. and Skegg, J. L. (1974), 'Control of smoking and price of cigarettes – a comment', *British Journal of Preventive and Social Medicine*, vol. 28, pp. 45–8.

[6] Azariadis, C. (1981), 'Implicit contracts and related topics: a survey', in Z. Hornstein, J. Grice and A. Webb (eds.), *The Economics of the Labour Market*, London, HMSO.

[7] Elster, J. (1979), *Ulysses and the Sirens*, Cambridge, Cambridge University Press.

[8] Feldstein, M. S. (1980), 'A contribution to the theory of tax expenditures: the case of

charitable giving', in H. J. Aaron and M. J. Boskin (eds.), *The Economics of Taxation*, Washington, DC, The Brookings Institution.

[9] Hammond, P. J. (1976), 'Endogenous tastes and stable long-run choice', *Journal of Economic Theory*, vol. 13, pp. 329–40.

[10] Hammond, P. J. (forthcoming), 'Utilitarianism, time, uncertainty and information', in A. Sen and B. Williams (eds.), *Utilitarianism and Beyond*, Cambridge, Cambridge University Press.

[11] Harris, J. E., 'Cigarette smoking in the United States, 1950–1978', in *Smoking and Health: A Report of the Surgeon General*, Washington, DC, US Government Printing Office.

[12] Harris, J. E. 1(980), 'Taxing tar and nicotine', *American Economic Review*, vol. 70, pp. 300–11.

[13] King, M. A. (1981), 'The distribution of gains and losses from changes in the tax treatment of housing', Discussion Paper 20, *SSRC Programme on Taxation, Incentives and the Distribution of Income*, London School of Economics.

[14] Mirrlees, J. A. (forthcoming), 'The theory of optimal taxation', in K. J. Arrow and M. D. Intriligator (eds.), *Handbook of Mathematical Economics*, Amsterdam, North-Holland.

[15] Pollak, R. A. (1976), 'Habit formation and long-run utility functions', *Journal of Economic Theory*, vol. 13, pp. 272–97.

[16] Seade, J. K. (1981), D.Phil thesis, University of Oxford.

[17] Small, K. A. 'Review', *Journal of Economic Literature*, vol. 18, pp. 1592–4.

[18] Stigler, G. J. and Becker, G. S. (1977), 'De gustibus non est disputandum', *American Economic Review*, vol. 67, pp. 76–90.

[19] Vickrey, W. S. (1971). *Agenda for Progressive Taxation*, (2nd edn), Clifton, New Jersey, Augustus M. Kelley.

16   Housing Allowances, Income Maintenance and Income Taxation*[1]

1   Introduction

Housing policy is a complex and controversial subject. The purpose of this chapter is to concentrate on one particular aspect of this problem: the provision of individual housing allowances and their relationship to income maintenance and income taxation. Housing assistance in this form has become increasingly popular in recent years.

Section 2 of this chapter describes the main issues to be examined, and discusses their relationship to recent housing policy in Britain and the United States. Although the motivation for the chapter stems from a concern with important policy issues, it should be stressed at the outset that the analysis is based on a number of strong assumptions (described in section 3) and that the results derived in sections 4–6 are largely theoretical in nature. The main emphasis is on isolating the essential issues rather than with making policy recommendations, and section 7 describes some of the further research necessary in this area.

2   Housing Allowances: Some of the Issues in Britain and The United States

Housing policy in Britain and the United States in the post-war period has been concerned with both the supply and the demand sides of the housing markets. Here attention is focused on the latter, and in particular on the relationship between housing subsidies and income maintenance/income taxation. The overlap between these policies has long been recognised in the case of the income-tax treatment of housing outlays; the overlap between housing assistance programmes and income taxation is a more recent problem and one that has not received sufficient attention.

Tax treatment of housing outlays
In both countries home-owners enjoy, under the income tax, substantial concessions, which in effect allow the deduction of housing costs from taxable income.[3] It has been argued that these concessions give rise to horizontal inequities[4] and many proposals have been put forward for their abolition.

*   Reprinted from *The Economics of Public Services*, 1977.

These proposals involve, ideally, the taxation of imputed rent accruing to owner-occupiers (as was the case in Britain until the abolition of Schedule A in 1963–4), but, in the event of this being administratively infeasible, it has been suggested that one could correct the horizontal inequities between owners and renters by permitting the deduction of rent for income tax purposes.[5]

Housing subsidies and income redistribution

The choice between the two policies just outlined may be seen in terms of the relative treatment of housing and other expenditure. A general subsidy to housing may also be given directly by reducing the cost of housing, and it has been argued that – given a low income elasticity of demand – a general subsidy of this kind would supplement the redistributive impact of income taxation. In section 4, we examine whether a case can be made for a general housing subsidy as a purely income-redistributive measure. Such a general subsidy would involve an equal reduction in the price of housing to all households. This may be contrasted with tax deductibility, where the price of housing depends on the household's marginal tax rate, so that, if the marginal tax rate rises with income, the rich derive greater benefit. It may also be contrasted with the housing assistance schemes, in which the subsidy is *reduced* as income rises, and to which we now turn.

Housing assistance schemes

The growth of interest in these schemes stems, in large part, from a desire to link housing subsidies to individual income and circumstances. In the 1960s, critics of British housing policy pointed to the fact that 'the assistance which a family obtains depends, to a large extent, on the housing sector in which it finds itself, and total housing costs often depend more on history than current ability to pay' (Cullingworth [5], p. 109). In the United States, Tobin argued similarly that housing 'subsidies are available only for an accidentally or arbitrarily selected few. The result is that some low income taxpayers are subsidising the rents of families with equal or higher incomes' (Tobin [12], p. 275).

In Britain, these considerations led to the Conservative government's Housing Finance Act, 1972, which was aimed at securing 'fairness between one citizen and another in giving and receiving help towards housing costs'. The mechanism by which help is to be channelled to 'those most in need' is the rent rebate (or allowance) scheme, which covers all tenants.[6] There is a national scale of allowances,[7] and, making a few simplifying assumptions, the formula for the rebate paid can be written as:

$$S = \max[0, \beta h X - \gamma Y] \tag{1}$$

where Y denotes income, X quantity of housing assumed, h cost of housing (so hX = rent), and β and γ are constants.[8] It should be noted that hX is actual housing outlay, but in certain circumstances (for instance, where the authority thinks that the house is larger than needed) the administrator may substitute a specified X^*.

The widespread introduction of housing assistance may eliminate some of the inequalities of previous housing subsidies, which themselves have been the subject of criticism. The first line of criticism concerns the relationship with the income tax system. In the American discussions of welfare reform, attention has been drawn to the high marginal rates of taxation resulting from the combined effects of unco-ordinated schemes (see Aaron [2]). In Britain, the rent rebate system means, for example, that a household on average earnings may face a marginal tax rate which is not reached on the positive income tax scale until well into the top 1%.[9] The design of housing assistance has to be considered, therefore, in relation to income taxation; the optimal value of γ has to be chosen in the light of the income tax structure.

A second important criticism of housing assistance schemes concerns the problem of administration and its effectiveness in reaching eligible families. Experience in Britain with similar rebates for rates (local property taxes) suggests that benefits reach only half of those entitled to them.[10] In the United States, this problem of 'take-up' has received less attention, but evidence for the food-stamp programme suggests that it may be important. Steiner [11] has referred to 'consistent evidence of client non-participation' (p. 197). The reasons for this failure are not fully known, but they result, in part, from an administrative structure in which the benefit paid depends on both the income and the housing expenditure of the family. The fact that both items are required to compute the benefit that is due means that the allowance can neither be paid automatically through the income tax (negative income tax) machinery, nor can it be provided via the landlord (in the case of rented accommodation). This raises the important issue of how far a unified rent-allowance/income-maintenance policy is required. Under what conditions can the administration be decentralised into separate – if co-ordinated – programmes for housing subsidies and income maintanence? These questions are discussed in a preliminary way in section 6.

3 The Framework for the Analysis

Household behaviour
Households are assumed to have identical utility functions[11] $U(C, X, L)$, where C denotes other consumption and L labour supplied (as a fraction of the total hours), but to differ in their wage per hour (w). C is taken as the numéraire. Households have no income apart from labour income ($Y = wL$).

Housing supply
As was indicated earlier, the model makes a number of strong assumptions, particularly in the case of the supply side of the housing market. It is assumed that the cost of housing (h) is determined exogenously, although it may vary among individuals. This assumption is made not on the basis of realism, but because it allows us to focus on the elements of the demand side that are of importance.

Policy instruments

The policy instruments examined in this chapter may be written in the general form $H(h, hX, Y)$ where the household budget constrain becomes:

$$C + hX = Y - H(h, hX, Y) \tag{2}$$

If the joint distribution of w and h across households is given by $f(w, h)$ then the government budget constraint is given by:

$$\int_0^\infty \int_0^\infty H(h, hX, Y) f(w, h) \; dw \; dh = 0 \tag{3}$$

(assuming that no net revenue is required). This general formulation contains a number of special cases, including:

(a) $H = H(Y - hX)$ which is the case where housing outlays are tax deductible;
(b) $H = H_1(Y) - H_2(hX)$, which is the case where housing outlay is subsidised independently of the income of the recipient; and
(c) $H = H_1(Y) - H_3(h)X$, which is the case where the unit cost of housing is subsidised.

Policy objectives

It is assumed that the government's objectives are represented by a social welfare function of the form:

$$W = \int_0^\infty \int_0^\infty G\{U(C, X, L)\} f(w, h) \; dw \; dh \tag{4}$$

where G is a concave function. It may be noted that this formulation allows for a range of concern from the strict utilitarian case $(G = U)$ to the Rawlsian case $(G = \min U)$, but that it excludes specific egalitarianism as defined by Tobin [12], and that we have ruled out interdependencies between individual utility functions.

In approaching questions of housing policy, it is clear that recommendations often diverge because of differing views of the sources of inequality in the housing market. Most importantly, one must distinguish between situations where, in the long run, everyone faces the same housing cost per unit (h is equal for all households) and situations where there there are long-run inequalities in access to housing. In the latter case, one is saying, in effect, that housing is different in this respect from most other commodities. In sections 4 and 5, the former case (equal h) is considered; section 6 deals with the case where housing is 'different'.

4 A General Subsidy for Housing

The view that there are no long-run inequalities in access to housing, and that it is only inequalities in incomes that are of concern, is held by a wide variety of authors.[12] As we have seen however, this does not mean that there is no role to be played by housing assistance. In particular, where the scope for direct taxation is restricted,[13] it has been argued that housing subsidies, given a low income elasticity of demand, can supplement the redistributive impact of income taxation.

In order to examine this argument, let us consider first the case where the government subsidises housing outlay at rate β, in addition to imposing a linear income tax (with a negative tax component). The household budget constraint becomes:

$$C + h(1-\beta)X = w(1-t)L + \alpha \tag{5}$$

and the government revenue constraint[14]:

$$\alpha = \int_0^\infty [twL - h\beta X]f(w)\,dw \tag{6}$$

The government chooses α, β and t to maximise:

$$W = \int_0^\infty G[U(C,X,L)]f(w)\,dw \tag{7}$$

subject to (6). We may form the Lagrangian:

$$\mathscr{L} = W - \lambda\left[\alpha - \int_0^\infty [twL - h\beta X]f\,dw\right] \tag{8}$$

and obtain[15]:

$$\frac{\partial \mathscr{L}}{\partial \alpha} = \int_0^\infty \left[G'U_C - \lambda + \lambda\left[tw\frac{\partial L}{\partial \alpha} - h\beta\frac{\partial X}{\partial \alpha}\right]\right]f\,dw = 0 \tag{9}$$

$$\frac{\partial \mathscr{L}}{\partial \beta} = \int_0^\infty \left[G'U_C hX - \lambda hX + \lambda\left[tw\frac{\partial L}{\partial \beta} - h\beta\frac{\partial X}{\partial \beta}\right]\right]f\,dw = 0 \tag{10}$$

$$\frac{\partial \mathscr{L}}{\partial t} = \int_0^\infty \left[-G'U_C wL + \lambda wL + \lambda\left[tw\frac{\partial L}{\partial t} - h\beta\frac{\partial X}{\partial t}\right]\right]f\,dw = 0 \tag{11}$$

If we define (where $\lambda > 0$):

$$\Omega(w) = \frac{G'U_C}{\lambda} + \left[tw\frac{\partial L}{\partial \alpha} - h\beta\frac{\partial X}{\partial \alpha} - 1\right] \tag{12}$$

the first-order conditions (9)–(11) may be re-written as:

$$\frac{1}{\lambda}\frac{\partial \mathcal{L}}{\partial \alpha} = \int \Omega(w) f(w)\, dw = 0 \tag{13}$$

$$\frac{1}{\lambda}\frac{\partial \mathcal{L}}{\partial \beta} = \int \Omega(w) X f(w)\, dw + \int \left[tw S_{LX} + h\beta S_{XX} \right] f\, dw = 0 \tag{14}$$

$$\frac{1}{\lambda}\frac{\partial \mathcal{L}}{\partial t} = \int \Omega(w)(-wL) f(w)\, dw + \int w \left[tw S_{LL} + h\beta S_{XL} \right] f\, dw = 0 \tag{15}$$

where S_{ij} denotes the Slutsky terms (and L is measured negatively for this purpose).

The expression $\Omega(w)$ is of central importance. It can be seen that the first term is a declining function of w (given the assumptions about G and U); the last term is more problematical, since it depends on how the marginal propensities to consume change with w (and on the signs of t and β). If we define $R(w) = twL - h\beta X - \alpha$, then a sufficient condition for Ω to be a declining function of w is that $\partial R/\partial \alpha$ (the marginal tax paid as lump-sum income increases) be a non-increasing function of w.[16] Let us also assume that all goods are normal and are Hicksian substitutes ($S_{ij} > 0$ for $i \neq j$). These assumptions, which do not seem unreasonable for the broad commodity groups considered here, imply that X is an increasing function of w and, hence, that the first term in (14) is non-positive. From this it may be deduced that $\beta < t$. Suppose $\beta \geqslant t$, then:

$$\left(\frac{1-t}{t}\right)\left[tw S_{LX} + h\beta S_{XX} \right] = \left[w(1-t) S_{LX} + h(1-\beta) S_{XX} \right] + \frac{(\beta - t)}{t} h S_{XX}$$

$$= -S_{CX} + (1-t)\frac{(\beta - t)}{t} h S_{XX}$$

(using the properties of the Slutsky terms). This expression is strictly negative, and it follows that $\partial \mathcal{L}/\partial \beta < 0$.[17] We thus have:

Proposition 1
If Ω is a non-increasing function of w, and all goods are normal and Hicksian substitutes, the optimal rate of subsidy on housing is strictly less than the rate of income taxation.

It is an immediate corollary of proposition 1 that, where those conditions are satisfied, the tax deduction of housing outlay is not optimal, since it would involve:

$$C + hX = \alpha + wL - t[wL - hX]$$

or $\beta = t$. The optimal policy could be achieved only if the deduction were limited to a certain proportion of housing outlays. We can also see that, if the income tax were to be replaced by a value-added tax, with a rate τ' on housing and a rate τ on other consumption, so that the budget constrain became:

$$C(1+\tau)+hX(1+\tau')=wL+u$$

then, where the conditions for proposition 1 are satisfied, the optimal tax on housing is positive $(\tau'>0)$. In other words, there may be a case for a reduced rate of value-added tax on housing, but there would not be a case for complete exemption.[18]

The case for subsidising housing $(\beta>0)$ depends on the nature of the demand for it. As noted earlier, it is commonly felt that the relevant factor is that housing is a necessity, in the sense that the income elasticity is less than unity. The empirical evidence does not, in fact, provide strong support for this,[19] but even if it were true, it would not necessarily provide a case for subsidies where other instruments for redistribution are available. This may be seen from (14). Suppose that we evaluate $\partial \mathscr{L}/\partial \beta$ at $\beta=0$. This will be positive where:

$$\int\Omega(w)Xfdw + \int twS_{LX}fdw > 0$$

The first of these terms incorporates the distributional considerations. We have already seen, however, that, where α is chosen to satisfy (13), together with the not unreasonable conditions that X is a non-decreasing, and Ω is a non-increasing function of w, then the first term is non-positive. In this situation, the case for a subsidy depends on the second (efficiency) term, which is positive where the goods are Hicksian substitutes.[20] Under quite reasonable conditions, therefore, there will be no 'equity' case for housing subsidies. The reason here is quite simple: where housing is a normal good, a housing subsidy is less progressive than a uniform per capita payment (α).

This point may be illustrated by reference to the Stone–Geary utility function commonly assumed in empirical demand studies:

$$U=b_C\log(C-C_0)+b_X\log(X-X_0)+b_L\log(1-L)$$

where $b_C+b_X+b_L=1$. The resulting demand relationships (where $L\geqslant0$) may be written:

$$C-C_0=b_CM \tag{16}$$

$$h(1-\beta)(X-X_0)=b_XM \tag{17}$$

$$w(1-t)L=w(1-t)-b_LM \tag{18}$$

where:

$$M=w(1-t)+\alpha-C_0-h(1-\beta)X_0 \tag{19}$$

denotes 'full income'. From (13)–(15), we obtain:

$$\frac{\partial \mathscr{L}}{\partial \beta} \sim \int \left[\Omega(w)b_X + \frac{t}{1-t}b_L b_X - \frac{\beta}{1-\beta}b_X(1-b_X) \right] M f \, dw$$

$$\frac{\partial \mathscr{L}}{\partial t} \sim \int \left[\Omega(w)(b_L - 1) + (b_L - 1)\frac{t}{1-t}b_L + \frac{\beta}{1-\beta}b_X b_L \right] M f \, dw$$

so that $\partial \mathscr{L}/\partial \beta, \partial \mathscr{L}/\partial t = 0$ implies $\beta = 0$. In this case, a subsidy on housing is not desirable, even though housing may have an income or expenditure elasticity of less than unity.[21]

5 Tax Deductibility and Non-linear Tax Schedules

In the previous section it was demonstrated that the need for housing subsidies depends on the other possible means of redistribution. Where the uniform subsidy α is chosen optimally, there is no equity argument for housing subsidies. In this section we examine further the relationship between subsidies and the scope for income taxation, examining the desirability of subsidies and tax deductions where the tax schedule may be freely varied (i.e. is not constrained to be linear, as it was in the previous section).

This question may be posed in general terms, allowing for non-linearity of both the income-tax and housing-subsidy schedules:

$$C + H(hX) = Y - T(Y) \tag{20}$$

This problem may be solved using the same approach as that of Mirrlees [9].[22] The household maximisation is equivalent to maximising $U(C, X, Y/w)$ subject to (20) and gives the first-order conditions:

$$U_X = hH'.U_C, \qquad (-U_Y) = (1 - T')U_C \tag{21}$$

The government maximises (7) subject to the overall constraint:

$$\int_0^\infty (C + hX - Y)f(w)\,dw = 0 \tag{22}$$

Heuristically, this can be solved by introducing a multiplier δ associated with (22) and a multiplier $\mu(w)$ associated with the differential equation:

$$\frac{dU}{dw} = U_w = -\frac{U_Y Y}{w} \tag{23}$$

U is a state variable: X and Y are control variables; and C is determined from (21). The Hamiltonian may be written:

$$H = \{G(U) - \delta[C + hX - Y]\}f + \mu U_w \tag{24}$$

and the following necessary conditions obtained:

$$\frac{\partial H}{\partial X} = -\delta f\left[h + \frac{\partial C}{\partial X}\bigg|_U\right] + \mu\left[U_{wX} + U_{wC}\frac{\partial C}{\partial X}\bigg|_U\right] = 0 \tag{25}$$

$$\delta f h[1 - H'] = \frac{Y\mu}{w}[U_{YC}hH' - U_{YX}] \tag{26}$$

From this it is clear that $U_{YC} = U_{YX} = 0$ implies that $H' = 1$ (since the right-hand side is zero and $\delta > 0$); in other words, we have:

Proposition 2
Where the utility function is additively separable in X and C, taken together, and L, then the optimal policy does not involve a subsidy on housing.

It should be emphasised that this result requires separability only between labour and all goods taken together; it does not require separability between housing and other goods.[23] Since the tax deductibility of a fraction θ of housing outlay would modify the household maximisation conditions to:

$$U_X = h(1 - T'\theta)U_C$$

so that the left-hand side of (26) became $\delta f h T'\theta$, we have the corollary that, where the utility function is additively separable (as above), the deduction of part or all of housing outlay from taxable income is not optimal.

Where the only intrinsic differences between individuals are those related to earnings, and where the government can levy any desired non-linear income tax, then separability of the utility function between labour and other goods implies (a) that housing outlays should not be tax-deductible; and (b) that housing outlays should not be subsidised. More generally, we have seen in this and in the previous section that the case for a general subsidy on housing for income-redistributive reasons is likely to be limited to situations where the government's income tax possibilities are restricted. This conclusion may, however, critically depend on the assumption that there are no intrinsic inequalities in access to housing, and we now examine this question.

6 Unequal Access to Housing

In this section, we consider the case where the price of housing varies across individuals, so that they are distinguished both by earnings possibilities (w) and by housing costs per unit (h).

The analysis of the optimal design of a general tax and housing allowance schedule raises a number of problems of considerable technical difficulty. In order, therefore, to make some limited progress with the question, I have made the following simplifying assumptions:

(a) that the income tax system is of the linear form examined in section 4; and
(b) that the housing allowance is paid on the basis of housing costs per unit (h) rather than on the basis of housing expenditure (hX).

The first of these assumptions clearly rules out the aspects discussed in section 5, but in fact a linear tax schedule closely approximates that in force in a number of countries.[24] The second of the assumptions limits attention to one of the two types of housing allowance scheme outlined in section 3, but, given the power of the authorities to substitute a reasonable rent for actual housing expenditure, it may be the closer approximation at least to the British system.
The housing allowance schedule examined here is of the form[25]:

$$C + hX = \alpha(h) + \{1 - t(h)\}wL + \beta(h)hX \qquad (27)$$

In other words, the housing subsidy consists of a payment $\alpha(h)$ related to rent per unit, plus a payment related to actual housing outlay (βhX), minus an adjustment related to income (part of $t(h)$).
The government aims to maximise:

$$\iint G\{U(C, X, L)\} f(w, h)\, dw dh \qquad (28)$$

subject to the revenue constraint:

$$\iint [\alpha - twL + \beta hX] f(w, h)\, dw dh = 0 \qquad (29)$$

with which is associated a multiplier λ. For any given $\hat{h}$ we obtain the first-order conditions (for $\lambda > 0$):

$$\int \left[\frac{G'U_C}{\lambda} - 1 + tw\frac{\partial L}{\partial \alpha} - \beta h\frac{\partial X}{\partial \alpha} \right] f(w, \hat{h}) dw = 0$$

or:

$$\int \Omega(w, \hat{h}) f(w, \hat{h}) dw = 0 \qquad (30)$$

$$\int \left[\left(\frac{G'U_C}{\lambda} - 1 \right) \hat{h}X + tw\frac{\partial L}{\partial \beta} - \beta\hat{h}\frac{\partial X}{\partial \beta} \right] f(w, \hat{h}) dw = 0$$

$$\int \left[\left(\frac{G'U_C}{\lambda} - 1 \right) wL - tw\frac{\partial L}{\partial t} + \hat{h}\beta\frac{\partial X}{\partial t} \right] f(w, \hat{h}) dw = 0$$

For the case of the Stone–Geary utility function considered earlier, the last two equations reduce to:

$$\int \left[\Omega(w) + \frac{t}{1-t} b_L - \frac{\beta}{1-\beta}(1 - b_X) \right] Mf(w, \hat{h}) dw = 0 \qquad (31)$$

$$\int \left[\Omega(w) + \frac{t}{1-t} b_L - \frac{\beta}{1-\beta} \frac{b_x b_L}{1-b_L} \right] M f(w, \hat{h}) dw = 0 \tag{32}$$

where $M = \alpha + w(1-t) - C_0 - h(1-\beta)X_0$ as before.

By the same argument as in section 3, $\beta(h) = 0$ for all h. We are interested in how α, t vary with h. In order to consider this, let us assume that $G' = 1$ and that the distribution is of the form $f(w)g(h)$. It then follows that Ω is independent of h, and hence M. To ensure this, α is determined so that $\alpha(h) - hX_0 = $ constant (i.e. the lump-sum subsidy should fully compensate for variations in housing costs at the level of the 'committed expenditure' X_0) and $t(h)$ is the same for all h.[26] We have, therefore:

Proposition 3
If the distributions of h and w are independent, and the utility function is Stone–Geary in form, then the optimal policy is to compensate for variations in housing costs at the 'committed' level of expenditure and for a uniform tax rate to be applied.

While based on very special assumptions, this result is of interest,[27] since it comes close to the policies put forward as alternatives to the British Housing Finance Act. In particular, the rate of income tax would be independent of housing costs. The income tax would be operated independently of the housing situation, and the housing subsidy would not depend on income. In this way, the administration of the two schemes could be separated, thus contributing to the elimination of the problem of a low rate of 'take-up'. The housing subsidy would be set at a level that levelled out differences in housing costs at a minimum standard of housing (X_0), which does seem to accord with views often expressed.

7 Concluding Comments

It will be clear that this chapter only scratches the surface of an important range of problems, and that only very limited guidance can be given to policy makers on the basis of this analysis. Two areas in particular may be mentioned. First, the importance of the case for housing subsidies depends very much on unequal access to housing, and the argument of section 6 needs to be extended to allow more definite conclusions to be drawn. Second, the whole question of administrative costs, borne both by tax authorities and by individuals, needs much more careful attention. Especial reference should be made to the problem of low 'take-up'; this was referred to at the beginning of the chapter and in the previous section, but, clearly, needs to be incorporated more explicitly into the analysis.

Notes

1 The author is most grateful to participants in the conference where this was first presented for their helpful comments. These have led to definite improvements.
2 See Welfeld [14].

3 Strictly speaking, taxable income excludes net rent plus interest payments plus (in the United States) property taxes. See Aaron [1] for the United States.

4 It is, of course, necessary to examine the incidence of these concessions in a general equilibrium framework.

5 This has been suggested, for example, in Britain (see Chapter 17) and in Canada (see Bossons [4]); in the United States it was permitted under the Civil War income tax (see Simons [10], p. 115).

6 Since 1930, local authorities have been able to apply differential rents for council (public housing) tenants. The number of schemes grew substantially after the mid-1950s, and by 1963–4 they were employed by 40% of the local authorities. Although the central government issued guidance, in the form of a model scheme, the central direction of rent rebates came only with the 1972 Act.

7 There is some minor scope for local discretion.

8 In broad terms, $\beta = 60\%$, and $\gamma = 17$ or 25%.

9 E.g. income tax of 30%, social security contribution of $4\frac{3}{4}\%$, withdrawal of rent rebate of 17%.

10 See, for example, Townsend [13] and Meacher [8].

11 U is assumed to be continuously differentiable and strictly concave. It is assumed that U_C, $U_X > 0$, and $U_L < 0$.

12 For example: 'Public housing is proposed not on the ground of neighbourhood effects but as a means of helping low-income people. If this is the case, why subsidise housing in particular?' (Friedman); 'The rent agreement is quite an ordinary commodity transaction which is... of no greater and no lesser interest to the worker than any other commodity transaction, with the exception of that which concerns the buying and selling of labour power' (Engels [6]).

13 It will be assumed throughout that lump-sum taxation, $T(w)$, is not possible and that the government is restricted to income taxation. Wage taxes are also assumed to be ruled out.

14 The distribution is normalised so that $\int \int f \, dw \, dh = 1$, or, in the present case of constant h, $\int f \, dw = 1$.

15 Using the fact that $\partial U / \partial \beta = U_C h X$, $\partial U / \partial t = - U_C w L$.

16 This does not seem unreasonable; it is ensured, for example, in the Stone–Geary case. It may be noted that the same problem arises in trying to determine whether R rises or falls with w. It can be shown that the first-order conditions imply that:

$$\int \Omega(w) R(w) f \, dw \leqslant 0$$

but this does not imply that $R' \geqslant 0$.

17 This requires $t < 1$, but the assumptions on the utility function ensure that $\partial \mathcal{L} / \partial t < 0$ for $t \geqslant 1$.

18 There may, of course, be a case for total exemption where both value-added tax and an income tax are in effect.

19 For the United States, see, for example, Aaron [1], Appendix C.

20 The relationship to the second-best results (for example, Green [7]) will be clear. Where $\beta > 0$, there is a further, negative term.

21 The expenditure on X relative to C rises or falls with M as:

$$\frac{b_X}{h(1 - \beta) X_0} \gtrless \frac{b_C}{C_0}$$

22 The argument given here is only heuristic; for a fuller treatment, see Atkinson and Stiglitz [3].

23 This kind of 'second-best' result has an intuitive appeal. The reason why a first-best optimum cannot be attained is because of variations in w (and limited tax instruments); if the utility function is separable in w and other elements, then one should not introduce a distortion between choices in the separable sector.

24 The British income tax system involves a constant marginal tax rate for all but the top few per cent of taxpayers. Under the tax credit proposals it would be extended to a negative income tax with the same marginal tax.

25 This form differs from the British scheme in that the latter embodies a non-linear tax on income, the marginal tax rate falling from 25%, to 17%, to zero.

26 The constancy of t can be seen from (31) and (32) to follow from the independence of M and Ω from h.

27 In the case of the assumption about the distribution, it is not clear whether h would be positively or negatively correlated with m; there are arguments in both directions.

References

[1] Aaron, H. J. (1972), *Shelter and Subsidies*, Washington, DC, The Brookings Institution.
[2] Aaron, H. J. (1973), *Why is Welfare So Hard to Reform?*, Washington, DC, The Brookings Institution.
[3] Atkinson, A. B. and Stiglitz, J. E. (1980), *Lectures on Public Economics*, Maidenhead and New York, McGraw-Hill.
[4] Bossons, J. (1970), 'Value of comprehensive tax base', *Journal of Law and Economics*.
[5] Cullingworth, J. B. (1976), *English Housing Trends*, London, Allen & Unwin.
[6] Engels, F. (no date), *The Housing Question*, Martin Laurence.
[7] Green, H. A. J. (1961), 'The social optimum in the presence of monopoly and taxation', *Review of Economic Studies*, October.
[8] Meacher, M. (1972), *Rate Rebates*, London, Child Poverty Action Group.
[9] Mirrlees, J. A. (1971), 'An exploration in the theory of optimum income taxation', *Review of Economic Studies*, April.
[10] Simons, H. (1938), *Personal Income Taxation*, Chicago, University of Chicago Press.
[11] Steiner, G. (1973), *The State of Welfare*, Washington, DC, The Brookings Institution.
[12] Tobin, J. (1970), 'On limiting the domain of inequality', *Journal of Law and Economics*.
[13] Townsend, P. B. (1973), 'Everyone his own home', *Royal Institute of British Architects Journal*, January.
[14] Welfeld, I. H. (1972), *European Housing Subsidy Systems*, Washington, DC, US Department of Housing and Urban Development.

17 Housing Policy, Taxation and Reform*

Few areas of government activity have so direct an impact on each citizen as housing policy. Housing is a major item in family budgets, and its cost is considerably influenced by the pattern of government assistance through tax relief, direct subsidies, and rebates. The sums involved are large, but government support often appears haphazard or ineffective. As a result, the cost of similar housing varies a great deal from one household to another. For some families, paying for accommodation imposes a heavy burden, and is a major reason for dependence on supplementary benefit; for other families, the tax system means that owner-occupation is a most attractive form of investment. The deprivation on the one hand, and the incentive for over-investment on the other, are both signs that the time is ripe for a re-examination of government policy towards housing assistance.

Housing finance has been a recurrent source of concern in Britain. Successive governments have searched for solutions, but the experience of the Rent Acts of 1957, 1965 and 1974, and of the Housing Finance Act 1972 has not been an especially happy one. It was perhaps for this reason that the *Housing Policy Review of 1977* (HMSO, Cmnd. 6851) rejected any root and branch reform. However, the problems cannot be expected to disappear of their own accord, and are likely to intensify if no action is taken. In our view, the difficulties with the earlier legislation arose to a considerable extent from the enormous variety in the housing circumstances of different families and from the divergent interest of different groups. As we have noted, housing costs differ greatly, and this applies both across and within tenure types. Council rents vary from one local authority to another; rents in the private sector exhibit even greater diversity. The position of owner-occupiers depends very much on when they stepped onto the house price escalator; for some families housing represents a substantial part of their net wealth, for others mortgage repayments absorb a sizeable fraction of their income.

In section 1, we describe in greater detail the diversity of housing circumstances in Britain. We then consider the principles underlying government assistance to housing and the comparison of the cost of accommodation

* Reprinted from the *Midland Bank Review*, 1980.
A. B. Atkinson and M. A. King.

to different tenure groups. This leads into an examination in the last sections of the chapter of possible reforms of the tax treatment of housing and of the system of local authority rents and rent rebates/allowances. In our opinion, it is important to view such reforms in the context of the housing problem as a whole, recognising that there are divergent concerns and interests.

We should stress that there are many aspects of housing policy not covered. Among these are the sale of council houses, rent control and security of tenure. Of particular significance is the level of house-building and the condition of the housing stock. Over the past thirty years, there has been significant progress, but there remain major problems. The *Housing Policy Review* estimated that in 1976 there wers some 1.8 million households in accommodation which was unfit or sub-standard or in overcrowded conditions, and that houses were becoming unfit at a rate of 50,000–70,000 a year. *The National Dwellings and Housing Survey* (HMSO, 1979) showed that in 1977 over 1 million households still lacked an inside WC. Any reform must be considered in relation to the contribution which it can make towards improving the quality of housing – and towards solving the continuing problem of homelessness. We return briefly to this at the end of the chapter.

1 Diversity of Housing Circumstances

The most striking development in housing tenure in Britain since the beginning of the century has been the growth of owner-occupation. Before the First World War about 90% of the housing stock in England and Wales was rented privately. The position in 1977 was that 56% of dwellings were owner-occupied, 31% rented from local authorities, and the remaining 13% were other tenures (principally rented from private landlords). In the absence of any change in policy, the trend towards owner-occupation seems likely to continue.

The popular impression is that owner-occupiers tend to be better-housed, both absolutely and relative to the size of the household, and that they typically have higher incomes. That this is on average true is confirmed by the first part of Table 1. Both average rooms per person and average number of bedrooms were higher for owner-occupiers than for local authority tenants in 1977. The median household income of owner-occupiers was significantly higher than that of tenants, particularly those renting unfurnished from private landlords.

What is less commonly appreciated is the great diversity within each tenure category, and this is illustrated in the second part of Table 1. The proportion with less than two-thirds of the overall median income is higher for tenants, but is still 19% for owner-occupiers. A sizeable minority of owner-occupiers was dependent on supplementary benefit. (At the other extreme, 21% of owner-occupiers had gross household incomes of £150 a week or more in 1977, compared with 8% of local authority tenants.) On average, standards of physical amenities may be higher for owner-occupiers, but overcrowded or sub-standard dwellings are to be found in all sectors. It is therefore highly misleading to think solely in terms of an 'average' owner-occupier or tenant.

Table 1 *Housing circumstances and tenure 1977*

	Average standards			Indications of diversity				
	Average rooms per person	Average number of bedrooms	Median gross normal weekly income of household (£)	% below the bedroom standard*	% lacking one or more basic amenities	% built before 1919	% with less than 2/3 median gross normal weekly income	% receiving supplementary benefit
Owner-occupiers	2.0	2.8	103	3.1	3.8	30.9	19	4
Renting from local authority	1.6	2.4	68	6.8	3.5	4.0	42	22
Renting from private landlord:								
unfurnished	2.0	2.4	55	6.0	21.2	60.8	51 }	18
furnished	1.6	1.6	86	12.4	7.7	63.2	34 }	

* The bedroom standard is used in surveys to illustrate overcrowding and the standard number of bedrooms depends on household composition.
Sources: National Dwellings and Housing Survey (HMSO, 1979), Tables 2, 4, 6, 19; *Family Expenditure Survey*, 1977; Supplementary Benefits Commission, *Annual Report*, 1978.

The same diversity is to be found when we turn to housing costs. The measurement of costs poses a number of problems, and these are discussed in more detail below. Initially we consider simply the cash out-goings in mortgage payments or in rent net of rebates.

In the case of local authority tenants, evidence from the *Family Expenditure Survey* (see *Housing Review*, Technical Volume I, Chapter 4) shows that the median rent first rises with income and then levels off. This pattern is not unexpected, but what is striking is the considerable dispersion around the median within an income group. For people with similar income the rents paid vary substantially. It is not of course suggested that all the variation in outlays reflects variation in the effective price of housing faced by different households, since there will be some association between expenditure and the quality and quantity of housing. If one takes the gross rateable value as a crude indicator of the quantity of housing services, then the cost, after rebates, per unit of rateable value for local authority tenants in 1973–4 had a coefficient of variation (standard deviation divided by the mean) of 0.36, which is not far short of the comparable index of dispersion for *earnings*. On this basis, the variation in unit housing costs appears quite appreciable. Moreover, for those in unfurnished rented accommodation, the coefficient is even higher (0.53). (These calculations are derived from the *Family Expenditure Survey*.)

In the case of council tenants, the dispersion reflects in part the differing *accounting* cost to local authorities of providing accommodation. Rents are governed by the requirement that each authority's housing revenue account should balance. Since interest charges depend on the size and age distribution of the housing stock, rent levels vary in a manner which bears little relationship to the *economic* cost of providing housing. The wide geographical variation in average (unrebated) rent is well known: in April 1976 it was, for example, £3.75 in Ipswich and £4.23 in Stoke, but £6.19 in Portsmouth and £6.50 in Southend. In part the dispersion of housing costs reflects rent rebates and their incomplete take-up. Despite the claim in the *Housing Policy Review* that 'rent rebate schemes ... protect low-income tenants from the full impact of rent increases' (p. 27), official estimates indicate that in October 1976 around 20–25% of those eligible did not receive rebates (*Royal Commission on the Distribution of Income and Wealth, Report No. 6*, p. 96). For private tenants, the take-up of rent allowances was even lower.

In the owner-occupied sector, cash outlays on housing tend to increase more markedly with income, but the dispersion within income ranges is even larger. A major factor is the pattern of mortgage payments by age of owner-occupier. Given the high rates of increase in house prices, the 'front-end loading' problem has become much more serious; and the average payment falls sharply with the occupier's age and with length of residence at present address.

This front-end loading, coupled with other sources of variation, such as that across regions, means that households may have quite different cash outgoings for equivalent accommodation. The age-pattern is similarly exhibited by the household's net wealth. In the early years, the value of the house is offset, or even more than offset, by the mortgage liability, but over time the family acquire equity in the house and it comes to represent a major component of net wealth. For the personal sector as a whole, dwellings have increased from 20% of net wealth in 1960 to nearly 50% in 1976 with borrowing to finance house purchase representing less than 10% of net wealth. This means that total mortgage liabilities amount to about one-fifth of the value of the privately-owned housing stock, a much smaller fraction than is commonly supposed. (*Sources:* J. R. S. Revell, *The Wealth of the Nation*, and Royal Commission on the Distribution of Income and Wealth, Report No. 7.)

2 Housing Costs and Public Policy

The differences in housing costs, both across and within sectors, are much influenced by public policy. By the same token, the financial burden of housing on central and local government – whether directly in the local authority sector or indirectly via tax relief for owner-occupiers – is very considerable. The national accounts record for 1978 direct subsidies from central and local government to housing revenue accounts of £1.6 billion, and current and capital grants to the private sector of £1.4 billion (*National Income and Expenditure*, 1979 edn, Table 9.4). The Inland Revenue estimated that in 1978–9 mortgage interest relief cost £1.1 billion (*Inland Revenue Statistics* 1978, p. 10) and that the relief on capital gains on owner-occupied houses cost £1.5 billion. (The latter figure, given in *The Government's Expenditure Plans 1979–80–1982–3*, Cmnd. 7439, does not allow for roll-over relief, but even allowing this relief the revenue would be substantial if the tax were charged on deemed realisation at death.)

These items, which total around £5½ billion, are not directly comparable; the figures are however sufficient to provide a guide to the magnitudes involved. First, it is clear that the sums are enormous, and it would be surprising if they were not to come under careful scrutiny in the near future. It may help put the amounts in perspective to note that £1 billion is approximately equivalent to a 2p reduction in the basic rate of income tax. Second, the figure which many people have in mind when discussing housing 'subsidies' – the payments to the housing revenue accounts – is large (£1.6 billion), but only one of several large numbers.

To go beyond these figures and to give an assessment of the extent of subsidy to housing is a difficult task. It was no doubt for this reason that the *Housing Policy Review* avoided the question and sheltered behind such negative statements as that 'the interactions in the housing market are so complex that no satisfactory estimate of the effective incidence of subsidies and tax relief has ever been made or probably ever could be made' (p. 16, Technical Volume II). Policy has, however, to be made, and the basis for analysis developed below, albeit crude, appears better than none.

Estimates of housing costs and subsidies have in the past usually been based on a comparison with the private rented sector. In our view this is not a sensible approach in the current state of the housing market. Whatever the future of the private rental sector, the rents paid do not provide a satisfactory foundation for a comparison of housing costs in other sectors. It is necessary to compare directly the position of the two *major* tenure groups – owner-occupiers and local authority tenants.

Our analysis of housing costs is based on three main elements. The first is the concept of a 'target' rate of return on capital invested in housing. The choice of this target is relevant to both the level of investment in housing and the pricing structure (rents in the local authority sector and tax relief for owner-occupiers). The second element concerns the relative treatment of different tenures, an issue which is relevant to both equity and allocational considerations (since it will influence decisions about choice of tenure). The third is the relationship between housing costs and income, and the design of forms of assistance to help low income families to meet high housing costs. We discuss these elements in turn.

3   The Return to Investment in Housing

In analysing housing finance in terms of the return to capital invested, we are not suggesting that housing should yield a market return. There are a number of important reasons why the target rate of return should be set at a low level: for example, because of the effect of bad housing conditions on health and educational attainment. Many would agree with the Governor of the Bank of England that 'preferential treatment of housing is justified as a matter of social priority' (Bank of England, *Quarterly Bulletin*, June 1978). The point that we are making is that the target rate of return is a social decision, and in this decision is implicit the extent of subsidy to housing as a whole.

We shall apply the concept first to the local authority sector. A significant fraction of the nation's capital stock is invested in local authority housing. At the end of 1978 the value of this stock of dwellings at current replacement cost was £58.7 billion (*National Income and Expenditure 1979*, Table 11.11). This represented 38% of the total stock of housing of £153.9 billion. More significantly, local authority housing accounted for 46% of the total fixed assets of central and local government and 12% of the total fixed capital stock of the country. Even these figures omit the value of land on which the stock of housing is built.

Table 2 shows the rates of return which have been earned on local authority housing over the last ten years. The first line gives the gross rate of return before depreciation on the stock itself, and the second line the rate of return net of capital consumption, management costs, and repairs and maintenance. These figures are, however, incomplete in two respects. First, the capital base excludes the value of land and we have made an approximate adjustment for this. Secondly, the figures take no account of any real capital gains accruing on the housing stock. An assumed real capital gain of 1% per annum (based on the experience of the post-war period, with an allowance for quality change) is incorporated in the estimates shown in the third line of Table 2. It can be seen that, on these assumptions, the real rate of return on the local authority housing stock was 2.8% per annum in the late 1960s and early 1970s before falling in 1974–5 to around 2%. Over the period as a whole it averaged $2\frac{1}{2}$%. In these calculations, we ignore rent rebates in view of their income maintenance

Table 2   *Rate of return on local authority dwellings (%)*

	1968	1969	1970	1971	1972	1973	1974	1975	1976	197~	1978
Gross return	4.09	4.17	4.25	4.14	4.19	4.26	3.50	3.05	3.08	3.26	3.22
Return net of capital consumption and management costs	2.34	2.44	2.50	2.40	2.44	2.43	1.63	1.25	1.29	1.47	1.45
Net return allowing for land and capital gains	2.76	2.83	2.88	2.80	2.83	2.82	2.22	1.94	1.97	2.10	2.09

Sources: National Income and Expenditure, 1979, Tables 8.3, 11.9, 11.11, and 1978, Table 11.11.
Notes:
(1) In lines 1 and 2 the capital base excludes land and the return excludes capital gains (see text). In line 3 the base includes an approximate a▢ t ment for land and allows for real capital gains of 1% pa.
(2) Management costs relevant to the running of the local authority housing stock have been assumed to be 0.2% of the value of the stock, ar▢ ⁻ pairs and maintenance (in addition to the estimate of capital consumption) to be 0.3% of the stock.

function. In fact, if the rate of return is calculated net of rebates, the values shown in the last row of Table 2 would be little changed in the earlier years but reduced by some 0.5% in 1976–8.

The estimates of the rate of return shown in Table 2 are based on a number of strong assumptions, and must be treated with considerable caution; none the less, we feel that they provide at least a starting point for the analysis. As may be seen, the return is significantly lower than in other sectors of the economy. For example, between 1974 and 1978 the average real rate of return earned by industrial and commercial companies was 4.1% (Bank of England, *Quarterly Bulletin*, June 1979), and this was substantially below the rates of return of about 9% during the late 1960s and early 1970s. There is, however, no reason why housing should yield a comparable return. Even ignoring social considerations, housing is a very secure investment; and, as we have argued, there are likely to be strong social arguments for setting a relatively low rate of return.

The choice of the target rate of return may be seen as determining the extent to which housing is 'subsidised' relative to other forms of investment. A change in the target implies a change in the level of housing costs to the occupier. In the case of local authority rents (we turn to the position of owner-occupiers below), if the target rate of return had been 3% rather than the 2.09% achieved in 1978, it would have been necessary to increase rents on average by 38% (rents do not increase in proportion to the target rate of return because of the role of management and maintenance costs and of real capital gains). With a target rate of return of 4%, the level of rents would have to have been some 79% higher on average.

In considering the socially desired rate of return, it may be helpful to relate the level of rents to average earnings. In the mid-1970s rents averaged around 7% of gross average earnings. For a family occupying a house worth $3\frac{1}{2}$ times its gross earnings, this ratio corresponds to a real return of about 2% – roughly that achieved in recent years. If the target return were raised to 3%, this would imply a rise in housing costs from 7% to nearly 10% of gross earnings. On average, families would have to find another 4% of their disposable income to pay the rent.

4   The Position of Owner-Occupiers

The target rate of return is the first parameter of housing subsidy policy; the second key element concerns the relative treatment of local authority tenants and owner-occupiers. For the owner-occupier his house both provides housing services and forms an attractive asset in his portfolio. Since 1963 owner-occupiers have paid no tax on the imputed rental income of their property, and no capital gains tax is charged on the increase in the value of the house. But mortgage interest payments are tax deductible up to the permitted ceiling. At the same time the capital held in the form of equity in the house could be invested by the home owner in alternative assets which would yield some rate of return.

Thus the true cost of housing services (excluding depreciation and repairs) to the owner-occupiers is the sum of the income which he sacrifices by investing in his house rather than in alternative assets (the 'opportunity cost') and the mortgage interest he actually pays minus the (tax-free) capital gain that he enjoys on the investment in his house. The cost of housing services to owner-occupiers depends on the interaction between these three elements. On the other hand had he been living in a local authority house of the same market value, he would have been paying a rent which can be expressed as the rate of return actually earned on local authority housing. For owner-occupiers and tenants to pay the same amounts for equivalent accommodation the rate of return on local authority housing must be equal to the capital costs (net of capital gains) paid by owner-occupiers. The argument is set out in terms of algebra below:

Consider an owner-occupier in a house with market value V and an outstanding mortgage liability M. Let the annual rate of increase of house prices be denoted by π, his marginal tax rate by t, and the mortgage interest rate by r. Suppose the opportunity cost of the capital held in the form of equity in the house is $R(1-t)\%$ after tax. Then the true capital cost of housing services (i.e. excluding depreciation, repairs and rates) is given (in real terms) by:

$$R(1-t)(V-M) + r(1-t)M - \pi V \qquad (1)$$

This may be compared with the target real return on a comparable investment in the local authority sector of ρV. The cost is greater to the owner-occupier than to the local authority tenant if:

$$(1-t)\left[\left(\frac{V-M}{V}\right)R + \left(\frac{M}{V}\right)r\right] - \pi > \rho \qquad (2)$$

This analysis shows the complex set of factors which influence relative housing costs. In order to compare the position of owner-occupiers with that of local authority tenants, we need – even in this highly simplified framework – to make assumptions about the tax rate of owner-occupiers, the size of the mortgage, the rate of increase of house prices, the mortgage interest rate and the opportunity cost of the house-owner's equity. In addition, we need to know the target rate of return on investment in local authority housing. To illustrate the results we show in Table 3 a range of cases, but assuming throughout a mortgage interest rate of 12% and an average annual rate of increase of house prices of 8%. In these calculations we are concerned with plausible long-run values. These are obviously hard to guess: the values we have taken imply a 'real' interest rate of 4%, which appears high in relation to the experience of the 1970s and tends to overstate the true costs of owner-occupation.

If we compare the numbers on cases A and B in Table 3 (where the mortgage is below the £25,000 ceiling) with the last row of Table 2, it can be seen that the calculated housing costs are typically lower for owner-occupiers who pay tax than they are for local authority tenants. In fact, for owner-occupiers paying a marginal tax rate of 40% or more, and with an opportunity cost less than 12%,

Table 3　*Capital costs of owner-occupiers (per cent per annum) – illustrative calculations*

	Marginal tax rate of owner-occupier (per cent)				
	25	30	40	50	60
A Mortgage 80% of value of house					
Opportunity cost of owner's equity:					
9%	0.55	−0.02	−1.16	−2.30	−3.44
12%	1.00	0.40	−0.80	−2.00	−3.20
15%	1.45	0.82	−0.44	−1.70	−2.96
B Mortgage 20% of value of house					
Opportunity cost of owner's equity:					
9%	−0.80	−1.28	−2.24	−3.20	−4.16
12%	1.00	0.40	−0.80	−2.00	−3.20
15%	2.80	2.08	0.64	−0.80	−2.24
C Mortgage above ceiling					
Marginal cost with 50% mortgage finance					
Opportunity cost of owner's equity:					
9%	1.4	1.2	0.7	0.3	−0.2
12%	2.5	2.2	1.6	1.0	0.4
15%	3.6	3.3	2.5	1.8	1.0

Note: Mortgage interest rate assumed to be 12%, and the rate of increase of house prices to be 8%, p.a. Cases A and B assume mortgage below £25,000 ceiling.

housing has a negative capital cost; the only positive costs are those associated with depreciation, repairs and rates. For basic rate taxpayers, the capital cost only reaches 2% when the opportunity cost approaches 15%. In case C we have shown the effect of the £25,000 mortgage ceiling on the *marginal* cost, where an additional housing investment, half mortgage-financed, is being considered. The cost is now positive in most cases, but less than 2% where the opportunity cost is less than $11\frac{1}{2}$% and the tax rate is 30% or higher.

The relative cost of housing for owner-occupiers is sensitive to the assumptions made concerning the rate of inflation and the mortgage interest rate – a feature of which politicians are only too aware. On the other hand, a long-term mortgage rate of 15% does not raise the capital cost to owner-occupiers on the basic rate of tax above 2.5%, even when they have no equity stake, unless house prices rise on average by less than 8% per annum. High money interest rates do of course lead to cash flow difficulties – the 'front-end loading' problem – particularly for those with a low equity stake in their house. This may in turn be a serious deterrent for would-be owner-occupiers. These difficulties have received a great deal of attention and bring out the need for measures to change the timepath of payments; they should not, however, be taken as representing the generality of experience of owner-occupiers.nor as indicative of the effect of inflation on the long-term cost of housing. A rise in the rate of inflation, accompanied by a rise in money interest rates, so that real interest rates are unchanged, does in fact lower the capital cost of housing, since it is *nominal* interest payments that are tax deductible. Suppose that the mortgage rate is equal to the rate of inflation plus 3%, and that house prices rise 1% faster than the rate of inflation. Then if the rate of inflation increases from 7% to 12%, the capital cost, with 100% mortgage, would be reduced by $1\frac{1}{2}$% per annum for a basic rate taxpayer. One consequence of the high rates of inflation which have characterised the 1970s is that the capital cost to owner-occupiers has fallen significantly.

These calculations are only inteded to be illustrative; they do how-ever provide some insight into the determinants of housing costs and subsidies in the local authority and owner-occupied sectors. (A similar analysis can be applied to private sector tenants, taking account of the tax treatments of landlords, but space does not allow us to discuss this aspect here.) To the extent that owner-occupiers face a higher (or lower) capital cost than the socially determined target rate of return, they are enjoying less (more) subsidy than local authority tenants. The analysis also highlights some of the factors responsible for variation in costs of accommodation within the owner-occupied sector. To the extent that the cost of housing varies with the tax rate, with the size of the mortgage, and with the opportunity cost of investment, this means that different groups of owner-occupiers may fare quite differently. The calculations confirm the picture of diversity described earlier.

In making a full comparison of the costs in the two sectors, there are a number of other factors which should be taken into account. We have not, for instance, included the transaction costs associated with moving house. We have estimated that in 1975 the average transaction costs for an owner-occupier, moving from one house to another costing 25% more, amounted to some 6% of the price of the new house. This is a substantial addition to the housing costs of a family which moves regularly (perhaps for career reasons). Since many owner-occupiers move only infrequently, transaction costs are a further factor causing diversity. (We do not wish to go into the legal and institutional arrangements for the transfer of housing, but it should not be beyond the wit of man – though apparently of the Royal Commission on Legal Services – to devise a less expensive process for buying and selling homes. In particular, we see little justification for the continuation of Stamp Duty on the transfer of housing.)

The transaction costs of owner-occupiers must be compared with those faced by local authority tenants, who, if they wish to move from one area to another, must either participate in an exchange with a family moving in the opposite direction or join the waiting list. Since it is not obvious that the number, or composition, of families wishing to move from Barnsley to Brighton, for example, will be exactly matched by those trying to move the other way, it may be necessary for a household to spend some time in private rental accommodation, if it can be found. In 1973 the average cost of housing in the furnished rental sector was twice that of local authority housing, so that it is not clear that on average transaction costs would be lower for tenants (and the variation is probably higher).

5 Housing Costs and Income

The third key element in analysing the impact of government policy is the variation of housing costs with income. We have seen (Table 3) that for owner-occupiers the capital cost falls quite markedly with the marginal tax rate, and hence with income. In contrast, in the case of rented accommodation, the scheme of rent rebates and allowances is designed to reduce housing costs for those with low incomes. Families qualifying for rebates, and who claim, face a marginal cost of housing (i.e. the cost of additional housing services) equal to 40% of the unrebated rent. For those whose income is higher, and for those who do not claim, the marginal cost is 100% of the unrebated rent. With rented accommodation, therefore, the marginal cost of housing rises with income – the reverse of the situation for owner-occupiers.

Rent rebates have been only partially successful on account of the problem of incomplete take-up described earlier; moreover, they aggravate very considerably the 'poverty trap', which means that it is extremely difficult for low-paid employees significantly to increase their net income by increasing their gross earnings. To illustrate this, we show in Table 4 the net weekly income of a household consisting of a married man with a non-employed wife and two children, at different levels of gross earnings. Even though we ignore all means-tested benefits other than Family Income Supplement and rent and rate rebates (there are over forty other benefits), the predicament facing the low paid is clear to see. Consider a mean earning £50 a week. In order for him to raise his family's net income by £5 a week, he would have to increase his gross

Table 4   *Net weekly household income at various earnings levels, January 1980 (£ per week)*[1]

Earnings	50.00	55.00	60.00	65.00	70.00	75.00	80.00	85.00	90.00
Less tax	3.81	5.31	6.81	8.31	9.81	11.31	12.81	14.31	15.81
national insurance	3.25	3.58	3.90	4.23	4.55	4.88	5.20	5.53	5.85
Take home pay	42.94	46.11	49.29	52.46	55.64	58.81	61.99	65.16	68.34
Add Child benefit	8.00	8.00	8.00	8.00	8.00	8.00	8.00	8.00	8.00
FIS[2]	5.25	2.75	0.25	0	0	0	0	0	0
Rate rebate	1.72	1.52	1.36	1.08	0.78	0.48	0.18	0	0
Rent rebate	4.58	3.95	3.51	2.70	1.85	1.00	0.15[3]	0	0
Net income	62.49	62.33	62.41	64.24	66.27	68.29	70.32	73.16	76.34
Implicit marginal tax rate[4] (%)	98.6	103.0	98.4	63.4	59.5	59.5	59.5	43.2	36.5
Approximate % of male earners in earnings range[5]	1½	4	5	5	7	7	7½	7	7

Notes:
[1] Household consists of a married man with non-working wife and two children aged twelve and fourteen and pays rent of £6.50 and rates of £2.50.
[2] Because Family Income Supplement (FIS) is included in relevant income, the addition to the effective tax rate resulting from rebates is reduced by one-half when a family is entitled to FIS.
[3] Would not be paid because it is below the minimum figure of 20p for rent rebates.
[4] Calculated over the £5 ranges below.
[5] In range £50.00–£54.99, etc.
Source: Kay, J. A. and King, M. A., *The British Tax System* (2nd edn), and own calculations.

earnings to over £73 a week. He must find the stronger incentives to effort allegedly afforded by the recent tax cuts a remote, not to say academic, proposition.

The implicit marginal tax rate faced by our hypothetical earner is shown in the penultimate row of Table 4. The rates are close to 100% for part of the range (indeed exceed 100% at £55 per week) which is just another way of saying that it is impossible over a wide band of earnings significantly to improve one's lot by working harder or changing to a more highly paid job.

Of course, these high implicit tax rates are the result of the combined effect of income tax and means-tested benefits, and cannot be blamed on any one benefit. Nevertheless, rent and rate rebates play a significant role at the levels likely to be relevant to many male workers (see the last row in Table 4). The effect of rent and rate rebates together is to add 23 points to the effective tax rate at earnings levels where relevant 'income' is above a household's 'needs allowance' (33 points where income is below the needs allowance), which for our hypothetical family is £60.95.

One aspect of the poverty trap not illustrated by Table 4 is that – despite a cut in the basic rate of tax in June 1979 – the implicit tax rates on the low paid rose. This is due in no little measure to the change in rent and rate rebates made in November 1979. A new £5 earnings disregard for husbands was introduced to help reduce disincentives for those on low incomes to remain in work, and to restore the real value of rebates for earners (though not pensioners) to that set when the national rebate scheme was introduced in 1972. While it is true that the change did increase the relative attractiveness of employment, it also increased the marginal tax rates of many in work. In fact it is only when entitlement to rent and rate rebates is exhausted that the marginal tax rate on earnings falls below 59.5%; this figure represents the combined effect of income tax, national insurance contributions, and rent and rate rebates. The percentage is strikingly close to the top income tax rate on earnings, and is presumably also worthy of the chancellor's attention.

Just as the tax system impinges on the housing decisions of owner-occupiers, so too the rent rebate schemes operate like an implicit income tax. Both indicate the needs for a reconsideration of the way in which housing subsidies are related to income.

6 Proposals for Reform

We have argued that there are three key elements in determining policy towards housing subsidies: the target rate of return, the relative treatment of different tenures, and the variation of housing costs with income. These govern the degree of subsidy to housing as a whole, relative to other forms of investment, and influence the distribution of the subsidy according to housing circumstances. We now examine how these three elements are likely to be affected by proposals for the reform of housing finance.

In our analysis, we considered first local authority housing and the return on capital in that sector; we then compared this with the capital costs of owner-occupiers. In discussing possible reforms, we reverse the procedure. We examine first proposals to change the tax treatment of owner-occupied housing, and then go on to the level of rents and the role of rent subsidies. Although we treat the two aspects – tax policy and rents – separately, we have tried to emphasise the way in which they are interdependent. In the past, these two areas of reform have typically been viewed in isolation. Both Conservative and Labour governments have been most concerned with the level of council rents; their critics have often concentrated on the tax relief to owner-occupiers. In our view, these two major sectors must be seen in conjunction, and any reform should be based on a systematic treatment of the degree of subsidy in both sectors. Moreover, there are signs that the time is ripe for such a concerted policy – with the present Treasury ministers being aware that there is scope for cutting tax rates via a reduction in tax reliefs as well as via a reduction in public spending.

The analysis of changes in housing policy is complex, and we shall not be able to provide an exhaustive treatment. As we have seen, different households are in very different circumstances, and they will be affected in very different ways. The removal of tax relief for mortgage interest, for example, would have different implications for the family who bought ten years ago than for the young married couple who bought at the top of the recent house price boom. The impact on local authority tenants of changes in the principles governing rents will depend on the previous policies pursued by the particular council, and on whether or not they were claiming rebates.

The analysis is further complicated by the fact that changes in policy may be capitalised in house prices. If tax relief is removed, this may cause house prices to drop. The extent of such capitalisation is difficult to predict, but the analysis requires that assumptions be made regarding the reaction of house prices. (Much of the discussion of housing policy in the past has been based on the assumption of no capitalisation.) A decline in house prices would, for example, lead to a fall in the level of rents implied by any given target rate of return in the local authority sector. This illustrates the point made above concerning the inter-relations between different elements of housing policy.

7   Tax Treatment of Owner-Occupied Housing

Ideally, reform of the tax treatment of housing would be based on an appeal to a fully articulated set of principles. Unfortunately, theoretical principles have played little role in the evolution of the British tax system; and this means that it is extremely difficult to propose a systematic plan for reforming the treatment of housing which is consonant with all other aspects of taxation. For example, the fact that existing taxation is neither consistently on an income basis nor consistently on an expenditure basis implies that it is hard to appeal to considerations of comparability with other areas. Any reform of the tax treatment of housing alone is likely to eliminate some inconsistencies at the expense of creating others. Our primary focus will not, therefore, be on discussing reforms in terms of their coherence with the tax treatment of other forms of income; rather we shall seek to identify those features which have the most significant impact on the cost of housing.

Our analysis of the capital costs of owner-occupiers indicated two aspects which warrant special attention. The first is that the cost of housing to owner-occupiers is a declining function of their marginal tax rate. There appears to be no strong justification for this situation, which increases the incentive for high income families to invest in housing, and which runs counter to that obtaining in the rented sector. The second is that the cost of capital is a declining function of the rate of inflation, for any given level of real interest rates. Both of these considerations stem from the fact that the imputed rental income from housing is tax-free, whereas mortgage interest is tax-deductible (in nominal terms). This brings us to the two main reforms which have been proposed for the tax treatment of housing: the taxation of imputed income and the abolition of mortgage interest relief. We consider these in turn.

The introduction of a tax on the imputed income of owner-occupiers is widely regarded as both impracticable and politically unfeasible. The latter is a question of political judgement, and depends on whether governments are going to continue to regard owner-occupiers as 'sacred cows'. The former is far from being self-evident. A tax on imputed income was levied under the old Schedule A. This was abandoned in 1963, but the decision was based in large part on political grounds. It should be noted that the Royal Commission on the Taxation of Profits and Income had concluded in 1955 that the tax on imputed income was quite justified and recommended its continuance. Similar taxes are levied in other European countries. The method of administration of a new tax on imputed income would probably differ from that under the old Schedule A; we envisage that it would be levied on capital values as proposed for the rating system by the Layfield Committee. Given that the valuation for rating purposes has been postponed, it would be difficult to bring in the tax at all speedily, and we return below to the problems of the transition, but once the capital assessments have been made the introduction of a tax on imputed income does not appear an administrative impossibility.

The tax on imputed income is here being considered, not as a means of securing horizontal equity with other forms of income, but in relation to the capital costs of housing. From our earlier analysis it may be seen that, given that capital gains are not taxed and that nominal interest payments are deductible, the appropriate imputed rent would be based on the money rather than the real return. If the opportunity cost of capital were equal to the mortgage interest rate, then this would be equivalent to taxing the equity element alone, and it would mean that the cost of housing was independent of both the individual tax rates and the rate of inflation.[1] It should be noted that the tax deductibility of mortgage interest would be retained, so that a person with no equity (a mortgage equal to the value of the house) would have no net tax liability.

With the kind of money rates of return which have applied in recent years, the tax charge on imputed income on this basis would be quite considerable. A return of 12%, for example, would imply for a basic rate tax payer with a house valued at £20,000 an additional tax payment of £13.85 a week. The revenue would be correspondingly large, and would allow a sizeable reduction in the rates of income taxation or a sizeable increase in the tax threshold. The fact that the amounts are so big is a reflection of the sensitivity of the tax system to high rates of inflation because of the failure to adopt indexation.

The figures for imputed rents may seem very high; this may well be because they have been thinking in terms of *real* rates of return. If the tax system were to be indexed, then the imputed rental income for tax purposes would indeed be much less. But the deduction for mortgage interest would also be much smaller, since only real interest payments would be tax-deductible. Unfortunately, such a position is simply incompatible with the tax treatment of interest elsewhere in the system. In recent years, real interest rates have been negative, and when this is the case, deduction of mortgage interest at its *real* rate would be less favourable than no deduction at all. If the payment of interest for house purchase were indexed for tax purposes, borrowers would desert building societies and borrow elsewhere on a non-deductible basis. Without a comprehensive tax reform, this does not seem a possible route to follow.[2]

It may also be argued that local authority rates, particularly if converted to a capital value basis, are equivalent to the taxation of imputed rental income. However, this ignores the fact that rates are levied on both owner-occupiers and tenants. Moreover, if rates are viewed as a tax on housing – rather than as a subscription for locally provided services – we would prefer to regard them as a substitute for VAT (which is not levied on housing services). In 1978 the level of domestic rates was roughly equivalent to a 22% rate of VAT on housing expenditure as recorded in the national accounts. But since recorded housing expenditure does not measure the factor cost of housing (because of subsidies), the calculation is misleading. Making a very approximate adjustment, we estimate that rates are broadly equivalent to the standard rate of VAT (15%).

The effect of the introduction of the tax on imputed rental income would depend on the extent to which the exemption had been capitalised and the speed with which capital values reacted. Suppose that the opportunity cost of capital is equal to the mortgage interest rate of 12% and that house prices rise at 8% per annum. For a basic rate taxpayer, the effect of the tax on imputed income is to raise the capital cost from 0.4%–4%; i.e. from £80 a year to £800 for a house valued at £20,000. If the capital value were to fall to, say, £16,000, then the capital cost would be £640 rather than £800 a year. All existing owners would suffer a capital loss, but new entrants would face a smaller increase in annual housing costs. The unbalanced timepath of payments associated with the front-end loading problem would be moderated.

A tax on imputed rental income would represent a substantial departure. The necessary adjustment of expectations could however be greatly eased by a phased introduction. There is indeed much to be said for announcing in advance the decision to bring in the new charge, in which case the delay in carrying out the capital valuation may not be a handicap. There would be an immediate effect on house prices, but the impact on cash-flow would be smoothed.

The second proposal for the reform of the tax treatment of housing is the alternative of reducing or eliminating mortgage interest relief. Two possibilities suggest themselves, both having certain administrative and legislative attractions. The first is simply to maintain the £25,000 ceiling in money terms and allow it to fall in real terms. This would probably be the easier step to take, and would, if inflation persists, lead in the limit to the complete withdrawal of interest relief. The second is to restrict the relief to a common rate of tax, possibly (but not necessarily) the basic rate. This would allow interest to be paid net of tax – as with life insurance premia – and permit considerable simplification in the operation of both tax relief and option mortgage subsidies. Moreover, the rate at which relief was given could be varied easily, thereby offering an alternative route to the phasing out of tax relief.

The effect of these changes may be analysed in terms of the impact on the marginal and average cost of housing. If at the margin housing is financed by borrowing, then with the withdrawal of interest relief the cost would become independent of the tax rate, and the outcome would be the same as with a tax on imputed income. On the other hand, where the owner has an equity stake in his house, he would continue to enjoy tax relief. The average cost of housing would still therefore fall with the tax rate and with the rate of inflation.

As with the tax on imputed rental income, it is important to consider the impact of interest relief on capital values. The Building EDC suggested that 'if tax relief was withdrawn, only mortgagors would be affected' (*Housing for All*, HMSO), but this ignores the possible capitalisation effect. If house prices fall, then existing owners suffer a capital loss, irrespective of their mortgage position.

Both tax reforms we have considered would increase the cost of housing to owner-occupiers as a class; this in turn raises the question of the relative treatment of owner-occupiers and tenants, which is the subject of section 8. The tax changes would also have rather different effects on different social groups, and we may for this reason want to make accompanying changes to the provisions for income maintenance, e.g. to reduce the net burden on pensioner households. We come back to this in section 9.

8 Rents and Housing Allowances

The tax changes discussed above would raise the cost of housing to owner-occupiers overall; and we need therefore to consider the position *vis-à-vis* other sectors. As we have stressed, one must view the housing market as a whole. It does not, however, follow that rents should necessarily be raised, since it is possible that the cost of housing would still be lower for owner-occupiers than for tenants. In the example taken for illustrative purposes, with the mortgage interest rate and the opportunity cost of capital equal to 12% and the annual rate of increase of house prices equal to 8%, the capital cost did indeed rise to 4% with the introduction of the tax on imputed income (or the withdrawal of mortgage interest relief with 100% mortgage finance). The capital cost would be the money interest rate minus the rate of increase in house prices. On the other hand, we noted that in recent years this 'real' mortgage rate has been close to zero or negative; so that the example was in this sense misleading.

During the 1970s, the Building Societies Association's recommended mortgage interest rate ranged between 8–12% and the average rate actually paid was 10%. Over the decade, retail prices rose on average by 12% per annum and house prices by some 14%. Therefore even with the increased taxation, the real mortgage cost seems likely to have been less than the overall rate of return on the local authority housing stock indicated in Table 2 (even allowing for the qualifications concerning these estimates). Allowance must be made for the opportunity cost of the owner-occupier's equity, and the diversity of capital cost which that introduces. On the other hand, the conclusion would be reinforced when one allows for the possible capitalisation of tax changes. A fall in the value of the local authority housing stock would impose a capital loss on the public sector, but would mean that a given level of rents would generate a higher rate of return on capital.

It is not therefore immediately apparent that the fiscal reforms we have been considering imply that there should be a corresponding increase in the target rate of return on local authority housing. The real return in the public sector, as estimated for recent years, may be quite high relative to that in the owner-occupied sector even with a tax on imputed rental income. (The divergences which this implies between different rates of return are a reflection of the institutional rigidities of the capital market, as well as such tax-induced distortions as would remain.)

The overall level of rents is not however the only issue, and we have emphasised the great variation that exists in unit housing costs within the local authority sector (and even more in the private rented sector). One of the aims of policy must be to bring about a more systematic relationship between rents and housing services. A national rent pool for local authorities is an idea which was rejected in the Housing Policy Review but which in the context of the overall reform of policy considered here seems worthy of further consideration. A scheme of this kind would extend nationally the pooling in the existing housing revenue account system. It may not be thought desirable, or practicable, to offset all sources of variation across authorities, but differences such as those associated with the age of the housing stock could be evened out. At the same time, we must recognise that such measures are likely to take time and that certain forms of variation in unit housing cost are likely to remain. This brings us to the subject of housing allowances.

Earlier we argued that the present rent rebate scheme fails to reach a substantial fraction of those entitled and that it now contributes significantly to the high marginal tax rates faced by wage-earners. In view of this, there are strong grounds for rejecting the means-testing approach, so we shall go on to consider housing allowance schemes which are not income-related.

Some proposals for a housing allowance would reject both means-testing and the view that the allowance should be related to housing costs. In this form, the allowance would be based on family composition, and other indicators of need (e.g. disability), but not on housing costs. As such, the allowance is more properly seen as a reform of the income maintenance system, a reform which may in itself be desirable but which does not deal with the problem of variations in rents.

In our view, it is of the essence of a housing allowance scheme that it should include an element related to housing costs. The precise form of this relationship is more debatable. Housing outlays may vary because of the quantity of housing services (over which the family may have limited control) or because of the cost per unit. The latter in turn may vary because of differences in capital costs (e.g. regional variations in house prices) or because of the way in which rents are related to capital values. Depending on the view taken, the relevant housing element could be defined as actual rent or in terms of an appropriately defined index of the cost of a specific minimum of housing services. The formula would presumably be a percentage of the housing element in excess of a prescribed level and subject to an overall maximum.

There is not space to discuss in detail the working of the housing allowance scheme. We envisage that it would be operated by local authorities in conjunction with national rent pooling. It may be objected, as in the Housing Policy Review, that it is unreasonable to expect local authority tenants, rather than the community as a whole, to bear the cost of helping those with high housing costs. However, it follows from the logic of our treatment that it is the overall level of rents *net* of the housing allowance which would be determined by the target rate of return. This illustrates once again the need to see housing policy as a whole.

9   Concluding Comments

The proposals discussed above would mean significant changes in the tax treatment of owner-occupiers and in the system of determining local authority rents. The aim would be to reduce the dispersion of housing costs both within and between different categories of tenure. As we have argued, housing costs vary with income in a manner which has no clear rationale, and the proposals would lead to a more systematic allocation of whatever level of subsidy it is felt should be given to housing as a whole. The serious impact of inflation on housing finance in the context of an un-indexed tax system would be reduced.

A main theme of this chapter has been that reform of housing finance will be successful only if the problem is viewed as a whole, and a consistent set of principles applied to each major sector. We have examined ways in which this might be achieved. Equally, the prospects of general agreement on the implementation of reforms would be much enhanced by explaining the need for change as part of an overall policy, and not as a series of unrelated actions affecting particular forms of tenure.

Even so, the magnitude of the change in policy required may make pause even those who feel that a reform of housing finance is long overdue. There are several reasons for proceeding cautiously, and we have emphasised the need for a gradual transition. First, the diversity of circumstances means that within tenure categories different groups of occupiers may be affected rather differently. The proposals would therefore have to be accompanied by measures to ease the burden on certain of those adversely affected: for example, a rise in the tax threshold and age exemption could reduce the number of pensioners liable to the tax on imputed rental income. The very substantial revenue – several billions – which could be raised by the tax changes would enable the government both to do this and to cut the rates of personal taxation if it so wished. The sheer size of the revenue should indeed be emphasised, since the higher benefits and lower taxes which could be financed would be the *quid pro quo* for the rise in housing costs.

Secondly, we have stressed the difficulties in piecemeal reform of the tax system. We have viewed the issues in terms of the impact on housing costs, but we appreciate that the proposals would intensify other problems. The favourable tax treatment of owner-occupation would be eliminated, but the position of other privileged assets, such as pension schemes, would remain unchanged. Such anomalies are bound to arise unless a more coherent approach is adopted to personal taxation as a whole.

Thirdly, we have to consider the effect on the level of investment in new and improved housing, given the priority attached to dealing with the problems of sub-standard housing and homelessness. Some investment would undoubtedly be deterred. Indeed one of the starting points of the analysis was the incentive for those with high tax rates to over-invest in owner-occupied housing; hence there may be less spent by the well-off (who are already typically well-housed). On the other hand, access to owner-occupation could be eased for those on lower incomes. To the extent that tax changes are capitalised in reduced house prices, this might enable some would-be buyers, currently unable to obtain a sufficiently large mortgage, to embark on house purchase. Moreover, as the demand for housing would be less dominated by the investment motive, construction would come to reflect more accurately people's desired consumption of housing. In other words, even if the level is reduced, it is quite conceivable that the *pattern* of investment would be more attuned to social priorities.

Finally, there will be those who dismiss the proposals discussed here as unrealistic. To them we would reply that it is no less unrealistic to suppose that one can reasonably continue with a system of housing finance which is greatly distorted by taxation and inflation and which leads both to patent inequities and to a bizarre pattern of incentives.

Notes

1 In terms of the algebra p. 345, taxing an imputed return of R, where this is equal to r, would add
   tRV to the cost (equation (1)). The cost then becomes $(R - \pi)V$, which is independent of t and of
   variations in the rate of inflation which leave $(R - \pi)$ unchanged. Where R is not equal to r, the
   cost varies with the tax rate, to a less marked extent, but it is still independent of the rate of
   inflation.
2 An alternative reform would be to levy a tax directly on the owner's equity stake in the house
   calculated at some real interest rate, but it does not ensure that housing costs are independent of
   the rate of inflation.

18 The Income Tax Treatment of Charitable Contributions*

Introduction

One of the many areas in which Vickrey has been a pioneer is that of the economics of charitable contributions. His essay 'One economist's view of philanthropy' [19] presented, among other things, an analysis of the motives for charity, and a critique of the tax treatment of contributions. The conclusion he drew was that the 'haphazard array of subsidies that result from present special tax privileges call for replacement with more uniform and explicit' arrangements' (p. 56). One particular recommendation for reform which he had made fifteen years earlier [18] was that the deductibility of contributions under the United States personal income tax should be replaced by a flat-rate tax credit (p. 131), a proposal which has received widespread attention (see, for example, Andrews [1], McDaniel [10], Pechman [12], and Surrey [16]). The aim of this chapter is to describe a simple theoretical model of contributions to charity. This embodies some of the insights contained in Vickrey [19] and pays particular attention to the redistributive consequences of philanthropy. The model provides in turn a framework for examining the income tax treatment of contributions, and whether tax deductibility should be replaced by a proportional tax credit as Vickrey proposed.

1 Redistribution and the Motives for Charitable Contributions

There are many motives for charitable contributions, and this is reflected in the wide variety of types of charities. People give to support religious institutions, to provide educational or medical facilities, to encourage cultural and scientific activities, or to help disadvantaged groups. These forms of charity may have quite different distributional consequences, and indeed Vickrey [19] has argued that in many cases the redistributive impact of philanthropy may be relatively slight. In what follows we consider two rather different views of the motives for contributions and their role in redistribution. The first is that individuals give to charity solely on account of the utility associated with the act of giving. They are not concerned with the end use of the funds, although it

* Reprinted by permission of the publisher from *Public and Urban Economics* (1976), Ronald E. Grieson (ed.), Lexington, Mass., Lexington Books, D. C. Heath & Co.

may be the case that some part performs a redistributive function. At the other extreme is the view that charitable activity is purely redistributive. Individuals give because they are concerned about the welfare of disadvantaged groups.

In the model described here, this is formalised as follows: There are two groups in society, the first is the working population, who consume X, spend a fraction L of the day working, and make charitable contributions G. They are assumed to have identical utility functions, but differ in the wage rate they can earn (w), and this is continuously distributed with density $f(w)$ and $w \geqslant \underline{w}$ where $\int_{\underline{w}}^{\infty} f dw = (1 - \mu)$. The second group has zero earning power, and is reliant on state financial provision and on private contributions. A proportion μ of the population is in this group, which is denoted as group A (for the *A*ged).

On the first view of the motives for charity, the level of contributions G enters the individual utility functions of the working population, and they maximise:

$$V^{I}(w) \equiv U(X, L, G). \tag{1}$$

The resulting total of contributions by the working population is given by:

$$\Gamma = \int_{\underline{w}}^{\infty} G(w) f(w) \, dw \tag{2}$$

and of this some fraction may go to group A, whose utility is denoted by U_A.

The second view – that charity is purely redistributive – means that G does not enter the individual utility function; on the other hand, individuals are concerned about the level of consumption of those in the disadvantaged group A. This concern may be represented by individuals in the working population maximising:

$$V^{II}(w) \equiv U(X, L) + \delta U(X_A, O) \tag{3}$$

where X_A denotes the consumption of group A.[1] Their altruism is limited in that only the welfare of group A enters their maximand (they are unconcerned, for example, about fellow workers with a lower wage) and that the utility of group A is 'discounted' by δ (where $0 \leqslant \delta < 1$). It is then assumed that individuals perceive X_A as being related to their charitable contribution G according to:

$$X_A = \gamma G + G_0. \tag{4}$$

It should be emphasised that this is the *perceived* and not the *actual* relationship between X_A and G. This formulation of charitable behaviour is based on Vickrey [19], who emphasises the importance of interdependence between donors:[2]

[it might be claimed] that in the case of a voluntary contribution the donor, on balance, gains in satisfaction at least as much as he would by spending the money in other ways ... in practice however we are in a situation akin to that of monopolistic competition where one's own behaviour is expected to influence that of others. ... A will expect that B and C may also be induced by his gift to contribute. ... The combined effects of A's original gift plus that of the induced gifts ... will provide for A a level of satisfaction equal to what he would have obtained had he kept the amount of his contribution for himself (pp. 46-7)

Two comments should be made about this formulation of the two views of charitable motives. First, it is clear that (3) and (4) together are a special case of (1), so that in a formal sense the analysis is equivalent. The difference lies in the interpretation of the results, as is discussed later in the chapter. Secondly, this representation of charitable behaviour is obviously not the only one which could be adopted, and the reader is referred to the discussion by, among others, Boulding [4], Hochman and Rodgers [8], Ireland and Johnson [9], and Becker [2]. But although the model is a rather special one, it seems worth exploring and, as shown below, it can lead to equations determining the level of contributions which are not dissimilar to those estimated in econometric studies by Feldstein [5] and others.

2 The Framework for Policy Decisions

Much of the previous discussion of the policy implications has been concerned with the 'efficiency' of alternative tax treatment of contributions, where this is measured by the amount of additional contribution received by charities per dollar of potential tax revenue forgone. In the case where there is a constant marginal tax rate t and full deductibility, this focuses on the level of $(1-t)\Gamma$ and it is for this reason that particular attention has been paid to whether the elasticity of Γ with respect to $(1-t)$ is greater or less than minus one. In the present context however we take the rather broader view of the government's objectives represented by the additive social welfare function:

$$\mu U_A + D \int_{\underline{w}}^{\infty} V(w) f(w) \, dw \tag{5}$$

where $0 \leqslant D \leqslant 1$. The case $D=1$ corresponds to a utilitarian objective, whereas $D<1$ means that the government attaches greater weight to the utility of group A. In what follows it is assumed that the transfers to group A are never sufficient to raise their utility (U_A) to the level achieved by a worker with wage $\underline{w}$:

$$U_A < V(\underline{w}). \tag{6}$$

This means that $D=0$ corresponds to the Rawlsian case where the government is concerned *only* with the welfare of the least advantaged group (Rawls [13]).

The consumption of group A is financed by the revenue raised from income taxation (R) and by charitable contributions (Γ). (It is assumed that the only government expenditure is on transfer payments to group A.) In both cases administrative costs and inefficiencies in allocation may mean that the total received is less than that collected. Denoting the relative effectiveness of charitable contributions by h, we have:

$$\mu X_A = \eta(R + h\Gamma) \tag{7}$$

where $0 < \eta \leqslant 1$ and $h \geqslant 0$ are constants.[3] A number of considerations are likely to affect the value of h, and two of the most important here are the type of charity supported and the effectiveness of charitable organisations. In the former case, the value of h is likely to reflect the motives for charity. Where individuals are motivated by the utility derived from giving, and where the redistributive consequences of philanthropy are limited (as argued by Vickrey [19]), the value of h may be very low. On the other hand, where the main motive for charity is redistribution, the value of h depends on the efficiency of the charitable organisations. Those who attach great importance to the disbursement of funds by private bodies rather than state agencies may feel that h is greater than 1. On the other hand, those who are concerned about the high proportion of collection costs in private charities, or about their patterns of allocation, may argue that h is substantially less than 1. To sum up, h is only likely to exceed 1 if most charitable activity is redistributive and if it is at least as effective as state income maintenance programmes.

The main aim of the subsequent analysis is to examine the desirability of tax preference for contributions in the light of the social welfare function (5) and differing views about the value of h. This may be contrasted with the 'efficiency' objective usually considered, which in the present context is equivalent to assuming that $h = 1$ (i.e. private charity and tax revenue are perfect substitutes) and that $D = 0$ (a Rawlsian objective).[4]

As explained in the Introduction, the principal question with which we are concerned is the choice between tax deductibility and a tax credit. This means that the assumption of a constant marginal tax rate, frequently made in the literature on income taxation, would rule out the interesting aspects of the question, since the two approaches would then be equivalent. At the same time, there are advantages in adopting a relatively simple form. For this reason, we assume that the tax system is given by:

$$T(Y) = Y - Y^\beta E^{1-\beta} \qquad \text{for } Y \geqslant E$$

$$= 0 \text{ otherwise}$$

where Y denotes income (wL) and $0 \leqslant \beta \leqslant 1$. The adoption of this function is particularly appropriate in view of its use in Vickrey [18]. As he showed, it has the property that if M denotes the marginal tax rate, then $1 - M = \beta(1 - T/Y)$, so that the marginal rate starts at $(1 - \beta)$ where $Y = E$ and rises as Y increases. If we now introduce the possibility of deducting a proportion Θ of charitable contributions, and a tax credit rate ρ, then the tax schedule becomes (for $Y - \Theta G \geqslant E$):

$$T = Y - (\Theta + \rho)G - (Y - \Theta G)^\beta E^{1-\beta} \tag{8}$$

where $0 \leqslant \Theta \leqslant 1$ and $0 \leqslant \rho < 1$. The cost of a gift of \$1 in terms of a loss of net income is \$$(1 - \rho)$ with the tax credit, and \$$(1 - \Theta M)$ with the tax deduction, so that the cost declines with income in the latter case.

3   An Explicit Model

In order to simplify the analysis we shall consider the special case where the function $V(w)$ takes the following form (identical for all individuals):

$$V(w) = \log X + b \log(1-L) + \delta \log G. \tag{9}$$

Although a special case, it is of some interest. Not only does it allow an explicit solution which throws light on the issues involved, but also it leads to a price elasticity close to that estimated in recent studies. The relationship to $V^{\mathrm{I}}(w)$ and $V^{\mathrm{II}}(w)$ may be seen as follows. On the first view of charity, V is a logarithmic individual utility function with δ the exponent associated with gifts and U_A equals $\log X_A$. On the second view, $U(X, L) = \log X + b \log(1-L)$, and it is assumed that $G_0 = 0$, so that δ is the discount attached to the utility of group A as perceived by the donors.

The maximisation problem for a person in the working population subject to tax may be written in terms of the Lagrangian:

$$\mathcal{L} = \log X + b \log(1-L) + \delta \log G + \lambda\{(wL - \Theta G)^\beta E^{1-\beta}$$
$$+ (\Theta + \rho)G - X - G\}$$

(the consumption good is taken as the numeraire). This gives first-order conditions:

$$X^{-1} = \lambda$$
$$b(1-L)^{-1} = \lambda w(1-M)$$
$$\delta G^{-1} = \lambda[(1-\Theta-\rho) + \Theta(1-M)] = \lambda(1-\rho-\Theta M)$$

To avoid unnecessary taxonomy, we assume that all the working population are subject to tax: i.e. $\underline{w}$ is sufficiently high to ensure $T > 0$ for all w. It may be verified that the second-order conditions are satisfied.

It follows that the level of G may be written as:

$$G = \frac{\delta X}{(1-\rho-\Theta M)}. \tag{10}$$

This equation for G in the case of tax deductibility ($\Theta = 1$, $\rho = 0$) may be compared with the empirical evidence in the United States. Analysis of the data presented by Vickrey [20] shows, for example, that the ratio of the net cost of gifts ($(1-M)G$ in the case of tax deductibility) to disposable income (here taken as X) was broadly constant over the range from $10,000 to $200,000 of adjusted gross income in 1970. As Vickrey pointed out, the evidence is consistent with both the price and the income elasticities being unity, and although he himself felt that the price elasticity was less than 1.0 (and the income elasticity greater than 1.0), more recent econometric studies which have attempted to isolate these elasticities give results close to those implied by equation (10).[5] The equation used, for example, in Feldstein and Clotfelter [6] to examine alternative tax policies (equation (6)) has a price elasticity of 1.15 with a standard error of 0.20. Some of the estimates obtained by Feldstein [5] indicate a price elasticity significantly greater than unity; on the other hand, those found by Schwartz [14] were typically rather less than unity.[6] It should also be noted that our formulation implies that all those in the working population are donors. In the sample used by Feldstein and Clotfelter [6] 'almost every individual' made gifts. Their sample excluded a number of groups, and therefore was not representative of the population as a whole. However, the excluded groups corresponded at least in part to group A in our model (e.g. they omitted the lowest fifth of households by income), so that the assumption made here may be unreasonable as a first approximation.

Solving the first-order conditions gives the following results for the two cases of particular interest:

Full tax deductibility, no tax credit $(\Theta=1, \rho=0)$

$$X = \frac{w(1-\tau)}{(1+(\delta+b)/\beta} \equiv X_1 \tag{11a}$$

$$L = \frac{1+\delta/\beta}{1+(\delta+b)/\beta} \equiv L_1 \tag{11b}$$

$$G = \frac{w\delta/\beta}{1+(\delta+b)/\beta} \equiv G_1 \tag{11c}$$

No tax deductibility, tax credit $(\Theta=0, \rho\geqslant0)$

$$X = \frac{w(1-\tau)}{1+\delta+b/\beta} \equiv X_2 \tag{12a}$$

$$L = \frac{1+\delta}{1+\delta+b/\beta} \equiv L_2 \tag{12b}$$

$$G = \frac{\delta w(1-\tau)}{(1-\rho)(1+\delta+b/\beta)} \equiv G_2 \tag{12c}$$

where τ is defined as the average tax rate, expressed as a percentage of taxable income, before allowing for the credit $(\tau=(T(Y)+\rho G)/(Y-\Theta G))$.

4 The Optimal Level of Tax Credit

In comparing the tax deductibility of contributions with the alternative of a tax credit, we have to consider the rate at which the credit would be set. Most of the discussion has assumed either a zero rate (the complete abolition of tax preference for contributions) or an arbitrary positive rate, typically around 20–30% (Vickery [18] suggested 25%). In this section we consider the optimal choice of the rate of credit (ρ).

The government's objectives are assumed to be represented by the social welfare function (5), and in the present context this is equivalent (using (7)) to maximising:

$$Z \equiv \mu \log (R + h\Gamma) + D \int_{\underline{w}}^{\infty} V(w) f(w) \, dw \tag{13}$$

where R and Γ denote total revenue and gifts respectively.

Differentiating with respect to ρ, we obtain (in the case $\Theta = 0$):

$$\frac{\partial Z}{\partial \rho} = \frac{\mu \Gamma}{R + h\Gamma} \left(\frac{h-1}{1-\rho} \right) + D \int_{\underline{w}}^{\infty} \lambda G f \, dw \tag{14}$$

where use has been made of the relationships:

$$\frac{\partial \Gamma}{\partial \rho} = \frac{\Gamma}{1-\rho} \quad \text{and} \quad \frac{\partial V}{\partial \rho} = \lambda G$$

and it may be noted that the labour supplied is independent of ρ.

It is clear from equation (14) that where $h \geqslant 1$ we want to have the largest tax credit possible. The subsidisation of charitable contributions is Pareto-improving, since it raises both the income of group A (the aged or handicapped) and the utility derived from giving by the donors. It is assumed that there is an upper bound to the possible level of credit, and in particular that the net revenue received by the government is always positive. The credit is therefore set at the upper bound ρ_{max}, and:

$$\rho_{max} < \frac{R_0}{R_0 + \Gamma_0} \tag{15}$$

where R_0, Γ_0 denote the total revenue and gifts when $\rho = \Theta = 0$ (the no tax preference case).

To see what happens where $h < 1$, that is charitable contributions are less 'efficient' than state provision or are not directed at redistribution, we may rewrite (14) using (12a) and (12c):

$$(1-\rho)\frac{\partial Z}{\partial \rho} = D\delta(1-\mu) - \mu(1-h)\frac{\Gamma_0}{(1-\rho)R_0 + (h-\rho)\Gamma_0}$$

so that $\partial Z / \partial \rho$ has the sign of:

$$\gamma - (1-\gamma)(1-h)\left[\frac{\Gamma_0}{(1-\rho)R_0 + (h-\rho)\Gamma_0} \right] \tag{16}$$

where $\gamma = D\delta(1-\mu)/(\mu + D\delta(1-\mu))$. This is a decreasing function of ρ (for $0 \leqslant \rho \leqslant \rho_{max}$). It follows that the optimal value of ρ is given by:

$$\max\left[0, 1 - \frac{(1-h)}{\gamma(1+R_0/\Gamma_0)}\right] \qquad \text{subject to } \rho \leqslant \rho_{max}. \qquad (17)$$

The term γ has the following interpretation where charity arises for redistributive reasons. In that case, the welfare of the disadvantaged group may be seen as entering Z both directly with weight μ and indirectly via the utility functions of the working population with weight $D\delta(1-\mu)$ (i.e. incorporating both the social discount factor D and the private discount δ). The value of γ is a measure of the indirect importance of group A relative to their total weight in the social welfare function. If the government's concern arises largely because of private charitable feelings (γ is high) then the credit will be higher than if the weight attached to group A arises largely from their direct effect on social welfare (γ is low). If the government is concerned solely with the disadvantaged ($\gamma = 0$), then there should be no tax credit.

The condition for a positive tax credit may be written as:

$$h > 1 - \gamma\left(1 + \frac{R_0}{\Gamma_0}\right) \qquad (18)$$

The possibility that a positive tax credit may be desirable even where $h = 0$ (i.e. that the right-hand side of (18) may be negative) can be ruled out where the following conditions hold[7]:

$$X_A < X(\mathbf{w}) \quad \text{and} \quad \eta = 1 \qquad (19)$$

If therefore charities perform no redistributive function ($h = 0$), the case for any tax preference has to be based on the inefficiency of transfers through taxation ($\eta > 1$) or on the marginal utility of consumption of group A being lower than that of the lowest paid worker.

From (17) it may be seen that the optimal rate of tax credit is higher, (i) the larger the value of h (the more effective charitable contributions), (ii) the greater the indirect importance of group A (γ), and (iii) the smaller are gifts as a proportion of tax revenue when there is no tax preference (Γ_0/R_0). To give some idea of the magnitudes involved, suppose that gifts in the absence of tax preference would be one-quarter of revenue (bearing in mind that this relates to revenue raised for redistributive purposes), and that the proportion of the population in group A is one-fifth. A value of 0.05 for δ would imply that net gifts constituted 5% of consumption. With these values, $D = 1$ implies that γ equals one-sixth and that a positive tax credit is desirable where $h > 1/6$. Where $h = \frac{1}{2}$, the optimal level of credit would be 40%. On the other hand, $D = 1/3$ would mean that the optimal policy was one of no tax preference where $h \leqslant 11/16$.

5   The Choice Between Tax Deductibility and a Tax Credit

The choice clearly depends on the value of D, or the relative weight attached to the welfare of the two groups. The simplest case to consider is the Rawlsian case $D = 0$, where the government is only concerned with the disadvantaged group A. The difference, denoted by Δ, between the level of social welfare in the situation with tax deductibility and that in the case of a tax credit is then given by (using (13) and the fact that total gifts with the tax credit are $\Gamma_0/(1-\rho)$):

$$\Delta = \mu \log \left[\frac{R_1 + h\Gamma_1}{R_0 + \dfrac{h-\rho}{1-\rho}\Gamma_0} \right] \tag{20}$$

The effect of the different tax treatment on the income accruing to group A from the two sources may be seen from the equations (11) and (12). In particular[8]:

$$wL_1 - G_1 < wL_2 < wL_1 \tag{21a}$$

$$(1-\rho)G_2 < G_1 \tag{21b}$$

In other words, gross income is higher with the tax deduction but *taxable* income (net of gifts) is lower. Revenue would therefore be lower than with a zero tax credit ($R_1 < R_0$). On the other hand, the level of gifts is higher with the tax deduction than with a zero credit ($\Gamma_1 > \Gamma_0$).

The government has therefore to balance the effect on revenue against that on charitable contributions. As noted in section 2, this is typically done by considering the total of revenue and gifts, i.e. the case where $h = 1$. The present tax deduction is then preferable according to the 'efficiency' criterion where[9]:

$$R_1 + \Gamma_1 > R_0 + \Gamma_0 \tag{22}$$

(although in empirical applications it is typically assumed that Y is unchanged, so that no allowance is made for the effect on the tax base). As argued earlier, h is only likely to equal or exceed 1 if most charitable activity is redistributive and it is at least as efficient as state income maintenance. Where $h < 1$, the optimal rate of credit is zero (since $D = 0$), and Δ is reduced as h falls below 1. In the limiting case where $h = 0$, Δ is clearly negative, since $R_1 < R_0$. Condition (22) implies therefore that there is a critical value of h below which tax deductibility ceases to be desirable. The critical value:

$$h^* \equiv \frac{R_0 - R_1}{\Gamma_1 - \Gamma_0} = \frac{\text{loss of revenue from deduction}}{\text{increase in gifts from deduction}}.$$

This and condition (22), depend on the effect of the tax deduction on pre-tax incomes and on the degree of progressivity (β). (It is assumed throughout the chapter that β is unchanged, although variation in the tax treatment of contributions might well affect the optimal degree of progression.)

In the case where $D \geqslant 0$, that is the government attaches some weight to the welfare of the working population, the difference between the level of social welfare with the deduction and that with the credit is proportional to:

$$\Delta = (1 - \gamma) \log \left(\frac{R_1 + h\Gamma_1}{R_0 + \dfrac{h - \rho}{1 - \rho} \Gamma_0} \right) + \gamma I \tag{23}$$

where:

$$I = \int_{\underline{w}}^{\infty} \frac{\hat{V}}{\delta(1 - \mu)} f \, dw \tag{24}$$

and $\hat{V}$ denotes the difference in utility between the tax deduction and tax credit situations (and is a function of ρ).

We are interested in the conditions under which $\Delta = 0$, or the government is indifferent between the two policies. It may be shown (see Appendix) that condition (22) implies that the possible contours for $\Delta = 0$, regarded as a function of h and γ, are shown in Figure 1. Where $\gamma = 0$, we have the case discussed in the previous paragraph with $\rho = 0$. Condition (22) means that the top left-hand corner has a Δ positive, and $\Delta = 0$ at h^* as indicated. Where $\gamma > 0$, we have to allow for the possibility that the optimal level of credit determined by (17) is positive. In the figure it is assumed that the conditions (19) hold, so that the boundary $\rho = 0$ is given by the lower dashed line. The value of ρ is zero to the left of this line, and then rises as one moves in a counter-clockwise direction around $(\gamma = 0, h = 1)$, until it reaches ρ_{max} at the upper dashed line. Where $\rho = 0$, $I > 0$ (see Appendix) and the $\Delta = 0$ contour slopes down from h^*. Two possible paths are then shown. If there is a feasible level of credit such that $I = 0$ (i.e. it compensates for the abolition of the deduction), then the contour cuts the line $\Delta_\gamma = 0$ horizontally and rises as indicated on Path I. In such a case, the tax credit would be preferred to the tax deduction in the upper right-hand corner. This would not imply that the credit made everyone in the donor population better-off; indeed one of the features of the credit is that it redistributes *within the donor class*. Where this level of credit cannot be attained, then we have Path II and Δ is positive in the upper right-hand corner. These results may be summarised as follows:

	Low γ	High γ
High h	Tax deductibility desirable on basis of condition (22)	May be case for tax credit at maximum rate to secure equity among donors
Low h	No tax preference	?

The above analysis suggests that the case against the tax deductibility of charitable contributions can be made in two main ways. First, if the

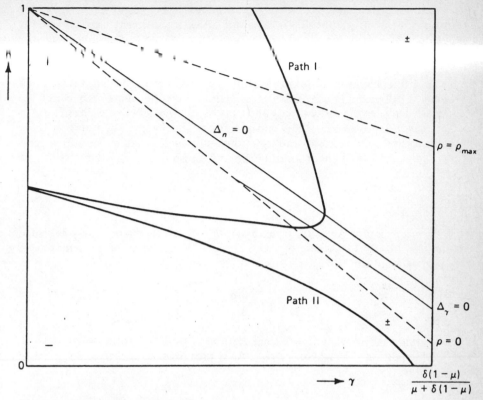

Figure 1   *Possible Contours for* $\Delta = 0$.

government is largely concerned with the welfare of the disadvantaged group (γ is low) and if it believes that the redistributive effectiveness of charitable contributions (as measured by h) is low, then there should be no tax preference for contributions. Secondly, if the government attaches more weight to the welfare of the donors (γ large) and believes that charitable contributions are both directed at redistribution and reasonably effective (h is high) then there *may* be a case for a tax credit at a relatively high rate to bring about greater equity between donors. The replacement of the deduction by a tax credit benefits the middle and lower income donors at the expense of the wealthy, and if this can be achieved without a serious reduction in total giving, then such a redistribution may be considered desirable.

6   Concluding Comments

The aim of this chapter has been to provide a framework within which the arguments concerning the income tax treatment of contributions may be made more precise than is commonly the case. At the same time, it hardly needs emphasising that the model considered here is a very special one. As recognised earlier, the model incorporates only some of the considerations influencing charitable behaviour, and it focuses on charities as redistributive agencies. More specifically, it does not allow for different views about the stimulus to giving provided by tax preferences, since it is assumed that the price and income elasticities are both unity. While this is consistent with recent econometric evidence Vickrey himself has argued that the price elasticity is less than 1.0. The reason for taking the unitary elasticity case is that it is clearly a critical value, and that it allows us to focus on the other elements affecting the choice between tax deductibility and a tax credit. In particular we have tried to go beyond simple 'efficiency' considerations (in the present notation these correspond to $h=1$, $\gamma=0$) and to set the analysis in an (albeit simple) general equilibrium model, incorporating the impact on decisions other than those about giving.

Appendix

The contours for $\Delta=0$ are given by $\Delta_h dh + \Delta_y dy = 0$ (where it may be noted that $\Delta_\rho d\rho = 0$). Differentiating with respect to h, it may be seen that Δ_h is proportional to:

$$(1-\rho)\left(1+\frac{R_0}{\Gamma_0}\right)-\left(1+\frac{R_1}{\Gamma_1}\right)$$

which is positive where $\rho=0$ (since $R_0>R_1$, $\Gamma_0<\Gamma_1$). Substituting for $(1-\rho)$ from equation (17), where $\rho<\rho_{\max}$, Δ_h is proportional to:

$$1-h-\gamma\left(1+\frac{R_1}{\Gamma_1}\right)$$

The line $\Delta_h=0$ passes through $(\gamma=0, h=1)$ and:

$$\gamma=\left(\frac{\Gamma_1}{R_1+\Gamma_1}\right), \quad h=0.$$

The contours $\Delta=0$ cut this line vertically. Differentiating with respect to γ, and evaluating at $\Delta=0$, the curve $\Delta_y=0$ is given by:

$$(1-\gamma)(R_0+\Gamma_0)=R_1+h\Gamma_1 \quad \text{for } \rho>0 \text{ and } h=h^* \quad \text{for } \rho=0.$$

Where condition (22) holds, this has the form shown in Figure 1. The $\Delta=0$ contours cut $\Delta_y=0$ horizontally. (The intersection of $\Delta_h=\Delta_y=0$ is at $\gamma=1$, $h=-R_1\Gamma_1$.)

Since V is a strictly increasing function of θ, it follows that $\hat{V}>0$ for $\rho=0$ and hence that I is strictly positive for the region where $\rho=0$.

Acknowledgement

I am grateful to A. J. Culyer, M. S. Feldstein, R. E. Grieson and M. K. Taussig for their helpful comments on an earlier version of this chapter.

Notes

1 This formulation has certain similarity to equation (1) in Mirrlees [11]; see also Sen [15]. The treatment by Mirrlees emphasises the role of charities in the provision of collective goods, an important aspect which is not discussed here.

2 It is of course only one aspect of interdependence and more generally we might expect G_0 to depend on the gifts by others. For interesting attempts to test this empirically, see Schwartz [14] and Feldstein and Clotfelter [6].

3 The assumption that h is constant is not necessarily realistic, since the effectiveness may depend on factors such as the size of gifts.

4 It also assumes that pre-tax incomes are independent of the tax treatment of contributions. For further discussion, see Boskin [3].

5 There have been a number of papers following the early econometric study by Taussig [17], including Schwartz [4], Feldstein [5], Feldstein and Clotfelter [6], and Feldstein and Taylor [7].

6 The results of the different studies using income tax data are compared in Feldstein [5], where he explains why the earlier finding of a low price elasticity (around 0.1) by Taussig [17] is likely to be misleading.

7 At $\rho=0$, $\delta(1-\mu)=\int(G/X)f dw \leqslant \Gamma_0/X(\mathbf{w}) < \Gamma_0/X_A$ where the first part of (19) holds. From (7) where $h=\rho=0$, $\Gamma_0/X_A=\mu\Gamma_0/\eta R_0$. It follows that $\gamma/(1-\gamma)<(\Gamma_0/R_0)$ where $\eta=1$, so from (16) $\partial Z/\partial\rho<0$ at $\rho=0$.

8 The second of these is obtained from (11c) and (12c), where for any given w:

$$G_1 \gtrless (1-\rho)G_2 \quad \text{as} \quad \frac{\beta+\delta\beta+b}{\beta+\delta+b} \gtrless 1-M$$

or:

$$M \gtrless \frac{\delta(1-\beta)}{\beta+\delta+b}.$$

Since $M \geqslant 1-\beta$ it follows that $G_1 > (1-\rho)G_2$.

9 Where $D=0$ and $h=1$, the government is indifferent about the level of credit, since the price elasticity is minus one.

References

[1] Andrews, W. D. (1972), 'Personal deductions in an ideal income tax', *Harvard Law Review*, **86**, pp. 309–85.

[2] Becker, G. S. (1974), 'A theory of social interactions', *Journal of Political Economy*, **82**, pp. 1063–94.

[3] Boskin, M. J. (1976), 'Estate taxation and charitable bequests', *Journal of Public Economics*, vol. 5, pp. 27–56.

[4] Boulding, K. E. (1962), 'Notes on a theory of philanthropy', in Dickinson, F. G. (ed.), *Philanthropy and Public Policy*, New York, Columbia University Press.

[5] Feldstein, M. S. (1975), 'The income tax and charitable contributions', *National Tax Journal*, vol. 28, pp. 81–99, 209–26.

[6] Feldstein, M. S. and Clotfelter, C. (1976), 'Tax incentives and charitable contributions in the United States', *Journal of Public Economics*, vol. 5, pp. 1–26.

[7]   Feldstein, M. S. and Taylor, A. (1976), 'The income tax and charitable contributions', *Econometrica*, vol. 44, pp. 1201–22.

[8]   Hochman, H. M. and Rodgers, J. D. (1969), 'Pareto optimal redistribution', *American Economic Review*, vol. 59, pp. 542–57.

[9]   Ireland, T. R. and Johnson, D. B. (1970), *The Economics of Charity*, Blacksburg, Centre for the Study of Public Choice.

[10] McDaniel, P. R. (1972), 'Federal matching grants for charitable contributions', *Tax Law Review*, vol. 27, pp. 377–413.

[11] Mirrlees, J. A. (1973), 'The economics of charitable contributions', Paper presented at the European Meeting of the Econometric Society, August.

[12] Pechman, J. A. (1971), *Federal Tax Policy*, New York, W. W. Norton.

[13] Rawls, J. (1972), *A Theory of Justice*, Cambridge, Mass., Harvard University Press.

[14] Schwartz, R. A. (1970), 'Personal philanthropic contributions', *Journal of Political Economy*, vol. 78, pp. 1264–91.

[15] Sen, A. K. (1966), 'Labour allocation in a cooperative enterprise', *Review of Economic Studies*, vol. 33, pp. 361–71.

[16] Surrey, S. S. (1972), *Federal Income Taxation*, Mineola, N.Y., Foundation Press.

[17] Taussig, M. K. (1967), 'Economic aspects of the personal income tax treatment of charitable contributions', *National Tax Journal*, vol. 20, pp. 1–19.

[18] Vickrey, W. (1947), *Agenda for Progressive Taxation*, New York, Ronald Press.

[19] Vickrey, W. (1962), 'One economist's view of philanthropy', in Dickinson, F. G. (ed.), *Philanthropy and Public Policy*, New York, Columbia University Press.

[20] Vickrey, W. (1973), 'Private philanthropy and public finance', unpublished mimeo.

19 Smoking and the Economics of Government Intervention[1]*

1 Introduction

A recent review of the evidence concerning the relationship between smoking and the incidence of cancer stated that 'it is now clear that smoking plays a significant role in the production of most cancers of the upper digestive tract, the respiratory tract, and the bladder' (Doll [1], p. 10). More generally, the prospective studies of Doll and Hill [4], Hammond and Horn [3] and others have shown a substantially higher mortality rate from all conditions. A selection of the evidence from the Hammond and Horn study is presented in Table 1 and Figure 1. How far this excess mortality can be attributed to smoking has been the subject of controversy, but in the case of the specific conditions mentioned by Doll, the relationship appears to be well established. In the case of lung cancer, the excess mortality is very substantial (see Table 2).

If the existence of a relationship between smoking and the incidence of disease is accepted, we should then consider the desirability of government intervention to reduce tobacco consumption, and the form which this intervention should take. It is with the economic aspects of these questions that this chapter is concerned. Section 2 reviews the empirical studies which have been made of the costs of smoking in Britain, and suggests that the underlying welfare economic framework has not been adequately considered. As a first attempt to remedy this deficiency, a theoretical analysis of the case for intervention (by taxation or by health education) is presented in sections 3 and 4. This analysis is based on a highly stylised model of smoking behaviour,[2] but the starkness of the assumptions made may serve to demonstrate the need for further research, and this need is discussed in the final section.

2 Estimates of the 'Cost' of Smoking

A number of estimates have been made in recent years for the 'cost' of smoking in Britain, including those by Peston [1], the Royal College of Physicians [2] and the Department of Health and Social Security.[3] The use of inverted commas is justified on the grounds that these studies appear to view cost in a rather different light, and it is with these differences that this section is primarily concerned.

* Reprinted from *The Economics of Health and Medical Care*, 1974.

Table 1   *Mortality ratio (non-smokers = 1.00), United States*

Lifetime smoking history	Men aged 45–54	Men aged 65–74
Pipe only	0.96	1.06
Cigar only	1.17	1.05
Cigarettes only	2.20	1.58
Cigarette and other	1.88	1.36

Source: Hammond [1] Table 1.

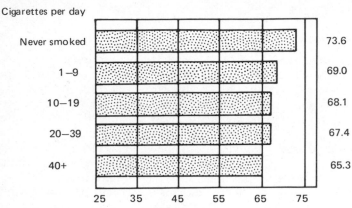

Figure 1   *Life expectancy at age twenty-five (male).*

Table 2   *Mortality ratio for lung cancer (non-smokers = 1.00)*

Study	Current cigarette smokers	Current pipe/cigar smokers
British doctors	16.9	4.6
US veterans	12.1	1.7
US nine counties	10.0	–
Canadian veterans	11.7	–

Source: Doll [1] Table 1.

The most straightforward approach – and one commonly adopted by doctors – is to view the problem as parallel to that of vaccination against, say, polio. For the expenditure on vaccination (health education to publicise risk involved in smoking) there is a return in reduced health costs, reduced sickness absence, the value of the lives saved, etc. It is this approach which appears to be the basis of the estimate of a total cost of £150 million made by Peston, which is made up of the following items:

	£m
Treatment cost	50
Lost production as a result of sickness	290
Cost of premature death	160
Fires	20

The analogy with vaccination is not, however, valid, since campaigns against smoking may impose costs on those giving up smoking (or, indeed, on those continuing) which have no parallel in the case of vaccination. A much more natural approach for an economist is that based on the divergence between social and private benefits and costs. In the extreme case where smokers are assumed to possess full information about the health risk, and where there are no habit effects, the argument for intervention would have to be based on the costs imposed on others, e.g. health costs and the net tax contribution.[4] It would be possible to interpret the Department of Health and Social Security figures as being concerned with these divergencies, and they estimate that a 100% reduction in smoking would lead, in the long run, to the following reduction costs imposed on others:

	£m
Health costs	$-12\frac{1}{2}$
Social security payments	-60
Taxes paid	$+210$

(The net *increase* in health costs arises from the fact that the savings on smoking-related disease are offset by the higher subsequent health costs for survivors.)

The approach just considered meets with resistance from the medical profession, but it has the merit of treating smoking in the same way as other activities in which individuals voluntarily assume risks, such as skiing. It would not be suggested that the social desirability of the latter should be assessed simply in terms of the working hours lost and the health costs, without any reference to the consumption benefits from skiing, and if smoking is to be treated differently, then an argument has to be made to this effect. At the same time, the extreme form of the approach outlined above is clearly not a realistic basis for policy-making, and allowance has to be made for imperfect information, for the addictive nature of tobacco, and for the social forces influencing its consumption. In the following sections an attempt is made to incorporate these factors, and to see under what assumptions different approaches to the measurement of the costs of smoking would be valid. The analysis is also concerned with the relative merits of two main forms of intervention: publicity concerning the health hazard, and taxation. The advocates of increased government intervention tend to assume that these two approaches are perfect substitutes, but it is far from clear that this is necessarily so.

3   The Individual Smoking Decision

(1) The basic assumptions
(i) A person plans his consumption of cigarettes C in period t and his consumption of other goods X_t subject to the budget constraint:

$$X_t + p_t C_t = E_t$$

where E_t is exogenous and p_t denotes the price of cigarettes (inclusive of tax).
(ii) A person maximises the expected utility derived from consumption over the remainder of his lifetime: i.e. at time V:

$$\max W_V = \sum_{t=V}^{t=T} U[X_t, C_t, Z_t] F_t$$

where F_t is the probability of his being alive in period t, Z is a variable reflecting past consumption (the effect of habit) and U is a concave function.[5] It is assumed that $U \geqslant 0$ for the relevant E_t.
(iii) The survival rate F_t depends on the death rates from smoking-related diseases δ_t^s and other causes δ_t (exogenous):

$$F_t - F_{t-1} = -(\delta_t^s + \delta_t) F_{t-1}.$$

The deaths from smoking-related diseases are assumed to be a function of age and current cigarette consumption. This assumption is not fully consistent with the evidence of Doll, which suggests that past consumption is also important, but may be a reasonable first approximation.
(iv) The person is covered by a state health service which is financed by a uniform tax (unrelated to the incidence of illness).
  On the basis of the four assumptions described above, it is possible to characterise the utility-maximising behaviour of the individual. In order to simplify the analysis we shall, however, add the following extra assumptions:
(v) The person lives for only two periods ($t = 1, 2$) and $E_1 = E_2 = E$.
(vi) The survival rates are given by:

$$F_1 = e^{-A_1^* C_1}, \qquad F_2 = e^{-A_2^* C_2} G_2$$

where G_2 is the survival rate for a non-smoker, and it is assumed that $A_1^* (1 + G_2) < A_2^*$.[2]

(2) Smoking behaviour: No habit formation and perfect knowledge
We consider first the case where U does not depend on Z_t, and where the person has perfect knowledge of the relationship between smoking and mortality.
  At the beginning of period 1, he maximises:

$$W_1 = U(C_1) e^{-A_1^* C_1} + U(C_2) e^{-(A_1^* C_1 + A_2^* C_2)} G_2 .$$

where $U(C)$ denotes $U(E, pC, C)$. If he survives to consume in period 2, he chooses C_2 to maximise:

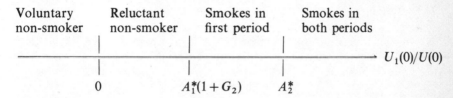

so that his plan is intertemporally consistent (i.e. he carries out at the beginning of period 2 his consumption planned at the beginning of period 1). The first-order conditions for maximisation are:

$$\frac{\partial W_1}{\partial C_1} = e^{-A_1^*C_1}[U_1(C_1) - A_1^*\{U(C_1) + U(C_2)e^{-A_2^*C_2}G_2\}] \leqslant 0 \tag{1}$$

with equality if $C_1 > 0$ (and $C_1 = 0$ if $\partial W/\partial C_1 < 0$):

$$\frac{\partial W}{\partial C_2} = G_2 e^{-(A_1^*C_1 + A^*C_2)}[U_1(C_2) - A_2^*U(C_2)] \leqslant 0 \tag{2}$$

with equality if $C_2 > 0$ (and $C_2 = 0$ if $\partial W/\partial C_2 < 0$).

We may characterise the solution in terms of the value of $U^1(0)/U(0)$:

Voluntary non-smoker	Reluctant non-smoker	Smokes in first period	Smokes in both periods
0	$A_1^*(1 + G_2)$	A_2^*	$U_1(0)/U(0)$

'Voluntary' non-smokers are those who would not choose to do so even if there were no health risk ($U_1(0) < 0$). For those people with $U_1(0) > 0$, we have either $C_1 = C_2 = 0$ ('reluctant' non-smokers), or $C_1 > 0$, $C_2 = 0$ or $C_1 > 0_2$, $C_2 > 0$ (as shown in Figure 2).

(3) Imperfect knowledge

Suppose that the individual believes the risk to be determined by A_1 and A_2. If $A_2 < A_2^*$ (the true value), it is clear that the number of smokers is higher. Moreover, for a person who previously was ignorant of the health risk, knowledge that $A_2 > 0$ will lead him to cut down the amount smoked (from $\bar{C}$ in Figure 2). At the same time, it is not necessarily true that increasing knowledge of the risk leads to reduced consumption. If A_2 increases, then C_2 falls; but if A_1 is constant while A_2 increases, then C_1 rises. A person in period 1 knows that expected utility in period 2 is lower, and therefore there is less incentive to cut down in period 1.

These results show that the spread of information about the health hazard reduces the number of smokers, but may increase consumption among young continuing smokers where the publicity is directed particularly at the risks in later life (as with lung cancer).

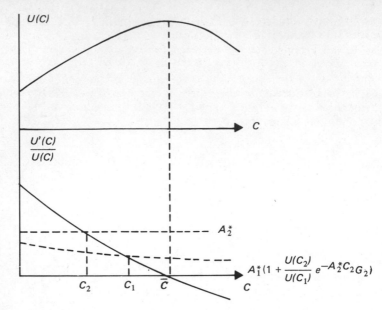

Figure 2.

It may also be noted that increased knowledge about the health risks may reduce the responsiveness of consumption to price change. If:

$$U = C^{\alpha}(E - pC)^{1-\alpha} \qquad (0 < \alpha < 1)$$

the elasticity of demand in period $2(\varepsilon_2)$ is given by:

$$\frac{1}{\varepsilon_2} = 1 + \frac{A_2 C_2 (1 - \alpha)}{(1 - A_2 C_2)(\alpha - A_2 C_2)} .$$

On the assumption that $A_2 C_2 < \alpha$, the elasticity falls as A rises above zero, e.g. if $AC = 0.05$ and $\alpha = 0.10$, the elasticity would be halved.

(4) Habit formation

The introduction of habit via the dependence of utility in the second period on C_1 is straightforward. On the assumption that $\partial U/dZ < 0$, the person must allow, in period 1, for the reduction in the later utility as he becomes habituated to tobacco consumption. If the person behaves myopically, and ignores this interdependence, then he will later 'regret' his earlier decision and may (depending on the form of U) raise his planned consumption C_2.

This formulation of the habit-forming effect of tobacco is similar to that put forward by Peston [9], Pollack [10] and von Weizsäcker [11], but it may not fully capture its addictive nature. Peston, for example, referred in the case of tobacco to the 'widespread evidence of large numbers of people who recognise its dangers and would like to give up, but are unable to do so'. Moreover, it can be argued that the habit may be transmitted to others (e.g. across generations). These considerations may be incorporated by supposing that individuals inherit a level of consumption C_0, that there are substantial costs of adjustment involved in reducing this level, and – in an extreme form – that the consumer is intrinsically indifferent about the allocation of his expenditure,[7] i.e.:

$$W = U[E, g(C_1/C_0)]e^{-A_1 C_1} + U[E, g(C_2/C_1)]e^{-(A_1 C_1 + A_2 C_2)}G_2$$

where g represents the cost of adjustment, having a shape similar to that shown in Figure 3, and $\partial U/\partial g < 0$. With suitable modifications, the analysis can be carried out as before.

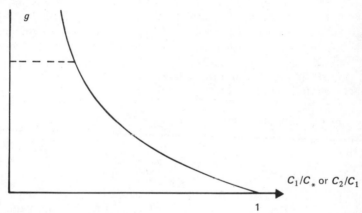

Figure 3
Note: there is assumed to be discontinuity at zero.

(5) Relationship with empirical demand studies

An analysis of the demand for tobacco in Britain in the period 1951–70 suggests the following conclusions [8]:

(a) The price elasticity is low, in line with earlier studies. It is around 0.4 for women and is not significantly different from zero for men.

(b) The spread of information about the health risks following the report of the Royal College of Physicians in 1962 led to no reduction in the consumption of cigarettes by women, but a fall of around 10% in the case of men (although this tended to disappear over time).

The second of these findings could be explained by the fact that women smokers tend to be younger, and – as shown above – increased knowledge about the risk at older ages may lead younger people to increase their smoking. Alternatively, it could be explained by the health education campaign having been less successful in reaching women. This would be consistent with the difference in price elasticities, since we have seen that increased awareness of risk may lower the price responsiveness.

4   The Welfare Economics of Government Intervention

On the assumption that social welfare can be regarded as a sum of individual utilities, we can distinguish between changes affecting the welfare of the smoker and those representing transfers between the smoker and others. In the latter category come health costs (with a national health service), the excess of consumption over production (benefits received less taxes paid and savings), the emotional burden borne by relatives and other externalities. This corresponds to the kind of method used to value lives by Weisbrod [13] and others, and the theoretical issues involved are not considered further here.

If we focus on the effect on the welfare of the individual smoker, the relevant component of the social welfare function W^* coincides with the individual lifetime utility W where $A_1 = A_i^*$ and there are no habit effects. In that case there is no divergence between private and social decisions. With this extreme case as a bench-mark, we may consider the effect of more reasonable assumptions.

Suppose first that $A_i < A_i^*$ but that there are no habit effects. In such a case, the social welfare function could take (at least) two forms:

$$W_{\mathrm{I}}^* = U(C_1)e^{-A_1{}^*C_1} + U(C_2)e^{-(A_1^*C^* + A_2^*C_2)}G_2$$

and:

$$W_{\mathrm{II}}^* = U(C_1)e^{-A_1C_1} + U(C_2)e^{-(A_1{}^*C_1 + A_2C_2)}G_2.$$

The rationale of the first is that social welfare depends on individual one-period utilities defined *ex post* (i.e. an individual not surviving to consume is supposed to have zero utility). In this case, the individual's expectations with respect to his survival are not relevant. In the second, on the other hand, the social welfare depends on individual one-period utilities defined *ex ante*, so that the survival rates expected by the individual (e^{-AC}) are relevant. The product $U(C_i)e^{-A_iC_i}$ represents individual expected utility, and this is summed across the survivors at the beginning of each period to give social welfare W_{II}^*.

In the case where $A_i = 0$, the individual chooses $C(P)$ determined by $U_1(C) = 0$. If there is a value p^1 such that $C(p^1) = 0$, we can calculate the associated change in welfare on criterion I from increasing p to p^1.[8]

$$\Delta W_{\mathrm{I}}^* = U(0)(1 + G_2) - U(\bar{C})e^{-A_1{}^*C}(1 + e^{-A_1^*C}G_2)$$

$$= U(0)(1 + G_2)(1 - e^{-A_1{}^*C}) + U(0)G_2e^{-A_1{}^*C}(1 - e^{-A_1^*C})$$

$$- [U(\bar{C}) - U(0)]e^{-A_1^*C}(1 + e^{-A_2^*C}G_2)$$

Since $1 - e^{-A^*C}$ is the death rate, the first two terms represent the value of the lives lost as a result of smoking-related disease, where this value equals $U(0)$

times the life expectancy of non-smokers. The final term represents the loss of utility (if $U(\bar{C}) > U(0)$) to surviving smokers from being forced to give up smoking. If we were to take the second criterion, then:

$$\Delta W_{II}^* = U(0)G_2(1 - e^{-A_i^* C_1}) - [U(\bar{C}) - U(0)](1 + e^{-A_i^* C}G_2)$$

which is clearly smaller than ΔW_I^*. This reflects the fact that the improvement in their survival prospects will not be recognised by those who are unaware of the risk in any case.

Let us now suppose that the change in smoking is brought about by health education, rather than by taxation, i.e. A_i is increased from 0 to A_i^*. If this is sufficient to ensure that the person does not smoke, then the change in welfare over the initial state is identical to that given before for both criteria. At the same time, the change in W_{II}^* may be decomposed into:

$$\Delta W_{II}^* = \Delta W_I^* - U(\bar{C})[1 - e^{-A_i^* C}] - U(\bar{C})G_2 e^{-A_i^* C}(1 - e^{-A_i^* C}).$$

The last two terms represent the change in welfare brought about by the individual perceiving the true value of A_i^*; the effect of health education is to change the evaluation of any given state under W_{II}^*. This brings out the differences between W_I^* and W_{II}^*. The former does not allow for the cost imposed on individuals through their awareness of the risks they are running – or, in the case of taxation, that they do not perceive the improvement in their survival prospects.

If we now turn to the model incorporating the effects of habit, as represented by the cost of adjustment, we can see that the value of g may depend on the method by which the reduction in smoking is brought about. If it involves individual response to health education campaigns, then there would undoubtedly be costs associated with giving up and, as a consequence, $U(0) < U(\bar{C})$. If there were to be (effective) prohibition, the psychic costs of the willpower involved might be avoided, but there would still be personal withdrawal costs. It seems unlikely that – in this model of habit formation at least – $U(0) \geqslant U(\bar{C})$ for those who are currently smokers, and we cannot on these grounds ignore the last term in ΔW_I^*.

Choice between taxation and health education

Let us suppose that the government wishes to reduce the consumption by a representative smoker to a certain level $C_2 = \hat{C}$ in the second period of his life, and that it has a choice between achieving this through an increase in p and through increasing A. If we assume for convenience that U has the simple form:

$$U = (C + \gamma)^\alpha (E - pC)^{1-\alpha}$$

the first-order conditions give:

$$\frac{\alpha}{\hat{C} + \gamma} - \frac{p(1 - \alpha)}{E - p\hat{C}} = A_2.$$

On the assumption that there are values of p and A satisfying this condition (and $A \leqslant A^*$), then the trade-off between them is given by:

$$\frac{dA_2}{dp}\bigg|_{C \text{ constant}} = -\frac{(1-\alpha)E}{(E-p\hat{C})^2}.$$

On the first criterion, we can see that:

$$\frac{dW_1^*}{dP}\bigg|_{C \text{ constant}} = \frac{\partial U}{\partial p} e^{-A_2{}^*C}.$$

If the revenue is handed back in lump-sum form, then $\partial U/\partial p = 0$ and the level of welfare is unchanged. On the other hand, with the second criterion,

$$\frac{dW_{II}^*}{dp}\bigg|_{C \text{ constant}} = \frac{\partial U}{\partial p} e^{-A_1\hat{C}} - \hat{C}W_{II}^* \frac{\partial A_2}{dp}$$

which will be positive (for $\hat{C} > 0$), so that tax measures are clearly preferable in this case. If we further assume that the costs of health education exceed those of tax collection (as certainly seems reasonable at the margin), the case for tax measures is even stronger.

This analysis brings out the important point that more information about the health risks of smoking is not necessarily socially desirable (even if it can be disseminated costlessly). There is a tendency for economists to believe that more information is always desirable (although doctors have, of course, always been aware that this is not so). Under the second criterion, for example, we have:

$$\frac{\partial W^*}{\partial A_1} = \frac{\partial W^*}{\partial C_1}\frac{\partial C_1}{\partial A_1} - C_1 U(C_1) e^{-A_1 C_1} + \frac{\partial W^*}{\partial C_2}\frac{\partial C_2}{\partial A_1}$$

$$\frac{\partial W^*}{\partial A_2} = \frac{\partial W^*}{\partial C_1}\frac{\partial C_1}{\partial A_2} - C_2 G_2 U(C_2) e^{-(A_1^* + A_2)C_2} + \frac{\partial W^*}{\partial C_2}\frac{\partial C_2}{\partial A_2}.$$

From the conditions for individual maximisation of W (interior solution) $\partial W^*/\partial C_2 = 0$, so that the last term vanishes and:

$$\frac{\partial W^*}{\partial C_2} = \frac{\partial W}{\partial C_1} + U(C_2) e^{-A_2 C_2} [A_1 e^{-A_1 C_1} - A_1^* e^{-A_1^* C_1}]$$

which is negative if $A_1^* C_1 < 1$ and approaches zero as $A_1 \to A_1^*$. It is clear, therefore, that if there are people who would continue to smoke even if they were fully aware of the health risk,[9] then there is a point beyond which further information is not desirable even if it can be provided at no cost.

5 Implications for Future Research

In section 2, I suggested that there were two approaches to the measurement of the cost of smoking, and from the analysis in sections 3 and 4 it can be seen that they represent two polar cases:

	Individual knowledge of health risks	Habit formation
Pure divergence approach	Perfect knowledge by individual	No habit formation
'Vaccination' model	Individual perception of risk not relevant	Allocation explained solely by habit, no costs of adjustment

The progression from one to the other can be seen as follows. With perfect information and no habit effects, it is only the costs imposed on others which are relevant, and in broad terms these can be measured by the loss of net production (present value of contribution to production minus consumption) and the health costs. An approximate estimate of the costs in this form in 1971 is that they would amount to £200 million.

If we now assume that people are unaware of the health risks and that the correct criterion of social welfare is W_I^*, then we have to add the elements under ΔW_I^*: (i) plus the intrinsic value of the lives lost, and (ii) minus the costs to smokers from giving up. If, following conventional practice, item (i) is approximated by the value of consumption plus an allowance for 'the value of life as such' (Peston), the total cost equals that calculated on the vaccination approach (approximately £500 million in 1971) minus item (ii). This latter item can be neglected only if we assume that the addictive nature of tobacco is such that individuals are, in fact, indifferent about the allocation of their expenditure and if the elimination of smoking could be achieved with no personal adjustment costs. If this is not the case, then the true costs under the first criterion would be less than those calculated on the vaccination model. Some idea of the difference is provided by the fact that there are over 20 million smokers, so that if the cost to each of giving up smoking were only £5 per annum, then the cost is reduced by £100 million. To reduce the total cost to that obtained on the pure divergence approach would require a cost per smoker of only £19 per year. Moreover, we have seen that the second criterion, ΔW_{II}, which takes into account the individual's perception of risk in evaluating different outcomes, would lead to a still lower estimate.

The main purpose of this chapter has been to argue that the 'cost' of smoking is far from being a straightforward issue, and that it raises a number of difficult questions in addition to those, such as the valuation of human lives, which usually arise with cost-benefit analysis in the health field. These questions include the determinants of smoking behaviour and the correct formulation of the social welfare function;[10] and there are other important issues not discussed here, such as the redistributional consequences of measures to reduce smoking.[11]

Notes

1 This paper grew out of a joint project on the economic consequences of smoking between the MRC/DHSS Epidemiology and Medical Care Unit, Northwick Park Hospital, and the Department of Economics, University of Essex. Many of the ideas arose from discussion with Joy Skegg, Senior Research Officer working on the project; and I am grateful to C. C. von Weizsäcker and C. J. Bliss for their comments.
2 Some readers may conclude that only a non-smoker could put forward such a model!
3 Estimates have been made for other countries (see, for example, [5]), but these are not discussed here.
4 In this case, no allowance would be made for the risk to the smoker. As it is put by Mishan [6]: 'If smoking tobacco causes 20,000 deaths a year, no subtracting from the benefits, on account of this risk, need be entered, in as much as smokers are already aware that the tobacco habit is unhealthy.'
5 The cardinal nature of U is clearly important. It should be noted that other formulations of the individual's objective function may be more attractive, e.g. maximising the expected average flow of utility.
6 Empirically, it appears that for constant C, $F = e^{-pct^5}$ where t denotes number of years smoking (Pike and Doll [7]), so that this assumption does not appear unreasonable.
7 Although the model would clearly be valid only within a limited range of variation in p. This formulation has some similarity with the model of Becker [12].
8 Where the revenue is handed back in a lump-sum form.
9 In this case, the only term in $\partial W/\partial A_1$ and $\partial W/\partial A_2$ which is relevant is the middle one, and this is negative.
10 For a discussion of this question in the context of the rather similar problem of decisions about family size, see Mirrlees [14].
11 Between 1958 and 1971, the proportion smoking cigarettes among social class I (professional, etc.) fell from 54% to 37%, whereas the proportion for social class V (unskilled) fell only from 61% to 59%.

References

[1] Richardson, R. G. (ed.) (1972), *The Second World Conference on Smoking and Health*, London, Pitman.
[2] Royal College of Physicians, (1971), *Smoking and Health Now*, London, Pitman.
[3] Hammond, E. C. and Horn, D. (1958), 'Smoking and death rates', *Journal of the American Medical Association*.
[4] Doll, R. and Hill, A. B. (1964), 'Mortality in relation to smoking: ten years' observation of British doctors', *British Medical Journal*.
[5] 'The Estimated cost of certain identifiable consequences of cigarette smoking upon health, longevity and property in Canada in 1966', mimeo.
[6] Mishan, E. J. (1971), *Cost–Benefit Analysis*, London, Allen & Unwin.
[7] Pike, M. C. and Doll, R. (1965), 'Age at onset of lung cancer', *Lancet*, **27**, March.
[8] Atkinson, A. B. and Skegg, J. L. (1973), 'Anti-smoking publicity and the demand for tobacco in the UK', *Manchester School*, vol. 41, pp. 265–82.
[9] Peston, M. (1967), 'Changing utility functions', in Shubik, M. (ed.), *Essays in Mathematical Economics*, Princeton University Press.
[10] Pollak, R. A. (1970), 'Habit formation and dynamic demand functions', *Journal of Political Economy*, August.
[11] von Weizsäcker, C. C. (1971), 'Notes on endogenous change of tastes', *Journal of Economic Theory*, December.
[12] Becker, G. (1961), 'The economics of irrational behaviour', *Journal of Political Economy*.
[13] Weisbrod, B. (1961), *Economics of Public Health*, Philadelphia, University of Pennsylvania Press.
[14] Mirrlees, J. A. (1972), 'Population policy and the taxation of family size', *Journal of Public Economics*.

20 Capital-Growth-Sharing Schemes and the Behaviour of the Firm[1]*

1 Introduction

There are good reasons for believing that policies designed to reduce the concentration of wealth in Britain have not been especially successful, and that we need to look beyond purely fiscal means of achieving redistribution. On the continent similar considerations have led trade unions to propose that wage negotiations should be extended to include a capital element. These proposals, described in detail in an OECD report, *Negotiated Workers' Savings Plans for Capital Formation* [5], would involve unions bargaining not simply about earnings but also for a capital payment to the workers which would be paid not in cash but into a workers' investment fund, where it would be accumulated (until, say, the worker retired). In this way, the continental proposals would appear to fulfil the purpose of increasing the wealth held by those in the bottom 90% without a fall in the rate of saving. It has also been suggested that the schemes could play an important role in the formulation of a successful long-term incomes policy. For these reasons, the proposals seem to merit further examination; they have, however, received relatively little attention in Britain.[2] Moreover, the discussion that has taken place has not been based on any formal analysis of the effect of the schemes on the behaviour of the firm; and indeed, there has been surprisingly little written on the micro-economic implications of profit-sharing of any form.

The aim of this chapter is to examine the effects of the introduction of such proposals on the behaviour of the firm, and in particular on its price and investment policies. These aspects are of central importance in assessing the distributional and other consequences. It has been argued, for example, that the firm would raise its price, so that there would be no real increase in the remuneration of labour. An attempt is made here to see how far this is likely to be true at a micro-economic level. Similarly, opposition to the continental proposals has often centred on their adverse effect on capital accumulation; however, it has not been demonstrated that this is a necessary consequence of their introduction.

The continental proposals have been of two main types: where the capital payment is fixed in advance ('investment wages'), and where the payment

* Reprinted from *Economica*, 1972.

depends on profits ('capital-growth-sharing'). This chapter is concerned with the latter scheme, and the way in which is would work is described in section 2. Section 3 sets out the basic model underlying the analysis; sections 4 and 5 examine the effect of capital-growth-sharing under the assumptions of long-run profit maximisation and 'managerial' growth maximisation; and section 6 discusses the likelihood of such schemes being introduced by collective bargaining.

2 Capital-Growth-Sharing Defined

The central feature of capital-growth-sharing is that a proportion of the excess of profits over a 'reasonable' return on capital is paid by the firm into a workers' investment fund. This fund is invested on behalf of the workers, and an individual can only withdraw the amount to which he is entitled after a number of years. This can be made more precise as follows:

(a) *Proportion of profits paid to workers* (α). This is negotiated at the outset of the scheme and is assumed to remain constant over time.

(b) '*Reasonable*' *return on capital* (j). The basis on which this is determined is likely to prove a major source of disagreement, and, as will be clear, the effects of the scheme depend sensitively on this parameter. It is assumed that workers do not receive any payment if the rate of profit falls below j. (They do not share any losses.)

(c) *Form of payment.* The payment by the firm to the fund could be in a number of different forms: cash, fixed-interest obligations or shares. It is assumed initially that a proportion β is paid in fixed-interest obligations and $(1 - \beta)$ in cash.[3] The former are assumed to be non-marketable and to yield a cash return r in perpetuity. Later we consider the effect of payments being made in the form of shares.

(d) *Workers' investment fund.* The assumption that a proportion of the capital-sharing payment is in the form of non-transferable fixed-interest obligations means that part of the portfolio of the fund is pre-determined. If the amount involved is denoted by S_t,

$$\dot{S}_t = \alpha\beta(P_t - jK_t), \tag{1}$$

where P_t denotes current profits, and K_t the capital stock at time t.[4] The form in which the remainder of the portfolio is invested is left open for the present.

(e) *Relationship with wage negotiations.* The proposals for capital-growth-sharing are assumed to involve acceptance by the unions of a slower rate of growth of wages in the year in which the scheme is introduced, so that as a result of the scheme the level of wages would be reduced by a proportion $\theta(0 \leqslant \theta \leqslant 1)$.

3 The Basic Model

As will become clear, the traditional theory of the firm is not a fully adequate tool for examining the effects of capital-growth-sharing; for this reason, the analysis is based on the more recent theories of the growth of the firm, and particularly on the presentation by Solow [8]. The assumptions follow closely those made by him.

(i) *Production.* To simplify the analysis, it is assumed that there are fixed coefficients of production. There is labour-augmenting technical progress at rate u:

$$Y_t = AK_t = BL_t e^{ut}, \tag{2}$$

where Y_t denotes output and L_t the labour force employed.

(ii) *Demand.* The firm faces a downward-sloping demand curve for its output. This demand curve shifts outward over time at a 'natural' rate g_0; however, by expenditure on sales promotion, the firm can expand its sales (for any given price) at a faster rate g. The net revenue depends on the price chosen and on the rate of growth (since selling costs have to be subtracted).

(iii) *Firm's decision variables.* It is assumed that the firm makes a once-for-all decision about the level of output (as represented by Y_0, or equivalently by K_0) and its rate of growth (g). This assumption is in a number of respects unappealing, and it precludes any discussion of the initial effects of capital-sharing; however, it does allow considerable simplification. The net revenue of the firm can be represented as:

$$R_0 e^{gt} = F(Y_0)T(g)e^{gt}. \tag{3}$$

The function F represents the gross revenue, and $T(g) = 1 - s(g)$, where $s(g)$ represents the selling or expansion costs as a proportion of sales revenue.[5] It is assumed that the elasticity of demand with respect to Y_0 is constant. The assumed shape of $T(g)$ is shown in Figure 1.

(iv) *Wages.* It is assumed that the level of wages (w_0 at time 0) is determined by collective bargaining, but that the rate of growth is equal to the rate of productivity increase.[6] Labour costs are therefore aw_0K_t, and net profits may be written as:

$$P_t = R_0 e^{gt} - aw_0 K_0 e^{gt}. \tag{4}$$

(v) *Dividend policy.* Of the investment carried out at time $t(gK_t)$, part is

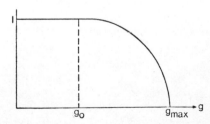

Figure 1   *Shape of T(g)*

financed by new issues (N_t) and part by retained earnings. The dividends paid to shareholders at time t are therefore:

$$D_t = D_0 e^{gt} = P_t - (gK_t - N_t). \tag{5}$$

It is assumed that the stock market valuation of a share is equal to the present value of dividends at a discount rate i. If the rate of growth of the number of shares outstanding is h, then the dividend per share grows at a rate $(g-h)$ and the present value for existing shareholders is $V_0 = D_0/[i-(g-h)]$. In other words, the shareholders receive a return i on their holdings made up of dividends D_0/V_0 plus capital gains at rate $(g-h)$. Since $N_t = hV_t$, we have[7]:

$$V_0 = (P_0 - gK_0)/(i-g). \tag{6}$$

4 The Long-run Profit Maximising Firm

The Fisherian firm is assumed to maximise the difference between the stock market value of the firm and the cost of the capital employed:

$$Z_0 = V_0 - K_0 = (P_0 - iK_0)/(i-g). \tag{7}$$

The first-order conditions for maximisation therefore give:

$$\partial P_0/\partial K_0 = \partial R_0/\partial K_0 - aw_0 = i; \tag{8}$$

marginal revenue is equated with marginal cost; and:

$$-\partial P_0/\partial g = (P_0 - iK_0)/(i-g), \tag{9}$$

the marginal cost of expansion is equated with the present value of profits in excess of the cost of capital at an interest rate i (or Z_0).[8]

The introduction of capital-growth-sharing into the model means that there will be (i) current payment of part of the agreed profit share in cash, and (ii) interest payments on the holdings of the workers' fund. It is assumed – in keeping with the steady growth assumption – that capital-growth-sharing has been in force from time immemorial. This means that the fixed-interest obligations held by the fund are growing at rate $g(\dot{S}=gS)$; so that, from (1):

$$S_0 = (\alpha\beta/g)(P_0 - jK_0). \tag{10}$$

The dividends paid to the shareholders at time 0 are therefore:

$$D_0 = P_0 - gK_0 + N_0 - \alpha(P_0 - jK_0)[\beta r/g + 1 - \beta],$$

and:

$$Z_1 = [(P_0 - iK_0) - \alpha\gamma(P_0 - iK_0)]/(i-g);$$ (11)

where $\gamma = (1-\beta) + \beta r/g$, and $P_0 = R_0 - aw_0(1-\theta)K_0$.

Effect on pricing policy

Let us consider first the effect of capital-growth-sharing on pricing policy – or (equivalently) the choice of K_0. The first-order condition becomes (for given g):

$$(\partial P_0/\partial K_0)(1-\alpha\gamma) = i - \alpha\gamma j,$$

or: (12)

$$\partial R_0/\partial K_0 - aw_0 = i + \alpha\gamma(i-j)/(1-\alpha\gamma) - \theta aw_0.$$

(It is assumed that $\alpha\gamma < 1$.) Comparing equations (8) and (12) we can see that where $\theta = 0$ the scale of operation of the firm increases or decreases according as $j \gtrless i$. If the rate of return allowed by the scheme as 'reasonable' is greater than the shareholders' rate of discount, the firm expands its scale of operation and lowers its price even where no reduction in wages accompanies the introduction of capital-sharing. (It should be noted that $P_0/K_0 > i$, so that $j > i$ may be quite consistent with positive capital-sharing payments being made.) If there is a once-for-all reduction in the level of wages ($\theta > 0$), the price may fall even where $j < i$.

As far as the individual firm is concerned, the case $\beta = 0$ is equivalent to ordinary profit-sharing – a straightforward cash payment as a proportion of profits in excess of 'reasonable'.[9] From (12) we can see that capital-growth-sharing differs only in the magnitude of the effect (through γ). If $r > g$, then γ will be larger with growth-sharing, and hence the price change larger than under profit-sharing. This is so, for example, where the return paid on the fixed-interest obligations held by the fund is equal to the total return received by ordinary shareholders ($r = i$).

From this analysis it is clear that there is no presumption that firms necessarily would increase prices as a result of capital-growth-sharing. Even with no compensating reduction in the level of wages, prices could be decreased; and to the extent that wages are reduced, the price decrease is the more likely. Moreover, it should be emphasised that this conclusion in no way depends on any such assumption as that it 'cannot be passed on in the form of higher prices because the amount of the employers' contribution is not known until after the event' ([5], p. 49). It is interesting to compare the conclusion reached here with the statement by Föhl [3]; 'Those who can pass on profits taxes can also pass on profit sharing via prices to the consumer. This applies in the first place to firms with a dominant market position and steep price-demand curves.' Although the parallel with a profits tax is an illuminating one, Föhl's conclusion is incorrect. For the firm a profit-sharing scheme ($\beta = 0$) has considerable similarity with a profits tax (at rate α); there is, however, an important difference in the extent to which the cost of capital can be deducted. With a profits tax, only bond interest can in general be set against tax, so that:

$$Z_0 = [(P_0 - iK_0) - t(P_0 - i\mu K_0)]/(i-g),$$

where t denotes the tax rate and μ the proportion of capital financed by bonds. Comparing this expression with (11), it can be seen that a profits tax is equivalent to assuming $j < i$ (for $\mu < 1$), so that it leads to a fall in K_0 and hence a rise in price. With capital-growth-sharing, however, it is quite possible for j to exceed i and for Föhl's conclusion to be reversed. This result is further strengthened by allowing for the compensating reduction in wages.[10]

Effect on investment

The principal differences between capital-growth-sharing and profit-sharing only emerge when we consider the growth of the firm, and it is for this reason that a dynamic analysis is necessary. Let us consider the firm's choice of g (for a given K_0).[11] The first-order condition is:

$$-\frac{\partial P_0}{\partial g} = \frac{P_0 - iK_0}{i-g} + \frac{\alpha\gamma(j-i)K_0}{(1-\alpha\gamma)(i-g)} + \frac{\alpha\beta r(P_0 - jK_0)}{g^2(1-\alpha\gamma)}. \tag{13}$$

From this it is clear that, if $\beta = 0$, the rate of growth of the firm is increased where $j > i$ (where no allowance is made for the fall in wages). However, where $\beta > 0$ (capital-sharing), the third term on the right-hand side is positive (providing positive capital-sharing payments are paid), which tends to increase the growth rate still further. The reason why capital-sharing in the form described here leads to a faster rate of growth than straightforward profit-sharing is that the firm can effectively spread the commitment to the fund further by growing faster. Despite its title, capital-growth-sharing means that the faster the firm grows the smaller is the share of the workers' fund in profits (in steady growth).

Alternative method of payment

At this point, we should consider the consequences of the fund receiving not fixed-interest obligations but shares identical with those held by other shareholders. The fund's holding (S_t) would then grow on account of capital gains and of the current profit share, $\dot{S} = (g-h)S + \alpha\beta(P-jK)$, so that in steady state $S_0 = \alpha\beta(P_0 - jK_0)/h$. Since the cash payment per share equals $D_0/V_0 = i - (g-h)$, the dividends paid to the shareholders (apart from the fund) become:

$$D_0 = P_0 - gK_0 + N_0 - \alpha(P_0 - jK_0)[1-\beta] - (i-g+h)S_0,$$

and the value of the holding of the original shareholders:

$$V_0 = \{(P_0 - gK_0) - \alpha(P_0 - jK_0)[1 - \beta + \beta(i-g+h)/h]\}/(i-g). \tag{14}$$

It is clear that V_0 is now an increasing function of h: new issues effectively allow the firm to gain by diluting the capital of the workers' fund. It seems reasonable to suppose, however, that there is a limit to this process, and in particular it seems unlikely that h would fall below g (since this would imply a falling share price).[12] It will be assumed therefore that $h=g$. This means that γ reduces to $1-\beta+\beta(i/g)$, and the analysis goes through as before (with $r=i$).

5   Capital-Sharing and the Managerial Firm

The theory of the firm underlying the analysis of the previous section represents the natural extension of the traditional profit-maximising assumption to a dynamic context. In this section, we consider how the results would be affected by alternative assumptions about the objectives of the firm.

The model of the 'managerial' firm discussed here is based on the work of Marris, as developed by Solow [8]. Managers are assumed to maximise the rate of growth of the firm subject to a takeover constraint, where this is formulated in terms of the valuation ratio, $V_0 \geq mK_0$, where m is a constant $(0<m\leq 1)$. If the stock market value of the firm falls below a certain proportion of the value of its assets, it runs the risk of a takeover bid. As it is put by Solow, 'the notion of a minimal safe valuation ratio comes from the idea that a firm with too low a value will be taken over and sold for scrap' ([8], p. 330). This constraint will in fact hold with equality, and can be written using equation (6) in the absence of capital-sharing as:

$$P_0/K_0 = mi + (1-m)g. \tag{15}$$

For any given K_0, the rate of growth is determined in the way shown in Figure 2. As Solow has pointed out, in this form the theory provides no adequate explanation of the choice of scale, since the firm can approach arbitrarily close to g_{max} by choosing its initial capital stock sufficiently close to zero.[13] It will therefore be assumed here that K_0 is given historically, and attention will be focused on the effect of capital-growth-sharing on the rate of growth.

The introduction of capital-growth-sharing means that the stock market value of the firm becomes:

$$V_0 = [(P_0-gK_0) - \alpha(P_0-jK_0)(1-\beta) - rS_0]/(i-g), \tag{16}$$

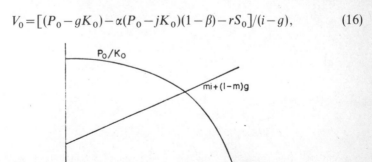

Figure 2   *Growth rate of managerial firm.*

where $P_0 = R_0 - aw_0(1-\theta)K_0$. At the same time, the valuation constraint is affected. A takeover bidder would acquire the assets of the firm (K_0) but also a liability to the workers' fund, which for the present is written as δS_0. The constraint becomes therefore:

$$m[K_0 - \delta S_0] = [P_0 - gK_0 - \alpha(1-\beta)(P_0 - jK_0) - rS_0](i-g),$$

or:

$$P_0/K_0 = mi + (1-m)g + \alpha(1-\beta)(P_0/K_0 - j) + (S_0/K_0) \times [r - \delta m(i-g)]. \quad (17)$$

In the case where $\beta = 0$ (so $S_0 = 0$), an increase in α increases the right-hand side and hence reduces the rate of growth. This is offset by the fall in w_0; but for the growth rate to increase it would be necessary for θaw_0 to be greater than $\alpha(P_0 - jK_0)$ – i.e. the current payment to labour would be decreased. In the case where $\beta = 1$, the effect depends on the value placed by a potential bidder on the liability to the fund. Since the view of takeover bids underlying the valuation ratio constraint is that the bidder is interested in the physical assets, it seems reasonable to suppose that the capital-sharing scheme would not be continued by him. The compensation payable would depend on the precise form of the agreement. If the compensation would be simply $S_0(\delta = 1)$, then the last term in (17) is positive where $r > m(i-g)$ (which is clearly satisfied, for example, when $r = i$). In general the growth rate is reduced unless:

$$\theta aw_0 > (r + mg - mi)(S_0/K_0). \quad (18a)$$

If, on the other hand, the fund has to be compensated at its own valuation of the flow of interest on S_0, the condition becomes:

$$\theta \alpha w_0 > r\left[1 - \frac{m(i-g)}{i'}\right](S_0/K_0), \quad (18b)$$

where i' is the discount rate applied by the fund.[14] If i' is less than i, it is possible for the right-hand side to be negative – so that the growth rate would be increased even if there were no compensating reduction in wages.

The case is rather more straightforward where the capital-sharing payments are made not in fixed-interest liabilities but in shares. To acquire complete control of the firm the bidder has to buy the shares of both shareholders and the fund, so that the valuation constraint becomes (taking $\beta = 1$):

$$mK_0 = V_0 + S_0 = [P_0 - gK_0 - S_0(i-g+h)]/(i-g) + S_0$$
$$= (P_0 - gK_0 - hS_0)/(i-g) \quad (19)$$

(from (14)). The total stock market valuation $(V_0 + S_0)$ is depressed because the shares issued to the workers' fund are 'given away'. The growth rate is reduced unless the reduction in wages $(\theta aw_0 K_0)$ exceeds hS_0. Under the assumptions made about the limits on new issues, $h = g$; so that the condition for g to be increased is:

$$\beta_{aw_0} > q(S_0/K_0),\qquad(18b)$$

This condition is the same as that obtained from (18a) if $r = i$ and $m = 1$.

As in the case of a Fisherian profit-maximising firm, there is, therefore, no presumption that the introduction of capital-growth-sharing would necessarily lead to a fall in the rate of growth. It is interesting to compare this conclusion with the less formal analysis of the OECD report ([5], pp. 123–4):

With self-financing, managers may undertake investment in projects which do not have a rate of return high enough to have attracted funds from the market. If part of the profits are to be taken away from the shareholders, it does not follow therefore that managers will be reluctant to undertake investment ... The crucial determinant becomes the rate of return set by management on its own use of internal funds, or the rate of return accepted as a minimum by the Investment Fund.

The role of the second of these factors is clear from our conditions (18a) and (18b). A low value of r (the return received by the Fund) or i' (its rate of discount) makes it more likely that the growth rate will be increased. The first determinant is, however, not relevant; it is not the 'return set by management' that is important as much as the *change* in this target return caused by the introduction of capital-growth-sharing. If its introduction depresses the firm's stock market value, the managers will have to raise their target return to avoid being taken over.

6 The Scope for Bargaining over Capital-Growth-Sharing

It would be possible for capital-growth-sharing to be introduced by legislation; however, it is interesting to examine the conditions under which it could be introduced through collective bargaining. Clearly a precondition for this to happen is that there exists a form of capital-sharing which would offer benefits to both sides in the negotiations. In this section we see what can be said about this in the light of the earlier analysis. It should be emphasised, however, that there are a number of factors not discussed here which are likely to influence the negotations. On the part of the employers, it might be expected that profit-sharing would provide an incentive to increased productivity; and this has certainly been considered an important factor by earlier writers (see e.g. [1]). On the part of the unions, capital-sharing might be seen as a means of acquiring greater control over industry (through the workers' investment fund).

In the earlier analysis, it was assumed that capital-growth-sharing had been in force forever; when considering the scope for negotiations, it is convenient to replace this by an alternative assumption. The scheme is supposed to begin at time 0; but at the outset the firm establishes a fund $S_0 = \alpha\beta(P_0 - jK_0)/g$, so that steady growth can be maintained thereafter.

In the case of the profit-maximising firm, there are two parties involved: the shareholders and the unions. If the latter are concerned with the present value

U of payments received per worker at a discount rate i', there will be no scope for bargaining.[15] With the introduction of capital-growth-sharing, U is changed from $w_0/(i'-u)$ to:

$$a(i'-u)U = aw_0(1-\theta) + \alpha\gamma[R_0/K_0 - aw_0(1-\theta) - j]$$
$$= aw_0 + \alpha\gamma[R_0/K_0 - aw_0 - i] - (1-\alpha\gamma)X, \qquad (20)$$

where $X = \theta aw_0 - \alpha\gamma(i-j)/(1-\alpha\gamma)$. For the union to be better-off with the scheme, we require that:

$$X(1-\alpha\gamma) < \alpha\gamma[R_0/K_0 - aw_0 - i]. \qquad (21)$$

The effect of the scheme on Z is:

$$Z = \frac{(1-\alpha\gamma)(R_0 - aw_0K_0 - iK_0)}{(i-g)} + \frac{(1-\alpha\gamma)XK_0}{(i-g)}.$$

If there were a scheme such that (21) was satisfied, we should have $Z < (R_0 - aw_0K_0 - iK_0)/(i-g)$, which implies that Z is less than the value obtained in the absence of capital-sharing, and hence that the employers would reject the scheme.

If the unions are interested not only in the payment per worker but also in total employment, there may be scope for bargaining. Suppose for simplicity that the union maximises the wage bill (this probably attaches too much weight to employment but serves to illustrate the possibilities), and that g is taken as given. Then the modified objective function of the union is:

$$U' = aw_0K_0 + \alpha\gamma[R_0 - aw_0K_0 - iK_0] - (1-\alpha\gamma)XK_0$$

and we have:

$$Z(i-g) + U' = R_0 - iK_0. \qquad (22)$$

The possibilities for Z and U' are, therefore, as shown in Figure 3. In the absence of capital-sharing, $\partial R_0/\partial K_0 = aw_0 + i$, so that if capital-sharing leads to a rise in K_0, the right-hand side of (22) will be increased. We may expect that negotiations will lead to K_0 such that $\partial R_0/\partial K_0 = i$, and from (12) this can be seen to require $X = aw_0$. The value of $\alpha\gamma$ then determines the distribution of the gains, i.e. the point reached on the segment AB.[16]

The requirement $X = aw_0$ means that $aw_0(1-\theta) = [\alpha\gamma/(1-\alpha\gamma)](j-i)$, so that the agreement will involve $j > i$ (since $\theta < 1$). Employment will be expanded (and the firm will reduce the extent to which it exploits its monopoly power). This will, however, be achieved at the expense of a fall in the payments per worker.

In the case of a profit-maximising firm, a scheme for capital-growth-sharing will only be negotiated if the unions are interested in expanding employment at

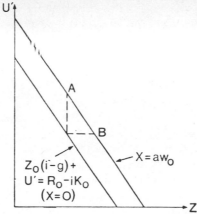

Figure 3 *Scope for negotiation.*

the expense of reducing payments per worker. Where, however, the firm is controlled by managers interested in maximising the rate of growth, there may be scope for negotiation even in the case where the unions are concerned only with payment per worker.

In the case of the managerial firm, there are three parties involved – workers, managers and shareholders – but the last group only affects the negotiations through the valuation constraint. The question is therefore whether the managers and the workers can agree on a scheme that leads to an outcome satisfying the valuation constraint and providing benefits to them both. By assumption managers are interested only in growth, so that they would favour any scheme that increased the rate of growth. If it is assumed that the unions are concerned with the present value U of payments per worker, they would be willing to agree to a scheme where:

$$\theta a w_0 \leqslant \alpha(P_0 - jK_0)[(1-\beta) + \beta(r/g)] = gS_0[r/g + (1-\beta)/\beta]. \qquad (23)$$

If $\beta = 0$, this becomes simply $\theta a w_0 \leqslant \alpha(P_0 - jK_0)$, which is the condition for g to be reduced; so there is no possibility of agreement on a purely profit-sharing scheme. Suppose, however, that $\beta = 1$ and that in the valuation constraint $\delta = 1$. The scheme will satisfy (23) and lead to a rise in g where:

$$[r - m(i-g)]S_0 \leqslant \theta a w_0 \leqslant rS_0, \qquad (24)$$

so that there will be a reduction in wages which would be less than the capital-sharing payment but sufficient to lead to a rise in g. Both managers and unions would be better-off with a scheme satisfying (24); the losers would be the shareholders.[17] If $m = 1$ and $r = i$, the left-hand side reduces to gS_0, and the same result appears with (18c) in place of (18a). Condition (18b) gives a slightly different version of (24), but the result is essentially unchanged.

It is possible therefore that in a managerially-controlled firm a scheme could be negotiated between managers and workers which would redistribute from the shareholders to the workers and would still meet the valuation constraint. This can be done because the capital-sharing scheme allows the workers to capitalise part of their future earnings and to demand compensation if the scheme is withdrawn.[18] In this case, the introduction of capital-growth-sharing would increase the payment per worker.

7   Concluding Comments

The aim of this chapter has been to examine the consequences at a micro-economic level of the introduction of profit-sharing and capital-growth-sharing schemes. The analysis has demonstrated that a number of the earlier views are incorrect. For example, profit-sharing does not necessarily have the same effect on firm behaviour as a profits tax, and it is quite possible that it can lead to a fall in price. Similarly, the view of Crossley that 'there is nothing ... to give us grounds for believing that the percentage mark-up of prices over wage costs can be reduced directly by altering the form in which employees are paid' ([2], p. 347) is not borne out by the finding that firms may be willing to negotiate capital-sharing agreements (to the benefit of the unions) which affect their price or investment policy. At the same time, it is important to emphasise the limitations of the analysis. The restrictiveness of the partial equilibrium framework will be apparent. The assumptions about the form of capital-sharing and the behaviour of the different agents (particularly unions and managers) are highly stylised. No account has been taken of the effect of capital-sharing on the choice of technique by the firm. The introduction of uncertainty into the discussion of negotiations about capital-sharing would have an important effect.

Notes

1 Based on a special university lecture given at the London School of Economics, November 1971.
2 Among the few references are the OECD report [5], Crossley [2], Forsyth [3], a brief passage in Pen [6], and the recent discussion of incomes policy by Jones [4].
3 As Prevoo (Supplement to [5], p. 113) has pointed out, payment in shares is unlikely to be practicable for firms without a stock market quotation. Payment in the form of fixed-interest obligations could therefore be more widely introduced.
4 Taxation is ignored in what follows. Exemption of contributions from company taxation may, however, be an important means of stimulating the spread of capital-growth-sharing.
5 For discussion of the normalisation of selling costs with respect to sales revenue, see Solow [8], p. 321.
6 The analysis can be extended simply to cover the case where wages grow at a different rate from the rate of productivity increase in the particular firm.
7 New issues do not, therefore, affect the stock market value (as demonstrated by Williamson [9]).
8 With the appropriate assumptions about the form of $T(g)$ and F, the second-order conditions will be satisfied.
9 Although for the workers it would not necessarily be the same, since the payment would be 'frozen' in the workers' fund until they retired.
10 In combining a 'tax' on profits with a 'subsidy' on wages, capital-growth-sharing has considerable similarity to the fiscal device proposed by Robinson ([7], pp. 164–5) for the control of monopoly.

11 The results can readily be extended to cover the simultaneous determination of g and K_0.
12 In practice, allowance would have to be made for the preferential tax treatment of capital gains, etc.
13 Solow [8], p. 330. This problem can be overcome if the utility of the managers is assumed to be an increasing function of both g and K_0 (as with Williamson's long-run sales maximisation hypothesis [9]).
14 It is assumed that the remainder of the fund's portfolio is invested in assets yielding i'.
15 At this point it is assumed that the discount rate applied by the individual worker is equal to the rate of return i' earned by the fund on its other assets.
16 In the absence of capital-sharing, there would be only one variable in the negotiations (w_0) and the level of K_0 could not be determined independently of the distribution between Z and U'. A situation with $X = aw_0$, for example, would imply $U' = 0$, which would clearly not be acceptable to the unions.
17 It should be noted that this result depends on the particular assumptions made about take-over bids. With an alternative theory of takeovers, such as that adopted by Williamson [9], the results could be rather different.
18 Capital-growth-sharing could provide workers with some of the benefits accruing to managers through service contracts.

References

[1] Bowie, J. A. (1922), 'Profit-sharing and copartnership', *Economic Journal*, vol. XXXII, pp. 466–76.
[2] Crossley, J. R. (1970), 'Incomes policy and sharing in capital gains', *British Journal of Industrial Relations*, vol. III, pp. 336–52.
[3] Forsyth, M. (1971), *Property and Property Distribution Policy*, PEP Broadsheet 528.
[4] Jones, A. (1972), 'A policy for prices and incomes now', *Lloyds Bank Review*, January.
[5] OECD (1970) *Workers' Negotiated Savings Plans for Capital Formation*, Paris, and Supplement.
[6] Pen, J. (1971), *Income Distribution*, London, Allen Lane.
[7] Robinson, J. (1933), *The Economics of Imperfect Competition*, London, Macmillan.
[8] Solow, R. M. (1971), 'Some implications of alternative criteria for the firm', in Marris, R. L. and Wood, A. (eds.), *The Corporate Economy*, London.
[9] Williamson, J. H. (1966), 'Profit growth and sales maximization', *Economica*, vol. XXXIII, pp. 1–16.

21 Unemployment, Social Security and Incentives in Britain*

1 Introduction

Unemployment is likely to remain a major social and economic problem in Britain for several years. Even without subscribing to the more alarmist views about growing technological unemployment, there seems little prospect, on current policies, of returning in the immediate future to the levels of activity of the 1950s and 1960s.

The first priority in government policy towards unemployment is the steady expansion of demand, at both national and international level. However, even sustained growth at the rate of 5% per annum – a minimum target – will have only a gradual impact. So that while we strongly endorse measures to reflate demand, and thus bring unemployment down to a more tolerable level, we feel that it is necessary to consider the implications of unemployment as a medium-term phenomenon and it is to these that the present chapter is addressed. In particular, we concentrate on the issues raised for income maintenance policy – the adequacy of social security, incentives to work, and the interplay between taxation and benefits.

The social security provisions for the unemployed in Britain have attracted a great deal of public attention, and the debate – as in earlier periods of high unemployment – has highlighted the conflicting principles underlying policy in this area. On the one hand, social security should guarantee a reasonable level of income to those out of work, on the other hand, it should not be provided in such a way that people have little incentive to seek or accept jobs. In this chapter we begin by considering how successful the present system of national insurance and supplementary benefits has been in reconciling these objectives. It is widely believed, for example, that unemployment is less serious financially than it used to be – that benefits prevent the unemployed and their families falling far below their usual incomes. How far is this true? Similarly, it is often claimed that much of the increased unemployment since the mid-1960s is 'voluntary' associated with a rise in benefit incomes relative to those in work. In section 2 we examine this view.

* Reprinted from the *Midland Bank Review*, 1978.
A. B. Atkinson and J. S. Flemming.

From this examination of the performance of the present system it is clear that there is scope for improvement, both to reduce the incidence of low incomes and to remove possible disincentive effects (actual or potential). In section 3 we discuss a range of reforms. These include the taxation of benefits, the restructuring of the national insurance system, and the wider role to be played by universal provisions such as the child benefit scheme.

2 Unemployment

As a background to answering these questions, it may be helpful to review briefly the main evidence about recent unemployment in Britain. The aggregate picture is probably well known. It is, however, highly misleading to regard unemployment simply as an aggregate. To begin with, Figure 1 brings out the relatively much larger increase in recorded unemployment for women, which rose from 136,000 in March 1972 to 375,000 in October 1977 (both figures seasonally adjusted). This is in part a genuine phenomenon, arising

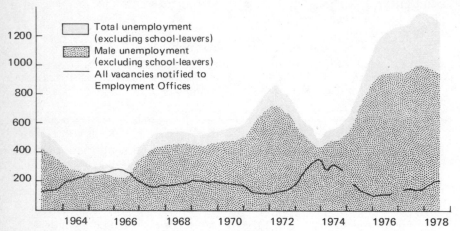

Figure 1   *Unemployment and vacancies in Great Britain.*
Three-month moving averages, seasonally adjusted (000's).
Source: *Department of Employment Gazette*, January 1968, February 1978.

from increased participation and reduced employment in areas such as the public sector, but is in part simply a reflection of the increase in the proportion registered.

Considering men alone, the increase is still very marked. The seasonally-adjusted total at successive peaks has been 465,000 (1968), 700,000 (1972) and 1 million (1977). This growth is to a substantial extend concentrated among those with longer durations and among younger workers.

The incidence of unemployment is very uneven. Many workers never become unemployed at any time in their careers; others suffer repeated spells – in extreme cases as many as ten in a year. The unevenness is underlined by the fact that a uniform distribution of unemployment would mean that an individual could expect (at 1978 levels) to be unemployed for an average duration of 3–4 months once every six years. The actual picture is of course very far from this.

Unemployment varies with occupation, and in particular is much higher for unskilled workers. Thus in December 1977 there were 463,000 unemployed in the category 'general labourers'. Although the figures need careful interpretation, the ratio of unemployed to vacancies appears much higher for this category, which is in sharp contrast to 'craft and similar occupations' where there is evidence of potential shortages of particular skills. For example, there were in December 1977 more vacancies for toolmakers than there were unemployed.

Within each occupation the incidence of unemployment varies with age. Young people are overall more likely to become unemployed: the rate of inflow for the age group 18–24 being estimated by Cripps and Tarling (*Economic Journal*, 1974) to be about double that for all males. On the other hand, younger workers are less likely to be unemployed for as long as a year and more likely to have had short spells (see Figure 2). In January 1978, one-

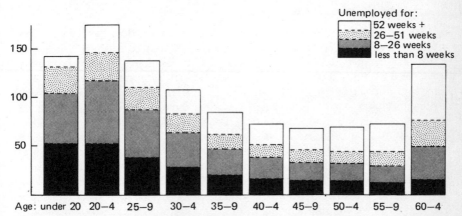

Figure 2 *Unemployment by age and duration. Males, January 1978, Great Britain (000's).*
Source: Department of Employment Gazette, February 1978, p. 205.

third of unemployed males aged under twenty-five had been out of work for less than eight weeks, compared with a quarter overall and 11% for men aged 60–4. At the other extreme, only one in eight of males aged under twenty-five had been unemployed for more than a year, compared with 43% of those aged fifty-five and over. In these older age groups unemployment may well be associated with ill-health or disability.

In addition to these factors, there is the well-known variation of unemployment by region and by industry. In March 1978, seasonally-adjusted unemployment ranged from 4.2% in the south-east, through 5.2% in the west midlands, to 8.0% in Scotland and 8.4% in the north. (The figure for Northern Ireland was 10.9%.) The 2:1 differential between the north and the south-east is in fact rather smaller than in 1972, when the ratio was nearly 3:1; the south-east now accounts for a larger proportion of total unemployment than previously. There are substantial differentials when classified by industry in which last employed, ranging in February 1978 from 2.5% in gas, electricity and water to 15.1% in construction. Manufacturing (rate 4.6%) accounted for one-quarter of total unemployment, compared with one-third in 1972 (a fall which can be explained in small part by the reduction in the total size of the manufacturing sector).

The experience of unemployment is likely therefore to be very different for different groups. The position of a skilled craftsman in manufacturing redundant for the first time is very different from that of a labourer in the building trade who has had repeated spells of unemployment. The situation of a younger worker in the south-east unemployed for eight weeks is likely to be different from that of a man aged sixty in the north who has been out of work for a year or more. These differences are important when we turn to the questions on which this chapter focuses.

3 Incomes When Unemployed

It is commonly asserted that people are 'better-off on the dole', with employers complaining that even with high unemployment they cannot attract labour because work provides little financial advantage. Such arguments are usually illustrated by hypothetical examples. Thus a married couple with two children aged four and six, where the man earned £55 a week and the wife did not work would, in November 1977, have had a net income of £45.55, after allowing for income tax, national insurance contributions, child benefit and working expenses of £2 a week. If the man had then lost his job, he would have continued to draw child benefit, have been entitled to £30.30 flat-rate national insurance benefit, and have received, after two waiting weeks, the earnings-related supplement (ERS). The amount of ERS is related to his earnings in a past tax year (for details, see the Technical Note on Benefits below), which are referred to as 'reckonable' earnings. On the assumption that the man had been in work throughout the relevant year and that his pay had risen in line with average earnings, the ERS may be calculated as approximately £8.50 a week. His net income would then be £41.30, or 91% of that in work. On top of that there are refunds of income tax after a month of unemployment, which can be quite substantial.

These calculations illustrate one aspect of the so-called 'poverty trap' – that at-work incomes are considerably reduced by income tax and national insurance contributions (nearly £10 a week) even at this low level of earnings. Moreover, the position is further exacerbated by means-tested benefits. Table 1 shows calculations of total 'net resources' (income plus benefits net of tax and housing outlays, allowing for rent and rate rebates) when unemployed relative to that when working. (The assumptions about rent etc. are explained in the notes to the table.) The ratio of net resources out of work to that in work,

Table 1 Replacement ratios, earnings, family type and unemployment duration: November 1977 (total income support[2] as percentage of that when working)

Family type	Duration (weeks)	Weekly gross earnings at work (£)							Percentage of male NI beneficiaries[3]
		25	35	45	55	65	75	85	
Single person	3–28	107	97	83	70	61	54	49	52 (including married men not claiming for dependent wives)
	29–52	88	72	59	48	40	34	30[1]	
	53–	87[1]	71[1]	59[1]	47[1]	39[1]	34[1]	30[1]	
Claimant with dependent wife	3–28	110	96	101	92	80	71	64	14
	29–52	110	90	79	70	59	52	46	
	53–	109[1]	89[1]	79[1]	69[1]	59[1]	51[1]	45[1]	
Couple with one child (age three)	3–28	115	99	99	98	89	79	71	7 (with one child)
	29–52	91	86	86	79	70	61	54	
	53–	89[1]	84[1]	84[1]	77[1]	69[1]	60[1]	53[1]	
Couple and two children (age four and six)	3–28	120	102	97	101	95	88	79	13 (with two or three children)
	29–52	95	86	88	84	77	70	62	
	53–	95[1]	86[1]	87[1]	83[1]	77[1]	70[1]	62[1]	
Couple and four children (age three, eight, eleven and sixteen)	3–28	130	110	98[1]	99[1]	98	95	93	4 (with four or more children)
	29–52	118[1]	102[1]	98[1]	99[1]	93[1]	88[1]	86[1]	
	53–	118[1]	102[1]	98[1]	99[1]	93[1]	88[1]	86[1]	
Percentage of full-time adult males earning less than amount shown at top of column[4]		0.2	1.1	5.5	18.2	36.6	54.6	69.0	

Notes:
[1] Includes supplementary benefit.
[2] Total income support is defined as gross earnings or benefit, plus child benefit, FIS, value of free school meals and free welfare milk, tax, NI contributions, work expenses and net rates and rent (after rebates). It is assumed that ERS is calculated on the basis of 'reckonable' earnings equal to 80% of current gross earnings. It is assumed that wives are not at work nor in receipt of benefit income. The take-up of means-tested benefits is assumed to be 100%. Where payable in employment, FIS is assumed to continue for six months into unemployment. Tax refunds are not included. Gross rent is assumed to range from £4.70 (single person) to £6.30 (couple with four children), and gross rates from £1.85 to £2.50. *Source:* Royal Commission on the Distribution of Income and Wealth, Report No. 6, Table 4.3.
[3] Data supplied by DHSS for May 1977. The balance consists of men with dependent children but not dependent wives.
[4] New Earnings Survey, April 1977.

referred to commonly as the 'replacement ratio', is close to 100% for the family described earlier for the period when it is receiving ERS (weeks 3–28). Moreover, for a family with lower earnings, or more children, eligibility to Family Income Supplement may continue into unemployment, depending on the date of assessment.[2]

The example given above is similar to those quoted in the press and in parliament. It is important to emphasise, however, that it is far from typical of actual recipients, and the concept of a 'representative' unemployed worker may be quite misleading. The case of a couple with two children is not the norm, and if one must take a representative example, then it should be the single man, or at least a man with no dependants. Of the men receiving unemployment benefit in May 1977, half did not claim for any dependants (see the last column in Table 1), and a further 14% claimed for an adult dependant only. From the family composition data in the 1976 Family Expenditure Survey and the 1977 New Earnings Survey, it can be estimated that at most 2% of men headed households with potential replacement ratios above 100% even in weeks 3–28, and the actual numbers with these replacement ratios is likely to be considerably smaller. The replacement ratio tends to fall with the duration of unemployment. A substantial proportion of the unemployed have been out of work for twenty-nine weeks or more, and as Table 1 shows the fall in income is then considerable for all except the family with four children (or earning £25 a week). Moreover, this table is calculated on the assumption that the family claims all means-tested benefits for which they are eligible. If, like many families, they did not claim free school meals and free welfare milk, then the replacement ratio would tend to be lower. If they do not claim supplementary benefit, then their position is considerably more serious. In all cases marked [1] in Table 1, the family is entitled to supplementary benefit, and this has been included in the replacement ratio.

The lesson to be drawn is that a hypothetical calculation of the replacement ratio for a supposedly typical case may provide little guide to the actual levels of income of the people actually unemployed. This is underlined by the evidence on benefit entitlement. In November 1977, well under half of the registered unemployed were receiving national insurance benefit:

	Number	Per cent of total
NI benefit only	470,000	33
NI benefit and supplementary benefit	129,000	9
Total receiving NI benefit	599,000	42
Receiving supplementary benefit only	574,000	40
Others unemployed registered for work	265,000	18
Total registered unemployed (including school-leavers)	1,438,000	100

Source: Department of Employment Gazette, April 1978, Table 112.

The most privileged in terms of benefits are those receiving the earnings-related supplement in addition to the basic national insurance benefit. They numbered however only about one-quarter of a million (245,000 in May 1976), or some 40% of those receiving NI benefit. The remainder did not receive the supplement because they were not yet entitled (weeks 1–2), had exhausted entitlement (weeks 29–52), did not meet the qualifying conditions (because of low paid or interrupted employment in the relevant tax year), or were cut off by the 85% rule (see Technical Note on Benefits). The important point is that quite a small proportion – around one in six – could have enjoyed the most generous replacement ratios shown in Table 1. (Reference should also be made to redundancy payments, but the number receiving statutory payments has been relatively small – of the order of 20–30,000 per month.)

What is very striking is that over half the unemployed were not receiving national insurance benefit at all. This may be because they failed to qualify on their past employment record or were disqualified (e.g. were dismissed for industrial misconduct), but a very important factor is the exhaustion of entitlement. In May 1976, 222,000 unemployed had exhausted flat-rate benefit. With the increased numbers unemployed for a year or more, this has become an even more pressing problem, but it may also apply to shorter durations where there are repeated spells of unemployment. If one spell is followed by another within thirteen weeks, then these are linked, so that many unemployed find that they have exhausted the year's benefit well before the current spell has reached twelve months.

For those who do not receive national insurance benefits, their main recourse is to supplementary benefits and very large numbers are now claiming (twenty years ago the figure was 55,000, one-tenth of the present total). There are however a sizeable number, the last category, not receiving any benefit at all. This group consists of some not entitled to claim supplementary benefit, such as married women, of some who are retired, and of some who have been employed for only a short time and whose claims have not yet been decided. On the other hand, there are those who are breadwinners and have been unemployed for long periods, and who do not claim supplementary benefits. According to the estimates of the Supplementary Benefit Commission, about one in five of the unemployed entitled to supplementary benefits do not claim, with the average benefit unclaimed being £9 a week in 1975 (*Royal Commission on the Distribution of Income and Wealth*, Report No. 6, p. 94). This group is particularly likely to fall below the poverty line, and we turn now to this aspect.

4   Unemployment and Poverty

In any analysis of the incidence of poverty, the unemployed constitute a fairly small number. This is illustrated by the study recently carried out by the *Royal Commission on the Distribution of Income and Wealth* Report No. 6, which defined lower incomes as those below the lowest quartile of net equivalent *per capita* incomes. Not surprisingly, the single largest group of households which had low incomes in 1976 was that headed by pensioners. On the other hand, although the number of unemployed with low incomes may be small, the *incidence* of poverty is high. A substantial proportion of the unemployed have low incomes: according to the Report, half the unemployed men were in the lowest quartile in 1975.

A more severe poverty standard is the supplementary benefit level itself, which in 1975 was some one-quarter to one-third lower than the Royal Commission cut-off. According to estimates based on the Family Expenditure Survey, there were in December 1975 60,000 families with a male head who had been unemployed for three or more months and were below the supplementary benefit level. These families were not receiving supplementary benefit, and there were a further 70,000 estimated to be eligible who had been out of work less than three months. By now the numbers are likely to be substantially higher. There is therefore a significant minority with incomes below a level which the Supplementary Benefit Commission recently described as 'barely adequate to meet their needs at a level that is consistent with full participation in the ... society in which they live'.

The evidence about the economic circumstances of the unemployed is deficient in a number of respects. We do not know for example enough about the relationship with the earnings of other family members. One of the reasons why family incomes of the unemployed are low is that wives are less commonly in work (which may of course be associated with the conditions under which benefits are paid for dependent, i.e. non-working, wives). For example, according to the Department of Employment (*DOE Gazette*, June 1978), probably no more than 10–15% of married couples with the husband out of work for more than a year, and on supplementary benefit, have a working wife. We do not know enough about the relationship with potential earnings. A study of unemployed men receiving supplementary benefit showed that over one-half had less than 60% of their disposable income at work, and it would be valuable to know the corresponding figure for other groups of unemployed, as well as evidence on potential, as opposed to past, earnings. We do not know enough about repeated spells of unemployment and the relationship of unemployment to job history.

There are therefore serious gaps in existing knowledge and new sources are badly needed. None the less, there can be little doubt that many of the unemployed have low standards of living. Although the conditions are not those of the 1930s, the national insurance system is only partially successful in guaranteeing incomes. Only one in six of the unemployed are receiving the ERS; fewer than half receive the basic NI benefit; and supplementary benefit does not provide a fully successful safety net.

5 Incentives and Benefits

We have suggested that only a relatively small proportion are actually better-off when unemployed. Moreover a replacement ratio close to 100% does not necessarily mean that people would be unwilling to take jobs when offered. For reasons of pride or fulfilment, a person may prefer to work even if it offers little immediate financial advantage; to obtain all the benefits making up the hypothetical replacement ratios is neither automatic nor straightforward; and there are administrative constraints on drawing benefit while 'voluntarily' unemployed.

None the less, the possibility that people are better-off when unemployed, or not much worse-off, has led to a great deal of popular speculation about the disincentive effects. It is frequently claimed that much of the increased unemployment since the mid-1960s is due to 'scrounging' and that there has been a shift in the 'natural' rate of unemployment. Where evidence is adduced in support of this view, it is usually based on the fact that increased unemployment has been associated with a rise in the replacement ratio, particularly following the introduction of the earnings-related supplement in 1966.

Figures comparable to Table 1 are not available for earlier years and, in any case, the information presented by a dozen or so such compilations would be difficult to absorb. In Table 2 the standard benefits for sickness and unemployment are compared to average earnings net of tax and family allowances/child benefit, for the years 1965–77; this represents a less extensive measure of the replacement ratio than used earlier (Table 1) since Table 2 excludes means-tested benefits, housing costs and work expenses. The ratios all jumped up sharply in 1966, with the introduction of ERS, and there have been a number of time-series studies attributing the rise in unemployment in part to the 1966 increase in the replacement ratio. These results are however far from fully convincing. As we have seen earlier, the great differences in the circumstances of the unemployed mean that it is very difficult to summarise the effects of benefits in a single indicator. The fact that the results do not appear to be consistent with the decline in the replacement ratios in recent years (they have fallen some ten percentage points between 1971 and 1977) suggests that the studies may have failed to separate the effect of benefits from other changes in the labour market. Indeed, there seems little hope of identifying the effect from time-series evidence, at least without the aid of much more fully-specified models of the aggregate labour market than have so far been used.

The cross-section evidence on benefits and incentives is more promising. The most careful study to date, by Nickell (*Economic Journal*, 1979), uses an average replacement ratio and data on duration from the 1972 General Household Survey. He finds a significant effect, but one modest in size and limited to those unemployed for less than twenty weeks. It would have implied a rise of about one-tenth in the level of male unemployment in Great Britain as a result of the 1966 increase in the replacement ratio. This is very much less than has been claimed as the rise in 'voluntary' unemployment by some writers. It may indeed be an over-estimate, since the job opportunities not taken by those deterred by benefits may well be taken, at a time of high unemployment, by other unemployed men. The *Department of Employment Gazette*, October 1976 put an upper bound of 50,000 on the male ERS effect when considering reasons for the change in the relationship between unemployment and vacancies (shown in Figure 1). They also attributed less than 20,000 to the Redundancy Payments Act. These figures may be compared with the shift between 1966 and 1974 which the Department described as

Table 2　*Comparison of benefits and average earnings 1965–77*

Year (October)	Average gross weekly earnings plus family allowances/ child benefit before tax and NI[1] £ (1)	Average net income[2] £ (2)	Standard rate of unemployment or sickness benefit plus family allowances/child benefit[3] £ (3)		Net income in col. (2) as percentage of gross earnings in col. (1) %	Benefits in cols. (3) as percentage of net income in col. (2)	
			excl. ERS	incl. ERS		excl. ERS %	incl. ERS %
Single person							
1965	19.59	14.82	4.00	4.00	75.6	27.0	27.0
1966	20.30	15.25	4.00	7.75	75.1	26.2	50.8
1967	21.38	15.87	4.50	8.55	74.2	28.3	53.9
1968	23.00	16.93	4.50	8.95	73.6	26.6	52.9
1969	24.82	18.15	4.50	9.45	73.1	24.8	52.1
1970	28.05	19.98	5.00	10.65	71.2	25.0	52.3
1971	30.93	22.18	6.00	12.75	71.7	27.1	57.5
1972	35.82	26.31	6.75	13.75	73.5	25.7	52.3
1973	40.92	29.67	7.35	14.35	72.5	24.8	48.4
1974	48.63	33.63	8.60	16.36	69.2	25.6	48.6
1975	59.58	39.98	9.80	18.35	67.1	24.5	45.9
1976	66.97	44.64	11.10	20.85	66.6	24.9	46.7
1977	73.34	50.37	12.90	24.00	68.7	25.6	47.6
Married couple with no children							
1965	19.59	15.77	6.50	6.50	80.5	41.2	41.2
1966	20.30	16.21	6.50	10.25	79.8	40.1	63.2
1967	21.38	16.82	7.30	11.35	78.7	43.4	67.5
1968	23.00	17.88	7.30	11.75	77.7	40.8	65.7
1969	24.82	19.10	7.30	12.25	76.9	38.2	64.1
1970	28.05	21.09	8.10	13.75	75.2	38.4	65.2
1971	30.93	23.22	9.70	16.45	75.1	41.8	70.8
1972	35.82	27.36	10.90	17.90	76.4	39.8	65.4

Year (October)	Average gross weekly earnings plus family allowances/child benefit before tax and NI[1] £ (1)	Average net income[2] £ (2)	Standard rate of unemployment or sickness benefit plus family allowances/child benefit[3] £ (3) excl. ERS	Standard rate ... incl. ERS	Net income in col. (2) as percentage of gross earnings in col. (1) %	Benefits in cols. (3) as percentage of net income in col. (2) % excl. ERS	Benefits in cols. (3) ... incl. ERS %
Married couple with no children							
1973	40.92	30.71	11.90	18.90	75.0	38.7	51.5
1974	48.63	35.15	13.90	21.66	72.3	39.5	51.5
1975	59.58	41.86	15.90	24.45	70.3	38.0	58.5
1976	66.97	46.99	18.00	27.75	70.2	38.3	59.5
1977	73.34	53.71	20.90	32.00	73.2	38.9	59.5
Married couple with two children							
1965	19.99	17.74	8.75	8.75	88.7	49.3	49.3
1966	20.70	18.23	8.75	12.50	88.1	48.0	58.5
1967	21.78	18.92	9.80	13.85	86.9	51.8	73.2
1968	23.90	19.98	10.10	14.55	83.6	50.5	72.3
1969	25.72	21.20	10.10	15.05	82.4	47.6	71.0
1970	28.95	23.19	11.20	16.85	80.1	48.3	72.7
1971	31.83	25.85	13.40	20.15	81.2	51.8	77.0
1972	36.72	29.98	15.10	22.10	81.6	50.4	73.7
1973	41.82	33.30	16.50	23.50	79.6	49.5	70.5
1974	49.53	38.47	19.30	27.06	77.7	50.2	70.3
1975	61.08	45.72	22.10	30.65	74.9	48.3	67.0
1976	68.47	51.66	25.00	34.75	75.4	48.4	57.3
1977	75.84	58.60	29.00	49.10	77.3	49.5	58.4

Notes:
[1] Average earnings of adult male manual workers in manufacturing and certain other industries. The 1977 figure is provisional. It is assumed that for married couples the wife has no employment or other income.
[2] After allowing for income tax and NI contributions.
[3] Earnings related supplement calculated using average earnings in October of the relevant tax year.
Source: Royal Commission on the Distribution of Income and Wealth, Report No. 6, p. 299.

equivalent to an increase of about 300,000 in unemployment.

There is, however, reason to believe that the figures in Tables 1 and 2 may *understate* the disincentive effects of benefits in one important respect, which may bias Nickell's results. In each case the net income attributed to a man 'in work' is that associated with a full year's earnings, and the income when unemployed is calculated with any regard to tax rebates or the effect of unemployment on subsequent tax liabilities. However, in deciding how hard to try for a job, or how choosy to be about one offered, an unemployed person might reasonably ask what it is worth to him to start work this week rather than next. In this connection taxes have a very different impact, as a result of the tax base being total annual earnings excluding unemployment benefit. While in Table 2 a married man with two children is shown as having an average tax rate of 22.7% in 1977, an extra week's earnings would raise his tax bill for the year by the equivalent of 34% plus NI contributions – say 40% – of that week's earnings and also lead to work expenses of, say, £3. Thus, marginal net earnings for an extra week's work are considerably lower than average net earnings, and it is the former which really ought to be compared with the tax-free unemployment benefits when deciding not *whether*, but *how long*, to stay unemployed.

Although the duration of unemployment which would maximise net income can be calculated, it is of little relevance to workers who cannot plan the precise date of job loss and re-employment.[3] Table 3 sets out the upper limits of the ranges of earnings in November 1977 for which a ten-week spell of unemployment would raise net income both allowing for the fact that ERS is not paid for the first two weeks (case A), as would a man planning such a spell of unemployment, and ignoring it (case B), as would a job-loser still out of work after three weeks. There is no particular significance to the choice of a ten-week spell, which is intended simply to be illustrative. The basis for the calculations is described in the Technical Note on Calculations.

While Table 1 shows that a man with a dependent wife and two children, eligible for ERS and earning £55 a week was in November 1977 fractionally better-off in the third to twenty-eighth week of unemployment than in a full year's employment, Table 3 brings out that taking into account the difference between average and marginal tax rates raises the 'break-even' point to around £70. The difference is important since many more men (27%) earned at that time between £55 and £70 a week than earned less than £55 (18%). In fact such a man earning £65 a week would gain nearly £4 for each of the third to twenty-third weeks of unemployment (after twenty-three weeks' unemployment he would not pay tax on $29 \times £65 = £1885$ as his threshold was £1891). The quite bizarre way in which the marginal replacement ratios may vary with earnings are shown, again for an illustrative ten-week spell, for two different family types in Figure 3 (this relates to case A).

These calculations of marginal replacement rates suggest that the effect could potentially be important. If all workers were cynically to 'play the system', and could plan their involuntary unemployment, then calculations similar to those in Table 3 (case A) suggest that 15% of men would be unemployed for an average of six months every three years. However, we have

Table 3 *Limit of earnings up to which unemployment would raise net income (as at November 1977)*

Type of dependants	Working men in this position[2] %	Basic benefit November 1977 £ week	Upper limit if ten weeks unemployment are to raise net income (case A)[3] £ week	Upper limit if, having been out of work for three weeks, a further ten weeks of unemployment are to raise net income (case B)[3] £ week	Men earning (— April 1977)[4] less ... (case A) %	(case B) %
No dependants	36	14.70	38.00	40.70	1.9	2.4
One dependent child[1]	9	18.20	45.00	48.00	5.5	3.2
Two dependent children[1]	14	21.20	50.90	54.20	11.0	5.0
Dependent wife	13	23.80	56.10	59.70	20.0	25.0
Three dependent children[1]	6	24.20	56.90	60.50	21.0	27.0
Four dependent children[1]	2	27.20	62.80	66.70	31.8	30.0
Wife and child	6	27.30	63.00	66.90	32.0	35.0
Wife and two children.	8	30.30	69.00	73.20	43.6	40.0
Wife and three children	3	33.30	74.90	79.40	54.0	52.0
Wife and four children	1	36.30	80.90	85.70	62.5	60.0

[1] Plus non-dependent wife.
[2] Estimates based on Family Expenditure Survey, 1976.
[3] Rounded to the nearest 10p. Based on average reckonable earnings of 80% of current weekly earnings and work expenses of £3 a week.
[4] From April 1977 New Earnings Survey.

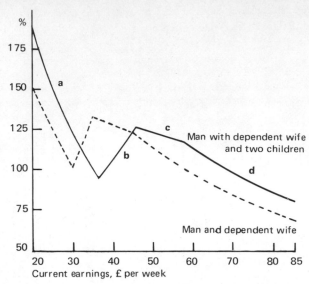

Figure 3   *Ratio of benefit to work income 'marginal replacement ratio' for 10-week unemployment spell (November 1977).*

Source: See Technical Note on Calculations.

no reason to believe that people either can or want to behave in this way. To begin with, whether the incentives offered by the tax/benefit system are translated into an actual effect on the level of unemployment depends on the perceptions of the workers concerned. The worker may not, either before or after becoming unemployed, do the (quite complicated) calculations necessary to determine his marginal replacement rate. Moreover, the calculations require him to make assumptions about his earnings and employment prospects for the rest of the tax year, about which there may be a considerable degree of uncertainty. Secondly, there may be serious problems in putting such a strategy into practice. Planning both dismissals and re-engagements is not easy. For some workers it may be difficult to take an 'extended holiday' without jeopardising their careers; for others it may lead to disqualification from benefit. The costs of being unemployed longer than intended may be high, and individuals may be risk-averse.

It is our view that – even if more widely known – the disincentive effect of high marginal replacement ratios is not likely to be great as far as voluntary job quits are concerned. What is a more plausible pattern of behaviour is that involuntary job-losers, knowing that 3–6 months' unemployment would maximise their net income, may decide not to search actively for the first 4–6 weeks. With an average duration of fifteen weeks, a five week extension by, say, 15% of job-losers (suggested by Table 3, last column) would raise unemployment by 5% (e.g. from 4–4.2%). This may be an underestimate, since job-losers tend to be concentrated more among the lower paid, with higher marginal replacement ratios. On the other hand, they may also be concentrated among those with fewer dependants, which will work the other way. Even if one-third of all job-losers extended duration by five weeks, the rise in unemployment would only be equivalent to going from 4 4.5%; and as we have suggested there may be other factors which mean that the actual effect is less. It should also be noted that the effect is likely to vary with the state of demand.

To sum up, we have argued that the disincentive problem may be potentially more serious than indicated by consideration of average replacement ratios as used in earlier studies. At the same time, there are a number of reasons why the potential effect is not necessarily translated into an actual increase in unemployment and the quantitive importance is, as far as we can judge at present, probably quite small relative to the rise in unemployment since the 1960s.

The relatively small quantitative importance means that the popular views about disincentives are not well-founded. It must however be recognised that beliefs about the financial advantages of unemployment colour the attitudes of the employed population and have a disproportionate effect on policy makers. Moreover, it would be hard to give any clear rationale for the structure of replacement ratios illustrated by Figure 3. The incentive problem – whether actual or perceived – cannot therefore be ignored.

6 Implications for Policy

The present system of benefits, taken in conjunction with the impact of taxation, gives rise to concern on grounds both of adequacy and of incentives. The benefits are in some cases ineffective in guaranteeing a minimum income at the supplementary benefit level; in others they may appear to be high in relation to marginal income from working. In part this reflects an inevitable conflict between income maintenance on one hand and incentives on the other, but there are features of the present structure which suggest that improvements may be possible on both fronts, particularly when we allow for the differing position of different groups of unemployed workers. We turn now to some possible reforms.

7 Income Taxation and Benefits

The structure of incentives described above has existed since the introduction of earnings related supplement in 1966, but has been particularly influenced in recent years by the fall in tax thresholds relative to average earnings. The relationship between these variables affects the duration for which unemployment can raise net income as well as the range of earnings over which this applies. If the tax threshold is £T per annum, a man earning £E per week needs to work for T/E weeks to become a taxpayer. His 'optimal' unemployment duration is typically $(52 - T/E)$ weeks, or the twenty-eight weeks up to the expiry of ERS, whichever is the less. Table 4 sets out the ratio of the tax threshold for various types of family to average annual earnings at different dates, together with its value at constant prices. It is interesting to note that the decline in tax thresholds since the mid-1950s is *not* attributable to inflation in

Issues of Public Policy

Table 4   *Tax thresholds, average earnings, and prices 1949–77*

					Family type					
			Married couple		*Married + one child*		*Married + two children*		*Married + three children*	
Year	*Single*									
	a	*b*	*a*	*b*	*a*	*b*	*a*	*b*	*a*	*b*
1949–50	36	91	59	97	79	91	98	88	118	87
1955–6	31	89	53	99	75	99	97	100	120	100
1966–7	27	100	41	100	58	100	75	100	92	100
1968–9	24	93	37	93	52	93	63	87	74	84
1972–3	32	147	41	124	54	114	63	104	73	98
1973–4	28	134	36	113	47	104	55	95	64	88
1974–5	25	119	34	107	45	100	54	92	62	88
1975–6	22	103	31	95	40	86	47	79	54	74
1976–7	21	97	31	93	41	86	49	80	57	76

Notes: Children assumed to be aged over eleven and under sixteen. The thresholds take account of earned income relief.
a = tax threshold as a percentage of average annual earnings
b = tax thresholds at constant prices (index 1966–7 = 100)
Sources: 1955/6–1976/7 *Royal Commission on the Distribution of Income and Wealth*, Report No. 6, pp. 311 and 314. 1949/50 *Annual Report of the Inland Revenue, Key Statistics of the British Economy.*

the case of single people and childless couples, but to real earnings growth. In families with children this effect has been increased by the fall in value of child tax allowances (and their merging with family allowances in the new non-taxable child benefit). For a married couple with two children the tax threshold has fallen 20% at constant prices, and 50% relative to average earnings since 1956.

The decline in the tax threshold has meant that many more of those who become unemployed have been taxpayers and hence face a substantial tax rate on an extra week's earnings. The figures in Table 4 show however that it would require a very large increase in personal allowances to improve things significantly. More promising is the reduced rate band introduced in the April 1978 Budget, and this has lowered certain of the break-even points shown in Table 3. On the other hand, it would need to be extended quite a lot beyond £750 in order to reduce the marginal replacement ratios of families with children where the wife is dependent. For example, for a family with four children, it would mean extending the band to over £1000, and this clearly involves a substantial revenue cost.

The raising of the tax threshold, and the extension of the reduced rate band, would provide benefits beyond those of reducing the marginal replacement ratios, and in particular would help raise the net incomes of the low paid. These measures are, however, because of their general effect, very expensive in terms of revenue. A much more limited measure, directed at the incentive problem, would be to make benefits taxable, as indeed they were in 1948–9. Many radical reforms, such as the Conservatives' tax credit scheme, or a general social dividend scheme, would, incidentally, by abandoning cumulation, have this effect. However, here we consider more piecemeal approaches.

The failure to tax short-term NI benefits which replace earnings lost due to unemployment or sickness, does not arise from failure to recognise the problem but from the administrative difficulties. The question of taxing them was not significant in 1949 when the tax threshold was so much higher (see Table 4) that the number of benefit-recipients who would have been liable to tax was unimportant, but even then the Revenue found the task unmanageable. The administrative problem of collection arises from two considerations – that PAYE is (almost uniquely in the world) a cumulative withholding system, and that it relies on those making payments to do the withholding. This means that in the case of job changes it is crucial that the new employer knows his employee's code number (representing the value of his allowances) and his pay (and tax withheld) in previous employment. For this reason a form (P.45) has to be completed in triplicate by the old employer and until the form reaches the new employer, tax will be over-withheld from the employee under an 'emergency coding'.

If this procedure were applied to the unemployed, the paying office would pay out little more than half the benefit to which they were entitled in the early weeks, which would be quite intolerable. There are, however, alternative procedures. The most straightforward would be to operate the normal P.45 procedure with the difference that offices paying benefits would never use penal emergency codings; when their information was incomplete they would withhold nothing. If even this method of taxing the full benefit were to prove impractical, it would be possible to use the information already available to the relevant parties to make minimum estimates of benefit received and to take those into account in making tax refunds or withholding from subsequent earnings. If the system is not to treat those unemployed late in the year, who draw refunds, more harshly than those unemployed early in the year, whose accumulating personal allowances reduce the tax withheld by their employer from the earnings of subsequent employment, it is necessary that only information available both to the Revenue and to an employer be used.

This means that only the basic benefit of the individual worker could easily be taxed; at £14.70 this benefit is less than the personal allowance of £18.17 so that benefits would always be paid in full; however tax refunds, or subsequent net earnings, would be reduced. Even this proposal requires *either* that employers know whether a newly engaged employee has previously been receiving benefit and if so for how long, *or* that *all* job-takers, including unemployed men disqualified from benefit, be assumed to have received benefit in every week of the current fiscal year since the end of their previous employment as indicated on their P.45. The latter step would be a substantial move away from the cumulative principle and would, for instance, increase the prospect of students working in vacation paying tax. The decision whether or not to take this step towards abandoning cumulation depends on the balance of advantage in increasing taxes on temporary participants on the one hand and the administrative difficulty in distinguishing them from genuine temporary benefit-recipients on the other.

The effect in November 1977 of taxing the basic individual benefit in most cases have been to reduce by £5 a week (34% of £14.70) the maximum net advantage of being unemployed. It is equivalent to exempting the first £14.70 of earnings in a marginal week from tax. It would thus eliminate 'optimal' spells for most of those who would benefit from them now, although it might raise the duration of those that remained. The proposed reform would largely eliminate the problem of those with marginal, but not average replacement ratios, in excess of 100%.

The taxation of benefits has been discussed so far in relation to the effect on marginal replacement ratios, but we need also to consider the impact on the incomes of the unemployed. Is it not inappropriately regressive to tax only the basic benefit since this amounts, in comparison to the *status quo*, to a poll tax of £5 a week on each unemployed basic rate taxpayer? First it is important to emphasise that this deduction applies only to those whose unemployment duration is sufficiently short, and their earnings sufficiently high, for them to be liable for tax. Thus for a married man entering the 29th week of unemployment the full £5 deduction would only apply if his earnings exceeded some £64 a week. For a duration of nine months the corresponding figure is £112 a week, and for those unemployed more than a year there would be no reduction in net income.

The second point is that the taxation of benefits would provide additional revenue and we would strongly urge that this be used for the improvement of benefits, to which we now turn.

8   Reform of Unemployment Benefit

The burden of taxing national insurance benefit in the way described above would fall on those with relatively short durations. We would now like to argue that the benefits for the long-term unemployed should be improved. As we have seen, many of the unemployed have exhausted entitlement to national insurance and are forced to depend on supplementary benefit. This latter scheme, called upon to play a much larger role than originally intended, does not provide a fully adequate safety net. We would recommend, therefore, that the present maximum of twelve months for national insurance benefit be extended to twenty-four months in the first instance, and ultimately to an indefinite period.[4] The gross cost of this reform is quite substantial, but against this must be set the saving on supplementary and other benefits. Moreover, the substantial reduction in the number claiming supplementary benefit would reduce the administrative costs (the administrative costs of the Supplementary Benefits Commission amount to some $13\frac{1}{2}\%$ of benefits paid, compared with 4% for national insurance). For those remaining on supplementary benefit, we recommend that those out of work for two years or more should be entitled to the long-term rate of benefit (while preserving the requirement to register for employment). This would put the unemployed on the same footing as other groups such as the sick and disabled, and would have increased the benefit for a couple by £4.80 a week in November 1977.

In the case of the ERS, it has been suggested that this could be abolished, with the saving being used to augment the basic benefit. This would contribute both to reducing any possible disincentive effect and to helping the long-term ⬛⬛⬛⬛⬛⬛⬛⬛⬛ If ⬛⬛⬛ in felt to be too drastic a step, then the structure of the supplement could be reformed in ⬛⬛⬛⬛⬛⬛ ⬛⬛⬛⬛⬛⬛⬛ ⬛⬛⬛ ⬛⬛⬛⬛⬛⬛⬛ ⬛⬛ ⬛⬛⬛⬛⬛ ⬛⬛ possible to make the schedule more progressive, providing larger benefit to those with lower earnings, while reducing the higher 'break even' points in Table 3. Thus, if the percentage supplement were increased in the first range (less than £30) and reduced on earnings above this, the schedule would 'tilt' in favour of the lower paid. A second example is provided by the lag in the calculation of reckonable earnings, which means that benefits fall behind in times of accelerating inflation and, conversely, rise relative to prospective earnings if inflation is brought down. This suggests that steps should be taken to shorten the administrative lag. Even if it really is impossible to supply the individual's average earnings in the tax year to 5 April before 31 December, it should be possible to apply an index adjustment at that point as well as making index adjustments to ERS in payment.

9   Universal Benefits

Many of the issues discussed here arise from the tension between low incomes in employment and the need to guarantee a reasonable standard of living when out of work. This tension is especially marked in the case of families with dependants, where marginal replacement ratios are particularly likely to be high. In the case of children this is brought out clearly by the level of benefits. A man in work in November 1977 received £1.00 child benefit for the first child and £1.50 for subsequent children; a man who was unemployed received a total of £4.50 for each from national insurance and child benefit combined. If the child benefit had been raised substantially to a rate of £4.50 a week for each child in all families, and the special national insurance benefit abolished, the unemployed would have been no worse-off than under the present rules and some of the working poor, and others with children, would have been better off. By absorbing the special child allowances for short-term benefit-recipients into the general child benefit most of the extreme cases of marginal replacement ratios would have been eliminated. (The lowest supplementary benefit scale for children would also be increased.) We would therefore like to see the increases in child benefits taken further than in the April 1978 Budget (welcome though that increase was). Such a policy is expensive (the recent increase to £2.30 cost over £300 million) but it is important to recognise how provision for children has been eroded over the post-war period. The Beveridge Report recommended that family allowances should be paid at the same rate for all with no special rate for the unemployed (except that the first child was excluded where the responsible parent was at work) and that the allowance should be eight shillings (40 pence) a week. This represented one-third of the recommended single person's insurance benefit. A comparable figure in November 1977 would have been £4.90.

This measure would leave the allowance of £9.10 for a dependent wife as the source of any remaining difficulties, including the very low participation rate of the wives of unemployed men when the family receives supplementary benefit. A home responsibility payment payable to all women with necessarily home-based dependants, as advocated by the Meade Committee, should make it possible to reduce this allowance as well as the married man's tax allowance.

10 Concluding Comment

In this chapter our concern has been with the implications of high levels of unemployment, and we have suggested some ways in which the tax and social security systems could be reformed. It is however well to bear in mind the warning given by Beveridge in 1930 when he described a more generous scheme of unemployment insurance: 'The dangers ... lie not so much in the risk of demoralising recipients of relief, so that they do not look for work, as in the risk of demoralising governments, employers and trade unions so that they take less thought for the prevention of unemployment.' In our view the single most important objective is to reduce unemployment.

Technical Note on Benefits (in 1977)

There are three main social security benefits available specifically for the unemployed. The first of these is the contributory national insurance flat-rate benefit. This benefit is paid to those registered as available for work and is subject to contribution and other conditions (a person may, for example, be disqualified for up to six weeks in cases of misconduct or leaving a job voluntarily). Benefit is paid after three waiting days for a maximum period of one year in any spell of unemployment (spells not separated by more than thirteen weeks count as one period for this purpose). The benefit covers a person's wife or other adult dependants (but not normally a husband) and dependent children.

The second benefit is the earnings related supplement (ERS), which is paid in addition to the flat-rate benefit for a period of six months after two waiting weeks. The supplement is related to 'reckonable earnings' in the relevant income tax year, defined as average weekly earnings in the year ending in the April before the calendar year in which the claim is being made. As a result, reckonable earnings may lag very considerably behind recent earnings (with the maximum lag from the start of the base period to the end of the benefit period being thirty-nine months). Moreover, any period of unemployment in the relevant tax year will reduce reckonable earnings. The benefit formula has changed periodically, but in 1975–6 (the tax year relevant in November 1977) there was an earnings floor of £11 a week, and if reckonable earnings fell below this no supplement was payable. For reckonable earnings between £11–30 a week, the ERS was one-third, plus 15% of earnings thereafter, up to a ceiling at reckonable earnings of £69 a week. The supplement does not vary with the number of dependants, and is subject to the condition that the total of flat-rate benefit and ERS must not exceed 85% of reckonable earnings. Where the flat-rate benefit alone exceeds 85% of earnings, no ERS is paid but the flat-rate benefit is payable in full.

The third benefit is that paid by the Supplementary Benefit Commission. Supplementary allowances (often referred to as supplementary benefit) are paid either as the sole benefit or as an addition to the national insurance benefits. The basic condition is that the person's resources are less than the requirements laid down in the benefit scale. The requirements include payment of rent or, in the case of owner-occupiers, mortgage interest, rates, repairs and insurance. There are no waiting days and no general limit on the period for which benefit may be received. The basic scale, before allowing for rent, was in November 1977 £14.50 for a single person and £23.55 for a couple, plus £4.10 to £8.90 per child depending on age. The unemployed are not entitled to the higher long-term scale payable after two years for others under pension age.

Technical Note on Calculations

This note sets out some of the details of the calculations underlying Table 3 and Figure 3. All amounts relate to November 1977. The additional income received when out of work for ten weeks is the basic benefit (BB) plus the earnings related supplement (ERS). For reckonable earnings between £30–69, the ERS (paid for eight of the ten weeks) is equal to £1.83 plus 15% of reckonable earnings (subject to the 85% rule). We assume that average weekly reckonable earnings are 80% of current weekly earnings; this percentage does in fact vary with inflation as well as varying between applicants. Denoting current earnings by E, this gives a total benefit over the ten weeks of:

$$10BB + 8(1.83 + 0.12E)$$

The 85% rule means that the supplement is reduced, or no supplement payable, where the total benefit exceeds 0.85×0.8 ($=0.68$) of current earnings. For a man with a dependent wife this applies below £45.77; for a couple with two children it applies below £57.38. The supplement is extinguished when $0.68 \times E$ is less than BB, which occurs at £35 for a man with a dependent wife and £44.56 for the two-child family.

The net income from working ten weeks rather than being unemployed depends on earnings in relation to the tax threshold. (In the example, it is assumed that the wife does not work and that there is no investment or other income.) If the person is not liable to tax even working a full year (i.e. below £27.98 a week for a couple and £36.37 a week for a couple and two children aged 11–15), then the net income from ten weeks is $9.4E - 30$, where the national insurance contribution rate has been rounded to 6% and work expenses taken as £3 a week. Where the person is liable for tax even working only forty-two weeks in the year (above £34.64 for a couple, and £45.02 for the couple with two children), the net income from working the extra ten weeks is $6E - 30$. For earnings in the intermediate range, the income tax liability is less than 34% of additional earnings.

Table 3 (case A) shows the (highest) earnings levels at which the total benefit equals the net income from working the ten weeks. It may be checked that these are above the tax threshold when working forty-two weeks and that the 85% rule does not apply. They are obtained therefore by solving the equation:

$$10BB + 8(1.83 + 0.12E) = 6E - 30$$

(Case B has to be modified to allow for three weeks already spent out of work.) Figure 3 shows the variation in the marginal replacement ratio with earnings and consists of four main segments (the letters correspond to those on the line for a man, wife and two children):

(a) basic benefit only payable, no income tax liability on earnings from marginal ten weeks,
(b) basic benefit only payable, income tax payable on part of earnings from marginal ten weeks,
(c) basic benefit plus supplement equals 85% of reckonable earnings, income tax payable on all earnings from marginal ten weeks,
(d) basic benefit plus supplement equal to £1.83 + 15% of reckonable earnings per week, income tax payable on all earnings from marginal ten weeks.

(Note: The point of extinction of the ERS does not quite coincide with the point at which all marginal earnings become liable for tax, so that there is a very small segment between b and c not shown in the figure.)

The calculations in such examples are complicated by the interaction of husbands' and wives' tax treatment and by the reintroduction, in the April 1978 Budget, of a reduced rate band of income tax. The former means that the husband's effective tax threshold falls pound for pound as his wife's earnings exceed the wife's earned income allowance (£945 per annum in 1977–8). If the wife earned more than £2836 all the husband's earnings would be taxed and it would pay him to be unemployed for three or six months, if at all, depending on his earnings. The reduced rate band means that some people will have a marginal net wage of 69% of the gross rather than the 60% assumed above.

Notes

1 The official unemployment statistics are based on registered unemployment and have been criticised for being both too high and too low. Thus reference has been made to fraudulent claims (although the numbers involved are likely to be small in relation to those shown in Figure 1). Working in the opposite direction is the fact that people may not register as unemployed, even though they are available and looking for work. Evidence from the *General Household Survey* suggests that around one-fifth of those who consider themselves unemployed may not register. Adjustments for such factors may affect the interpretation of given levels of unemployment; moreover, their significance may vary with economic activity. At the same time, they are unlikely to change the general picture of a very substantial rise in unemployment.
2 Although it should be noted that fringe benefits at work are not taken into account, which would tend to reduce the replacement ratio.
3 Typically this 'optimum' is either zero or three months (January to April) every second year or six months (January to June) every third year.
4 The original Beveridge proposal was that unemployment benefit be paid without limit so long as the person remained available for work, but subject to attendance at a work or training centre. (Social Insurance and Allied Services, p. 128.)

22 Unemployment Benefits and Incentives in Britain*

1 Introduction

Popular attitudes to unemployment and unemployment insurance in Britain are much influenced by the widespread belief that benefits act as a serious disincentive to work. Such beliefs are scarcely new. Following the 1930 Unemployment Insurance Act, which provided more generous benefits and conditions, Winston Churchill claimed that it had led to 'an avalanche of new claims' (Skidelsky [35]). Nor were these opinions confined to politicians. As noted by Benjamin and Kochin [2], economists such as Rueff and Cannan argued that the dole was an important factor leading to prolonged unemployment.

In the post-war period, discussion of the possible disincentive effect of benefits was renewed with the introduction of the earnings-related supplement to unemployment benefit in 1966, and the rise in unemployment after that date. This is well illustrated in the following commentary by Feldstein [12]:

In October 1966, one month after the change in unemployment insurance, British unemployment began rising dramatically. The number of registered unemployed rose from 340,000 in September to 436,000 in October and 543,000 in November. The registered unemployment rate for males rose from 1.6% in August to 3.3% in January. It is, of course, difficult to know how much of this increase should be attributed to the change in unemployment compensation. Other macro-economic and tax policies occurred at approximately the same time. It is noteworthy, however, that unemployment rates above 3% had been seen only once before in the post-war period (during an unusually bad winter) and that such a rapid rise in the rate of unemployment had not been seen before. Moreover, the male unemployment rate has remained over 3% ever since then. The previous relation between the unemployment rate and the vacancy rate ceased to hold after 1966. An examination of the occupational composition of unemployment shows that the proportional rise in unemployment among skilled manual workers was greatest and among the lower paid unskilled workers (who would benefit less from the earnings-related supplement) was least. Although there are problems in interpreting each piece of data on the British experience, the evidence as a whole clearly indicates that the new method of earnings-related unemployment compensation has raised the level of unemployment.

With the rise in unemployment during the 1970s to levels far above those described by Feldstein, the belief in the disincentive effect has gained great currency. The (largely incorrect) view that the unemployed are better-off receiving benefits and tax rebates than at work has led many to conclude that

* Reprinted from *The Economics of Unemployment in Britain*.

unemployment insurance is responsible for a substantial degree of 'voluntary' unemployment.

The aim of this chapter is to review the evidence about unemployment levels and durations, to see how far it supports the popular opinion. Does the existence of unemployment benefit in fact lead to higher unemployment? If so, how large is the effect? What was the impact of the earnings-related supplement and what is likely to be the effect of its abolition?

As a basis for assessing the evidence, section 2 sets out a simple analytical framework. Since there is no fully adequate theory of the determination of unemployment, the approach is intentionally eclectic and seeks to sidestep some of the controversies which do not bear directly on the issue in question. It is also restricted in scope in several significant ways. First, it concentrates on the behaviour of *male heads of households* and does not examine in any detail the effects on other workers. This is a serious limitation since, for example, the response of wives to the unemployment of their husbands may be quanti-tatively at least as important as that of the men. Secondly, it considers only *whether or not a person is in employment* and does not deal with the kind of employment (e.g. whether it is well matched to the person's level of skill), the hours of work, or other dimensions of the job. Thirdly, there is no treatment of the possibility that the unemployment insurance provisions may shift the *demand curve* for labour. It has been suggested that improvement in benefits relative to incomes in work made employers more likely to declare people redundant; in the United States it is argued that unemployment insurance increases the incidence of temporary lay-offs (e.g. Feldstein [13]).

The empirical evidence reviewed here is of two main kinds. The first, discussed in section 3, is based on aggregate time-series data. In other words, inferences are derived from the observed variations in the overall rate of unemployment (as in the quotation from Feldstein above). The second, considered in section 4, makes use of cross-section data on individual durations of unemployment. Both sources of evidence have strengths and weaknesses, and the final section weighs the conclusions which can be drawn. It should be emphasised at the outset that the survey of the evidence is not intended to be comprehensive, and that little attention is paid except, in passing, to research for countries apart from Britain.

2   Framework for the Analysis

The model of the labour market set out here is a simple one; some of the necessary qualifications are set out at the end of the section.

On the demand side of the labour market it is assumed that there is a structure of jobs on offer, dependent on the state of demand and on technology, and that with each job is associated a specified gross wage. The structure of vacancies is assumed in the short run to be independent of the supply of labour. Employers try to fill the vacancies with those who apply, either offering them a job or not. There is no attempt to tailor the jobs to the applicants by making an offer at a lower wage. This feature differentiates the model from that of a perfectly competitive labour market, and it is caused by a variety of factors: 'Equity, custom, internal labour markets, union bargaining agreements, legal constraints, morale factors and difficulties in measuring individual productivity all combine to associate a particular wage with a particular job in any firm' (Nickell [29], p. 1250).

On the supply side, it is assumed that each worker has a *reservation wage* (or a series of reservation wages for different jobs). If when unemployed he is offered a job at a wage equal to, or in excess of, his reservation wage, he accepts. In any period of unemployment he may of course receive no offer of a job, despite any efforts on his part to seek work. When employed, he quits a job when the wage paid falls below his reservation wage: for example, when he becomes aware of better prospects elsewhere, or his benefit income rises. The reservation wage will be adjusted over time, depending for example on the worker's experience in the labour market, changes in taxation, benefits and wage levels.

Bringing together the demand and supply sides of the market, allowance must be made for the fact that these are not perfectly matched at the micro-level. At any time there are likely to be both vacancies and unemployed people who would accept a job if it were offered to them. The extent of the mismatching depends on several factors, including the efficiency of employment exchanges, and the availability of information. The resulting level of unemployment is governed by the number of vacancies (dependent in turn on the conditions of demand), the structure of wages offered, the structure of reservation wages, and the extent of mismatching.

In this simple model the impact of unemployment benefit and taxation depends on the way they influence the reservation wage. It is quite conceivable that this wage is independent of benefit levels, but those who argue that there is a disincentive effect take the view that the reservation wage increases with the level of benefits. In its simplest form, this can be modelled in terms of the benefit income, B, and the net of tax wage, Y, with the job offer being accepted if Y exceeds some critical proportion of B. (The proportion may be greater or less than 100%; nothing can be deduced simply from the observation that B is larger than Y.) The ratio of B to Y, referred to as the 'benefit/earnings ratio', or the 'replacement ratio', plays a central role in the empirical studies.

If the reservation wage is not affected by the level of benefits, then that is the end of the matter. Suppose, however, that the reservation wage is an increasing function of B. A rise in benefits consequently means that an unemployed worker is more likely to refuse a job offer (the constraints on making such a refusal are discussed below) or to look less intensively for a job. Whether this change on the supply side is translated into any actual effect on the level of unemployment depends on the conditions of demand. If demand is high then it is possible that he is offered a job with a wage well in excess of the reservation wage, so that small changes in the latter do not in fact affect his decision. Conversely, if demand is low he may receive no job offer at all, in which case the rise in the reservation wage is again irrelevant. Moreover, it is possible that a rise in the reservation wage has no effect on the overall rate of unemployment even where decisions are affected for some people. If jobs are being rationed, and jobs can be quickly re-offered, then a diminution in the pool of potential workers (i.e. those who would accept) may not have an impact on the employment rate:

Some of those who are now 'voluntarily' unemployed take the place of the 'involuntary' unemployed. The reason why there are N people unemployed can be due to cyclical and structural factors, but which particular individuals are unemployed could be determined by the existence of unemployment benefits and interpersonal differences in tastes and situations (Sawyer [32], p. 136).

To sum up, it is quite possible in theory that the level of unemployment is influenced by benefits. There is, however, no theoretical necessity that there must be a disincentive effect. It is sometimes suggested that this conclusion is simply an implication of basic price theory (e.g. Grubel and Walker [18]), whereas it depends on assumptions about individual motivation and about the operation of the labour market. The *existence* of a disincentive effect, and not merely its magnitude, is a matter for empirical demonstration.

The model described above is highly stylised. There is not space here to consider all possible elaborations, but three points in particular should be noted. First, the assumption that a worker is free to accept or reject a job offer ignores the constraints on 'voluntary' unemployment imposed by the social security system. The fact that a person can be disqualified for refusing a job 'without good cause' or for neglecting to avail himself of 'a reasonable opportunity of suitable employment', is not given much weight in the literature, but clearly is a major consideration for both claimants and the government departments. (For discussion of the 'genuinely seeking work test' in the 1920s and 1930s, see Deacon [9]; on present day control measures, see Field [14] and Fulbrook [16].) To the extent that such administrative controls are effective, the possibility of a disincentive effect is reduced. Secondly, the effect of unemployment insurance has been discussed in terms of the current benefit level, but workers may take a less myopic view. Future benefit entitlement may influence decisions about whether to seek a job or to accept an offer. This may be particularly important when the operation of the tax system is taken into account. With income tax levied on annual earnings excluding unemployment benefit, a person may calculate the implications for the remainder of the tax year: that is, he may be concerned with the 'marginal' cost of additional periods of unemployment. The interaction of taxation and benefits is quite complex (see Atkinson and Flemming [1]). Thirdly, the chance of receiving a job offer may be related to the characteristics of the worker (see, for example, Daniel [8]), including how long he has been unemployed, and the previous offers he has refused. These considerations may in turn affect the worker's decision.

3   Aggregate Time-Series Evidence

One of the bases for the popular beliefs about unemployment insurance is that both the generosity of benefits and the level of unemployment appear to have risen over the post-war period. Figure 1 shows the unemployment rate for men, U, and the ratio of benefits, for a married couple with two children, to average net earnings, B/Y, in October of each year. Both series show a substantial rise

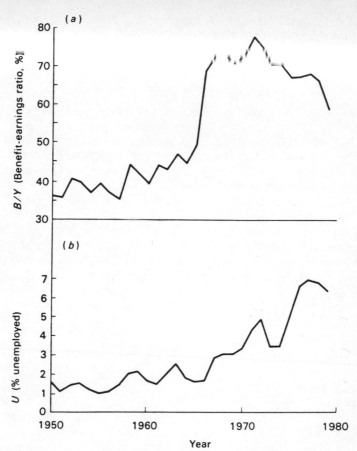

Figure 1   *Benefit/earnings ratio and unemployment rate 1950–79.*

Notes:

1 The unemployment rate relates to males in Great Britain and expresses the annual average total unemployment (excluding school-leavers and adult students) as a percentage of the mid-year estimate of total employees (employed and unemployed).

2 The benefits earnings ratio is calculated for a married couple with two children, where the husband has average earnings for adult male manual workers in manufacturing and certain other industries, and it is assumed that the wife does not work. The benefit includes earnings-related supplement, calculated on the basis of average earnings for the relevant tax year. The figures relate to October of each year.

Sources:

(*U*) Department of Employment, *British Labour Statistics*, 1886–1968, Table 166, with subsequent data from the *Department of Employment Gazette*, (*B/Y*) Maki and Spindler (1975) Table 1, *Social Security Statistics* 1977, Table 46.05, and the author's own calculations.

over the period 1950–79 as a whole, although the timepath has been rather different. In particular, the benefit/earnings ratio jumped sharply in 1966, with the introduction of the earnings-related supplemented (ERS), and has, if anything, declined since then, whereas of course the unemployment rate has increased significantly since the mid-1960s.

Before considering the conclusions (if any) which can be drawn from such changes over time, the definition of the benefit/earnings ratio should be clarified. This ratio is given by:

$$\frac{B}{Y} = \frac{\text{national insurance benefit (incl. ERS and child benefit)}}{\text{average gross earnings} - \text{tax} - \text{NI contribution} + \text{child benefit}}$$

Thus in October 1978, average gross earnings, including benefit for two children, came to £83.50, and after tax and NI contributions this was reduced to £67.28. At the same time, unemployment benefit, including child benefit and ERS (calculated on the assumption of average earnings in the relevant tax year), came to £44.41. This gave a benefit/earnings ratio of 66%. Without ERS, the ratio would have been 49%.

In considering changes in the ratio (B/Y), it should be borne in mind that there are several factors at work. The role of unemployment benefit has received most attention, but the decline in the tax threshold has also been a major factor. This is brought out clearly by the figures in Table 1.

Table 1   *Changes in the benefit/earnings ratio*

	(1) Benefit (B) ÷ gross earnings (%)*	(2) Net income (Y) ÷ gross earnings (%)*	(1)/(2) (B/Y) (%)
October 1966	60.4	88.1	68.6
October 1978	53.2	80.6	66.0

* Including family allowance/child benefit.

Over the period 1966–78, the level of benefits fell relative to gross earnings; it was the decline in net income relative to gross that kept the benefit/earnings ratio fairly constant. The ratio depends on the level of child benefit. If in October 1978 this had been set at £4.50 per child, which was the total paid per child under unemployment benefit, for both employed and unemployed alike, then B/Y would have been 62%. It must similarly be noted that there are other elements which should enter the calculation. A more extensive measure of 'total income support' in and out of work would include supplementary benefit, Family Income Supplement, rent and rate rebates, free school meals, free welfare foods, and would allow for work expenses and tax refunds. Finally, it must be remembered that benefits are adjusted at discrete intervals, and the date of up-rating may influence the timepath indicated (Figure 1 relates to October of each year). A clear example is provided by 1971 when the benefits were increased on 23 September, compared with 1979 when the increase dated from November. Taking the pre-increase figures for 1971, then the ratio would have been 69% rather than 78% as shown in Figure 1. Conversely, taking the post-increase figures for 1979 would give a ratio of 66% rather than 58%.

In terms of the earlier model, the benefit/earnings ratio may be seen as an indicator of the relationship between reservation wages and the wages offered. Other things being equal, this has led to the inference that B/Y and the unemployment rate would move together. It is not, however, the case that other things do remain equal, as recognised in the quotation from Feldstein given in section 1. The fact that the two series move together – if only in broad terms – does not mean that one can attribute the increase in unemployment to the changing benefit/earnings ratio. To draw any firm deductions it is necessary to construct an adequate model of the determinants of unemployment. Only by examining unemployment at dates which are comparable in other respects, or where the effect of other variables has been allowed for, can one draw conclusions about the response to B/Y.

There are broadly two methods which can be adopted. First, attempts may be made to construct a full-scale model of the determinants of unemployment. Alternatively, this may be short-circuited by trying to relate unemployment to a variable which incorporates the other influences but is itself unaffected by B/Y. The second is the simpler, and is well illustrated by the studies which have sought to explain the changed relationship between unemployment (U) and vacancies (V) since 1966. These studies in effect assume that the demand influences are captured by V, so that 'while unemployment has risen very steeply, the vacancy series has remained a better measure of the "true" level of demand pressure' (Bowers et al. [6], p. 75). For example, Gujarati [19] fitted a linear–logarithmic relationship between U and V for the pre-1966 period, and used this to measure the deviation of post-1966 unemployment from its predicted level. He concluded that actual unemployment (total male and female) was some 44% higher than predicted (although see the criticism by Foster [15]); and Bowers et al. [6] estimated that the shift in mid-1971 was about 2%.

The existence of such a shift does not, however, mean that it can be attributed to particular changes on the supply side. Gujarati argued that it reflected the Redundancy Payments Act 1965 and the introduction of ERS; but apart from the timing he produced no evidence in support of this assertion. There are several other possible explanations, and these have been discussed by Bowers et al. [6], Bowers [4], Taylor [38 and 39] and the Department of Employment [10]. The last adopted a 'constructive' approach to see how far the different factors might in fact have contributed to the shift (taken to be about 300,000 relative to vacancies). The Department first pointed out that many of the unemployed are not receiving ERS, so that the increase in the B/Y ratio applied only to a minority of claimants. Assuming that ERS doubles the length of an individual's spell out of work (which was considered 'likely to be on the high side'), the Department estimated that the resulting increase in the level of unemployment was probably less than 50,000. This is only some one-sixth of the total shift. (The validity of the underlying assumptions is discussed in the context of the cross-section evidence in section 4.) The Department concluded that 'evidence ... on the numbers receiving these benefits at relevant dates suggests that statutory redundancy payments and earnings-related supplements could have accounted for only a small part of the observed shift' (p. 1098).

The first, more ambitious method, via the estimation of a full model of the determinants of unemployment, is illustrated by the work of Maki and Spindler [28]. They estimated an equation to explain the rate of unemployment (U) which incorporated B/Y and two variables designed to capture the structural and cyclical factors. The latter are:

Structural: X_{1t} = total labour force multiplied by output per person (i.e. labour supply in efficiency units), expected sign positive.

Cyclical: X_{2t} = ratio of GNP to trend (exponential function), expected sign negative.

The results for male unemployment were:

$$\ln U = -2.0 + 1.3B/Y + 0.00018X_{1t} - 12.2\ln(X_{2t}) - 4.6\ln(X_{2t-1})$$
$$\quad\quad\quad (3.2)\quad\quad (4.9)\quad\quad\quad (6.6)\quad\quad\quad\quad (2.9)$$

where the figures in brackets are t-statistics; $\bar{R}^2 = 0.965$, $DW = 1.62$.

The unemployment rate, as in several other studies, is expressed relative to the civilian labour force rather than total employees as in the published statistics. The equation is estimated simultaneously with another equation expressing B/Y as a function of U and other variables.

The precise status of this equation was not made very clear by the authors. It is presumably a reduced form, obtained from a set of labour market equations, but the full derivation from a theoretical model is not given. This makes it difficult to interpret the results, and the question of specification is taken up below. Moreover, it must be remembered that U relates to *registered* unemployment, so that the effect may represent in part an increased propensity to register rather than a lengthening of actual durations. Accepting for the present the equation as it stands, one can calculate the response of U with respect to B/Y. For example, the introduction of ERS raised B/Y from approximately 50–70% (see Figure 1). From the estimated coefficient (1.3), it can be deduced that this would have led to an increase in the unemployment rate of some 30% (i.e. exp. (1.3×0.2)). In terms of male unemployment at the end of 16, this would be some 110,000 – or over twice the Department of Employment estimate.

There are a number of criticisms which have been made of the Maki and Spindler results and of their general approach, which has been applied to a wide variety of countries (see Grubel and Walker [18]). Attention is focused here on three major problems: the specification of the unemployment equation, its interpretation as a reduced form equation, and the appropriateness of the aggregate benefit/earnings ratio.

In commenting on the evidence for Canada, which includes a similar paper by Grubel, Maki and Sax [17], Diewert [11] has argued the need for a 'theory of the effect of unemployment insurance which is built up on micro-foundations, since the rigorous use of consumer theory in constructing the model to be estimated imposes discipline on the choice of variables to be included as controls'. This sets a demanding standard, but it does point out the essentially arbitrary choice of 'control' variables $(X_{1t}, X_{2t}, X_{2t-1})$ in the estimated equation. What reason is there to believe that these, and not other possible variables, should be included? The sensitivity of the conclusions reached regarding the influence of the benefits variable has been shown by several authors. The coefficient of B/Y may be reduced by the introduction of a time trend (Taylor [40]) or of permanent income (Cubbin and Foley [7]).[1] The difficulties are recognised by Spindler and Maki in their reply [35]. Nickell [30] has summarised the position as follows:

Much of the statistical impact of the replacement ratio in the post-war studies arises because both it and the level of unemployment have risen secularly over most of the last twenty years. The inclusion of any other variable which moves monotonically over time will ... tend to reduce this impact. Given also that the theoretical basis of these equations is weak, we are then left with virtually no statistical or prior criteria for choosing between results (p. 35).

The second problem is related: the interpretation of the equation as a reduced form. A number of authors have expressed their unease: for example, Helliwell [20] noted that 'from the point of view of a labour-market economist, or anyone concerned with micro-economic specifications, the use of a reduced-form unemployment equation is intrinsically unsatisfactory. One simply does not know how to work back to the micro-behavioural parameters.' The unemployment relation should indeed be seen in terms of a larger model of the labour market, which considers explicitly employment, hours of work and the supply of labour. Only in such a context can one attempt to explore whether any observed response to variation in B/Y is associated with an increase in labour supply (more workers registering) or with a reduced acceptance of jobs. In the United States and Canada a number of full-scale models of the labour market have been constructed. For instance, Black and Kelejian [3] estimated a five-equation system covering the demand for man hours, the division of man hours into employment and hours, the determination of average wages, and the supply of labour by primary and secondary workers. A similar approach is adopted in a number of macro-economic models, including, for example, that of the National Institute (Ormerod and Whitley [31]).

The appropriateness of the benefit/earnings ratio used by Maki and Spindler has been questioned by several critics. Sawyer [32] argues, for example, that the appropriate scale prior to 1966 is not the flat-rate national insurance benefit but the national assistance scale; the latter was higher and its use tends to reduce the size of the jump in B/Y. In an alternative approach, Taylor [40] uses a variable for the average benefit actually received. This statistic needs careful interpretation (for example, because of the interaction with national assistance/supplementary benefits), but it has the advantage of avoiding the difficulties which may arise because of the differences in dates of up-rating. As indicated earlier, the variation due to slight differences in timing (e.g. from 69–78%) can be large in relation to the variation in the series as a whole.

More generally, the choice of benefit/earnings indicator must be related to the underlying model, and it may be helpful to draw a parallel with other types of aggregate analysis. This is typically justified by reference to an 'average' consumer or household; a procedure which is strictly valid only under strong assumptions but which may be an adequate approximation where the relevant variables change smoothly and where the aggregation is over a representative cross-section of the population. In the present case these conditions are not met. The benefit/earnings ratio varies sharply with earnings and with the duration of unemployment. For a 'representative' worker on £88 per week (including child benefit) in October 1978, the ratio with ERS was 66% (for a married couple with two children). With earnings of £65 a week, the ratio would have risen to 78%; but if there were no entitlement to ERS, then it would have fallen to 52%. In addition, the studies are not concerned with a simple cross-section of the population. By this is meant not just the fact that the unemployed are atypical of the population as a whole, tending to have below-average wages when in work, but also that the B/Y ratio relevant to the analysis is not necessarily that of the representative unemployed. The response to the benefit/earnings ratio depends on the interaction with demand, and on the constraints faced by the individual. If, for instance, it is those with a high B/Y for whom the reservation wage is close to that offered, then it may be reasonable to take the ratio including ERS, even though it is received only by a minority of the unemployed. It may be the more skilled workers for whom the demand exceeds the supply, and hence their decisions which are relevant, not those of the lower paid who make up a greater proportion of the unemployed. What is needed is an indicator of B/Y for the 'marginal' unemployed. Here the micro-economic evidence may be of assistance, and this is the subject of the next section.

4   Cross-Section Evidence

Cross-section studies make use of information on individual unemployment and its relation to the individual's characteristics and position in the labour market. In their most simple form, the studies seek to explain the differential duration of unemployment for individual members of a sample, with one of the explanatory variables being the B/Y ratio. In considering this kind of evidence, it must be borne in mind that one can never hope to explain all the variation in such data. Because of the 'mismatching' referred to in section 2, the duration of unemployment is a random variable, and even a 'perfect' model will only be able to explain a certain fraction of the variance.[2] What the studies should be seeking to explain, therefore, are the differential probabilities of different individuals remaining unemployed.

There are many factors likely to influence such probabilities: they include age, previous work career, qualifications, family circumstances, and local labour market conditions. These may affect the reservation wage of the individual or the probability of receiving a job offer. This means that any model designed to test for the effect of the B/Y ratio must incorporate these factors. Conversely, their omission may lead to biased estimates of the effect of B/Y. This may be illustrated by the work of Hill *et al.* [22], who analysed unemployment duration in relation to receipt of ERS. They concluded that this comparison 'produced no evidence in support of the hypothesis, and in fact, in one area, Newcastle, there was a statistically significant tendency for those without earnings-related supplement to remain unemployed the longest' (Hill [21]). However, as Hill goes on to point out, this comparison is not meaningful since those receiving ERS are not typical of the unemployed. Among other things, they are likely to have better employment records and by definition have been out of work less than six months. These features may well make them more attractive to employers. The second point, therefore, is that it is necessary to include in the estimated relationship those factors likely to influence the probability of re-employment.

Among the studies which have attempted to do this (again no attempt is made to give a comprehensive survey) are those of MacKay and Reid [27] using a sample of redundant workers in 1966–8, of Lancaster [25] using a national sample of unskilled unemployed workers in 1973, and of Nickell [30] using the 1972 *General Household Survey*.

MacKay and Reid [27] carried out a regression analysis of the unemployment experience of 613 male workers declared redundant from twenty-three engineering plants in the West Midlands. The essential aspects of their results may be summarised in terms of the regression equation:

$$
\begin{Bmatrix} \text{Unemployment duration} \\ \text{(including observations} \\ \text{of zero) (mean 11.8} \\ \text{weeks)} \end{Bmatrix} \begin{matrix} \text{DEPENDS} \\ \text{ON} \end{matrix} \begin{Bmatrix} \text{Personal characteristics (age} \\ 55+, \text{ marital status} \\ \text{significant)} \end{Bmatrix}
$$

$$
+ \begin{Bmatrix} \text{Demand characteristics} \\ (\% \text{ vacancies significant)} \end{Bmatrix} + \begin{Bmatrix} \text{Search activity (whether} \\ \text{looked for work before} \\ \text{redundancy, employers} \\ \text{contacted, etc.)} \end{Bmatrix}
$$

$$
+ \begin{matrix} 0.42 \\ (2.0) \end{matrix} \begin{Bmatrix} \text{weekly unemployment} \\ \text{benefit in £} \end{Bmatrix} + \begin{matrix} 0.005 \\ (1.4) \end{matrix} \begin{Bmatrix} \text{reduncancy} \\ \text{pay in £} \end{Bmatrix}
$$

Figures in brackets are *t*-statistics.
Source: MacKay and Reid [27] Table III.

The effect indicated by the coefficient of the benefit variable is rather smaller than found in the aggregate studies: 'while unemployment benefit may have had some impact in raising the level of unemployment, the small partial regression coefficient does not indicate that workers were "living off the state" for long periods' (p. 1269). The coefficient implies that a person receiving the maximum £7 ERS (in 1966–8) would have had a longer expected duration by 2.9 weeks. This is smaller than the hypothetical doubling assumed in the Department of Employment calculation quoted in the previous section, and the overall estimate of the impact of ERS made by MacKay and Reid is correspondingly smaller. Taking an average ERS of £3, they estimate the increased total unemployment to be about 12,000 men. On the other hand, MacKay and Reid include as a separate variable the intensity of job search. Since the effect of benefits is supposed to operate partly through reduced search activity, the total impact may therefore be understated by the coefficient on their benefit variable.

For most of the MacKay and Reid sample, the observations relate to *completed* spells of unemployment. In contrast, the data analysed by Lancaster [25] relate to 479 workers some of whom had returned to work by the date of the interview but others of whom had not yet completed their spell of unemployment. The development of the appropriate estimation technique is described in Lancaster [25] and Lancaster and Nickell [26]. Lancaster assumes a re-employment probability which is a loglinear function of the benefit/earnings ratio for the individual, of other characteristics, and of duration. He notes the problems which may arise because of unobserved differences in re-employment probabilities, particularly in relation to estimating the effect of duration. Thus individuals with higher probabilities will be less strongly represented at longer durations. Making different assumptions about the extent of such unobserved differences between workers, he concludes that the elasticity of unemployment duration with respect to the benefit/earnings ratio is around 0.6. A rise in the ratio from 50–70%, as with the introduction of ERS, would on this basis lead to an increase in average duration of some 22%. This is again considerably less than the doubling assumed in the Department of Employment calculation.

The evidence from the *General Household Survey* employed by Nickell [29 and 30] is more limited than that available to Lancaster in that it is based on uncompleted spells recorded at a single interview, but it can be used in a similar way to estimate the conditional re-employment probabilities. The data relate to the 426 males in 1972 who had been out of work for more than one week and claimed either that they were actively seeking work or that they would have been doing so but for temporary sickness or that they were waiting to take up a job. The B/Y ratio used by Nickell is a more extensive measure including supplementary benefits, rent and rate rebates, family income supplement, free school meals and tax rebates. The results are illustrated by the following estimates of the re-employment probability, p, for a person who has been unemployed s weeks:

$$\ln\left(\frac{p}{1-p}\right) = \text{quadratic terms in } s$$

$$+ \text{personal characteristics (marital status, age, family needs, ill-health)}$$

$$+ \text{local demand and other variables}$$

$$-1.58B/Y \text{ [for } s \leqslant 20] + 0.31B/Y \text{ [for } s > 20]$$
$$\quad (0.43) \qquad\qquad\qquad (0.55)$$

where the figures in brackets are asymptotic standard errors (see Nickell [29], Table 1, equation 2).

In the case of the benefit/earnings ratio, Nickell argued that the effect is likely to vary with the duration of unemployment and allowed the coefficient to vary (continuously) at different durations. The likelihood was fairly flat between cut-offs of fifteen and twenty-five weeks but the hypothesis that the coefficient was the same for all durations was convincingly rejected. The implication is that the coefficient is highly significant for durations less than twenty weeks but insignificantly different from zero after that. It is possible that this arises because of unobserved differences between workers, there being a changing 'mix' of unemployed with duration, as noted earlier, but the experiments with different assumptions by Lancaster and Nickell [26] suggest that this is not the explanation. The overall implications of the estimated coefficient may be seen from the effect of different replacement ratios on the expected duration for a 'typical' man in Table 2.

Table 2 *Expected duration of unemployment*

Benefit/earnings ratio	Weeks of unemployment
0.4	6.7
0.7	10.5
0.8	12.1
1.0	16.3

Source: Nickell [29], Table II.

On the basis of this analysis, and the more extensive treatment of the benefit variable in Nickell [30], he concluded that the elasticity of expected duration with respect to the benefit/earnings ratio is between 0.6 and 1.0. In interpreting this, it must be remembered that the B/Y measure is a more extensive one, including other benefits apart from unemployment pay, so that the proportionate impact of a change in unemployment benefit is smaller. For this reason, Nickell himself summarised the results in terms of an elasticity of 0.6, which is the same as that found by Lancaster.

The conclusions from the cross-section evidence in Britain indicate therefore that the effect of benefits on unemployment duration is significant but small in magnitude. In this they seem in close agreement. At the same time, there are a number of possible criticisms. First, the studies described concentrate on the probability of leaving employment once a person has entered. They do not allow therefore for the possible effect on the flow into unemployment. Hence they tend to understate the elasticity to the extent that the propensity to quit increases with B/Y. Nickell [30] argued that this effect is of minor importance, on the grounds that the rate of flow into male unemployment has changed little since 1967 and that the *General Household Survey* shows only about 20% leaving their last job voluntarily. This may be correct, but evidence about reasons for entering unemployment needs careful interpretation, and the conclusion requires confirmation from a study of the incidence of unemployment.

Secondly, one cannot immediately draw conclusions about aggregate unemployment from the estimated individual probabilities of re-employment.

As pointed out in section 2, a rise in the reservation wage for one group of workers may simply mean that another group are employed – with aggregate unemployment remaining unchanged. Thus, the introduction of ERS could have led to an increase in the number out of work for less than twenty-eight weeks, but a decrease in longer durations; or it could have led men with a taste for leisure to quit and be replaced by unemployed men with no hobbies. The re-employment probabilities of different individuals are interdependent.

Thirdly, one of the strengths of micro-economic data is that they contain information on individual benefit entitlement, but in practice this information is not complete. For example, the *General Household Survey* contains relatively little information on the actual unemployment benefits received, and calculations in Nickell [29] are based on the assumption that all unemployed received ERS and full NI benefit in the relevant periods. Moreover, the earnings relevant to ERS were calculated from predicted earnings. In his later paper [30], Nickell does examine the effect of using actual past earnings and actual current benefits, but it is not apparent that the earnings relate to the relevant period for determining ERS and there is no information on past benefits. It is also assumed in the calculations that the take-up of means-tested benefits is 100%. For benefits such as rent/rate rebates and free school meals, this is a dubious assumption; and for supplementary benefit it is also open to question (the estimated take-up rate by the unemployed in 1975 was 78% – see Supplementary Benefit Commission, [37]). The benefit/earnings indicator may therefore be measured with considerable error, and the error may be correlated with relevant unobserved characteristics. For example, those more 'motivated' to search for a job may be more (or less) likely to claim means-tested benefits.

Fourthly, the benefit/earnings ratio used in these studies compares the benefit income with that of a man in work for a full year. However, in deciding on a job offer, an unemployed person may reasonably ask what it is worth to him to start this week rather than next. In this connection the effect of income taxation may be crucial. In a system where the tax base is total annual earnings excluding unemployment benefit, the *marginal* net earnings for an extra week's work may be considerably lower than *average* net earnings. As Atkinson and Flemming (Chapter 21 in this volume) suggested, it may be more appropriate to use a marginal rather than an average benefit/earnings ratio.

Finally, the evidence used by Lancaster and Nickell relates to the early 1970s, when unemployment was considerably below its level at the start of the 1980s. The framework described in section 2 indicates how the impact of the benefit variable might depend on the demand conditions, and it is not clear that the findings can be applied to current conditions. (This applies even more to the results of MacKay and Reid for the mid-1960s.)

5 Conclusions

This chapter has reviewed some of the findings about the possible effect of unemployment benefit on the rate of unemployment. The review has not attempted to be comprehensive, concentrating on aggregate time-series and on cross-section studies, and selecting certain of these for special attention. There are a number of other potentially fruitful sources of evidence, including longitudinal studies of the kind being carried out by the Department of Health and Social Security, and the pooling of cross-section data for several years (as in the *General Household Survey* or the *Family Expenditure Survey*).

The results may be summarised usefully in terms of the implications for the effect of the earnings-related supplement (ERS), and many of the studies have focused on the consequences of its introduction in 1966. The quotation from Feldstein [12] in section 1 drew attention to the rise in unemployment after that date, and argued that the introduction of ERS was one of the factors responsible. The time-series analysis by Maki and Spindler [28] was seen by them as confirming this, and they estimated that the resulting increase in male unemployment was some 110,000. This was more than twice the 'constructive' estimate made by the Department of Employment on the basis of the assumption that the average duration of unemployment for ERS recipients was doubled. Put in reverse, and applied to the abolition of ERS at much higher levels of unemployment, the Maki and Spindler estimated relationship would imply a fall in male unemployment from (say) 1 million to 775,000.

This time-series study has been heavily criticised, and there are several reasons for regarding the findings with considerable scepticism. The specification of the unemployment equation, and its interpretation as a reduced form, raise serious problems. The difficulties of representing the impact of benefits in a single indicator, and of separating it from other trended variables, are substantial. Maki and Spindler themselves agree that 'it is probably the case that the insurance-induced unemployment hypothesis has not yet been adequately tested or the magnitude of the effect exactly measured' (p. 159). Indeed, there seems little hope of identifying the benefit effect at all precisely from time-series evidence, and it will at the very least require much more fully specified models of the labout market.

The cross-section evidence appears to find a significant effect of benefits on individual probabilities of re-employment, but the magnitude is relatively small. Indeed, the results of all three studies reviewed indicate that the assumption by the Department of Employment of a doubling of the duration may considerably overstate the impact. Nickell, for example, concluded that ERS would only have increased expected durations for ERS recipients by about a quarter. Again there are problems with the methods employed. In some cases these are intrinsic to the cross-section approach: for example, the aggregation of individual probabilities where these may be interdependent. In other cases, the analysis can be refined: for example, the treatment of the benefit variable and the examination of different demand conditions. The conclusions to be drawn must therefore be qualified, and may need to be modified in the light of subsequent research. There does however seem to be little ground to suppose that the introduction of ERS led to an 'avalanche' of claims or that its abolition will dramatically reduce the level of unemployment.

Writing about the 1930s, Benjamin and Kochin recently concluded that 'the army of the unemployed standing watch in Britain at the publication of the *General Theory* was largely a volunteer army' ([2], p. 474). This conclusion is open to question for reasons similar to those discussed in section 3 (their approach resembles that of Maki and Spindler). More importantly, there is at present no strong evidence that there are a large proportion of volunteers among the unemployed watching the monetarist experiments of the early 1980s. It does indeed appear to be a 'conscript' army.

Acknowledgements

This paper is a revised, and shortened, version of a paper prepared at the request of HM Treasury in February 1978.

Notes

1 Other writers have argued (e.g. Sawyer [32] and Junankar [23]) that the equation is not stable over the period for which it was estimated, the coefficients having shifted.
2 This point is made clearly in Lancaster [24] who shows that where the probability of re-employment is constant over time for a person, but differs across individuals, then the R^2 recorded in a least squares regression of duration is strictly less than 0.5.

References

[1] Atkinson, A. B. and Flemming, J. S. (1978), 'Unemployment, social security and incentives', Chapter 21 in this volume.
[2] Benjamin, D. K. and Kochin, L. A. (1979), 'Searching for an explanation of unemployment in interwar Britain', *Journal of Political Economy*, **87**, pp. 441–78.
[3] Black, S. W. and Kelejian, H. H. (1970), 'A macro model of the US labor market', *Econometrica*, **38**, pp. 712–41.
[4] Bowers, J. K. (1976), 'Some notes on current unemployment', in *The Concept and Measurement of Involuntary Unemployment*, Worswick, G. D. N. (ed.), London, Allen & Unwin.
[5] Bowers, J. K., Cheshire, P. C. and Webb, A. E. (1970), 'The change in the relationship between unemployment and earnings increases', *National Institute Economic Review*, No. 54, pp. 44–63.
[6] Bowers, J. K., Cheshire, P. C., Webb, A. E. and Weeden, R. (1972), 'Some aspects of unemployment and the labour market 1966–71', *National Institute Economic Review*, No. 62, pp. 75–88.
[7] Cubbin, J. S. and Foley, K. (1977), 'The extent of benefit-induced unemployment in Great Britain: Some new evidence', *Oxford Economic Papers*, **29**, pp. 128–40.
[8] Daniel, W. W. (1974), *A National Survey of the Unemployed*, London, PEP.
[9] Deacon, A. (1976), *In Search of the Scrounger*, London, G. Bell.
[10] Department of Employment (1976), 'The changed relationship between unemployment and vacancies', *Department of Employment Gazette*, pp. 1093–9, October.
[11] Diewert, W. E. (1978), in *Unemployment Insurance*, Grubel, H. G. and Walker, M. A. (eds.), p. 89, The Fraser Institute, Vancouver.
[12] Feldstein, M. S. (1973), *Lowering the Permanent Rate of Unemployment*, pp. 47–8, Washington DC, US Joint Economic Committee.
[13] Feldstein, M. S. (1976), 'Temporary layoffs in the theory of unemployment', *Journal of Political Economy*, **84**, pp. 937–57.
[14] Field, F. (1977), 'Control measures against abuse', in *The Conscript Army*, Field, F. (ed.), London, Routledge & Kegan Paul.
[15] Foster, J. I. (1973), 'The behaviour of unemployment and unfilled vacancies: A comment', *Economic Journal*, **83**, pp. 192–201.
[16] Fulbrook, J. (1978), *Administrative Justice and the Unemployed*, London, Mansell.
[17] Grubel, H. G., Maki, D. and Sax, S. (1975), 'Real and induced unemployment in Canada', *Canadian Journal of Economics*, **8**, pp. 174–91.

[18] Grubel, H. G. and Walker, M. A. (1978), *Unemployment Insurance*, Vancouver, The Fraser Institute.

[19] Gujarati, D. (1972), 'Behaviour of unemployment and unfilled vacancies: Great Britain, 1958–1971', *Economic Journal*, **82**, pp. 195–204.

[20] Helliwell, J. F. (1978), 'Discussion', in *Unemployment Insurance*, Grubel, H. G. and Walker, M. A. (eds.), pp. 113–19, Vancouver, The Fraser Institute.

[21] Hill, M. J. (1976), 'Can we distinguish voluntary from involuntary unemployment?' in *The Concept and Meaurements of Involuntary Unemployment*, Worswick, G. D. N. (ed.), p. 172, London, Allen & Unwin.

[22] Hill, M. J., Harrison, R. M., Sargeant, A. V. and Talbot, V. (1973), *Men Out of Work*, London, Cambridge University Press.

[23] Junankar, P. N. (1981), 'An econometric analysis of unemployment in Great Britain, 1952–1975', *Oxford Economic Papers*, vol. 33, pp. 387–400.

[24] Lancaster, T. (1976), 'Redundancy, unemployment and manpower policy: A comment', *Economic Journal*, **86**, pp. 335–8.

[25] Lancaster, T. (1979), 'Econometric methods for the duration of unemployment', *Econometrica*, **47**, pp. 939–56.

[26] Lancaster, T. and Nickell, S. (1980), 'The analysis of re-employment probabilities for the unemployed', *Journal of the Royal Statistical Society*, vol. 143, pp. 141–65.

[27] Mackay, D. I. and Reid, G. L. (1972), 'Redundancy, unemployment and manpower policy', *Economic Journal*, **82**, pp. 1256–72.

[28] Maki, D. R. and Spindler, Z. A. (1975), 'The effect of unemployment compensation on the rate of unemployment in Great Britain', *Oxford Economic Papers*, **27**, pp. 440–54.

[29] Nickell, S. (1979a), 'Estimating the probability of leaving unemployment', *Econometrica*, **47**, pp. 1249–66.

[30] Nickell, S. (1979b), 'The effect of unemployment and related benefits on the duration of unemployment', *Economic Journal*, **89**, pp. 24–49.

[31] Ormerod, P. A. and Whitley, J. D. (1977), *National Institute Model 2: The Labour Sector*, National Institute of Economic and Social Research, Discussion Paper No. 10C.

[32] Sawyer, M. C. (1979), 'The effects of unemployment compensation on the rate of unemployment in Great Britain: A comment', *Oxford Economic Papers*, **31**, pp. 135–46.

[33] Sinfield, A. (1968), *The Long Term Unemployed*, Paris, OECD.

[34] Sinfield, A. (1976), 'Unemployment and the social structure', in *The Concept and Meausrement of Involuntary Unemployment*, Worswick, G. D. N. (ed.), London, Allen & Unwin.

[35] Skidelsky, R. (1970), *Politicians and the Slump*, p. 167, Harmondsworth, Penguin.

[36] Spindler, Z. A. and Maki, D. (1979), 'More on the effects of unemployment compensation on the rate of unemployment in Great Britain', *Oxford Economic Papers*, **31**, pp. 147–64.

[37] Supplementary Benefit Commission (1978), *Take-up of Supplementary Benefits*, p. 2, London, HMSO.

[38] Taylor, J. (1972), 'The behaviour of unemployment and unfilled vacancies: An alternative view', *Economic Journal*, **82**, pp. 1352–65.

[39] Taylor, J. (1976), 'The unemployment gap in Britain's production sector 1953–73, in *The Concept and Measurement of Involuntary Unemployment*, Worswick, G. D. N. (ed)., London, Allen & Unwin.

[40] Taylor, J. (1977), 'A note on the comparative behaviour of male and female unemployment rates in the United Kingdom, 1951–76', Discussion Paper, University of Lancaster.

Index of Names

Full references to economists and other writers cited in the text are given at the end of each chapter.
See also the Bibliography to Chapter 1, pp. 32–6.

437

Subject Index